Economics of an Islamic Economy

Themes in Islamic Studies

VOLUME 6

Economics of an Islamic Economy

By

Rauf A. Azhar

BRILL

LEIDEN • BOSTON
2010

This book is printed on acid-free paper.

Library of Congress Cataloging-in-Publication Data

Azhar, Rauf A.
Economics of an Islamic economy / by Rauf A. Azhar.
p. cm. —
Includes bibliographical references and index.
ISBN 978-90-04-17937-0 (hardback : alk. paper)
1. Economics—Religious aspects—Islam. 2. Islam—Economic aspects. I. Title.
BP173.75.A935 2010
330.917'67—dc22

2009036799

ISSN 1389-823X
ISBN 978 90 04 17937 0

PRINTED IN THE NETHERLANDS

قُلْ إِنَّ صَلَاتِي وَنُسُكِي وَمَحْيَايَ وَمَمَاتِي لِلَّهِ رَبِّ ٱلْعَـٰلَمِينَ

Say: "Behold, my prayer, and (all) my acts of worship, and my living and my dying are for God (alone), the Lord of all the worlds"
(Qurʾān, 6:162)

CONTENTS

PREFACE

I am thankful to God for making it possible for me to finish this work against considerable odds. It has taken the better part of the past decade for it to reach the stage of publication. Some of the difficulties related purely to lack of logistical support for research at the university where I worked, while others, even more daunting, related to my lack of formal training in the required areas of Islamic studies. In the late 1990s, when I held a position at what subsequently came to be known as the University of Central Punjab, I started to offer a course on the subject of money and finance to MBA students. In view of the ongoing debate on the issue of *ribā*, I felt obliged to include a section on Islamic finance in the course. As it happened, this roughly coincided with the time when the famous *ribā* case was being adjudicated at the Supreme Court of Pakistan, and as a result of the various issues that came under scrutiny there the section on Islamic finance grew to about one third of the course. Some of the material included in the lectures was not readily available in the form I presented it while other bits were scattered around. The students naturally felt some difficulty in handling the material, and asked for a more easily accessible source but none was available, even in the writings of Islamic economists, that would satisfy the demands as I saw them. The main difficulty stemmed from the way the theory of financial intermediation in view of the profit-sharing through *muḍāraba*, the contractual arrangement that was supposed to be the workhorse of Islamic finance, needed to be expounded. In this, financial intermediaries were viewed as pure intermediaries, and the conventional model's severance of the link between their assets and liabilities, through their issuing of independent, or rather autonomous, liabilities of their own, and thus as a result holding similarly independent assets, as happens in conventional financing, was in principle inadmissible. In view of the students' difficulties, I felt the need for a text that they could use for this section of the course. I often thought of writing one myself but every time abandoned the idea in the face of the obstacles in the way of writing one; this required, beyond surmounting the logistical problems, a working knowledge of a number of fields in Islamic studies, such as *tafsīr, ḥadīth*, and *fiqh*, which I lacked at the time, and time went on.

My own reading of the material on Islamic economics made me aware of some of the logical deficiencies in its exposition. Over the years, I had somehow collected considerable reading material on Islamic economics, but had not read it in any serious manner. A serious reading now suggested that it was worthwhile exploring the idea of writing the book despite all the problems. It took several years of toiling on my own to obtain a sufficient grounding in the required areas before I felt comfortable to proceed with the project. A bit of a boost to this disposition was provided by the reopening of the *ribā* case in the Supreme Court in 2002.

As often happens with the writing of books, what I have ended up writing turned out to be quite different from what I had intended to write. When I decided to go ahead with the project, I had an outline of about six chapters in my mind, roughly, but only roughly, corresponding to material that is presented in Chapters 1, 3, 4, 6, and 9, and a paper of my own that presented a model of intertemporal choice under the *muḍāraba* form of profit-sharing. I did not realize how complicated the issue of *ribā* was, even though when I had read, for instance in ʿAbdullah Yūsuf ʿAlī's commentary on the Qurʾān, that it was perhaps the most difficult issue in *fiqh*. I had believed what the Islamic economists had been saying following a particular modernist interpretation of *ribā*. I thought that I could present their position in one of the later chapters in the book that would reveal that what was needed was a profit-sharing system and then I would present my own model, followed by a concluding chapter.[1] I saw some problems with the optimality conditions as derived in my own model: in its exposition in Islamic economics, the *muḍārib*'s input was not viewed in an intertemporal setting. I thought this difficulty could be overcome by considering his input as an application of human capital rather than labor, and thus easily derive the optimality conditions. As it turned out, that paper became largely irrelevant for the book as it took its final form: the confidence I reposed in the writings of Islamic economists on the subject of *ribā* turned out to be misplaced. The chapter

[1] Eventually the paper was published in 1992, five years after the seminar in which it was presented, in Ausaf Ahmad and Kazim Raza Awan (eds.), *Lectures on Islamic Economics*, Jeddah: Islamic Research and Training Institute, Islamic Development Bank, 1992, pp. 217–42. I was not sent the galleys of the paper for final proof reading, and when I finally received a copy of the book, I noticed a few typing errors.

I intended to write on the subject now metamorphosed into the two longest chapters in the book.

I started writing the book in late 2004, and by the end of 2005 had completed ten chapters. Chapter 11, was written in March 2009 after the manuscript had gone through the process of reviewing at Brill. The ten completed chapters were submitted to Brill in March 2006. As a result of a misplacing of a communication, eight months were lost. The displacement caused by my move back to Canada prevented me from finding out what had happened. The reviewing process took two and a half years. The first review report came quickly, within a few months, but a long time elapsed before the second reviewer's report came through, possibly because of the difficulty of locating a suitable person with the multi-disciplinary expertise required for the task. Thus the first ten chapters of the book, except for some revisions of an editorial nature, appear here as they were originally written. Admittedly Chapter 4, and some parts of Chapter 8 that relate to it, could have been revised in view of later events, but since my analysis in those chapters in a way anticipated what has transpired, I have not felt it necessary to add anything. Had the subject been one of a topical nature, this long a lag between writing and publication would have rendered the book obsolete. Luckily, that is not the case: the issues explored in this work, specifically those relating to *ribā*, will be discussed and debated for a long time.

Writing this work has been a lonely journey, though it is to be hoped a worthwhile one, for it was difficult to locate individuals having similar interests and bent of mind with whom to discuss the outline, and the questions that I wanted to articulate. Those who could readily understand what was to be presented in the first part of the book, roughly up to Chapter 4, namely those who are trained as economists, could hardly understand what was to follow. In fact, they might have even failed to see the whole point of this part, especially the material in Chapter 3. And those who could understand the exposition of some of the issues in the latter part of the book, beginning with Chapter 5, would generally not even be familiar with what was presented in the first part, let alone connect the arguments of the two parts. The only group who would readily get the drift of the argument, and thus could connect the material of the two parts, was that of the Islamic economists, but in their case I thought they may not be well disposed to the critical view this work takes of their own articulations, or the articulations with which they may have come to sympathise even though when this may simply be for sentimental reasons. Thus I had to rely entirely on my own judgment as to how the material was to be arranged and expounded. It is therefore clear that the responsibility for any errors of omission or commission is entirely mine, and *wa-Allāh-o-ʿalam* (and God knows best).

It may appear to Islamic economists, and perhaps some others, especially those who may have come to sympathize with their opinions but are not fully initiated in their writings, that I have been somewhat harsh in my treatment of some of the exponents of Islamic economics. To them, some of whom I have known personally, I only wish to say that whatever I have said has been said in all sincerity. I have not doubted their sincerity either; my disenchantment has broadly to do with the lack of care in their expositions, especially if what was being offered was offered as an Islamic position on a specific matter. Yet, in all that follows, if some of them feel that I have overstepped the bounds of legitimate criticism, I ask for their indulgence.

It is customary to thank people who may have helped in some way in an undertaking such as this . In any work of this nature, one is indirectly indebted to all those on whose shoulders one needs to stand. To all the scholars, of old and of not so old, whose contributions to our common heritage of intellectual knowledge shaped my own thoughts, I happily acknowledge, even without mentioning any names, my gratitude. I am thankful to Professor Syed Ahmad of McMaster University, my alma mater, for having read some of the chapters, for his kind words after having read them, and for always inquiring about the status of its publication. For editorial help, to improve the clarity of presentation, I am thankful to Brill. Finally I must say that given the circumstances, it would not have been possible for me to write this book, at least in its present form, without the help of the Internet and the search engines available. Without knowing any one of them, I am thankful to all the souls who contributed to these developments, notwithstanding the misuse this technology, like any other, can be, and has been, subjected to.

I have often used the term "classical times" when referring to the Islamic literature in various areas of Islamic sciences. Different scholars may mean different time periods when they use this term, and there may be further refinements such as early, middle and late classical periods. I have not felt it necessary to introduce such refinements. In this work, the classical time period is interpreted quite broadly, from the beginning of the Islamic sciences down to Suyūṭī's time at the end of the fifteenth century. In transliteration, which is mostly from Arabic, I have followed the system used in the *International Journal of Middle East* Studies, in using diacritical marks and omitting *tāʾ marbūta* except in the construct state. Only words that would be capitalized in English are capitalized in transliteration, except at the beginning of titles. I have not used the definite article *al* at the beginning of proper names in the text but I have included it in the lists of references. Place names that are commonly used in English, except for Mecca where the departure from its original pronunciation is too pronounced, are given in their usual form. As for the use of the word God instead of Allah, I agonised for a while, but then decided to use the former in the context of the vernacular being used for the book, recognizing, as He himself says in the Qurʾān, that all beautiful names belong to Him.

I hope I have been able to raise some questions on the subject of Islamic economy, for that is the best a single work of this nature can expect to accomplish. Much needs to done, only some of which I point out in the concluding chapter, and I hope and pray that those and other related questions will be taken up by others to advance the subject of Islamic economy to a higher plane of scholarly discourse. Most of all, I record my profound gratitude to the creator of everything that exists by noting His words from the Qurʾān: *wa-mā tawfīqī illā bi-ʾllāh.*

Rauf A. Azhar
April 6, 2009

CHAPTER ONE

INTRODUCTION

Great expectations were attached to the idea of "Islamic economics" by its exponents at the time the venture was launched some four decades ago. They thought of themselves as embarking on an intellectual endeavor that aimed at nothing short of presenting an entirely new paradigm in the field of economic thought, and they were quite convinced that once the new paradigm established its roots, it would usher in a Kuhnian paradigm shift in the existing discipline of economics. And, regardless of how it might be received in the established circles of economics, it was at any rate supposed to represent an unparalleled development in the Islamic sciences, for hitherto these did not possess a distinct and well articulated body of economic thought at par with the contemporary Western economic literature. Now, several decades later, nothing of the sort is visible on the horizon; indeed it seems that the original ardor has run somewhat dry. As this enterprise progressed, and more of their writings became available, it became increasingly clear that the protagonists of Islamic economics were not just overshooting, they were somewhat overstretching themselves in their zeal to advance what was purported to be an Islamic cause. It is this zeal that explains the adjective 'Islamic' in the nomenclature selected for the endeavor, and in their vision it was not just the discipline of economics that was to undergo this transformation: all modern disciplines were, with the passage of time, to be subjected to a similar process of change in order to make them a part of the modern Islamic sciences.[1] Economic paradigm shift was thus just a small, albeit

[1] This has fallen under the rubric of what has come to be known as "Islamization of knowledge" in recent years. The term was originally coined by Ismail Ragi al-Faruqi of Temple University, in a book of the same title (Herndon, Va.: IIIT, 1982), presumably to motivate Muslim scholars to integrate Islamic outlook into various modern academic disciplines. It is not clear whether Faruqi intended it to be used as an epithet to be used in the titles of various disciplines as they came under study, but that possibility was eagerly seized upon by those who were engaged in exploring various dimensions of an Islamic economy—a rightful subject in my view—to launch what was henceforth to be called "Islamic economics." Clearly, in so doing, they paid scant attention

important, part of a wider metamorphosis that the stock of humanity's accumulated knowledge was supposed to undergo.

In the West, not unexpectedly, this enterprise has generally gone unnoticed except for an opportunistic response to what has become known as Islamic banking. As far as the theoretical writings are concerned, because of a preponderance of *fiqh* (Islamic jurisprudence) contents in them, the enterprise has been viewed as an internal Islamic affair. With the exception of a session here and a session there in the learned societies meetings, over the past quarter of a century, mainstream economics has maintained an attitude of bemused silence in view of the enormity of the task those writers had set for themselves. But surprisingly, the West was not alone in maintaining this stance. A large majority of Muslim economists, both in the West and the Islamic world, also decided to remain silent at least until the initial percolation was over, and a clearer picture of the contours of the new paradigm emerged. But, equally, it must be recognized that there was a small minority of young Muslim economists who were quite enthusiastic about the idea and what it may eventually lead to, though not all of them could, for one reason or another, formally join the enterprise. Participation or not, this latter group wholeheartedly accepted whatever was offered in the name of Islam by the leading proponents of the paradigm shift more or less at face value, without any critical eye as to its substantive contents. No wonder then that, following their lead, the sympathizers of the Islamization of knowledge across a broad spectrum of disciplines accepted the new vision of economics equally uncritically.

The task of evaluating what was thus offered was, and still is, not very easy; the offerings were overlaid by the terminology and language of *fiqh*, a language that has always retained a reverential aura among Muslims, and the intricacies of which can be mustered only with a

to the inappropriateness of applying the same procedure to sciences (and thus the possibility of titles such as *Islamic Botany, Islamic Physics, Islamic Astronomy*, etc.). Even if one follows Faruqi's advice faithfully—for he stated that scientific disciplines did not fall under the scope of his argument—one has to contend with titles such as *Islamic Psychology, Islamic Accounting*, and so forth. What is more disconcerting is that in Islamic Economics Faruqi's original intent came to be read as a plea to discard or disregard the existing pool of knowledge created by non-Muslims, as we will see in the following pages. This is contrary to how Muslims responded to the prevailing stock of knowledge in the early centuries of Islam, a response that contributed to the rise of a brilliant civilization.

great deal of effort and time by anyone not formally trained in that discipline, such as an economist. If economists were ill-equipped to deal with the language of *fiqh*, the *fiqh* scholars were equally ill-prepared to deal with the discipline of economics and the working of the modern economy; indeed most of the *fiqh* scholars have lacked even an elementary knowledge of economics as well as the issues that it deems important. It is thus that those few who could occupy the middle ground—at the confluence of *fiqh* and economics—were able to set a course of their own liking for a discourse that was to be known as Islamic economics.

I have felt that this uncritical acceptance by those who are considered to be better informed of whatever is offered in the name of Islam is problematic, to say the least. Experience suggests that whatever is offered in the name of Islam is taken seriously by not only lay Muslims, but also those who may otherwise be well informed but do not know the intricacies of a particular discipline. In absence of any critical evaluation, whatever is thus offered is likely to become established as a genuine Islamic position by default. And history is replete with instances where, for example, a purely local cultural norm acquired this status in the minds of concerned Muslims, leading to unnecessary dogmatism. I consider it important to review the Islamic credentials of what is being offered in the name of Islam in the area of economics: what is being offered is supposed to represent the universal articulation of the Islamic position, and not just one of the possibilities admitted by the universal norms of Islam. As for the application of those norms, I have been mindful of two things: first, some of the norms may afford a degree of flexibility, and thus may get articulated in diverse manners across time and space. Second, specifically in the context of the march of time, applicability of the universal norms of Islam requires a very careful consideration of the contemporary conditions that are so far removed from the corresponding socioeconomic conditions prevailing at the time when those norms were entrusted to mankind. This in turn means that one must keep a sharper eye on the spirit and not just the letters of particular enunciations, letters that may not lend themselves to ready applicability in the changed circumstances. An exclusive focus on letters may result not only in the loss of spirit behind them, but in the stifling of those norms in the minds of even the sincere adherents of Islamic values simply because of the practical inoperability of the exact words. One must recognize that a great deal of water has flowed under the bridge, so to speak, in the intervening centuries, especially the past few that have seen such a phenomenal change and during which Islamic thought has remained more or less dormant.

When it comes to the main thrust of the arguments presented by Islamic economists, I have come to the conclusion that to the extent they have a point, it relates more to the structure of what could be regarded as an Islamic economy rather than the discipline of economics as such. As far as I can see, it would have been much better for the exponents of Islamic economics to focus on the former, that is to say, on the subject of Islamic economy, or for that matter Islamic economic system, for such an economy may well be quite different from any other in a number of important respects. Much confusion arises when economics is not distinguished from an economic system. It is interesting to note that a number of sympathizers of Islamic economics, on a closer look, turn out to equate it to an argument for a distinct form of Islamic economy rather than reading it as new economic paradigm, as its exponents would have it. There is no doubt that economics as a discipline of study draws its *raison d'être* from its applicability to an economy, yet there are advantages in keeping the theory separate from practice, for practice can always fall short of the underlying theory. Though in principle it is possible that the economics of an Islamic economy may differ from conventional economics, the explorations in the following pages show that there is no compulsion for it to be so in light of the original sources of Islamic values, namely the Qurʾān and *Sunna*. Indeed, most of the premises on the basis of which the so called Islamic economics is supposed to represent a new paradigm are either the middle period *fiqh* developments or the result of modernist articulations based on *ijtihād* (Islamic legal interpretation) by its exponents. These articulations often represent unwarranted extrapolations to which the original sources do not lend explicit support.

The writings on Islamic economics can be split into two distinct though related strands: First, following the Qurʾānic sanction against *ribā*, one strand of writings explores the various Islamic financing alternatives to interest on the presumption that interest is precisely the same thing as *ribā*. Some of these alternatives are based on the idea of variable returns on capital—and therefore stipulate some sort of profit sharing arrangements—while others, in sharp contrast allow fixed returns to capital that are supposed to be compatible with Islamic *Sharīʿa*. It is this strand of writings that, understandably, provided the initial impetus to the venture of Islamic economics. The task of constructing a financial system without the institution of interest could not possibly be considered a mean one, had it been what the Islamic economists were content to do. After all, it would amount to eliminating a system that had evolved over a period of several centuries, and is so well entrenched that dislodging it seems inconceivable to most concerned professionals. Such a task would have required building the relevant institutions, developing the attendant structure of property rights, along with an obvious attention to updating the modes of financing available in the *fiqh* literature in view of modern conditions. It is not difficult to see that a plethora of issues would need to be sorted out, pointing to an arduous journey for those attempting the task. Yet that is not what the Islamic economists chose to do. As though this would be well below their intellectual dignity, they vastly expanded the scope of their discourse by taking on the entire edifice of the "degenerate" economics in an attempt to "reform" it in the light of what they thought was necessarily a different set of values, the values espoused by Islam.

While one can easily discern that this expansion of the scope was primarily motivated by a profound mistrust of, and therefore a desire to reject, the capitalist system, it is equally true that Islamic economists did not confine their attack to just the capitalist institutions. We observe them launching an all out assault, though a less than careful one, as it turns out, on more or less everything in conventional economics barring certain elements of the analytical toolkit that were to be reluctantly spared the chop in absence of any alternative offerings. As far as they were concerned, there was no difference between the capitalist economic system and economics. Nothing of the conventional economics was *de facto* acceptable, for nothing in it was supposed to conform to their perceived value system. What draws our specific attention, though, is a two-pronged attack that goes directly to the roots of the whole economic analysis. One prong of this attack attempts to take care of the Pareto criterion, and thereby tries to dismantle the entire basis of the focus on economic efficiency, and thus the theoretical foundations of much of economic policy; the second centers on the irrelevance of the assumptions of the benchmark model of economic analysis, namely the perfectly competitive model, and from there moves on to discredit the central place of competition in the ideology of the market system. Both Pareto and Smith must be eradicated from the new paradigm.

No doubt both of these assaults exploit the well-known weakness of capitalism, that is to say its inability to insure what would be generally acceptable as an equitable distribution of income. Thereupon, Islamic economics hastily proceeds to indict conventional economics for this sociopolitical failing as though the blame for it could be squarely laid at the door of an academic discipline. When it charges economics with not paying sufficient attention to this important issue, the charge turns out to be patently uncalled for, for economics has treated the distributional issues in all earnestness. So much so that some of the best minds in the discipline have devoted their energies to this rather intractable problem—intractable because of its normative nature, not to mention the breadth and depth of the vast cornucopia of writings on the issue. Islamic economists then proceed to offer as an alternative their own version of the criteria that would be in accord with the value system of Islam. An overwhelming feature of the alternative offered is its more or less exclusive focus on the issue of equity to the total neglect of the efficiency considerations; thus it is not the size of the pie that is of any concern but only the way it is distributed. Once that perspective is advanced as the legitimate Islamic one, the fundamental concern of welfare economics, centering on the conflict between efficiency and equity, can be easily cast aside as irrelevant. Indeed, the way this issue is dealt with raises even deeper concerns, for often it is not even pointed out that such a conflict exists. The unwary reader—for not all students of economics, and particularly of Islamic economics, are quite well versed in the subject—is quite likely to get a distorted picture of the relevant issues. Beyond that, not much attention is paid to the internal consistency among the various elements of the set offered as an alternative. These issues are discussed in detail in the next chapter in order to assess whether the alternative offered could discharge the task entrusted to it.

Things would have been much simpler for the proponents of the new paradigm had matters come to rest there, for then it would be a matter of removing the internal inconsistencies of the set, inconsistencies that would be encountered in any initial articulation of a new position, and as such could be overlooked as the usual teething problems. With the passage of time, those difficulties would be expected to be resolved, thus firmly establishing the new paradigm, provided its roots were firmly implanted in the original fonts of Islamic values. But when we explore this latter issue, we run into a serious difficulty: Upon a closer examination, it turns out that what is being offered as *the* Islamic position is rather an interpretation of the value system of Islam—an *ijtihād* effort of sorts—which, incoherence apart, turns out to be less than warranted. This issue is more fully explored in Chapter 5.

All in all, our inquiry there shows that what is made to appear like the Islamic position in these writings turns out to be either pure and simple rhetoric, or a less than cogent representation of some of the strands of thought in the literature of conventional economics, the ones that seem to address the discontent with capitalism felt by the exponents of Islamic economics. But before we reach that stage of the argument (i.e. Chapter 5), a number of related issues need to be sorted out, issues about which the new paradigm has created enormous amount of unnecessary confusion for a student of Islam and economics, or should we say of Islamic economy.

To begin with, the discontent with the conventional paradigm led, perhaps unwittingly, to another serious consequence. The rejection of capitalism quickly became a rejection of the market system, and this because capitalism was unequivocally equated to the market system. One would admit that a part of the blame for this confusion must be apportioned to economics, for economics has conventionally not thought it necessary to explicate a distinction between capitalism and market economy. Once the Islamic economists thought it necessary to discredit the market mechanism, if not totally discard it, the vacuum so created needed to be filled: it was then filled by either an overwhelming reliance on government for performing every conceivable economic function, or an appeal to a conceptualization of man as *homo Islamicus*, a human agent par excellence, who is supposed to be "perfectly imbued" with the values of Islam. Often both of these perspectives are used as complementary to each other—as two cogs in the same wheel—without any attention to the contradictions involved in this conceptualization. Once we postulate the existence of homo Islamicus, not much is left of what economics conceives as an economic role of government. On the other hand, when reliance is placed on the government, the striking thing is that the contours of the underlying Islamic state, and its form of government, are hardly ever articulated; an ideal Islamic state and the attendant government are presumed to be already in place. As far as the practical implications drawn from the existence of such a state are concerned, one is hard pressed to differentiate them from what would obtain under a socialistic system. In their zeal to advance this hypothesis—of an all-pervading state—as a fundamental ingredient of an Islamic economy, some of the writers do not even feel it necessary to draw a distinction between the state and economy. For them, an Islamic economy is simply an extension of the Islamic state. On a closer look, each of these solutions, working complementarily or otherwise, not only exhibits internal contradictions and inconsistencies but also fails to establish a firm connection with a set of relevant values that emerges out of the original sources of Islam. In view of the relevance of this issue to the subject matter of Chapter 2, I shall delve a little further into it at this stage instead of postponing its coverage to Chapter 5.

Consider the appeal to the idea of "homo Islamicus," which is set in sharp contrast to "homo economicus." Whereas the social behavior of the latter is assumed to be regulated by nothing less than greed, the behavior of the former is supposed to be in total conformity with the moral norms set by Islam, someone who is totally God-fearing, and therefore a social agent *par excellence*. One could hardly resist translating this vision of homo-Islamicus as an economic agent characterized by perfect responsibility. If the assumption of a perfect competition seems troubling to Islamic economists, as it does (their rejection of the market mechanism is not a qualified one—but more on this a little later), the assumption of perfect responsibility may be equally problematic. To lay stress on individual responsibility is one thing, to assume perfect individual responsibility is quite another matter. There is no question that an Islamic social order, including the economic one, has to be predicated on the doctrine of individual responsibility—as indeed all revealed moral systems are—for it is obliged to be if the idea of free will is to have any eschatological significance. To stretch the doctrine of individual responsibility to the limits by assuming that all economic agents would behave in *total* conformity with the Divinely ordained moral imperatives goes contrary to the Divine plan as enunciated in the Qur'ān. Since free will is corruptible, some souls are bound to fall prey to it—indeed, a very large number, according to the Qur'ān—and thus the assumption of total conformity is untenable. In the Divine plan of human existence, humanity is destined to live, if it may be expressed thus, in the shades of gray rather than in black or white; and this without, in any way, belittling the import of that fundamental Divine commandment, namely the endeavor to achieve as much of the white as possible. It is only in the choices represented by the various shades, indeed an inexhaustible continuum, of gray that economics becomes relevant and important. The purity of white and the utter bleakness of black render the question of such choices meaningless. The vision of perfect responsibility could serve as an ideal, but the puritan's "ideal or nothing" approach fails to recognize that ideals are not meant to stifle the ground reality but to serve as a source of inspiration. They are meant to be vigorously pursued—to be as closely approximated as possible—even as they are never fully attainable. The moment one admits less than perfect responsibility—even in one economic agent, let alone in large numbers—the distinction between homo Islamicus and homo economicus becomes irrelevant for all *practical* (social) purposes. One fish can spoil the whole pond.

If that sounds like an unwarranted assertion, let us approach this issue from a slightly different perspective by asking what exactly it is that is offensive in homo ecomomicus from the Islamic point of view. It would be asserted that the behavior of homo economicus is too self-centered, too selfish. In short he is given to an *unbridled* pursuit of pleasure (utility and profit maximization, in the technical parlance of economics). This charge is unfounded not only because it is not what economics assumes—what it assumes is self-interested behavior, and self-interested behavior is not *necessarily* selfish behavior (although, no doubt, these two terms are, at times, carelessly equated in the economic literature)—but for another related reason: any unbridled behavior, be it in pursuit of pleasure or whatever, is tantamount to anarchy that no society—built, as it necessarily must be, on a social contract—can endure for very long.[2] Individual behavior in any society is circumscribed by that society's social contract, be that in the form of its formal legal corpus or, even prior to that, its religio-cultural norms. The fine details of this social contract can vary from society to society. An Islamic society would have its own legal corpus (based upon *Sharīʿa*), and its own religio-cultural norms. It is these that delineate the boundaries of individual behavior. Once these boundaries are defined, the individual is free to exercise his free will within those boundaries regardless of whether we call him homo Islamicus or homo economicus.

At any rate, the appeal to homo Islamicus is not made in recognition of some governmental failure—that question never comes up for discussion—and therefore, it is perforce made in spite of no such failure. It is seldom, if ever, realized that if one had the kind of government that is presumed to exist, it would not matter one way or another whether one had to deal with homo this or homo that, and if, on

[2] I have used the term 'social contract' in the strictly Hobbesian sense of underscoring the need for order, or to avoid his 'war of all against all', but without in any sense implying the existence of a particular form of government.

the other hand, one assumed the human agent to be homo Islamicus, one would not need a government to do all those things that Islamic economists want it to do anyway. This circularity in the logic is pushed to the limits by a hard core of Islamic economists who assign the government an explicit responsibility of *daʿwa* (evangelism, if you will) to convert the non believer, or waiverer, that the homo economicus happens to be to the cause of homo Islamicus, without expounding the underlying political theory—a theory that must explain how such a government will come into being in the first place. In the black and white world of this hard core, if we assume all human agents to be homo economicus, the only possibility of such a government ever coming into existence is in the form of some foreign implant (such a course of action will not be objectionable to the exponents of Islamic economics, indeed reading between the lines suggests that they would be happy to fill the spot themselves). On the other hand, if we assume all human beings to be homo Islamicus, there is no need of *daʿwa* to begin with. And if we assume that there are both varieties of homo in the society at any given time, then the inescapable first question centers on the institutional form of the Islamic government, and assuming that question is answered satisfactorily, the government will be liable to discharge any responsibilities assigned to it, be it *daʿwa* or whatever. But in the economy of things, one would wish to keep the *daʿwa* function quite separate from the economic functions of the government. What, however, is inescapable in the final analysis is the fact that if that government is to emerge out of the indigenous soil, rather than being a foreign implant, it is bound to reflect the underlying convictions, the values, held by that society.

Once that is granted, we can look at the idea of reliance on the state for performing all sorts of economic functions somewhat more closely. The rejection of the market mechanism argument is buttressed by pointing out that the assumptions of the "perfectly competitive" model are not realistic, and therefore the model is not applicable in real life. The fact that the perfectly competitive model, even when it is unrealistic, serves as a benchmark, a background against which the outcomes obtained in the other market forms are compared and contrasted, is simply ignored. More seriously, the role of prices as signals for allocation of resources is hardly ever recognized. Consequently, in absence of price signals, the corresponding allocation function is entrusted to the government. This blind trust is, at best, misplaced. There is no appreciation of the fact that markets, as long as, and to the extent, they are subject to the price-taking behavior, are necessarily *impersonal* in nature. Yes, granted that they may, at times, lead to what one may regard as unacceptable outcomes, and while arguably one may call such outcomes cruel, these could not be deemed as unjust. And nobody needs to be blind to the fact that governments can be, as they often are, equally, if not more, cruel. And this time the cruelty may well amount to "injustice"—injustice because it may well be the result of the play of the *free will* of government functionaries who invariably are entrusted with some discretionary power. An impersonal system can hardly be unjust in the sense that injustice necessarily involves a personal dimension connected to the play of free will. A system that perpetrates personal, in contrast to impersonal, cruelty, even when not explicitly condoning it, is necessarily unjust, but an outcome which may be deemed as cruel may not necessarily be unjust. Nobody deems the vagaries of elements as unjust. As a matter of fact, the administration of justice in itself may be deemed cruel by someone repulsed by the severity of a particular punishment. This distinction has important implications as will be seen later. Here we need only to note that the rejection of a primarily, if not wholly, impersonal system in favor of one that inherently involves a personal dimension may well not, as is likely if the evidence of history is anything to go by, deliver the goods its proponents confidently presume it will. One almost gets the feeling that the fire ignited by Islamic economists creates some heat, a lot more smoke, but hardly any light. Confusion abounds.

It is by no means easy for a student of Islam, particularly one who has some interest in the economic system of Islam, to find a way through this confusion. One would think that in light of the value system of Islam, the Islamic economists would stress the significance of the institutional economics, and put the issue of property rights squarely at center stage of their discourse. Alas, nothing of the sort is in sight in these writings except for a haphazard attempt at establishing a connection of *fiqh* with economics, and even that without any reference to the rich recent literature on the subject of property rights. To my mind, the way to clear the smoke is to follow this approach. This I have done in Chapter 3, which begins with a clean slate to define what an economic system is supposed to be. It focuses on the minimum set of characteristics that would define an economic system. Once that is done, it then goes into the institutional set-up needed to render an economic system a market system. There, while the exposition revolves around the characteristics of a market system, the primary focus is to clarify that while positive economics could by and large be labeled as value-free, an economic system could hardly ever be so. The well-known debate as to whether economics is value-free (i.e. objective, and therefore positive) is at best sterile, in the sense that economics becomes relevant only when there exists an economy. And an economy is primarily characterized by a set of institutions that help a society organize and regulate its economic relations, and these institutions could hardly fail to reflect the value system subscribed to by the society. An economic system that is based on these institutions is bound to be value-loaded, and since capitalism is an economic system, though a form of market system, it reflects the underlying values held by the society. In light of this, it would be natural to ask what gives a market economy that distinctive hue which transforms it into capitalism. The answer to this question must focus on those additional institutions, and therefore the attendant structure of property rights, that would convert the market economy of Chapter 3 into that specific form that has come to be known as capitalism. I have explored this question in Chapter 4 on the assumption that once this is done, the student of Islamic economy would be in a much better position to appreciate the similarities and differences between capitalism and what he would then be able to recognize as an Islamic economy.

All we need to note at this juncture is that an economic system that primarily relies on price signals (primarily, but not exclusively, since the market mechanism has its own well-known failings), for both allocation and distribution purposes—as any economic system that sanctions the institution of private property must—will essentially be a market system, but not necessarily capitalism. And to the extent its institutions and the structure of property rights conform to the 'Islamic' norms, the economy could be characterized as an 'Islamic economy' regardless of whether it is labeled as such or not. What, however, must also be noted is that in this economy, the extent to which issues such as externalities, public goods, efficiency, economic growth, inflation—to mention only a few—are considered relevant, as they must be, the existing paradigm of economics as we know it today, will remain equally relevant. The premise that an Islamic economy is necessarily a market economy is substantiated in Chapters 6 and 7, following the exposition of the fundamental axioms of such an economy in Chapter 5. What the exposition of these chapters strikingly brings forth is that the attack on the market mechanism launched by the Islamic economists is not very sure-footed, finding no echo whatsoever in historical Islam. Unable to muster any support from the classical Islamic literature, the detractors of market mechanism find themselves sailing totally uncharted waters. A rejection of the market mechanism is something the classical Islamic literature hardly ever contemplates, let alone proposes, except for a possibility of intervention in cases of monopoly power. The institution of market was condoned by the Prophet (upon whom be peace and blessings, *always*) when he refused the request, on a number of occasions, to intervene in the market when certain prices were thought to be too high adding that it all comes from God, thus underscoring the impersonal nature of the market mechanism. The primary focus of exposition in Chapters 6 and 7 is to clarify the role of competition and price signals in an Islamic economy, and a critical evaluation of the position taken by the Islamic economists on these subjects. The presumption is that once the Islamic position on these fundamental issues is made clear, since that is where most of the confusion resides, the remaining issues can benefit from the rich and varied economic literature on those subjects. I have, however, felt that the issue of factor pricing needs an explicit treatment in light of a great deal of focus on it in Islamic economics. This I have done in Chapter 8.

Before moving on to the specific issue of *ribā*, the perspective of those who wish to see Islamic economics as a new paradigm can be summed up as the following: anxious to disown what they consider to be an alien system, they end up disowning economics, as though economics, as it were, could be held responsible for the crimes committed in its name. A large majority of these may actually subscribe to this notion simply because they fail to draw a distinction between economics and an economic system and thus the detractors of a particular form of economic system—capitalism—quickly become detractors of economics. For the puritans among them, economics must undergo a paradigm shift for it to become Islamized. In this new garb, economics becomes nothing more or nothing less than another platform of *daʿwa* for the conversion of the unbelievers, with the obvious implication that once the conversion is complete, economics will cease to be meaningful any more—no economic problem will be able to survive this transition.[3] This will usher in the golden age, and thus one would reach Fukuyama's "End of History"—via a slightly different route.

---

[3] To avoid any misunderstanding, let it be said that I am not by any means belittling

One can easily understand that exploring the implications of the prohibition of *ribā* would naturally form an important, perhaps the most important, dimension of the endeavor of Islamic economists. This would obviously require a precise definition of the term *ribā*. Islamic economists, from the word go, have proceeded on the assumption that *ribā* was precisely the same thing as interest. This presumed equality has not turned out to be trouble free, as the proceedings in the Supreme Court of Pakistan on the subject in the recent past amply attest to. Part of the problem, *but only a part*, relates to the alternatives to interest proposed by the Islamic economists that more or less resemble interest, in all but name. Although these alternatives come from the classical writings on *fiqh*, most of them do not have any explicit roots in the original sources of Islam, namely the Qur'ān, and *ḥadīth*. In other words, these were the alternatives accepted by different *fuqahā'* that then became part of the *fiqh* literature, commonly referred to as Islamic *Sharī'a*. And while a large part of the effort of the Islamic economists, at least in terms of the volume of literature produced, has quite understandably gone into this subject, nevertheless it has not as yet produced a coherent and satisfactory outline of the Islamic financial system.

This effort, naturally, begins by going back to the roots, to the classical writings on the subject, mostly translating these writings into the vernaculars of modern discourse, primarily English, collating this material from diverse sources, and identifying the various positions taken by the *fuqahā'* on different financing arrangements prevalent at the time of those writings. While there may be slight differences in the technical terms used by different schools of *fiqh*, the main financing arrangements include *muḍāraba, mushāraka, murābaḥa, bay' mu'ajjal, bay' salam*, and *ijāra*. Since these were all permissible contractual arrangements, the focus in the classical writings was on the legal stipulations inherent in these contracts. Though a reader gets fairly detailed information on the structure of property rights associated with these contracts, there is no discussion with regard to a unifying principle common to all these arrangements. In absence of the unifying principle, the knowledge of the legal strictures that once

the significance of *da'wa*; though it must be noted that as things stand, it has come to mean sermonizing more than anything else: words have come to speak louder than actions and deeds.

prevailed is quite obviously of limited relevance in the changed times and circumstances. Those societies were primarily trading societies. Whatever manufacturing activity did occur had a simple production and organizational structure not unlike agriculture. Thus the contractual arrangements that are readily available in those classical writings are inapplicable to most modern business practices, both manufacturing and trading, without a serious rethinking of the fundamental principles that underpin those legal stipulations, and then applying the principles derived to formulate contractual arrangements that satisfy the demands of current enterprise. Those who are engaged in this effort have not paid much attention to this fundamental point, and have strived more at a ready application of the aforementioned classical contracts to modern business organization. Such efforts, while admittedly leading to instances of success in odd and restricted cases, raise more questions than they answer, leaving a bad taste in the mouths of serious students, quite apart from creating confusion in the minds of uninitiated readers.

One instance of the kind of difficulties one faces when reading this literature relates to how the term *ribā* is defined. Is it to be defined with reference to *bayʿ* (sale) transactions—as the traditional *fiqh* writers down to the present have done, or is it to be defined with reference to loan contracts—as the Islamic economists do. If it is defined as any increase in the amount of loan, the first thing that would then be required would be to precisely define what a loan is. Is it the same thing as *qarḍ*, and if yes, what is the difference between *qarḍ* and *qarḍ ḥasan*, or is *qarḍ* equivalent to another Qurʾānic term, *dayn*? And regardless of what the answer is, what is the relationship, or interrelationship between these terms? Another class of issues is related to the possibility of all of the foregoing being in either nominal terms (i.e. in the form of money) or in real terms (i.e. on the basis of real assets). One can hardly turn to the classical writings to find an answer to this question for at the time the classical writers expounded these issues, no meaningful distinction could be made between the real and monetary variables in that era of commodity money. The complexity attendant upon the introduction of paper money cannot be simply wished away as the Islamic economists are wont to do. Introduction of paper money adds an entirely new dimension to the whole range of such issues that requires a careful consideration before any meaningful generalizations, or principles, can be derived from what turns out to be writings that belong to the middle period of *fiqh* development. In the final analysis, the contradictions in the writings on the subject of alternatives to interest cannot be resolved until there is clarity on the issue of *ribā*.

In other words, the issues raised by the alternative modes of financing cannot be resolved until one is clear about the meaning of the Qurʾānic term *ribā*. The blanket tendency in the writings on Islamic economics, following upon the recent writings of some influential *fiqh* scholars, to equate it to interest, turns out to be much less cut and dried than it is made out to be. Indeed the closer one looks at the classical writings on the subject, the more one gets the feeling that these writers have not done justice to it. The issue of *ribā* turns out to be much more complicated than is ordinarily believed by both lay and well-informed readers, even those who profess to be Islamic economists. The major complications relate to the seemingly irreconcilable interpretations of *ribā al-ḥadīth* and the *ribā al-jāhiliyya* (or the Qurʾānic *ribā*), the contradictory evidence with regard to the timing of the prohibition of *ribā*, and the attendant issue of whether or not the Qurʾān provides a legal definition of the term, and finally the rationale behind the prohibition. Undoubtedly, these issues require very careful attention to details about historical narratives that are not devoid of contradictions. Chapter 9 attempts to present a coherent account of these issues, and in the light of the evidence presented, evidence that comes from the classical works on Qurʾānic exegesis, arrives at a definition of the term that, while retaining a connection with interest in so far as it may give rise to what the Qurʾān calls *ʿaḍʿāfan muḍāʿafa* yet is quite different from its straightforward equality with interest that the influential group of *fiqh* writers insists upon.

It so happened that *fiqh* from the very beginning focused on *ribā al-ḥadīth* to provide a legal definition of *ribā* on the assumption that the Qurʾān did not provide a workable definition, and that the term was therefore ambiguous and thus needed an interpretation through *ijtihād*. The exploration in Chapter 9 and particularly Chapter 10 shows that the *fiqh* position that emerged in the due course of time, spanning a period of several centuries, not only disregarded very important Qurʾānic imperatives on the issue, but also ended up needlessly extrapolating the meanings of some of the phrases that occurred in the relevant *ḥadīth* reports. This, in turn, was done on the presumption that the *ḥadīth* perspective had a greater degree of clarity besides being more comprehensive. And by virtue of its being broader, it must form the starting point of providing a legal definition of *ribā*. This course of action led to ever-increasing complications with the passage of time; for once the correspondence between the Qur'ānic and *ḥadīth* perspective was broken, it could not be easily re-established. This raises an obvious question as to why *fiqh* took this position. This question is taken up in Chapter 10 and a number of factors are identified that might have contributed to perpetuating the progression of *fiqh* on a path that could not be easily reconciled to the Qur'ānic perspective on the issue—a perspective that was faithfully adhered to by the classical works on exegesis. We will also see that in the complex and confusing picture that emerged over the centuries, the fundamental Qur'ānic imperative, that is the imperative of justness in the corresponding social dealings was side-tracked. On the whole, this exploration shows that the original *fiqh* response represented a somewhat simple solution to a complex problem. We will also see that while the traditional *fiqh* scholars have stuck to the original position down to the present, the dominant group of *fiqh* scholars has not remained faithful to that position. For one, it contradicts the traditional position by asserting that Qur'ān provides a clear definition of the term, but then circumvents the difficulties faced by the classical writers by totally ignoring the Qur'ānic term *ʿaḍʿāfan muḍāʿafa*, as we will see in that chapter. Yet, while this group discards the classical methodology of defining *ribā*, it finds it difficult to shed the weight of history—or should we say *fiqh* literature—in so far as it keeps all other elements of the classical discourse intact, including a neglect of the issue of injustice implied by *ribā* transactions. As a result, what is presented as the true interpretation of *ribā* in the context of contemporary reality—a reality that has changed in several significant ways, particularly relating to institutionalized credit, from the historical one in which *fiqh*'s position was articulated—makes this new articulation not only simple but rather simplistic.

The discussion in Chapter 10 also focuses on what is represented as the alternative modes of financing by the Islamic economists. Specific attention is paid to the historic origins of these alternative modes. From that perspective, two modes of financing draw our specific attention, the modes the origins of which can be traced back to the Prophetic times: *salam* and *qirāḍ*, although admittedly the latter term may have evolved in the post-Prophetic period. We will see that *salam* is the precursor of what has now come to be known as *bayʿ muʿajjal*, and *qirāḍ* the precursor of what subsequently became *muḍāraba*. We will note that *salam*, or the complications arising out of its unequivocal permissibility, played a crucial role in the evolution of *fiqh* position on *ribā*. As far as *muḍāraba*, the star of modern Islamic finance, is concerned, we will observe that the *fiqh* position on it did not remain faithful to its precursor, the *qirāḍ*. And we will see that this lack of faithfulness, again, was the result of the specific course of interpretation of *ribā* that *fiqh* had embarked upon from the very beginning of its evolution in the eighth century. As a result of the inquiry in Chapters 9 and 10, we come to the conclusion that any consistent interpretation of the prohibition of *ribā* cannot be divorced from the fundamental Qur'ānic imperative of justness in the dealings that involve an intertemporal dimension, in exactly the same way that justness forms the foundation for all social dealings (*mu'amalāt*, in the language of *fiqh*) in the value system of Islam. As such, the prohibition of *ribā* cannot be understood without referring to the Qur'ānic term *'aḍ'āfan muḍā'afa*. Once that connection is established, surprisingly most of the difficulties in the interpretation of *ribā* disappear, and all the apparent contradictions between the various Islamic modes of financing become irrelevant.

In the light of what has gone before, the concluding chapter, Chapter 11, poses the obvious question: how far would an Islamic economy differ from other economies, particularly those that are reviled by Islamic economists as the capitalistic ones? Our exposition in the earlier chapters, beginning with Chapter 5, leads to the inescapable conclusion that an Islamic economy is fundamentally a market economy. In that sense, an Islamic economy would resemble capitalist economies, for these are also market economies. But then how far it would depart from those economies depends on the additional institutions that render a market economy capitalist, as shown in Chapter 4. Since the existing capitalist economies are not monolithic with regard to those additional features, and since different Islamic economies may by themselves not turn out to be monolithic, the differences between the two forms may ultimately become just a matter of degree. Indeed, it is possible that they may exhibit a greater degree of diversity among themselves than their differences from the capitalist economies as a group.

When all is said and done, no economy can fail to reflect the underlying values held by the society in which it operates. If Islamic values are significantly different from the values held by the capitalist economies, as is believed by the proponents of Islamic economics, such differences must be reflected in the structure of property rights and the institutions of Islamic economies. And the most important institution in any economy happens to be the institution of government. Governments, however, can be tyrannical, especially if there are no checks and balances on the exercise of their executive power. If there is one power that can stifle the values held by a society, it is that of the government, and the evidence on that score is not very encouraging throughout the Islamic realm. Thus it is that we invariably return to that fundamental unanswered question, a question never touched by the proponents of the new paradigm, and the one that recurs throughout this book: what would be the political system and thus the institutional form of the government of an Islamic society?

CHAPTER TWO

FUNDAMENTAL AXIOMS OF ECONOMICS

Introduction

An important, perhaps the most important, task the new paradigm set for itself was to undermine the foundations of economics. These foundations rest on the twin concepts of equity and efficiency, and a crucial element of economic analysis is the tension between these two, for often a conflict arises between a simultaneous achievement of the objectives relating to them. Such conflicts cannot be resolved without an appeal to the values (norms) upheld by the society. Indeed those concepts cannot even be defined without a reference and appeal to those norms. That any pronouncement regarding equity requires a value judgment is well understood by even those who have barely an elementary training in economics. What is, however, not commonly understood is that even the concept of efficiency requires a criterion if it is to proceed beyond an empty conceptualization to become an operative principle. This requires a value judgment. In economics, this value judgment is incorporated in a criterion—the Pareto criterion—that has come to command such a universal acceptance, at least in the home turf of economic thought, that often one is not even aware of its presence in the backdrop of economic discourse. That universal acceptance became a unifying principle that led to the growth of a vast yet coherent body of economic literature over time. Away from the home turf of economics, in the territory of the new paradigm, a vocal majority of its proponents insist that Pareto is quite irrelevant as per the norms that must prevail in that territory, or should we say in an Islamic society. Their hope was that once the Pareto criterion is dismantled, it will perforce establish the paradigm they propose as its rightful alternative. This, at the very least, obliges us to toss the Pareto criterion up in the air to see whether it can land safely, and find a place for itself in this landscape supposedly quite alien to its spirit. This I intend to do in Chapter 5, which focuses on the fundamental axioms of an Islamic economy once the requisite groundwork has been laid in the intervening chapters. Here, I confine myself to a somewhat sharper focus but only on what those Islamic economists have to say about Pareto criterion, and a brief but critical assessment of what is offered as its replacement in the new paradigm. Even this limited task requires some spadework, a spadework whose contours—and I urge the reader to take a note of this—are essentially determined by numerous misrepresentations of welfare economics (though primarily relating to its second fundamental theorem) by the Islamic economists. I felt that not all elements of this warranted an explicit treatment in the formal assessment that concludes this chapter, but which nevertheless, it is hoped, will make it easier for a reader, who at some stage may visit that literature, to better appreciate the nuances of what is said there.

The Present Offerings

While economics could be defined in a variety of ways, and indeed there may be as many definitions as writers, all definitions ultimately focus on the twin concepts of efficiency and equity. Efficiency relates to the allocation of a society's scarce resources to the production of various goods and services, as equity relates to the distribution of those goods and services among its citizens. Economics, no doubt, by necessity had to focus on the social organization, or should we say the institutional mechanisms, which are put in place to discharge these twin functions, namely the allocation and distribution functions. Market mechanism represents an array of such institutional arrangements where prices serve as signals to both the producers and consumers, to the effect that resources are allocated to the production of various goods and services that a society demands, and subsequently rationed back to various members of that society in light of their individual preferences, preferences that formed the basis of the allocation of resources in the first place. But once the market mechanism, or for that matter any other alternative array of institutions that is meant to discharge these twin functions, is assumed to exist, the concern of economics shifts to efficiency and equity of the resultant outcome, and thereby also to any inter-relationship between these two with regard to the outcome. It shifts to efficiency because once a given amount of resources is available to a society, that society is *bound* to allocate these resources one way or the other. Struggle for survival obliges it to do so. There is nothing peculiar in that for homo sapiens; even the lesser species of animals do the same, that is, they allocate their labor (i.e. their time), the only resource at their disposal, to various activities such as gathering food, playing, tending to their offspring, resting, etc. The real question, the one that makes economics interesting, and indeed a distinct discipline in its own right, is firstly whether or not those resources are allocated efficiently, and secondly, whether the resulting distribution of income satisfies the society's sensibilities with regard to what it considers equitable.

From the efficiency viewpoint, the real question boils down to whether a society ends up doing the best it can within the constraints imposed by its resource endowment. But what ought to be the criterion of efficiency, or "doing the best"? This question led Wilfredo Pareto, towards the end of the nineteenth century, to develop a utilitarian criterion, called, after him the Pareto criterion, according to which an economic outcome is not efficient if someone in the society *could* be made better off without at the same time making someone else worse off. Pareto's idea was not only very simple but also seemingly very potent. No one would have any qualms with the Pareto criterion if and when it could be implemented as such. But that is where the trouble lay, for Pareto's idea was as simple as it was irrelevant in practice; most economic situations do not lend themselves to its ready applicability. Rarely does a situation arise where a change makes someone better off without at the same time making someone else worse off. Most of the time one encounters situations where when one person, or group, is made better off, it happens at the expense of another person, or a group. This can happen either because the relevant utility functions may be interdependent, or the relevant outcomes may be interdependent in the sense that the lot of one party could not be changed without at the same time changing the lot of the other. In all such situations, the Pareto criterion, as such, had not much to say. It goes to the credit of all those souls who struggled to lend relevance to Pareto by coping with the difficult subject of interpersonal comparisons that were inescapable if the criterion were to become an operative principle in economics. It took economics more or less the first half of the twentieth century to sort out these two issues, i.e. interdependent utility functions and interpersonal comparisons of utility. Reading Islamic economics, one gets the impression that these efforts are either ignored or not appreciated. It is hoped that what follows in this chapter will provide a clearer picture of the relevant issues and a better understanding of what the new paradigm offers as an alternative.

The Italian Recipe and Occidental Cuisine

Economics, quite fruitfully, split the concept of efficiency into two distinct categories: technical efficiency, and allocative efficiency. Technical (or productive) efficiency is used in economics to highlight engineering efficiency in production. This is to rule out any wastage of valuable resources. Technical efficiency in production would obtain, according to the Pareto criterion, when maximum output is produced from some given amount of resources, or alternatively when a given output is produced at the lowest possible cost, i.e. by using the minimum possible quantities of various required resources. Consider the following scenario: producing a larger output from given amount of resources by satisfying the dictates of technical efficiency, when these were not previously satisfied, would represent a Pareto improvement. It would make at least one person better off without making anyone else worse off, and this according to self-assessment of the relevant economic agents, where better off and worse off are adjudged on the basis of their respective utility levels. But this will be true only if there was no interdependence between the utility functions of the individuals concerned. When we introduce this complication, the Pareto criterion becomes irrelevant, and if it becomes irrelevant in such an innocuous case, it is bound to become so in more complex situations. The point is that all such cases would give rise to the same analytical difficulty that would need to be tackled if Pareto were to become relevant to economics. But let us continue with the so-called innocuous case.

When a higher quantity of even one good becomes available as a result of satisfying technical efficiency conditions, *ceteris paribus*, the society as a whole is supposed to be better off than before, because some individual/s could be made better off without making anyone else worse off. The whole argument hinges on the validity of the *ceteris paribus* assumption. When that assumption becomes inherently unrealistic, as would happen in the case of interdependent utility functions, or the interdependence between the quantities accruing to various individuals as a result of some change, the straightforward application of the Pareto criterion becomes, at the very least, problematic. Obviously, in the case of independent utility functions, one person could be made better off without making someone else worse off as adjudged on the basis of the quantities of the goods and services available to them. But what if there are feelings of jealousy, envy or, for that matter, altruism among the individuals involved? Of these cases, ignoring altruistic behavior leads to the serious charge that economics assumes human behavior to be too self-centered, indeed selfish. The interdependence of the utility functions would imply that gains would necessarily be accompanied by losses. The same problem crops up when a change in the quantities of various goods and services accruing to one individual cannot occur without at the same time causing a change in the quantities available to others, earlier referred to as a situation where two economic states are interdependent. It may be fruitful to keep in mind that the concerned changes may be either policy induced or the result of the working of the market mechanism—a point that will recur a number of times in what follows in this chapter. Every relative price change, regardless of its origins, changes the distribution of income thereby giving rise to gains and losses. The Pareto criterion would now require a modification where these gains and losses must somehow be compared to arrive at any conclusion with regard to the superiority or otherwise of the new state as compared to the old. We will turn to that question a little later.

The problem of interdependent utility functions often gives rise to the following misunderstanding: since economic theory generally proceeds with the analytics of optimization—utility maximization, for instance—under the assumption of independent utility functions, this creates the impression, as it does in Islamic economics, that such an analysis is irrelevant to the extent that the assumption of independent utility functions is unrealistic. That conclusion, however, requires a closer scrutiny. In principle, utility maximization can proceed under the assumption of interdependent utility functions provided the relevant functions are specified in goods rather than utility space. Calculus of optimization requires an objective quantification, which would not be possible in the case of a subjective measure that utility happens to be. Once that is done, the implications of the interdependent utility functions are not difficult to deduce. For instance, in the context of altruism, this would mean that the concerned individual's utility is not only a function of his/her own consumption of different goods and services but also those of one or more of other individuals, in which case his utility maximization behavior would imply that he would be willing to contribute some positive quantities of goods to the other individuals' consumption. The first order conditions would then determine his optimal amount of what could be regarded as charity. Conversely, in the case of envy, the other individuals' consumption levels would be negative arguments in the utility function of the concerned individual, implying that he would be willing to pay (sacrifice some consumption of his own) to effect a reduction in their levels of consumption. All this could be considered as a matter of personal tastes (a catch-all in consumer theory), and the positive economic theory could proceed with its Marshallian analysis of market equilibrium, recognizing that whenever these feelings come into play, the equilibrium position would change through a shift in the corresponding demand curves. If the literature, nevertheless, makes the assumption of independent utility functions, it does so more for the sake of convenience rather than as a matter of conviction. What is more important, and perhaps more relevant, is a focus on the constraint/s, under which the optimization proceeds. Presumably if nothing can be done about the objective—i.e. the utility function—the budget constraint can be subjected to appropriate manipulations. In fact, any change in economic states necessarily manifests itself in a change in the constraint/s that individuals face, either through a change in the relative factor prices, which changes their income, or the relative prices of goods and services they consume. The real question is whether these relative price changes, particularly when they are brought about through a policy change, are justified. It is here that a modified Pareto criterion had something to offer. But before analyzing that issue, let us turn to the idea of allocative efficiency to see, for one, that a society confronts the same sort of dilemmas in applying the Pareto criterion.

The concept of allocative efficiency relates to the problem of defining efficiency in due recognition of the possibility that a society's given resources lend themselves to innumerable uses. More appropriately, it relates to making choices in the face of unlimited wants that cannot all be satisfied with the limited resources at the disposal of a society at any given time. Ultimately, it boils down to ensuring that every good and service is produced in the right quantity: it may be noted that this right quantity may turn out to be zero for some of the goods and services. (Indeed, for a very large proportion of goods and services that could be produced, the right quantity will turn out to be zero, leading to corner solutions in the technical jargon of economics.) It is here that the Pareto criterion helps to define the right quantity for each good as that quantity from which no reallocation of resources will make anyone better off without, at the same time, making someone else worse off. In other words, an allocation of resources will be efficient if no Pareto improvement remains possible. Any economic system must perform the task of allocation of resources. A market economy does so through the price signals. However, the market mechanism, by itself, is blind to any efficiency considerations. It is blind to any value judgment including the one that forms the basis of the Pareto criterion. All it does is to ensure a state of equilibrium on the basis of an interaction between the forces of demand and supply, provided, of course, that the well known conditions with regard to existence and stability of such equilibrium are satisfied. What is interesting is that under certain conditions this equilibrium output also turns out to be the "right" output—as per the second fundamental theorem of welfare economics—and thus the conclusion that under those conditions, the market system leads to an efficient allocation of resources. These conditions include: first, that all goods and services be of the "private" variety (more appropriately exclusion must be possible at relatively low cost even if the goods or services may be jointly consumed); second, that prices be set equal to the respective marginal costs of those goods and services, which necessarily happens when assumptions with regard to perfect competition are satisfied; and third, that there be no external effects in either consumption and/or production. The last condition ensures that the demand and supply curves represent Marginal Social Benefits (MSB) and Marginal Social Cost (MSC) respectively, and since the Pareto criterion holds true when there is equality between the MSB and MSC, the competitive equilibrium that ensured an equality between quantity demanded and quantity supplied also ensures satisfaction of the Pareto criterion. This, in turn, ensures that total surplus, comprised of the consumers' and producers' components, is maximized. This is another way of saying that net social benefits to society are maximized. Whenever relative prices change, the system ensures a reallocation of resources such that net social benefits are again maximized. The new outcome is optimal from society's point of view provided the attendant redistribution is deemed as socially acceptable. Let us look at this process somewhat closely.

When a prevailing equilibrium—for the sake of argument, let us assume that it is allocatively efficient and distributionally acceptable—is disturbed as a result, for instance, of an increase in demand for good "x," *ceteris paribus*, resulting in an increase in its price, the market mechanism leads to a reallocation of resources in favor of this good at the expense of some other good/s and ensures that the new allocation of resources is Pareto optimal. Although the allocation of resources is efficient in both the cases, as compared to any situation in both instances where the marginal conditions were not satisfied, yet the society may not be indifferent between these two cases because of the accompanying changes in the distribution of income. Clearly, the reallocation of resources that ensures satisfaction of the Pareto criterion also changes the distribution of income (a case of interdependence between the two situations). The producers' surplus for "x" increases at the expense of such a surplus for the other goods, although we are not quite sure what happens to the consumers' surplus. There are gains and losses, arising out of a change in the distribution of income, this time as a result of a relative price change, rendering Pareto inapplicable without some sort of modification as earlier remarked. Regardless of how the gains and losses arise, what is important is that these be somehow compared to arrive at any conclusion with regard to the superiority, or otherwise, of the new state as compared to the old. Such a comparison would require an interpersonal comparison of utility unless a way could be found to neutralize the distributional effects through some sort of compensation payments to those adversely effected by those who are favorably effected by the change. In other words, the crucial question is whether the gainers could compensate the losers. If the gainers could compensate the losers and yet be left with some benefits, the result would be a Pareto improvement. It is to this important question—underscoring the modification required in the Pareto criterion—that the profession devoted its energies to after the publication, in 1920, of Professor Pigou's *The Economics of Welfare* culminating, in 1956, in the publication of Professor Hicks's *A Revision of Demand Theory*.

This effort was important in the sense that if the Pareto criterion were to be abandoned because of its practical irrelevance, any other criterion that would be needed to replace it, and needed it would be, could hardly be expected to involve a value judgment any less controversial than the one needed in the present case. Supplanting it with another criterion would involve the same difficulty, as is clear from the difficulties faced when it came to specifying a welfare function, as we will see shortly. But the issue of possible compensation, in turn, required an answer to another question: could those gains and losses be *accurately* measured in terms of some consistent unit of measurement, a numerare. The hairsplitting analysis that ensued no doubt enlightened the economic discourse but did not yield a fully satisfactory answer, and has indeed eluded economics to this day.

The law of demand is predicated on the law of diminishing marginal utility. Utility, being subjective, is not amenable to an operationally meaningful aggregation across different individuals. If, however, the individual utilities could be converted into a measurable numerare, such as money (it need not be money, yet money is the most convenient one), it would then lend itself readily to required aggregation. This can be done quite easily once utilities are translated into money at the concerned individuals' selected evaluation rates. This converts the individual marginal utility (MU) curves into individual demand curves, which could now also be called marginal benefits (MB) curves, but this procedure is impeccable only if the MU of money, the measuring rod, is constant. Notwithstanding the fact that economic analysis frequently made, and still makes, this assumption for the sake of convenience, the assumption is problematic at the least. The search for a solution to this problem led to the development of an alternative approach, the neoclassical ordinalism, which used the indifference curve analysis to derive the individual demand curves. But the problem now resurfaced in a slightly different guise. When the price of a good changes, it gives rise to two quite distinct effects: the substitution effect and the income effect, the latter arising as a result of a change in real income occasioned by the price change. Thus, for instance, a price decrease makes a consumer better off by raising his/her real income. Consequently, estimates of changes in consumers' surplus on the basis of the Marshallian demand curve do not accurately reflect the resulting benefits (gains) or harms (losses) to individual consumers. Professor Hicks (1939) started working on the issue, and labored over several years (1944, 1956) to sort out the complex underlying arguments. He derived the compensated demand curve in order to provide an accurate measurement of the consumers' surplus, but ended up with four alternative measures of such surplus depending on i) the level of utility the concerned consumer was *entitled* to receive, and ii) the degree of flexibility allowed him in adjusting his consumption pattern after the price change. Consider, for the sake of illustration, the case of a price decrease. When the price of say good x decreases, the individual increases his consumption of the good according to the Marshallian demand curve, thus leading to an increase in his consumer's surplus. If he is allowed to consume that larger quantity but his right to increased surplus is not recognized, and therefore his income is now reduced, say through a lump sum tax, by an amount sufficient to put him back at his original indifference curve (level of utility), this amount of tax, in the Hicksian terminology, will be called the "compensating surplus" of the price decrease. If, however, as soon as the individual attempts to increase his consumption in response to price decrease, he is taxed to always keep him at the same level of utility, his consumption of x will not increase to the same extent as in the previous case, and the resulting amount of tax will be called the "compensating variation" of the price decrease. On the other hand, if the individual's right to higher utility, occasioned by the price decrease, were to be recognized, there again are two possibilities of compensating him in the form of, let us say, a subsidy that will put him at the higher level of utility without there being a decrease in price. One possibility would be an amount of subsidy, calculated at the original level of consumption of x, which would be sufficient to give him the higher utility, or put him at the higher indifference curve. This gives us the Hicksian "equivalent surplus" of the price decrease. On the other hand, if he were to be allowed to vary his consumption continuously as his real income rises, due to payment of subsidy, he will consume a larger quantity of x than in the previous case, and the amount of subsidy based upon this new quantity would represent "equivalent variation" of the price decrease.

The same four measures of consumers' surplus could be estimated for a price increase. It may be noted that the compensating surplus of a price increase turns out to be equal to the equivalent surplus for a price decrease, while the compensating variation of a price increase turns out to be equal to the equivalent variation of a price decrease. Similarly, the equivalent surplus of a price increase turns out to be equal to the compensating surplus of a price decrease, while the equivalent variation of a price increase turns out to be equal to the compensating variation of a price decrease. These four measures give us four different answers with respect to changes in surplus depending upon first, the property rights delineation, namely, whether individual's right to higher/lower utility is accepted or not, and second, whether the amount of surplus is calculated on the basis of the original, or changed quantities of consumption, as noted above. And none of these measures coincides with the Marshallian measure of the consumers' surplus (which happens to be the most convenient basis of estimating such surplus) except in the special case where the income effect turns out to be zero, or equivalently, when the income elasticity of demand is zero. If the income elasticity of demand is zero, the compensated demand curve coincides with the Marshallian demand curve, and all four of the Hicksian measures coincide with the Marshallian one. Therefore it is only when the income effects are assumed to be zero that the consumers' surplus would represent an accurate measurement of the gains and losses arising out of price changes.[1] The New Welfare Economics' assumption of zero income effect is somewhat less stringent than the Old Welfare Economics' assumption of constant MU of money, but an unrealistic one all the same. Yet these theoretical niceties, while clarifying the complications involved, did not deter economics from proceeding to highlight the practical possibilities of making compensation payments if and when they were deemed necessary. But even there things turned out to be fairly complicated.

Ever since Marshall developed the concept of consumers' surplus, and notwithstanding the initial reservations of his contemporaries, its potential as a useful tool in the area of applied welfare economics as a measure of gains and losses was never in doubt. Professor Kaldor (1939) proposed that if the gainers could compensate the losers as a result of a change, social welfare will increase. This came to be known as the compensation principle or, later on, as Kaldor-Hicks criterion. As it turned out, the question as to whether the gainers *could* compensate the losers was just one, albeit the first, of a number that needed to be answered to arrive at the conclusion that a particular change resulted in an increase in social welfare. There followed a somewhat involved discourse on the issue, the contours of which could be summed up thus: obviously, the first thing that got underlined, reflecting a faithfulness to Pareto, was that it was not sufficient that a compensation *could* be made, it actually *should* be made. However, the question of practical implementation of this dictum got entangled in the complications that arise in the correct estimation of the needed compensation payments. Professor Hicks (1940) pointed out that it was not sufficient that the gainers could compensate the losers; it was equally important that the losers be unable to compensate the gainers to affect a reversal of the change, or in other words, bribe the potential gainers to block implementation of the change. This possibility could not be dismissed in light of his proof that the compensating variation of a price decrease may be different, as it generally would be, from the compensating variation of a price increase, as we saw earlier. Thereupon, Professor Scitovsky (1941) showed the possibility that the Kaldor-Hicks criterion may be satisfied both ways: for a change as well as against it. This time

[1] An interested reader may find an extended discussion on these measures of surplus, and the compensation principle in general, in Little (1957) or Winch (1971).

the problem arose because of the possible inequality between the corresponding compensating and equivalent variations of price increase and decrease. As if that was not enough, in the aftermath of Bergson's (1938) formulation of the welfare function, it became abundantly clear that all of the foregoing debate about the compensation criteria related only to the constraint (the utility possibility frontier) at the neglect of the objective (the welfare function), and that it was quite possible that even when none (all) of those criteria were satisfied, the change may yet be (not) desirable purely on distributional (equity) grounds depending upon the positioning of the welfare function (this is further elaborated in the discussion pertaining to Figure 1 below).

To sum up the arguments so far: the cases where compensation payments not only could but would actually be made to neutralize the redistribution effects posed no particular difficulty, and whether these payments were estimated on the basis of Hicksian or Marshallian measures could be regarded as a matter of expediency. But in the large proportion of cases where, for one reason or another, no compensation could be made, a puritanical application of the Pareto criterion eluded economics. Nevertheless, as a result of this penetrating analysis, economics became somewhat wiser than before. After all, recognition of one's limitations happens to be a precondition for wisdom. Apart from a more clear thinking at the conceptual level, this wisdom is reflected in a number of policy relevant inferences economics was able to draw.

First, it recognized that in some cases no compensation payments would be advisable on purely practical grounds. After all, such payments involve implementation of a redistribution policy, which, at times, may itself be quite costly. To ignore these costs in order to clarify the underlying issues is one thing but to treat them so in reality is quite another. If the benefits of affecting a particular redistribution are only marginal, relative to the costs, social welfare may actually decrease as a result of implementing the policy. For instance, one may consider a redistribution arising out of a price change undesirable, and may wish to reverse its effects through compensatory payments, but this may be counterproductive in the face of prohibitively high costs of doing so. Second, the redistributive effects that arose out of a free functioning of the market system were, in general, considered to command social approval (that important issue is discussed at length in the next chapter). Exceptions to this rule were admitted but must be evaluated in the light of the first point. One may put this argument slightly differently. If the income effects arising out of a particular change are relatively small in the backdrop of a vast canvas that an economy happens to be, the resulting redistributional effects may be ignored. Economics tends to view the redistributions arising out of changes in market forces, each being quite insignificant in relation to the larger economic background, precisely in this light. More importantly, this idea forms the theoretical foundations of the cost-benefit analysis, which is extensively used for evaluating the consequences of all sorts of economic changes, including project evaluation, and without which public policy will be forced to operate on a purely ad hoc basis. Last, and related to the foregoing points, economics emphasizes that when a change is not insignificant in relation to that background, as happens in the case of large public works projects, the redistributional consequences could not be ignored.

Disaffection and Alternative Offerings

It is against the backdrop of the foregoing perspective that the writings of the Islamic economists must be assessed. These economists have criticized the relevant body of economics on two counts, and on both those counts the argument turns out be less than cogent, bordering more on rhetoric than being a genuine critique. To begin with, there prevails a confusion about the distinction between positive economics and normative economics, which in turn is accompanied by an equal degree of confusion as to where the concepts of efficiency and equity belong in economics. Let us consider the position Dr. Umer Chapra, one of the leading authorities on Islamic economics, takes on these questions. Chapra (1996, p. 13) asserts that, "Conventional economics has set before itself two different sets of goals. One of these is what may be termed positive, and relates to the realization of 'efficiency' and 'equity' in the allocation and distribution of scarce resources. The other is what may be called normative, and is expressed in terms of the universally-desired socio-economic goals...." At the outset, one faces the difficulty of comprehending his distinction between "positive" goals and "normative" goals as though the idea of goals could somehow be divorced from the societal norms that need to underpin them. No goal could possibly be devoid of normative content, a content that alone could render it a goal. One is forced to proceed on the assumption that Chapra, in fact, is referring to the distinction between "positive" and "normative" economics. If that were to be the case, then one has to contend with his troubling inclusion of the concepts of both efficiency and equity in positive economics. Economics may be riddled with conflicting opinions on a variety of issues, but I am not aware of any confusion as to where the concepts of efficiency and equity belong in economics. Both of these concepts involve value judgments, and therefore indisputably belong to normative economics as the foregoing discussion has shown. The former, needless to say, involving the one that underpins the Pareto criterion, as has been the main burden of the exposition throughout this chapter, and the latter requiring a value judgment either besides Pareto's, thereby supplanting it, or over and above Pareto's, thereby over-riding it, as will become clear a little later in this chapter in the discussion pertaining to Figure 1.

Further confusion is created when Chapra makes the following statement about the second fundamental theorem of welfare economics (Chapra, 1992, p. 19, emphasis added), "Every competitive equilibrium is considered to be a Pareto optimum—it is not possible to make anyone better off without making someone else worse off—which *must* be accepted as both efficient and *equitable*." There are a number of fatal misconceptions in this statement. To begin with, the idea of competition has no inherent links with the concepts of efficiency and equity. What it is inherently linked to is the ideology of the market system, and in that system it may become a means to achieve efficiency. (This is not the place to go into the role of competition in a market economy, a subject that is taken up comprehensively in the next chapter). By bundling competition with efficiency and equity, what Chapra ends up doing is either to extend his perceived grievances about the concepts of efficiency and equity to competition, or to hold competition responsible for those grievances. Neither of these viewpoints stands up to an elementary scrutiny. Part of the reason he runs into the confusion is that a statement such as "a competitive equilibrium is Pareto optimal and therefore 'efficient'" could be taken as a positive statement. But then it must also be recognized that it would be a positive statement only when viewed with respect to the outcome of a competitive economic system, and not with respect to the idea of efficiency itself. The concept of efficiency will still require a definition such as provided by the Pareto criterion. But whatever that definition may happen to be, it need not be considered as inherently linked to a market system. After all Pareto's ideas are not restricted to a market system; a non-market (command) system could equally satisfy the Pareto criterion, an idea that will not be adjudged as the least explored in economics. What is troubling is the assertion that economics requires that such an outcome "must be accepted as efficient and equitable." Economics makes no such claims and imposes no such requirement. Dr. Chapra equates every Pareto optimum to optimum optimorum, and completely disregards the plethora of writings that focus precisely on the conflict between the efficiency and equity objectives, a conflict which is now well articulated even in the elementary textbooks of economics.

Chapra's disregard of what economics has to say about the conflict between efficiency and equity requires a little more attention. He feels that economics has helped perpetuate a status quo in favor of the rich, and thus is responsible for the distributional inequities prevailing in Western societies. In all fairness it must be admitted that this criticism is directed more against capitalism, which happens to be just one form of market system as will become clear in the next chapter, and particularly in Chapter 4; but since he does not feel obliged to take the distinction between economics and the economic system into consideration, it can equally be taken as a criticism of economics. Chapra (1992, p. 49) continues: "the concept of Pareto optimality confirmed the 'undesirability' of any effort to change the existing distribution. It was argued that any redistribution would make the *rich somewhat* worse off even though it would make the *poor substantially* better off. Redistribution would take the economy away from the point of 'bliss' as indicated by Pareto optimum," and again (1992, pp. 29–30, emphasis added), "The 'Pareto optimum', identified with 'economic efficiency' [note that this time Pareto optimum is identified with only efficiency and not equity, as was the case a little while ago], became a favorite child of welfare economics. If a *million persons* felt themselves to be better off but there was *one person* who felt he was worse off as a result of a proposed policy, then the economist was compelled to suspend value judgment about the desirability of that policy measure." One would tend to disregard such statements as superfluous had they not been made by a very well recognized authority on the subject of Islamic economics, and therefore likely to be taken seriously by an unwary reader. The moment one takes them seriously, one is compelled to note a number of serious flaws, and innuendos. To begin with, there is the problem of logical inconsistency whereby Chapra condemns the conclusions implied by a statement one way and, by the force of his own logic, would take a contrary position with regard to what the opposite of that statement implies. For instance, if "the economist" was compelled (if that is the right word) to suspend value judgment when a million persons, supposedly the poor ones, as is clear from the first part of the quote, felt better off but one, the rich, felt worse off, he was equally "compelled" to suspend value judgment in favor of a policy that will make a million poor persons worse off by making one rich person better off. And this is precisely what Chapra would require him to do in that situation. Related to this is the unwarranted blanket statement that *any* redistributive departure from Pareto optimality would make only the rich worse off and the poor better off, and further, any such redistribution is supposed to make only the rich "somewhat" worse off while making the poor "substantially" better off. And what about the possibility of "substantial" gainers, whoever they may happen to be, compensating the "somewhat" losers, whoever they may happen to be, as per the foregoing discussion on the compensation principle. This should not be difficult since not only are the gainers and losers clearly identified but the magnitude of gains and losses are also quantified. In any case, it is not necessary that any redistribution from *a* Pareto optimal point will necessarily imply a violation of Pareto optimality conditions. It is quite possible that both pre- and post-redistribution points may lie *on* the utility possibility frontier, and all points on the utility possibility frontier satisfy the Pareto optimality conditions. Figure 1 helps clarify the point.

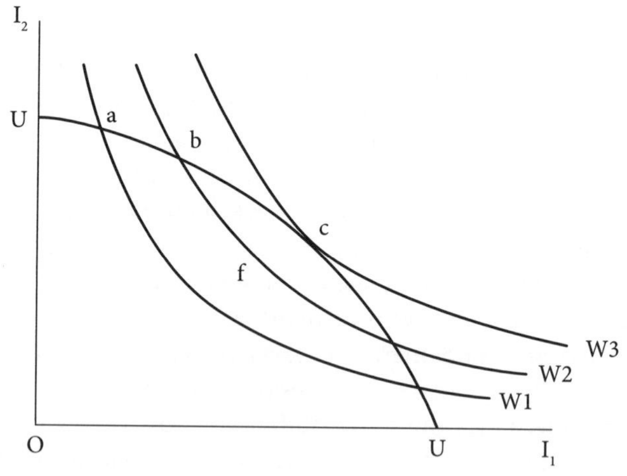

Figure 1

In Figure 1, UU represents the utility possibility frontier, and W1, W2, and W3 are the welfare contours. (I have drawn the utility possibility frontier and the welfare contours as smooth, but they do not necessarily have to be so). Assume I_1, and I_2 represent the million poor and the rich person respectively, and assume that the economy was at point a to begin with, being on the utility possibility frontier and welfare contour W1. If now a redistribution is affected in favor of the million poor, the economy may move from point a to either of the other points such as b, c, or f. This means that it is not necessary that the economy must move to a point such as f, which lies inside the utility possibility frontier, and therefore violates the Pareto optimality conditions. Nevertheless, economics has no problem in accepting the superiority of a point such as f as compared to point a on distributional grounds, although it also likes to point out that a move to a point such as c may be, and indeed is, possible as per the second theorem of welfare economics, a point that is even superior to point f on distributional grounds, and the one which also satisfies the Pareto optimality conditions.[2] At any rate, if a move from point a is made

[2] Mannan (1992), in a paper quite heavy on rhetoric and marred by a number of analytical shortcomings (for one, he draws indifference curves in an Edgeworth box that eventually become positively sloped as well as violate the continuity assumption) dismisses the possibility of a move to a point such as c through "direct transfer payments to the poor so that they can enter the market" because such a redistribution "is based on the implicit assumption that the market mechanism will automatically ensure equitable redistribution of goods and services through the invisible forces of demand and supply." Thus he begins with the failure of the "invisible hand" to ensure equitable distribution of income, considers the possibility of whether the "not-so-invisible hand" of the government could rectify the failure through direct transfer payments, and then goes on to argue that this will not be possible because the invisible hand will fail to act even after the transfer payments have been affected. Just how the invisible hand will do this, he does not say. Does he mean that the invisible hand will not let the government affect the transfer payments? It is hard to say, but if we assume that that is what he means, just how will the invisible hand do this? No explanation of that either. So, we don't quite know what he is trying to say. But then he continues: "Secondly, we have already noted that effective need is a far broader concept than 'effective demand'. The market is either inefficient, ineffective, or indifferent in providing all aspects of basic needs." His "effective need" includes the unexpressed demands of those who do not have the purchasing power to back their demands. But what happened to the direct transfer payments if they did not get expressed in effective demand? Which black hole they disappeared into, he does not say. And beyond his "effective needs," there are the "all aspects of basic needs" that the market is "inefficient, or ineffective" in providing for. Thus it is that even when his "effective needs" have been satisfied, there are still "all aspects of basic needs" that still need to be addressed. (Though the idea of "needs" as stressed by Islamic economists is discussed later in this chapter, a more detailed investigation is offered in Chapter 6.) "Lastly," Mannan tells us, "there is no

to any point on the utility possibility frontier, any point such as b or c, a Pareto enthusiast will have no difficulty accepting the outcome, and therefore no cause to declare it "undesirable," unless he makes a distributional value judgment in favor of the rich, a possibility Chapra himself rules out as is clear from what we have quoted from him—i.e. "the suspension of judgment."

Then there is the problem with his presumption that an economic system operates in a political vacuum, and if so, that somehow economics is responsible for this unfortunate turn of events. Exactly how a status quo that kept a million persons away from a substantial gains at the expense of a slight loss to a rich person would be politically sustained in a democracy is beyond anybody's comprehension, and Chapra does not bother himself with that question except to emphasize that Pareto has everything to do with it. In a non-democratic society—such as most of the Islamic countries—such a possibility cannot be ruled out, but then that is not exactly what he has in mind. And last, but not least, is the issue of empirical evidence that he must contend with. The evidence from the Western democracies over the past century paints a picture that could hardly be identified with his assertion about the status quo. The policies with regard to welfare payments, unemployment insurance, agricultural support

guarantee that transfer payments will be made available to the poor on a permanent basis [just why? he does not say]. Even if the transfer payments are used to increase the productivity of the poor, they may not guarantee an increase in their income." One wonders how the transfer payments will increase productivity of poor without effecting their income, unless he has some sort of slavery in mind. At any rate, in the very next paragraph, he contradicts himself by declaring, "While the role of direct transfer payments cannot be denied for the bottom 10 to 15 per cent, i.e. the absolute poor or unemployable, the fact is that the market cannot always supply wage goods, particularly public services such as education, health care, safe water, sanitation etc. It is essential to expand and redistribute public services so that the poor have access to such services. A part of the income of the rich will have to be transferred to ensure this expanded and equitable redistribution of public services" (all citations are from p. 213). So, transfer payments are no solution, but then transfer payments are necessary. Never mind the question as to how 'wage goods' are to be equated to public services, and never mind the idea of 'redistribution' of public services that were to be provided by the government to begin with. It is possible, although Mannan does not make it clear, that initially he was talking about private transfer payments, and therefore weighed against their inadequacy, and subsequently showed his heavy interventionist bias to make up for this shortfall, but had he introduced the policy initiated transfers to begin with, he would not have to deny the move to a point such as c. There is further discussion on transfer payments (charity) in an Islamic context in Chapters 6 and 7.

prices, food coupons, commitment to full employment, student loans, health care programs, child support programs, etc. do not portray the picture of a society where issues relating to distribution of income were ignored, or where the distribution of income remained static.

But let us be clear as to what exactly it means when economics makes the statement that a competitive system satisfies the Pareto optimality conditions. What it means is that if the system moves from a position of sub-optimality to optimality, the gainers *could* compensate the losers and still be better off than before, and therefore the conclusion that satisfaction of Pareto optimality conditions leads to an increase in social welfare. The foregoing discussion about the compensation principle tells us that economics took the task of estimating these gains and losses very seriously, so that when it made the statement that social welfare will increase as a result of satisfaction of the Pareto criterion, it made this statement in all earnestness. It also tells us that, when the compensation cannot be paid for one reason or another, no conclusions can be drawn as to what will happen to social welfare according to Pareto, and that in such instances, since inter-personal comparisons are involved, the society will have to make a decision as to whether to implement the change on the basis of an additional value judgment notwithstanding Pareto. This latter point underscores the possibility that from the welfare point of view, satisfaction of the Pareto optimality conditions does not ensure that the outcome will necessarily be superior to the position prior to change when the Pareto conditions were not satisfied. It all depends on the position of the welfare function in the utility possibilities space. It is not very difficult to show that, depending on the position of the welfare contours, a point that does not lie on the utility possibility frontier, and hence does not satisfy the Pareto optimality conditions, may be superior to a point on the frontier (this can be quite clearly seen in Figure 1 when we compare points a and f). And all this because of a value judgment that reflects the society's concerns with regard to distributional equity. Yet welfare economics also shows that for any such sub-optimal point, there will always be a point in its north-easterly direction, such as point c—the optimum optimorum—lying both on the utility possibility frontier as well as the welfare function, which will be superior to it on both efficiency and equity grounds provided the required compensation payments were *indeed* made. It is patently wrong to accuse economics of neglecting distributional issues or sanctifying the competitive outcome as necessarily distributionally equitable, as maintained by Chapra.

What ought to be the nature of this overriding value judgment, or, in other words, what should be the shape of the welfare contours? Economics agonized over this issue for a while and came, somewhat reluctantly, to the conclusion that *it* does not need to specify what this ought to be. For instance, Bergson (1938, p. 323), while noting his disagreement with Professor Robbins (1932) who strongly felt that economists need to take these values as datum (read: it was none of the business of economics), wrote: "But the determination of prevailing values for a given community, while I regard it as both a proper and necessary task for the economist, and of the same general character as the investigation of the indifference functions for individuals, is a project which I shall *not undertake* here" (emphasis added). The Cambridge School's initial forays in this area, culminating as they did in the development of the compensation principle, did not bear fruit in that economics did not quite follow the Pigovian prescriptions in this regard, i.e. to get involved in the issues pertaining to specification of welfare function. Ever since, economics has maintained that such distributional value judgments must be distilled through political process or, at the very least, that they do not fall in the domain of economics. This, by itself, could be considered a value judgment, which some may accept while others reject. If economics kept its hands off such additional value judgment issues, it was to acknowledge that distributional issues very quickly become emotive, and that there may be as many opinions as the number of people, and consequently it is something that is best handled through a mass participation process. Yet, for its part, economics has considered it important to identify those instances where such a value judgment may have to be made, and discharged this responsibility accordingly as the intricacies of the discourse on compensation principle makes amply clear.

But let us now turn to the alternative Chapra has to offer us in terms of efficiency and equity. In his 1996 paper he repeats what he wrote in his 1992 volume:

> The total shift in paradigm [i.e. to Islamic economics] should enable us to move away from the *abstract* mainstream definition of efficiency and equity in terms of Pareto optimality to a more down-to-earth definition [as though there was nothing down to earth in Pareto] in conformity with the normative goals. An economy may be said to have attained *optimum* efficiency [as though the idea of efficiency per se could be divorced from the concept of optimization] if it has been able to employ the total potential of its scarce human and material resources in such a

> way that maximum feasible quantity of *need-satisfying* goods and services has been produced with a reasonable degree of *economic stability* and *sustainable* rate of future growth. The test of such efficiency lies in the inability to attain a *socially more acceptable* result without creating prolonged macroeconomic imbalances, and without unduly upsetting the ecological balance. An economy may be said to have attained *optimum equity* if the goods and services produced are distributed in such a way that needs of all individuals are *adequately satisfied* and there is an equitable distribution of income and wealth, without adversely affecting the *motivation* for work, saving, investment and enterprise (1996, p. 31, emphasis added).

What does it all mean? We can begin by considering his concept of efficiency in order first to contrast it with the conventional concept, and then to explore its implications. As far as technical efficiency is concerned, the new concept seems to accord perfectly with the conventional one in so far as it requires that maximum output be produced from given amounts of resources. But then it is not that simple. One cannot determine the maximum of something that has not yet been defined, and that is where we run into a number of problems. It may be helpful first to see how economics handles this question. It begins by determining what goods and services are to be produced through an expression of demand for these in the market. It is the consumers who determine what goods and services are to be produced. Call it the postulate of consumer sovereignty or freedom of choice or what have you. It is only when the issue of the allocation of resources has been settled that the issue of technical efficiency becomes relevant. If the selected goods and services are produced at the minimum possible costs, i.e. by using the minimum possible quantities of resources, we will say that technical efficiency conditions have been satisfied. This would also mean that against the resources being used in the production of goods and services, maximum quantity of each of those goods and services has been produced, and therefore for the given overall quantity of resources, the output of the economy has been maximized.

But what goods and services are to be produced under the new paradigm? Chapra defines these as "need-satisfying" goods and services. But then which goods and services are need-satisfying and which ones are not? If such things as non-need-satisfying goods and services do indeed exist, who is supposed to consume these, and why? Who is to determine whether a particuar good or service qualifies as need-satisfying or not? And do these need-satisfying goods and services vary across time and space? All these questions arise because he opts to depart from the conventional terminology of "wants," where all goods and services are assumed to satisfy human wants. So, apparently, want-satisfaction and need-satisfaction are two different things as far as he is concerned. Are not wants a reflection of needs? A look at the dictionary may be helpful. The Webster's Encyclopedic Edition, 1988, defines a need as "a condition necessitating supply of relief" or "a requirement for subsistence," and it defines a want as "the state or fact of having too little of something desirable or needed" or "a need" or "privation because of poverty." This does not help much except for the word "desirable" occurring in the definition of wants. From that one may infer that the word "want" has a broader meaning than the word "need." It is safe to say that all needs are also wants but all wants do not necessarily qualify as needs. If that is what Chapra has in mind, then we can infer that he wishes to restrict the feasible production, and therefore consumption, set. But which goods and services are to be included in this set, and exactly how, he does not say. In the final analysis, until he answers these questions, his down-to-earth conceptualization of efficiency turns out to be more abstract than that of Pareto. Yet the question as to whether Islam imposes any restrictions on the feasible set is important in its own right, and since this is essentially a question of property rights specification, I will take it up later when I discuss the contours of an Islamic economy in Chapters 5 and 6.[3]

When it comes to equity, Chapra requires that the goods and services produced be distributed in such a way that the needs of all individuals are adequately satisfied. This, according to him, will be "optimum" equity. But, then, on top of that he requires that there be an equitable distribution of income and wealth, but one that does not adversely affect the motivation for work, saving, investment and enterprise. Whether optimum equity is something different from equitable distribution of income, he does not say. If the two are assumed to be the same, then the second statement is redundant. If they are not the same, then either he is saying that the economy will end up producing more goods and services than required for need-satisfaction, or that other goods and services are produced along with the need-satisfying

[3] In Chapter 6, we will also encounter further classifications of goods into need-complementing and need-ameliorating as defined by some other Islamic economists.

ones. Both of these interpretations betray logical inconsistencies. In the first instance, if the society has resources that are more than sufficient to produce his need-satisfying quantities of goods and services, then to force it to keep producing those goods and services beyond the quantities required for the optimum equity amounts to wastage of resources. And if the society does not produce those additional quantities beyond need-satisfaction, some resources, including labor, will remain unemployed. If, on the other hand, we grant him the production of goods and services beyond the need-satisfying ones to resolve this problem, then his conceptualization of efficiency is incomplete in so far as it does not encompass those additional goods and services. Actually, his definition of efficiency rules this option out when it requires that a "maximum feasible quantity of need-satisfying goods and services" be produced. Therefore, only need-satisfying goods and services are to be produced. As a result, if a society possesses resources over and above what is required for the production of need-satisfying quantities, his definition of efficiency would become inconsistent with his definition of optimum equity. Indeed, in that case his definition of optimum equity would become redundant.

But even if we suppose that Chapra answers that this basket of need-satisfying goods and services is variable with respect to time and space, and consequently manages to accomplish the gigantic task of defining this basket at all times and in all places in such a way that only sufficient quantities are producible by the given resources, he still is not out of the woods. He now faces another thorny question. Would he allow *individual* needs to vary across different individuals? If the answer to this question is "no"—after all it could be argued that all individuals are equal in the eyes of the law—then his optimum equity is reduced to equal distribution of income. This would mean that his second stipulation, the one about equitable distribution is redundant, whatever may then happen to the various "motivations" that he worries about. And if we admit the answer "yes," then the question arises as to who will define those variable needs. If it is left to the concerned individuals, and this perhaps is what he has in mind, since at another place he rules out coercion (Chapra, 1996, p. 32), his whole argument about the new paradigm, in redefining efficiency and therefore equity—based as these were on the possibility of defining a basket of need-satisfying goods and services, as noted above—becomes irrelevant. Given all these difficulties, one wonders whether there would be any point in asking what exactly he means by a "reasonable" degree of economic stability, or "sustainable" rate of economic growth, or "socially more acceptable" result without "prolonged" macroeconomic "imbalances," etc. etc. that he requires his economy to exhibit besides efficiency and equity.

Beyond this crucial issue relating to the norms as they have prevailed in the economic discourse and the ones that are supposed to prevail in an Islamic economy that are the subject of the present chapter, other dimensions of economic discourse have also come under attack in varying degrees by Islamic economists, which gives a general impression that economics as we know it today is unsuitable, if not totally irrelevant, for an Islamic society. I have assessed this premise in the four chapters that follow Chapter 4. That discussion requires laying down the basic framework which clarifies what an economic system is supposed to be. That is the subject to which we now turn in the next chapter.

CHAPTER THREE

ECONOMIC SYSTEM AND MARKET ECONOMY

Economic System: General Framework

For the various criticisms directed at capitalism, and thus indirectly at a market economy, by Islamic economists, only some of which—though potentially the most lethal ones for being directed at the foundations of economics yet not requiring a fuller comprehension of an economic system—have been covered in the previous chapter, one is forced to begin with a clean slate, and ask the following question: what exactly is an economic system, and what tasks is it supposed to perform for the society? I am quite convinced that a student of Islam and Economics needs a clarity of mind on these issues, in order to be in a better position to evaluate the literature on Islamic economics knowing well what issues any society—be it Islamic or otherwise—needs to pay attention to in the economic sphere of its life. I define an economic system as an integral structure of a society characterized by a set of institutions established to enable it to accomplish the twin tasks of allocation of resources at its disposal, and distribution of the goods and services thus produced among its citizens (the latter could be referred to as distribution of income). Following the jargon of economics, we will call these tasks allocation and distribution functions respectively. For the sake of formality, we note that an institution is defined as something that has been established by society to perform certain tasks. Establishing the institutions needed for an economic system, it must be noted, presupposes the existence of a commonly held *set of values* (norms) that provide the foundation on which those institutions are erected. Since these institutions can vary across time and space, it is not possible to define a unique set of institutions that could help us define 'the' economic system. Furthermore, the set of institutions that may impinge on the allocation and distribution functions is likely to be quite large. This forces us to be somewhat selective in our choice of what is to be included in our exposition in order, if nothing else, to keep it manageable. One would naturally like to start with the most fundamental of these institutions and then proceed to the others with a view to include only the ones that are indispensable in performing the two aforementioned functions. This means our focus is essentially on the *minimum* set of such institutions. This minimum set must include:

i. an institutional mechanism for delineation of property ownership, or more appropriately of resources, at the disposal of the society. This mechanism provides us with what will be referred to as the *ownership postulate* in the following pages; and
ii. an institutional mechanism to effect the allocation of resources to the production of various goods and services and distribution of those goods and services among citizens—call it the *signaling postulate*.

This irreducible set of institutions requires a number of additional postulates for a sustained operationalization of what then would be called an economic system. These postulates are grounded in the same, given, set of values that led to the establishment of the set of institutions, thereby implying a close connection between these two components. This connection is likely to be so strong that the institutional postulates would not make any sense without these additional, complementary postulates. The *minimum* set of such postulates, therefore, is as much an integral part of the economic system as the former set of institutions. This set must include the following elements:

iii. a postulate relating to "rights" and therefore "responsibilities" associated with (i) above, call it the *freedom of choice postulate*, or at a deeper level the free will postulate.
iv. a motivation postulate for economic agents, both consumers and producers; a sort of a propulsion force needed for a sustained operation of the system, call it the *motivation postulate*; and
v. a *criterion, or a criteria set* to evaluate the performance of the system. The resulting evaluation may require use of the existing or new institutions to address any deficiencies, inherent or otherwise, in the ones included in (ii) above.

In the following pages I attempt to show how these five pieces fit together to form a system—an economic system. However, the following remarks must be kept in mind to fully appreciate what follows.

Although I have felt it necessary to begin with a clean slate to present the essential elements of an economic system, I do not present anything new in so far as the contents of this exposition go: indeed, I have drawn on the rich economic literature only to present the material in a pedagogical form that should be easily assimilated by a student of Islam and economics. I have come to the conclusion that in view of the centrality of *fiqh* in Islamic sciences, particularly social sciences, a Muslim reader can best understand the material once it is cast in what in economics would be regarded as the property rights framework. However, it may be noted that the detailed specific elaborations, particularly on the subjects of freedom of choice, self-interest, and competition are conditioned by my overall reading of where the confusion in the literature on Islamic economics lies. Here, I have not cited any specific writer or any particular viewpoint, for that would unnecessarily complicate the exposition. As for specific writers on, and issues in, Islamic economics, this is covered in a number of subsequent chapters, beginning with Chapter 6, in the hope that once the basic framework has been laid down in this chapter, it may be drawn upon from time to time for any discussion relating to a specific point in those chapters. Furthermore, a meaningful discourse on any specific point in Islamic economics requires clarity with respect to issues that are covered in the intervening chapters, especially Chapter 5. Finally, it should also be noted that one chapter cannot do justice to the vast subject at hand; it can provide nothing more than its bare bones coverage. Yet I feel that the sketch that emerges is adequate, as it ought to be, for adding the necessary colours for details in the later chapters. We can now turn to the individual components of the system as noted earlier.

With regard to the ownership postulate, it may be noted at the outset that some well recognized categories of resources are embodied in human beings, such as labor, human capital, and entrepreneurial talent, and therefore their ownership cannot be divorced from the agents in whom these are embodied, except through the institution of slavery, something which will not be entertained in this work. Thus the concept of ownership will be restricted, as is the case in economics, to disembodied resources, namely property ownership, which includes the two well-known remaining factors of production, namely land and physical capital, although, in recent years, another variety, hitherto neglected, has come to occupy an important place in the property hierarchy, namely intellectual property. In all these cases, property has a separate existence, and hence an identity, quite distinct from that of its owner. Leaving aside the possibility of coercive ownership, the moment we consider the question of property ownership, that is to say its ownership in an orderly society, we are forced to presume the existence of a social contract, and, therefore, an institution that is charged with the responsibility to ensure compliance with that contract by all members of the society.[1] This institution also happens to be the one which has historically enjoyed the power, or has come to be vested with the authority, to delineate the structure of property ownership: call it the state, or, for that matter the government of the concerned society; the latter, at any rate, being the operational manifestation of the former. While a government performs myriad functions in a society, our focus here is primarily on its economic role. The existence of the institution of government immediately implies two possibilities with regard to ownership of property: a) private ownership, b) state ownership. There is also, however, a third form of ownership, which antedates state ownership, namely c) communal ownership, which must also be taken into consideration. Although both b) and c) involve some sort of collective ownership, yet there is a world of difference as far as their economic implications are concerned, an issue to which we will turn somewhat later in this chapter.

What is noteworthy at this stage of the argument is the fact that the concept of ownership is not meaningful without due regard to the contents of that ownership, namely the rights, or perhaps better the freedoms, associated with it. This is the subject of the postulate of rights, or the freedom of choice postulate. The connection between freedom of choice and property ownership is so intimate that each in isolation from the other hardly makes any sense. The word freedom, however, is liable to misinterpretation arising as a result of according the idea of freedom an air of absoluteness. One can entertain the idea of absolute freedom for a Robinson Crusoe, but in a societal context, the idea is nothing short of meaningless. Absolute freedom for one individual would amount to absolute oppression of others. Granted to all individuals, it would quickly lead to anarchy, which no society could endure for long. Absolute freedom actually implies absolute lack of freedom. In orderly societies, one individual member's freedom is

[1] While one would normally attribute the idea of social contract to Hobbs, it could equally be attributed to Ibn Khaldūn's concept of *ʿaṣabiyya*, or group solidarity.

underwritten by the other members on the basis of anticipated reciprocity. One undertakes to protect the freedom of others, which means one circumscribes one's own freedom, in the anticipation that others will reciprocate. One accepts the attendant responsibility in order to claim the corresponding right for oneself. There can be no such thing as rights without corresponding responsibilities, in exactly the same way that no one accepts any responsibility voluntarily without a corresponding right. Viewed from the angle of property ownership, in orderly societies there can be no such thing as absolute freedom pertaining to, or unbounded rights to, the use of property.

A society may deem it necessary to impose upon itself, that is, upon its individual members, certain reciprocal constraints regarding the utilization of any piece of property. The differences between different forms of property ownership, and their economic significance, cannot be fully appreciated until those restrictions, or conversely the rights, associated with each ownership structure are spelled out. The process of defining those rights culminates in a structure of property rights for the society—a structure that ends up going much beyond the idea of mere ownership, by encompassing all the regulations ordering the collective life of a society, at least at the formal, or should we say at the legal, level. No economic system could be comprehended without an understanding of the corresponding structure of property rights that underwrites it. Indeed no societal system can be.

Given the structure of prevailing property rights, a society must ensure that the resources at its disposal are productively utilized. Utilization of resources generally requires an effort on the part of the economic agents—agents who will always be individuals, acting either as principals or agents as in the principal-agent scenario—that may not be pleasant for them. People may not like to exert themselves without some motivating force. This obliges us to pay close attention to what motivates economic agents, the subject of the motivation postulate. As a starting point, this postulate may be conceived as signifying survival. In order to ensure their survival, the individual economic agents are compelled to utilize the resources at their disposal to sustain an ongoing resource replenishing process, call it the process of production. While survival may well be recognized as the fundamental motivating postulate, no individual, and thereby the collectivity that he is a part of, has ever been content with bare survival as an ultimate goal and achievement. Man has always striven to go beyond bare survival to enjoy the richness that life offers in its various dimensions. This point forces us to go beyond bare survival to search for a broader behavioral postulate, broad enough to be applicable in all the diverse situations that economic agents are bound to confront in the course of their daily lives. It is here that the postulate of 'self-interest' suggests itself, or rather forces itself upon us. This postulate has been much maligned in the literature on economics, and not only economics, because of self-interest's tendency to overwhelm an individual soul. Here, two points may be noted: first, self-interest is a broader postulate than survival in the sense that survival can be viewed as an expression of self-interest, but then self-interest may go much beyond bare survival, which is to say that survival implies self-interest whereas self-interest may imply much besides bare survival. Second, and more substantively, the intimate connection between property ownership and freedom of choice becomes meaningful only when viewed against the backdrop of self-interest. Freedom of choice is conditioned by self-interest, exactly as it is by the idea of survival. It may be noted that when individuals voluntarily accept constraints on their freedoms, they might be viewed as doing so precisely under the motivation of self-interest, as mentioned earlier under the idea of reciprocity in the social context. We may sum up the discussion by saying that the three elements discussed so far, i.e. property rights, freedom of choice, and self-interest are so intertwined that the jigsaw puzzle that an economic system happens to be cannot be appreciated, indeed even understood, until these elements are placed at their respective places in that puzzle. Yet fitting these elements together gives rise to certain difficulties, difficulties that are primarily, if not exclusively, centered on the play of self-interest, the end result of which is the possibility of a divergence between individual (or private) and collective (or social) interests.

One would readily admit that the idea of self-interest is liable to misinterpretations, both of omission and commission: of omission when the idea is unwittingly interpreted out of context, and of commission when it is deliberately taken out of context. In both the cases, the misinterpretation revolves around an unqualified equating of self-interest with selfishness; after all both of these are manifestations of the play of self or human free will. A commonly used statement, that economic agents try to "do the best" (or some variant thereof) for themselves lends itself readily to be as much a manifestation of self-interest as of selfishness. That such a blanket statement could give rise to misunderstanding or misinterpretation is beyond any doubt. But this is mostly a result of the lack of care on the part of someone making the statement. The carelessness arises out of either non-recognition, or non-explication, of the *objective conditions* (the constraints) under, and/or the *manner* in, which "the best" is supposed to be accomplished. It is such unguarded statements that make easy prey for those who may wish to exploit, if nothing else, the sloppiness in which the argument may be presented. Such criticism, pervasive though it may be, does not negate the fact that in a societal setting one cannot possibly conceive of economic agents "doing the best" for themselves without regard to the objective conditions under which they are confined to operate—they do the best for themselves but only under given circumstances. It is, however, worth keeping in mind that some times the postulate of self-interest is criticized when in fact the disenchantment is with the prevailing objective conditions, including a lack of enforcement of property rights—a theme that will recur later in this chapter.

Before taking up the issue of the 'manner' in which self-interest is pursued, two additional points relating to the analytical treatment of self-interest in economics must be noted. First, economics is often castigated for its treatment of self-interest in the form of utility and profit maximization. (In this twin maximization, profit maximization is actually only a manifestation, albeit an easily quantifiable one, of utility maximization, and utility, in turn, is assumed to be a manifestation of self-interest). It is, however, not clear whether the critics are unhappy about the concept of "utility" or the idea of "maximization." And if the unhappiness is associated with utility, is it because utility for them is not a good indicator of self-interest, in which case it is like someone saying: I agree with the idea of self-interest, but I am not quite convinced if utility is the right variable that measures it; or: Forget about the issue of equating utility with self-interest, I don't quite think that human agents ought to have self-interest in their focus to begin with. The former is purely a matter of semantics, although sometimes people become enamored with semantics—after all, on this sensitive subject, people have often ended up focusing less on Smith's "self-interest" than on Jevons' "pleasure and pain machine." And in that, it may very well be the word pleasure that is the cause of irritation. But then the critics often forget that pleasure does not necessarily have to be hedonistic. In the latter case, the critics are usually less worried about what it is that is being maximized as compared to the idea of maximization itself. It seemingly worries them when economics assumes that economic agents maximize utility, because it seems to them to condone an unbridled pursuit of self-interest. This, however, ignores the fact that economics assumes no such thing as unconstrained maximization. At any rate, when economics is criticized for making such an assumption, most of the times it is the result of not distinguishing between simplifying assumptions and behavioral assumptions. Utility maximization is not a simplifying assumption, as some critics take it to be. It is a behavioral assumption. And if economic agents do indeed maximize utility, it does not change anything regardless of whether it is recognized as such or not. Surely it is not economics that taught economic agents to be self-interested.

The other line of criticism focuses on the idea of "rational" economic behavior, or the postulate of rationality, which runs something like this: If economic agents are self-interested, and therefore maximize utility, their behavior must exhibit certain minimum consistency requirements such as continuity and transitivity. It needs to be realized that this transition from utility maximization, or more appropriately from self-interest, to rational behavior was motivated more by a desire to use mathematical models in economics to derive more firm or robust conclusions rather than anything else. If economic agents, in reality, did not quite pass this test of rationality, it was well recognized in economics as the work of Professor Herbert Simon (1957, 1991) on the postulate of bounded rationality clearly demonstrates. Of course there are those who take Simon's work as an indictment of the postulate of self-interest, without taking into consideration the fact that when, at times, economic agents exhibit seemingly inconsistent behavior, they do so only in view of their self-interest. If they do not have the accurate, or complete, information available to make the right decisions, they may end up making the wrong ones. Self-interest may not always lead to rational behavior if the informational requirements are not satisfied. The excesses of mathematical modeling in economics point to the failings of a specific methodology in positive economics instead of being an indictment of the self-interest postulate.

As for the manner in which the best is accomplished, there are more serious grounds for concern. If, and when, self-interest is viewed as an unbridled horse, there may well be genuine reasons for equating it to selfishness. There is hardly any doubt that self-interest is easily given to blind pursuits; one is quite likely to ignore the possible consequences of one's actions for others. Admittedly, it is difficult to define selfishness in a rigorous manner but it is not essential to do so for the argument to proceed further. It suffices to note that, in the ultimate analysis, selfishness amounts to excesses committed in the name of self-interest, that is to say a self-interest that is pursued at the expense of others. There is hardly any doubt that given room, and there often is a plenty of that, as we will see later in this chapter, self-interest does indeed quickly degenerate into selfishness. It all depends on the room afforded to it to play itself out, and that brings us back to the issue of property rights, and their enforcement. But before we move on to that issue, two things must be noted. First, selfishness implies (indeed emanates from) self-interest, but equally, and this must be emphasized, self-interest does not necessarily imply selfishness. Second, that "doing the best" in given circumstances without harming anyone else provides us with a possible principle to delimit the sphere of self-interest. Interestingly, this delimiting may provide us with a criterion for evaluating the performance of the system, as indicated in point (v) above and recall Pareto in the last chapter. We now turn to the issue of property rights, an issue of fundamental importance in economics, notwithstanding the fact that it has conventionally not been accorded its due importance at least in the textbook treatment of the subject.

As already noted, a society may always impose various restrictions on the use of property. The ambit of property rights is much broader than mere property ownership, reaching far beyond that to encompass all goods and services. When a good or service is exchanged—and exchange is what economics is all about—it is in fact a bundle of property rights that is exchanged. The goods and services merely serve as tokens of what is being exchanged. As a result, it is the bundle of property rights associated with goods or services that essentially determines their economic value. A few examples may help clarify the point. The value of a given plot of land, for instance, will be the highest of its alternative use values. But if some alternative uses are not permitted it, its value will be the highest of the now restricted uses to which it can be put. The value of a car will depend, inter alia, upon whether or not one can drive it to the central business district of a city every working day. The value of a house will be influenced by whether one is required to keep the pavement clear of snow, and by the traffic noise level in its vicinity, and a host of other factors in each one of these cases. The value of a particular skill will depend, among other things, on the working environment in which the acquirer expects to work. The value of an intellectual endeavor, or research and development activity, will depend upon whether the resultant benefits can be appropriated by the person performing it, and so on. In the final analysis, what is important is not just the ownership of property, goods or services, it is the bundle of property rights associated with them which is.

It is, therefore, quite clear that the importance of the institution of property ownership, relating to the ownership postulate, is crucially dependent upon the institutional set-up that defines the property rights. This institutional set-up includes all the societal institutions that help define and enforce property rights. The word define is meant to underscore the entire process of formulation and delineation of property rights, which culminates in enactment of laws, rules, and regulations that regulate the collective life of a society, at least at the formal level. This entire body defines a society's structure of property rights at any given point of time, and may be called its legal corpus. It is this corpus that is supposed to impose the necessary constraints on individual behavior to insure that self-interest does not degenerate into selfishness. To turn the argument around, a system that defines the constraints on behavior of economic agents at the same time defines the corresponding freedoms by delineating what is thereby permissible from what is not; namely, it defines the sphere in which freedom of choice is to operate.

While economics has now come to regard the subject of property rights with the attention and seriousness it deserves, the other crucial dimension of that issue, pertaining to its effective enforcement, is still left untouched. A structure of property rights is only as good as its effective enforcement. Lack of effective enforcement of a structure of such rights amounts to the same thing as absence of those rights. There is a tendency in economics to presume that whatever structure of property rights a society defines, as given by its legal corpus, will be effectively enforced. Such a position is clearly untenable as experience in a vast majority of countries demonstrates. The disenchantment with self-interest and freedom of choice may indeed be the result of insufficient enforcement of property rights; self-interest is now afforded more room and may turn into selfishness. Enforcement by itself is a resource using activity; thus an efficient level of enforcement is conceivable on the basis of corresponding benefits and costs at the margin. But then it might be reasonable to ask: why would a society end up with a structure of property rights which, or some elements of which, it would not effectively enforce based on the costs and benefits of enforcement? An answer to this question requires a slight digression, involving a somewhat closer look at the connection between the process of property rights evolution in a society and the corresponding costs of enforcement.

A society's property rights structure is not something static, and therefore fixed for all time. It is always subject to change, the pace of which may vary across time and space. Yet in all societies it contains some elements that are enduring, and others that are more ephemeral. Enduring elements conform to a subset of values that is more cherished by the society—all of the societal values could not possibly be held in equal esteem. This enduring set will necessarily be a part of the set of values referred to earlier. Notwithstanding mankind's recent experience, historically the structure of property rights of a society evolved gradually in the spirit of social contract as pointed out by Professor Harold Demsetz (1967). This gradualness helped assimilation of the new elements in the existing structure, thus bestowing upon them general societal acceptability, and thereby ensuring that the new structure continues to command the respect so essential for it to remain an effective social institution. As a society adapts to changes thrust upon it, it absorbs new elements in its structure of property rights. Some changes are adopted quickly, others take longer, and there may be yet others that are rejected, all depending upon the required departures from the set of values, particularly the cherished elements in it. It is here that contemporary Islamic societies have faced ever new challenges.

The most enduring elements of this structure of rights, the ones that most closely conform to the cherished set of values, become social norms and conventions of a society—sort of its unwritten laws. These are no less a significant source of property rights than the formal corpus, actually more so. In the multi-society global village that we have increasingly come to live in, the changes thrust upon a particular society may not be indigenously rooted. They may have alien origins, and thus may not easily conform to the society's set of values. The process of assimilation may take a long time while also perhaps requiring adaptation to conform to the values the society holds. What is important for the argument at hand is that such changes may, for whatever reasons, become part of the legal corpus, i.e. the formal structure of property rights, prior to their assimilation and necessary adaptation. These elements of the property rights structure fail to draw the allegiance of, and respect from, the citizens, and are therefore relatively difficult to enforce, in contrast to those elements that are in harmony with the society's set of values. The more removed an element of property rights is from those values, either because of borrowing or imposition, the higher would be the enforcement costs. It is no wonder then that a society's unwritten laws are self-enforcing in contrast to the formal laws that require enforcement machinery. For instance, certain items of apparel, while in harmony with indigenous values of one society, may amount to obscenity in some others, and regardless of whether a formal prohibition against them is enshrined in the law, will not be worn under the social taboos. Ultimately, any structure of property rights derives its strength, and therefore effectiveness, from the degree of social acceptance it can command, which, in turn, is rooted in the enduring values upheld by the society. We may note in passing that in the past two centuries the pace of change, in general, and therefore that of introduction of alien elements, in the property rights structures of various societies, including Islamic ones, has been very rapid when judged by the historical standards primarily as a result of technological changes. Earlier, trade and colonization played a more important role, which is not to suggest that these might themselves not have been influenced by technological change.

In any case, the important thing is that the greater the degree of change, the more demanding the task of upgrading the structure of property rights in any society. This fact is amply demonstrated by current experience as well as the turmoil of the past century in all countries, and this regardless of the issue of imposition. When the pace of technological change is too fast, a society's legal corpus breathlessly runs to catch up with it. In the present context, to the extent the legal corpus lags behind the changes taking place in a society, self-interest is afforded more space to pursue its own ends. The same will be true if the changes are not rooted in the indigenous values and are exogenously thrust upon a society, and this irrespective of whether these are formally incorporated into the legal corpus, as long as the required process of assimilation or adjustment remains incomplete. This may leave significant areas of social life in a state of flux for a prolonged period of time during which self-interest can indulge itself.

Beyond these difficulties, property rights will often not be effectively enforced because of the rent-seeking behavior of those responsible for enforcement; the self-interest of the enforcers is also liable to degenerate into selfishness. Arguably, no society can achieve full compliance with a given structure of property rights, for discreet excesses always remain possible; but equally no society can afford to turn a blind eye to the possibility of such excesses, and thereby to the problem such neglect may give rise to, a problem that may be referred to as the process of adverse selection. The problems of moral hazard and adverse selection are well-known in the economics discourse. I use these terms in a somewhat broader context, and tie the two in a manner slightly different from how they are used in financial economics. I define moral hazard as a situation where self-interest degenerates into selfishness regardless of whether a direct principle–agent relationship is involved or not. Thus, moral hazard covers the familiar principal–agent scenario but beyond that to also include willful violations of the structure of property rights. But it must be recognized that the moment this happens in connivance with those responsible for the enforcement of the property rights, as it often does, the principal–agent scenario becomes relevant, for after all a government is nothing more than an agent of the citizens (the principals), at least under any form of representative government. Moral hazard, to the extent it goes unchecked is likely to give rise to a process of adverse selection whereby it generates additional instances of moral hazard; for a violation of the property rights by one member of the society is bound to be considered by others as violation of the social contract which after all is the basis of an orderly society. If one member violates the social contract with impunity, others find it difficult not to reciprocate in a similar manner. One violation begets another, with the end result that this process becomes a self-perpetuating geometric progression, leading to chaos that may become increasingly difficult to reverse as time goes by. In a sense, unchecked repeated violations erode the commitment to the social contract, and thus lead to what I call the process of adverse selection. The more this process continues without society paying due attention to it because of the vested interests of those who benefit from this chaos, the more difficult it becomes to enforce the property rights, thereby geometrically increasing the costs of enforcement. In addition, no economy can flourish in an environment of chaos, for economics is all about exchange, and every act of exchange is a contract (a subject to which we will return shortly), and when contracts are discouraged, economic performance is bound to suffer. Economics would neglect this issue at the peril of becoming irrelevant to the extent a society undergoes this process of adverse selection.

At this stage, we may take a brief stock of the main points that emerge from the discussion about the interplay between the elements of the economic system discussed so far, namely property ownership, freedom of choice, and self-interest. First, freedom of choice, conditioned as it is by self-interest, is meaningless without the attendant property on which such freedom is to be exercised, in the broadest sense of that term, in so far as it forms the basis of defining property rights. Conversely, property ownership is meaningless without the relevant freedom of choice. Second, though this point is generally neglected in economic discourse, the social value of a structure of property rights is limited to the extent of its effective enforcement. In the final analysis, a structure of property rights without its effective enforcement amounts to absence of property rights. Third, it is during the state of flux, when the structure of property rights is coping to adjust to the changes brought about by technological change or otherwise, that self-interest is more likely to degenerate into selfishness, but more on that issue a little later. And finally, the legal corpus of a society, which defines its structure of property rights, cannot fail to reflect the underlying values, be those indigenous or alien impositions. There can be no such thing as a value-free economy or economic system.

And the Market System

We now come to the signaling postulate. The signaling system is meant to effectuate the allocation and distribution functions, and the practical form an economy takes, namely the economic system, essentially depends upon the institutionalized form of this signaling system. The signaling system adopted by a society must be consistent with the structure of property rights it has come to adopt. After all, the signals are meant for the holders of property rights. For instance, if all property rights are vested in the state, the signaling system will have to be very different from the case where they are vested in individual members of the society qua private citizens. If all property rights are vested in the state, there ensues socialism in its pure form (although it seems to me that we actually do not need to add the adjective). In this system, there may be a divestiture of state property rights down to even the individual level, but this is simply a matter of convenience rather than of conviction. It amounts to an acknowledgment of the inability of the state to cope practically with all the property rights vested in it. To illustrate the point: if prices existed in socialist countries, and we have observed that they did, this was merely to handle the complexity of distribution (rationing) without their support, and not to perform the allocation function (prior to that distribution). It was purely for the sake of convenience in the face of the enormity of the attendant task, and thus nothing more than an acknowledgment of the impossibility of, say, delivering everybody's breakfast on time every day. As long as allocation decisions are made by the state through an administrative fiat, the element of arbitrariness can hardly be ruled out from this process, if for no other reason than the enormous informational requirements attendant upon the required task. In this system, it is the state that, for instance, decides which hospitals people are born in, if indeed they are born in one, where they lived after leaving hospital, if they manage to do so, which schools they attend, what apparel they wear, what professions they adopt, where they worked, where they go for holidays, where they die, and finally where they are buried, if not cremated. The sarcasm here is meant to underscore the fact that at the individual level, there can be no freedom of choice because such is not possible without the existence of private property. In socialism, freedom of choice is the prerogative of the state. At the individual level, the system does not afford any room for the play of self-interest (apart from the result of some convenient divestiture), something which is an inherent property of the human psyche. But when property rights exist, as they must in any social setting—never mind the possibility that they may be defined through the law of the jungle—someone is bound to exercise the power associated with them. In socialism, it is the state functionaries. And since these functionaries are likely to be a law unto themselves, in absence of any checks on their behavior, their self-interest cannot but degenerate into selfishness. Socialism, or any system of authoritarian government, apart from its oppression, is bound to come to grief because of the scuttling of the motivation force at the private individual level.

But Then It's a Mixed Bag

If it is difficult to conceive of pure socialism for the foregoing reasons, it is equally difficult to conceive of a pure private economy (laissez faire, in its pure sense), defined as a situation in which all property rights are privately held with no state property rights. This amounts to absence of state and therefore of government, which is tantamount to anarchy. Leaving aside primitive times, a pure market economy has never existed, and is not likely to do so in future. What has always existed is a mixed system, where all three forms of property ownership have coexisted side by side. The hallmark of all such economies is their reliance, to varying degrees, on prices as signals for both allocation and distribution functions. Different names have been used to describe these economies, such as free-enterprise economies, capitalist economies, or market economies. At this level of generality, the most appropriate epithet is the last one. This is because a market economy can take various forms depending upon certain special features in its structure of property rights in addition to the minimum set under consideration here, and the name capitalism is in fact more a reflection of those features on the presumption that such an economy is necessarily a market economy.

The bare-bone distinguishing characteristics of a market economy are already clear. We may sum them up as:

a. private property, though not necessarily to the exclusion of state, and communal, property,
b. self-interest as the motivating force,
c. constrained freedom of choice as defined by the structure of property rights, and finally,
d. the use of price signals for performing both the allocation and distribution functions.

In such an economy, the structure of property rights which demarcates the permissible from the non-permissible is supposed to hold self-interest in check—it is another matter that it may not always succeed in doing so for the reasons already noted. But, and this is quite important, the property rights structure alone cannot accomplish the task under consideration because of the impossibility of devising a structure of property rights so detailed, and exhaustive, that it could rule out the possibility of excesses that may be committed in the name of self-interest by certain economic agents at the expense of others. This requires an elaboration.

Self-interest always feels the urge to circumvent, or bypass, the constraints imposed on it. Quite often this is because it is difficult to see where the boundaries of self-interest end. The laws may not be clear-cut enough to make this distinction clearly visible. In addition, each individual member, in his private capacity, may not see eye to eye with the society at large on the demarcation of these boundaries when it comes to his own self-interest. He would normally tend to stretch these boundaries when it comes to his own interests as compared to those of others in similar situations. "Self" has an inherent tendency to indulge itself, in self-praise and aggrandizement, and therefore assert itself at the expense of others. Individual self always feels itself to be somewhat special in relation to other members of society. As a result, people do not normally see it as such when they behave in a selfish manner. One could reasonably dismiss this worry by simply pointing out that the societal laws are oblivious to such individual blind spots, presuming that those laws are effectively enforced. This point would have considerable force provided the legal corpus was all that was required to regulate the social life of a society. That, however, is hardly ever the case. We have already noted that when it comes to that part of social life that is governed by unwritten laws, or where the legal corpus lags behind the changes thrust upon it, discreet excesses of self-interest are always present, and to the extent they become pervasive, they are likely to damage the social fabric of the society. What is more pertinent in the present context can be put in the form of the following question: is it possible to devise a legal corpus so comprehensive as to rule out any possibility that self-interest might cross into what the society would regard as selfishness? Putting it slightly differently, is it possible to precisely delineate the boundaries for the play of self-interest for every member of the society in every conceivable societal contingency? A little reflection would suggest that it is not possible to proffer an affirmative answer to this question even in a static society, for the number of attendant possibilities may well be infinite. One can dispense with the next question: even if we admit this possibility, could such a structure of property rights be effectively enforced at a reasonable cost?

This point could be explained in a number of ways even within the confines of economic discourse. The easiest one is to recognize that every act of exchange implies a contract. Such a contract could be explicit, in which case it could be either formal, and therefore written, or informal, and therefore verbal; or it could even be implicit, and therefore unspoken or unarticulated. To rule out the possibility of self-interest degenerating into selfishness in every individual act of exchange, which amounts to specifying property rights for each possible case, is beyond the capacity of any legal corpus, if not theoretically then at least practically, simply because of the enormity of the task involved. It is another matter that even if it were possible to devise such a legal corpus, it may not be advisable. Granted that it may be desirable to have as detailed a legal corpus (laws, rules, and regulations) as possible in situations where a misuse of free will (for instance in the exercise of discretionary power) is feared, such details may be undesirable where initiative and drive would be considered as a positive attribute, such as would be the case in business dealings. In the context of an economic system, the function of the legal corpus is to restrain excesses of self-interest and not to unduly constrain the freedom of choice. But it is impossible for the legal corpus to draw a line between restraint, and undue constraint. As far as the legal corpus of a society is concerned, self-interest will always enjoy some room for maneuverability, and while this may have an intrinsic merit in business dealings, at times this maneuverability may give rise to excesses.

The prolonged medieval debate on the idea of "just price"—an idea that is still with us, if not in so many words—can only be understood in the context of this point. That an individual or a group could be unjust to another individual or group is beyond any doubt. A few words on the idea of injustice are in order before we proceed any further. The idea of injustice is something that cannot be divorced from the play of free will. When an individual or group is deemed to be unjust to another individual or group, through the play of collective or individual free will, there is no hesitation judging the resulting price unjust. But consider the possibility where an individual or group outcome seems unjust, but where no malice (unjust intention) on the part of any individual or group can be deemed as the cause. Clearly, such a possibility cannot be ruled out, but should such an outcome be called unjust notwithstanding the fact that it is commonly labeled as such? To my mind, words such as "harsh" or "cruel" may be more appropriate provided, of course, that it can be ascertained that no individual bad intention came into play to influence the outcome.

Evaluation of the justness or otherwise of a market price entails the difficulty that any price can be considered just and unjust at the same time, depending on who is looking at the crystal ball of the market. From the buyer's point of view, any price is excessive—after all he/she gazes at the ball through the lens of his/her own self-interest—and from the seller's point of view, no price may be unjust, for precisely the same reasons. The two groups do not use the same lens while looking at the crystal ball. No legal corpus, no matter how broad an agreement, even consensus, it may command on other social issues, is going to resolve this difficulty. Is there another objective way, apart from the legal corpus, to resolve this difficulty? It is this riddle that Adam Smith (1776) conceptually resolved by underlining the role of competition in a market system that eventually led to its incorporation in the fundamental tenets of a market economy. Smith's well known argument is very simple, and very potent. There is no need to worry about individual exploitative behavior as long as there is sufficiently large number of participants in the marketplace, i.e. numbers large enough to impose conformity on the price-taking behavior on the part of all the participants. To continue with the previous analogy, when so many lenses are piled up, one on top of the other, and everyone is forced to view the crystal ball through their combined opaqueness, nobody would be able to even see the ball clearly, let alone working out what it held out for any individual viewer. In other words, nobody would have the power to influence the price that prevailed in the market, and therefore, nobody would be in a position to exploit anybody else. There would be nothing personal about the market outcome, and when that is true, the question of an individual free will succeeding in exploiting, and therefore inflicting injustice on others, through voluntary transactions does not arise. That is to say that while every seller may wish to exploit the buyers, competition makes it impossible for him to do so. We must, nevertheless, consider the question: could a price determined through this impersonal process be considered unjust? It is possible for such a price to seem excessive to some, or even to all, members of the society? This is another way of admitting the possibility that competition itself at times could be considered unfair by some. But it must be recognized that this will essentially be because of the existing distribution of factor endowments, or more appropriately the existing structure of property rights, rather than an inherent weakness of the idea of competition. This may require a change in the structure of property rights. At any rate, it may be better to deem such a price "harsh" rather than "unjust" in exactly the way one would hardly judge harshness of the elements as unjust.

But what is the exact nature of connection between competition, *per se*, and the number of participants in a market? Is it necessary that there be large numbers for there to be competition, and therefore an absence of possible individual exploitative behavior? Competition can ensue even when the number of participants is as small as two; indeed, in such cases it is likely to be of a cutthroat variety, which means that the price may even be below what would be regarded as its "just" level—provided one could somehow find that level—even if that phenomenon may occur only transitorily. But the possibility of collusive behavior between the two sellers is so strong that such cases of cutthroat competition may be regarded as aberrations from the norm. Yet it is important to note that any collusive behavior involves a play of free will motivated by selfishness, unless it is in response to an equally selfish behavior by an agent or agents on the other side of the transaction. As the number of economic agents in a collusive arrangement increases, it becomes increasingly difficult to reach a mutually satisfactory collusive arrangement, which, in turn, means a corresponding decrease in the likelihood of self-interest degenerating into selfishness. When the numbers involved on both the demand and supply sides are large, the selfish collusive behavior becomes a practical impossibility. It is therefore clear that presence of large numbers on both sides is a *sufficient*, but not *necessary*, condition for absence of exploitative behavior. Perfect competition necessarily rules it out, but the other market forms, which involve more than one economic agent on both the demand and supply sides, i.e. excluding monopoly and monopsony, do not *necessarily* imply exploitative behavior, although the smaller the numbers, the greater the likelihood of such an occurrence as a result of either the relative ease of collusive behavior, or the presence of significant market power with one or more firms. But when it comes to monopoly, or for that matter, monopsony, things are altogether different, and in view of the preceding discussion, there is no need to belabor the point that exploitative behavior will be the rule rather than exception.

It may, however, be noted that apart from collusion, exploitative behavior can also arise out of informational asymmetries, a situation where economic agents on opposite sides of a transaction do not have access to the same information. That one may get exploited out of ignorance is obvious, yet it may be noted that the implications of asymmetric information become serious only in the intermediate market forms such as oligopoly and monopolistic competition. In the extreme market forms, they are unimportant either because they are difficult to sustain, as in the case of perfect competition, or they do not matter one way or the other, as in the case of monopoly or monopsony. In the latter case, the exploitation is not a function of such an asymmetry.

The foregoing discussion boils down to the following summary statement. In a market economy, prices serve as signals to both producers and consumers. As a result, the resources are allocated to the production of various goods and services by economic agents—citizens *qua* producers—and these are then distributed back to those economic agents—citizens *qua* consumers. The allocation and distribution functions are actually two sides of the same coin, as long as the two functions are performed through the same price signals. Possibility of exclusion at a negligible, or relatively low, cost (the transaction costs) underscores the fact that prices can serve as a mechanism to enforce property rights, with competition serving as an additional and complementary check on the play of self-interest to cover the contingencies where the property rights could, or would, not be so meticulously specified as to ensure an absence of exploitative behavior.[2] To clarify the point, consider the example of a homogeneous product being sold at various locations in a given city. Since different locations can have different rents, theoretically there could be as many prices as locations, each representing a just price for a specific location. Once it is admitted that a homogeneous product can have different prices, then in practice which products are at their just level and which are not is clearly beyond the capacity of any legal corpus to handle effectively. But once competitive conditions are ensured, there is no need to lose any sleep over the possibility of exploitative behavior. The role of competition in a market economy cannot be over-emphasized. The signaling system when erected on the foundation of market determined prices requires the support of competition to establish its acceptance and prestige in the societal ethos, that is, to become an essential part of the society's set of values. In absence of that, or rather in absence of institutionalization of competition, prices are likely to be perceived as instruments of tyranny by one or another section of the society, and so would be the corresponding market economy. It is this role that has secured a lasting place for competition as an additional tenet or postulate, besides the previously noted four, in the minimum set of characteristics of a market economy; it has led in the corresponding societies to assign to their governments the responsibility for ensuring that markets remain as competitive as possible. In this, the role of the government is conceived of either as an arbiter, a referee, an adjudicator, if you will, between the two groups of players, i.e. the buyers and the sellers, or that of a regulator, to insure, *inter alia*, that there are no barriers to entry into the markets. But, then, there is much more to the institution of government in a market economy than ensuring competition, as we will see.

---

[2] It will not be lost on the reader that my emphasis on property rights and transaction costs here and later underscores the significance of the New Institutional Economics (NIE) that began with the publication of Coase's (1937) seminal article. For a relatively recent focus on NIE, see the proceedings on the same subject in a roundtable discussion as published in American Economic Review (May 1998), especially Coase (1998), and Williamson (1998).

Before proceeding any further, however, it will be helpful to link this discussion to that of the last chapter on the subject of fundamental axioms of welfare economics. Markets only ensure equilibrium between the demand and supply forces provided certain conditions relating to existence and stability are satisfied. The question now is: how does the equilibrium outcome fare with respect to efficiency (the allocation function) and equity (the distribution function)? Though the relevant points have already been discussed, we do, however, need a fresh look at them from the perspective of a market economy. In light of the preceding discussion, it is clear that an answer to this question crucially depends on the assumed market structure. Consider, first, the issue of equity, and assume perfectly competitive markets. Given the structure of property rights, which is predicated on the initial distribution of factor endowments, each factor gets a reward according to its marginal productivity, which, in turn, will be used as an expression of demand for various goods and services, leading to the corresponding allocation of resources. Once the relevant goods and services have been produced, these will be distributed back to the individuals according to the demands they had expressed. This process is conceived to have a simultaneous character as is stressed by the general equilibrium models. Once the markets have discharged these functions, one is entitled to ask the important question: is the resulting distribution of income socially acceptable, or in the common parlance of welfare economics, equitable? An answer to this question that exclusively focuses on the market prices—whether those of inputs or outputs is quite immaterial since both sets are interrelated—misses the point that these, in turn, are crucially dependent upon the initial distribution of factor endowments. If that distribution is regarded as just, then the result is *ipso facto* just. If, on the other hand, the prevailing distribution of income is considered unacceptable, it is because the initial distribution of factor endowments was not just, rather than the resulting prices being unjust. Under the assumptions of perfect competition, if the prices cannot be unjust, the distribution of initial factor endowments may well be so. It is for this reason that a value judgment at the societal level is inescapable. Such a value judgment may require implementation of a policy of redistribution in favor of a certain groups, in which case it may be appropriate to orient such a policy to changing factor endowments through, for instance, affirmative action—recall the charge of competition being unfair—education and retraining, instead of market intervention that focuses only on input/output prices. In any case, a society cannot ignore the fact that redistribution is not a costless activity. Besides the administrative costs, which would need to be subjected to requirements of technical efficiency, a policy of redistribution may, and ordinarily does, introduce additional costs in the form of deadweight losses due to the accompanying misallocation of resources. The societal objectives with regard to equity and efficiency may come in conflict with one another. It is, therefore, quite possible, in certain cases, that while redistribution is adjudged to be desirable *in principle*, a policy of redistribution may not be implemented in view of the associated costs. It all depends on these *costs* in relation to the expected *benefits* of redistribution. Alternative redistribution policies that achieve the same goals may have different administrative costs. Technical efficiency would require that these costs be minimized. Neither can one avoid Pareto nor inter-personal comparisons of utility even when it comes to deciding which policy is the best and most efficient in achieving a particular redistributive objective. (Since Pareto optimality is the universally accepted objective criterion in economics, I have thought it reasonable to invoke it in the present chapter, pending answers to the question of its suitability or otherwise for an Islamic economy in Chapter 5).

When it comes to market forms other than perfect competition, the same arguments remain valid except for one additional dimension. This time the distribution of income may become unacceptable not only because the initial distribution of endowments was deemed to be unjust, but because the market prices may also be so, as a result of the possibility of exploitative behavior. If that turns out to be the case, the appropriate policy response might as well focus on that portion of the structure of property rights that made such exploitation possible. One may here refer to the anti-trust, or anti-monopoly, legislation that is part of the legal corpus of various countries, and which is meant precisely to rectify such excesses. It may be pointed out that these market forms do not, in general, satisfy either the technical or allocative efficiency conditions. Exceptions to this statement are noted later in the discussion of the issue of natural monopoly.

Let us now turn to the allocation function. Here the market mechanism has a number of well-known failings. These can be split into two broad classes, depending upon the cause of failure. In one of these classes, the cause pertains to the difficulties relating to property rights and resides in either i) the difficulty of enforcing the related structure of property rights through prices, as in the case of externalities and public goods, or ii) the way those rights are specified, as happens in the case of common property resources. In the other class, the cause is purely technical, that is the unexhausted economies of scale, leading to the problem of natural monopoly. In all these cases, market mechanism fails to satisfy allocative efficiency conditions. We will briefly take up each of these cases in order.

Consider perfect competition, and assume an absence of external effects—the question of unexhausted economies of scale, by definition, does not arise in the case of perfect competition. The demand curve, when viewed from the perspective of the quantity axis, represents the willingness to pay at the margin for each possible quantity, and can be labeled as Marginal Private Benefits (MPB) curve. Under the assumed absence of external effects on the consumption side, the curve becomes identical to Marginal Social Benefits (MSB) curve. Similarly, on the supply side, the supply curve, namely the Marginal Cost (MC) curve, becomes identical to Marginal Social Costs (MSC) curve. The equilibrium outcome now satisfies marginal conditions relating to efficiency, namely the equality between MSB and MSC, with the result that the allocation of resources is Pareto optimal. At the same time, it also satisfies the technical efficiency conditions by forcing each of the firms to produce an output level that conforms to the lowest possible unit cost. The long run equilibrium price in a perfectly competitive industry is determined by its correspondence to the minimum point on the long-run Average Cost (AC) curves of the relevant firms.

Economic Role of the Government

When external effects on either the production and/or consumption side are present, the supply and/or demand curves fail to represent the corresponding social values at the margin, which means the equilibrium outcome does not satisfy the Pareto optimality conditions. Externalities, variously called external, neighborhood, spillover, or third-party effects, arise when production or consumption activities give rise to beneficial or harmful effects—benefits or costs—that are not reflected in the corresponding supply and demand curves. These benefits and costs generally accrue to individuals who are not a direct party to the relevant production or consumption activities, although it is possible that a part of these may accrue to those who are directly involved in the relevant activities, as, for instance, would happen in the case of a common property externality, to be discussed later, or in the case of reciprocal externalities. Market mechanism fails to allocate resources efficiently in the face of externalities. But this failure is a qualified one; market mechanism does not necessarily fail in all such cases. The real culprit is to be found in either an absence of clear property rights delineation, and/or a difficulty in the enforcement of the corresponding structure of property rights through price mechanism. Professor Ronald Coase (1960), in the now celebrated path-breaking paper, showed that market mechanism will satisfy allocative efficiency conditions by internalizing an externality provided certain conditions are satisfied. Accordingly, in a situation of externality, negotiations among the concerned parties will lead to a mutually satisfactory resolution of the problem, provided i) the property rights are clearly defined, and ii) the transaction costs, including the negotiation costs, are relatively low. Some writers add a third condition, that the number of parties involved be small. But if it is recognized that the transaction costs, defined broadly as the costs of concluding an exchange, are directly related to the number of parties that must agree to the settlement, the third condition becomes redundant and can therefore be dropped, particularly in view of the difficulty of defining how small is small. This helps us draw certain conclusions. When considering the resolution of an externality problem, the first thing that needs to be looked into is whether or not the property rights, i.e. who has the right to do what, are clearly defined. Defining them more clearly, when they were not clearly spelled out, may resolve the problem, provided the second condition is satisfied.

If that is not the case, and the transaction costs are relatively high, relative to the benefits of internalization that is, and this in all probability will happen when the number of parties is large, a negotiated, or market, solution will not emerge even if the property rights had been clearly defined. In all such situations, government will have to directly intervene if the externality is to be internalized. It may be noted in passing that such an intervention may, and generally would, have distributional consequences. A well-delineated structure of property rights implies a clear liability for damages, and therefore internalization foreseen by Coase anticipates compensation payments for damages if the underlying structure of property rights accords a sanction to the rights of the affected party. When a government intervention is accompanied by the required compensation payments, such an intervention is in principle equivalent to private solution, and the government intervention purely an attempt to economize on transaction costs. No change in the structure of property rights is attendant upon such an internalization. The outcome honors the prevailing structure of property rights in exactly the same way as it did in the case of private solution. If, however, the required compensation payments are not affected, for instance for lack of detailed information, the internalization will actually amount to an alteration in the structure of property rights in favor of the government. Those who are at the receiving end of the externality will continue to suffer the harms attendant upon the now optimal level of output because of the difficulties associated with affecting the compensation payments. The distribution of income changes as a result of the high costs of making compensation payments that would be required to maintain the property rights status quo.

Returning to the argument, the foregoing discussion by no means implies that government ought to intervene in each and every situation of externality that escapes a private solution. If there are high transaction costs in the case of private solution that lead to an impasse, and necessitate a solution through the government, the required intervention will have its own counterpart costs, in the form of administrative costs. These costs must be taken into consideration to assess the viability of an intervention, to ensure that as a result the society does not end up with negative net social benefits. It goes without saying that if different alternatives for internalization are available, *ceteris paribus,* the one that maximizes net social benefits must be selected. Either we go back to Pareto to get some idea of what happens to social welfare, acknowledging that this answer may not always be precise as a result of informational problems, or abandon him, in which case we would have no idea of the changes in social welfare that result from the goings-on in what would then become a black box economy.

The second difficulty arises when for certain goods/services that a society wishes to consume, the transaction costs are not relatively low, either because exclusion is impossible (implying infinite transaction costs), or difficult, in which case it implies relatively high transaction costs, that is, relative to the benefits of exclusion. Since transaction costs, just like any other cost, are reflected in the price of goods/services, the market mechanism breaks down. It fails in the former case because the price will be infinite, and in the latter case because the minimum supply price will be higher than the maximum demand price. In both cases, market mechanism leads to corner solutions, i.e. zero output, simply because of the relatively high transaction costs. This is the familiar public goods problem. Prices cannot now serve the function of enforcing the attendant structure of property rights. Such goods, whether of pure (infinite transaction costs) or impure (relatively high transaction costs) variety, must be provided through non-market mechanism, a mechanism that will reduce the transaction costs sufficiently to make their provision economically viable. That alternative is the political mechanism (costs associated with collection of taxes to pay for these goods could now be considered the relevant transaction costs). This implies that the government is now not just an uninterested third party as far as allocation of resources is concerned; it is actively involved in that process, as actively as it would be in the case of externalities when Coasian conditions are not satisfied.

The third difficulty arises because of the way the property rights may have come to be entrenched in the structure of property rights from the times when property, or more appropriately a resource, was abundant and its ownership—that is exclusive rights to the benefits derivable from it—did not matter one way or the other. Everyone in the community had an equal access to the property for the purpose of deriving private benefits. There were now rights pertaining to the use of the property but there were no corresponding responsibilities for its upkeep. It goes without saying that abundance renders the issue of upkeep irrelevant. But when the resource became scarce with the passage of time, and the question of its ownership became pertinent, at times the prevailing practice of open access for everyone was recognized, leading to its entrenchment in the structure of property rights, and so led to what has come to be known as communal ownership. Because of the scarcity of the resource, the question about its upkeep now assumed a crucial significance. But since rights in communal property come without the corresponding responsibilities for the upkeep of the property, it leads to the well-known "tragedy of the commons" or the common property externality. The resulting overuse or over-exploitation ultimately causes the destruction of the property. Until the right of exclusion is incorporated in the structure of property rights, through either privatization or transfer of at least some property rights to the state, the dilemma of the commons cannot be resolved. The transfer of property rights to the state does not necessarily mean state ownership, as it normally would be understood, and therefore non-recognition of the traditional communal rights. It must, however, lead to some sort of controlled access through regulation by state or a cooperative arrangement as must happen in the case of global commons where the alternatives of privatization or state ownership are simply not available. Regulation must also be resorted to, as is discussed later, in the case of natural monopoly.

This massive appeal to the government to resolve the allocational difficulties faced by a market economy obliges us to attempt an elementary understanding of the nature of state property rights. We can get a glimpse of what is involved by confining ourselves to the nature of rights associated with state property under a representative form of government. This will also help us to formally note the differences between "private," "state," and "communal" forms of ownership in light of the remarks made at the beginning of this chapter. Conceptually, the most important right associated with ownership of property is the right to exclude others from the use of that property. The problem with communal property arises precisely from an absence of this right. That this "right to exclude" is the hallmark of private property goes without saying. It is through this exclusion principle that a society acknowledges the right of its individual members, or, for that matter, grants them the right, to exclusively claim the benefits derivable from the property under consideration. Individuals, in their capacity as owners, appropriate whatever benefits are derivable from the property, and therefore are correspondingly held responsible for whatever costs may be attributable, or may ultimately come to be attributed, to the property. In the case of state property, and state being a collective organ (an agent) of the society, the benefits derivable from the property are supposed to ultimately accrue to the individual members of the society (the principals)—who are ultimately the real owners of the property—though the individual members concede the right of exclusion to the agent. What is important to note is that individual members agree to circumscribe their private rights in favor of the state. The end result of this is a divorce of ownership from control, which gives rise to the familiar "principal and agent" problem. We will have occasions to discuss this important issue at length later in this work. Here it suffices to note that this leads to the familiar problems of moral hazard and rent-seeking behavior that have very serious economic consequences. And beyond all that, when a society also bestows additional powers of market interference on state, in all this it attempts to solve one set of problems but, then, ends up facing another, and it is not quite clear whether, in the final analysis, it becomes any better off as a result.

Let us now turn to the problem of natural monopoly. Conceptually, the issue of natural monopoly regulation poses no difficulty, especially in light of the consonance between equity and efficiency considerations. When regulation imposes a price ceiling, which leads to an increase in monopoly output, it reduces the associated deadweight loss at the same time that it would be distributionally commendable. But on the practical side, devising a policy that is equitable to parties on both sides of the divide, i.e. the producers and the consumers, turns out to be fairly complicated. This requires a brief look at the issue of monopoly in general. There are several sources of monopoly. Besides what are known as technical reasons, a monopoly may arise as a result of barriers that are rooted in the structure of property rights. These include barriers such as ownership of strategic raw materials, and the legal barriers including grant of patents, copyrights, registration and trade marks, and permits and licenses to operate particular businesses. Theoretically, there may be quite sound economic reasons (dynamic efficiency) for granting of these exclusive rights. However, at times granting of such rights may be motivated more by rent-seeking behavior, particularly in the case of permits and licenses, not to mention the spurious granting of patents and trade marks, etc., than sound economic considerations. To the extent the resulting excesses are widespread owing to the weaknesses of the political system, we are back to the government itself being a major part of the problem. Other than that, monopoly, when rooted in the structure of property rights, could be thought of as enjoying some sort of tacit social approval with the exception of a monopoly that is based upon the ownership of some strategic resource, and even in that case it may be tolerated in deference to the institution of private property. Correspondingly, while in these cases regulation may or may not be an irresistible imperative, in the case of natural monopoly, which arises for purely technical reasons, it can be taken for granted. Of course, it is possible that a particular monopoly may arise as a result of a combination of these two sets of reasons, i.e. a natural monopoly enjoying patent rights is quite possible. An appropriate regulatory response will have to take both of these reasons into consideration.

The technical reasons that give rise to natural monopoly include things such as high set-up (fixed) costs, and economies of scale over the relevant range of output. Generally, the literature attributes the rise of natural monopoly to economies of scale contingent upon indivisibilities on the production side. A careful look reveals that, in fact, there may be two conceptually distinct reasons for the rise of natural monopoly, one relating to increasing returns to scale, and the other to indivisibilities on the production side. As far as economies of scale are concerned, the rise of natural monopoly does not require unbounded economies of scale—any scale economies are bound to be exhausted eventually—but only that such economies prevail in the relevant range of output as determined by the existing demand conditions, or rather market size. If their exhaustion point lies beyond the relevant range of output, the long-run AC curve will be negatively sloped in that range, and hence the corresponding MC curve will lie below the AC curve. In such a case, even if the industry were to start with a large number of firms, only one will eventually survive, thus becoming a natural monopoly. An equally plausible way in which a natural monopoly could arise would be a delay in the operation of the law of diminishing returns. This will happen if the minimum plant size (set-up costs) was so large in relation to the relevant range of output that in that range AC would still be falling, and therefore the corresponding MC curve would lie below the AC curve. In this case, it is the minimum plant size, arising out of indivisibilities on the production side, which becomes critical in giving rise to a natural monopoly. Either natural monopoly arises due to such indivisibilities, in which case the question of scale economies does not apply, or the cause is to be found in the unexhausted economies of scale, in which case the question of indivisibilities becomes irrelevant.

At any rate, a monopoly, natural or otherwise, is open to objections on both equity and efficiency grounds. A monopoly will generally be technically inefficient in the sense that it will rarely achieve the lowest possible AC of production. If it ever achieves that result, which will happen when its MC curve crosses its Marginal Revenue curve at the minimum point on its AC curve, it will be purely a matter of coincidence. Even in that case, the possibility of the entire configuration of AC curves being located on a higher plane than would be the case under perfectly competitive conditions, because of X-inefficiency, cannot be ruled out. This may be just a reflection of the lack of competitive pressure on the monopolist, leading to somewhat complacent behavior on his part, rather than an indication of intentional exploitative behavior. As far as allocative efficiency is concerned, monopoly does not satisfy the marginal conditions except in the theoretically extreme, and practically impossible, case of perfect price discrimination. Practically speaking, there will always be a deadweight loss of monopoly. These inefficiencies are bound to be reflected in the higher price, making monopoly, whether natural or otherwise, objectionable on distributional grounds. In any case, it must be kept in mind that the issue of natural monopoly regulation cannot be divorced either from technical change, which leads to a change in the configuration of cost curves, or from the prevailing demand conditions. Today's monopoly may be tomorrow's competitive industry, to put it in somewhat stark terms. It is therefore clear that any solution to the natural monopoly problem must be subject to a continuous review to ensure that up-to-date changes in demand and supply conditions are duly taken into consideration.

The regulation policy must not only ensure a price considered fair from the consumers' point of view but also a fair return to the monopolist. This may not always be easy. Determining a fair return to the monopolist may be complicated when there are multiple reasons for the existence of a monopoly, i.e. a natural monopoly enjoying a patent protection. And determining a fair price from the consumers' point of view may be tricky when there are inherent technical and X-inefficiencies. A monopolist who is guaranteed a particular return, and no more than that, has no incentive to be technically efficient, that is, to build a plant size that leads to output being produced at the lowest possible point on the AC curve. Besides, he has no incentive to eliminate any X-inefficiency that is likely to creep in.

Any government that is responsible for regulation of the various monopolies that are bound to arise; given the task of resolving the misallocation of resources that is bound to occur as a result of the all-pervasive externalities; held responsible for the provision of a plethora of public goods; liable to efficiently enforce the existing property rights as well as adjudicate fairly in situations involving conflicts; and that is then asked to ensure that the distribution of income conforms to certain socially sanctioned norms of equity is bound to find itself struggling in the best of times. But this is precisely what economics requires a government to do, and do it persistently against a background that is continuously shifting. Needless to say, there are myriad other responsibilities that a government is required to shoulder. The puzzling factual observation that governments quite readily accept all these responsibilities does not give one the impression of an institution straining under the demands of the job. For an explanation one would need to turn to the other side of the page. With responsibilities come corresponding rights—the property rights. While it is easy to accept or even acquire, if not usurp, rights, it is much more difficult to discharge the corresponding responsibilities. If individuals can misuse their power (conferred upon them by property rights), so can the governments, particularly when the government itself happens to be a monopoly, rather a natural one. If a society feels compelled to restrain its individual members' behavior through its structure of property rights, it would logically wish to do the same for its government. For this purpose, it may introduce additional safeguards in the form of checks and balances within the structure of its government. Yet the fact remains that these checks and balances are inherently internal to the government. A government is then a self-regulated monopoly, and howsoever conscientiously it may impose upon itself those regulatory constraints, it still remains a monopoly, given to possible excesses. It is this point that must be taken into consideration when assessing the reliance Islamic economists are wont to place on an undefined form of government as will be seen at a number of places in various chapters of this work.

To conclude this chapter, an economy cannot fail to reflect the values of the society whose constituent part it happens to be, and these, at the formal level, are enshrined in its structure of property rights. Consequently what form an economy takes depends to a large degree on this structure. Since this structure can vary across time and space, economies of various societies will reflect the corresponding differences, although there may be certain general traits that may endure across time and space and for a prolonged period of time. A market economy is one such general form whose broad contours have been the subject of this chapter. It goes without saying, that a market economy is not inherently a monolith, and may assume various forms subject to the additional relevant details contained in the structure of society's property rights. These details will be reflected in the additional economic institutions, institutions in addition to those discussed earlier. It is these additional institutions that make a market system capitalism, and it is these that, in my judgment, will make a market economy an Islamic economy. Capitalism is necessarily a market economy, but a market economy does not need to be a capitalistic one. I will discuss the institutions that render a market economy capitalist in Chapter 4, and then turn to the fundamental axioms of an Islamic economy in Chapter 5. Further explorations about the structure of such an economy in Chapters 6 to 8 show that an Islamic economy is necessarily a market economy.

CHAPTER FOUR

A PERSPECTIVE ON CAPITALISM

Introduction

The market economy, an outline of which was the subject matter of Chapter 3, has existed in a crude or refined form for millennia. But as it entered the modern epoch, spanning the past few centuries, it began to evolve into a unique form that eventually came to be known as capitalism. The epithet capitalism, though of a relatively recent origin, has gained such a currency that economics literature mostly does not even bother to make a distinction between the two, with the end result that market economy and capitalism have become synonymous. Perhaps there was no imperative to delve into this distinction; it seemingly would not have made much of a difference, one way or another, given the sociocultural milieu in which the discipline of economics gained increasing level of maturity in the second half of the nineteenth century. For our purpose, however, this distinction is pivotal for the reasons noted in Chapter 1, reasons that formed the basis of coverage in Chapter 3. The evolution of any institution naturally reflects the environment in which it evolves. Since the modern market economy was molded into its present form in the West, it could hardly fail to take on its hues. It was bound to reflect whatever homogeneity and diversity Western civilization had to offer the world, diversity in the sense that capitalism assumed many shades, and homogeneity in so far as all these shades had a certain number of common abiding features. One important focus of this chapter is to highlight that while capitalism is necessarily a market economy (though admittedly not of the pure variety—and indeed that fact becomes the second focus of this chapter), a market economy is not necessarily the same thing as capitalism. A market economy must possess certain additional characteristics, and thus also the attendant institutions—besides the ones noted in the previous chapter—to render it capitalist. In what follows, I intend to identify what in my view is an irreducible set of these additional characteristics, with a specific view to how the discipline of economics came to terms with their gradual evolution—an evolution that embedded these characteristics in the structure of property rights in more or less all the countries of the world, albeit following the lead of the West. From the viewpoint of Islamic economics, economics ended up condoning, and even lending respectability to, this structure of property rights. (The commonly accepted stance that economics generally does not concern itself with the issue of what ought to be the property rights structure of a society is in reality not quite tenable, for there are instances—in the area of environment and international trade—where it has vigorously attempted to influence that structure. We may recall our discussion in the previous chapters to see the rationale behind the positions thus advocated). What is important in the context of the following exposition is that Islamic economists have failed to realize that a considerable part of what they would regard as the objectionable structure of property rights is actually vested in the government. The second focus of this chapter, therefore, is to show that what they are objecting to as far as capitalism is concerned flows more from the governmental interference in the economy rather than being an inherent feature of capitalism or a market economy. This fact becomes somewhat ironic in view of the enormous powers Islamic economists would readily vest in the government, as we will see in Chapters 6 and 7, and specifically in Chapter 10 in the context of material covered in the present chapter. We now turn to the first issue and in passing note here that an Islamic economy will depart from capitalism to the extent its own variants of these attendant institutions differ from those of capitalism.

This new set includes two characteristics: (i) the commoditization of money, which in turn facilitated the eventual instrumentalization of interest (though this was predicated on the prior existence of the institution of interest), and (ii) the institution of limited liability, with the caveat that the first of these institutions is the fundamental, the defining, institution of capitalism, while the second is an attendant institution, an institution that supports and complements it.[1] The nature of this symbiotic relationship can be appreciated only when one recognizes that the institution of limited liability would not make any

[1] I would, however, like to point out that the institution of limited liability may exist in a market economy which is not capitalist in light of the liability that may arise in response to consumer protection laws. But then that is quite a different matter, and something that is not relevant to the discussion at hand.

sense without the institution of interest, and the institution of interest will not proceed very far in the context of modern financing requirements of business, especially in the corporate sector of the economy, without the institution of limited liability. By the institution of interest, I mean a contractual arrangement about debt where the liability of the debtor is fixed (beforehand) in nominal terms, i.e. in terms of money, without necessarily paying any regard to how or where the funds that gave rise to the debt under consideration may be utilized. By the commoditization of money I mean a situation where money becomes an object of inter-temporal exchange in its own right without any regard to the price paid for its use (the interest) and the expected profits as determined in the real sector of the economy. The term "instrumentalization of interest" means the same thing, except that in this case the government becomes one of the parties to the transactions and thus the severance of relationship between interest and the expected profits occurs as a result of its use of the rate of interest as a policy tool to achieve certain stabilization objectives. A structure of property rights that sanctions the use of such contracts, and where, as a result, the financial system of the economy is overwhelmingly grounded in such contracts, would mean that the economy has commoditized the money, and to the extent it permits the government's use of the rate of interest as a policy tool, it would be deemed to have instrumentalized the interest. In the following pages we will see that while classical economists were careful in maintaining the link between interest and the expected profits, such has not been the case beginning with Keynes, and while a strong voice did emerge against instrumentalization of interest in the past four decades, not much attention has been paid to the problem of commoditization of money. To the extent economics has lent respectability to these two institutional developments, it shares the blames for the excesses of capitalism.

The institution of interest gives rise to a number of difficulties at the conceptual level, not to mention the obvious ones relating to the Scriptures because of the association of interest with usury in the Judeo-Christian context and *ribā* in the Islamic context. At the conceptual level, the West, and consequently economics, has come to see interest in a very different light from Islamic economists. Islamic economists have seen interest as a predetermined fixed return on money, and as such a risk-free return not at par with profit where the latter is viewed as legitimate return on investment of the same money.

Issues such as the real rate of interest, which cannot be known with certainty *ex-ante*, the risk of default, and *fiqh*'s permissibility of fixed returns in certain transactions are brushed aside as unimportant in view of the presumed equality between interest and *ribā*. How far this presumption is justified is a subject that will be treated at length in Chapters 9 and 10. Here we would confine ourselves to the issues already identified, and begin by noting that while the institution of interest has existed from time immemorial, and not just in the West, economics came to terms with it only gradually, and somewhat grudgingly I feel, but when it eventually did, during the first half of the twentieth century, it smoothed the way to a process already underway of instrumentalization of interest. The following pages trace a brief outline of this story, with an eye to the relationship between interest and profits, as well as the related conceptual difficulties that lay on the way. Towards the end of this chapter, I also attempt to underscore the economic implications, both distributional and allocational, that flow from the instrumentalization of interest under its attendant structure of property rights.

Capitalism can mean different things to different people, yet one way or the other all shades of meanings revolve round the concept of capital. For some, it may be understood to highlight the significance of capital as a factor of production, particularly in view of the important role capital accumulation has played in the process of growth, specifically in roughly the past two and a half centuries. Others may focus on the capitalist mode of production, but again this relates to capital as a factor of production. And yet others may underscore the dimension of accumulation as such, the unscrupulous concern with accumulation of wealth, recognizing that capital, particularly of the physical variety, is a major component of such wealth. I take a somewhat broader and fluid view of capital and define it to include, besides physical capital, the financial capital—the putty that awaits transformation into clay, or is at least directly linked to that transformation, primarily, if not exclusively, through the support of financial institutions, and therefore *capitalism as a market economy with a distinct financial system that relies, primarily if not exclusively, on the institution of interest to channel financial capital without necessarily imposing any binding (usually legal) restrictions for it to undergo a transformation or at least be directly associated with an existing or new process of transformation.* While the concept of transformation is readily understood in economics, for the sake of clarity let it be noted here that it refers to transformation of present goods into future goods, and in the present context, of financial capital into productive assets, primarily physical capital—of putty into clay—with the aim of producing goods and services in future.

According to this definition, the distinguishing feature of capitalism at the practical level is its use of debt finance based, it should go without saying, on institutionalized interest. It is only when this feature is made an integral part of the minimum set of institutions defining a market economy that the market economy is transformed into capitalism. This way of defining capitalism comes quite close to how Joseph Schumpeter (1928, p. 362) saw it when he wrote, "we have to define what we mean by 'our economic system': We mean an economic system characterized by private property (private initiatives), by production for a market and by the phenomenon of credit, this phenomenon being the *differentia specifica* distinguishing the 'capitalist' system from other species, historic or possible, of the larger genus defined by the two first characteristics." This places the financial institutions of capitalism right at the center of our analysis, and it also obliges us to pay a closer attention to who controls those institutions or, for that matter, whose interests these institutions end up serving.

It is tautological to say that capitalism serves the interests of capitalists. But who exactly belongs to this class? It seems natural to include the owners of capital, but then things are not as simple as that, or rather they have not turned out to be as simple as that. The structure of property rights associated with capital in a particular society may well confer, as it has for reasons that need not detain us here, its control on part owners or even non-owners, giving rise to the well known principal and agent problem. In the final analysis, it is the agent who has come to exercise more or less complete control over capital, and who, therefore, more than anybody else is the most prominent member of the capitalist class.

Terminological Minefield

When it comes to sorting out the issue of rewards associated with capital, things become fairly complicated through the fact that capital comes in a variety of forms, including working or circulating capital, inventory capital, physical capital, human capital, not to mention the latest addition, namely intellectual capital. And beyond all these there is the loosely used term, financial capital. The trouble is that some of these forms can hardly be distinguished from money, and therefore when one talks about the reward for capital, it becomes difficult to figure out whether one is talking about reward for capital or a return on money pure and simple. Therefore, it is important to be clear as to what these terms mean before proceeding any further. Working or circulating capital is defined as the liquidity any business would need to manage its receipts and payments; physical capital is defined as the stock of produced means of production; inventory capital is the stock of inventories more or less every business is required to keep to iron out any discrepancies between its production and sales profiles during any specified period of time; human capital is the acquired skills and knowledge embodied in human beings; and intellectual capital, while conceptually equal to humanity's stock of knowledge, has come to mean knowledge secured through intellectual property rights such as patents, copyrights, etc. The term financial capital can take a variety of meanings depending on the context in which it is being used. Sometimes it is used to denote the stock of financial instruments in circulation, at others it refers to the surplus (i.e. savings) available during a specified period of time for conversion into any one of the other categories of capital, and at yet others it may denote the working capital of a firm. I have avoided using this term, but if I do use it, it is in the second sense, to underscore the surplus available for investment purposes—a surplus which is essentially in the form of money. I may hasten to add that defined thus, financial capital could be conceived of as a flow variable (hence the caveat "during a specified period of time"), unlike the other conceptualizations and the other categories that are essentially stock variables. Sometimes it may be convenient to subsume inventory capital under working capital—both required for the same purpose, a smooth running of business. I follow this convention in the following exposition. As far as human and intellectual varieties of capital are concerned, these are not directly relevant to the subject at hand. This means the circulating and physical varieties of capital form the core of our discourse throughout this essay. Of these, the former, at least in its strict sense, namely excluding inventory capital, is indistinguishable from money.

When it comes to the structure of rewards associated with capital, the degree of complexity increases greatly. Here, one is forced to find one's way through a confusing array of terms including profits, interest, natural interest, returns, dividends, yield, capital gains, not to mention the corresponding rates associated with some of these terms. And since all of these, except natural interest, are expressed in nominal terms, there are also their corresponding real values to be reckoned with, and to add to the confusion, there are their expected values to worry about. And beyond those, there are the concepts like marginal productivity of capital, marginal efficiency of investment, marginal efficiency of capital, marginal internal rate of return, and marginal rate of return over cost that one must contend with. Jargon aplenty. Notwithstanding the fact that some of these terms are used interchangeably, one can easily get lost in the process of sorting out the interrelationships and connections between them. Luckily, it is not necessary to sort all these details out for our argument to proceed. What, however, we do need to note is that some of these terms have historically been associated with money, while others are one way or another related to capital, to identify either its rewards or its productivity. The one which has always been intimately related to money, and which eventually came to be so associated in the discipline of economics, is interest. Though it has its roots in the Latin word *interesse*, the original meaning of the word is quite different from a return on money per se (the original meaning is quite close to the meaning of the term *ribā*, as we will see in Chapters 9 and 10). What it represented was a compensation to the creditor in the case of a default or delay in the repayment of a loan. How the term acquired its new meanings is by itself an interesting question, but this is not the place to go into that subject (though in Chapter 10 we will touch on the subject). What is important here is that the term, as far as economics is concerned, was quite clearly connected to the returns to capital at least until the first half of the twentieth century. In the same vein, profits, in so far as they were considered as reward to factor services, not only became related to capital and to money through its connection with capital, but also to entrepreneurship and, when they were not justified as reward for such services, they became akin to rent, but then one was never quite sure whether they were to accrue to capital or entrepreneurship. The inseparable connection between money and capital was never going to be trouble-free. If the invention of money was motivated by the vagaries of barter exchange, it also meant that anything that served as money automatically became a store of value. Being perfectly liquid, the link it established between present and future got elevated to an altogether higher plane of economic significance—a link that, no doubt, was also served by other goods but only tenuously. What this discussion highlights is that when one encounters the term interest, one is never quite sure whether it is to be taken as a return on money or a reward for capital, and when profits come under consideration, one is not quite clear whether these are to be taken as accruing to capital or to entrepreneurship. We may now turn to the story as it evolved beginning with Adam Smith in the last quarter of the eighteenth century and ending with Keynes and Knight around the middle of the twentieth century.

Smith and the Latter-day Saints

At the time Adam Smith wrote *The Wealth of Nations* (1776), the distinction between various varieties of capital had yet not crystallized in the economic thought of the day. Indeed, much else in the conceptual framework of economics that we now take for granted did not exist at the time—a point that will become clear as we proceed. Smith recognized the importance of what later came to be known as physical capital—his emphasis on "division of labor" makes that amply clear—yet his focus was primarily on circulating capital. The process of accumulation, accumulation of savings, generates a stock of circulating capital, the wages fund, which sustains manufacturing employment. No surprise there, for the process of production he observed in a pre-industrial revolution economy was drastically less capital intensive than what it increasing turned out to be in the post-industrial revolution economies. Interestingly, Smith did not regard circulating capital quite at par with the two main factors of production, land and labor. What we observe in Smith is a capitalist-employer, who was the residual claimant; the distinction between capital and entrepreneurship as two distinct factors of production was still a century away, though obviously the capitalist-employer performed the functions that the entrepreneur was entrusted with once the theory drew a distinction between capital and entrepreneurship later on. In such a frame of analysis, no distinction could be expected between the returns to capital and returns to entrepreneurship. What is interesting, however, is that these combined returns were sometimes called profits and sometimes interest. If we associate interest with capital, it is then quite obvious that the interpretation being given to interest by Smith, and his followers over the next century or so, represented a conceptual break with the historical interpretation of that term. It was no longer just a return on money. Money was now presumed to be associated with the process of transformation, and if much could be earned by the use of money, much could be paid for its use, as Smith would have it. From a slightly different angle, especially when viewed in light of the subsequent developments in the analytical framework of monetary economics, it is the store of value function of money, beyond its being merely a medium of exchange, which takes the center stage in economics discourse. Smith was primarily concerned with the possibility of the process of accumulation coming to a halt as a result of a continuous decrease in the rate of profit, which when it ultimately reaches zero ushers in a stationary state. Thereafter, no further accumulation, and therefore growth, occurs in the economy.

This line of thought continued in a somewhat more systematic way over the next century with David Ricardo (1817), and John Mill (1848), by which time the industrial revolution had manifestly established an unprecedented pre-eminence of physical capital in the process of industrialization. It was not just that accumulation appeared increasingly in a different guise, i.e. physical capital, but rather that it was accompanied by technological change, in fact a technological change that was embodied in it, that propelled it on to the center stage of not only economic growth but also economics discourse, leading understandably to an upheaval that took more than a century to subside. The immediate effect, however, was that it rendered the classical worries relating to accumulation, in the form of an ultimate onset of the stationary state, irrelevant, at least for the time being, indeed for a long time to come, as it turned out. It was now realized that current labor could be used not only to produce goods and services for current consumption but could also be congealed into something that would produce goods and services in future. Diminishing returns to capital, and thus to the attendant circulating capital as well, could now be postponed more or less indefinitely. This switch of emphasis from circulating to physical capital gave rise to certain conceptual difficulties that were resolved primarily in the writings of the Austrian School, particularly those of Professor Bohm-Bawerk (1889) who used the concept of a roundabout method of production to explain the significance of capital deepening to the process of growth. As a result, capital came to be defined as a "produced means of production." But that is running a bit too fast. Let us return to Ricardo and Mill.

Ricardo kept the Smithian connection between interest and profits intact in his framework. Writing some forty years down the road (1817), while explaining rent, he wrote: "Rent is that portion of the produce of the earth, which is paid to the landlord for the use of the original and indestructible powers of the soil. It is often however confounded with the interest *and* profit of capital, and in the popular language the term is applied to whatever is annually paid by a farmer to his landlord" (p. 33, emphasis added). Here we see profit and interest as two separate entities, but both are attributed to capital. Ricardo did not bother to tell us why two distinct rewards are to be attributed to capital. Was one of these to be attributed to the circulating, and the other to the physical variety of capital? That, however, is not how it appears in his subsequent argument when he continues, "If, of two adjoining farms of the same extent, and of the same natural fertility, one had all the conveniences of *farming building, and, besides, were properly drained and manured, and advantageously divided by hedges, fences, and walls*, while the other had none of these advantages, more remuneration would naturally be paid for the use of one, than for the use of the other; yet in both cases this remuneration would be called rent. But it is evident, that a portion only of the money annually to be paid for the improved farm, would be given for the original and indestructible powers of the soil; the other portion would be paid for the *use of the capital* which had been employed in ameliorating the quality of the land, and in erecting such buildings as were necessary to secure and preserve the produce" (p. 33, emphasis added). There is no trace of "wages fund" in what he lists. Indeed, there could not be any, simply because it was the farmer who is supposedly running the business and not the landlord, and even if there is any circulating capital, it will necessarily be contributed or arranged by the farmer since circulating capital, by definition, cannot be divorced from the day-to-day running of the business. This time it is the rent paid that includes returns to capital, albeit in two forms, i.e. interest and profit, but only to the physical variety. If Smith attributed interest and profits to circulating capital, perhaps subsuming interest under profits, Ricardo now quite clearly attributed both of them to physical capital, even though the idea of "wages fund" retained its echo in his writings.

This confusion continues in John Mill another thirty years later (1848). Focusing on the issue of continued accumulation leading to a fall in the rate of profit and on to the onset of the stationary state,

Mill, in the chapter 'Of the Tendency of Profits to a Minimum' now equates the rate of profit to the rate of interest when he argues, "For these two reasons, [namely] diminution of risk and increase of providence, a profit *or* interest of three or four per cent is as sufficient a motive to the increase of capital in England at the present day, as thirty or forty per cent in the Burmese Empire, or in England at the time of King John. In Holland during the last century a return of two per cent, on government security, was consistent with an undiminished, if not with an increasing capital" (para. 3, emphasis added). Yet one can also discern an element of confusion in this equality. For instance, Mill observes, "In England, the ordinary rate of interest on government securities, in which the risk is next to nothing, may be estimated at a little more than three per cent: in all other investments, therefore, the interest or profit calculated upon (exclusively of what is properly a remuneration for talent or exertion) must be as much more than this amount, as is equivalent to the *degree of risk* to which the *capital* is thought to be exposed" (para. 4, emphasis added).[2] Mill quite rightly notes that profits are somehow linked to the risk of an undertaking—and in this he may be considered as a precursor to Frank Knight—but then goes ahead to equate profits to interest. And then there is yet another rate of interest—the ordinary rate of interest—which is quite distinct from the rate of profit, being actually the rate of interest as would be understood in the historical sense, a return on money borrowed by the government. How is this rate supposed to be determined? Yes, it is determined by the government, but on what basis? And to the extent it is purported to be risk-free, it could not possibly be identified with a rate of profit as no rate of profit could be risk-free. So we see that the interest was equated to profits but then it really was not quite the same thing as profits. Supposing this rate was determined on the basis of some minimum risk rate of profit, did the government know what that rate was supposed to be at any given time? The theoretical foundations that provide an answer to this question did not exist at the time. After all, the beginnings of the marginalist revolution were still a generation away. It may, however, be added that government borrowing at the time was primarily for public works investments and thus its link to profits

[2] Both citations from the said chapter (Mill, 1848, Chapter IV) in Book IV: "Influence of the Progress of Society on Production and Distribution."

was not as tenuous as it became as capitalism matured in the first half of the twentieth century, a point that must be kept in mind to fully appreciate what follows. At any rate, when we read about the rate of interest and rate of profit in the classical literature, we do not quite know what they stand for: for instance, it begs the question as to whether we are supposed to take both of them as returns on capital, and if so, which form of capital; or is one of them a return on capital, of some variety, and the other a return on money, pure and simple?

Marginalism and Time Preference

Capital, whether of the circulating or physical variety, has been an integral part of the production process ever since man invented the most primitive tools. Bohm-Bawerk (1889) did not invent the roundabout method of production, he only underscored its significance, and provided an analytical framework in which issues relating to physical capital could be fruitfully explored. Human civilization discovered the advantages of using a roundabout method of production in exactly the same way it discovered the advantages of using money as a medium of exchange at a somewhat later stage. But not all societies using roundabout method of production could be labeled capitalist. There is something more to the term capitalist than just the existence and therefore ownership of capital. Ownership is but one dimension of property rights associated with a piece of property. A look at the structure of reward associated with capital may be helpful in unraveling the complications associated with the question of who is entitled to the epithet capitalist.

The marginalist revolution, admittedly, changed economics beyond recognition, but did not resolve all the difficulties. Its onset heralded the transformation of the hitherto political economy into economics with a claim to some degree of scientific objectivity. The spirit of rigorousness started to pervade the discipline. One of the major crystallizations of this revolution was the formulation of the law of diminishing returns, a law that provided the much-needed foundation for the theory of distribution. But the application of this law required a degree of clarity about conceptualization of various factors of production, which was hitherto lacking. This placed capital right at the center stage of the economics discourse. It is at this stage that

Eugene von Bohm-Bawerk (1889) and John Bates Clark (1899), among others, devoted their energies to clarify the concept of capital. Their efforts bore lasting fruits as far as the concept of physical capital was concerned. Both Bohm-Bawerk and Clark inherited the age-old concern with falling profits as a result of continued accumulation, and this provided the umbrella under which issues relating to capital were discussed. Conceptually, Bohm-Bawerk used the idea of "roundaboutness," while Clark used that of "abstinence" or "waiting" to underline the same essential characteristic of physical capital. Increased roundaboutness, where labor, the original factor of production, was employed over an extended period of time to make increasingly sophisticated machines and plants, meant increased postponement of the final consumable product. Bohm-Bawerk postulated a positive, but diminishing relationship between this roundaboutness and the final consumable product. With a few hiccups relating to sorting out the dynamic (that admitted technological change) from the static (that did not) considerations that necessitated the invoking of the *ceteris paribus* assumption in the formulation of the law of diminishing returns, the law meant that marginal productivity of physical capital would decrease as capital deepening progressed. But at the same time it was recognized that this onset of diminishing returns could be postponed as long as technological change continued apace. The law of diminishing returns lent itself satisfactorily, but barely so, to physical capital—there are here problems as attested by the well-known Cambridge controversies (more on that in Chapter 8)—but the circulating variety did not lend itself readily to the marginal analysis. One could meaningfully talk about the marginal product of a machine but what exactly was the marginal product of liquidity? Both Bohm-Bawerk and Clark were aware of this problem, and did try to come to grips with it, but without much success. In Bohm-Bawerk, labor is progressively congealed into physical capital as the process of roundaboutness progresses, but at the final stage of production when labor is applied, the end result is production of the consumables without any further addition to the process of roundaboutness. The wages paid at this stage, the circulating capital, could hardly be treated as identical to the wages paid in the construction of machinery and plant that resulted in additions to the physical capital stock. Leaving aside the possibility of an inventory accumulation, there is no further waiting involved once the consumables have been produced. Bohm-Bawerk tried to get around this problem by a continued appeal to his idea of "advances" to labor. Clearly, the advances to labor have an altogether different significance when the end result is roundaboutness from when it produces the consumables at the final stage of production without any further increase in it. Clark, on the other hand, after drawing a distinction between "capital" and "capital goods," tried to handle this difficulty of justifying returns to circulating capital at par with physical capital by resorting to a synchronizing function performed by circulating capital, in his terminology "capital." That there was this problem is quite clear from the exchange that occurred between Bohm-Bawerk and Clark in the various issues of the *Quarterly Journal of Economics* during 1906 and 1907. That this exchange was quite heated is clear from Professor Samuelson (1943, p. 64) referring to it as "Bohm-Bawerk's polemic against Clark." Participating in this exchange, Professor Frank Taussig underlined the problem in the May 1908 issue of the same journal. In his introductory remarks, besides noting the well-known problem of decline in interest as a result of continued accumulation, he tersely remarked that, "There is another problem even more important, and no less unsettled, in the background,—the grounds on which the receipt of interest can be defended as part of the social order... To some of these unsettled problems I propose to give attention" (Taussig, 1908, p. 334). When it came to giving his attention to this issue, he did not say much. In a thirty-page article, he devotes less than a page to it, leaving the reader guessing as to what exactly he had in mind:

> The value of a distinction lies in its pointing to propositions which hold good of one of the things distinguished and do not hold good of the other. The particular propositions or conclusions which Professor Clark deduces from his distinction between capital and capital goods seem to me quite untenable,—thus, as to the "synchronizing" of labor and its product, or the replacement of capital without abstinence. There may be other conclusions from *this sort of distinction*, as to the social merit or *justification* of return on "capital goods" as distinguished from returns on 'capital.' I suspect, however, that the conclusions which might be deduced on such social questions would be very different from those which run through Professor Clark's writings. They would point not to the *same justification for all kinds of "capital"* (such of course is the drift of Professor Clark's reasoning), but to a discrimination between "capital" and "capital goods," and to a still further discrimination between those capital goods which are fashioned by man and those agents which are the free gifts of nature. But these are matters not pertinent to the subject of present discussion. So far as this is concerned, the distinction between capital and capital goods only beclouds the situation, in no way clarifies it (Taussig, 1908, pp. 343–44, emphasis added).

On the one hand, Taussig did not quite approve of drawing a distinction between the circulating (capital) and physical (capital goods) categories of capital as these related to the process of production, yet, on the other, he felt uncomfortable with Clark's justification of returns to circulating capital at par with physical capital. Neither did he say as to what he meant by a still further discrimination between capital goods and "free gifts of nature." There he may be echoing Marshall (8th ed., 1890, p. 430) who insisted that, "land is but a particular form of capital from the point of view of the individual producer."[3] Obviously, liquidity can be used for the acquisition of land. Should there therefore be a "rate of rent" as return to land? Taussig, for the most part, occupied himself in differing with Clark's interpretation that capital accumulation and technological change necessarily went hand in hand (and this was the "present discussion" referred to in the quotation above), and did not delve further on the question he raised. Was he concerned about the Clarkian identity between returns to the two categories of capital serving as a justification for the institution of interest, which subsequently led to its complete instrumentalization in the aftermath of the so-called Keynesian revolution? It is difficult to be sure but at least an affirmative answer resolves the apparent contradiction in his position in the sense that a legitimacy of a return to circulating capital could be used to justify a return on money, and therefore his insistence that no distinction be drawn between the two categories of capital.

Be that as it may, at this stage the question of returns for capital became fairly complicated. Up to now, even in the post-marginalists writings on the subject, terms such as returns, interests, as well as profits were used rather loosely to denote the marginal product of physical capital. This is quite understandable when we consider that economic discourse was still couched in the background of a capitalist-employer and "entrepreneurship" as a distinct factor of production had yet not made its appearance on the economic scene. If the marginal productivity theory was to become relevant, capital must be assigned a distinct return. It could no longer be considered a residual claimant, as it had been up to that point in time. This, in turn, meant that the residual could not now be expressed as a rate, be that of profit or whatever. This forced the introduction of a new factor of production in economics, the fourth one, namely the entrepreneur,

[3] For an extended discussion on this issue, see Robbins (1930).

who now assumed the status of the "residual claimant" once all other factors of production had been compensated according to their respective marginal productivities. This obviously drew a wedge between profits (the residual), and interest, which somehow remained connected to capital, and destroyed the conceptual identity between profits and interest that classical economics had maintained, however imperfectly.

The concept of marginal productivity is intimately connected with the idea of opportunity cost, in the sense that equality between the two becomes the necessary condition of equilibrium. But what was the entrepreneur supposed to do and what was, therefore, the opportunity cost of entrepreneurship, were the new issues that now needed to be sorted out. What Professor Joseph Schumpeter, and later Professor Frank Knight had to say on this issue was still in the distinct future. Marshall, having thrust entrepreneurship on to the stage, skirted the issue, however, by introducing the troubling notion, at both conceptual and practical levels, of "normal profits" as a component of the cost of production—as the opportunity cost of entrepreneurship. We come to that issue a little later. What is of interest to us at the moment is that it was at this time, in the early part of the twentieth century, that Professor Irving Fisher (1907) paved the way to the neoclassical theory of investment by extending the marginalist analysis to an inter-temporal setting. Fisher emphasized the interaction between the demand and supply sides of the saving-investment process (investment being the flow variable that corresponded to the physical capital as the stock variable), and showed that in equilibrium the Wicksellian natural or real rate of interest, which ultimately is supposed to be determined in the real sector of the economy, and the marginal rate of time preference will be equalized. By drawing a distinction between the real and nominal rates of interest, Fisher tied the former to the real rate of return as determined in the real sector of the economy. At a purely conceptual level, neoclassical economics removed the classical confusion between rate of profit and rate of interest. Money was now first to be transformed into physical capital, and it was the marginal product of physical capital that was now to be equated to the real rate of interest. But then the real rate of interest was conceptually not the same thing as either the classical rate of profit (or rate of interest) or the age-old rate of interest—the latter now to be called the nominal or money rate of interest. The elegance of the neoclassical approach lay in its combining the demand

and supply forces to explain the existence of returns to capital. In any demand and supply analysis, absence of one side renders the other practically meaningless. In the absence of a supply curve, what practical significance could be attached to the infinite possible prices, each corresponding to a unique quantity, and thereby to the idea of a price? However, this elegance becomes more or less irrelevant the moment it is realised that the real rate of interest is not observable. What is observable is the nominal rate of interest, and it is that rate which must be appealed to in order to establish the neoclassical equilibrium. Neoclassical economics rescued the concept of the rate of interest, but what was rescued was a phantom that could not be readily pressed into service. Defining it in real terms connected it to the rate of return on capital, but exposed it to the vagaries of inflation in an economy which was, by that time, increasingly moving away from real money to much more volatile paper money. The real rate of interest cannot be known at the time debt contracts are entered into. Those contracts are necessarily based on the nominal rate, and to the extent the nominal rate may be arbitrarily influenced by monetary authorities, and given that the required adjustment in price level may not be instantaneous in Wicksell's (1935) "cumulative process," the nominal rate of interest may never converge with the real rate of interest. In the much later developments, an appeal to the expected rate of inflation to arrive at an *ex-ante* real rate of interest does not rescue the ship except to introduce considerable haze in the already choppy waters, though admittedly the idea has some merit when one is addressing questions of individual optimization rather than macroeconomic policy. An economy-wide expected rate of inflation is again an unobservable—more on these issues later. To continue with the story, if capital was now to be paid according to its marginal product, who was to be the residual claimant?

Theory Thickens

Capitalism around this time, towards the end of the nineteenth and the beginning of the twentieth century, underwent a number of important changes at both the theoretical and practical levels. At the practical level, these changes represent an entrenchment of the institutions that made the economic system a truly capitalist one, and interestingly it is at this time that we encounter the term capitalism for the first time. This new version of capitalism was a great deal more complicated than the older, simpler one. While the theoretical answer to the question as to who was a capitalist in the older version was fairly straightforward, it was not so any more. In the times of Smith and his immediate followers, capital was created primarily out of the surplus accruing to what I have earlier called the capitalist-employer. And whether the economic discourse of the time called the residual accruing to this capitalist-employer profits, interest, or returns did not matter a great deal. But as the nineteenth century progressed, particularly as it entered its latter half, this structure began to change. The industrial revolution, underway for more than a century, progressively increased labor productivity. Labor now became increasingly well off as compared to the corresponding historical standards. It could now afford to save, and as time went on, saved an increasing proportion of its income. These savings, while individually small, became collectively quite large, and represented an increasing proportion of total savings available for capital accumulation. The financial institutions helped channel these savings into investment, and the primary mode selected for this channeling turned out, for whatever reasons, to be debt-financing. Since debt-financing is, by definition, based on nominal interest rate, signifying a fixed liability in monetary terms, the conceptual distinction between rate of return and rate of interest could no longer be fudged.

Economic theory responded to this change by introducing the fourth factor of production (entrepreneurship); the entrepreneur was now to be the residual claimant. This meant that the surplus, which was previously synonymous with profits, would now have to be split into two components: return to capital, and profits, where the latter itself needed to be conceptually split into two components, a component that would somehow be deemed as normal, and profits over and above this were to be reckoned as economic or pure profits. It may be said that previously capital enjoyed these pure profits and for that matter suffered losses if and when these accrued, for there was no distinction between capital and entrepreneurship. Under the new scheme of things, it was the entrepreneur who became entitled to these profits at the expense of capital, necessarily when such profits were positive, but not necessarily when these were negative. This happened not because of the presence of the fourth factor of production per se, and not even because of the fact that there were now two distinct sources of capital accumulation available to what could be called the equity-capitalist-entrepreneur, the old equity capital now being supplemented by debt capital, that is capital created out of debt-financing, but because the latter was coupled with the institution of limited liability. That the equity-capitalist-entrepreneur was able to secure a legal protection against claims arising out of debt financing through the new institution was his real triumph, and it is this triumph that secured the foundations of capitalism.

While the equity-capitalist-entrepreneur might have wished to resort entirely to debt capital, for then he would lose nothing of his own in the case of a loss, that would have been too blatant a scenario to survive. His own equity—which could be tucked away in the safest of the assets available—was required to establish the credibility of capitalism. Anyway, the result was that he was now entitled to surplus created not only by his own capital but also the capital created by the savings of the others, including the small savers, primarily the wage earners. Debt capital was entitled to returns determined by the productivity of the marginal unit of capital, and it does not require much imagination to see which of the two forms of capital this marginal unit would turn out to belong. It was the debt capital that became marginalized. The capital created by the entrepreneur's own savings, while theoretically treated at par with that created by the other savers, and subject to marginal productivity hypothesis, practically always retained a status of infra-marginality by virtue of its ownership association with equity-capitalist-entrepreneur; though it is only fair to say that the equity-capitalist-entrepreneur received the corresponding additional surplus *qua* entrepreneur and not *qua* capitalist. If now the entrepreneur, instead of the capitalist, became the hero of capitalism, it obliges us to look at the fourth factor of production somewhat closely. But before that we need to note that in this exposition, while the debt capital is assumed to receive a return determined by the marginal product of capital, in reality, however, it received only an interest, determined by the nominal rate of interest—a rate that was not necessarily equal to the Wicksellian real rate of interest. This obviously added a complication as far as the strict application of the marginal productivity hypothesis was concerned, but due to its insolubility economic theory decided to disregard it.

Back to the Future

Economic theory's acceptance of the rate of interest as being a purely monetary phenomenon owes much to Keynes (1936). Marking a U-turn from his earlier position, as enunciated in *A Treatise on Money* (1930), Keynes criticized the classical writers for obscuring the concept of interest, which, according to him, was quite clearly understood by their mercantilist predecessors to be a return on money loans. Keynes went straight to the heart of the problem created by the existence of money by focusing on the link it provides between the present and future through its role as a store of value. No doubt, the primary function of money remains the medium of exchange, but anything that serves as a medium of exchange automatically becomes a store of value; a bridge between the present—where the decisions regarding consumption and saving are to be made—and a future, which is unknown, and indeed unknowable with certainty. Admittedly, all assets provide this link between present and future with varying degrees of ease depending on how readily they can be converted into other assets, or for that matter into other goods and services when so needed at a future date, i.e. by the degree of their liquidity. Money, however, acquires a pre-eminence on this count by virtue of being the medium of exchange: it is the most liquid of all assets. Putting the matter slightly differently, while conversion of other assets from one form into another would entail a transaction cost, money could be so converted at virtually zero transaction cost. However, money suffers from a disadvantage vis-à-vis other assets. Other assets, being generally productive or utility yielding, offer the holder a promise of return or satisfaction (utility); money holds no such promise. But since money can be readily converted into a productive asset, it naturally gives rise to the question: shouldn't a transfer of its control offer its owner something in return? By the time Keynes came to write his *General Theory*, his frame of mind required that such returns, in the form of interest, be quite independent of the returns to the underlying productive assets: interest must now be considered a purely monetary phenomenon. For this Keynes invented an ingenious explanation. One cannot but suppose that the difficulty of justifying the productiveness of, and therefore demand for, liquidity per se would not have escaped Keynes's genius. He couldn't have been unaware of the Aristotelian dictum that money was barren. Instead, he gave the idea of demand for money a novel twist to provide a justification for a reward (interest); he made the concept of liquidity preference the central pivot of his explanation. According to the liquidity preference theory, people somehow prefer to hold money instead of real, or should we say productive, but less liquid assets, and parting with liquidity required compensation in the form of interest payment. So money was not productive per se, and its holding was therefore non-interest-bearing, but then it was to be interest-bearing in the sense that parting with it required a compensation in the form of interest. This requires a little elaboration.

To begin with, one needs to be quite clear about the meaning of the term liquidity, and therefore liquidity-preference. Keynes was being quite consistent when he noted that "the concept of hoarding may be regarded as a first approximation to the concept of liquidity-preference (Keynes, 1936, p. 174)" because the income which was hoarded in the form of money represented a leakage from the circular flow and therefore a decrease in aggregate demand. And he concluded the argument by saying, on the same page, that "the habit of overlooking the relation of the rate of interest to hoarding may be a part of the explanation why interest has been usually regarded as the reward of not-spending, whereas in fact it is the reward of not-hoarding." This may seem somewhat confusing, and a reader unfamiliar with this debate may well believe that not-spending is the same thing as hoarding, and consequently conclude that somehow Keynes was attacking a position where interest was considered to be a reward for hoarding. Clearly that was not the case, for in the classical economics, not-spending actually meant saving and thus investment by the capitalist employer, as we have seen earlier. One can now see that not-hoarding would be investment once the savings, now also made by labor, was entrusted to a financial institution, which would undertake the investment. Viewed in this light, interest under both of those scenarios was, in the final analysis, linked to the process of transformation. The natural question now is: so what was new in Keynes? To answer that question, we need to ask another: if people do indeed hoard, then the crucial question is why? Why would anyone hoard if there existed a reward in the form of current rate of return through process of transformation (call it waiting or not-spending), and therefore what was one to make of the Keynes's "speculative balances"? Keynes' explanation was quite straight forward: People held speculative balances because they like to take advantage of the possible changes (actually, a rise) in the rate of interest in future. This way, the current rate of interest was made to be the opportunity cost of holding money—the liquidity. And whenever one parted with money by making a money loan, one was entitled to receive an interest payment. This restored the conventional meaning of the term interest. It was Keynes, more than anybody else, who helped instrumentalization of interest by removing any inhibitions of the Taussig variety associated with that concept. Keynes was at least frank to admit that liquidity preference, in the context at hand, arose out of "speculative motive" in contrast to the later Keynesians who attempted to soften the impact of this somewhat charged term by opting to call it "asset demand" for money.

But this begs another crucial question. Where would the expected changes in the rate of interest (people holding different expectations about the future course of the rate of interest) emanate from, which the holders of liquidity would like to take advantage of? Would these emanate from the real sector of the economy, namely would they be the result of changes in the real rate of return to capital? But then is the real sector of the economy so volatile as to give rise to the needed fluctuations in the rate of return such that people would forego those existing returns, however low, and hold on to their savings in the form of hoarding, i.e. speculative balances, to take advantage of these fluctuations? Such fluctuations would imply an unstable investment demand curve thus rendering the notion of an equilibrium rate of return meaningless. We do have a somewhat volatile investment demand in Keynes but only as a result of changing expectations about future profitability during an economic downturn. Part of this volatility indeed comes from the changes in the rate of interest itself. Rate of interest enters as a cost of production, the cost of borrowed funds, in the Keynesian framework. Any change in it causes a change in the profitability of an enterprise, thereby changing the investment demand via its effect on his marginal efficiency of capital. That line of argument is not what Keynes had in mind because of the obvious circularity in the reasoning. And if he was not thinking along those lines, then was it the possibility of government tinkering with the rate of interest, supposedly to pursue certain stabilization objectives that would tempt the savers to hold on to their savings in liquid form to take advantage of such tinkering? In reality that is exactly what happens in a system where the rate of interest becomes a purely monetary phenomenon. More on this a little later. What we need to note, at the moment, is the fact that Keynes makes us realize the economic existence of the government, and thereby the role—whether desirable or undesirable is another matter—that it can play in making interest a monetary phenomenon against the backdrop of a debt-finance economy.

The transition from primarily equity-financed economies to predominantly debt-financed economies had important theoretical implications. In the equity-financed economies, one could presume, as Jean-Baptiste Say did, a theoretical symmetry between the act of saving and the act of investment. This presumed symmetry disregarded the possibility of hoarding of saving, which could reduce aggregate demand thus nullifying the Say's law. If Keynes criticized Say on this count, Say could equally wonder why somebody would hoard in the face of productive investment opportunities. Of course this argument may well turn out to be somewhat more complicated than that. For one, a farmer saving part of his corn produce as seed could well be thought of as making an investment in Say's terms at the same time that Keynes would consider this an act of hoarding. And he may well take it quite seriously if his primary concern is a sufficiently short period of time. Under a debt-financed scenario, on the other hand, the act of saving is necessarily divorced from the act of investment. When the savers and investors are not the same people, one could hardly presume an *ex-ante* automatic synchronization between savings and investment. If Keynes could appeal to the efficiency of the financial system to underwrite such interpersonal synchronization, or coordination, it was unfair on his part to deny such a possibility, indeed at a much easier individual level, to Say. Let us now turn to the fourth factor of production, entrepreneurship.

Knight and Free Riders

When debt finance forced in a distinction between capital as a factor of production and the ownership of an enterprise, economics responded by introducing the entrepreneur as a new factor of production; he was the owner of the enterprise but not the sole contributor to the capital employed by the enterprise. He was supposed to be a scarce factor and therefore had an opportunity cost, which entitled him to command a reward in the form of normal profits. But in actual fact, he was the new residual claimant, earning not just the normal profits but receiving whatever profit accrued to the enterprise. The conceptual split of actual profits into the normal and abnormal categories was unavoidable simply because of the fact that while actual profits could be negative, one could not conceive of an opportunity cost being negative. But what was the function of the entrepreneur for which he was entitled to receive normal profits? Several answers were offered with the passage of time, all attempting to cover an ever-changing entrepreneurial landscape. Initially, beginning with Marshall (1890), he was thought of as the organizer of the process of production. But soon it became clear that, for the most part, this conceptualization referred to only a particular kind of labor when one talked thus about the entrepreneur. A better explanation had to be offered.

Schumpeter (1942), formulating his ideas at the time the new system was facing its gravest crisis yet, realized that a worthwhile role for the entrepreneur could not be secured in the static conditions of a stationary state. It was only in the dynamics of the system that a role, and a very important one, could be vouchsafed to the entrepreneur. Regardless of whether we call his entrepreneur a leader, an innovator, a visionary, or whatever else, he was essentially a catalyst for change, for improvement, the one who forced the system to take on a new course, the destroyer of the status quo. He was the leader who forced others to follow his lead. He was entitled to a reward in the form of profits, but only during the period when his advantage had not yet been eroded by a whole host of run-of-the-mill entrepreneurs whom he forced to adapt to the change for their own survival. Profits were only a dynamic surplus. In a stationary state there could not be any profits. But a stationary state never arrived regardless of the romance with which the classical, and later some neoclassical, economists entertained that idea. Real life never conformed, and is never likely to conform, to the dictates of a stationary state. It represents a dynamic process, full of surprises and unexpected turns of events, requiring creative responses and initiatives that though they may not fit the Schumpeterian bill of innovation would still not be the stuff for the faint-hearted. Any business is bound to be effected by the vicissitudes of life; life is uncertain, the future is unknowable. Past experience may provide some clues as to the future course of certain events, and this forms the basis of a distinction, in economics, between uncertainty and risk; yet the unknowable remains essentially unknowable. Current decisions link the present to that future which always retains its capacity to spring surprises. A business that would like to make a profit, and is admittedly motivated by that prospect, can always run into losses. It is always exposed to a risk of loss. It is this idea that caught the attention of Professor Frank Knight (1921). According to him, the entrepreneur is the one who is supposed to bear the ever present risk, and therefore normal profit was supposed to be the necessary payment to compensate him for the risk undertaken. Since the Schumpeterian entrepreneur is also exposed to the same risk, the distinction between his and the Knightian entrepreneur is essentially one of degree only.

But how were the normal profits to be determined, or in other words, what exactly was the opportunity cost of the entrepreneurship? Normal profit, being a conceptual variable, was not directly observable. There could not be any objective measurement of the opportunity cost of entrepreneurship for two inter-related reasons. First, a marginal product of entrepreneurship could not be conceptualized simply because marginal increments to entrepreneurship in a given firm were inconceivable. The appeal to an entrepreneur varying his input of time could not satisfactorily resolve this difficulty of indivisibility. Second, there could not be a market for entrepreneurial services. The textbook treatment that the opportunity cost of entrepreneur was the amount of income he could earn when he worked as an employee in some other enterprise is problematic for the following reasons: when someone offers his services in the labor market, he could not possibly be an entrepreneur; labor is not the same thing as entrepreneurship, and the moment a person assumes the role of an entrepreneur, he could hardly earn wages for that function. In other words, no one would assume the risks associated with an entrepreneur's actions for a payment. Professor Knight, however, pointed out that an individual entrepreneur might be able to insure himself against certain future contingencies, thereby reducing his exposure to risk. In such cases, something that would previously have been a part of the profits—the insurance premium, for example—may now be reckoned as a component of explicit costs. While this may provide certain clues as to the opportunity cost of some of the entrepreneurial decisions, no insurance firm could provide a comprehensive coverage for all the contingencies associated with entrepreneurial function. Though the question about the opportunity cost of entrepreneurship was not satisfactorily answered, and perhaps could not be so answered, Knightian analysis did succeed in linking risk to returns. The higher the risk of an enterprise, the higher ought to be the actual profit either because the explicit costs will be higher because of the inclusion of insurance premium, or the implicit costs will be higher because of the higher normal profits. But the connection between risk and return became more complicated because of the changes in the structure of property rights relating to the institution of interest. For one, the risk premium began to be built into the rate of interest. These changes made it difficult to work out who the entrepreneur was, and who, therefore, was the legitimate recipient of the residual.

Historically, entrepreneurship has always been tied up with management. Indeed entrepreneurship was so thoroughly mixed up with management that it was difficult to sort out where the management function ended and the entrepreneurial one began. The Schumpeterian argument can be interpreted as drawing a distinction between the ordinary, day-to-day management of the business and its more dynamic aspects that lead to innovations as a result of the leadership and dynamism of one who is regarded as his true entrepreneur. Admittedly, much of what an entrepreneur did in the ordinary run of the events was nothing more than labor, involving tasks that could easily be delegated to, and thus performed by, hired managers. It is also clear, given the structure of business in the nineteenth century, that there was a core of decisions that would be considered the sole prerogative of the entrepreneur, and would not be delegated either because of the practical reasons or because of business traditions. But as capitalism matured and spread its wings, and the modern corporate form of business took firm hold on the business world at the start of the twentieth century, the organic link between entrepreneurship and management started to come apart. As the new system planted its feet firmly, virtually a complete delegation of entrepreneurial function took place. Now almost all decisions, even those that would give the Schumpeterian entrepreneur a pause, started to be made by professional managers, decisions that were previously supposed to be an exclusive prerogative of the equity-capitalist-entrepreneur. This divorce of ownership from control could not but have profound implication for the business landscape, indeed changing it beyond recognition for a nineteenth-century would-be visitor. While the decisions made by the professional managers determined the profits and losses of the business, those who took them had no claims, at least not in any formal sense, to the resulting profits, and by the same token were not liable for any losses that may accrue, except for the possibility of losing their jobs. But then there was a conundrum. Their formal rewards in the beginning were puny when compared to the powers vested in them. (It is another matter that eventually they became the masters of determining their own rewards—power could not fail to show its true colors—an analogy with the powers of government, as we saw in Chapter 3, would be quite suggestive here). The perceptive minds in economics did realize quite early on the trouble that lay ahead in this principal and agent drama where the agent was handed a blank check with which to enrich himself. But let us not move too fast.

It is in this panoply of confusion arising out of the divorce of ownership from control that we hear radical suggestions, for example that offered by W. L. Crum (1938), that the wages of the management workers should not be considered economic costs but, instead, be reckoned as profits, or the one offered by J. H. Strauss (1944) that the firm itself be regarded as an entrepreneur. What became clear now was that it was not the residual claimants who ought to be the focus of our attention but rather the residual controllers. The story that began with capitalist-employer, moved on to the equity-capitalist-entrepreneur, now entered a new phase in what Schumpeter (1928) called "trustified capitalism," for which, later, the more popular term turned out to be "managerial capitalism." The hallmark of this new system was that not all residual claimants were residual controllers, and not all the residual controllers were residual claimants, at least in the beginning, though eventually they all have become residual claimants, *de facto* if not *de rigueur*. I have called this group "trustee capitalists," its defining characteristic being the control over the *distribution* of residual. It may include equity holders, professional managers, outside directors, or others, but with agency being its necessary condition. It goes without saying that this group necessarily includes all those at the helm of affairs in the corporate sector of an economy. It is not difficult to imagine the implications of this new set-up in favor of the residual controllers in a system where information asymmetries abound. I will touch upon this issue towards the end of this chapter. Let us turn to the Knightian connection between risk and returns in this new environment.

Consider the somewhat pedantic issue of any enterprise running the risk of loss. It sometimes makes unusual profits, economic profits if you will, at others it may just break even, earning just the normal profits, and at yet other times it may run into losses. In the comparative static models, a firm may make normal or abnormal profits, or, for that matter, losses, in the short run. In any given short run, a loss is considered to be a loss pure and simple, and so is the profit, without any regard to the time-frame of the firm, which is necessarily dynamic. The theoretical treatment of the short run, where it is treated only at the conceptual level—in that it may vary from industry to industry, indeed from firm to firm—while satisfactory when a firm is doing well and wishes to expand, leaves a crucial question unanswered when a firm runs into losses. It explains the shut down but does not explain close down of the firm. How long would the shut down continue before a firm decides to close down is anybody's guess. When profits are regarded as profits pure and simple, and losses as losses pure and simple, we run into the difficulty that no consideration could be given to the possibility that abnormal profits during a given period of time may actually be viewed by the firm as offset to losses at other times, and that a firm may actually view both of those as transitory phenomena. When losses do occur, the normal response of the firm is to try to recoup those losses from expected future profits, and it may succeed in doing so. When a firm suffers losses its value decreases, but then the value may rebound as it recovers from the temporary difficulties. Even if its value is not restored to some previously attained level, the firm may continue its operations. The incidence of this decrease in value, a capital loss, falls on the equity holders. At any rate, a firm must be, and always is, mindful of the possibility of losses that at times it may run into, and would need to take appropriate precautions to weather such eventualities. Whether this is done through an insurance coverage against at least some of the contingencies, or through self-insurance by keeping aside a portion of the profits of good times or, barring those, through additional capital or finances, is quite immaterial. In the final analysis, what is important is that losses may be recoupable. As long as a firm can ride out these ups and downs, and makes what it considers to be normal profits—these may be difficult to measure objectively, but it is safe to assume that the entrepreneur knows what they are—over an extended period of time, or in the long run, it will stay in business even if there may be occasional shut downs. As long as the firm stays in business, the Knightian correspondence between risk and returns is not difficult to appreciate, although more appropriately in the ex-post sense rather than an ex-ante sense, i.e. not to justify higher ex-ante returns for all times to come but to recognize the shock absorbing role of abnormal profits. In other words, it is to recognize that a business with higher risk must have larger abnormal profits, either in a particular period (some short run) or spread over a number of such periods, to insure a *given* level of normal profits in the long run. That is all fine in view of the risk taking role of the entrepreneur. But now introduce the government with its not too uncommon tax credits provisions to offset losses, and guess who ends up paying for at least a part of the losses, and therefore bearing the corresponding risk. There is even more.

Let us now consider the ultimate eventuality to which any business is subject, where losses may continue period after period and the firm, after some time, whatever that may happen to be, becomes insolvent, and as a result is forced to close down. It is in view of such an eventuality of Knightian nightmare that risk becomes the fifth column that a firm needs to really worry about, but whether economics should worry about it is an entirely different question. Such an eventuality can, of course, arise for all sorts of reasons, not least of which could be internal problems such as bad management, strike and strife, failure to adopt up-to-date technology, etc., or external factors such as changes in market conditions in a dynamic economy subject to structural changes, where some industries become obsolete and their place is taken up by newer ones that show a greater promise of growth. None of these reasons warrant a particular concern from the social point of view. If anything, this process needs to be looked at in a positive light as a process of weeding and pruning essential for healthy growth, or as being an inherent feature of a dynamic economy. But leaving aside this social dimension, there is the question as to who actually suffers the losses in such cases. The answer is not just the equity holders, but most of the time also the debt-capitalists, small and large, by virtue of the institution of limited liability, and then the taxpayers, particularly if the firm happens to be a financial institution (fear of systemic risk) or is deemed to belong to a strategic industry that needs to be rescued in the name of supreme national interest. Practically speaking, therefore, again there is no strict correspondence between risk bearing and entrepreneurship, however defined, unless one is willing to include the creditors as well as the taxpayers in that definition. But in all fairness to Knight, it was not his insight that was faulty: the shock-absorbing function that profits perform must be recognized. It was rather the march of history, the change in the structure of property rights, that rendered it irrelevant, if not wholly than at least partly. When all is said and done, it is not easy to define who an entrepreneur is, even if the idea seems sound; and even when we succeed in identifying him, the property rights structure of a capitalist economy vitiates against the Knightian correspondence between risk and returns, and it is the trustee-capitalists that come on top through marginalization of not only the small saver but also of the small equity holder. Let us now turn to the equity and efficiency implications of the institution of interest as these emerge in this environment.

From Equity to Equity

To understand the equity implications of the institution of interest, we need to go back a little. At the time Smith wrote, workers were supposed to be paid a subsistence wage. There could hardly be any savings out of these wages. If one could contemplate any such savings at all, it was only during a time of an aberration from the Malthusian norm. Virtually all savings were made by the capitalist-employer, whose sole purpose in making these savings was to undertake further accumulation, namely to make investment. Jean-Baptiste Say could safely assume that supply created its own demand. But as workers became increasingly well-off, they also started to save. Keynes recognized that this not only meant an absence of automatic synchronization between savings and investment, for which the financial system could be pressed into service, but also that such workers' saving may not be motivated expressly with a view to capital accumulation. What if a part of income that was saved was squirreled away, away from the financial sector, for whatever reasons? In such a situation, Say's law will be violated due to a deficiency of aggregate demand. Supply would not create its own demand, not at least immediately. Inventories would then accumulate, and the result may be laying-off of workers. What was to be done in such a situation? Instead of focusing on the reasons why the squirreling away from the financial system (hoarding) occurred, and to suggest appropriate remedies, Keynes decided to take a short cut, and suggested that a fiscal stimulus by the government would remove the deficiency. But where would the resources for such a stimulus come from if the hoarded savings were not available, as they would not be, by definition? Keynes offered a mesmerizing suggestion. This was to create artificial credit by increasing the supply of money, which was supposed to lower the rate of interest, a rate that was now a purely monetary phenomenon divorced from the rate of return in the real sector of the economy. In the Keynesian logic, this would dupe the economy into bypassing the deficiency of aggregate demand, restore the lost jobs, and re-establish full employment, as though increase in money supply was the same thing as increase in savings, and thereby investment. In the heady days of the 1930s, economics was looking for a Messiah, and it got one in Keynes. And the Keynesian message was quite intoxicating. A culture that understood the dictum that there is no such thing as a free lunch marveled at the possibility of having its cake and eating it. Parenthetically, it may not be out of place here to mention the euphoria it created in the newly emerging development literature—if not in the less developed countries themselves, at least in the beginning—at the prospect of the Keynesian multiplier working its magic to lift the poor countries out of their poverty quickly and without much pain and sacrifice. After all, money could be created costlessly under the pure paper standard towards which the global economic order was inexorably drifting. All it required was an administrative fiat. At any rate, the interest rate theory that was divorced from the real sector of the economy was in fact a rent-seeking theory of interest, and those who could, and would, appropriate the surplus loved it.

To see this, let us continue with the case of a decrease in aggregate demand, assuming for the sake of simplicity that it is occasioned by an act of hoarding, although this may very well be the result of a setting aside of some surplus by the businesses for prospective investment operations—a prospect which Keynes (1937) himself admitted in an exchange with Professor Bertil Ohlin (1937). This provides a pretext to the government to increase the supply of money, resulting in a decrease in the rate of interest. Would anything happen in the real sector of the economy as a result of this purely monetary change, i.e. an increase in the supply of money? Keynes thought that this would increase investment and therefore national income, and the increase in the latter would take care of the increased savings required for the investment that had already occurred. This would offset the impact of hoarding that was the cause of the deficiency in aggregate demand to begin with. But what really happens cannot be fully understood until the Keynesian liquidity preference theory is combined with Professor Dennis Robertson's (1940) loanable funds theory of interest rate determination. The increased demand for monetary assets, namely bonds, occasioned by government purchases, required to implement an increase in the supply of money, causes an excess demand for bonds in the bond market. The resultant increase in bond prices is of course the other side of the same coin, the coin that showed a decrease in the rate of interest under the liquidity preference theory that uses the demand and supply of money framework. The increase in bond prices, an asset price inflation, *ceteris paribus,* means an immediate capital gain for the bond holders, a largesse distributed by the government. Nothing has happened in the real sector of the economy. This fact is not negated by the Keynesian play with the idea of marginal efficiency of capital, which is now supposed to increase because of this artificial decrease in interest costs. Economics remained forgetful of the asset price inflation at its peril, as it has come to discover, but only after a lag of half a century. For a long time it did not realize that this asset price inflation leaves the real rate of return unchanged through the compensating capital gains. And inflation, particularly when not anticipated—leaving aside the question as to whether it can ever be correctly anticipated—causes an arbitrary redistribution of income regardless of whether it is of the conventional variety or of the asset-price variety. The cost of this redistribution, as a result of a deliberate interest rate policy, falls on the taxpayers in general, who are required to foot this bill in the name of stabilization policy.

But that is not the end of the story. An increase in the money supply will eventually show up as an increase in the conventional price level, and at that time the nominal rate of interest rises to reverse the original fall, thus leaving the real rate of interest unchanged. Inflations of the two varieties will eventually cancel each other out as far as the real sector of the economy is concerned. But the redistribution that occurs in the interim cannot be reversed. The scramble for surplus will have its gainers and losers. An objection may be raised against this argument that the kind of redistribution we are talking about always occurs whenever the price of any good changes in a market economy, as discussed in Chapter 2, and, after all, the rate of interest is supposed to be the price (opportunity cost) of money. Under the market mechanism, when the price changes occur in the opposite direction, the redistribution effects are also reversed. This leads to the following argument: if a decrease in the rate of interest causes a loss to the taxpayers, wouldn't a rise in the rate of interest at other times lead to offsetting gain to them, such that the taxpayers are, on the balance, neither better nor worse off? Not so in the present case, as a closer look at this argument reveals. When the government follows a contractionary policy, and increases the rate of interest, it does not secure any gains for the taxpayers but indeed ends up distributing largesse once again. This time it sells bonds at prices lower than their existing prices. When a government sells bonds, it leads to an increase in the supply of bonds. The resulting excess supply in the bonds market reduces their equilibrium prices, which amounts to an increase in the rate of interest. This time the largesse does not show up in the form of capital gains but in the form of higher yields the government promises to pay until the maturity of those bonds. Every time the government meddles to change the rate of interest, it redistributes income in the economy. And beyond all this there is another question that needs to be considered. If the government is successful in increasing the aggregate demand by decreasing the rate of interest through not the Keynesian but the monetarist transmission mechanism, what would happen if the hoarded savings, that started the stabilization ball rolling, were to return to the circular flow at the time aggregate demand was increased, which can happen in view of the lags in the implementation of the policy, or during the time when the expansionary policy was playing itself out?

In the Keynesian transmission mechanism where a decrease in the rate of interest is supposed to increase investment, a remarkable confusion arises when the relationship between the stocks variables and the corresponding flow variables is not kept in focus. At any particular time, there exists a given stock of financial assets in circulation. The Keynesian framework includes only two such assets in the analysis: money and bonds, the former non-interest bearing, the latter interest bearing. The two assets are considered to be very close substitutes for one another, and by virtue of the Hicksian (1937) reconciliation of the liquidity preference and loanable funds theories, a formal analysis can proceed on the basis of either the money or bond markets, the two being opposite sides of the same coin. However, the analysis in terms of the bond market possesses certain advantages: it is not only more transparent as compared to the corresponding analysis focusing on the money market, but also more appropriate, as it directly relates to the open market operations conducted by the central bank of a country to influence the rate of interest. Let us suppose that the existing demand and supply of the stock of both the government and private bonds is represented by the curves D and S respectively in Figure 2. This identifies E to be the equilibrium point, with the corresponding equilibrium price and stock of bonds being

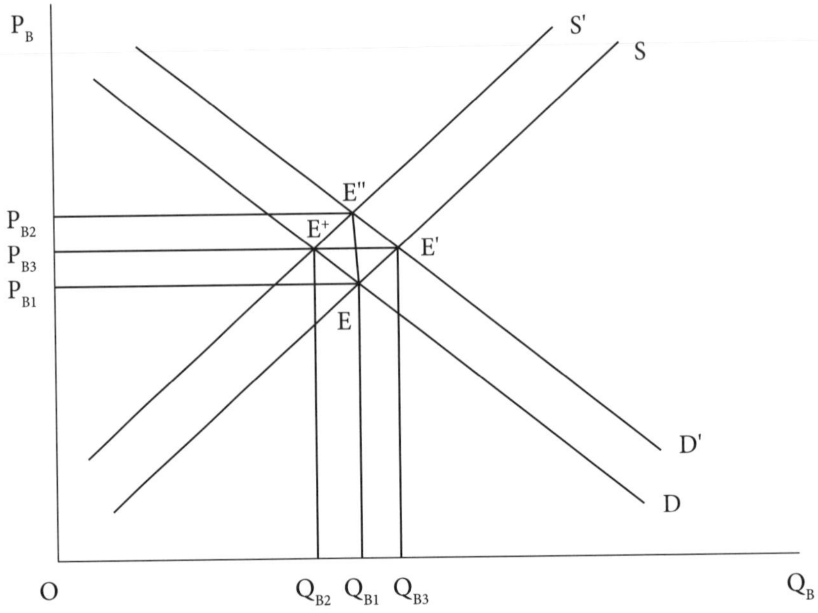

Figure 2

P_{B1} and Q_{B1} respectively. Once the equilibrium price of bonds is determined, the corresponding equilibrium rate of interest is also determined. Let us assume, for the sake of exposition, that this rate, i_1, is 10%. Let us further assume that the marginal rate of return in the real sector of the economy, call it marginal efficiency of capital, is also 10%, and that there are no intermediation costs. Under these assumptions, a 10% interest rate, or, for that matter, the corresponding 10% coupon rate on bonds, is sustainable indefinitely. Now suppose the government decides to follow an expansionary monetary policy to achieve a Natural Rate of Unemployment, which it thinks has gone down from its previous level. It now purchases bonds from the private sector of the economy, thus leading to an excess demand for bonds, causing a shift in the bond demand curve from D to D'. The end result of this process is that the equilibrium is established at point E' in the figure, with equilibrium price of bonds increasing to P_{B3}, and thus the corresponding equilibrium rate of interest decreasing to some level less than i_1, let us say, i_3. The corresponding equilibrium stock of bonds is now Q_{B3} and, we are told, this increased stock corresponds to a higher capital stock in the economy than was the case previously. A decrease in the rate of interest led to increased investment that resulted in the higher capital stock. The economy now reaches a new equilibrium at the lower rate of interest that now corresponds to a lower rate of return in the real sector of the economy as per the law of diminishing returns as applied to the higher capital stock. The economy has achieved a higher output level, and is now sitting pretty at the new lower Natural Rate of Unemployment. End of the story. Or is it?

There are several problems with this line of argument, not least of which is the complication that arises because of a perpetual link between the existing stocks and the ongoing flows, which implies that the stocks remain in a state of continuous flux. At any given time, there exists a given stock of bonds held by either the public at large or the central bank of the country. Generally, most of these bonds are government bonds. At any particular time, or more appropriately, during a given period of time, be it a day, a week, or whatever, a part of these financial assets matures and gets retired, and at the same time a new bunch is issued, both of these being the flow variables that would normally change the existing stock except when both these magnitudes are exactly equal. In terms of Figure 2—drawn in terms of the stock variables—the supply curve, S, continuously flutters around S, from S to something like S' and back again as the two flows play themselves out every time period. The first difficulty that may arise is that when the central bank of a country implements an expansionary monetary policy by buying bonds from the public at large, it generally buys the existing government bonds, a part or all of which may actually be the ones maturing during the time period under consideration. The end result is a decrease in the stock of government bonds held by the public at large. As far as the total quantity of bonds is concerned, nothing has happened except for a reshuffle of existing bonds between the central bank and the public at large, with the public at large now holding only a smaller quantity than was the case previously. In the case of private bonds, it is not quite clear whether this policy should be viewed as an increase in bond demand, causing an excess demand in the bond market, and thereby increasing the price of bonds, or a decrease in the supply of bonds, causing an excess demand, and thereby increasing the price. As far as the price of bonds is concerned, the end result is the same, although with regard to the equilibrium stock of bonds, the result is very different. In other words, it is not quite clear whether this policy action should be interpreted as an equilibrium at point E' (in which case it would be interpreted as an increase in demand), or at E* (a decrease in supply) in Figure 2, with the corresponding equilibrium quantities being Q_{B3} and Q_{B2} respectively. If, on the other hand, it is argued that the central bank is very careful and purchases only the private bonds, the policy could be interpreted as an increase in demand for bonds to insure an outcome at E', but that leads to another problem. There is no guarantee that this increase in demand will necessarily elicit an increase in quantity of bonds supplied by the private sector and thereby establishing an equilibrium at point E' as desired by the government. The private bondholders may be quite happy to sell the replacement bonds i.e. the new bonds that would have been issued in lieu of the maturing ones in the ordinary course of the events in the private bond market, but to the government at a higher price than would have been the case had the government done nothing. In other words, it is quite possible that an equilibrium would now be established at a point such as E", or some such point directly above E, instead of E' as the expansionary policy would have us believe. The maturing low price private bonds now get swapped with the high price ones, and the bond issuers are quite happy to accept this windfall before they contemplate issuing new bonds over and above those maturing, and the ones that needed to be replaced in the ordinary course of the events. Indeed, it is also possible that the private bond issuers may issue some new bonds over and above those that just matured during the period under consideration to replace the low price ones that are to mature in near future. Put slightly differently, the debtors are happy to swap their existing 10 percent debt for a less than 10 percent one to the maximum extent permitted by the central bank in pursuit of its expansionary policy.

This is the redistribution discussed earlier, and this much is certain to happen, implying a shift in the equilibrium point from E to a point such as E" directly above E, as already pointed out, but whether this will now encourage additional investment to fulfill the Keynesian promise of equilibrium at E' is an altogether different matter. The additional investment must come out of additional savings, and the question now is whether the system that was content to save a particular amount previously can be enticed to undertake additional savings for the new investment. The Keynesian answer that the additional money will serve as a temporary bridge to this effect, and that this bridge will generate additional income to ensure the required additional savings is, at best, a shaky bridge. What this bridge is more likely to lead to is an increase in the conventional price level, leading to a downward revision of the monetary magnitudes, namely the bond prices and the rate of interest, back to their original *real* levels, the levels from where we started off. The point such as E" may well become a permanent new equilibrium point instead of a temporary staging point, as the Keynesians would have us believe. Keynes actually came face to face with reality when he had to consider the theoretical possibility of his monetary-sector determined rate of interest hitting the zero floor level. He now had to admit the failure of his suggested remedy when his liquidity preference becomes a liquidity trap, a situation where whatever amount of money was supplied by the government will itself somehow sit as idle balances (or hoarding) in the economy.

Let us put the matter slightly differently: in an economy with a well developed financial system, people do not put whatever money (actually their savings) they wish to hold under their mattresses. These savings are entrusted to the financial system, and the financial system is supposed to invest these savings except for an amount needed to meet the reserve requirements, statutory or otherwise. In such an economy, there could hardly be any private hoarding as Keynes would have it. So who would be doing the hoarding, liquidity trap or not? The answer is quite clear. It is the financial system which is now sitting with excess reserves, but why? Again, the answer is not difficult to find: it is because there is no demand for credit at even the zero rate of interest (actually the banks could hardly charge zero rate of interest determined by the central bank of the country due to intermediation costs, but that is besides the point). And this could happen only if the rate of return in the real sector of the economy was so low that businesses were not now willing to borrow at even the near zero rate of interest. That a rate of interest that was delinked from the real sector of the economy, and was a purely a monetary phenomenon, determined by the monetary authorities, can run into a brick wall should now be quite clear. The economic instabilities, including the liquidity traps, are primarily created by a misconceived stabilization policy to begin with. One only needs to look at what happened in Japan in the 1990s and what is underway now in the United States and other Western countries to appreciate what has been said.

To the extent Keynes had a point, it was only this much: at times, a judicious use of government fiscal policy could resolve such difficulties by investing those excess balances in building public infrastructure. It is possible that infrastructural bottlenecks may have rendered further private investment unproductive and thus unprofitable. Private sector will not be able to remove those bottlenecks on its own—it cannot handle the provision of public goods. It goes without saying that such infrastructural investment is a routine public sector activity, it is only that at times such investment may lag behind economic growth in the economy, thus creating bottlenecks. It must be recognized that this route out of economic troubles may not be available if the infrastructure happens to be up to date. In that case, the government may end up building roads and bridges to nowhere as happened in Japan in the 1990s. The danger of this happening becomes real when the fiscal stimulus is used to resolve the difficulties that were themselves created by the government's monetary policy to begin with. One may add here that the classical economists' worry about the onset of a stationary state was not entirely misplaced, and that if such an onset could be delayed, it was thanks to technological change which raised the productivity of the factors of production.

Though the Keynesian revolution suffered an early death, the Keynesian legacy in legitimizing, if sanctifying be too strong a word, the instrumentalization of interest is likely to endure much longer. Money became a commodity, which in turn made what were supposed to be investment instruments, now to be known as financial instruments, likewise commodities, all having their own independent utilities for their holders, and to be traded just like other commodities. But this commoditization meant day-to-day fluctuations in their prices with the prospect of asset price inflation, not to mention the attendant problem of speculative activity. In a more formal way, this can be stated as follows.

The Keynes–Hicks framework worked satisfactorily when there were two such commodities (financial assets), money and bonds, under its umbrella. The resulting model was thought to depict reality fairly adequately. The Hicksian reconciliation of the liquidity preference and loanable funds theories of interest rate showed that one of the equations in the models was redundant, and therefore either the money market or the bond market equation could be dropped from the model for it to become a determinate system. In other words, when there are only two financial assets that are more or less perfect substitutes for one another, equilibrium in the market for one of those assets implied equilibrium in the other. If the money market was in equilibrium, it implied equilibrium in the bonds market, and vice versa. For a while it seemed to work, but then the trouble inherent in such a scheme of things began to surface. A system that made one form of investment instruments commodities was bound to do the same to any others. Once bonds became a commodity, there was no stopping equities or stocks becoming commodities too, sooner or later. Once that happened, as it resoundingly did towards the end of the twentieth century in at least the United States, the foundations on which the Keynes–Hicks analysis was built were equally eroded, or rather crumbled. The presence of three financial commodities destroyed the notion of an automatic equilibrium in the remaining markets once one of those was in equilibrium. Now a zero excess demand in the money market did not imply zero excess demand in both the bonds and stock markets. An absence of excess demand in the money market could coexist with an excess demand for stocks and an equal magnitude of excess supply in the bonds market. What this means is that an equilibrium in any one of the markets could coexist with disequilibria in the two remaining markets. What was even more devastating was what it implied for the transmission of monetary impulses to the real sector of the economy. The transmission mechanism now becomes even more transparent as equities are directly related to the real sector of the economy.

Continuing with the previous example, which would imply a 10% return on equities assuming all profits are distributed as dividends, an "easy money" policy, pushing down the rate of interest to, let us say, 5%, would mean people would borrow at that rate to buy equities that promise to pay 10%, creating an excess demand for equities and thus pushing up their prices. Yes, the marginal product of capital goes down to 5% but not because of an increase in investment. It goes down as a result of an increase in asset prices. Excess supply in the money market implies excess demand in the equities market. Once the equilibrium is restored, the equity prices shoot up by 100% to accommodate the 50% reduction in the rate of interest. A $100 equity that previously fetched $10, thus giving 10% dividend, is now priced at $200 to yield the required 5% return. This asset-price inflation can at times get out of hand depending upon how easy the easy money policy turns out to be, and may lead to asset-price bubbles, be it the property bubble of late 1980s in Japan, or the Unites States equities bubble in the late 1990's, or, for that matter, the more recent property bubble in the United States, and not only there. Diffusing such bubbles then becomes the main worry of the concerned monetary authorities, authorities that created the bubbles in the first place. The asset price inflation feeds into the conventional inflation sooner or later, and we are back to square one as far as the real sector of the economy is concerned. But recall that the redistributive effects associated with expansionary and contractionary monetary policy are not reversible, as pointed out earlier.

Before proceeding to the efficiency implications of the instrumentalization of interest, we may now pause to ask, in the presence of an ever-obliging government, who are the major beneficiaries of this rent-seeking theory of interest? It is these beneficiaries who are the rightful claimants to the title trustee-capitalists. Since the redistributive effects that we have discussed operate through the financial markets, it is quite clear that those who are the movers and shakers, the so-called 'players', in these markets, markets that have never been thought to fall under the purview of perfect competition for reasons that need not detain us here, that would without any doubt fall in the first rank of trustee-capitalists. It is they who exercise control over the flow of financial resources in general, and debt capital in particular, in the economy. Also included, of course, are the residual controllers in the corporate sector that get ready access to the debt capital by virtue of their being the members of the "big boys" club. These are the insiders, so to speak, who include the top management and directors. The ordinary equity holders fall in this group only as tail-enders, beholden to any redistributive largesse that may come their way, particularly during periods of asset price inflation, and who, no doubt, have become more interested in such capital gains in this rent-seeking environment rather than in exercising their voting power at annual general meetings. After all, the system is geared to considering shares as just another commodity rather than an investment. The tax-payer, in general, is at the other end of this inherently zero-sum redistributive game played in the name of certain presumed stabilization gains.[4]

[4] This chapter was written towards the end of 2004. Subsequent events, and especially those starting in the summer of 2008, attest to the scenario presented here.

And On to Efficiency

The financial system of any economy is crucial for both mobilization of resources and an efficient functioning of the payments system. There is no doubt that sickness of an industry, whatever its detailed institutional structure, which is central to the process of saving and investment in an economy is likely to have serious repercussions for the health of the other industries, and thereby the over-all health of the economy. An unhealthy financial services industry cannot spawn a healthy clutch of offspring. Inefficiencies in that industry are tantamount to inefficient allocation of resources throughout the economy. This obviously means that the financial services industry requires special attention. One ignores the vital organ of a body, such as the heart, at one's peril. Under capitalism the financial services industry has naturally come to occupy the commanding heights of the economy. The industry has successfully exploited its vital position in the resource allocation mechanism to extract favors that would ordinarily be denied to other industries. The danger of systemic risk obliges governments, it is argued, to provide protection to the financial industry in the form of deposit insurance, or finality of payments in the settlement system, etc., to avoid any contagions that can have devastating effect on the real sector of the economy. And that is the reason for an elaborate system of protection, coupled with regulation that characterizes the capitalist financial industry throughout the world. But protection has its own down side. It gives rise to another set of problems: for instance the system of deposit insurance makes both the depositors and financial institutions less careful in the knowledge that if anything goes wrong, the government will come to their rescue. The depositors become less vigilant in the selection of the financial institution that they entrust their savings to, and the financial institutions become less careful in the selection of customers or firms they extend loans to. This, as in any other form of protection, leads to less than prudent behavior that gives rise to the well known moral hazard problem, which in turn leads to the process of adverse selection—here I have used these terms as they are conventionally used in financial economics, a special case of the broader meanings given to them in the previous chapter—with serious consequences for allocative efficiency. The safeguards put in place in the form of regulatory regimes hardly ever work satisfactorily for all sorts of reasons, including political considerations. The heavy hand of regulation, which coordinated its decision in fifty-six countries of the world to shut down the Bank of Credit and Commerce International (BCCI) in 1991, was unprecedented in the history of financial regulation, and is likely to remain so for a very long time to come, unless the regulators can once again find a despised financial institution without any domestic constituency in the heartland of capitalism as a scapegoat. In general, financial regulation can best be described as theatrics of proverbial cat and mouse—the latter has become the clicking sort in recent decades, with the clicking having global implications far beyond the domestic regulatory jurisdiction—in a game of hide and seek. In this game, on one side there is a powerful industry, populated by the brightest in the land, attracted there by the lure of appropriable surplus, facing, on the other side, the *typical* bureaucrats operating a regulatory regime that is always one step behind its times. There is an increasing recognition that this vicious circle, beginning with the danger of systemic risk leading to protection, leading on to moral hazard and back to an even greater degree of systemic risk needs to be broken somehow, but the proposed solutions hardly ever go far enough. That at the heart of this problem sits the issue of moral hazard is recognized all too well. What is not recognized, at least openly, is that the problem is not likely to go away in a financial system built on the instrumentalization of interest, centered on a rate that is nothing more than a monetary phenomenon in an age of paper, plastic, and electronic money, and supposedly controlled by a government that can hardly resist the play of powerful special interests, and is subject to the pressures of the pressure groups. No wonder, then, that the capitalist financial system, despite all efforts, has evaded stability and has failed to deliver the goods expected of it. The patient, in spite of the most generous medical benefits, continually runs a fever with occasional bouts of severe headache coupled with flu that exhausts his vital fluids, his "liquidity," requiring costly intensive care treatment at the taxpayers' expense.[5] The largesse distribution,

[5] If that seems too harsh a pronouncement on capitalist financial system in light of the evidence that the system worked with fair degree of stability after the safety net was put in place in 1934 in the United States in the aftermath of the spectacular crash of 1929, up until the 1970's, one needs to take into consideration a number of factors that contributed to this period of relative calm. Briefly these would include: (i) the second World War; (ii) the shift of global financial capital across Atlantic to New York, which meant the new players would take some time to learn the tricks of the trade; (iii) the crash of 1929 invoked a greater degree of caution among the

or rent seeking, theory of interest rate determination always comes home to roost whenever the vigilant eye blinks because of fatigue or winks because of moral hazard.

An important implication of this system in the international context may be briefly noted here before closing this chapter. This relates to the harm that the developing countries have suffered when credit, in the name of foreign aid if the donor was a government, was extended without any regard to where the proceeds were to be used. More often than not the funds were embezzled by the government functionaries, or wasted on grandiose projects to project the image of the rulers, or simply used to defray current expenditures, with the end result that the recipient countries were saddled with unbearable debt burdens without any economic uplift.

In the final analysis, capitalism is a reflection of the financial institutions of the concerned society, which in turn is a reflection, as all institutions including the institution of government are, of the structure of property rights prevailing in that society. This structure of property rights is embedded in the set of values held by the society, as was pointed out at the outset in Chapter 3. To what extent the market-based economic system of a society may depart from capitalism is crucially linked to the extent the financial institutions and the rules pertaining to those institutions differ from those prevailing in the capitalist economies. For an Islamic economy, this question cannot be answered until the issues relating to *ribā* are sorted out. This I have done in Chapters 9 and 10. In Chapter 11, I take up the question as to how far an Islamic economy is likely to differ from a capitalistic one.

participants; (iv) the ongoing technological revolution that created more surplus, and provided a greater degree of cushion; and (v), and perhaps most importantly, the threat of Communism which imparted a missionary zeal in capitalism to succeed. No wonder, then, that as soon as the threat receded, it started to progressively show its true colors beginning with the decade of 1980's. The financial services industry, in turn, blames, with considerable justification, the erratic interest rate policy of the government for some of the major problems it faces. Accordingly, it is the government, which creates a problem by its erratic interest rate policy to begin with that it then clamors to resolve by providing the needed safety net, a net that creates its own problems in the form of moral hazard, and this vicious cycle continues.

CHAPTER FIVE

FUNDAMENTAL AXIOMS OF AN ISLAMIC ECONOMY

Some Preliminaries

The exposition in this and the following three chapters is crucially dependent on the conceptual framework for an economic system laid down in Chapter 3. That framework was built upon a set of essential elements of an economic system, and these elements can be, and often are, referred to as the characteristics of an economic system or simply an economy. It may be noted that the set of elements discussed there was comprised of the minimum set of such elements. One element of this set was referred as the criterion, which was supposed to form the basis on which the economic performance of the system was to be adjudged. We also note that the set of characteristics presented there was predicated on the existence of a set of values, and more than any other element, it was this criterion that reflected these values. Understandably this criterion forms the foundation of what has come to be known as normative economics. This criterion is more or less universally acknowledged to be the Pareto criterion, at least in the market economies, and the discussion in Chapter 2 revolved around this criterion. What this means is that the set of values held by the market economies is supposed to approve, tacitly or otherwise, the use of this criterion to judge the efficiency of the system as well as to sort out the issues relating to conflict between efficiency and equity. It must be emphasized that regardless of what form an Islamic economy takes, the question as to how the performance of that economy will be evaluated cannot be ignored. The present chapter focuses exclusively on this subject, while the remaining characteristics form the subject matter of the next two chapters. To be somewhat more specific, since the Pareto criterion in principle can be invoked only when the benefits and costs associated with different economic outcomes are assumed to be measurable, towards the end of this chapter special attention is paid as to what the value system of Islam has to say about such a procedure. The relevance of the entire edifice of welfare economics to an Islamic economy crucially depends upon that answer.

A search for what the pioneers of Islamic economics had to say about the issues of efficiency and equity, and the conflicts between these two, reveals surprisingly very little. It is only when the scope of the enterprise was expanded to stop nothing short of a paradigm shift that the perceptive exponents of Islamic economics felt obliged to address the relevant questions. But the results of this undertaking have turned out to be far from satisfactory as we saw in Chapter 2, where, at least explicitly, only the exposition by the leading writers on the subject came under review. These writings normally presume that the existing economic systems exhibit serious flaws, particularly relating to the distribution of income, and that once an economy is Islamized, these distributional anomalies will be automatically resolved. Leaving aside the question of the validity of such claims, for that would require empirical evidence which is never presented, there is the further presumption in these writings that distributional issues are, indeed ought to be, the only ones that are worthy of our attention, as we saw there. The main reason for this tendency is discernable. Either because of a genuine desire to ground their arguments in the classical Islamic soil, and/or to lend an air of legitimacy to them, all writers on the subject of Islamic economics find it convenient to appeal to the classical literature on Islamic sciences. There is, of course, nothing wrong in doing that; if anything it is commendable, provided it is realized that history has moved on, and a one to one mapping of the concepts and terminology of the classical times into the contemporary discourse may not always be fruitful. One important implication of this unconsidered resorting to the past is the absence of any concern with the idea of economic efficiency: the classical literature does not have much, if anything, to say on that issue. At the most, one can glean a concern with technical efficiency, but then the concept of allocative efficiency is an altogether different matter. An idea which has its roots in twentieth-century welfare economics could hardly be found to have an echo in the intellectual discourse of a millennium before.

Ignoring the issues relating to efficiency seriously restricted the space in which Islamic economics was then confined to operate. It amounted to worrying about the distribution of a pie without there being any concern about the possible changes in its size due to improvements in efficiency. Even more seriously, in principle it robbed it of what one would recognize as any positive economics contents. I may add that one does indeed find abundant use of positive economics terminology in the discourse on Islamic economics but this opportune use does not negate the fact that such terminology is not provided any firm moorings from either the Islamic lexicon, or its social norms. In what follows, we pay special attention to the Islamic value system in order to explore whether it lends its support, as claimed, to the positions taken by the proponents of Islamic economics in general, and of those who would like to see nothing short of a complete paradigm shift in particular.

The Minimum Set

We begin by posing an elementary question: what are the fundamental value axioms of an Islamic economy, indeed of any Islamic social system? It is interesting to note that a vast majority of writers on Islamic economics do not concern themselves, at least directly, with this question. Instead they focus on what seems to them to be the right question, and that is: what are the objectives of an Islamic economic system? And their answer is surprisingly simple, indeed simplistic. It is to achieve the so called *maqāṣid al-Sharīʿa*, (objectives of the *Sharīʿa*) as expounded a millennium ago. These are five in number, and their original exposition is traced back to classical writings on *fiqh,* particularly in the writings of Imam Ghazālī in the second half of the eleventh century. A detailed discussion of this subject follows a little later. Here we only note that, in the final analysis, their focus and concern boils down to enforcing what are presented as the Islamic injunctions. The only writer, that I am aware of, who addresses this question at the doctrinal level, and in a systematic way, is Syed Nawab Haider Naqvi (1981). He attempts to enlist a set of fundamental axioms of an Islamic social system, and having an acute mind, recognizes that this set ought to include just the minimum number of internally consistent elements. His selection of the elements, as well as his claim that the set includes a minimum irreducible number of elements (he has four), must draw our careful attention, for the implications of including an unwarranted element in such a set could be nothing short of far reaching. Naqvi's set includes:

a. The axiom of Unity,
b. The axiom of Equilibrium,
c. The axiom of Free Will, and
d. The axiom of Responsibility.

After a careful consideration of the theological foundations of the various elements in the list, one is forced to conclude that Naqvi's otherwise fine exposition suffers from a serious flaw, which relates to the inclusion of the fourth element, the axiom of responsibility.[1] The reason for this is the way he conceptualizes the idea of responsibility. He forces an idea which inherently cannot be divorced from individual actions into a collective imperative. This is plainly unwarranted. Thus, I argue in what follows that his set goes beyond what he claims to be a minimum number of internally consistent elements in so far as he includes the axiom of collective responsibility. No doubt the idea of individual responsibility is fundamental to any doctrinal formulation in Islam, but then as such it is necessarily a part of the axiom of free will. The inclusion of the fourth element in the list is either unwarranted or redundant. We now turn to a closer look at the set of axioms.

The axiom of unity underscores Islam's uncompromising stance towards Divine Unity. Much has been written on that subject, and yet no human endeavor could possibly do justice to the subject, for there is no common measure between the finite, that creation happens to be, and the Infinite that He happens to be in all His conceivable grandeur and glory. It is only in the name of His grace and mercy that man approaches the subject of His Unity, and it is only in view of His commandments, revealed through the offices of His Messengers that he endeavors to explore the implications of the Infinite coming into contact with the finite. It is thus that the universe is a unity for it could not be otherwise, being His creation, and so is man, for the same reasons. In the immensity of serial time and cosmic space, man may seem like less than a speck of dust, yet he sits, thanks

[1] The use of the word "theological" is liable to give rise to misunderstanding, for it may be taken in its technical meaning relating to other religions, for example as in Christianity. I am not using the word in any such sense, for Islam does not have any such theology, and when it is used in Islamic discourse to roughly denote *kalam* it does not have the same connotations that are meant in the present discourse. More specifically, I use the word to highlight the doctrinal contents of Islam, contents that are obviously rooted in Divine revelations.

to His plan, at the summit of creation. He has something of theomorphic in his nature; nothing less than that would be worthy of his station. It is because of that that he is capable of soaring beyond the Angelic realms, but then at the same time he is equally capable of sinking to the unfathomable depths, for the concomitant acceptance of free will entailed that danger. The Qur'ān narrates it thus: "Verily, We did offer the trust (of reason and volition) to the heavens, and the earth, and the mountains: but they refused to bear it because they were afraid of it. Yet man took it up," adding "for, verily, he has always been prone to be most wicked, most foolish" (33:72).[2] The first sentence of the Qur'ān, after the brief first *sūra, al-Fātiḥa* (The Opening), which serves as a preamble, and which the Prophet himself called *Umm al Kitāb* (The Essence of the Qur'ān), in the second *sūra* enunciates the philosophy behind its revelation declares: "This book—let there be no doubt about it—is (meant to be) a guidance for all the God-conscious who believe in (the existence of) that which is beyond the reach of human perception, and are constant in prayer, and spend on others out of what We provide for them in sustenance; and who believe in that which has been bestowed from on high upon thee (O Prophet), as well as in that which was bestowed before thy time: for it is they who in their innermost are certain of the life to come! It is they who follow the guidance (which comes) from their Sustainer; and it is they, they who shall attain to a happy state!" (2:2–5). But then the story of man's predicament is narrated in a highly allegorical manner in a *sūra*, which was quite appropriately given the title *al-Aʿrāf*, probably by the Prophet himself (it is commonly translated as "The Heights" but in my view Muhammad Asad's translation as "The Faculty of Discernment" seems more appropriate), which expounds the issue of free will, among other things. Let us see what the Qur'ān has to say on the subject and why it would emphasize the need for guidance at the very outset:

> Yea, indeed (O men), We have given you a (bountiful) place on earth, and appointed thereon means of livelihood for you: (yet) how seldom are you grateful! Yea, indeed, We have created you, and then formed

[2] The first number in parentheses refers to the Qur'ānic *sūra*, and the second to the verse number. Throughout this book I have used the English rendering of the verses by Muhammad Asad, *The Message of the Qur'ān*, Gibraltar: Dār Al-Andalus, 1980. On rare occasions, however, I have used ʿAbdullah Yūsuf ʿAlī's translations, *The Meaning of the Glorious Qur'ān*, Cairo: Dār al-Kitāb al-Miṣrī, where I thought it made the meanings clearer.

you; and then We said unto the angels, "Prostrate yourselves before Adam!"—whereupon they (all) prostrated themselves, save Iblīs: he was not among those who prostrated themselves. (And God) said: "what has kept thee from prostrating thyself when I commanded thee?" Answered (Iblīs): "I am better than he: Thou hast created me out of fire, whereas him Thou hast created out of clay." (God) said: "Down with thee, then, from this (state)—for it is not meet for thee to show arrogance here! Go forth, then: among the humiliated shalt thou be!" Said (Iblīs): "Grant me a respite till the Day when all shall be raised from the dead," (And God) replied: Verily, thou shalt be among those who are granted a respite." (Whereupon Iblīs) said: "Now that Thou hast thwarted me, I shall most certainly lie in ambush for them all along Thy straight way, and shall most certainly fall upon them openly as well as in a manner beyond their ken, and from their right and from their left: and most of them Thou wilt find ungrateful." (And God) said: "Go forth from here, disgraced and disowned! (And) as for such of them as follow thee—I will most certainly fill hell with you all! And (as for thee), O Adam, dwell thou and thy wife in this garden, and eat, both of you, whatever you may wish; but do not approach this one tree, lest you become evildoers!" Thereupon Satan whispered unto the two with a view to making them conscious of their nakedness, of which (hitherto) they had been unaware; and he said: "Your Sustainer has but forbidden you this tree lest you two become (as) angels, or lest you live forever." And he swore unto them, "Verily, I am of those who wish you well indeed!"—and thus he led them on with deluding thoughts. But as soon as the two had tasted (the fruit) of the tree, they became conscious of their nakedness; and they began to cover themselves with pieced-together leaves from the garden. And their Sustainer called unto them: "Did I not forbid that tree unto you and tell you, "Verily, Satan is your open foe'?" The two replied: "O our Sustainer! We have sinned against ourselves—and unless Thou grant us forgiveness and bestow Thy mercy upon us, we shall most certainly be lost!" Said He: "Down with you, (and be henceforth) enemies unto one another, having on earth your abode and livelihood for a while: there shall you live"—He added—"and there shall you die, and thence shall you be brought forth (on Resurrection Day)!" O children of Adam! Indeed, We have bestowed upon you from on high (the knowledge of making) garments to cover your nakedness, and as a thing of beauty: but the garment of God-consciousness is the best of all. Herein lies a message from God, so that man may take it to heart. O children of Adam! Do not allow Satan to seduce you in the same way as he caused your ancestors to be driven out of the garden: he deprived them of their garment (of God-consciousness) in order to make them aware of their nakedness. Verily, he and his tribe are lying in wait for you where you cannot perceive them (7:10–27).[3]

[3] This story recurs in Qur'ān in fragments depending upon the stress intended for the occasion. It recurs with more or less the same elements as above in 20:115–121,

Thus it is that man accepted free will at his peril but then he was not left alone, alone to his own devices, thanks, once again, to the Divine mercy. "Does man, then, think that he is to be left to himself, to go about at will?" (75:36) The Creator provided the necessary guidance for the free will to actualize all the latent possibilities that were commensurate with man's theomorphic endowments. This Guidance could not possibly be less than sufficient. "Say: Behold my Sustainer has guided me onto a straight way through an ever-true faith—the way of Abraham, who turned away from all that is false, and was not of those who ascribe divinity to aught besides Him" (6:161), and then as though enclosing oceans in the palms of man's hands raised up in prayer and supplication, the next verse provides the ultimate statement of what ought to be man's orientation in his terrestrial life: "Say: 'Behold, my prayer, and (all) my acts of worship, and my living and my dying are for God (alone), the Sustainer of all the worlds'" (6:162).

If man is a unity, his terrestrial life must reflect that unity by being whole and not divided into all sorts of compartments. This is one of the profound, if not the most profound, implications of His unity for man's terrestrial existence, and what it means is that his earthly life cannot be split into mundane and profound, material and spiritual, secular and religious, or any such categorizations. His life is to be lived in such a way where all these dimensions—dimensions that he is given a liberty to label variously for his own reference, to organize his life—are to be balanced and harmonized in a symphony that can be characterized as a Divinely ordained equilibrium, the equilibrium that sanctifies even the seemingly most mundane of the mundane, at the same time that it reminds him that the loftiest of his thoughts and works, and the most acute of his spiritual experiences are incapable of releasing him from his earthly concomitances. Thus it is that the Divine remains Divine and man remains man. Nothing can release man from his earthly responsibilities, and by implication

and thereafter the following is added; "Thereafter (however), his Sustainer elected him (for His grace), and accepted his repentance, and bestowed His *guidance* upon him, saying: 'Down with you all from this (state of innocence, and be henceforth) enemies unto one another! None the less, there shall most certainly come unto you guidance from Me: and he who follows My guidance will not go astray, and neither will he be unhappy. But as for him who shall turn away from remembering Me—his shall be a life of narrow scope; and on the Day of Resurrection We shall raise him up blind'" (20:122–124, emphasis added).

nothing ought to take away from him his Divinely sanctioned freedoms. Freedoms, or rights, can only be enjoyed by accepting the corresponding responsibilities. As far as man is concerned, there is no absolute freedom save God's. Man's predicament can be summed up by noting that he wishes to enjoy rights without accepting the corresponding responsibilities, after all free will is subject to a thousand temptations, temptations that primarily, if not exclusively, lead man to trample on or usurp the rights of the others for his own indulgences, his own aggrandizement. It is thus that the final revelation for the guidance of mankind introduces the concept of "collective man" side by side with "individual man," the former addressing the inescapable social dimension of human existence. It is not difficult to see that in view of the 'equilibrium' it envisages for man's collective existence, it could hardly fail to introduce the concept of collective man.

If God is *al-ʿAdl* (justness), as per the Qurʾān (6:115), man's theomorphism could not be divorced from that Divine attribute. In the affairs of man, this dimension essentially relates to his participation in the collective existence. No doubt, man can do violence to himself, for at the personal level he can always ignore his station in the Divine scheme of things, and in that case he risks forfeiting his possible lofty station in the life to come. But that is not the only way he faces damnation in the hereafter. Beyond the haughtiness, which is implied in the foregoing, there is his attachment to the life here and now, and the possibility of his losing a sense of proportion with regard to that attachment, which is bound to lead to greed, avarice, and viciousness. "And they should not think—they who niggardly cling to all that God has granted them out of His bounty—that this is good for them: nay, it is bad for them. That to which they (so) niggardly cling will, on the Day of Resurrection, be hung about their necks: for unto God (alone) belongs the heritage of the heavens and of the earth; and God is aware of all that you do" (3:180). The Divine guidance in such cases, apart from issuing warnings to the individual man of reparations in the hereafter, also makes it incumbent upon the collective man (i.e. him being a member of the society) to institute retribution at the societal level for the excesses committed by the individual members, for not doing so will disturb the social equilibrium, and if the equilibrium could be disturbed by someone with impunity, this would carry the danger of acquiring its own momentum, resulting in chaos, which is an antithesis of Divine universal order. Thus the need for a

Divinely sanctioned code of conduct, both at the individual and collective levels, and hence *Sharīʿa*. Once the Creator decided to bestow on man His blessing of guidance, no sphere of his action, or of the deployment of his will, could possibly be left unattended. At the level of individual man, the code requires shunning of the extremes, and thus following of the middle path, and at the collective level it necessitates *ʿadl* in all dealings, dealings that may not always fall within the domain of what is commonly understood as law. For matters that do not fall in the domain of law, it demands fairness, just as for those dealings that would fall within the purview of the law, it would insist on such being based on justice.[4] Any societal institution concerned with man's collective dealings cannot but be required to dispense justice. While it goes without saying that man neglects these ethical imperatives at his peril, it must be emphasized that when he voluntarily accepts the responsibility of dispensing justice among other men, his willful failure to discharge this responsibility would necessarily amount to his negation of Divine Unity.

So everything begins and ends with Divine Unity, for He is the First (*al-Awwal*) and the Last (*al-Ākhir*), and "Verily unto God do we belong and, verily, unto Him we shall return" (2:156). In reality, as far as Islam is concerned, there is only one ethical axiom, both in the legalistic and principial senses of that term: in the legalistic sense because Islam is a distinct religion with its own *Sharīʿa*, and in the principial sense in so far as Islam is the only religion ever revealed by God, notwithstanding different *Sharīʿas*[5] given to different prophets, presumably in view of the different temperaments of different people, "that they may vie with one another in doing good works" as the Qurʾān says (5:48). The doctrine of Divine Unity is universal in so much as it is common to all revealed ethical systems, and is limited only to the extent of its non-acceptance by the free will, but then at the same time it may be viewed as particularistic in so far as it may allow for different crystallizations under different codes of conduct

[4] Generally the term fairness is used in the same sense that I use the term justness. Since in the conceptualization here, fairness is used to highlight the subjective dimension of a person's behavior towards others, I have opted to use the term justness somewhat broadly to include fairness. Though at the operational level, it would coincide with the general conception of fairness.

[5] For an explicit reference to different *Sharīʿa*(s) for different people, see verse 5:48 (also cited below in this Chapter), and for an explicit statement about different forms of worship for different people, see verse 22:67, also cited below in this Chapter.

(systems of law, *Sharīʿas*) followed by different people. Interestingly, when free will denies Divine Unity, it wishes to usurp the related privilege for itself to masquerade as that universal axiom by itself, and in that case it could hardly be likely to accept any responsibilities. And as a consequence, there could be no hope for the axiom of justness or equilibrium. For a Muslim, again in the principal sense, there are no morals that are not grounded in the immutable Divine Unity. The so called axiom of responsibility derives its essence, and thereby existence, from the acceptance by the free will of the axiom of Divine Unity. Once the free will accepts that axiom, there is no need to include the axiom of individual responsibility as an independent entity in the minimum set of axioms. For when it does so, it perforce accepts the axiom of justness, with all its demands at both the personal and inter-personal levels. As a result, the collective man must endeavor to institute a system of justice at the societal level. Let us repeat that at the operational level, either the individual man accepts the axiom of Divine Unity by deploying his free will, and the collective man then ends up with the axiom of justice or, alternatively, the free will rejects the axiom of Divine Unity, and in that case what is left is just the axiom of free will, and thereby an insuperable moral void.

In light of this discussion, it is difficult to miss the significance of the metaphysical doctrine of Unity along with the place of the free will in the cosmic drama, and thereby the imperative of justness at the personal and justice at the collective level. Combine the latter two into one axiom and call it the axiom of equilibrium, if you will, as Professor Naqvi would do. But what is the place of his axiom of responsibility in this scheme of things? If it is to pinpoint individual responsibility, it turns out to be redundant for the axiom of free will necessarily implies such individual responsibility. But if it is to introduce an imperative in the form of 'collective' responsibility, as he does, very serious conceptual as well as theological problems are encountered. It must be kept in mind that collective responsibility is not the same thing as responsibility of a collectivity, in exactly the same way as rights of a collectivity could not be construed as collective rights. When a responsibility is assigned to a collectivity, it actually amounts to assigning it to none, or at the very least, to no one in particular. If the idea of responsibility is to have any practical implications, such an open ended formulation is nothing short of inviting trouble. The idea of holding someone responsible implies, first of all, a prior conferring of rights, and second, a punishment commensurate with the seriousness of the negation of that responsibility. We know that the idea of collective rights (read communal rights) is fraught with trouble (the tragedy of the commons), but the idea of collective responsibility may indeed turn out to be tyrannical. Humanity has suffered immeasurably from the actions taken in the name of collective rights, or for that matter responsibilities, be that under the umbrella of nationalism or in the guise of sectarianism. The possibility of excesses that may be committed in the name of collective responsibility simply cannot be ignored. Yet, admittedly, the issue of collective responsibility cannot be easily dismissed in a societal setting. Islam handled this issue in a rather daring manner by wedding the idea to individual responsibility, in what has been called a *farḍ al-kifāya* (roughly communal responsibility, but without necessarily any corresponding rights) where when one or a few members of a collectivity discharge the responsibility voluntarily, it is considered to be discharged for everyone. Interestingly, *farḍ al-kifāya*, upon a closer look, turns out to be the precursor to the twentieth century developments in the theory of public goods. We will touch upon that subject later in this chapter, as also in the next. What is significant at this stage of the argument is that in Islam, the idea of collective responsibility is made subservient to the idea of individual responsibility, for it could not be otherwise in a Divinely ordained system. It is the individual will, and therefore responsibility, that remains the pivot of any social system in Islam. An individual free will that accepts the axiom of Unity and strives earnestly to discharge the attendant responsibility, including that of instituting justice at the collective level—an onerous task, without doubt—could not be held responsible for any lack of success in such an endeavor. For, in the final analysis, it is the striving of the individual free will that counts, and indeed ought to count. We clearly know from the Qurʾān that the strivings of the various prophets were never judged on the basis of the results obtained at the societal level.

The question now is: what should we make of Naqvi's extrapolation of individual responsibility into collective responsibility? His firm commitment to the philosophy of dirigisme—and thereby his surprising faith in the institution of government, contrary to the historical as well as contemporary evidence in the Islamic realm—leads him to subsume individual responsibility under the collective one, never mind even if the theological edifice of Islam had to be thus turned upside down. Recognizing the inherent difficulty of reconciling his twin commitments, one to dirigisme and the other to his faith, he argues, "Although, according to the Islamic teachings, the 'individual man' comes before the 'collective man', at least '*historically*', there is an essential reciprocity between these two aspects of man. In the all-comprehending vision of Islam, everything must be assigned a proper place" (Naqvi, 1981, p. 46; emphasis added). One is surprised at this relegation of Islamic teachings (if a fundamental theological doctrinal point could be termed as such) to be a phase in some perceived historical progression, only to find out later in his book that the idea of collective responsibility—that historical evolution—is to be used to justify all sorts of collectivist (i.e. government) interferences in the economy in the name of equalizing the distribution of income.[6] One would indeed sympathize, as one must, with Naqvi's concern with the plight of the poor, and one may find some merit in the policy of redistribution that he so eloquently advocates, but the introduction of an unwarranted theological position, that is the collective responsibility axiom is unacceptable: the framework of *Sharīʿa*, as it stands, without this addendum, is flexible enough to

[6] At the end of Naqvi's citation, we are given to understand, through a footnote, that "the distinction between man as such and 'the collective man'" and thus the collective responsibility he enunciates is affirmed by Frithjof Schuon's exposition of the same (Schuon, pp. 26–27). In his use of Schuon's exposition, Naqvi does not do justice to what Schuon had to say on the subject. It is only fair to let Schuon speak for himself, to see if what he has to say leads to any notion of collective responsibility:

> If there is a clear separation in Islam between man as such and collective man, these two realities are none the less profoundly linked together, given that collectivity is an aspect of man—no man can be born without a family—and that conversely society is a multiplication of individuals. It follows from this interdependence or reciprocity that anything that is done with a view to collectivity, such as tithe for the poor or the holy war, has a spiritual value for the individual and conversely; this converse relationship is the more true because the individual comes before the collectivity, all men being descended from Adam and not Adam from men (Schuon, 1963, p. 26).

And to understand the context in which Schuon said this, we must refer to his next paragraph:

> What has just been said explains why the Moslem does not, like the Buddhist and the Hindu, abandon external rites in following some particular spiritual method which can compensate for them, or because he has attained a spiritual level of a nature to authorize such abandonment. A particular saint may no longer have need of the canonical prayers since he finds himself in a state of being steeped in prayer, in a state of "intoxication"—none the less he continues to accomplish the prayers in order to pray with and for all and in order that all may pray in him (1963, pp. 26–27).

accommodate his distributional concerns—an issue taken up later in this chapter. At any rate, the value framework of Islam begins at the metaphysical level with the axiom of Divine Unity, goes through the axiom of free will, and ends up with the operative axiom of justness, which at the social plane of man's earthly existence boils down to axiom of justice, or of equilibrium if one likes.

The question now is to find out if this operative axiom would have any connection with the Chapter 2's axioms of efficiency and equity or, in other words, with the concepts of Pareto optimality and the optimum optimorum as used in welfare economics. But before we move on to that subject, we need to consider what the leading writers on Islamic economics have to say on the issue of the value premises of an Islamic economy.

Value Premises in Islamic Economics

In light of the distinction that we have drawn between individual and collective man, several points need to be kept in mind to get a correct perspective as to where Islamic economics stands with regard to value axioms. When it comes to individual perspective, Islamic economists use the idealistic but practically problematic perspective of homo-Islamicus that we met in Chapter 1. Leaving that idealistic rhetoric aside, we may now turn to more specific issues, recognizing that Islamic economics—indeed any social Islamic discourse—cannot divorce itself from the imperatives of the guidance we have discussed. Here we encounter a number of serious difficulties. As far as the individual man is concerned, Islamic economists seem to endorse the general perspective of *fiqh*- though perhaps unlike the more careful *fiqh* writers- where often no clear distinction is drawn between what is incumbent (*wājib*, pl. *wājibāt*) and what is supererogatory (*al-iḥsān*), and where, as a result, sometimes supererogatory acts are viewed as something that must be legally enforced, as we will see below. It goes without saying that this creates a confusion about the correct boundaries of state action. But then interestingly, and this is the second problem, when it comes to collective man, that is to say the societal level, they hardly ever emphasize the fundamental imperative of instituting justice. This may be an inadvertent result of the lack of a theory of government. In consequence, the functions of government are something that the society is held responsible to perform in some sort of a vacuum. No wonder then that the subject of efficient enforcement of property rights is quite alien to their discourse. It is another matter that the institution of government mysteriously reappears in their writings when such is deemed convenient. Beyond that, as briefly touched upon earlier in this chapter, Islamic economists generally do not feel obliged to address the subject of values in terms of the fundamental axioms of an Islamic economy. For them it is sufficient to state that the objective of an Islamic economy is the fulfillment of the so called *maqāṣid al-Sharīʿa*.

The term *Sharīʿa* has also occurred in my exposition of the axioms of an Islamic economy. It is important that the meaning of this term is sufficiently, but only sufficiently, spelled out for a clear understanding of what then follows. Earlier, it was referred to as a code of conduct encompassing both the personal and interpersonal spheres of free will's operation. When Islam claims that it is a complete way of life, this is what it purports to signify. But then *Sharīʿa* is often referred to as Islamic law. While this is true to some extent, it may lead to the wrong impression that all of its injunctions are enforceable, for that is how the term law is commonly understood. Admittedly, while *Sharīʿa*, which is in principle based on the original sources of Islamic values, namely the Qurʾān and *ḥadīth*,[7] is quite specific as to the details of conduct in particular situations, it often provides only broad guidelines in others. This flexibility is Divinely ordained, for it cannot be otherwise if *Sharīʿa* is to have universal applicability with regard to time and space. These broad guidelines were subsequently codified into specific rules, and this science of codification was given the name *fiqh*. This process of codification required a certain degree of precision, specifically with regard to the principles used to ground the rules so derived in the original sources of Islamic

[7] A vast majority of Muslim writers would include *sunna* instead of *ḥadīthʾ* in the original sources. The term *sunna* originally meant the sayings and actions of the Prophet, which were subsequently included in the compilations of *ḥadīth* treatises. Later on, the scope of the term *sunna* was extended to include the sayings and actions of the closest companions of the Prophet (*al-Ṣaḥāba*), and sometimes even those of the pious Muslims of the later generations. A vast majority of Muslims are unaware of this crucial extension, for it must be noted that the Prophetic *sunna* is necessarily a part of the *ḥadīth* literature. My choice of *ḥadīth* is dictated by the fact that the sayings and actions of persons other than the Prophet himself could not be vested with the same authority in the context of legal formulations in changing times.

values. The science of *fiqh* required a science of the *uṣūl al-fiqh* (principles of *fiqh*). Those who participated in this undertaking differed with regard to these principles, or details pertaining thereto, and thus Islamic *fiqh* ended up with a number of *madhāhib* (sing. *madhhab*), or schools of *fiqh*. This process eventually crystallized into five major schools, Ḥanafī, Shāfiʿī, Mālikī, Ḥanbalī, and Jaʿfarī, and the leading exponents of each of these schools were, and still are, commonly given the honorific title of *Imām*. With the passage of time, the terms *Sharīʿa* and *fiqh* came to be used interchangeably, though formally the term *fiqh* is more appropriate, being the formally codified body of Islamic law (in the remaining part of this work, I have mostly used the term *fiqh* rather than *Sharīʿa* for that codified body of law). The question now becomes: is *fiqh* the same thing as law in the commonly understood meaning of that term? The answer is no, for if *Sharīʿa* encompassed more than what would be considered as the sphere of law, its codification could hardly remain confined to that sphere. It is thus that we see detailed discussions not only on issues pertaining to interpersonal relations but also on personal conduct. With the passage of time, the codification evolved into more and more refined branches, and now we see it split, *inter alia* into: *fiqh al-ʿibādāt* (*fiqh* of religious rites); *fiqh al-munākahāt* (family law); *fiqh al-muʿāmalāt* (rules covering social relations including contract law); *fiqh al-taʿzīrāt* or *fiqh al-jināyāt* (criminal law); *fiqh al-ḥukm* (procedural law); and *fiqh jihād al-siyar* (rules pertaining to war and international relations).[8] According to *Sharīʿa*, strictly speaking, an action was either *ḥalāl* (permissible) or *ḥarām* (forbidden, pl. *ḥurum*). But, then, the ethical framework of *fiqh* for understandable reasons, as will become clear a little later, divided *ḥalāl* actions into four categories: *wājib* (incumbent, and therefore necessarily meritorious); *mustaḥabb* (meritorious); *mubāḥ* (indifferent); and *makrūh* (not recommended). This graduated system evolved under two distinct imperatives.

First, it was inspired by the Qurʾānic term *al-iḥsān*, which can be roughly translated as a highly meritorious or benevolent act, and thus the term *mustaḥabb* (pl. *mustaḥabbāt*). To appreciate the true significance of this concept, the following remarks are in order. One can

---

[8] It may be noted that except for the first three of these, there are differences in categories and terminology used in different schools of *fiqh* and even within a given school across different countries.

see that if the individual man was conceived to be capable of a soaring flight by the deployment of his free will, the corresponding guidance, as the Qur'ān provides, had to be vouchsafed him, for otherwise the individual soul will be liable to its own flights of fancy. One may also note that it is not the juristic writings of the *fuqahā'* but the writings in the *Taṣawwuf* (Islamic mysticism) genre that do true justice to this concept. More significantly, every Muslim may dearly wish to go beyond the minimum demands of his faith, as identified by the *Sharī'a,* and try to accomplish some of the multifarious dimensions of *iḥsān* but whether he is able to meet the corresponding demands is another matter.[9] An ordinary soul may be more concerned with meeting the minimum demands of *Sharī'a* rather than the rigors of *iḥsān,* and such a right cannot be denied, being Divinely adequate, and therefore efficacious. The less careful *fiqh* expositions usually put *mustaḥab* on a level with *wājibāt* and thus misrepresent the true place of the former in the Divine scheme of things (more of this problem in the next two chapters).

An ordinary Muslim, however, is likely to pay more attention to the abiding elements and prohibitions of the *Sharī'a,* which means that the terms *wājib* and *ḥarām* have a special resonance in his psyche. The Qur'ānic term *farḍ* (pl. *farā'iḍ*) is necessarily related to the term *wājib* of the *fiqh,* where, as per the juristic precision, a given *farḍ* may have a number of *wājib* elements individually spelled out. By the inherent nature of *Sharī'a,* these elements encompass both personal conduct—relating to man as such—and interpersonal relations—pertaining to the collective man. But it must be noted that both *farā'iḍ* and *ḥurum* are explicitly stated in the Qur'ān, and therefore it is the *farā'iḍ*, rather

[9] Underscoring the significance of *al-iḥsān,* Schuon writes, "Islam as we have already seen proceeds through 'sincerity in unitary faith' and we know this faith must imply all the consequences logically following from its content—which is Unity, or the Absolute. First there is *el-imān,* the accepting of Unity by man's intelligence; then, since we exist both individually and collectively, there is *el-islām,* the submission of man's will to Unity, or to the idea of Unity, this second element relating to Unity considered as a synthesis on the plane of multiplicity; and finally there is *el-ehsān,* which expands or deepens the two previous elements to the point of their ultimate consequence. Under the influence of *el-ehsān, el-imān* becomes 'realization' or 'a certitude that is lived'—'knowing' becoming 'being'—while *el-islām,* instead of being limited to a certain number of prescribed attitudes, comes to include every level in man's nature; in the beginning faith and submission are hardly more than symbolic attitudes, although none the less efficacious at their own level" (Schuon, 1963, pp. 118–19).

than *wājibāt*, *per se*, that have special resonance. What this means is that all *farāʾiḍ* are necessarily *wājibāt*, but all *wājibāt* are not necessarily *farāʾiḍ*. More significantly, some of the *wājibāt*, including the *farāʾiḍ* of course, are enforceable while others are not: some are intended to appeal to man as such, and others are essentially related to the conduct of the collective man. And if it is so by the nature of things, and it could not be so unless it was the Divine Will, then the collective man, or society, has no reason to intrude upon the corresponding preserve of man as such, that is to say the individual man. If this point is not recognized, it is bound to create a lot of confusion, for then the collective man may attempt to accomplish something that is not only well nigh impossible, but also unwarranted, since it implies voluntary acceptance of some responsibilities that could not be discharged. If there are areas of personal conduct pertaining to *wājibāt* that a society simply cannot enforce, there are also areas where it *ought not* to make any attempt at enforcement. And this is the sphere of *al-iḥsān*, the area of *mustaḥabāt*, for it simply cannot be divorced from the play of individual free will, and therefore from the actions of man as such.[10] It may not be out of place here to mention that for an individual, the voluntary performance of a *farḍ al-kifāya* essentially falls in the domain of *al-iḥsān*.

The second point is related to the *fiqhī* concept of something being *makrūh*. The actions that are explicitly forbidden in the Qurʾān are necessarily labeled *ḥarām* but when something is not explicitly forbidden yet disliked, often according to *fiqh* interpretations, it is deemed *makrūḥ*. Therefore, there are actions that are worth censuring yet legally permissible. Nevertheless, the term *ḥarām* has given rise to considerable difficulties as a result of its indiscriminate use in the *fiqh* literature. The acts that are *ḥarām* are explicitly stated in the Qurʾān, and the Qurʾānic reading also clearly suggests that no one else has the authority to declare anything *ḥarām* that has not been declared so explicitly by it. It is here that the collective man runs into a difficulty.

---

[10] Marshall Hodgson illustrates this issue in an interestingly peculiar manner: "For instance: Muhammad used a toothpick after meals (sunnah); there is a report to that effect (hadīth) transmitted through a chain of reporters (isnād); the mūjtahid studies this report (ijtihād) and decides that the use is recommended not only for the Prophet but for the ordinary believer (fiqh); it is therefore to be included in the Sharīʿa, the established way of life; and a mufti may deliver a fatwā to an inquirer, telling him he should do it; but as it is merely recommended, the qāḍī will assess no penalty if he does not" (Hodgson, 1974. vol. 1, p. 338).

His earthly imperatives of time and space require that certain additional actions be disallowed from time to time, besides the ones that have been declared forbidden for all time in the Qur'ān. But the actions so forbidden, reflecting changes in man's earthly contingencies, cannot be considered at par with the lasting Divine prohibitions. It is in the context of this flux of time, and this ever-changing tide of events across space that we need to appreciate the efforts of the *fuqahā'*, their differences of opinions reflecting the contingencies of time and space, differences that may be thought of as part of a Divinely sanctioned flexibility as enunciated in a famous *ḥadīth* to that effect.[11] These efforts proceeded under the framework of certain principles, as noted earlier, and led eventually to the development of a corpus of *qānūn* (from Greek kanon, rule) that was meant to regulate the affairs of collective man.[12] This corpus included what was enforceable at the societal level, and therefore it is this corpus that is equivalent to the term law as it is commonly understood. It is this that in large part came to define what was permissible and what was not permissible in the interpersonal domain, i.e. formal property rights, in the Islamic realms. But the relationship between *qānūn* and *fiqh* has not been a smooth one. Beyond the problems associated with an indiscriminate use of the term *ḥarām*, we specifically note two points relating to this relationship.

First, what was *ḥarām*, and related to the public domain, was necessarily impermissible (*ghayr qānūnī* or illegal) in the *qānūn* corpus, but what was declared illegal from time to time in view of the contingencies of time and space could not, understandably, be deemed *ḥarām*. Thus there may be actions that are intrinsically *ḥalāl* but may

[11] Though this *ḥadīth* report, where the Prophet is supposed to have said that the differences of opinion among his community would be a blessing, is referred to very frequently, yet it may be noted that its authenticity was debated right from the beginning. This may be because of the apprehensions of its being taken out of context and applied to fundamental doctrinal points, a misuse that history attests to, rather than the day-to-day *fiqh* formulations—the spirit in which it is interpreted here. At any rate, my argument regarding the issue of flexibility remains valid even in the absence of support from this report because of the Qur'anic sanction for the use of *'urf* (something which is commonly acceptable). The interested reader may see a brief discussion on this subject by G. Fouad Haddad at http://www.themodernreligion.com/basic/madhab/mercy.html.

[12] The nomenclature of such a corpus may vary across different Muslim countries. The earlier commonly used term is *aḥkām al-sulṭaniyya* (legal decrees, or literally the decrees of the ruler), but here I have opted to use the term *qānūn* in view of its contemporary relevance.

be declared illegal. This, of course, creates much confusion. The second point requires some elaboration.

The *qānūn* corpus, by virtue of its being associated with state power, for it requires enforcement, has always lived in uneasy coexistence with the *Sharīʿa*. In the early centuries of Islam, excluding the Prophetic period and the period of the *Khulafāʾ al-Rāshidūn* (the rightly guided caliphs), the *Sharīʿa* faced the thorny problem of according legitimacy to the institution of government as it crystallized at the time. The ground realities relating to the institution of prevailing government did not lend themselves readily to *Sharīʿa* legitimacy, and thus such a legitimacy was not forthcoming until the latter centuries of the ʿAbbāsid dynasty, and it eventually did so in such broad terms as to be of any practical relevance for the vast Islamic realm. The efforts of *fiqh* were directed more at circumscribing the arbitrary powers of the state. Besides the *Sharīʿa* courts, presided over by *qāḍīs* (judges well versed in *fiqh*) there also existed the court of the ruler; this often handed down summary sentences without any due process of the law. This was partly because the *Sharīʿa* requirements with regard to witnesses were very stringent, and partly because the *Sharīʿa* law, or *fiqh,* was still in the process of being formulated. Since the *Sharīʿa* law did not accord any recognition to case law, its attitude was that even if excesses were committed by the non-*Sharīʿa* courts, they would be rectified in due course as similar cases were brought before the *Sharīʿa* courts.[13] If the relationship between *Sharīʿa* and *qānūn* was troublesome, it was not just because of the *Sharīʿa*'s reluctance to lend legitimacy to the form of state and thus the government that evolved but also because of *fiqh*'s carefulness in the process of assimilation of *ʿurf* (something which is commonly acceptable, from the Qurʾānic exhortation: *al-amr bi al-maʿrūf wa-al-nahy ʿan al-munkar*, enjoin doing what is right and forbid doing what is wrong, 3:104) elements such that only elements that did not contradict or compromise its original sources were incorporated into it. This obviously required working out the *uṣūl al-fiqh*, a process that took some time to complete. At any rate, the relationship between *qānūn* and *Sharīʿa* at the time was one of uneasy coexistence rather than hostility that

[13] The interested reader may consult the masterly treatment of the subject by Marshall Hodgson (1974, vol. 1—The Classical Age of Islam).

later developed, particularly in modern times. A few words as to why this happened are in order here.

With the passage of time, alien accretions began to permeate the *qānūn* corpus, with the end result that it became increasingly divorced from *fiqh* and thus lost the allegiance of the masses, and thereby the respect that any legal corpus must command to remain effective. This happened for two distinct yet interrelated reasons. First, there was the intellectual inertia not only in the area of jurisprudence but in all sciences that began with the so-called "closure of the gates of *ijtihād*," which occurred gradually but had its roots in the thirteenth century. Life went on under its own imperatives for the Muslim communities. Second, with its ascendancy, the West started breathing heavily on the shoulders of Muslims, shoulders that had lost their capacity to bear the accompanying burden in the face of the intellectual torpor of centuries. The breathing became increasingly heavier as the 'West' ran at an ever faster pace with the advent of the industrial revolution, leaving the Muslims far behind their times. To push this analogy a bit further, this heavy breathing had mixed odors; there were aromas that were simply irresistible, but then there were smells that was considered, with considerable justification, obnoxious. The Muslims were (and still are) incapable of inventing a filtering system that could separate the two odors, especially when eventually the West came home to the Islamic lands to roost, beginning with the process of colonization, bringing its own laws to those lands. This started the process whereby the *qānūn* corpus began to lose legitimacy, and thus the allegiance of the Muslims masses. The West itself recognized the diversity of these odors but felt (and still feels) that these could not be separated. The bleary-eyed Muslim world keeps on insisting that this is something that must be accomplished, and that it is accomplishable. This love-hate relationship between the West and the Muslim world continues apace, and the West's antagonism towards Islam prevents Muslims from using *ʿurf* to formally incorporate the irresistible elements in their *Sharīʿa*. This discussion is directly related to the exposition of the issues pertaining to enforcement of property rights in Chapter 3. This perspective needs to be kept in mind while reading the remaining chapters of this work.

We now turn to the coverage of the norms of an Islamic economy as expounded by writers other than Syed Nawab Haider Naqvi. We observe these writers approaching the issue in a rather direct way in the sense of articulating the objectives of economic activity, or of an

Islamic economic system, within the overall context of a perceived Islamic system. The first economist to address this question, as far as I am aware, is Muhammad Nejatullah Siddiqi (1979), who argues that the principal goal of economic activity is *falāḥ,* by which he means "welfare of this life as well as that of the hereafter." *Falāḥ* is a Qurʾānic term commonly translated as "success" but primarily with eschatological underpinnings. Siddiqi struggles to handle the profound Qurʾānic connotations of this term, in the sense of bringing down to earth an idea that primarily belongs to the celestial realm—the realm of imponderables—without recognizing that such ideas are meant to be awe-inspiring rather than a subject of our earthly calculations, and that any such attempts actually end up doing violence to a sublime idea.[14] And, sadly, in this he is not alone in the area of Islamic economics. In his case though, after an unequivocal focus on *falāḥ*, he decides to discard it a little later by saying, "But to single out this factor [*falāḥ*] as the sole objective of economic activities would mean a callous neglect of all other factors and lead to a disintegration of the whole scheme of life envisaged by Islam" (Siddiqi, 1979, p. 8), and goes on to list five objectives (in his terminology "subends") that include: i) fulfillments of one's needs in moderation; ii) meeting family liabilities; iii) provision for future contingencies; iv) provision for posterity; and v) social service and contribution to the cause of Allah. One wonders how these subends could be divorced from the *falāḥ* of the individual under consideration, and why Siddiqi feels that a focus on *falāḥ* will lead to a "disintegration of the whole scheme of life envisaged by Islam." What is even more disconcerting is that he begins by promising to highlight the objectives of economic activity, but ends up, quite explicitly, listing man's economic responsibilities as, presumably, envisioned by the *Sharīʿa.* Never mind what he means by discharging of a responsibility "in moderation." But what about the rights corresponding to those responsibilities? No ethical system pertaining to the collective affairs of man can possibly ignore the other side of the coin.

---

[14] For instance, he thinks that "while the pleasure of the Lord is an abstract idea, beyond scientific analysis, *Falâh* is a tangible quality [?] which can be 'understood', and as such forms the only means through which the achievement of the Lord's pleasure can be ascertained and observed" (Siddiqi, 1979, originally published in 1972, p. 3, f. n.). What is perhaps is interesting to note is that he is not averse to the idea of using calculus to ascertain the possible benefits or costs that may result from following a particular course of action, something that may be useful when we come to that subject towards the end of this chapter.

Furthermore, since rights can be usurped and responsibilities can be evaded- because there will always be some black sheep in the collectivity- any ethical system must insist on instituting a system of justice to mete out appropriate punishment to the offenders. An ethical system would ignore this issue only at the peril of becoming irrelevant. Siddiqi has nothing to offer on these scores. We get a somewhat better coverage of this basic issue in Chapra's writings, either under his exposition of the so-called *maqāṣid al-Sharīʿa*, or else his articulation of what he considers the Islamic worldview.

For instance, more than a decade after Naqvi's exposition, Chapra begins by citing Ghazālī (d. 1111 CE) in his preamble to Chapter 1, which in a sense is a preamble to the entire book: "The very objective of the *Sharīʿa* is to promote the welfare of the people, which lies in safeguarding their faith, their life, their intellect, their posterity and their wealth. Whatever ensures the safeguarding of these five serves public interest and is desirable" (Chapra, 1992, p.1). It is only after he has enumerated the objectives of *Sharīʿa*—and in a sense the objectives of *any* legal system, Islamic or otherwise—that he cares to list the triad *tawḥīd* (Divine Unity), *khilāfa* (literally vicegerency of man, to signify the role of free will), and *ʿadāla* (justice) in his conceptualization of the worldview of Islam as though a part could somehow encompass the Whole, as though the creation could somehow take precedence over the Creator, as though the the finite could enclose the Infinite, or as though in the Islamic scheme of things cosmos issued forth from the earth. He now arrives at the right framework but in a theologically inadmissible manner. While one may differ with him with regard to the details of his treatment of *khilāfa* and *ʿadāla*, in the context of the fundamental axioms of an Islamic economy, one could not disagree with the general thrust of his arguments.

For instance, in his treatment of the office of *Khilāfa*, he rightly notes that it implies the fundamental unity, and therefore brotherhood, of mankind. He refers to the Qurʾānic verse: "O men! Behold, We have created you all out of a male and a female, and have made you into nations and tribes, so that you might come to know one another. Verily, the noblest of you in the sight of God is the one who is most deeply conscious of Him. Behold, God is all-knowing, all-aware" (49:13). The *sūra* from which this verse is cited primarily deals with social relations and sets out some of the norms of social behavior: be just and equitable; make peace between the brethren when they are at odds; do not deride others; do not insult others by using opprobrious epithets; avoid guesswork about others; do not spy on others; do not speak ill of others behind their backs, etc. The argument is then summed up by the verse under consideration. In the exhortations noted above, the address is to the believers, even though the summing up addresses the collective man (I am aware of some who would wish to restrict the universal applicability of these exhortations). But then in a remarkable but much less quoted passage, the Qurʾān, without which man's moral moorings remain anything but firmly grounded, goes on to say this: "Unto every one of you have We appointed a (different) law and way of life. And if God had so willed, He could surely have made you all one single community: but (He willed it otherwise) in order to test you by means of what He has vouchsafed unto you. Vie, then, with one another in doing good works! Unto God you all must return; and then He will make you truly understand all that on which you were wont to differ" (5:48).[15] And then again: "Unto every community have We appointed (different) ways of worship, which they ought to observe. Hence, (O believer,) do not let those (who follow ways other than thine) draw thee into dispute on this score, but summon (them all) unto thy Sustainer: for, behold, thou art indeed on the right way. And if they (try to) argue with thee, say (only): 'God knows best of what you are doing'" (22: 67–68). In Islamic morals, there is no place for sectarianism and disputations relating to metaphysical issues. What men are urged to do is to vie with one another in good works.[16]

---

[15] This *sūra* (*al-Māʾida*) is among the few where the numbering of the verses differs in various compilations of the Qurʾān. In some of these compilations, the verse number may be 51. Muhammad Asad writes in his introduction to this *sūra*: "Being one of the last revelations vouchsafed to the Prophet, it lays down a series of ordinances relating to religious rites and to various social obligations".

[16] Interestingly, here is some of what the Qurʾān has to say about the followers of earlier revelations: "(But) they are not all alike: among the followers of earlier revelations there are upright people, who recite God's messages throughout the night, and prostrate themselves (before Him). They believe in God and the Last Day, *and enjoin the doing of what is right and forbid the doing of what is wrong*, and vie with one another in doing the good works: and these are among the righteous. And whatever good they do, they shall never be denied the reward thereof: for, God has full knowledge of those who are conscious of Him" (3:113–15, emphasis added); "And, behold, among the followers of earlier revelations there are indeed such as (truly) believe in God, and in that which has been bestowed from on high upon you as well as in that which has been bestowed upon them. Standing in awe of God, they do not barter away God's messages for a trifling gain. They shall have their reward with their Sustainer—for, behold, God is swift in reckoning" (3:199). In a fascinating statement, the Qurʾān, underscoring its own finality and completeness, sums it all up: "You are

Chapra then goes on to cover the issue of man's trusteeship of resources—in here discussed in relation to the question of private ownership from an Islamic perspective in the next chapter. He says very little about the commendable Qur'ānic urgings towards a humble lifestyle, naturally because of the difficulties inherent in saying something universally concrete about it, and then moves on to the last element in his scheme of things, namely the issue of Divinely granted human freedom, stressing, again rightly, that no one can take away this freedom from man. Thus far into his argument he has not said a word about the *maqāṣid al-Sharī'a* with which he began his discussion. At this stage in the discourse, he moves on to *'adāla*. That the Qur'ān stresses the establishment of justice in numerous places goes without saying, for it could not be otherwise. But how should it be instituted at the societal level? The Qur'ānic conception of *'adl* (justness) is much more comprehensive than the concept of justice in the legal sense of the term, for it covers both dimensions of human existence, the individual dimension relating to man as such, and the social dimension relating to the collective man. And in the latter conceptualization, justice in the legal sense of the term essentially pertains to only some of the dimensions of the collective man, in the sense that it may not cover other dimensions of interpersonal relations. In other words, while the idea of *'adl* pervades the whole *Sharī'a*, the sphere of justice in the juridical sense is necessarily restricted to its enforceable part, or *qānūn*. When Muslims insist that Islam provides a complete code of life, the statement is justifiable in view of the comprehensiveness of the *Sharī'a*. While that is very reassuring, it has also given rise to certain indulgences, especially in the modern Muslim discourse. For instance, when Muslims castigate other value systems, what they assume, directly or indirectly, is that these systems are not ethically as well grounded as their own and that there are anthropomorphic elements in these systems, and as such these are subject to the whims and fancies of man. While there may be a point to this perception, often the argument is pushed beyond a reasonable

indeed the best community that has ever been brought forth for (the good of) mankind: *you enjoin the doing of what is right and forbid the doing of what is wrong*, and you believe in God. Now if the followers of earlier revelations had attained to (this kind of) faith, it would have been for their own good; (but only few) among them are believers, while most of them are iniquitous" (3:110, emphasis added). In the universalistic perspective of the Qur'ān, such statements cannot be considered as time-bound, as some writers tend to do.

degree of prudence which not only stifles it but also creates unnecessary antagonism. It also exposes them to a similar charge. In a sense, Muslims' criticism of other ethical systems, but primarily the Western one, boils down to the charge that Western man has not lived up to his theomorphic potential. Whether they themselves have lived up to that promise is hardly ever explored, and even when they come to a realization of their own failings, these are usually laid at the door of foreign forces, mostly of the West. But let us return to the issue of man-made elements in the ethical systems from the Islamic perspective.

The perspective of certainty that a Muslim takes for granted in his ethical system is well founded provided it is put in its proper context. A Muslim rightly feels that his system of values is grounded in the unchanging, or rather unchangeable, *Sharīʿa*. But he often forgets, if at all he realizes it, that the *Sharīʿa*, in fact plays two inter-related roles, one connected to the theomorphism of God, and the other appealing to the theomorphic nature of man. Put slightly differently, *Sharīʿa* not only provides the unchanging backdrop of the stage, but also participates actively in the drama enacted on that stage, the drama of history. It serves as the backdrop in so far as it provides the fundamental value axioms, and it acts on the stage by providing the detailed rules of conduct, since it encompasses the whole of *fiqh*, including the *qānūn* corpus. It goes without saying that man, or Muslim man, acknowledged this by participating in this drama through *ijtihād*, originally in the form of *raʾy* (personal opinion), which, in due course, came to be known as *qiyās* (analogical reasoning), and became one of the recognized source of *fiqh* formulations, or *ijmāʿ* (an *ijtihād* that eventually led to a consensus of the learned, another source of *fiqh* formulations).[17] This represented the Divinely sanctioned

[17] Actually *fiqh* also recognizes a number of other sources besides the Qurʾān (which is universally recognized as the "Principle of Principles"); *sunna* (see n. 7 above); *ijmāʿ*; and *qiyās*; and these are: i) *istihsān* (literally, goodness, but actually going beyond the surface interpretation to establish social or moral preferences within the context of *qiyās*); ii) *istidlāl* (reasoning); iii) *istiṣlāḥ or maṣāliḥ al-mursala* (roughly necessity in view of public interest, public welfare); iv) *taʿāmul* (the conduct of the companions of the Prophet); v) *ʿurf* (customs and social conventions); vi) *Sharīʿa ma-qabl* (*Sharīʿas* relating to earlier revelations); and vii) *qānūn* (laws of a particular land). Generally, however, these are not explicitly mentioned because they are subsumed under either *qiyās*, for instance, (i) to (iii), or *ijmāʿ*, such as (iv), (v) and (vii), or Qurʾān, (vi). For a fairly detailed discussion on this subject, see Muhammad Taqi Amini (1975). With regard to the principle of *maṣlaḥa* (pl.

flexibility referred to earlier. It is another matter that Muslims decided to abdicate the responsibility through a more or less complete closure of the gates of *ijtihād*. For those who believed in such a closure, the thirteenth century represented the end of history. What is important for the argument at hand is that Ghazālī's articulation of the *maqāṣid al-Sharīʿa* drew not only on the original sources of *fiqh* but also on the participation of man in *Sharīʿa*.

When Chapra eventually comes to discuss the *maqāṣid al-Sharīʿa*, he altogether abandons Ghazālī, to whom he appealed in the opening of his argument, and provides us with a list of his own, which includes: i) need fulfillment; ii) respectable source of earning; iii) equitable distribution of income and wealth; and iv) growth and stability. He shies away from claiming that this is his *ijtihād* and at the same time goes ahead to attribute some of these conceptualizations of the modern economic discourse to traditional Islamic scholars such as Mawdudi, Hasan al-Banna, Sayyid Qutb, etc. to lend his list an aura of *Sharīʿa* legitimacy.[18] On a closer look, he conceives 'need fulfillment' to be a *farḍ al-kifāya* (and thus nobody's responsibility in particular) and his 'respectable source of earning' (Respectable to whom? Why would there be an disreputable source of earning in an Islamic state?) turns out to be a matter of personal responsibility. Yet he draws the inference (How? he does not say) "that it is the collective obligation of a Muslim society to ensure for everyone an equal opportunity to earn an honest living" (Chapra, 1992, p. 211). And why should one even worry about need fulfillment if there were to be equitable distribution of income? He proclaims these goals to be 'absolute' (p. 213). Does he say anything, anything at all, about instituting a system of justice, about enforcement of property rights, in light of the vast injustice that exists in most of the Muslim

maṣāliḥ,), Muhammad Khalid Masud (Masud, 1991, p. 10), on the position of the Mālikī school of *fiqh*, writes that it "explained that the underlying purpose in the Quranic laws, the *Sunnah* of the Prophet, the practice of Madinah, the precedents and consensus of the Companions of the Prophet was the *maslahah*, common good or welfare of mankind. Therefore, whenever clear specific guidance was not available in the Qur'ān, the *Sunnah*, and the practice of the Companions, this object should serve as the guiding principle of reasoning and justification." It may, however, be noted that a certain section of *fiqh* writers tend to restrict the meaning of *ijmāʿ* to the consensus of the learned who belonged to the first few generations of Islam.

[18] He claims that all these scholars, and others in his list, are agreed (i.e. that there is *ijmāʿ*) on need fulfillment being a *farḍ al-kifāya*, but this does not lead to the conclusions he wishes to draw, for it must be remembered that a *farḍ al-kifāya* is not legally enforceable.

countries on account of the neglect of these areas? He never gets past the overall framework of *Sharīʿa* to reach the domain of *qānūn*, the domain of enforceable *Sharīʿa*, to look for answers to these questions. His conceptualization of *ʿadāla* has no room for such issues. The important thing now is to see whether such a position can be substantiated by the relevant classical writings. Here I have paid special attention to whether the conceptualization of *ʿadl* in those writings could possibly be related to the ideas of Pareto, or that of the *optimum optimorum* of economics. The matter of how the goals Chapra articulates are supposed to be achieved—his "strategy" (which is actually his parlance for an economic system)—is a theme that will recur. His peculiar conceptualization of efficiency and equity in an Islamic economy is discussed in Chapter 2, noting a number of logical inconsistencies in his arguments. The following exposition presumes those arguments to be fresh in the reader's mind.

ʿAdl *and Optimality*

In the classical Islamic writings, a connection between *ʿadl* and the idea of optimality is discernable. Indeed we run into an intriguing scenario where it appears that the ideas of social welfare and utility had their roots in Islamic *fiqh*, contrary to the hostility Islamic economists have shown against these concepts. They have, unwittingly it would seem, not only failed to read this connection but have gone on to mount a vociferous opposition to the relevance of utility and social welfare to an Islamic economy, never mind that the word *falāḥ* literally means welfare. There seem several reasons for this beyond the obvious one of missing the point in the *fiqh* literature: first, simply because these appear to them to be Western constructs, or rather constructs of certain Western men of, as far as they are concerned, doubtful personal convictions; and second, in doing so they were, ironically, doing nothing more than following the lead of some of the Western critics on those subjects.

Consider the idea of utility, associated in Western thought with the name of Jeremy Bentham (1748–1832). Let us, first, note that the word utility is derived from the Latin utilis (useful.) Bentham (1781) used it to build his utilitarian ethics, or utilitarianism, to argue that what is useful is good, and consequently, that the ethical value of conduct is determined by the utility of its results. Bentham then goes on to relate his idea to both man as such and collective man. He urges man as such to be a judge for himself as to what is useful for him or otherwise, without regard to any prior ethical norms. In this case, utilitarianism becomes ethics in itself. But whether a man accepts or rejects his suggestion is a matter over which Bentham has no control. If to a Muslim it seems that Bentham does not live up to his theomorphic potential, he at least needs to consider the context in which Bentham made his pronouncements: church hegemony, or rather theological authoritarianism, in both the individual and collective spheres of Western man's life, and the reaction to it in the form of the so-called Enlightenment movement or European renaissance. Nevertheless, for a Muslim it is disconcerting, to say the least, that Bentham was reacting to another Utilitarian philosophy as enunciated in its most characteristic form by the British theologian William Paley in *The Principles of Moral and Political Philosophy* (1785). His utilitarianism is linked to virtue, which he defines as the "doing [of] good to mankind, in obedience to the will of God, and for the sake of everlasting happiness."[19] Which utilitarianism one accepts is a matter of taste, or rather free will. Interestingly, what Paley said could equally come from any exponent of *fiqh*, or for that matter an Islamic economist.

What is perhaps more important, for the argument at hand, is the use Bentham tried to make of his doctrine at the collective level. Here, he was concerned, specifically, with the principles of legislation within the broader perspective of providing a normative criterion for all social institutions, and his utilitarian criterion was now translated into achieving the greatest happiness for the greatest number. In proposing this criterion, Bentham in a sense was rejecting a theology where a "fallen man" was supposed to redeem himself through heroic acts, necessarily involving pain, often in the form of asceticism. But was Bentham's contribution original? Contrary to what is generally believed in the West, the answer to this question is not unequivocal, for what he had to say about whether legislation should be subjected to certain moral imperatives, and what he proposes that imperative

[19] Paley's definition may easily be found in any encyclopedia, such as Encarta or Britannica. A reader interested in pursuing the subject further may be referred to an article by W. R. Sorley, "Paley and His Theological Utilitarianism" in A. W. Ward and A. R. Waller (eds.), *The Cambridge History of English Literature*, vol. 10, The Age of Johnson, XIV, # 20 (Philosophers), Cambridge: The Cambridge University Press, 1907–27.

should be, is nothing more than a rehashing of ideas that had been developed a thousand years earlier in the Islamic world, during the European Dark Ages.[20]

There is, however, a significant difference between the institutional mechanism through which Islamic *fiqh* evolved and the presumed institutional mechanism in Bentham. In the Islamic world, jurisprudence has historically been a private effort of *fiqh* scholars (more on that in Chapter 10), a tradition that is still alive today, though it is now recognized that some sort of more formal and collective arrangement is needed to address the complexity of modern life. In contrast, in Bentham it was the institution of government, or more appropriately the legislative branch of the government, which was supposed to perform this task. This in turn meant that whereas the Islamic *fiqh* scholars did not feel obliged to reckon the benefits, or for that matter, costs of a particular edict they offered, a representative government could not be presumed to be so relieved. But one would hasten to add that the sphere of *fiqh* is necessarily much wider than the scope of governmental legislation, at least as this field has come to be perceived in the West, and there were occasions in Islamic *fiqh* where such reckoning was, in principle, not warranted (for instance, in edicts relating to rituals), as there were occasions where such reckoning was practically uncalled for.[21] The Western conceptualization of this field roughly corresponds to the *qānūn*, which is just one part, admittedly a very important one, of the *Sharīʿa*.[22] But when we ask the question as to whether the Islamic *fiqh* scholars were mindful of the social benefit–cost implications of their exercise of *ijtihād*, we find that not only were they so mindful, they thought they could hardly be unmindful of them, for otherwise, they thought, they would be going against the spirit of the Qurʾān.

The Qurʾān is an amazing book in the profoundest meaning of that word, for it never ceases to open new vistas no matter how adept its student. When it comes to the principles that could govern man's

[20] For a brief historical perspective on the issue of principles of jurisprudence, see Muhammad Hameedullah (1992).

[21] In principle, a *fatwā* (juristic opinion), which could be an edict relating to personal conduct, and therefore could be, at times, relevant to only a particular individual at a particular time in history.

[22] The West, a newcomer to the area, takes the liberty of insisting, somewhat naively, that the scope of jurisprudence in all societies must be restricted to its own conceptualization of that sphere.

earthly sojourn, it assures us—for the last revelation could do no less than that—that it is comprehensive, and thereby imparts that crucial sense of certainty to the idea of justness, and therefore to the system of justice built on the foundations so provided. In *sūra al-Nahl* (The Bee), which deals with the subjects of man's haughtiness and social relations, among others, it characteristically states: "But if they turn away (from thee, O Prophet, remember that) thy only duty is a clear delivery of the message (entrusted to thee). They (who turn away from it) are fully aware of God's blessings, but none the less they refuse to acknowledge them (as such), since most of them are given to denying the truth" (16:82–83), "And thee (too, O Prophet) have We brought forth to bear witness regarding those (whom thy message may have reached) inasmuch as We have bestowed from on high upon thee, step by step, this Divine writ, to *make everything clear*, and to provide guidance and grace and glad tiding unto all who have surrendered themselves to God. Behold, *God enjoins justice, and the doing of good, and generosity towards (one's) fellow-men*; and He forbids all that is shameful and all that runs counter to reason, as well as envy; (and) He exhorts you (repeatedly) so that you might bear (all this) in mind" (16:89–90, emphasis added). And after emphasizing the sanctity of pledges, and oaths (v. 94), among other things, it continues: "And so, partake of all the lawful, good things which God has provided for you as sustenance, and render thanks unto His blessings, if it is (truly) Him that you worship" (16:114). And in anticipation of man's participation in jurisprudence, it unequivocally admonishes: "Hence, do not utter falsehoods by letting your tongues determine (at your own discretion), 'This is lawful and that is forbidden', thus attributing your own lying inventions to God: for, behold, they who attribute their own lying inventions to God will never attain to a happy state!" (16:116).

It is under these constraining imperatives that the *fuqahā*ʾ endeavored to undertake *ijtihād* to formulate new edicts to meet the challenges of changing times, and it is only in light of these imperatives that we can understand why a person like al-Shāfiʿī would worry about the possibility of unscrupulous use of *ijtihād*, and would feel the need to write the treatise *al-Radd ʿalā al-istiḥsān* (rejection of *istiḥsān*), *istiḥsān* being a particular principle of *ijtihād* generally associated with *Ḥanafī fiqh*. But then all the *fuqahā*ʾ were confronted by the same reality, the inevitable march of history, which somehow had to be addressed if the *Sharīʿa*, in its totality, were to remain relevant to the overall lives of the Muslims. This meant that *ijtihād* had to be provided with much firmer foundations, indeed had to be grounded, in the Qurʾān for it to become an acceptable and effective instrument of Islamic jurisprudence. When *fiqh* turned to the *Aṣl al-uṣūl* (Principle of principles, as the Qurʾān is referred to in *fiqh* literature), it found a number of guiding lights; thus: "Qurʾān was bestowed from on high as a guidance unto man and a self-evident proof of that guidance, and as the standard by which to discern the true from the false...God wills that you shall have ease, and does not will you to suffer hardship" (2:185); and after describing the method of ritual purification, it adds "God does not want to impose any hardship on you, but wants to make you pure, and to bestow upon you the full measure of His blessings, so that you might have cause to be grateful" (5:6); "God does not burden any human being with more than he is well able to bear" (2:286); "God wants to lighten your burdens: for man has been created weak" (4:28); and a statement that sums it up, "And strive in His cause as ye ought to strive (with sincerity and under discipline). He has chosen you, and has imposed no difficulties on you in religion; it is the cult of your father Abraham. It is He who has named you Muslims, both before and in this (Revelation); that the Apostle may be a witness for you, and ye be witness for mankind! So establish regular prayer, give regular charity, and hold fast to God! He is your Protector—the best to protect and the Best to help!" (22:78).[23] And in a very interesting passage providing another principle relating to what is permissible or otherwise, the Qurʾān says: "O you who have attained to faith! Do not ask about matters which, if they were to be made manifest to you (in terms of law), might cause hardship; for, if you should ask about them while the Qurʾān is being revealed, they might (indeed) be made manifest to you (as laws). God has absolved (you from any obligation) in this respect: for God is much-forgiving, forbearing. People before your time have

---

[23] In a statement comparing the new dispensation (*Sharīʿa*) with the older ones, the Qurʾān states: "those who shall follow the (last) Apostle, the unlettered Prophet whom they shall find described in the Torah that is with them, and (later on) in the Gospel: (the Prophet) who will enjoin upon them the doing of what is right and forbid them the doing of what is wrong, and make lawful to them the good things of life and forbid them the bad things, and lift from them their burdens and the shackles that were upon them (aforetime). Those, therefore, who shall believe in him, and honor him, and succour him, and follow the light that has been bestowed from on high through him—it shall be they that shall attain to a happy state" (7:157).

indeed asked such questions—and in result thereof have come to deny the truth" (5:101–102).[24] Also, "O Mankind! Partake of what is lawful and good on earth, and follow not Satan's footsteps: for verily he is your open foe, and bids you only to do evil, and to commit deeds of abomination, and to attribute unto God of something of which you have no knowledge" (2:168); and "O Children of Adam! Beautify yourselves for every act of worship, and eat and drink (freely), but do not waste: verily, He does not love the wasteful! Say: Who is there to forbid the beauty which God has brought forth for His creatures, and the good things from among the means of sustenance? Say: They are (lawful) in the life of this world unto all who have attained to faith—to be theirs alone on Resurrection Day. Thus clearly do We spell out these messages unto people of (innate) knowledge!" (7:31–32); and then again "O you who have attained to faith! Do not deprive yourselves of the good things of life which God has made lawful to you, but do not transgress the bounds of what is right: God does not love those who transgress the bounds of what is right" (5:87); and the stern warning in the following is noteworthy: "Say: Have you ever considered all the means of sustenance which God has bestowed upon you from on high—and which you thereupon divide into 'things forbidden' and 'things lawful'? Say: Has God given you leave (to do this)—or do you, perchance, attribute your own guesswork to God? But what do they think—they who attribute their own lying inventions to God—(what do they think will happen to them) on the day of Resurrection? Behold, God is indeed limitless in His bounty unto man—but most of them are ungrateful" (10:59–60).

These passages need no elaboration. It is on the basis of these and other similar passages that the *fuqahā*ʾ formulated the basic guiding principle referred to as *ḥikmat al-Illāhiyyā* (Divine wisdom), the seeking of profit (benefit) and removal of hurt, and it is this principle that

[24] This is a reference to the dialogue between Moses and his people after he returned from Mount Sinai and in view of the wrongs committed by them in his absence told them of the commandment to sacrifice a calf as an expiation, as it occurs in the Qurʾānic verses 2:67–71. Commenting on the present verse, Muhammad Asad (1992) writes, "Following Ibn Hazm's principles of jurisprudence, Rashīd Riḍā thus explains the above verse: 'Many of our jurists (*fûqahâ*ʾ) have, by their subjective deductions, unduly widened the range of man's religious obligations (*takâlîf*), thus giving rise to the very difficulties and complications which the clear wording (of the Qurʾān) had put an end to: and this has led to the abandonment, by many individual Muslims as well as by their governments, of Islamic Law in its entirety' (Manār vii, 138)." See also his commentary on (2:71), (2:168), (10:35-36) and (42:10).

all schools of *fiqh* have followed in their *ijtihād* regardless of the nomenclature under which this effort proceeded, or may proceed (a list of the nomenclature is given in n. 17 above; it essentially pertains to certain fine details with regard to emphasis on one thing or another). It goes without saying that the guiding principle is all-encompassing: it encompasses both the individual and collective spheres of man's life. At the collective level, it boils down to maximization of social welfare and minimization of social hurt, or should we say, social costs. No wonder then that when it eventually came to the codification of *fiqh* during the late Ottoman period, around 1868,[25] representing centuries of reflection on the issues, which was published as *Majallat al-aḥkām al-ʿadliyya*, commonly referred to as *Majalla*, 100 maxims of jurisprudence (*al-qawāʿid al-fiqhiyya*) were listed in its preamble, including:

- Severe injury is removed by lesser injury (no. 26).
- In the presence of two evils, the one whose injury is greater is avoided by the commission of the lesser (no. 27).
- The lesser of evils is preferred (no. 28).
- Injury is removed as far as possible (no. 30).
- Management of citizens' affairs is dependent upon public welfare (no. 57).
- The burden is in proportion to the benefit and the benefit to the burden (no. 87).[26]

Reading these maxims in an economic rather than legal context amply demonstrates that costs can be compensated by benefits, and *vice versa*, that the basic criterion for public policy should be the welfare of the citizens, and that whoever receives the benefits must bear the corresponding costs. In the parlance of welfare economics, these maxims squarely put the maximization of net social benefits at the center of public policy. But before moving on, let us specifically note at this juncture that the *maqāṣid al-Sharīʿa* listed by Chapra were in fact a sort of earlier crystallization of such maxims as a result of the efforts of the *fuqahāʾ*, and were listed under *maṣāliḥ ḍarūriyya*

[25] Though the Majallah was published that late, most of it was inspired by the work of Zayn al-ʿAbidīn ibn Nujaym (d. 1573), entitled *al-Ashbāh wa al-Nazāʾir*.

[26] For an English translation, see C. R. Tyser, et al. (1967).

(loosely, the essentials of human life), which by itself was a subcategory of *maṣāliḥ al-mursala* (see n. 17 above).

The crucial question now is: did *fiqh* meet all the societal challenges adequately? While this subject is discussed in greater detail in the following chapters, particularly Chapters 9–11, here we note only one glaring omission in the *fiqh* literature, which relates to absence of any substantive discussion about an appropriate institutional form of an Islamic government. Since the Qurʾān is silent on this issue—except for imposing the imperative of consultation (*sūra*) that must form the foundation as well as the building block of whatever form such an institution may take—*fiqh* seems to have used this as a pretext to let the untouched remain untouched.[27] But then one has a right to ask the following question: what is *fiqh* for, if not for elaborating the issues on which the Qurʾān opts to remain silent for the sake of flexibility? The issues on which the Qurʾān is silent are, in principle, left to the discretion of the collective man, and as such must be considered the natural domain of *fiqh*. What institutional form should the Divinely ordained requirement of consultation take,[28] what sort of checks and balances should be built into the system to ensure that the government stands up to its responsibilities, and what should be done if its functionaries fail, willfully or otherwise, to discharge their responsibilities, not to talk of willful scuttling of the consultative process by those in the position of power? These were, and still are, some of the many questions that would have required acute attention of the *fuqahā*ʾ. The indifference of the *fuqahā*ʾ seems to suggest these

[27] See, for instance, Chapra (1993, Ch. 5), and the citations therein for somewhat muted responses in favor of democracy in modern times. There is always the apprehension of vesting people with sovereignty lest they, the ignorant masses, misuse it to the chagrin of *fiqh*. While the influence of money in the political process of the Western democracies is rightly frowned upon, no concrete proposals are offered to circumvent its misuse in an Islamic polity. Likewise, no concrete suggestions are offered against the perennial misuse of military and political power in the Islamic realms down the centuries. Putting these elements together, and the attitude of the West, as noted below, the obstacles in the way of democracy would seem almost insurmountable. Educating Muslims would seem to be the only way out, and in that context, one would agree with Chapra (p. 121), and others, who interpret verse 4:58 in a broader manner to imply an exhortation to Muslims to entrust authority to only those among them who are genuinely entitled to it.

[28] The Qurʾān is very clear about this. Addressing the Prophet, it says, "Take counsel with them [your followers] in *all matters of public concern*; then when thou hast decided upon a course of action, place thy trust in God: for verily, God loves those who place their trust in Him" (3:159).

questions have nothing to do with *maṣāliḥ ḍarūriyya* or, for that matter, the dispensation of justice. The recent pronouncements by Muslim scholars in favor of a Western-style of democracy are more a knee-jerk reaction to the pressure emanating from the West rather than a well thought out program suitable for a ready implementation. As for the sincerity of the West in exerting that pressure, the less said the better. Democracy in Muslim countries must be such that it serves the interests of the West. It thus appears that Fukuyama's "end of history" charity begins at home, and unfortunately ends at home.[29] It is pertinent to note that while the West had to overcome many religio-cultural obstacles on its way to democracy, the Islamic religious milieu, for that is what counts in the ultimate analysis as far as a Muslim is concerned, and that is the backdrop in which *fiqh* evolved, is inherently democratic: it is totally egalitarian, and admits of no theological sanction for any terrestrial socio-religious hierarchy.[30]

If the Qurʾān did not impose a specific form of government in view of the earthly concomitances of man, it insists on *ʿadl* (justness): "Behold, God bids you to deliver all that you have been entrusted with unto those who are entitled thereto, and whenever you judge between people, to judge with justice. Verily, most excellent is what God exhorts you to do: verily, God is all-hearing, all-seeing" (4:58), and "O you who have attained to faith! Be ever steadfast in upholding equity, bearing witness to the truth for the sake of God, even though it be against your own selves or your parents and kinsfolk. Whether the person concerned is rich or poor, God's claim takes precedence over (the claims of) either of them. Do not, then, follow your own desires, lest you swerve from justice: for if you distort (the truth), behold, God is indeed aware of all that you do!" (4:135). One can hardly escape the fundamental purport of these exhortations, which at the level of collective man primarily reduces to establishing a system of justice. One must, however, recognize that any system of

[29] Witness the blatant manipulation by the West in the cancellation of the second round of elections in Algeria in the early 1990s when the so-called Islamists had won the first round and were poised to win the second. It is much easier to manipulate dictatorships of one form or another to serve the interests of the West than true democracies. The Muslims, in particular, now suffer from the law of the jungle both at the domestic as well as the international level.

[30] Barring the exception of Shiʿism. A perceptive reader may see the reasons for controversy about a *ḥadīth* report cited earlier in this chapter (see n. 11), for it could be used for the theological split that led to the development of Shiʿism.

justice the collective man institutes is necessarily linked to, or rather draws its vitality from, the individual man's perception of the idea of justness. And that is why the Qurʾānic route to collectivity passes through the individual, i.e. man as such, with the obvious connotation that the system of justice that he will institute will be only as just as he is himself. A man with a distorted idea of justness could hardly build a system of justice that will not reflect the underlying distortion. And this obliges us to give a brief account of the most recent conceptualizations of justice in the economic discourse, including among others the competing Rawlsian and Nozickian conceptualizations, to see to what extent these may accord with the Islamic perspective. It goes without saying that all collective institutions reflect the underlying values, and commitment thereto, held by the individual members of the society, including the institution of government. If this points to the dilemma that one cannot hope to end up with a just social system unless one begins with individual man who is just, it is only to make us realize that we cannot indiscriminately delegate responsibilities to collective institutions without paying close attention to the fact that a collective responsibility amounts to responsibility of no one in particular. It is quite likely that this delegation will become more like relegation, and will thus amount to abdication of individual responsibility. The more this happens, and the more the man as such abdicates his individual responsibility, the more ineffective will the collective institutions become. Man may wish to do so to have an easy conscience, but let us note that he has no right to ground it in the Qurʾānic message. Let us put the matter slightly differently in view of its importance.

One institution which is indispensable for the collective man, and is explicitly sanctioned by the Qurʾān, is the institution of governance, or government, for there are always dangers lurking both within and without a given polity: after all free will is corruptible. "O you who have attained to faith! Pay heed unto God, and pay heed unto the Apostle and unto those from among you who have been entrusted with authority; and if you are at variance over any matter, refer it unto God and his Apostle, if you (truly) believe in God and the Last Day. This is the best (for you), and best in the end" (4:59). For those twin dangers, the government must institute a system of safeguards, at both internal and external levels, and this may be taken as a categorical imperative, if one may be allowed to use Kantian terminology in the collective realm, as far as the governance in an Islamic society is concerned. Therefore, at the domestic level, the government must institute a system of justice, and must institute a system of defense against external aggression. Beyond these, what is in fact delegated to the government must be subjected to very close scrutiny. Even this minimum delegation may become problematic, for when responsibilities are delegated, the corresponding rights are also vested with the government. This in turn means that governments can themselves become instruments of oppression. Ibn Khaldūn (1332–1406) did not worry about this problem unnecessarily in his *Muqaddima*, and the subsequent historical evidence does not leave any room for doubt on that score. A system of checks and balances needs to be an integral part of whatever political dispensation the collective man may build for his governance. All that *fiqh* could manage to do was to insist that those charged with the adjudication responsibilities must be men of impeccable character, and if it could not proceed any further, it was because of its disregard for any specifics with regard to the system of governance. The question as to how those involved in the adjudication process would be chosen is fundamentally linked to how those in the system of governance would themselves be chosen. Yet we note that, along with emphasizing the universal dictum that the adjudication system must treat everyone equally, *fiqh* insists on independence of the adjudication branch from the administrative branch of government, and that is why some of the leading *fuqahā*ʾ always kept their distance from the rulers even though at times they were persecuted as a result. Be that as it may, when the *Sharīʿa* is envisaged as imposing collective responsibilities, the first thing it would require the collective man to do would be to institute a system of justice, that is to say enforce the enforceable part of *Sharīʿa*, namely *qānūn*, to the best of his abilities. And this could hardly be accomplished without first establishing a system of just governance.

Man's conceptualization of justness, and thus also justice, requires a continuous grappling with the prevailing objective conditions. In recent decades, a number of disciplines within social sciences have attempted to formulate a contemporary perspective on the subject. This effort has led to the development of a number of theories of justice with primary contributions coming from John Rawls (1971), Robert Nozick (1974), Richard Posner (1981), James Buchanan (1986). Broadly speaking, these efforts have led to formulation of three principles of justice: the Need Principle, primarily associated with Rawls; the Efficiency Principle associated originally with the name of Pareto and lately defended by Posner; and the Equity Principle associated with the names Locke (natural law), and Nozick's "entitlement" theory of justice. We have already seen the conflict that may arise between the equity and efficiency principles, and the efforts directed at resolving this conflict through the compensation principle in Chapter 2. One of the difficulties noted there was that at times it becomes impossible to affect compensation payments. The practical difficulties of affecting these payments by no means belittle the efforts at reconciling the equity and efficiency principles, for the idea of justice in the final analysis does not lend itself to a single-faceted interpretation. In similar vein, economics has begun to pay more attention to the needs of the least disadvantaged members of the society. It is here that Buchanan's heuristic approach helps in moving towards a unified theory of justice. According to Buchanan, four factors determine the distribution of income and wealth: effort, luck, choice, and birth, and he considers the inequalities caused by birth to be most controversial. Others have argued that inequalities based on luck, choice, and birth are all unjustified. Buchanan's contribution has led to considerable interest in the subject resulting in a flurry of research, both of theoretical and empirical nature, in the past two decades or so. As a result of these explorations, we have gained further clarity on the luck factor, resulting in a distinction between brute luck (that accounts for things completely beyond one's control), and option luck, where the outcome depends upon the choices made by individuals.

The Islamic position would appear to be somewhat eclectic.[31] Though some of the vocal Islamic economists, emphasizing needs would support the Rawlsian position, one could not ignore the lacunas in that position as noted specifically by Nozick. Nozick is critical of the Rawlsian "original position" and forcefully argues that the concept of justice must take into consideration the historical acquisition as well as transfer of property among individuals. While the Islamic concept of *zakāh* (mandatory redistribution) would conform to Rawlsian concerns, its individually based fairness (*ʿadl*) and respect for individual possessions, including those accruing through inheritance, "entitlements," would lend credence to the Nozickian position. As far as Buchanan's birth factor is concerned, it loses much of its force out-

[31] For a fairly comprehensive conceptualization of justice in Islamic context, see Khadduri (2002).

side the Western system of primogeniture. The Islamic system of inheritance is well recognized to be egalitarian. At any rate, the efforts at formulating a unified framework of justice have continued. On the basis of one such formulation (Elster, 1992), there are four lexicographic propositions that deserve a careful consideration in an Islamic economy. These in Konow's (2003, p. 1229) words are: "(1) maximize total welfare, (2) deviate from (1) if necessary to ensure a minimum level of welfare, (3) deviate from (2) if people fall below the minimum level because of their own choices, and (4) deviate from (3) if the failed choices are due to conditions beyond their control." And he continues: "Although our principles are not ranked, Elster's proposition (1) is a clear call for efficiency, and (2) is a statement of basic needs. Propositions (3) and (4) are reminiscent of desert, whereby individuals are rewarded or punished for the choices they control but not for the ones they do not" (Konow, 2003, p. 1229).

Islam's abiding emphasis on individual responsibility draws our attention to one interesting, though not altogether unexpected, result the recent empirical investigations have forcefully brought to our attention, and which is intimately related to the individual conception of justice, *ʿadl* or justness. These investigations highlight the importance of the so-called contextual effects in the individual evaluation of justness of an outcome. How individuals judge an outcome to be fair crucially depends, for instance, on how the question is framed (the framing effects), what information is contained in the question (the information effects), and the historical precedents (for one, it seems to me that even the unsanctioned property rights can at times become well-entrenched if left unattended), to mention only a few. Besides, the conception of fairness, or justness, varies across time and space, particularly the latter, because of the cultural effects, or the set of fundamental values held by different societies. Lastly, these studies also underscore the significance of the procedural justice, that is to say that not only should the outcome be just but also that the processes, such as rules of conduct, policies, practices, customs, laws, etc. be just.[32] In my view Islam's unwavering emphasis on individual responsibility would require procedural justice to be an essential element of the system of justice.

---

[32] See, for instance the survey of the literature by, Konow (Konow, 2003).

Interestingly, the Qur'ān keeps a separation between the demands of justice and the crucial idea of benevolence as far as the collective institution of governance is concerned. Although it often mentions the two in the same breath, i.e. *al-ʿadl wa-al-iḥsān* (justness and benevolence), the address, nevertheless, is to man 'as such'. There is no such thing as an involuntary collective *iḥsān* as far as the Qur'ān is concerned.[33] A collective institution, such as the government, is only bound to discharge the aforementioned responsibilities, and not exercise benevolence on behalf of individual members. The collective man is not permitted to trespass on the individual man's domain of *iḥsān*. In other words, the jurisdiction of the enforceable *Sharīʿa* does not extend to what falls under *iḥsān*. We see that when Qur'ān imposes a *ḥadd* (definite penalty), it at times gives the right of commutation against an agreed monetary compensation but only to the afflicted party and not to the government, or for that matter to any collectivity. The act of commutation falls under *iḥsān*. In a passage that discusses the issue of divorce, the Qur'ān ordains, "And if you divorce them before having touched them, but after having settled a dower upon them, then (give them) half of what you have settled—unless it be that they forgo their claim or he in whose hand is the marriage-tie foregoes his claim (to half of the dower): and to forgo what is due to you is more in accord with God-consciousness. And forget not (that you are to act with) grace towards one another: verily, God sees all that you do" (2:237), or "O you who have attained to faith! Just retribution is ordained for you in cases of killing: the free for the free, and the slave for the slave, and the woman for the woman. And if something (of his guilt) is remitted to a guilty person by his brother, this (remission) shall be adhered to with fairness, and restitution to his fellow-man shall be made in a goodly manner. This is an alleviation from your Sustainer, and an act of His grace. And for him who, none the less, willfully transgresses the bounds of what is right, there is grievous suffering in store: for, in (the law of) just retribution, O you who are endowed with insight, there is life for you, so that you might remain conscious of God" (2:178–79); or "And it is not conceivable that a believer should slay another believer, unless it be by mistake. And upon him who has slain a believer by

[33] This assumes that the mandatory contribution to redistribution, i.e. *zakāh*, does not fall under the purview of *iḥsān*.

mistake there is the duty of freeing a believing soul from bondage and paying an indemnity to the victim's relations, unless they forgo it by way of charity"(4:92). And there are a number of other offences, even in the domain of personal conduct, for which either a tangible penalty, or penance in lieu thereof, is either a must or recommended, as expiation according to the Qur᾽ān and thus the *Sharī῾a*.[34] In all such cases no state authority, low or high, has the power to commute the sentence, or the compensation payments, without the willing and voluntary consent of the aggrieved party; as a matter of fact, the demands of justice would require that the state must insure that no coercion has been used in winning the commutation, and that the agreed indemnity payments are indeed made. In the final analysis, as far as the adjudication process goes, the foremost responsibility of the state is to ensure that justice is carried out, nothing more and nothing less.

This is the most fundamental dimension of social justice as far as it can be related to an Islamic state according to the Divine revelation. (One may like to add a second component, and in a truly Islamic state one must, that is *zakāh*—a subject discussed in the next chapter—but historically, apart from the first few decades, the institution of *zakāh* retained its vitality without any support from the government). No wonder then that Ibn Taymiyyah felt compelled to say what might be somewhat disconcerting to many a modern-day exponent of Islam, "God upholds the just state even if it is unbelieving," and that "the world can survive with justice and unbelief, but not with injustice and Islam"[35] though this accentuation disregards the fact that Islam could not possibly be conceived of without justice.[36] In the final analysis, the following Qur᾽ānic admonition sums it all up: "O you who have attained to faith! Be ever steadfast in your devotion

---

[34] For instance, the Qur᾽ān says: "God will not take you to task for oaths which you may have uttered without thought, but He will take you to task for oaths which you have sworn in earnest. Thus, the breaking of oath must be atoned for by feeding ten needy persons with more or less the same food as you are wont to give to your own families, or clothing them, or freeing a human being from bondage; and who has not the wherewithal shall fast for three days (instead). This shall be the atonement for your oaths whenever you have sworn (and broken them). But be mindful of your oaths! Thus God makes clear unto you His messages, so that you might have cause to be grateful" (5:89).

[35] As cited in Chapra (1992, p. 209), see Muhtar Holland's (1967) translation of Ibn Taymiyya's, *al-Ḥisba fī al-Islām*.

[36] But, then, see Schuon (1969, Chapter 1), "The Use of Hyperbole in Arab Rhetoric."

to God, bearing witness to the truth in all equity; and never let hatred of anyone lead you into the sin of deviating from justice. Be just: this is closest to being God-conscious. And remain conscious of God: verily God is aware of all that you do" (5:8).

Those who wish to expand the scope of state-sponsored social justice beyond this, in the form of coercive charity—but beyond *zakāh*, for it could also be considered as coercive charity when an Islamic state may manage to institute it—have to justify it through *ijtihād*, with all the stringencies associated with that process. If the state is to encroach upon the domain of man as such, and attempts to substitute some sort of collective free will (!) for the Divinely ordained individual free will, its proponents would be obliged to begin by spelling out a theory of governance for an Islamic state, for without this no such redistributive effort, even when given a semblance of voluntary agreement through some sort of political process, could be accorded Islamic legitimacy. As far as the Islamic perspective is concerned, not only must the ends be legitimate, but the means to achieve those ends must also be equally legitimate. No amount of wishful thinking can be substituted for the principles that would be at stake. Furthermore, one would be required to establish the inadequacy of the private redistribution so characteristically urged by the Qur'ān, particularly in view of its specificity with regard to the beneficiaries of the redistribution. The Qur'ānic redistribution begins at home, and then gradually extends to include the kith and kin, neighbors, and the close community, and so on, for it says: "They will ask thee as to what they should spend on others. Say: 'Whatever of your wealth you spend shall (first) be for your parents, and for the near of kin, and the orphans, and the needy, and the wayfarer; and whatever good you do, verily, God has full knowledge thereof'" (2:215).

Assume now that all the foregoing issues have been sorted out, and that we proceed under the interpretation given to Qur'ānic verse (13:11) by Naqvi in favor of a state sponsored redistribution—over and above the mandatory redistribution through the *zakāh* funds, as instituted immediately after the Prophet's time by his successors—for the citizens of the Islamic state may well decide to do so, and one would have no reason to question such a choice.[37] Once all this is

[37] But let us note that the verse reads: "Verily, God does not change men's condition unless they change their inner selves; and when God wills people to suffer evil

done, then with a summing up of the arguments presented here, and the clarification of a few minor points, one cannot escape the conclusion that the welfare economics' perspective as discussed in Chapter 2 becomes not only relevant but quite meaningful as far as the Islamic economy is concerned.

Let us begin by repeating that the idea of something having utility is not only endorsed by *Sharīʿa*, it actually originally belongs to it, the West having borrowed it without acknowledgment. As to the concern that the idea is materialistic, one only needs to note that ideas are ideas pure and simple, and only the environment in which they are used determines a particular coloring on their surface. In the environment in which spirituality has a positive place, utility will take on a different hue. Those who worry that Islam is ultimately concerned with the hereafter, and therefore that a Muslim ought to have other-worldly aims, forget that those aims are not to be pursued in some "other" world, or the other world. Man is bound to a terrestrial existence, and whatever he pursues is to be pursued here and now, and he has a Divinely granted freedom to do so. It is the goods and services that he will decide to produce and thereafter consume that will achieve for him his objectives, be they this worldly—if they could ever be purely so in Islamic perspective—or other-worldly. It is all a matter of taste in the jargon of economics, or *dhawq* in Ṣūfī terms. Second, the *Sharīʿa* permits the use of benefits and costs; indeed the basic principle of *fiqh*, "Divine wisdom," has always been that issues pertaining to the collective realm can only be tackled in a just manner by resorting to this criterion. Third, the Qurʾān not only sanctions compensation payments but also insists that the state has no authority to condone them, and by inference to impose them, without the willing consent of the concerned individuals. Although human life is so precious that no monetary value could be placed on it *ex-ante*, yet the Qurʾān ordains that when human contingencies give rise to an injustice (in the present case, the killing of a human being), placing a value on even human life is necessary in view of the *ʿadl*.[38] The

(in consequence of their own evil deeds), there is none who can avert it: for they have none who can protect them from Him", and ignore the question as to whether it can be pressed into the required service.

[38] And let us not forget that this notwithstanding the *ex-ante* exhortation that; "We ordain unto the children of Israel that if anyone slays a human being—unless it be (in punishment) for murder or for spreading corruption on earth—it shall be as

religion which God Himself calls "the middle way" ("And thus have We willed you to be a community of the middle way, so that (with your lives) you might bear witness to the truth before all mankind, and that the Apostle might bear witness to it before you," 2:143) cannot be reduced to some idealistic improvisations in the face of possible human failings. And if as a result of a *fait accompli*, it would allow placing of value on human life, no other earthly contingency could be deemed an exception to this rule. If to the followers of other religious dispensations, this amounts to profanation of religion, a sort of "bringing God down to earth," let us note that in the Islamic perspective, if God comes down to earth, it is only in view of His infinite mercy that He does so. In *al-iḥsān*, Islam allows a vast space for the soaring of the soul; but it also understands that man can soar not because of his own efforts, *per se*, but because God comes down to earth, so to speak, to reduce the demands of the flight unto Him. Islam, however, does not impose the rigors of this flight on an ordinary soul for its salvation. For that purpose, meeting the minimum demands of the *Sharīʿa* is assured to be quite efficacious. In contrast to the skeptics who struggled to cope with their free wills through the 'philosophy of enlightenment, Muslims always felt enlightened through the Divine message, and never felt that they somehow had to be grounded in some categorical imperative except the categorical imperatives issuing out of Divine Unity. And if economics came to the conclusion in the twentieth century that contingencies of human social life required that a value be placed on even human life, it arrived at this conclusion in its own peculiar, roundabout way, when the Qurʾān had deemed it necessary more than fourteen centuries ago.

In the terminology of the "compensation principle" of Chapter 2, what our discussion a little earlier means is that it is not sufficient to conclude that compensation *could* be paid, it actually *must* be paid, as has been noted there. What we are now left with is the issue of efficiency, of both allocative and technical varieties. Although the previous discussion with regard to the maximization of benefits, following the maxims of Islamic jurisprudence (*fiqh*), is relevant here in the sense that what is applicable at the collective level could not become unacceptable at the individual level, the Qurʾān has the following:

---

though he had slain all mankind; whereas, if anyone saves a life, it shall be as though he had saved the lives of all mankind" (Qurʾān, 5:32).

"And We ordained for him in the tablets (of the law) all manner of admonition, clearly spelling out everything. And (We said:) Hold fast unto them with (all thy) strength, and bid thy people to hold fast to their most goodly rules" (7:145); and "Give, then, this glad tiding to (those of) My servants who listen (closely) to all that is said, and follow the best of it: (for) it is they whom God has graced with His guidance, and it is they who are (truly) endowed with insight" (39:17–18). And doing the best in given circumstances is what efficiency is all about. Interested readers, if they wish, may now go back to Chapter 2, and some relevant parts of Chapter 3, and refresh their reading of the intricacies of the conflict between efficiency and equity. Given the foregoing caveat about the compensation payments, the optimum optimorum of welfare economics, as explained in Chapter 2, is quite at home in an Islamic economy, as is Islamic economy, in turn, comfortable with it. Indeed, it can safely be said that the roots of welfare economics can be traced back to Islamic *Sharīʿa* notwithstanding its unwarranted disparagement by some of the Islamic economists. We may now move on to more particular issues, issues relating to the structure of an Islamic economy.

CHAPTER SIX

CHARACTERISTICS OF AN ISLAMIC ECONOMY

Introduction

Against the backdrop of the previous chapter, we can now proceed to address the issue of the essential elements of an Islamic economy. If the previous chapter can be thought of as a continuation of the subject covered in Chapter 2, the present chapter can be considered a continuation of the exposition of Chapter 3. There we began by first identifying the basic elements of an economic system, which essentially meant that anyone addressing the issue of as to what ought to be the form an economic system must weave the elements identified therein together to provide the requisite framework which satisfactorily responds to the basic economic functions that any society must address: that is, the allocation and distribution functions. The requisite framework was demonstrated to include a certain minimum number of institutions along with attendant postulates, again minimum in number, which would be needed to perform the required tasks. It was noted that these elements, whether in the form of institutions or postulates, could hardly fail to reflect the underlying values held by the society. Once that framework was established, the discussion moved on to a more concrete surface by identifying the minimum set of institutions and the corresponding postulates required for a market economy. It was understood that this framework was necessarily predicated on the presumption that the society's set of values underwrote the necessary sanction and commitment to the required elements. This set included five elements that were referred to as the characteristics of a market economy. For ready reference, these included:

1. private property,
2. constrained freedom of choice,
3. self-interest,
4. market system, or price signals, and
5. competition.

In addition, an important economic role was assigned to the government—an integral institution in any modern society—not just in the classical, Smithian, sense to define and enforce the structure of property rights as well as perform the adjudicating function, but much beyond that: to take care of all the market imperfections and failures. Furthermore, since the set contained only the minimum number of elements, it was recognized that the market economy could not be conceived of as a monolith; it could assume diverse shades, some of them marked and some not too marked, depending on the additional institutional arrangements deemed necessary for its detailed workings. Following that, one of the burdens of Chapter 4 was to identify the additional institutions that would render a market economy capitalist. The major drift of the argument in that chapter was that an Islamic economy, based as it necessarily would be on its own distinct set of values, may not condone those institutions, and therefore cannot *a priori* be conceived of as a version of the capitalistic system. But the more fundamental question is: would it be a market economy? The answer to that question depends upon what the value system of Islam has to say about the five elements of the set. It is to this question that we now need to turn.

Before that, a number of crucial issues need to be clarified. First, an efficient functioning of a market economy requires that all values be reckoned in terms of some numerare, usually money, in which all values (prices) are expressed. Once that numerare is deemed acceptable, all benefits and costs are then expressed through it; namely, it becomes the commonly acceptable measuring rod. It must, then, be presumed that its use does not go counter to the fundamental values adhered to by the society; that indeed this procedure commands a tacit approval, and therefore is grounded in those values. Besides the use of prices as value signals, a subject taken up in the next chapter, what this means is that the criterion to be used in evaluating the performance of the economic choices as per the framework developed in Chapter 3 must use the same numerare for reckoning the benefits and costs regardless of whether such monetary reckoning turns out to be the final arbiter of the choice a society may end up making. This is to recognize that there may be other imperatives besides the monetary benefits and costs that may dictate the final choice. But although there may be supplementary elements in the criterion, if the straightforward comparison of benefits and costs is to be rejected in a particular choice situation, the society needs to be quite clear as to why this has to be done. In other words, if either the benefits or costs, or a part thereof, need to be ignored, or discounted, there must be clear reasons for doing so. In general, the monetary benefits and costs must be the choice by default in implementing the criterion.

This was one of the subjects discussed in Chapter 5, to answer the crucial question as to whether the value system of Islam would permit the use of monetary benefits and costs, to be used as a criterion to evaluate the performance of the economy. The burden of the arguments presented there showed that indeed Islam's value axioms not only sanction this, but rather seem to insist on it. In that case, it requires no great leap of imagination to conclude that the existing contents of normative economics, as enshrined in the basic postulates of welfare economics, become eminently relevant for an Islamic economy.

A related point that needs to be kept in mind throughout what follows is to recognize that the scope of normative economics is much wider in an Islamic economy as compared to the so-called secular economies of the West. This is because the existing body of normative economics does not concern itself with the question of how an individual member of the society, i.e. man as such, comes to decide what he in fact decides. That is to say, it does not concern itself with the issue of the appropriateness of the individual choices. It is assumed that the rational man, operating within the constraints imposed by his environment, makes the right choices as to what is best for him. In the context of our exposition in the last chapter, conventional normative economics concerns itself with the collective man and not man as such. Islamic economists, on the contrary, insist that it is up to them to tell what the man as such ought to do at the personal level; that is to say, what his behavior ought to be if it is to be Islamically rational. In a sense this attitude is quite understandable in the context of an all-embracing *Sharīʿa*, which covers both dimensions of man's existence (individual and collective) as discussed, one would hope adequately, in the last chapter. In view of this, one would readily admit that *fiqh* and economics, or fiqhnomics, would be an important branch of inquiry in an Islamic economy, more than the area of law and economics in the conventional economic discourse. But beyond that, it is also somewhat disconcerting that fiqhnomics is often assumed to be more or less all that is actually needed as far as the economics of an Islamic economy is concerned. This, perhaps, is a reflection of the concern with "first things first," so to speak; it is thus to be expected that with the maturing of thought over time, fiqhnomics will settle down to assume its due place within the broad corpus of economics in an Islamic economy. Yet, it would seem useful, as far I can see, to split it into two branches: personal fiqhnomics, relating to the non-enforceable part of *fiqh* and collective fiqhnomics to cover what is, or rather ought to be, enforceable in it. *Fiqh*, *per se*, acknowledges this distinction in its manifold classifications, as we saw in the previous chapter; the trouble lies more in the realm of Islamic economics. Making this distinction is important in a number of ways.

To begin with, it has the advantage of delineating the sphere in which the government is supposed to operate: in light of the point just made, it will be required to define only what is illegal and thus indirectly what is not. In other words, it will define the property rights. In the last chapter, such a distinction was alluded to, but here we need to delve a little further. First, there are actions that are *ḥarām* (explicitly forbidden by the Qurʾān) but do not lend themselves to enforceability. Therefore, such actions need not be declared illegal, for it does not auger well for law to declare something illegal that it simply cannot enforce. Doing so would amount to making a travesty of the law, and thereby reduce the respect that it must command to make it an effective institution. Secondly, and this is where much confusion lies, there may be things that are not *ḥarām* as such but need to be declared illegal, as a result of either *ijtihād* or their alien origins, possibly in the form of foreign imposition. In the first case, a terminological confusion is bound to arise, and in the second case, the absence of the needed loyalty of citizens creates serious hurdles in effective enforcement. The latter issue is discussed in both Chapter 3 (with reference to the transaction costs) and Chapter 5 at a more fundamental level, relating to the loyalty of citizens. It is the former issue to which we need to pay somewhat closer attention at this stage.

Historically, as has been noted, the process of jurisprudence in Islam was the result of individual efforts of the *fuqahāʾ* who, being ordinary citizens, could not declare some act as legal or illegal in the sense of their enforceability. Generally, though not always, the *fuqahāʾ* kept a distance between themselves and the state, for they thought, with considerable justification, that the state was prone to being corrupt. They were generally quite scrupulous in their juridical pronouncements, i.e. the juristic opinions (*fatāwā*,—plural of *fatwā*) in the sense of not using the term *ḥarām* except for those cases where the Qurʾān was very explicit about the prohibition. But then, in later generations, the same scrupulousness was not adhered to, and often led to a rather indiscriminate use of the term *ḥarām*.[1] This problem was exacerbated by the fact that what was often declared illegal by the state, regardless of the terminology used, was often not accorded legitimacy by *fiqh*, either because different schools of *fiqh* had different positions on a particular issue, or because the legal decree was thought to be motivated by personal fancies of the rulers, or because the social significance of the prohibition was not fully appreciated. Much later, foreign elements in the legal corpus of different Muslim countries, that were as alien as the idea of a nation state itself, added additional complications.[2]

Then, there is the related problem of the religious authorities themselves not only recognizing but more often actively endorsing the idea of a split between religious (*dīn*) and secular (*dunyā*) realms of a Muslim's life, a split that is inconceivable in view of the unity of man's life. This split, it appears to me, began with a distinction between *fiqh*

---

[1] The more cautious *fiqh* scholars have not fallen in this trap. Consider, for instance, the following statement by one well-known contemporary *fiqh* scholar, Yūsuf Qaraḍāwī in his *al-Ḥalāl wa-al-ḥarām fī al-Islām* (The lawful and the prohibited in Islam): "The other group is frozen in its fixed opinions concerning questions about the *ḥalal* and the *ḥaram*, following a statement in a text which they assume to be Islam. They do not budge a hair's breadth from their position, nor do they try to weigh their opinion against the arguments of the others, and to arrive at the truth after a comparison and critical evaluation of all opinions. If one of them were to be asked his opinion concerning music, singing, chess, women's education, a woman's showing her face and hands, and similar matters, the most likely word to issue from his tongue would be *ḥaram*. This group has forgotten the caution exercised by our righteous forbearers in such matters, who never applied the word *ḥaram* to anything unless they knew it to be definitely prohibited. If there were the slightest doubt concerning the matter they would only say, 'We disapprove of it' or 'We do not like it', or some other similarly mild statement" (citation from the English translation, Indianapolis, Ind.: American Trust Publications, 1960, p. 3).

[2] Imagine the problems that arise when one considers the question of smuggling between two adjacent Muslim countries, for a people not attuned to thinking in terms of national boundaries arising out of the alien concept of nation-states, in contrast to the concept of Muslim *umma*, which is ingrained in their consciousness, and a historical experience that did not deviate much from that conceptualization regardless of the different political jurisdictions, jurisdictions that did not matter much as far as the life of a common man was concerned. Further complications arise when governments of the concerned state are not recognized as Islamically legitimate because they do not live up to the Islamic norms. Then there is the question of the legitimacy of the exorbitant rates of duty often imposed under one pretext or another. It is often observed that an otherwise God-fearing Muslim would entertain no qualms about breaking such a law simply because to him such laws do not make any sense from an Islamic perspective. This is just one instance of a plethora of similar dilemmas that need to be effectively addressed by *fiqh*.

al-ʿibādāt and *fiqh al-muʿāmalāt*; the latter dealt seemingly with profane matters that could not be considered at par with obligations relating to the Divine, and therefore perhaps not really worthy of the dignity of a sincere and committed Muslim's acute attention. It is also possible that the former category of *fiqh* was less encumbered as far as the ambit of the powers that be were concerned, and therefore *fiqh* felt less pressure to make pronouncements on those matters. At any rate, the first we read about this split, as far as I can see, is in a treatise by Māwardī (d. 1058) aptly entitled *Kitāb al-dīn wa-al-dunyā*.[3] Muslim interaction with the Christian world, which recognizes a theological split between these two spheres because of man's fallen nature, might have contributed to this dichotomy in Islam—indeed this factor may have been significant from the very beginning with the process of conversion of both the Christians and Persians. It is also conceivable that the aversion of the Ṣūfīs to the rulers, and the well-to-do in general, particularly those associated with the courts of the rulers, contributed to this dichotomy. Interestingly, it was Māwardī's better-known work, *al-Aḥkām al-sulṭāniyya* (Ordinances of government), which lent a *de facto* legitimacy to the Caliphal form of government during the ʿAbbāsid era and thereby, one would surmise, lent respectability to the *qānūn* corpus within the framework of *fiqh*. But this reconciliation remained tenuous, and indeed became untenable, though much later, in the aftermath of Western hegemony. Be that as it may, this dichotomy has persisted to the present; if anything, it seems to have become more pronounced, with the end result that a Muslim lives a dual life, that is, one part of the law that he lives under does not draw any inner commitment from him. And a law that is devoid of such commitment on the part of the populace is very difficult to enforce. The enforcement costs of doing so turn out to be very high. Do the Islamic economists, with their heavy reliance on fiqhnomics, have anything to say on the matter? Not much, at least nothing directly. As a matter of fact, the dichotomy between religious and secular spheres has been quietly accepted as a part of the Islamic value system, and much of what the Islamic economists end up saying is based on this presumption.

And, to top it all, there is the problem of rhetoric. Islamic economics is quite heavily influenced by Arabic writers or the non-Arab writ-

[3] al-Māwardī was associated with the ʿAbbāsid court as chief judge (*qāḍī*).

ers based in the Arabian Peninsula. Arabic literature has a long tradition of rhetoric (*balāgha*),[4] and while it insists on soundness of content, at least it used to, it now often boils down to a long winding argument attempting to belabor what would seem to be quite obvious. This problem becomes more serious in pure rhetoric, namely rhetoric of the spoken variety. As serious scholarship waned in the Islamic world after the closure of the gates of *ijtihād*, it was replaced by rhetoric of speech; a speaker would normally play with the emotions of the crowd to drive his point home without any obligation with regard to the internal consistency of the argument, and no obligation to provide citations in support of the argument. Pure rhetoric caters to the present moment: there is no need to establish a rigorous connection with the past, and no worry as to how it will be judged in future.[5] This sort of rhetoric spread to all Islamic lands, and farther in recent times, and has not always remained confined to the spoken word. Written material now shows a very strong imprint of this style in more or less all areas of Islamic discourse. The literature of Islamic economics bears this stamp in that the writers do not usually give the impression that they have an obligation to observe a logical consistency in their articulations, as though they owe nothing to posterity, if not to history. For readers who are not used to this style of writing, the encounter often leads to frustration, for often an elaborate argument ends up introducing a number of logical inconsistencies; obviously, the more that is said the more care must be taken in keeping track of the internal consistency of the argument. In the writings on Islamic economics, it is the case that the fuss, if that word may be excused, is less about the substance than the terminology. This springs from an unarticulated desire to use the Arabic lexicon. While it is possible to sympathize with this tendency, the translations rendered for the terminology used often deliberately avoid the commonly accepted terminology of economics with the intention of driving a difference for its own sake.

Consider, for instance, the word *falāḥ*—recall our discussion on it in the previous chapter—a word pervasively used in the *fiqh* literature. Its most appropriate translation into English is welfare, a word

[4] See, for instance, Schuon (1969, Chapter 1), "The use of hyperbole in Arab rhetoric" for an excellent treatment of this subject.

[5] Recording technology may have made the more cautious among them somewhat careful, yet ingrained habits die hard.

used equally pervasively in economics. But in their writings, the Islamic economists have increasingly come to ignore the word welfare, and instead use terms such as well-being, success, to thrive, to become happy, etc., as though these words had no relationship with welfare. Take the following example where the author after defining *falāḥ* as "the success in this life and in the hereafter" goes on to state: "Consumer behaviour in an Islamic society can be described as a maximization of success, *falah*. Success may be defined, in the narrow sense, corresponding with consumer choice, as the level of obedience to Allah (SWT) derived from the satisfaction of one's material wants and the exhibition of the effect of Allah's bounty by extracting enjoyment of the *mal* [wealth] given by Allah (SWT), and the enrichment of one's lifeafter."[6] And such statements abound. In what follows, I have generally discounted the rhetorical material, and have tried, instead, to focus more on the substantive part of the writings of the Islamic economists, though I am not sure to what extent this can be successfully accomplished. With these preliminaries out of the way, we may now turn to the main subject at hand.

Property Ownership

Consider the issue of property ownership. We begin by noting that the institution of private property finds an unequivocal sanction in the Qur'ān. Indeed it could not be otherwise, for the imperatives, or rather the operationalization, of the free will necessarily requires this to be so. Beyond private property, the *ḥadīth* literature sanctions, or rather commends, communal ownership for certain forms of property. Very early on in the history of Islam, we also observe the growth of another form of property commonly referred to as *waqf*—more appropriately *waqf fī sabīl Allāh*, property dedicated in the way of Allāh—the closest Western conceptualization of it being a charitable trust. As far as private property is concerned, the Qūr'ān not only sanctions it but rather sanctifies it, and the *ḥadīth* literature naturally supports that stance. In a speech that still retains the power to move people to tears, the Prophet, in what has come to be known as his farewell pilgrimage address (*khutba*) said, *inter alia*: "I do not know

[6] From Monzer Kahf (repr. 1980), p. 93 (only larger brackets added).

whether I shall ever meet you in this place again after this year. Your blood and your property is sacrosanct until you meet your Lord, as this day and this month are holy."[7] No wonder then that there was never any confusion on this count until the collectivist confusion of the twentieth century, created by socialist ideology, led a fringe section of Muslim writers to put forward stretched interpretations of some Qur᾽ānic verses to support their claims about the essentiality of nationalization of private property in Islam. Obviously such claims could not be taken seriously. On the contrary these writings actually force us to explore the question about the place of state ownership in the *Sharīʿa*. Apart from the public treasury, which originally was called *māl Allāh*, and subsequently came to be known as *bayt al-māl*, there is no tradition of public ownership of property during the Prophetic times. But there is considerable confusion on this issue because communal ownership is often equated to public ownership in *fiqh*, and thereby in the writings on Islamic economics. As far as communal ownership is concerned, there is evidence about it in the case of three things according to the only *ḥadīth* report cited in Sunan of Abū Dā᾽ūd: pastures, running water, and fire.[8] Accordingly the Prophet declared some lands that fell under his preserve as pastures for the horses that were used in military expeditions. Subsequently, the *fuqahā᾽* extended the scope of communal ownership on the basis of *qiyās* to include a number of other natural resources in its ambit.[9] It appears, however, that according to *Sharʿī* rules about *al-ḥimā* (relating to enclosures) a natural resource can be declared communally owned only if it did not fall under private ownership prior to such declaration; namely it was *mubāḥ*, open to everyone, before the question of enclosure arose. As *fiqh*, which felt uncomfortable with the prevailing institutional form of the government as it took roots in the era following the *Khulafā᾽ al-Rāshidūn* (the rightly guided caliphs), evolved, it did not recognize public ownership, even in those cases that in a classical sense fall under public ownership, such as streets, roads, and bridges, etc. Instead it opted to put these in the category

[7] Translation cited from A. Guillaume (1955), p. 651.

[8] Report No. 3470 in his *Kitāb al-ijāra*. Zarqa (see the next footnote) reports the same from Sunan Ibn Māja on the authority of Ibn ʿAbbās.

[9] For instance, Zarqa (1992, p. 148) mentions that Shāfiʿī *fiqh* used this report to include "a long list of items such as salt, sulphur, naphtha, etc. falling under the same category."

of communal ownership. Leaving aside the Islamic economists, who are supposed to know the distinction between state ownership and communal ownership—and never mind their unconsidered advocacy of public property in the name of *fiqh*—a classical *fiqh* scholar even today has difficulty distinguishing between these two forms of property ownership; his training naturally leads him to equate public property with communal property. Since *fiqh* has as yet not come to terms with the issue of the appropriate form of an Islamic government, notwithstanding Māwardī, no wonder it finds it difficult to recognize public apart from communal ownership. And this besides the fact that the *qānūn* corpus in most Muslim countries in the post-colonial era accords due recognition to the public ownership of property, but then the corresponding provisions of that *qānūn* seldom get enforced, again because *fiqh* does not provide the necessary support for such property rights to command respect and thereby for them to become part of the common ethos. These provisions obviously relate to the right of exclusion, which in the case of public properties is vested with the government, for otherwise public properties in principle belong to the citizens. And once that right of exclusion is thrown in practical abeyance, a public property becomes the same thing as communal property and is thus subject to the tragedy of the commons.[10] It needs to be reiterated that a law that is not felt by the citizens to be rooted in the values that they adhere to is difficult to enforce. Even for those elements which prove quite irresistible in public interest, special enforcement efforts may be required, at least initially, to embed them in the public psyche. It is here that *fiqh* (and therefore fiqhnomics) has an important role to play, for *fiqh* legitimacy makes acceptance of these elements easier.

This raises an interesting question. If the *Sharīʿa* did not accord any recognition to public property, how were the public goods provided in Islamic realms, for provided they were, as per the historical evidence. And this brings us to the idea of *waqf* property,[11] and its

---

[10] No wonder then that we commonly observe the tragedy of the commons playing out on the streets in most Muslim countries in the form of all sorts of excesses and encroachments, where everyone feels they have a right to the use of these properties for their personal gains.

[11] The tradition of *waqf* property goes back to the immediate post-Prophetic times as attested by a *ḥadīth* report, recorded in both Bukhārī and Muslim's chapters on *waṣāyā* (wills) where ʿUmar, the second caliph, is supposed to have given the proceeds from a piece of land in Khaybar as *ṣadaqa* (charity), and declared that the rel-

essential link with the idea of *farḍ al-kifāya* as discussed in the previous chapter. Once the idea of *farḍ al-kifāya* was grounded in the *Sharīʿa* in recognition of the fact that a society could not be effectively organized without meeting those requirements, requirements that were essentially collective by their very nature, the Muslims adequately responded to these imperatives through, but, and this must be emphasized, whatever they did in response was necessarily done in their private capacity in view of discharging a *farḍ al-kifāya*, for a *farḍ al-kifāya* could not be made legally binding on any individual. The discharging of the *farḍ al-kifāya* took a number of forms but two are especially significant. One was to declare certain private property as communal property as happened in the case of streets, roads, etc. The second was to declare certain private property as *waqf* property, and in this case, at times, the declarer could, and often would, stipulate conditions with regard to the management of the property. Most of the mosques, schools (*madāris*, sing. *madrasa*), hospices, etc., in Islamic lands were built in this manner.[12] Thus the provision of public goods was the result of an individual or group initiative to discharge a *farḍ al-kifāya*. There is no doubt that often the rulers also participated in this endeavor, but when they did so, it was more in spirit of discharging a *farḍ al-kifāya* in their private capacity rather than discharging a public duty that would be considered incumbent upon them. *Fiqh*'s individualistic framework did not admit any collective *farḍ al-ʿayn*. It is, however, possible that public funds may have been used in such provision, but in this context two things must be kept in mind.

First, the *bayt al-māl* (public treasury) funds are quite specifically earmarked for certain purposes as far as the *Sharīʿa* is concerned, and while there is some room for interpretation of this to undertake public works, generally these funds were understood to be meant for redistribution purposes. Second, we also get the impression that the rulers often used their private funds for such purposes, and that at

---

evant piece of land must not be sold or inherited or given away as gift. ʿUmar dedicated this *waqf* land to "the poor, the nearest kin, the emancipation of slaves, and in the way of God and guests." Based on his example, the *Sharīʿa* recognizes that the beneficiaries of a *waqf* property can be specified. The *ḥadīth* report, and thus *Sharīʿa*, also permits the defraying of the administrative costs from the income of the *waqf* property.

[12] For a recent evaluation of the institution of *waqf* in the provision of public goods, see Kuran (2001).

times these allocations were quite substantial. It is, however, not clear as to what the sources of rulers' income were, for we know fortunes were indeed routinely made. Perhaps there were sources of revenue other than those that were supposed to go to the *bayt al-māl*, in which case the rulers would have enjoyed considerable discretion about expenditure allocations. This impression is supported by Māwardī, writing in the latter part of the ʿAbbāsid era in his *Aḥkām al-sulṭāniyya*, listing several *dīwāns* (departments?), one of which happens to be *bayt al-māl*. It is tempting to think of it as the department of the treasury, but the problem is he also lists a separate *dīwān* for taxes. In any case, what must be particularly noted is that the pattern of governance set by the *Khulafāʾ al-Rāshidūn*, and followed subsequently for centuries, sometimes in spirit but often only in letter, was that the office of governance was seen by all concerned as the discharging of a personal responsibility rather than the holding of a public office responsible only for overseeing a vast bureaucracy in an impersonal manner. And regardless of what transpired thereafter, Muslims have always seen the issue of governance according to the tones set by the *Khulafāʾ al-Rāshidūn*, that is to say, as a matter of personal responsibility for the rulers.

What is fascinating is the daring manner in which the *Sharīʿa* combined individual responsibility with social purpose through *farḍ al-kifāya*, and how the Islamic societies rose to the occasion by establishing the required institutions to discharge the collective responsibilities, a tradition that continued over the centuries until these societies were overwhelmed by the new, and rather alien, technological age, in which the provision of public goods took on some altogether new colorings. Modern Muslim writers, of all stripes, have succumbed to the negative view of individualism that originated in the West, and is based on West's encounters with its own version of it. While it is quite likely that the idea of individualism in the West, with its roots in Italian humanism of the sixteenth century, was to a considerable extent influenced by Islamic individualism, when it was planted in the alien soil it lost its original mooring, the mooring of individual sense of responsibility in view of possible reckoning before God for failing to discharge communal responsibilities. Actually the Western collectivist soil was not entirely hospitable to the idea of individualism to begin with. Those who struggled to cultivate it had to do so against formidable odds, for the corporate church and the institution of serfdom could not take kindly to such a challenge to their deep seated interests. Though the Reformation did occur, and it represents a proof of commitment of those who struggled for it, as far as individualism is concerned the victory was never complete.[13] The collectivist psyche of the Western man strongly militates against such success.[14] One can see that, in general, Western man, conditioned as he is by the first Council of Nicaea, has trouble coming to terms with the idea of individual responsibility, for in doing so he must confront the starkness of the doctrine of Divine Unity, rather than seeking atonement through redemption; he either accepts it and thus becomes a Unitarian, to say the least, and ends up severing his emotional link

[13] Salim Rashid (1987) despairs at the paradoxes of individualism in America, and almost levels a charge of hypocrisy on the basis of a number of examples he cites where individual rights are not recognized in the interest of certain collectivity, including those that are not recognized in the name of nation-states. He goes on to record the disenchantment about individualism among some Western writers, primarily, and perhaps obviously, belonging to the clerical class. He cites W. K. Jordan's "detailed study of the patterns of voluntary donations" of protestants in the fifteenth to seventeenth centuries and writes, "Jordan found that the rich men of this age gave enormous amounts of their wealth to the *poor, to educational institutions, for hospitals and municipal works* and to the church," and wonders why Jordan regarded "these benefactions to be militantly and aggressively *secular* in temper and in purpose" (Rashid, p. 49, emphasis added). The difficulty he encounters is easily resolved if it is recognized that a corporate church could not look at such independent and individualistic acts of charity favorably. Salim Rashid further notes, rightly I think, that Western scientists in those days, in general, were men of religion, and provides a number of examples including that of Newton, but then fails to see the power of the collectivism which instilled fears in the hearts of these men. Consider the case of Newton, and see what this meant. I will let Encyclopaedia Britannica speak for itself: "In the early 1690s he had sent Locke a copy of a manuscript attempting to prove that Trinitarian passages in the Bible were latter-day corruptions of the original text. When Locke made moves to publish it, Newton withdrew in fear that his anti-Trinitarian views would become known." With regard to his concern where individual freedom (of movement) is denied in the name of national interests, Rashid should have gone to the logical conclusion of the argument to note the excesses, rather atrocities, perpetrated in the name of perceived national interests. But more than that to the recognition that the idea of nation state, by itself, is a reflection of the collectivist mentality. One may add that such an idea could hardly be conceived of in the individualistic climate of the Islamic culture. Granted that fragmentation often occurred in the Islamic realms, and we don't need to go into the reasons thereof, but yet it must be noted that an individual's freedom to move about from one jurisdiction to another on this earth of God was never conceived to be an alienable right in Islamic realms.

[14] When a Christian thinks of prayer (service, if you like), he instinctively thinks of the church and communion; he feels incapable of approaching God directly, here and now, with the possible exception of a Protestant. On the contrary, whenever a Muslim thinks of offering his prayers, he is certain that he can do so here and now, and if he feels the need to go to the mosque, it is to express his solidarity with the community as exemplified in the Prophetic times.

with the Pauline theology, or else rejects it for his long-established emotional security. But then he also exposes himself to the possibility of wandering in the maze of his own creating, and thus ending up in a God-less existentialism. When a Muslim disowns the idea of individualism, and therefore the idea of individual responsibility, he betrays a lack of familiarity with his own past. In a rather ironic turn of events, the West's failure to cope with its own variety of individualism seems to have led Muslims to abandon their admirable tradition of individualism—an individualism, let us note specifically to avoid any misunderstanding, that was wedded to collectivity in an admirable harmony—and blindly turn to Western collectivism. Witness the regrettable destruction of the venerable institution of *waqf* property through imposition of public (collectivist) administration in more or less all Muslim countries in the past century without a whimper of protest on the part of the Muslims in general, and the *fiqh* scholars in particular. What is important, and this must never be lost sight of, is that when the government appropriates such property, the individuals have a right to feel that they are relieved of the corresponding *farāʾiḍ al-kifāya*. Even if it is granted that there were cases of mismanagement of such property, it is a sad commentary on Muslims' intellectual paralysis, or even their perfidy, that they could not rise to the occasion, and acquiesced in this blatant nationalization, as though the *Sharīʿa* could somehow approve of property confiscation, even by the government, in the name of some national interest or under the pretext of some lawless behavior.

What this clarifies is that the concept of public property, as we know it today, does not have any roots in the classical sources of Islamic *fiqh*. One would be obliged to justify its existence through *ijtihād*, which in turn means putting the issue explicitly on the table and invoking some principle of Islamic jurisprudence, *uṣūl-al-fiqh*, to argue for its acceptance. While I feel this can be done, it must be noted that that this is not what the Islamic economists do. They treat public ownership as the same thing as communal ownership, or worse, take it for granted in light of modern practice in all the countries, and thereby create much confusion as far as its place in *Sharīʿa* is concerned.

Finally, in the context of private property ownership, it may be noted that when Islamic economists discuss it, they admit its sanction but only conditionally, adding that such ownership is by no means absolute, for according to the Qurʾān only God is the absolute owner of everything, everything that is "in the heavens and on earth." This is often expressed with the undertones, but then sometimes quite explicitly, that man could be denied such ownership or that such ownership could be usurped by a collectivity (read state) under certain conditions in the name of some collectivist imperative.[15] No such inference can be drawn from any Qurʾānic exhortations, making such innuendos totally unwarranted, for the Qurʾān is quite explicit about the issue: "And devour not one another's possessions [*amwāl*, pl. of *māl*) wrongfully, and neither employ legal artifices with a view to devouring sinfully, and knowingly, anything that by right belongs to others" (2:188); and then again, "O you who have attained to faith! Do not devour one another's possessions wrongfully—not even by way of trade based on mutual agreements—and do not destroy one another: for, behold, God is indeed a dispenser of grace unto you! And as for him who does this with malicious intent and a will to do wrong—him shall We, in time, cause to endure (suffering through)

[15] For instance, Monzer Kahf, a luminary of the Jeddah School of Islamic economics, and whom we met earlier, provides us with the theory of production in an Islamic economy: after a few introductory lines, he begins by drawing inspiration from a *Sḥīʿī fiqh* scholar of the twentieth century by quoting him thus: "The extraction of every particle of usefulness from the entire universe is an ideological objective of the Islamic society," goes on to say that "The legislative means taken by Islam to promote productivity and discourage idleness or non-utilization of resources will become clear in a summary of twenty clauses" some of which, for the indulgence of our reader, are "3) Non-privately owned natural resources [communally owned?, publically owned? One can see, in light of the above discussion, his predicament to be more specific on this score] are to be left unused. Non-use of them results in the invalidation of the private claims on them; 15) The discouragement of luxury in private consumption makes investment-biased spending more attractive; 16) It is a collective duty [*farḍ al-kifāya*] of the Islamic community to make available every useful branch of knowledge and industry; 17) It is the collective duty of the members of the Islamic community to participate in the leading industries and fields of knowledge in the world; 20) The state enters the field of economic activity as a central planner and supervisor," and then 3 pages later, he concludes the paper by giving us a list of six Islamic conditions for the "right of ownership" where the fourth item reads: "The object of the right of property is the opportunity of economic utilization. If this opportunity is not attended [why?, he does not say] or the utilization is diverted to non-economic purposes as defined earlier [the reference is those twenty conditions, some of which we saw above], the right will be reduced (to the limit of zero) in proportion to the 'oppression' [which oppression? he does not say] committed. This may mean foregoing the entire right in case of losing the opportunity, or the deprivation of control over one's property in case of misuse" (Kahf, 1978, reprinted in Sayyid Tahir et al. (eds.) (1992, pp. 113–14, 118, brackets added). If a reader wonders why the support for such a position, and on such a fundamental issue, had to be sought in the writings of a *Shīʿī fiqh* scholar, let it be noted that no such support could be had from any of the *Sunnī fiqh* schools, for only *Shīʿī* theology could permit such extravagant departures from the original sources of Islamic *fiqh*.

fire: for this indeed is easy for God" (4:29–30); and as though anticipating man's tendency to look for excuses, the exhortation continues, "Hence, do not covet the bounties which God has bestowed more abundantly on some of you than on others. Men shall have a benefit from what they earn, and women shall have benefit from what they earn. Ask, therefore God (to give you) out of His bounty: behold, God has indeed full knowledge of everything" (4:32).[16] When the Islamic economists misuse the verse reported above, namely that everything "in the heavens and on earth" belongs to God, and thus subject to appropriation by state, one may be forgiven for feeling a strong aversion against such excesses. What the Qur'ān reminds us is that an ephemeral being, man, cannot possibly be conceived of as an absolute owner of anything irrespective of whether he accepts the doctrine of Divine Unity or not.[17] And as such, it serves as a warning to man, in view of his possible haughtiness, that the freedoms associated with ownership can always be misused, in exactly the same way that they may be enjoyed as His favors. How man uses his freedoms is entirely up to him, for "There shall be no coercion in matters of faith. Distinct has now become the right way from (the way of) error." (2:256), but whatever he does with what he owns during his terrestrial life, he will be held accountable for it on the Day of Judgment, for then "every human being will be held in pledge for whatever (evil) he has wrought" (74:38). And that brings us to the issue of free will, and thereby to the second element in the list of characteristics noted above, namely the freedom of choice.

Free Will, Freedom of Choice and Self-Interest

Free will implies freedom of choice, for otherwise it does not make any terrestrial or eschatological sense. One of the things stressed in Chapter 5 was that free will was not left to its own meager resources

[16] Similar exhortations are repeated especially concerning the people of Madyan to whom Prophet Shū'āyb, considered to be the father-in-law of Moses (Jethro), was sent, who are especially charged with dishonesty with regard to weights and measures. See, for instances, Qur'ānic discourse beginning with verses 7:85, 11:84, and 26:176.

[17] As the Qur'ān says: "And now, indeed, you have come unto Us in a lonely state, even as We created you in the first instance; and you have left behind you all that We bestowed on you (in your lifetime)" (6:94).

to cope with its terrestrial existence, situated as it was in the enormity of time and space. Man, the Creator knew, accepted free will like a fool (33:72) and thus, in a sense, not realizing what he was getting into; a cosmic drama that had had its own history, the significance of which was not fully grasped by him, and perhaps was not meant to be fully graspable. The Divine plan appears to be to put only necessary and sufficient faculties at man's disposal. The why of this, of course, is a part of that incomprehensible ultimate mystery that the human mind has struggled to solve for millennia without any success. Man is told by the Qur'ān to contemplate it, and to reflect upon it, to realize the speck that his terrestrial surroundings represent in the vastness of the cosmos, but not to despair if a fuller comprehension eludes him. The sufficiency of the faculties placed at man's disposal was deemed to be contingent upon Divine guidance, for nothing in creation could be sufficient unto itself; it is only the Creator who is thus. It is only when man starts thinking that he is the measure of everything that he runs into trouble, as alluded to in the context of Western individualism and in Chapter 5 with reference to the Benthamite prescription. The guidance, as noted earlier, was comprehensive in the sense that it covered man's individual, private conduct, as well as his collective affairs.

As far as individual personal consumption behavior is concerned, the Qur'ānic position has been demonstrated, again in Chapter 5. There are prohibitions that are quite specifically noted in the Qur'ān, and beyond those everything is deemed to be permissible, though the *fiqh* position seems to be that certain things may be declared not permissible from time to time in light of social interest. (One needs to be careful here to draw a clear distinction between things that are *ḥarām* and things that are not so but yet may be illegal). While the Qur'ān does not impose many restrictions on the basket of goods and services that may be consumed beyond its explicit prohibitions ("They will ask thee as to what is lawful to them. Say: 'Lawful to you are all the good things of life'," 5:4), it does weigh against profligacy: "O ye who believe! Make not unlawful the good things which God hath made lawful to you, but commit no excess: for God loveth not those given to excess," 5:87. But then it leaves the question of what would count as profligacy to individual conscience, for what would count as profligacy at one time may not be at another, and what may be so for one individual may not be so for another who is differently endowed. The *ḥadīth* literature, however, provides further guidance on this issue. The Prophet (upon whom be peace and salutations, always) himself lived a very frugal life, and since his lifestyle is considered to be as *uswa al-ḥusnā* (best conduct) according to the Qur'ān (33:21), the Muslims have always drawn inspiration from his *faqr* (austere living). And this was perhaps not too difficult until the advent of the technological age that rendered that traditional pattern of living practically impossible to maintain. The Prophet, as a rule, disliked conspicuous consumption, particularly of the things that would be considered symbols of ostentatious living such as long robes, silk garments, or gold ornaments for men. What that meant was that modesty should be the norm in all spheres of a Muslim's life, though one is dismayed by the literalist bias of the *fiqh* that tends to restrict the scope of the Prophetic disliking to the specific things found in the *ḥadīth* reports; the emphasis in *fiqh* thus being more on the letter than the spirit. No wonder then that an ordinary Muslim feels a bit lost regarding any connection between his current and the Prophetic lifestyle.

Aware of the income inequalities that were ordained to prevail, for the temptation to accumulate wealth is an essential part of man's earthly trials, "and know that your worldly goods and your children are but a trial and a temptation" (8:28), the Qūr'ān links the individual consumption permissibility to social obligations, both at the compulsory (obligatory *ṣadaqa*, i.e. *zakāh*, though the latter word is often also used in the Qur'ān in its original meaning, i.e. charity in general), and voluntary (*ṣadaqa* beyond *zakāh*) levels. Indeed, the Qur'ān ties such expenditures to true piety by quite explicitly stating that "never shall you attain to true piety unless you spend on others out of what you cherish yourselves; and whatever you spend—verily, God has full knowledge thereof" (3:92). This emphasis on charity recurs in numerous places in the Qur'ān. Whenever the ritual prayer (*ṣalāh*) is mentioned, charity is mentioned alongside it. Specifically, 4:37, 13:22, 14:31, and 25:67 admonish man not be niggardly in his charitable spending, and to do it both openly and secretly. There is a comprehensive statement about charity in *sūra al-Baqara*. After a discourse on some of the legal injunctions, man is offered the following admonition:

> The parable of those who spend their possessions for the sake of God is that of a grain out of which grow seven ears, in every ear a hundred grains: for God grants manifold increase unto whom He wills; and God is infinite, all-knowing. They who spend their possessions for the sake of God and do not thereafter mar their spending by stressing their own

> benevolence and hurting (the feelings of the needy) shall have their reward with their Sustainer, and no fear need they have, and neither shall they grieve. A kind word and a veiling of another's want is better than a charitable deed followed by hurt; and God is self-sufficient, forbearing. O you who have attained to faith! Do not deprive your charitable deeds of all worth by stressing your own benevolence and hurting (the feelings of the needy), as does he who spends his wealth only to be seen and praised by men, and believes not in God and the Last Day: for his parable is that of a smooth rock with (a little) earth upon it—and then a rainstorm smites it and leaves it hard and bare. Such as these shall have no gain whatever from all their (good) works: for God does not guide people who refuse to acknowledge the truth. And the parable of those who spend their possessions out of a longing to please God, and out of their inner certainty, is that of a garden on high, fertile ground: a rainstorm smites it, and thereupon it brings forth its fruits twofold; and if no rainstorm smites it, soft rain (falls upon it). And God sees all that you do. Would any of you like to have a garden of date-palms and vines, through which running waters flow, and have all manner of fruit therein—and then be overtaken by old age, with only weak children to (look after) him—and then (see) it smitten by a fiery whirl-wind and utterly scorched? In this way God makes clear His messages unto you, so that you might take thought. O you who have attained to faith! Spend on others out of the good things which you may have acquired, and out of that which We bring forth for you from the earth; and choose not for your spending the bad things which you yourselves would not accept without averting your eyes in disdain. And know that God is self-sufficient, ever to be praised. Satan threatens you with the prospect of poverty and bids you to be niggardly, whereas God promises you His forgiveness and bounty; and God is infinite, all-knowing, granting wisdom unto whom He wills: and whoever is granted wisdom has indeed been granted wealth abundant. But none bears this in mind save those who are endowed with insight. For, whatever you may spend on others, or whatever you may vow (to spend), verily, God knows it; and those who do wrong (by withholding charity) shall have none to succour them. If you do deeds of charity openly, it is well; but if you bestow it upon the needy in secret, it will be even better for you, and it will atone for some of your bad deeds. And God is aware of all that you do. It is not for thee (O Prophet) to make people follow the right path, since it is God (alone) who guides whom He wills. And whatever good you may spend on others is for your own good, provided that you spend only out of a longing for God's countenance: for, whatever good you may spend will be repaid unto you in full, and you shall not be wronged (2:261–72).

If charity is one element of piety, it is perhaps worthwhile to note its other elements to provide an overall perspective of the Qur'ānic conception of piety. Again, while the explanation occurs in numerous places in the Qur'ān, the following is quite succinct: "True piety does not consist in turning your faces towards the east or the west—but truly pious is he who believes in God, and the Last Day, and the angels, and revelation, and the prophets; and spends his substance—however much he himself may cherish it—upon his near of kin, and the orphans, and the needy, and the wayfarer, and the beggars, and for the freeing of the human beings from bondage; and is constant in prayer, and renders the purifying dues; and (truly pious are) they who keep their promises whenever they promise, and are patient in misfortune and hardship and in time of peril: it is they that have proved themselves true, and it is they, they who are conscious of God" (2:177). In this, notice that the voluntary charity, *āṭ al-māl* (spending on others, as in the first part of the admonition) is mentioned separately from the compulsory charity, *zakāh* (the purifying dues, as in the latter part of the verse). Furthermore, the recipients of that charity are quite explicitly identified, hence the dictum: charity begins at home. Further clarity is provided by 2:215, which implies a hierarchy of beneficiaries as in the verse just cited, and the following verse, which reinforces the same but notes a few more categories: "And do good unto your parents, and the near of kin, and unto orphans, and the needy, and the neighbour from among your own people, and the neighbour who is a stranger, and the friend by your side, and the wayfarer, and those whom you rightfully possess. Verily, God does not love any of those who, full of self-conceit, act in a boastful manner" (4:36).[18] While the Qur'ān mentions parents explicitly, and then the near of kin in general, it is the *ḥadīth* literature that further clarifies what is meant by the near of kin. The Prophet, who understood the purport of Qur'ānic injunctions more than anybody else, is reported in a number of narrations included in all the canonical collections to have clarified that it is the nuclear family that has the first right to a person's charity, and thereafter the circle of beneficiaries is expanded on the basis of blood ties to that nuclear family.[19] As a matter of fact, one of the *ḥadīth* reports urges an individual to

[18] It is fascinating to see how the Qur'ān anticipates the modern age in which neighbors may be strangers, something inconceivable at the time of its revelation.

[19] See, for instance, Ṣaḥīḥ Mūslim, "*Kitāb al-zakāh*" (Book of charity), Chapters 366 to 370. It is interesting to note that all canonical collections of *ḥadīth* reports opt to name their relevant chapter "Kitāb al-zakāh" rather than "*Kitāb al-ṣadaqa*, for unlike the report under consideration, the Qur'ān uses the word *zakāh* in numerous a places to underscore charity in general, or *ṣadaqa*.

start with himself, and then his family, relatives, and the closer and wider circle of an individual's social relations.[20] It is interesting to note that when the Prophet was asked to explain the meaning of the word *ṣadaqa*, he is reported to have included all acts of supplication in its ambit, enjoining of the good (*amr bi-al-maʿrūf*), a courtesy smile for even strangers, removing a stone from people's path, assisting a man to ride upon his beast, and even discharging of conjugal obligations.[21] It is in this perspective of guidance to man, where his individual consumption behavior (a dimension of his freedom) is closely wedded to charity, and where the scope of charity is much broader than the commonly understood meaning of that term, that we must conceptualize the theory of consumer behavior in an Islamic perspective. What this means is that such a theory must presume interdependent utility functions, something that conventional economic theory already permits. There, the head of the household, the bread-winner, is assumed to make the decisions, often in concert with the other adult members of the family, that maximize the utility, not just his personal utility but that of the entire nuclear family and sometimes even of an extended family. In a sense, he is presumed to reckon the utility of his family his own.

But now let us come to the question of constraints on individual freedom. Man, as they say, is a social animal. But in a societal setting, individual freedom could hardly be conceived of as something absolute. Absolute freedom amounts to absolute lack of freedom; simply put, it would amount to anarchy. The Islamic perspective is no different. Man as such is presumed by the Qurʾān to live in a society, and the freedoms that are vouchsafed him are vouchsafed in that context; otherwise the freedoms would hardly make any sense. If the idea of absolute freedom is an anathema to any society, the society thus feels obliged to institute constraints on individual freedoms, which was the subject of what has previously been called the legal corpus of a society, a corpus that could hardly fail to reflect the underlying values upheld by that society. In the Islamic perspective, the legal corpus is quite explicitly supplemented by rules governing an individual's personal conduct. That is more or less true for other value systems as

[20] See ibid., Chapter 367. It may be noted that similar *ḥadīth* reports are also recorded in Saḥīḥ Bukhārī, Sunan Abū Daʾūd, and Sunan Ibn Majāh, all belonging to *Ṣiḥāḥ al-sitta* (the six canonical collections), in chapters entitled *Kitāb al-zakāh*.

[21] See ibid., Chapter 370.

well in the form of ethical constraints, although the emphasis may vary from one to another. In the Islamic perspective, there are the explicit prohibitions that are clearly spelled out by the Qur'ān, and then there is the *ḥadīth* literature, which is used to formulate elements of the legal corpus, but beyond that there is a whole wide area, an area that is bound to grow with the passage of time due to the changes in man's earthly environments, for legal formulations that is left to man's ongoing endeavors. The principle for such endeavors ought to be same as the exhortation to the individual given in the Qur'ān, *amr bi-al-ma'rūf wa-nahy 'an al-munkar* (command the doing of good and forbid the doing of wrong), admittedly in an environment of flux where good appears in ever new forms at the same time that evil takes on ever new guises, and to complicate matters even further where the simplicity of the pre-technological age has been rent asunder.

In an age where good and bad elements have increasingly been packaged in the same bundle, a faculty of discernment is required that is not habituated to thinking in terms of black and white. It is here that *fiqh* in particular, and thus Muslims in general, have found it increasingly difficult to handle the complexity of the modern times, although it must be recognized that this sort of complexity is attested to by a story commonly related to a famous *ḥadīth* report.[22] A peg was put in place in the passage outside the Prophet's mosque for tethering camels, i.e. a public service, by one of his companions. Another companion removed it in view of the possible harm that passers-by might have suffered by stumbling over it. The Prophet approved both actions. It was not the act of placing or removing the peg that was important, it was the intentions behind those acts, intentions that made them both meritorious. At any rate, it is the exhortation to command the doing of good that must provide the legislative framework, and thus provide the elements necessary for a legal corpus in the ever-changing climate of modern times to fill the vacuum in the existing legal corpus that defines property rights in an Islamic economy. This daunting task cannot be discharged in any satisfactory manner without a prior detailed articulation of the legislative process

[22] This *ḥadīth*, by itself a somewhat lengthy report with which Bukhārī opens his Ṣaḥīḥ, contains the well-known maxim *innamā al-a'māl bi-al-nīyyāt* (actions are to be judged by their intentions).

enshrined in the constitution of a society. The traditional process of *fiqh* formulations cannot adequately cope with this problem, with the exception of cases of personal conduct. The contours of an Islamic economy remain meaningless in absence of a well-defined theory of government.

Freedom of choice cannot be conceived of as absolute in any orderly society. As a matter of fact one can almost say that it was in anticipation of the possibility of one individual usurping the freedoms of all that the Divine guidance in the form of revelation was deemed to be necessary, a grace and a mercy that was supposed to liberate an individual from the tyranny of others. Admittedly the nature of constraints imposed on individual freedoms beyond those originating in the revelation itself may vary from one society to another. This depends on the set of fundamental values held by the society. Even a society not beholden to a Divine revelation necessarily has a set of values that serves as the starting point for its collective endeavor to construct its indispensable legal corpus. This was the point of departure in Chapter 3, and once it is recognized that an Islamic society has quite distinct elements in its set of values as compared to other societies, the rest of the analysis as presented in that chapter becomes relevant, with the proviso that an Islamic economy is a market economy, a subject to which we will turn in the next chapter.

Here what we do need to recall from Chapter 3 is how the idea of self-interest is related to freedom of choice; which is, that freedom of choice does not make any sense without some presumption of a motivating force. Economic theory recognizes this motivating force to be self-interest; self-interest is not necessarily the same thing as selfishness; and what the contents, or scope, of that self-interest happen to be is an issue that is left entirely to the discretion of the individual. It is the individual conscience that must determine what is and is not important to him, for there need not be any compulsion here except the constraints that individuals are supposed to agree to voluntarily, if nothing else, in view of the social contract. These are the constraints that are reflected in the legal corpus of the society, which an individual is supposed to abide by. Finally, since self-interest can degenerate into selfishness, the society must institute a system of efficient enforcement of its legal corpus, or what ultimately amounts to the same thing, its structure of property rights. Once these points are understood, all we should recognize is that what the individual conscience may dictate in view of its self-interest need not be, indeed could not be, even if an outsider had so wished, restricted to only the *terrestrial concerns*.

One last thing with regard to self-interest and therefore freedom of choice in an Islamic economy needs to be cleared up before we proceed any further. The foremost economic expression of a man's self-interest is reflected in his pursuit of livelihood, for consumption presupposes production, or individual consumption requires purchasing power. The Qur'ān recognizes this expression of self-interest, indeed deems it as one of His signs; "And among His wonders is your sleep, at night or in daytime, as well as your (ability to go about in) quest of some of His bounties: in this, behold, there are messages indeed for people who (are willing to) listen!" (30:23). It then goes on to tell us; "Are you not aware that God has made subservient to you all that is in the heavens and all that is on earth, and has lavished upon you His blessings, both outward and inward? And yet, among men there is many a one that argues about God without having any knowledge (of Him), without any guidance, and without any light-giving revelation" (31:20). Man is reminded: "thus, the two great bodies of water (on earth) are not alike—the one sweet, thirst-allaying, pleasant to drink, and the other salty and bitter: and yet, from either of them do you eat fresh meat, and you take gems which you may wear; and on either thou canst see ships ploughing through the waves, so that you might (be able to) go forth in quest of some of His bounty, and thus have cause to be grateful!" (35:12). Last but not least, as though to negate the man-made restrictions on the movement (freedom) of people in search of livelihood on His earth, it declares: "He it is who has made the earth easy to live upon: go about, then, in all its regions, and partake of the sustenance which He provides: but (always bear in mind that) unto Him you shall be resurrected" (67:15). In view of man's greed and insolence, besides verses 3:180 and 8:28, the Qur'ān admonishes: "Know (O men) that the life of this world is but a play and a passing delight, and a beautiful show, and (the cause of) your boastful vying with one another, and (of your) greed for more and more riches and children" (57:20), to which the following statement adds additional meanings: "For, if God were to grant (in this world) abundant sustenance to (all of) his servants, they would behave on earth with wanton insolence: but as it is, He bestows (His grace) from on high in due measure, as He wills: for, verily, He is fully aware of (the needs of) His creatures, and sees them all" (42:27). It goes without saying that individual freedom on the production side will also be subject to the constraints imposed by the legal corpus of the society, just as was the case on the consumption side.

At this stage, we need to take stock. There is a summary statement of the subjects covered here in *sūra al-Isrāʾ*, which, according to *ḥadīth* reports, the Prophet used to recite every night in his prayer vigils. In it we find a concise summary of surpassing eloquence and beauty with regard to man's predicament in his terrestrial life, presented at one place in an integrated manner, every word of which requires a reader's acutest possible attention:

> Verily, this Qurʾān shows the way to all that is most upright, and gives the believers who do good deeds the glad tidings that theirs will be a great reward; and (it announces, too,) that We have readied grievous suffering for those who will not believe in the life to come. As it is, man (often) prays for things that are bad as if he were praying for something that is good: for man is prone to be hasty (in his judgments). And We have established the night and the day as two symbols; and thereupon We have effaced the symbol of night and set up (in its place) the light-giving symbol of the day, so that you might seek to obtain your Sustainer's bounty and be aware of the passing years and of the reckoning (that is bound to come). For clearly, most clearly, have *We spelt everything*! And every human being's destiny have We tied to his neck; and on the Day of Resurrection We shall bring forth for him a record which he will find wide open; (and he will be told:) 'Read this thy record! Sufficient is thine own self today to make out thine account!' Whoever chooses to follow the right path, follows it but for his own good; and whoever goes astray, goes astray to his own hurt; and no bearer of burdens shall be made to bear another's burden. Moreover, We would never chastise (any community for the wrong they may do) ere We have sent an apostle (to them). But when (this has been done, and) it is Our will to destroy a community, We convey Our last warning to those of its people who have lost themselves entirely in the pursuit of pleasures; and (if) they (continue to) act sinfully, the sentence (of doom) passed on the community takes effect, and We break it to smithereens. And how many a generation have We (thus) destroyed after (the time of) Noah! For, none has the like of thy Sustainer's awareness and insight into His creatures' sins. Unto him who cares for (no more than the enjoyment of) this fleeting life We readily grant thereof as much as We please, (giving) to whomever it is Our will (to give); but in the end We consign him to (the suffering of) hell, which he will have to endure disgraced and disowned! But as for those who care for the (good of the) life to come, and strive for it as it ought to be striven for, and are (true) believers withal—they are the ones whose striving finds favour (with

God)! All (of them)—these as well as those—do We freely endow with some of thy Sustainer's gifts, since thy Sustainer's giving is never confined (to one kind of man). Behold how We bestow (on earth) more bounty on some of them than on others: but (remember that) the life to come will be far higher in degree and far greater in merit and bounty. Do not set up any other deity side by side with God, lest thou find thyself disgraced and forsaken: for thy Sustainer has ordained that you shall worship none but Him. And do good unto (thy) parents. Should one of them, or both, attain to old age in thy care, never say 'ugh' to them or scold them, but (always) speak unto them with reverent speech, and spread over them humbly the wings of thy tenderness, and say: 'O my Sustainer! Bestow Thy grace upon them, even as they cherished and reared me when I was a child!' Your Sustainer is fully aware of what is in your hearts. If you are righteous, (He will forgive you your errors): for, behold, He is much-forgiving to those who turn unto Him again and again. And give his due to the near of kin, as well as to the needy and the wayfarer, but do not squander (thy sustenance) senselessly. Behold, the squanderers are, indeed, of the ilk of the satans—inasmuch as Satan has indeed proved most ungrateful to his Sustainer. And if thou (must) turn aside from those (that are in want, because thou thyself art) seeking to obtain thy Sustainer's grace and hoping for it, at least speak unto them with gentle speech. *And neither allow thy hand to remain shackled to thy neck, nor stretch it forth to the utmost limit (of thy capacity), lest thou find thyself blamed (by thy dependents), or even destitute.* Behold, thy Sustainer grants abundant sustenance, or gives it in scant measure, unto whomever He wills: verily, fully aware is He of (the needs of) His creatures, and sees them all. Hence, do not kill your children for fear of poverty: it is We who shall provide sustenance for them as well as for you. Verily, killing them is a great sin. And do not commit adultery—for, behold, it is an abomination and an evil way. And do not take any human being's life—(the life) which God has willed to be sacred—otherwise than in (the pursuit of) justice. Hence, if anyone has been slain wrongfully, We have empowered the defenders of his rights (to exact a just retribution); but even so, let him not exceed the bounds of equity in (retributive) killing. (And as far him who has been slain wrongfully—) behold, he is indeed succoured (by God)! And do not touch the substance of an orphan, save to improve it, before he comes of age. And be true to every promise—for, verily, (on Judgment Day) you will be called to account for every promise which you have made! And give full measure whenever you measure, and weigh with balance that is true: this will be (for your own) good, and best in the end. And never concern thyself with anything of which thou hast no knowledge: verily (thy) hearing and sight and heart—all of them—will be called to account for it (on Judgment Day)! And walk not on earth with haughty self-conceit: for, verily, thou canst never rend the earth asunder, nor canst thou ever grow as tall as the mountains (17:9–37, emphasis added).

And with that, in light of the close inter-connection between the characteristics discussed so far, we may sum up as follows:

1. Private property is not only permitted, it is sanctified, both in the Qurʾān and the *ḥadīth* literature. It clearly becomes indispensable in view of the foregoing summary where man is exhorted to spend, including spending on charity, in such a way as not to become destitute tomorrow. Communal ownership is recommended for certain forms of property in the *ḥadīth* reports. The institution of *waqf* property evolved very early on in Islamic society with a view to discharging *farāʾiḍ al-kifāya* (which is in need of revival now); and public ownership, where the rights of exclusion are vested with the government, unlike communal property, may be instituted in view of public interest.
2. Property ownership is a precondition for freedom of choice in the economic sphere, and this freedom cannot be absolute. First and foremost, it is subject to Divine laws, and thereafter to the collective man's considerable leeway to curtail individual freedoms in view of societal contingencies (public interest), or in view of the imperatives of social contract. The overall structure of property rights will therefore reflect the explicit prohibitions of Qurʾān as well as what is deemed good along with what is considered as bad, what may be called the *nahīyāt* (prohibitions), but these additional elements cannot be considered equal to the explicit injunctions, and are subject to change and revision in light of changing circumstances. Furthermore, these additional elements ought not infringe on the individual domain of *iḥsān*. The general rule is that individual initiative and responsibility are given priority even as the discharging of the *farāʾiḍ al-kifāya* would require.
3. The property rights enshrined in the legal corpus must be effectively enforced, as is implied in the Qurʾānic exhortation, addressed in its proverbial style to man as such, in 4:59, with a view to institute justice at the societal level on the basis of equal treatment before the law of all citizens regardless of their position or power. In light of the emphasis on individual responsibility, the system of governance must be as decentralized as possible, thereby making the individual functionaries fully responsible for their actions within the purview of the legal corpus. The issue of effective enforcement simply cannot be neglected, for it is absolutely clear that lack of effective enforcement itself amounts to injustice. Besides, lack of

effective enforcement gives rise to a cascading effect whereby, over time, enforcement starts becoming increasingly difficult. This point has been discussed in Chapter 3.

It is in the light of the Qur'ānic perspective on individual economic freedoms, supplemented by the *ḥadīth* reports, and the foregoing stock-taking summary, that we are obliged to articulate individual economic behavior in an Islamic economy. At more than one place in the previous chapters it has been emphasized that these freedoms could not possibly be absolute for they are necessarily circumscribed by the legal corpus of the society. In an Islamic economy, as long as a Muslim abides by the constraints so imposed, he is free to do the best for himself, be it utility maximization or profit maximization within the limits imposed by his budget constraint. This is precisely what economic theory assumes without explicitly stating that the sphere of freedoms is constrained by the legal corpus of the society. It simply takes that for granted. And if someone wishes to read into that a sanctioning of limitless freedom, that clearly is a matter of individual choice, or rather it is itself a matter of freedom of choice. At any rate, it is in light of the foregoing discourse that we may evaluate some of the contributions of the Islamic economists to the so-called theory of consumer behavior and the theory of production in an Islamic perspective to provide the reader an opportunity to see for himself/herself to what extent these writings do justice to the fundamental Islamic imperatives relating to these issues, and which for a Muslim are totally inviolable.

Consumer Theory in Islamic Economics

In light of my remarks earlier in this chapter, I have here tried to leave out the rhetorical content in the writings of the Islamic economists to focus more on the substantive elements—though often this not easy to do—in what is articulated to be the conceptual framework for Islamic consumer theory. I have also kept an eye open for unarticulated suppositions, or presumptions, in these theoretical formulations, for often an understanding of these is more enlightening than what is explicitly stated. Once that is done, we will resume our discourse relating to the characteristics of an Islamic economy to focus on the remaining two elements in the next chapter.

The first thing one notes in these writings is a penchant for new terminology, a part of an effort to Islamize knowledge, in this case economics. Consider, for instance, Khan (1992) discarding the term utility and replacing it with *maṣlaḥa* in his effort to construct a theory of consumer behavior in an Islamic economy. The word *maṣlaḥa* can be translated as public interest, and is a well established term in *fiqh* denoting the same. We have previously encountered this term in Chapter 5 (n. 17) as a principle of *ijtihād*, i.e. *maṣāliḥ* (plural of *maṣlaḥa*) *mursala*, and it was on the basis of these that the *maqāṣid al-Sharīʿa* were constructed, as noted there. Thus the objective of consumer behavior is supposed to be public interest. But, then, that is not exactly how Khan follows through. He begins by saying that "*maṣlaḥa* is a more objective concept than the concept of utility to analyse the behaviour of economic agents. Analytically, the concept of *maṣlaḥa* can be more easily manipulated than the concept of utility," but why it is to be manipulated and by whom, he does not say. Then, in the next sentence he tells us: "Though *maṣlaḥa* will remain to be a subjective concept like utility, its subjectivity does not make it as vague as utility," and just what he means by not as vague as utility, he does not explain. But then, in the next sentence, he contradicts himself by saying: "Some of the superiorities of the concept of *maṣlaḥa* are" that it "is subjective in the sense that an individual will himself be the best judge to determine whether a good or service has *maṣlaḥa* for him," and again contradicts himself by continuing, "But the criterion to determine *maṣlaḥa* is not left to the subjective whims as it is in the case of utility." He moves on to enlighten the reader that different consumers may use different criteria to determine the utility of goods, and thereafter continues, "This is not so in the case of *maṣlaḥa*. The criteria are fixed for every one and the decision has to be made on the basis of these criteria." These criteria are supposed to be the same as *maqāṣid-al-Sharīʿa*, which he translates as "the welfare of human beings". What he is therefore implying is that somehow the concept of utility is counter to such welfare!

In the second "superiority" he notes that, "The individual *maṣlaḥa* will be consistent with social *maṣlaḥa*, unlike individual utility which will often be in conflict with social utility...For example, alcohol may have utility for several people because they like to drink it but it may not have social utility." When he uses the term utility, one would surmise that he is not talking about it in just an Islamic economy, but then he does not tell us why something which would have utility for individuals would not have social utility in such a society. And this leaving aside the fact that drugs have individual utility but are not recognized as having social utility in Western societies. The third "superiority" is that, "The concept of *maṣlaḥa* underlies all economic activities in a society. Thus, it is the objective underlying consumption as well as production and exchange [as though consumption and production occurred without exchange]. This is unlike conventional theory where utility is the objective of consumption and profit is the objective of production" (Khan, 1992, all citations are from p. 175, bracketed remarks are mine). This quite clearly betrays ignorance of the economic theory's use of profits as an objectively measurable proxy for utility. Furthermore, what he is then trying to imply is that there would be no profit maximization in an Islamic economy without any realization that the maximum profits could indeed be zero, or even negative, a subject to which we will return. As to the falsity of his last "superiority" that it is not possible to make interpersonal comparisons of utility, but that such comparisons are possible in the case of *maṣlaḥa*, the reader is referred to the coverage of this subject in Chapter 2. Incidentally, the discussion in that chapter also provides another example of the penchant for new terminology when it notes the replacement of the well established term "wants" with "needs" by Islamic economics. There the difficulty of distinguishing between wants and needs is discussed at some length. Khan insists on using "needs" but then informs the reader that there are actually "three levels" of needs: first, where the five elements of the *maqāṣid al-Sharīʿa* are "barely protected"; second, that protection is "complemented to reinforce their protection"; and finally "the five elements are either ameliorated or refined" (1992, p. 74). Whatever is then left of the distinction between needs and wants is left for the reader to judge. Besides, Khan gives the impression that the conventional consumer theory operates in a property rights vacuum.

A whole class of problems in the writings of the Islamic economists relates to a lack of appreciation of the essential background of economic discourse provided by a society's structure of property rights. This, in turn, means confusion with regard to the institution of government, for the existence of a structure of property rights is predicated on the existence of a government. If in one place in these writings one is forced to presume the existence of government in the background, for otherwise the argument would not make any sense, in other places the argument would seem to be broached in a governmental vacuum. If conventional economics takes it for granted that there is a given structure of property rights which is effectively enforced, an issue discussed at some length in Chapter 3, the Islamic economists take that presumption to mean an absence of such a structure, and thus an absence of the corresponding legal corpus. It is in this perspective that freedom of choice is understood to be absolute, and it is assumed that economics accepts this perspective, and therefore what economics does is quite dangerous. Reading between the lines, one cannot help feeling that Islamic economists seem to credit themselves for injecting a dose of order in an otherwise chaotic situation, if not a state of total anarchy, by placing an emphasis on fiqhnomics. Instead of stating the obvious, that the legal corpus of an Islamic society will necessarily be different from that of another society that does not subscribe to the same prohibitions, the Islamic economists create their own phantoms in order to destroy them, and thereby claim credit where otherwise no credit would be due. (Indeed Islamic economists thrive on the phantoms of their own making alongside the penchant for new terminology). It is only in light of these remarks that we can understand why every writer on the subject of consumer theory in an Islamic perspective emphasizes that the demand for alcohol and pork will be (or ought to be?—see n. 25) zero,[23] as though these could be deemed permissible by the legal corpus of such a society, or alternatively as though these societies were supposed to operate under an enforcement vacuum, or for that matter in a governmental vacuum, and therefore a pleading of the case is required on their part to convince those who would otherwise not abide by the Qurʾānic prohibitions.

But is it actually true that these writings presume an absence of government in a consistent manner to persuade the black sheep of an Islamic society to voluntarily abide by the Qurʾānic prohibitions?[24]

[23] See, for instance, Siddiqi (1979), and Kahf (1978).

[24] Indeed the Qurʾānic exhortations, apart from a few specific injunctions, are in the form of general moral precepts that are meant to appeal to the individual conscience. Timur Kuran (1986, 1989) takes up this subject, and rightly points out that even for the most devoted person it may not be easy to figure out what for instance a fair price or a fair wage rate may be (1989, p. 184). One would like to add, however, that social conventions on these variables may evolve over time, but then in the ever-changing social milieu that is the dominant characteristic of modern times, this difficulty may remain, because conventions take time to get established.

The answer is a definite no, for the existence of the institution of government is often quite explicitly recognized.[25] But if the existence of government is accepted, two inter-related difficulties are encountered: either it is then presumed that the government would not honor even the explicit Qur'ānic prohibitions, thus justifying their pleadings or, alternatively, if the government is assumed to abide by those prohibitions, in which case one would take it for granted that such prohibitions will be part of the legal corpus that will be effectively enforced,

---

[25] It is another matter that some of the writers try to avoid the word government and substitute the word state, presumably because of the difficulties associated with articulating an acceptable form of Islamic government. Some of them actually go some length to avoid the word 'government'. Witness the following: "These (the enforcement institutions) are established to force the individuals to refrain from activities that can create social or economic disorder in the society. Individual freedom is not allowed to disturb the peace and order of society [as though other societies encourage such behavior]. Such institutions are mainly state institutions [so there would also be non-state institutions to enforce prohibitions], which can intervene in the following activities of consumers in an Islamic economy: 1) consumption of prohibited goods, which amounts to violating the law and order of the society; 2) conspicuous consumption activities, which create a state of unrest, emotions of jealousy, depravity in the society; 3) israf or excessive propensity to consume...; 4) gross deviant or inconsistent behaviour from the point of view of Islamic principles, such as spending the bulk of the budget on the *taḥsīniyyāt* [recall his classification of "needs" as noted earlier, and note that those are to be prohibited now by someone who will figure out that the "bulk" of expenditure is going towards them] and ignoring the *darūriyyāt* [necessities; so someone else would know better as to what the necessities of a consumer are, but then why would somebody ignore his *darūriyyāt*, he does not explain]," and goes on to add that "non-market institutions thus have to play an important role, along with market institutions, in an Islamic economy" (Khan, 1992, p. 180). What is troubling is the way he proposes extra-governmental institutions to enforce prohibitions. He does not bother to tell us why governments, if I may use that word, within governments would be needed, and under what *fiqh* rule/s these would be sanctioned. No wonder he hesitates to use the word government, and instead uses the word state as though as a state could exist without a government. At any rate, this betrays his mistrust of government, something I take up next in this chapter. In another example of such a diatribe, Kahf (1978) extrapolates the *fiqh* position with regard to those who are mentally infirm and concludes his theory of consumer behavior in an Islamic economy by saying: "An important characteristic of Islam is that it not only changes the values and habits of people but also provides the necessary legislative framework to support and sustain these ideals and prevent their misuse. This feature of Islam also has its applicability to the case of the extravagant or the profligate. In Islamic jurisprudence, such a person would be restricted and, when appropriate, precluded and debarred from administering his own properties. In the eyes of Shari'ah (Islamic law), he would be treated as a *minor* and someone else would be assigned to administer his property on his behalf" (emphasis mine). Leaving aside his totally unwarranted extrapolation of the ambit of Sharī'a, how he would chose those members of the society who are "the extravagant or the profligate" to confine them to someone else's care is anybody's guess, for he has nothing to say on the issue.

then inclusion of such explicit prohibitions in economic discourse leaves the impression that those explicit prohibitions are conceivably the only ones that could be deemed as illegal, and thus excluded from the consumption basket, in such societies.

And beyond that, when they enter the domain of fiqhnomics, the Islamic economists have trouble confining themselves to what falls in the domain of enforceable *fiqh*, and invariably end up extending the scope of their coverage to encompass what falls in the personal domain relating to *iḥsān* (for one, recall the example of Prophetic use of toothpicks in the previous chapter [n. 10], and then the fulminations of an Islamic economist reported in the preceding footnote). This may be a reflection of the influence of *fiqh*, since the area of personal behavior does fall within the ambit of *fiqh*, but then such would blur the distinction between Islamic economics and *fiqh*. Further, a reader has trouble figuring out whether the discourse falls within the purview of positive economics or normative economics. Although it is not stated in so many words, it appears, as far as one can discern, that Islamic economists consider such a distinction to be irrelevant.[26] Should one draw the conclusion, therefore, that there is no room for the so-called positive economic analysis in Islamic economics? Later, this question is explored at some length. Here we note that these are some, and only some, of the difficulties encountered in the writings in just one area of Islamic economics. I have by no means tried to be exhaustive in reviewing the economic works cited here. Besides conceptual problems, these are also riddled with analytical ones, and focusing on all those difficulties will, I feel, unnecessarily occupy us for too long. Interested readers can always consult those writings on their own account.[27]

But there is one analytical problem, which is also related to the question just raised, that must be dealt with, and although this problem has previously been discussed in Chapter 2, I feel that it is worth dilating on it in the present context, for doing so now will also help

[26] It is interesting to note that at the end of the reprint of Khan's (1992) article cited in the text, the editors felt compelled to add the following note of their own to support the assertions noted in the preceding footnote: "It may be helpful to new students of Islamic economics to attempt to understand that the gap between the positive and the normative in an Islamic society will be minimized if 'what is' does not deviate far from 'what ought to be'"; see Sayyid Tahir et al. (eds.) (1992), p. 80. I return to this question a little later in this chapter.

[27] Some of these difficulties are taken up by Ausaf Ahmad (1992).

us in all subsequent encounters with Islamic economics. This difficulty has to do with the use of economic models by Islamic economists. Islamic economists mostly prefer the partial equilibrium models, and even there the norm is the use of diagrammatic models that obviously impose severe restrictions on the number of variables that can be accommodated. There is nothing wrong with this procedure; indeed it offers a number of advantages such as simplicity and pedagogical convenience, etc., provided one always keeps an eye open to the *ceteris paribus* nature of the explanation. This, however, is often forgotten. As a result, when they attempt to analyze the influence of more than one independent variable in such models, and get lost because they were unable to track the results, this weakness is attributed to economics, and quite often they have trouble visualizing the good use to which the *ceteris paribus* assumption can be put. This difficulty is particularly noticeable in their formulations of the theory of consumer behavior, and therefore in their discussion about the law of demand.

Consider the issue of values held by a society (or members of a society), and particularly the issue of altruism and therefore charity, and how this may be, and actually is, incorporated in consumer theory. The law of demand is stipulated under the *ceteris paribus* assumption where one of the variables thrown in the *ceteris paribus* bag is "tastes." This much is often recognized, but then the variable tastes is assigned an arbitrary and ad hoc interpretation without it being realized that the entire set of values held by a consumer, be these religious, cultural, aesthetic or anything else, is reflected in this one variable. Indeed the variable tastes is a catch-all variable, as is noted in Chapter 3. Furthermore, it is often not realized that consumption can be viewed as a function of purchasing power, i.e. disposable income and not income, and the wedge between income and disposable income may arise not only because of direct taxes but also voluntary surrender of some income under charity, and the individuals often do not like to quantify the rewards that are associated with their charity. Indeed, even a heathen would not like to put cent and dollar values on such acts, and a believer only knows that he is ordained to offer charity, and that the reward that he may get may well be beyond his wildest imaginings, for, as the Qurʾān says, "no eye can behold what is in store for the believers in the hereafter". The Islamic economists have trouble realizing that the postulate of utility maximization is subject to a budget constraint, and this budget constraint does not necessarily need to be specified in terms of total income; indeed in the presence of income taxes it is conventionally specified in terms of disposable income.

Let us look, for instance, at the contradictions in Nejatullah Siddiqi (1992), one of the main exponents of Islamic economics: "Though the conventional technique of focusing at the margin is helpful and the idea of substitution can be retained for commodities satisfying basic needs, generalized use of the utility analysis (including its indifference curve version) is not very helpful. It fails to take hierarchy of needs into consideration and ignores other factors influencing choice, *apart from the price changes*. Nevertheless, the notions of price elasticity of demand and income elasticity of demand are useful and helpful in analysis" (p. 21, emphasis added). Immediately before this, in the context of "Consumer Behaviour and Hierarchy in Human Needs" he begins by saying, "Given purchasing power and facing a market with goods and services available at specific prices, how does the consumer decide what to purchase and how much of it to purchase? It is reasonable to assume that the consumer will first try to satisfy his basic needs for food, clothing, shelter, medical care, education, transportation, etc. He will try to fulfill these needs for himself as well as his family and other dependent, if any. The quality and quantity of these purchases is determined, over a period of time, by habit and customary level of living (which in its turn is determined by the individual's level of income relative to the prices of goods concerned and by the social norms)." One may be forgiven if one thought that in this latter quotation he is articulating the conventional theory of consumer behavior, for what he says could easily come from some Principles textbook. But that is not what Siddiqi means.

He is actually trying to enunciate something new, something novel as far as conventional consumer theory is concerned, and something that he, as an Islamic economist, was offering to the world. For him, the conventional economics' position is represented by the first quotation. There, he begins by asserting that the conventional analysis fails to take the hierarchy of needs into consideration, and exclusively focuses on price changes, but then in the very next sentence he approves of the notion of the income elasticity of demand apart from the price elasticity of demand. So income is now another determinant of demand, but then where is his understanding of the conventional analysis defining goods as necessities versus luxuries on the basis of the "useful" concept of income elasticity being less or greater than one to satisfy his hierarchy requirements? Indeed, one could, if one so wished, classify goods and services in an endless array by using the coefficient of the income elasticity of demand, instead of the three that Islamic economists, including Siddiqi, argue for by following Shāṭibī (d. 790 H), and Khan could then go ahead and banish some, or many, goods from consumer preferences that are offensive to him, on the basis of some cut-off in income elasticity of demand through a government decree, or perhaps through some extra-government enforcement institutions of his likings (see n. 25).[28] And, this is just the beginning of the problems as far as Siddiqi's exposition is concerned.

One would think that he is trying to underline the "tastes" factor when he mentions habits and customary level of living in the second quotation, for earlier on in the paper, while commenting on the *ceteris paribus* tool used in conventional economic analysis, he writes, "Ceteris paribus, or 'assuming other factors to be constant' is a sensible way of tracing the impact of change in any one of the numerous factors likely to affect (sic) a situation. If we want to study a consumer's response to fall in price of a commodity he is interested in purchasing, we assume his income, his taste, and prices of related commodities to be constant... This method can be applied without any risk provided we keep remembering what factors are to be held constant, including the ones ignored by conventional economics" (p. 6). So what are we now supposed to make of his statement that the conventional analysis ignores other factors influencing choice apart from price changes? And what, in his view, are the factors ignored by the conventional economics? One such factor, according to him, is "need of others for the same commodity," and thus we are back to altruism, but this time in the form of "the same commodity." Siddiqi does not realize that economics is quite capable of handling altruism—a subject covered in Chapter 2—and charity, at any rate, is not the monopoly of any one system of morals. And if he does not wish to understand that the variable tastes is indeed used in a much

[28] One would sympathize with Shāṭibī (d. 790 H) who would have scarcely imagined that his idea of *taḥsīniyyāt*, literally the embellishments of life (the word is derived from the root ḥ-s-n (good) and thus related to *uswa al-ḥasan* referred to earlier), inspired by the Qur'ānic "good things of life," would be misused in this manner.

broader sense in economics than he recognizes, by interpreting it as simply covering changing fads and fashions, then that is entirely up to him, but it certainly is not a charge that he could legitimately level against economics.

As far as economics is concerned, it would gladly accommodate his concern by drawing a demand curve based on the disposable income before charity, and then happily conclude that a favorable change in taste for charity, *ceteris paribus*, would lead to an increase in demand for the good under consideration to reflect a concern for the need of others for the same commodity. As a result, if income is assumed to be given, demand for some other goods will decrease, presumably the ones he would classify as luxuries, and this is precisely what he would have wanted to see accomplished by his Islamic economics. One can also see that if the good under consideration was what he would regard as a luxury, and therefore the one that his consumer would not wish to offer in charity, its demand, *ceteris paribus*, would decrease as a result of a favorable change in tastes for charity. The result will be a transfer of purchasing power towards goods deemed suitable for charitable purposes, and thus their demand will increase, this time irrespective of whether the transfers are effected through cash payments or payments in kind.[29] The end result is the same, that is, a decrease in demand for luxuries and an increase in the demand for what he would regard as "needs." Indeed, he could go ahead and classify different goods as luxuries and needs on the basis of whether the coefficient of the charitable expenditures turned out to be negative or positive, and he could calculate the corresponding coefficients of the elasticity if he so wished. But it is at that stage that he will have to squarely confront the real issue; the issue of which expenditures are to be reckoned charitable and which ones not, in the context of Islam's broad conceptualization of charity as discussed earlier in this chapter.

For its part, economics was not content to let matters stand at that, and went ahead to explore the issue of optimal level of charity (Hochman and Rodgers, 1969), and from there to optimal level of voluntary (or private, in contrast to publicly administered) charity to argue that for the Cobb-Douglas form of utility function (inter-dependent, of

[29] At this stage, in light of our discussion here, a reader may like to skip back to Chapter 2, especially n. 2, to review Mannan's thoughts about the issue at hand.

course) used in that analysis, the level of charity will fall short of the Pareto optimum level primarily because charity is a pure public good, subject to the well-known free rider problem (Warr, 1982). Thus the conclusion, and all Muslims including Siddiqi will be happy to note, that the situation needs to be rectified through a program of compulsory (public) charity, or *zakāh*, provided of course that he is comfortable with the idea of Pareto optimum.

Siddiqi then moves on to inform us that, "The assumption that the consumer seeks to maximize utility or satisfaction implies that all goods and services have a common denominator called utility or satisfaction which can be measured or at least compared with one another. The idea is not acceptable in view of the hierarchy of human needs and the fact that the same commodity may serve a number of needs. This makes a generalized analysis of consumer equilibrium impossible. But it is not necessary to do so to arrive at the demand curve or to study changes in consumer's choice in response to changes in prices and income, which is what is actually needed in analysis of consumer behaviour. Conventional analysis gives an allusion (sic) of rigour and generality which have no basis in reality and divert attention from the real problems" (p. 21).[30] In absence of any elaboration on these issues, it is not easy to work out what Siddiqi is trying to say; he points to a number of issues, and it is unclear whether he is objecting to the notion of utility or satisfaction, or its measurability, or that these satisfactions are assumed to be comparable, or that a particular good may provide satisfaction in a variety of ways, his "number of needs." In view of his statement, "the consumer will first try to satisfy his basic needs," it would seem that he is not objecting to the idea of utility or satisfaction, but feels uncomfortable with measurement of these satisfactions, for that is what would be required for comparisons as well as aggregation when one good serves a variety of needs. But, then, it is surprising that he says all this is not necessary "to arrive at the demand curve" without explaining how that would then be done, for plainly it would not be possible without appealing to the law of diminishing marginal utility. It may be kept

[30] Siddiqi does not like the idea of generalizing, and that is perhaps why he rejects the general equilibrium analysis, for at another place in the same article, he writes, "the concept of the circular flow of economic life [he means circular flow of income] involves the idea of general equilibrium which is hardly admissible" [he means in Islamic economics], (1992, p. 8).

in mind that the use of the indifference curve analysis to derive the demand curve does not vitiate the law of diminishing marginal utility, for the convexity of the indifference curves incorporates that law in the analysis. And one would hope that he does not take a pedagogical device, which the indifference curve analysis is, too literally, and worry too much about its inability to handle two goods that are perfect substitutes, in which case the indifference curves turn out to be linear (and economics then says that practically the two goods are actually one), or perfect complementaries, in which case the indifference curves turn out to be L-shaped. Once a numerare is specified (usually money, M) that the corresponding mathematical specification of the model will handle any number of goods and lead to the condition $MU_1/MU_M = P_1/P_M$ for all goods, be these substitutes or complementaries, and that the simpler indifference curve analysis leads to the same condition, $MRS_{xy} = MU_x/MU_y = P_x/P_y$ for the two goods under consideration, x and y.

So how do we resolve the riddle Siddiqi's statement poses? It is quite possible that he had something else at the back of his mind. He may actually be worried about measurement of total utility rather than marginal utility, and therefore about the measurement of the area under the demand curve where there may not be a finite vertical intercept, particularly in the case of goods that are absolute necessities. This explains his acceptance of the demand curve without having to concern himself with measurement of the total utility, or benefits, or for that matter willingness to pay for a good. In that case, what he may actually be trying to say is that such total benefits are immeasurable for the necessities as compared to luxuries, and thereby alluding to the age-old "diamond-water" paradox, a paradox that was resolved only when economics recognized the necessity of combining the supply side with the demand, to determine the equilibrium price, the price that will prevail in the market. And luckily, thanks to the market mechanism, what the consumer actually pays for a particular quantity does not have to be equal to what he would have been willing to pay—the difference between these two being the familiar consumer's surplus, a surplus that may well be immeasurable in the case of absolute necessities. If Siddiqi is concerned only with the first glass of water, and feels a sense of revolt at the possibility that the consumer will forego his glass of lifesaving water to buy a diamond, and in the process lose his life, then nobody needs to deny him his right to worry, but one obviously has a right to ask him why he thinks a consumer would do a foolish thing like that, or more appropriately, why his Islamic consumer would wish to do such a thing.

There is one other possibility that may be the cause of Siddiqi's concern with this issue, but then again this can only be surmised, for he does not say so explicitly. And this has to do with government policy. What he may be *implying* through these concerns is that government policy may not pay much attention to the necessities in contrast to the luxuries. This premise is supported by what he has to say at another place:

"These effects—the elimination of certain goods and services from the demand schedule and decrease in demand for other goods and services—will in turn have a similar effect on the goods and services that are complementary to these. It would not be unrealistic to assume that the extent of complementarity amongst this group of goods and services is much more than that in the group that constitutes the necessities of life. The abandonment of 'wine, women and gambling' as a way of life will definitely affect (sic) a whole host of other goods and services attached to this way of life. The Islamic structures [sic; he probably means strictures] against extravagance and prodigality are a case in point. They imply that the Islamic individual, while consuming many luxuries and comforts, may feel obliged to limit his consumption quantitatively. Once again, this quantitative limit would be defined in any particular circumstance by the individual's own purse, and by social conditions. If social considerations require that the national resources should be applied to these goods only to a limited extent, the individual would willingly co-operate by limiting his own consumption before the state feels it necessary to impose restrictive measures" (1979, p. 93).

Reading this reminds us of the confusions about the existence of the government and the enforcement of laws, and apart from those, now that the state (government) is there to impose the "restrictive measures," the additional confusion: yes, luxuries are permissible, but then on second thoughts they may not be, and yes, a Muslim should voluntarily restrict himself from their consumption, for otherwise the state will have to jump in to discipline him, never mind as to where the state disappeared when the explicit Qur'anic prohibitions regarding "wine, women and gambling" were being flouted.[31]

---

[31] Somebody living a comfortable life in an affluent Arab country may feel obliged to say that the permissible luxuries will depend on consumer budget and social

A similar problem arises when Zaman (1992) proposes lexicographic preferences for Islamic theory of consumer behavior. He begins with a critique of Friedman's methodology of positive economics by pointing out that there is no such thing as value-free economics, that if nothing else, the questions a researcher asks and the issues that he explores are necessarily determined by the sociocultural milieu of the researcher, and gives the impression that in an Islamic economy the preferences will be lexicographic, i.e. first things first—like the letter a coming before b—a reference to the basic needs. There are a number of problems with his line of argument. First, he fails to tell us that the idea of lexicographic preferences originated in the same sociocultural milieu that he criticizes; it was first explored by Gerard Debreu (1959). Debreu's concern was that if people did indeed have lexicographic preferences, what would be the form of mathematical utility function that would capture such preferences? In a sense, it was a purely technical problem that he attempted to tackle, but what is significant is that the question was identified for anyone to pursue. A second difficulty arises when one tries to handle such preferences in empirical estimation; this requires a very complex ordering of preferences over a typical consumption basket that may include a very large number of goods and services. The necessary informational requirements are too over-bearing. No wonder that Zaman uses two utility functions, a primary one to represent lexicographic orderings (for the so called needs), and a secondary one to represent normal preferences over and above those needs. Even that does not relieve him of the informational weight required, which obliges him to admit that "when preferences are lexicographic, it appears that some additional assumptions to the conventional ones will be required for the existence of competitive equilibrium. This has not been explored fully [he means in his paper]" (p. 88). But the procedure of introducing two utility functions solves fewer problems than the complications it gives rise to. For one, how to handle altruism, or charity, in the primary function, which was to represent the

circumstances. All that is nice, but what exactly is an Islamic state, and where do its boundaries begin and where do they end from an Islamic point of view? And even if one accepts the idea of nation states, what about the historically new phenomenon of imposing restrictions on the movement of the believers who would wish to search for God's bounty on God's earth as per the Qur'ān? In a sense, the passage cited above reveals Siddiqi's narrow concern (wine, women and gambling), and as long as that concern is addressed, preferably through voluntary abandonment, everything else is fine.

predicament of the poor; he knew they may also undertake charity, although he feels that it is "a characteristic of basic needs that concern for others arises only after their fulfillment" (p. 86). As a result, he ends up introducing two forms of altruism, apparent and true, the latter relating to the primary utility function, and the former to the secondary one. The altruism relating to the primary utility function, he feels, vitiates utility maximization, because it is motivated by "expected rewards in the hereafter." His suggestion: "Several technical and methodological difficulties arise if we permit non-maximizing behaviour by consumers. For this reason, it is recommended that we ignore this possibility of altruism, at least in the initial phases of our analysis. We believe that this will cause no serious distortion since it is likely that most altruistic behaviour can be adequately modelled by supposing it is only apparently altruistic" (p. 87).

Unfortunately, his treatment of apparent altruism is not devoid of problems, at least in the conceptual if not in the practical sense. Leaving aside the connotation that such behavior is not motivated by a reward in the hereafter, it is supposed to be incorporated in the utility function as an externality. Similarly, he treats envy and conspicuous consumption as externalities. This obviously goes against the well-established definition of the term externality, which denotes a situation where benefits or costs remain external to the market, i.e. they are not reckoned in the market determined prices. I have not seen anybody referring to the "bandwagon" and "snob" effects as externalities. After all, Zaman has "*keeping up* with the Joneses" in mind and not just *observing* them enviously without following through with conspicuous consumption. And how is altruism to be treated as an externality? A pure public good, subject to the well-known free rider problem, yes, as we saw earlier but the externality conceptualization is inappropriate to say the least for in his analysis those who end up with what he calls a "warm glow" inside them actually pay for that warm glow.

Furthermore, how do we determine which goods are to be included in the primary and which in the secondary utility function for each and every consumer, both spatially and temporally? And finally, how do we handle the lexicographic orderings when we leave his deliberately selected two-good—bread, diamond—diagrammatic model (after all, all his axioms are stated in impeccable mathematical jargon), and introduce a large number of goods that may satisfy the basic needs. Imagine, as would be required in such orderings, a situation where one unit of bread could not be compensated for by an infinite quantity of rice in a consumer's preference orderings. A consumer theory could not be confined to the pedagogical device that the two-dimensional diagrammatic models happen to be. The large number of goods that an economy ends up producing in response to consumer preferences is what a consumer theory must contend with. Can we interpret his primary function to be defined over some composite commodity to represent a certain minimum standard of living? Perhaps yes, but in that case it becomes a question of income distribution rather than a subject of consumer theory, and reduces to the well-known argument for a redistribution of income, but in a fairly circuitous manner. It may be useful to keep in mind that following upon his articulation, and taking a cue from him, the lexicographic orderings have been used by some as though these represented some sort of well-defined basket of goods in the social orderings of a society to justify massive intervention, governmental or extra-governmental, in an Islamic economy, examples of which we have encountered. Be that as it may, one can always enjoy his conclusion that "we are firmly convinced that current microeconomic theory is a dead end (for both Muslims and non-Muslims) and salvation lies along the directions indicated" (p. 89).

Lastly, the entire discourse on Islamic economics is underwritten by a split of total expenditures between "this-worldly" and "other-worldly." Thus, we observe the dichotomy between religious (pertaining to *dīn*) and secular (pertaining to *dunyā*) working its way through into Islamic economics, whereby Islamic economists have not just been content to emphasize charity but have felt that an analytical split must be introduced between these two varieties of expenditure. In so doing, they end up taking a somewhat more restricted view of charity than is actually warranted by its conceptualization as it emerges out of the Qur'ān and the *ḥadīth* literature. In that conceptualization, expenditures on the immediate family, indeed even personal expenditures according to the *ḥadīth* report cited, are considered to be a part of charity. In light of this perspective, one wonders why the Islamic economists feel it necessary to introduce the analytical distinction between this-worldly and that-worldly expenditures, and how they would handle this problem when it comes, if ever, to empirical estimation of those expenditures.

It may well be that such a split is motivated by the *fiqh* (or legal) use of the term *zakāh*, where the term is reserved for compulsory charity, unlike its broader meaning in some Qur'ānic passages where it denotes charity in general, hence the title *Kitāb al-zakāh* used for the chapters on general charity in all canonical collections of *ḥadīth* reports (see n. 19). If that is the case, and I am not saying it necessarily is, then it amounts to comparing apples with oranges, for one is a tax—and never mind that often this tax has been paid privately and thus voluntarily by the faithful—and the other is a voluntary charity that falls in the domain of *iḥsān*, and is not therefore legally enforceable. Beyond paying his taxes, and recognizing that he is enjoined to be charitable in a very broad perspective, a Muslim has all the freedom to pursue what he perceives to be his self-interest (but not selfishness, it may be noted), and nobody needs to assume that his understanding of his own self-interest is necessarily confined to hedonism or restricted to his terrestrial existence only. All he needs to know is that if he follows the code of conduct enunciated in the *Sharīʿa* faithfully and in all sincerity, he will be blessed in the hereafter with rewards that are not quite quantifiable in earthly terms. In the mean time, the Islamic economists can follow their own fancies in quantifying these rewards, and in constructing models of charity; after all they have a freedom that nobody needs deny them.[32] Incidentally, once the Qurʾān and *ḥadīth* perspective on a Muslim's freedom of choice is understood, the entire argument about the wide gulf between economic rationality, whether bounded or not, and Islamic rationality loses its force.

In the foregoing assessment of the new paradigm that Islamic economics is supposed to be, I have confined myself to only a few cases to provide a flavor of the difficulties faced in trying to construct a coherent and consistent outline of this new paradigm in the context of the foundations on which this structure is supposed to be built. I have by no means tried to be exhaustive even in the elements of the

[32] With regard to quantification, we read the following in Kahf (1978), "Islam associates belief in the Day of Judgment and the life in the hereafter inextricably with the belief in Allah (SWT). This extends the Muslim's time horizon beyond death. Life before death and life after death are closely interrelated in a sequential manner. This has two effects as far as consumer behaviour is concerned. First the outcome a choice of action is composed of two parts, its immediate effect in this life and its effect in the life to come. Therefore, the utility [whatever happened to his obsession with the term *falāḥ* now] derived from such a choice is the total of the present values of these two effects," and he tells us this measurability is prompted by the Qurʾānic parable in 2:261 [note that this verse has been cited earlier in this chapter]. So now the Qurʾānic parables are to be used to estimate benefits, while Jevons was wrong in assuming that man is a pleasure and pain counting machine. As far as models of charity are concerned, Khan (1992) builds a diagrammatic one which barely spans a page, which also includes a diagram (p. 171).

outline that I have explicitly focused on, for this would require much patience and time, both on my part but more so on part of the reader that, I have felt, need not be endured. Other areas of Islamic economics will, of course, come under review in the remaining chapters, but one area that should, in principle, have been covered here relates to the supply side, namely the theory of production, which is covered in Chapter 7. In the mean time, the present discussion may be concluded by a brief reference, in the light of what has gone so far, to what Siddiqi thinks will be the basic difference between conventional and Islamic economics. He tells the reader that, "It is advisable to point out the significant differences between the above and the institutional [?] pattern assumed in the conventional textbooks [he means economics]. Four specific points can be easily emphasized: 1) a positive role for the state [but, then, how about going beyond the broader concept of state to the specifics with regard to the form of government, and in any case where does economics deny a positive role for the state]; 2) moral constraints to freedom [so, the legal corpus, and therefore, the structure of property rights that economics assumes to be given is necessarily amoral if not immoral]; 3) obligations attending upon rights [when did economics say there could be rights without corresponding responsibilities in a societal settings, or is he saying economics advocates discriminatory enforcement of property rights and now Islamic economics would correct that mistake?]; and 4) the emphasis on mutual consultation and cooperation [and all this to condemn an economics that presumes the existence of a democratic form of government—see discussion in Chapter 2—and as though economics assumed that an orderly societal system could be envisioned without cooperation]." He does not feel any contradiction when he adds that, "It may be also pointed out that despite these significant departures of our assumptions, conventional economic analysis still remains useful in view of the fact that the assumptions of private property, free enterprise, and competitions are not wholly rejected by us. They have been significantly modified" (Siddiqi, 1992, p. 4).

As far as I can see, once the penchant for new terminology is discounted, once the phantoms of their own making are eliminated, and once the rhetorical contents are washed out, not much of what is called Islamic economics survives as a distinct paradigm. But as far as Islamic economy is concerned, the substance of what I have maintained all along—which perhaps may well be what the Islamic economists try to articulate but in a rather cumbersome and round-about manner and which unnecessarily attacks and implicates the subject of what is called conventional economics—can be summed up by the following points: the fundamental values adhered to by an Islamic society and therefore the corresponding economy will obviously be different from that of any other society that does not subscribe to the same philosophy with regard to the origin and source of those values; and therefore both its legal corpus, which defines the structure of property rights, and its institutions will necessarily be different. It goes without saying that its taboos, social conventions, cultural patterns and its tastes will therefore also be different. One can also see that in such an economy, in light of those fundamental values, more emphasis will be placed on individual responsibility in general, and specifically in discharging of the *farāʾiḍ al-kifāya*, as compared to societies where the collectivistic instincts are stronger. If one feels that such differences represent a new paradigm, so be it, but then it must also be realized that there will be as many paradigms as there are societies, and indeed there may be a number of paradigms within the Islamic societies reflecting *fiqh* differences as well as cultural diversity in the Islamic realm.

In conclusion, we may note the following: one can discern that a considerable part of the disenchantment of Islamic economists with conventional economics, or rather economic paradigm, is indeed the result of equating economics with economic system, i.e. equating economics with capitalism. A similar misconception occurs in conventional economics, where market system is equated with capitalism, as pointed out in Chapter 3. It is not fair to criticize Friedman for not applying himself to the study of economic problems that may be specific to a sociocultural milieu different than his own. Economics, or rather positive economics—for without an adjective, that is what it denotes—merely represents an analytical toolkit, a rich one I may add, that has evolved over a long period of time as a result of efforts expended by a very large number of sharp minds whose sincerity we do not need to question without providing specific reasons. These efforts have provided us with a body of principles, laws, and theorems, each exhibiting a logical internal consistency. It is this toolkit that is used to understand "what is" before the decision is made to change things so they conform to what they "ought to be." If this body is to be rejected then Islamic economists must convincingly show why that needs to be done, providing logical argument grounded in the original sources of Islam that would warrant such rejection, and not through some careless and misdirected *ijtihād* efforts grounded, consciously or otherwise, in some defunct socialistic ideology, or influenced by the controversies of the same discourse they wish to reject. They need to go much beyond the current offerings that are masked in an unstitched cloth of new terminology, that reveals more than it embellishes, and are propped up by arguments that are heavy on a rhetoric that pays little regard to reason and logic (this is a recipe that repels serious students of economics even when they are committed to Islamic values). For instance, and just for instance, they will have to show why the law of diminishing marginal utility (the foundation of the law of demand) would be false in an Islamic society, or why the law of diminishing returns (the basis of the law of supply) would be inapplicable for a process of production used by Islamic economies, or why the Coase theorem would be invalid in a structure of property rights specification based on an Islamic system of values, or for that matter, how the riddle posed by Arrow's impossibility theorem would be handled in an Islamic form of democratic government, if they ever go beyond merely enunciating the principle of *sūra*, and come to propose some concrete democratic institutional form for that government. We can now turn to the remaining two elements in the set of characteristics.

CHAPTER SEVEN

THE STRUCTURE OF AN ISLAMIC ECONOMY

Market Mechanism and Competition

Continuing with the coverage of the subject that began in the previous chapter, here we focus on the institutional mechanism a society must put in place to discharge the two fundamental economic functions; that is allocation and distribution. It is this institutional mechanism that, in the ultimate analysis, becomes the most visible feature of the economy, and thus determines its structure. The economies that rely on price signals to perform these functions are called market economies, for the existence of markets imply price signals in exactly the same way that the existence of prices implies the institution of market. That an Islamic economy is necessarily a market economy is actually something that would ordinarily be taken for granted, and in the light of what has been said in Chapter 3, one would not need to belabor the point any further, except to note that it will be a mixed economy. And it would also be taken for granted that the voluminous economic literature that deals with myriad issues in such an economy would become relevant for such an economy. Unfortunately a student of Islamic economics cannot proceed on those lines because of the ferment created by the Islamic economists, to claim for themselves an originality of thinking in the stale world of so-called conventional economics. Those who have created this intellectual ferment have felt obliged to question everything conventional economics has to offer, including the strongest of its theoretical propositions, those pertaining to the theory of value and the role of competition. The market mechanism is grudgingly accepted either when it is heavily overlaid by their interventionist propositions and/or the idea of competition is thrown overboard to be replaced by nothing less than what is touted as "free cooperation" among economic agents.[1]

[1] Use of such terminology requires one to contend with the idea of non-free cooperation. But Kahf, who is fond of using this term, as we will see, probably means perfect cooperation as his Islamic alternative to the unacceptable idea of perfect competition.

Given this ferment, one is obliged to provide a critical review of what is being proposed as the true Islamic alternative on these issues. This requires a brief historical perspective on markets and prices, to be followed by what conventional economics might offer on the issues raised by the Islamic economists. Although the latter is so well understood by the students of economics that it seems somewhat pedantic and thus not worth repeating, I feel that it is only when that background is looked at afresh that we are able to fully assess the contributions made by the Islamic economists. Actually this procedure is not new to this chapter. It will not be lost on the reader that this is more or less the way our discourse has progressed so far. In a sense the entire structure of this book was determined by the naivety that has been offered in the name of Islam, or rather as part and parcel of Islam.

Markets and prices have existed from time immemorial, ever since man learned to conduct exchange. Exchange implies specialization, and specialization in turn implies exchange, with the end result that the parties involved become better off. But this was not always fully understood and appreciated. No wonder that exchange has always been a matter of anxiety and concern for those who tried to understand its economic implications, at least in the heartland of economics. The basic concern has always been with the possibility of an unequal exchange, where it would appear that one party benefited at the expense of the other. And although the act of exchange was supposed to be voluntary for both parties, misgivings arose that may lead to the impression that the consent of the weak party was dictated by force of circumstances. If exchange did not appear to be equal, obviously the price at which it was concluded could not be considered fair. The idea of "just price" was debated in mediaeval times for centuries beginning with Thomas Aquinas (1225–1274), and continuing vigorously down to the times of the physiocrats. Yet what is surprising is a total lack of concern with such an idea in Islamic civilization, a civilization that was in every sense far more advanced than its Western counterpart, at least up until the time Aquinas raised the issue. It appears that the democratic spirit of Islamic culture occasioned much less concern with the idea of exploitation through prices as compared to the hierarchical civilization of Europe. But equally, it may be the result of a general perspective on prices provided by a famous *ḥadīth*, reported in both Tirmidhī and Dā'ūd on the authority of Mālik ibn Anas, according to which, when a group of people complained about an increase in price of a number of goods and requested the Prophet to fix the prices for them, the Prophet responded by saying that "prices are determined by God," for "it is He who contracts or expands the sources of livelihood," and then surprisingly added: "And I hope to meet my Sustainer in a state that no one may raise a claim of injustice against me in respect of blood or money."[2] This very clearly shows an appreciation of the role of supply in price determination, but what is interesting is how the impersonal process of price determination in the market is visualized as something coming from God, and how the Prophet shunned the idea of intervention in that process, for such an action in his view amounted to an injustice. (We will come back to both these perspectives somewhat later in this chapter).

In the next five centuries, the time during which the Islamic culture flourished, and Islamic civilization achieved its florescence, we do not see any concern with the issue in the intellectual developments that occurred during that period, the first half of which was particularly productive as far as *fiqh* is concerned. Abū Yūsuf (d. 798), one of the two prominent students of Abū Ḥanīfa, reflecting on price changes, records his commitment to the *ḥadīth* report just cited in his *Kitāb al-kharāj* (Book on tax) by saying that "it all comes from God." Then in the eleventh century, Ghazālī (d. 1111), in his treatise *Iḥyā' 'ulūm al-dīn* (Revival of religious sciences), weighs against state interference in market determined prices. Thereafter, for another three centuries, we observe the same quiet. It was only in fourteenth-century post-Crusade Damascus, undergoing the Mongol turmoil, and long after the closing of the gates of *ijtihād*, that Ibn Taymiyya (d. 1328) wrote *al-Ḥisba fī al-Islām* (Market regulation in Islam) in which he discusses the issue of monopolistic practices and proposes some sort of regulation of such prices, yet endorses non-interference by the state in absence of any evidence about monopolistic excesses. Thereafter there descended on the Islamic lands a long period of intellectual brown-out in general and a total black-out as far as economics is concerned. But during this black-out, much water passed under the bridge in Europe, especially after the second half of the eighteenth century, and not just on the subject of economics. When the Muslims, including those who dubbed themselves Islamic economists, woke up from that deep slumber, they found themselves inhabiting a landscape that had changed

---

[2] Sunan al-Tirmidhī (No. 1314) in *Kitāb al-buyū'* and Sunan Abu Dā'ūd (No. 3443, and 3444) in *Kitab al-ijāra*.

beyond their recognition—there were areas of lush growth and there were marshes, and some of these marshes were perceived to be inundated by sewage. The water had also caused deluge in some areas. They found their civilizational heritage more or less reduced to an undergrowth struggling to survive. Its survival and re-flourishing required a creative response, and not just a knee-jerk reaction. But this was not easy for a culture that viewed everything new, particularly if it had alien origins with a great degree of suspicion, and had thus for centuries resisted even the adoption of the printing press. The West's colonial onslaught, and its general animosity towards Islam, contributed to this knee-jerk reaction. Nothing good could come out of the West, as far as the upholders of the faith were concerned.

Thus it is that market mechanism was looked upon by the proponents of the new paradigm with suspicion, as though it was a Western invention, notwithstanding their own classical heritage, and notwithstanding the historical fact that the Arabs were deft traders, and the masters of sea trade for centuries, till long after their intellectual springs had run dry; and notwithstanding the fact that it was the exemplary conduct of these tradesmen that contributed to the spread of Islam, be it to the east coast of Africa, the coastal areas of the Indian subcontinent, or the Indonesian and Malaysian archipelagos. And thus it is that the Smithian resolution of the riddle relating to just price through the idea of competition, as a check on the play of self-interest, as discussed in Chapter 3, was disowned even when due recognition was accorded to the anti-competitive concerns shown by Ibn Taymiyya. This is to say that rather than accepting the idea that a policy which would promote competition by removing restrictions on trade as a solution to the monopolistic excesses, they opt for a greater reliance on state intervention, contrary to the empirical evidence about the performance of the state in most Muslim countries, an experience that does not warrant any optimism in the ability of the state to handle the complex question of intervention in market mechanism, as we will see later in this chapter. What may be noted at this stage is that a large part of the criticism of the market mechanism is motivated by the possibility of excessive profits that could be made through market transactions, a possibility that is hardly lost on economics. The Islamic economists, however, have extended the arguments relating to imperfect competition to even perfect competition, and have thus created an atmosphere of confusion for the unwary student who might take their arguments seriously. In what follows, I have used a very simple conventional model of production and exchange to put issues relating to benefits of exchange, price determination, efficiency of the market system, and governmental interference in the market mechanism, etc., in their proper perspective, to help that student judge the merit of what is being offered as an alternative.

A Model of Production and Exchange

Consider a very simple two-individuals two-goods economy comprised of a farmer and a herder occupying adjacent properties, each of whom is capable of producing either wheat or meat from the given endowment of resources (primarily land) when combined with their labor, assumed to be applied at the rate of 50 hours per week by both individuals. Assume that the technology of production is given, and further assume, for the sake of simplicity, that the opportunity cost of wheat in terms of meat, or for that matter meat in terms of wheat on the production side, is constant. This, of course, violates the law of increasing opportunity cost, but for the purpose at hand this is inconsequential. Assume that when the farmer devotes all his resources to the production of meat, the best he can do is to produce 30 kgs of meat, and if he decides to produce just wheat, the maximum amount turns out to be 100 kgs. This means that technical efficiency conditions are satisfied, and therefore both these points happen to lie on his Production Possibilities Frontier (PPF), being its end points. Other possible combinations of the two goods that he can produce are identified by his PPF as presented in Figure 3. The corresponding numbers for the herder are assumed to be 55 kgs of meat and 110 kgs of wheat, and the other possible combinations of the two goods that he can produce are identified by his PPF.[3] The two can select any combination on their respective PPFs, and in absence of any trade, that is, under a regime of autarky, they will consume whatever amounts they individually decide to produce, or rather they will produce whatever combination they would like to consume as determined by their tastes for the two goods. Under autarky, their PPFs coincide with their respective Consumption

[3] These numbers have been selected to show that even when one of the parties, in the present case the herder, has an absolute advantage in the production of both the goods, the Ricardian argument about comparative advantage remains valid. It means that if neither party enjoys absolute advantage, the following conclusions will remain equally valid.

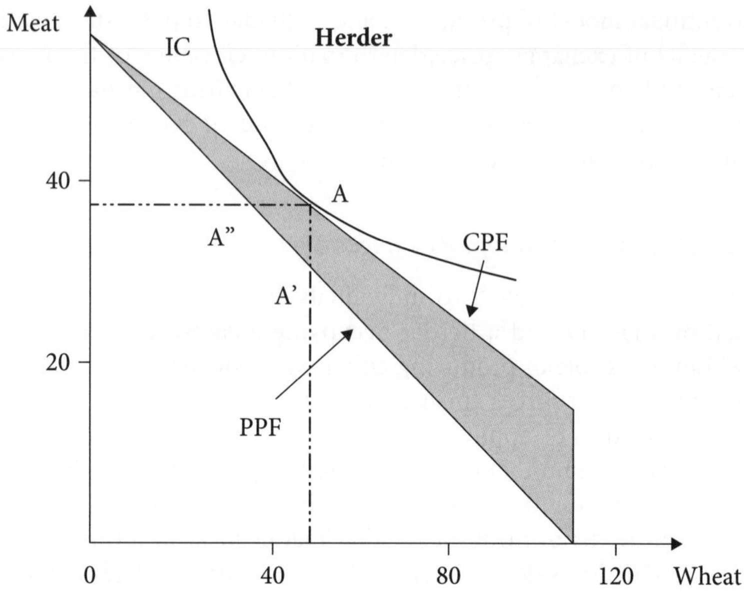
Meat
Herder
IC
40
A
A”
CPF
A’
20
PPF
0
40
80
120
Wheat

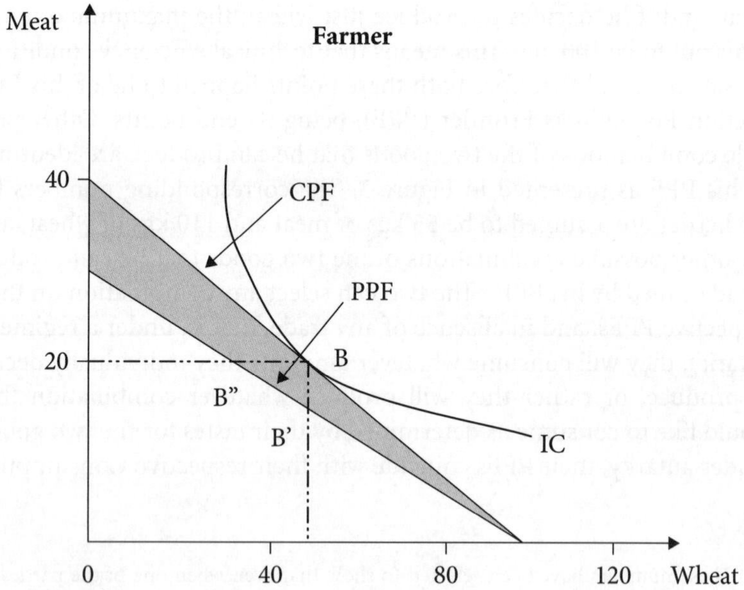
Meat
Farmer
40
CPF
PPF
20
B
B”
B’
IC
0
40
80
120
Wheat

Figure 3

Possibilities Frontiers (CPFs). The two gentlemen may live under a regime of autarky for a while, but sooner or later—sooner rather than later—they will find out the benefits of specialization and exchange, leading to each of them specializing in the production of one of the goods.

Who specializes in the production of which goods is crucially dependent upon their respective comparative advantages, which can be shown either in terms of their productivities or the opportunity cost of one of the goods in terms of the other, for each of the two individuals. Consider their productivities: the herder is more productive than the farmer in the production of both the goods, but his productivity advantage is greater in the production of meat (55/30 = 1.84) as compared to wheat (110/100 = 1.10). Therefore, he has a comparative advantage in the production of meat, and consequently the farmer has a comparative advantage, or comparatively less disadvantage, in the production of wheat. The same conclusion can be arrived at if we look at the opportunity cost of wheat in terms of meat, identified by the slopes of the two PPFs. Here we observe that the opportunity cost of 1 kg of wheat in terms of meat is lower for the farmer (0.3 kg of meat) as compared to the herder's 0.5. Whichever way we look at it, the conclusion is the same, i.e. that the herder should specialize in the production of meat, leaving the farmer to specialize in the production of wheat, and thereafter the two can trade meat and wheat to their mutual benefit. But the trading of wheat for meat, or meat for wheat, requires the existence of an exchange ratio (or the terms of trade, TOT, as used in the trade theory), a ratio which will determine how much of meat will trade for how much wheat. Once the exchange ratio is determined, the prices of the two goods will be automatically determined provided we assume the existence of a medium of exchange. For instance, if we assume the exchange ratio between wheat and meat to be 2, i.e. 2 kgs of wheat for one kg of meat, it automatically means that meat will be twice as expensive as wheat, and if the price of wheat is assumed to be $1 per kg, that of the meat will be $2 per kg. But how is the required exchange ratio, or price level, for goods determined for exchange to proceed?

Consumer theory tells us that the price level for goods is determined by the forces of supply and demand. A closer look at the supply conditions for the two goods determined by the productivity of the factors used identifies a range in which the exchange ratio must settle. We know that the farmer, whose opportunity cost of producing 1 kg of wheat is 0.3 kg of meat, will be happy to accept any amount of meat greater than 0.3 kg for 1 kg of wheat; the higher that number, the greater his benefit from trade. It goes without saying that he would not accept any amount less than 0.3 kg of meat for 1 kg of wheat, for we know that he himself can always produce that amount by foregoing 1 kg of wheat—that number happens to be his trade-off between meat and wheat on the production side. On the other hand, the herder would not like to surrender any amount greater than 0.5 kg of meat for 1 kg of wheat for exactly the same reasons. Any amount less than 0.5 kg will be acceptable to him; the smaller that amount, the better off he will be through trade. Therefore, we know that the exchange ratio (or Terms of Trade) between wheat and meat will have to settle between these two opportunity cost numbers, i. e. between 0.3 and 0.5 kg of meat for each kg of wheat.

Given the supply conditions, the price level for each good will be determined by its demand, and demand in turn is determined by the shape of the indifference curves. These shapes, in their turn, are a reflection of the tastes held by the consumers for each of the goods as compared to the other. An Arrow-Debreu process of *tâtonnement* leads to a utility maximizing equilibrium for the two individuals at points A and B respectively for the herder and the farmer with exchange ratio settling at 0.4 kg of meat for 1 kg of wheat, which implies that meat will be two and a half times more expensive than wheat. Once the exchange ratio is determined, we can construct the CPFs for the two individuals, and show that, except for the end points, those representing the actual production points under specialization—the herder producing 55 kgs of meat and the farmer producing 100 kgs of wheat—the entire CPF for each of the two individuals will lie outside their corresponding PPFs. The CPFs in Figure 3 are drawn on the assumption that the exchange ratio turns out to be 0.4 kg of meat for 1 kg of wheat, and thus the enhanced consumption possibilities are highlighted by the shaded area. One can easily visualize that this enhanced area will be larger for the farmer, the closer the exchange ratio to 0.5—actually at exactly 0.5 exchange ratio, the herder's CPF will coincide with his PPF, which means he does not derive any benefits from trade, and similar remarks can be made for the farmer when the exchange ratio is presumed to be exactly 0.3. It goes without saying that the closer the exchange ratio to 0.3, the greater is the enhancement of the herder's consumption possibilities.

Let us note some of the results of this process of specialization and exchange before proceeding any further. At point A, the herder attains a higher indifference curve as compared to any non-trade combination that he might have consumed.[4] We can measure his benefits from trade under certain assumptions about his pre-trade utility maximizing point. Normally his pre-trade utility maximizing point will lie between points A' and A" on the PPF, and therefore benefits of trade would accrue in the form of increased consumption of both the goods, but if we assume his pre-trade utility maximizing point to be A", the benefits in terms of wheat would turn out to be the distance A"A (this amount turns out be 10 kgs of wheat) or, alternatively, if his pre-trade point is assumed to be A', the benefits turn out to be the enhanced consumption of meat identified by the distance A'A (which turns out to be 4 kgs of meat, which at the market determined exchange ratio turns out to be precisely equal to 10 kgs of wheat)—call this an increase in surplus, and the question as to whether it should be reckoned as consumer's or producer's variety is immaterial in the circumstances at hand; and indeed one could call it profit if one so wished.[5] The corresponding numbers for the farmer turn out to be either 5 kgs of meat, or what amounts to the same thing, 12.5 kgs of wheat.[6]

If the benefits of trade seem to be fairly equally distributed—and it is obvious that they will be, for notice that the exchange ratio was assumed to settle mid-way between 0.3 and 0.5—then it must be noticed that this was because the tastes between meat and wheat were fairly balanced for both the consumers. A different pattern of tastes may, and indeed would, lead to a drastically different result with regard to the ensuing distribution of benefits of trade. For instance, if the indifference map of one or both the consumers is tilted towards the meat axis, giving us relatively flatter indifference curves, meat will be in greater demand, and therefore the exchange ratio will tend towards

[4] I have not considered the possibility of the indifference map being such that it leads to a corner solution. That of course, would mean that the herder likes his meat so much as compared to wheat that he consumes only meat, the only good he would produce in that situation of autarky. In this case no trade will occur. The analysis assumes that consumers prefer diversity as compared to monotony of consuming a fixed bundle of goods.

[5] At this stage of the argument, we would leave aside a number of questions that would need to be addressed, such as entry into the industry in which profits are high, or whether this increased profit may encourage technological change in the industry concerned. Once the basic issues relating to the market mechanism and competition have been sorted out, the remaining issues will automatically fall into place.

[6] These results could also be shown in the more commonly used general equilibrium model, using the famous Edgeworth diagram, even if the idea of general equilibrium is disparaged by some of the Islamic economists (see n. 28 in Chapter 5).

the lower value, i.e. 0.3, and in that case the benefits accruing to the herder will be relatively large, and vice versa if the tastes, or preferences, tilt towards wheat. There could hardly be any question as to whether such benefits are just or not, but there could be a question as to whether the resulting distribution is just or not. And this obviously depends on whether the exchange ratio is, or the prices are, considered to be just or not.

As far as Adam Smith, and therefore economics, is concerned, the answer crucially depends on the number of participants in the market. If there are a large number of herders and large number of farmers, none individually having any influence on the prices that prevail, one would not, in general, need to worry about the issue of the justness or otherwise of the prices. And if in particular circumstances one had a cause to worry, those circumstances would have to be very clearly spelled out and scrutinized. But the answer would not be as clear-cut if that condition (large numbers) was not satisfied, which is what would happen if we took the foregoing model as an accurate description of reality. In the case of small numbers, the justness of the outcome could not be taken for granted because of the possibility of strategic behavior on part of the participants. For instance, in our example, the actual exchange ratio may well be influenced by relative bargaining strengths, whatever their cause, social status, political power, etc., of the individuals, as well as the availability to only one of the individuals of information about the other's productivity and therefore opportunity cost. The two crucial issues, therefore, and thus the ones that we need to focus on, are small numbers and asymmetric information.

With this basic economic framework in place, let us proceed further and introduce government in this stylized world. This government could be conceived of as an external entity imposed on the economy, or an internal one, consisting of some member/s of the society. As far as an imposed government is concerned, such as an autocracy, benevolent or otherwise, we can hardly say much as to what the whims and fancies of such a government will lead to, although some of the points noted below may shed a little light on some of the possible scenarios. Let us therefore focus on an internal government, and assume for the sake of simplicity that there are no taxes to keep our analysis focused.[7] This internal government could be comprised of one of the two indi-

[7] Introduction of taxes is quite inconsequential as far as our results are concerned.

viduals, or both of them. In the case that one of them is deemed to be the government, and assuming there is no agreed upon constitution that lays down the rules of governance, there is no hope for the other party, the party outside the government. It will amount to being an internal dictatorship, and the results are not likely to be any different from those obtained in an imposed dictatorship. The exchange ratio will reflect the interests of the party in government. This will either lead to exploitation through an unjust price—consider the exchange ratio being set at 0.3 by the herder government, or a little above that to show a sense of benevolence—or it will lead to autarky when that ratio is set below even 0.3 under some pretext of justice; after all, the self-interest of those in governance can as easily degenerate into selfishness in exactly the same way as of those who participate in the market, as discussed in Chapter 3. The herder, who specializes in meat production, will quickly forget his own opportunity cost of producing wheat, and his sense of self-aggrandizement is likely to suggest to him that no amount of wheat can actually compensate for his efforts at producing meat. Any amount of meat that he surrenders is actually surrendered out of, in his view, a sense of charity. Similar results would obtain under the farmer government whereby the exchange ratio would turn out to be close to 0.5 if not any higher, although this latter scenario cannot be ruled out in light of the preceding remarks in the context of herder. Assume now that the government is comprised of both of them, sort of a representative government. In this case, the chances are they will always be at loggerheads as to what the right exchange ratio ought to be, and in all likelihood the end result will be autarky, each of them going his own way. In any case, there is either exploitation, or the benefits of specialization and trade are lost because of a lack of cooperation, or rather because of self-interest degenerating into selfishness, but this time in the political arena. Introduce a third party, either a herder or a farmer, and the chances of exploitation become even stronger, either because of one of them exploits not just one but two of them, or two gang up on one, depending upon who forms the government. The point is clear enough to need no further elaboration.

Now consider an internal government operating under a constitution—or a set of rules (rules of the political game)—agreed to by the members. One would surmise that one of the rules of the game would be rotating government, which may lead to an explicit rule or an implicit understanding on non-interference in the market determined exchange ratio, for we can reasonably assume that the participants would be aware of the scenario sketched above. Introduction of a third person, let us say a voter, complicates matters, for now one of the rules of the game may very well be the majority rule, and unless there is an explicit commitment to no unwarranted interference, the possibility of exploitation of the minority by the majority cannot be ruled out.[8] Large numbers in the political arena do not necessarily solve the problem, as happens in the case of markets. One must also note that what will constitute an unwarranted interference may, by itself, turn out to be a thorny issue, and cannot be settled without an appeal to the moral values held by the society. It may also be noted that the outcome may turn out to be the same if a dictator, whether internal or external, adhered to the same values, although the argument that there may be safety in large numbers remains forceful. The possibility of one "will" becoming corrupted, particularly when it has all the power at its disposal, as compared to a large number of wills, cannot be easily discounted. The apparent simplicity of these cases should not lead to the conclusion that they are not enlightening. At any rate, an Islamic government, mindful of the *ḥadīth* report cited earlier, along with the historical evidence on the confidence reposed in the market system, will have to think hard and fast, at the pain of introducing an injustice of its own, before it wields its interventionist stick. This is particularly significant in light of the redistributional alternatives that may be available to it to address any equity issues. We will return to this question later. Let us now leave this stylized world but continue with the pedagogy to consider the questions of efficiency and equity as far as the markets with large numbers of participants are concerned.

Consider the market demand and supply curves for bread (or wheat) in the Figure 4, and the resulting equilibrium established at quantity Q*, and the corresponding price, P. Given those demand and supply curves, is this the right quantity from the society's point of view? An answer to this question requires a criterion to judge the rightness or otherwise of any quantity that the market mechanism may end up producing, for the market mechanism is morally neutral, or blind, with respect to such normative considerations. Market is an institution that establishes a contact between the buyers and sellers

---

[8] This relates to the well-known cyclical majorities problem as shown in Arrow's "Impossibility Theorem." For a detailed statement, see Arrow (1963).

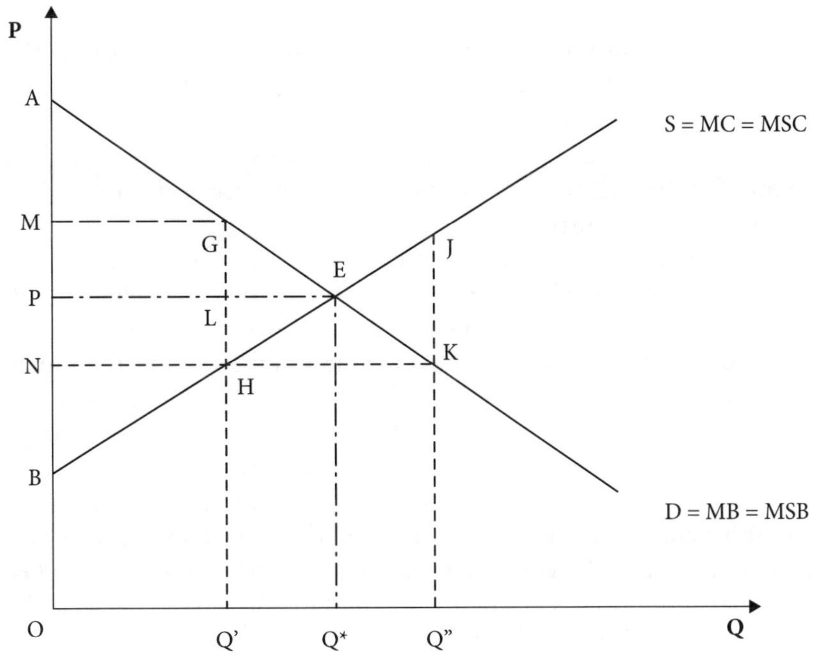

Figure 4

for exchange to take place, and as such it only reflects the disposition of the parties involved in exchange. If markets do seem to reflect certain moral bearings, these are a reflection of the moral values held by the participants. What matters most from the social point of view is whether an individual, or a group of individuals in consort, can influence this outcome to their own advantage at the expense of the others. To put the issue somewhat directly, the question is whether a degenerated self-interest, or selfishness, can exploit others to its own benefit through market mechanism. The answer in the case of small numbers has been elaborated upon, and is not only well recognized in economics but there is also a voluminous literature that deals with it. As for the large numbers, the answer, again well-established in economics, is in the negative, for regardless of the intent of the participants—and we are not given the authority to judge intentions, and at any rate, in the public domain it is the actions that are either permissible or reprehensible—the outcome with regard to prices is not effected, and it is this outcome that matters as far as the society is concerned. Let us turn to the question of criterion for the rightness of the market outcome, let us say with regard to the quantity, and keep in mind that once we establish the right quantity, we also end up establishing the right price, call it just price, for the price merely reflects the cost of production, and as long as the production process operates within the confines of the legal corpus of the society, one would have no reason to question the rightness of the corresponding price as determined by the market mechanism.

The demand curve, which identifies the willingness to pay, and is for that reason considered to be the marginal (private) benefits, MB, curve would be identical to marginal social benefits, MSB, curve in absence of externalities on the consumption side. Similarly, the supply curve, which represents the marginal cost, MC, of production becomes identical to the marginal social cost, MSC, curve under the assumption that there are no externalities on the production side. The conventional criterion used in economics is the maximization of total net social benefits, or total surplus, which is often conveniently split into two components: the consumers' surplus and the producers' surplus. This maximum occurs at point E where the MSB curve intersects the MSC curve, and the total surplus turns out to be area AEB, which is comprised of AEP, representing the consumers' surplus, and PEB, the producers' surplus. This means that the equilibrium quantity turns out to be the right quantity from the society's point of view. It obviously means that any quantity other than Q* will reduce total surplus. For instance, if the society ends up producing an output level less than Q*, such as Q', the surplus will be reduced by the area GHE, and similarly for any output greater than Q*, let us say Q", the surplus obtained at Q* will decrease by the area JKE. It is, therefore, at point E that the allocative efficiency condition is satisfied, that is to say no further increase in total net social benefits is possible by any reallocation of resources, either to or away, from the production of this good than the quantity determined by the market forces, i.e. the equilibrium quantity, Q*. It is thus that the outcome is Pareto optimal.

Now the first question that we need to address is whether in the value system of Islam the consumers (that would include both the herders and the farmers) and producers (that would include only farmers, but then in the case of meat, there would only be the herders) are entitled to enjoy their respective surpluses, as identified above. In the light of our discussion in the last two chapters, we have no *a priori* reasons to question these entitlements provided, of course, that there was nothing that violated the legal corpus of the society, an Islamic society. There could be a question about possible excessive profits (and those would show up in the respective producers' surplus), profits that the legal corpus would not deem illegal but yet could be regarded as excessive by some, a question to which we will return in a moment. That naturally leads us to the question of equity, the equity of the outcome just discussed. We know that there could be n-number of opinions on the question of equity where 'n' is the number of individuals in the economy. If the objective of discussing such an issue is to affect a redistribution at the collective level, there must exist a collective institution charged to do the needful. Therefore, let us assume that there exists an Islamic government, such that the problems raised earlier in the context of small number of parties do not arise. Let us also assume that the government is a bit concerned about the existing distribution of income, which is the distribution of meat and wheat, among its citizens as determined by the outcome in the market. Let us further assume that the government has looked at the private redistribution that occurred in this charity-minded society—after all we are talking about a society which takes the value system expounded in Chapter 5 seriously—and has found it insufficient, and let us further assume that this government has already redistributed income through *zakāh*, the compulsory charity, and found that the situation was not yet satisfactory according to its sense of equity. It is only in these circumstances that the government will have a justification to take additional action to redistribute income. But before we proceed with our argument, we need to pay somewhat closer attention to what our assumptions imply.

To begin with, it may seem a bit odd that a society which was so emphatically enjoined by the *Sharīʿa* to undertake charity at both the individual and collective levels, and yet failed to discharge that responsibility, would now end up with a government that is so concerned with redistribution. Was it because of the free-rider problem, noted in Chapter 5, that it failed to do so at the private level? Perhaps so. In that case it would understandably wish to institute a collective redistribution program such that everybody would contribute a fair share to this effort. This may well be one of the rationales for the Divine ordinance relating to compulsory charity that has come to be known as *zakāh*. This warrants a short but pertinent digression.

The Qur'ānic verse which forms the basis of the institution of *zakāh*, revealed in the ninth year of the Hijra,[9] very clearly spells out the expenditure heads for the revenues thus raised: "The offerings given for the sake of God are (meant) only for the poor and the needy, and those who are in charge thereof, and those whose hearts are to be won over, and for the freeing of the human beings from bondage, and (for) those who are overburdened with debts, and (for every struggle) in God's cause, and (for) the wayfarers: (this is) an ordinance from God—and God is all-knowing, wise" (9:60).[10] There are a number of fascinating implications of this verse that require our closest possible attention. The first is the use of *ṣadaqāt* (offerings given for the sake of God), a word commonly used in the Qur'ān for charity, for these compulsory levies, taxes in modern parlance, to establish an unequivocal connection between these levies and the redistribution of income, as read by *fiqh*. But the conceptualization of redistribution seems to be somewhat broader than is commonly recognized. The verse opens by declaring that these *ṣadaqāt* are meant for the poor (*fuqarā'*), and the needy (*masākīn*); the separate mention of the needy apart from poor, who obviously are needy, suggests that these funds may be used for relief of temporary economic distress. What is even more striking is the permission to use part of these revenues to defray the required compensation to "those who are in charge thereof." It is obvious that the existence of some sort of collective institution is presumed, an institution that is responsible for discharging the duty being imposed, and whose functionaries are the "in charge thereof." This collective institution could hardly be anything other than the government. The next expenditure

[9] While verse 9:60 is unequivocal on the imposition of compulsory *zakāh*, there are those who think that it was instituted much earlier, in the second year of the Hijra. This is perhaps because of the verse 2:177, which mentions more or less the same entitlement categories as 9:60 (though the words used are *āṭ al-māl*, spending) and which belongs to *sūra al-Baqara*, which is supposed to have been revealed in the second year of the Hijra. For more details, see Qaradāwī (1969, vol. ii).

[10] Incidentally, the term used for the compulsory charity in this verse is *ṣadaqāt* and not *zakāh*, but subsequently the latter term has come to be reserved for such compulsory charity in *fiqh*, one of the instances where the juridical meaning given to a Qur'ānic term differs from its original meaning in the Qur'ān. This may perhaps be in view of the verse 2:177 (see the previous note) which while elaborating on the elements of piety mentions the general spending on charity (*āṭ al-māl*) as well as *zakāh*, as noted in the previous chapter. There are scholars who think that parts of *sūra al-Baqara* were revealed much later, including those relating to prohibition of *ribā* that are supposed to have been revealed just before the Prophet's death. On this last issue, more in Chapter 9.

head relates to the dissemination of the message of Islam, for indeed in the universalistic perspective of Islam, every human being is a heart to be won over; the final revelation must be made as widely known as permitted by the available means. Next come two headings that represent one-off outlays that are meant to circumvent the possibility of prolonged human suffering: those of bondage (*rikāb*) and financial distress (*ghārimīn*, debtors).[11] Next comes a general heading, "in the way of God" (*fī sabīl Allāh*), and finally the wayfarers (*musāfirīn*). Interestingly, what is the purport of the general category "in the way of God" when a number of socially crucial specific heads have already been noted? The need for flexibility is obvious in view of any spacio-temporal contingencies that may arise, but what could be more in the "way of God" than provision of a system of justice, for He is "the Just" and loves those who are likewise just. Let us recall a Qur'ānic verse cited in Chapter 5: "O you who have attained to faith! Be ever steadfast in upholding equity, bearing witness to the truth *for the sake of God*, even though it be against your own selves or your parents and kinsfolk. Whether the person concerned is rich or poor, God's claim takes precedence over (the claims of) either of them. Do not, then, follow your own desires, lest you swerve from justice: for if you distort (the truth), behold, God is indeed aware of all that you do!" (4:135). There could not be a more explicit statement defining *fī sabīl-Allāh* with *li 'llāh* (for God's sake), as appears in this verse. In addition, defense of the entire community from external threats equally falls in this category when the occasion so arises. It is another matter that even after according recognition to the general purport of *fī sabīl-Allāh*, most of the *fiqh* scholars restrict its scope to meeting only defense needs. As far as the category relating to wayfarers is concerned, it perhaps could be interpreted as provision of roads and other amenities for travelers, public goods in modern parlance,[12] although such would seem to go

[11] Salama (1983, p. 115) notes that the Prophet allowed payment of debts of both living and deceased from the *zakāh* funds, more on this in Chapters 9 and 10.

[12] When Faridi (1983) presented this idea at a seminar on Islamic economics, he did not receive a favorable response and withdrew the suggestion in his revised version of the paper. See the comments on his paper that are published along with the revised paper. We may note though that the classical exegete Bayḍāwī (d. 1280) interpreted *fī sabīl Allāh* in that spirit and approved disbursement of *zakāh* funds for the expenses of building bridges for the benefit of poor people. A contemporary writer, Sa'adi (1986, p. 166), is also in favor of taking somewhat broader meanings of *fī sabīl Allāh* when he includes as entitled to *zakāh* disbursements "those involved in warfare,

against the Ḥanafī requirement with regard to *tamlīk*, i.e. earmarking of the beneficiaries. Yet one may note that the verse does not confine itself to any specific class of wayfarers, and therefore the issue of *tamlīk* does not seem quite relevant for this category of beneficiaries. One may add here that in the Mālikī interpretation, *zakāh* can be paid to even those who are *zakāh* payers themselves. It must also be kept in mind that "justice system" is a classic public good. At any rate, we see that apart from the first and the fifth categories, namely the poor and "those in bondage," the latter would be poor by inference, the Qur'ān does not restrict the beneficiaries to any specific economic class. Putting it slightly differently, these revenues are not meant to be restricted to only redistribution in cash, or even just redistribution, for it is not just the indigent that are supposed to be their beneficiaries under all the heads except the two noted above.

There exists a voluminous literature in *fiqh* that deals with these specifics and it is not my objective to go into those details. My focus is slightly different, yet equally, if not more, important. And that is to point out that if there ever was a Qur'ānic ordinance that explicitly stated any specific functions of the government, it would be this verse. The presumption about the existence of government in this verse does not leave any doubt on that score. It is significant to note that *sūra al-Tawba* in which this verse appears was revealed at the occasion of Prophet's expedition to Tabūk in view of the free rider problem that arose when some of the able-bodied Muslims avoided going with the Prophet under one pretext or another. This is the only *sūra* in the Qur'ān that does not begin with the customary invocation "In the name of God, the most Clement, the most Merciful," and seemingly a manifestation of Divine wrath as a result of the free rider problem. We are obliged to recognize all of the foregoing functions as necessary functions of an Islamic government without by any means implying that these may be sufficient in all circumstances. But an Islamic government must discharge these functions before it may take upon itself any additional responsibilities. Once that is understood, imagine the mindset of the state functionaries who are mindful, or must be made so, that their livelihood comes out from *ṣadaqāt*, as compared to the mindset of the typical haughty, self-conceited, irresponsible bureaucracy misusing its discretionary powers for its own enrichment to the

in social care, in provision of infrastructure, and indeed all those providing what is required for the peace and security of the Muslim community."

maximum extent possible. Be that as it may, it is at least clear that if there is to be compulsory collective redistribution in an Islamic society, it could not possibly be conceived of ex-*zakāh* in contravention to this explicit Qur'ānic injunction.

Returning to the argument, why is the redistribution through *zakāh* deemed insufficient, as is assumed by the Islamic economists? The answer, and a rather apologetic one, may be that either the rates of *zakāh* or its *niṣāb* (level of income at which *zakāh* becomes payable) or both were not high enough to accomplish the desired redistribution. This in turn raises the obvious question as to why one or both of these variables are not adjusted upwards to achieve what is needed? This, needless to say, would have the advantage of drawing the moral commitment of the contributors since they would have the satisfaction of discharging a Divinely ordained responsibility. If the answer is that *fiqh*, in deference to the rates set during the Prophetic times, would not allow any such revision, then what are the options open to the government?[13] For one, it may decide to abandon its additional redistributional programs, those that go beyond the existing *zakāh* regime. In that case, the whole interventionist argument of the Islamic economists about additional redistribution becomes irrelevant. It goes without saying that in that case we end up with what has been the case *de facto* for more or less the past fourteen centuries.

But suppose the government wishes to follow through its redistributive imperatives in any case: it then is confronted with a number of thorny questions regardless of the course of action it follows. One possibility is to go ahead and revise the *zakāh* rates, or *niṣāb*, or both to suit the redistributive requirements. But then the question is whether *fiqh* would accord legitimacy to such a government. If it did no such thing, which is what is most likely to happen, then we are left with a government which would have trouble establishing its Islamic credentials—there would not be anything new in that if history is any guide—and its collectivistic redistributive endeavors would lack the required moral legitimacy for these to be effectively enforced, as pointed out earlier, specifically in Chapter 3 but then also in Chapter 5. If, on the other hand, *fiqh* did acquiesce in this revision by the

[13] Qaradāwī (1969), a contemporary *fiqh* scholar, is sympathetic to the idea of adjusting the *niṣāb* upwards to accommodate a reasonable standard of living in modern times. But without an upward revision in the *zakāh* rates, this may lead to a reduction in *zakāh* revenues at the same time that the necessary disbursement increases.

government, then it would end up abdicating its historical role with regard to jurisprudence, something it would hardly like to do. (In a sense, *fiqh* has lived with this dilemma from the very beginning. Being a system of legal guidance directed at the individual [man as such], and individually articulated by the *fuqahā'*, it was not explicitly geared to be a system of law designed to be enforced by state [more on this in Chapter 10], with the end result that *fiqh* took its own historical course, and the governments of the Islamic realms always went their own way. The complexity of the modern, technological and cosmopolitan age requires a greater attention to the enforceable part of *fiqh*—the legal corpus—and therefore the historic pattern of each "going its own way" may not turn out to be as innocuous as it has been in the past.) In the former case we go back to history, and in the latter, we enter an entirely different universe as far as an Islamic society is concerned, and one without any precedence in Islamic history, a sort of "brave new world" of Islam. Is this what Islamic economists have in mind? Hardly. What they seem to have in mind is that the government does no such thing as tinkering with the rates and *niṣāb*, yet follows through with its redistributive agenda anyway, preferably through direct intervention in the market mechanism and not just through direct lump-sum transfers as would happen in the case of *zakāh*. The government, and its Islamic economic advisors, may be happy with this easy route, but on whom the incidence of such a redistribution will fall remains clouded. One cannot rule out the possibility that a below-*niṣāb* individual may be burdened with footing the bill of this redistribution. There is the other troubling possibility where a government may not be able to institute the system of *zakāh*, for whatever reasons, and yet may institute the redistribution. Quite apart from the question of Islamic legitimacy of such a course of action on the part of the government, an individual whose primary redistributive obligation is to discharge his *zakāh* payment would like to know whether such an obligation has been taken care of through whatever burden the government has imposed on him for this compulsory, as far as he is concerned, redistribution.[14] We still end up with a brave new world but this time one which is rootless. At any rate, in which direction this brave new world,

[14] Consider a person who is barely above the *niṣāb* level with a *zakāh* obligation of \$1x and has paid \$2x in taxes to the government some, or all, of which the government uses for redistribution purposes. Is his *zakāh* obligation still the same \$1x? The easy answer given by *fiqh* is 'yes'!

of whichever variety, cut-off from the nourishment from its roots, may go is anybody's guess.

A brief digression is in order here. Although laissez-faire doctrine had established itself after the publication of Ricardo's *Principles of Political Economy and Taxation* in the mid 1830s—with a little help from senior Mill, I presume—the doctrine was not yet firmly planted in the collectivistic soil of the West. And although trade restrictions were considerably reduced in the United Kingdom—thanks to the influence of people like Mill and Bagehot -the protectionist lobby kept appealing to the government not to proceed all the way to free trade. One dimension of this reliance on the government is seen in Jevons's presidential address to Section F (dealing with Economic Science and Statistics) of the Royal Society, the precursor to the Royal Economic Society, in Liverpool in 1870 on the subject of economic policy. Jevons rightly underscores the importance of public provision of education but felt impelled to rail against private charity:[15]

> I am glad to say that, in spite of all opponents, we have an Education Act. Three centuries ago the State recognized the principle that no person should be allowed to perish for want of bread; for three centuries the State has allowed the people to perish for want of mind and knowledge. Let us hope much from this tardy recognition of the greatest social need, but let us not withdraw our attention from many other causes of evil which still exist in full force. I wish especially to point out that the wise precautions of the present poor law are to a great extent counteracted by the mistaken humanity of charitable people. Could we sum up the amount of aid which is, in one way or other, extended by the upper to the lower classes, it would be almost of incredible amount, and would probably far exceed the cost of poor-law relief. But I am sorry to believe that, however great the good thus done, the evil results are probably greater. Nothing so surely as indiscriminate charity tends to create and perpetuate a class living in hopeless poverty. It is well known that those towns where charitable institutions and charitable people most abound are precisely those where the helpless poor are most numerous... Mr. Goschen and the poor-law authorities have of late begun to perceive that all their care in the administration of relief is frustrated by the over-abundant charity of private persons or religious societies... Far worse, however, than private charity are the innumerable small charities established by the bequests of mistaken testators [recall the *waqf* property of Chapter 5]. Almost every parish church has its tables of benefactions, holding up to everlasting gratitude those who have left a small patch

[15] In Smyth (ed.) (1963).

> of land or an annual sum of money to be devoted to pauperizing the population of parish throughout all times (pp. 27–28).

One is appalled at such an unbridled attack on Christian charity. It can only be understood in the context of revolt against the Church. What Jevons does is to spurn one form of collectivism in favor of another. I do not wish to comment on this passage except to note that such sentiments could only come from someone with an unbounded confidence in the ability of the state to deliver the goods, and all that against the backdrop of a three-hundred year history of the poor law. What happened to the modern formulation of the poor law in the form of welfare state does not require any explanation. How an Islamic state of the Islamic economists, whose institutional form is not yet articulated, would fare in this respect is something that can hardly even be guessed at.

We already have had glimpses of this world in, particularly in Chapters 2 and 5, but let us venture into this brave new world a little more in the present context. And let us assume that the proponents of this world have been able to institute a just government, perhaps in a society dominated by potential beneficiaries of the contemplated redistribution, the bill for which will fall on a rich minority. Just how such feat of representative government will be accomplished, where millions are likely to be spent by those who present themselves to public as the guardians of the society's moral values only to recoup the spent millions with added millions, is the real question confronting Islamic political thinkers including the *fiqh* scholars. The evidence with respect to the experience of the West in this regard is not very encouraging, and it is even worse in some Muslim countries where that system has been tried, albeit half-heartedly. But let us assume for the sake of argument that a truly Islamic government has been somehow instituted and established. Suppose this government feels that the farmers are not getting their due in the national income, that the price of wheat relative to meat is too low, that perhaps the herders are making too much profit—although this need not necessarily be the reason—and therefore something needs to be done to redistribute income in favor of the farmers. While this may be accomplished in a variety of ways, the options available to the market interventionists are rather limited. They may provide a support price to the farmers, i.e. set the price higher than the equilibrium price, or alternatively put a ceiling on the meat price; after all, they may well argue, quite convincingly, that during the Prophetic times meat was considered to be a luxury, and could use a potent mix of arguments to show that the producers of any luxury make excessive profits.

Assume that the policymakers of this economy, the Islamic economists, institute a price ceiling at price N in Figure 4—here I use the bread market diagram for meat instead of drawing a new one just for the sake of economy, without in any way impairing the validity of the results.[16] This implies that the quantity supplied is Q', presuming, of course, that no coercive force is applied on the herders to produce a quantity larger than what they would voluntarily produce—in other words, I am presuming that our Islamic state will abhor the idea of state-sponsored slavery. The first effect of this will be a reduction in surplus equal to area GEH, known conventionally as the deadweight loss of intervention, comprised of a reduction in consumers' surplus equal to GLE, and in producers' surplus equal to LEH. The society ends up losing these benefits and the losers include not only the producers, who are well understood to be the bearers of this redistribution burden, but also the consumers who are supposed to be its beneficiaries. There is of course a redistribution of surplus from the producers to the consumers given by the area PLHN, with the result that producers' surplus has shrunk to BNH, and the consumers' surplus has increased to AGHN. Are the intended beneficiaries any better off now than before? Well, the answer depends on a comparison of the areas PLHN (the gain) to the area GLE (the loss), and it is not *a priori* clear which of these two areas will be larger. But this is not the end of the story. At the price ceiling N, there will be an excess demand (shortage) equal to quantity HK which, in all likelihood, will lead to development of a black market, where the price that will prevail will be equal to M. If we assume that this black market is dominated by the suppliers (producers), as would usually be the case, then the policy will have backfired, for now the consumers' surplus will shrink to area AGM, while the producers' surplus will increase to BHGM, implying a further decrease in consumers' surplus equal to PLGM, which now gets appropriated by the producers. The total loss to the consumers is now given by PEGM. Actually the previous result, where the

[16] I am content to contemplate a meeker version of this brave new world as compared to Mannan (1992, p. 207) where he proposes that this world must admit negative prices—a world, therefore, where the producers will not only offer their products to the consumers for free but will also pay them a subsidy to consume their products. More on his Islamic vision later in this Chapter.

consumers' surplus increased by PLHN, is contingent upon the existence of such a black market, but the one dominated by the consumers, who would receive the good under certain rationing schemes, that must be instituted if the counter-productive result is to be avoided, and are able to resell their rationed amount at the price M. This is particularly true for those consumers whose demand is represented by the segment EK on the demand curve, and who actually are the real intended beneficiaries of the redistribution. They somehow must be enabled to buy at N and sell at M if the consumers' surplus is to be AGHN. Of course, in that case one would not like to call this secondary market a black market, and of course one would not expect an enforcement lapse in instituting a rationing scheme on the part of the Islamic government, for otherwise the policy will fail miserably.

The results for the alternative policy, that is to say the support price policy, can be shown to lead to a similar trade-off between equity and efficiency with the attendant deadweight losses to the society, although in that case the economic rationale is much stronger, particularly in view of the mismatch between demand and supply at the time of harvesting and the attendant danger of revenue loss for the farmers due to inelastic demand when the price plunges at that time. I have not here gone into the details of that policy—though it can be shown to be equally counter-productive if not implemented effectively—for the simple reason that it is not a possible redistributional alternative that Islamic economists contemplate. For them every producer is an affluent, unbridled profiteer who needs to be somehow restrained through market intervention.

But does every producer make excessive profits? And since the focus of Islamic economists would be the so-called meat producers, we can read this question straight away as aiming at the possibility of their making excessive profits as compared to the farmers. Assume the exchange ratio is close to 0.3 in our model, and therefore the herders benefit more from exchange as compared to the farmers. Let us also reiterate that this advantage was not the result of political power play, presumably because there is supposed to be an Islamic government in office. Now the important question is whether this situation can continue indefinitely to the advantage of the herders in a dynamic context where new producers may enter and the existing ones may leave, and tastes may change. We have already seen that if tastes change in favor of bread, the herders' advantage will be eroded. But if tastes do not change, which means the luxury of meat retains its hold in the imagination of both the herders and the farmers, then the question will boil down to entry and exit. Why would the existing farmers and the new entrants not acquire the herding skills to erode the excessive profits? Did the acquisition of the herding skills required more investment to begin with? If yes, is that additional investment entitled to a return that now shows up in the form of higher surplus or profits? And if no, were there any restrictions on entry? If yes, where was the government that allowed a perpetuation of these restrictions? And if no, was this advantage the result of certain innate or natural factors such as intelligence or physical attributes? If yes, should the government now necessarily stifle these attributes, or, indeed would it satisfy the demands of fairness if it did so? And if no, was it because of some initial distribution of land? And the litany of questions continues.

The answer to the dilemma depends upon the cause of the perceived inequality. Chapters 2 and 3 addressed these questions. In Chapter 2, we saw that if the distribution of initial endowments is unjust, the outcome of the market forces may well be considered unjust. In that case, the culprit is not the market mechanism but rather the initial distribution of factor endowments, and the problem must be addressed at that level instead of maligning the institution of market. Chapter 3 highlighted the role of competition, which necessarily means an absence of restrictions on entry and exit. The Smithian insight that as long as there are no such restrictions, the abnormal profits will be competed away is logically impeccable, and as long as the initial distribution of factor endowments is deemed as just, the outcome of the market mechanism cannot be considered as unjust on *a priori* grounds. When we leave this simple world of herders and farmers, and introduce a more complicated process of production where not all factors may be owned by the firm—the possibility where the herders and the farmers do not necessarily own the land and implements, etc. and where they may also hire other workers, besides using their own labor if they themselves work which by itself is not necessary—the present equality between producers' surplus and profits breaks down. It suffices here to note that the producers' surplus may now accrue to various factors of production, including, it may be noted, labor.

Finally in this regard it may be noted that, *ceteris paribus*, when tastes keep on changing, as indeed they do in reality, there will be abnormal profits in the short run, sometimes for the herders and sometimes for the farmers, and such profits are understood to offset losses whenever they accrue, as well as serving as signals for entry and exit that lead towards long-run equilibrium, a state where every firm earns just the normal profits. It is another matter that an industry may never reach that long-run equilibrium, since real life is complicated and subject to one change after another, such that the process of dynamic adjustment may be never-ending. Yet, this in no way militates against the fact that the short-run price movements will revolve around that long-run equilibrium price, which in the case of perfect competition is established at the lowest point on the long-run average cost curve. This of course ensures satisfaction of technical efficiency conditions to the advantage of the consumers in the form of lowest possible prices.[17]

We have touched upon a host of issues in the foregoing discussion, including that of technological change, and the role that abnormal profits may play in stimulating such change. Indeed, if there is a conceptual problem with the perfectly competitive model, it is precisely related to the issue of technological change, for an industry populated by small firms each just making ends meet could hardly afford to undertake the investment needed for research and development to propel the risky undertaking that the process of technological change happens to be. In any case, the analysis is not meant to be exhaustive by any means, and could not possibly be so within the space of one chapter. My objective is limited to highlighting the significance of the market mechanism and the role competition plays in a market economy in light of the anti-market, anti-competition slant in the writings on Islamic economics. As far as redistribution is concerned, which is what leads those economists to mistrust the market mechanism, I have tried to show that such intervention could in no manner be considered an abiding rule as per the Islamic values, and a better alternative may be a direct redistribution in the spirit of *zakāh*, where any additional needs may be met through corrective taxes imposed on the negative externalities, or through the least distortionary of taxes.

Two further points may be noted before we proceed to evaluate, in the light of our discussion, some of the significant contributions of Islamic economists in this area. The perfectly competitive model often comes under attack for its lack of realism, and Islamic economists seize on this supposed weakness, particularly relating to the assumption about perfect information. The first thing that needs to

[17] This will not be true for decreasing cost industries if the economies of scale in the source industry are not yet fully exhausted.

be noted is that the perfectly competitive model is considered to be a benchmark model; it serves as a reference model to judge the outcome obtained in the other market forms, monopoly, oligopoly, or monopolistic competition. The model provides a practical guideline in the form of marginal-cost pricing, and therefore the conclusion that the greater the divergence between marginal cost and price, the greater the efficiency, and therefore social, loss. Furthermore, the ultimate significance of the perfect information assumption boils down to information about price that is supposed to prevail in the market so that nobody is able to exploit the ignorance of the other participants. But when there is a very large number of participants, thousands upon thousands, to assume that everyone knows everything about everyone else is of course quite unrealistic. In the case of such numbers, it is more likely that nobody knows much about the others, much akin to perfect lack of information. But interestingly, when there is perfect lack of information, the results with regard to exploitation of one party by the other turn out to be exactly the same as when there is perfect information, since exploitation is a function of asymmetric information and not the absence, or otherwise, of information. When nobody knows anything about others, there may be arbitrary divergences from what would turn out to be the equilibrium price, but such divergences, leading to arbitrary gains and losses, are subject to cancellation, which is to say that one day you gain and the next you lose.

Second, an important sector of any economy, namely agriculture, in general still falls under the purview of the perfectly competitive model. Granted that this sector has become relatively small in the developed countries, but that clearly is not the case in the less developed countries, including most Muslim countries. In such countries, agriculture contributes between a quarter and one half of the GDP in contrast to the corresponding numbers for the developed countries that usually hover around 5 percent or even less. Besides, in the less developed countries, the informal sector (which may actually account for a significant proportion of the overall economic activity), as well as small retailing, also falls under the sway of perfect competition. Therefore, for these countries, the perfectly competitive model is not as practically irrelevant as it would appear in the developed countries.

In the final analysis, Islamic economists fail to recognize the significance of the Smithian idea of an invisible hand, and its role in the coordination of the market forces of demand and supply, that is to say a coordination between all the participants in the market, such that an order finally comes to prevail in the form of equilibrium. This is primarily because of a lack of appreciation of the deep-seated meanings of the surface terminology used in the academic discourse. The Occidental discourse has a tendency, for reasons that need not be examined, to keep the name "God" out of the discourse by substituting it with terms such as "nature," "natural," or "invisible hand." In the latter case, which is the one relevant in the present context, one should not forget that ultimately what is being underscored is an impersonal process where no particular individual will has any influence on the outcome obtained in the market. Had the Prophet himself not made it clear that "it all comes from God" and the leading lights of Islamic *fiqh* discourse down to Ibn Taymiyya's time not adhered to that dictum, there would be less difficulty understanding the commotion created by the Islamic economists on this score. I see no difficulty in interpreting what the Prophet said as being an endorsement of the idea of what has come to be called perfect competition.

Market Mechanism and Competition in Islamic Economics

Consider now the positions of some of the Islamic economists on the issues relating to market mechanism and competition. First, on those relating to market mechanism, which of course are crucially linked to the laws of demand and supply, Nejatullah Siddiqi (1992) has this to say:

> A study of functional relationships in economics sometimes results in laws, i.e. functional relationships of universal validity. Some laws relate to human behaviour, like the law of demand, whereas some relate to the physical world, such as the law of diminishing returns. The latter are acceptable since the world of nature has stable properties being governed by uniform unchanging rules. But the notion of a "law" in the context of human behaviour involving freedom of choice is unacceptable in principle. It is better to recognize propositions like the "law of demand" as tendencies of fairly general validity but subject to certain *ceteris paribus* conditions which need to be spelt out in detail in each situation" (p. 7).

He does not offer us any explanation as to why an economic law based on human behavior involving freedom of choice is not acceptable in principle in Islam. When he says it is not acceptable in principle, he is implying more than the qualification he spells out in the next sentence, for that sentence would be readily acceptable in what he would call conventional economics. Indeed, the law of demand is never stipulated without invoking the *ceteris paribus* assumption, and more or less all laws of economics can be thought of as "tendencies of fairly general validity" without by any means negating the freedom of choice. So, the question is what was at the back of his mind when he wrote the last sentence, which at any rate is out of place as far as his refutation of the freedom of choice is concerned? Is he unhappy with the idea of freedom of choice, or is he saying that Islam does not allow a freedom of choice to consumers, or is he worried that this freedom may turn out to be absolute? All these questions have already been dealt with in the context of herders and farmers, and in the past two chapters, and there is no need to repeat what has already been said. One would also hope that he is not refuting the law of diminishing marginal utility, or saying that this is not relevant for a Muslim consumer. And finally he may be unhappy, although this does not seem to be the case, about the assumption of constant marginal utility of money needed to translate the marginal utility curve into the demand curve, an issue which is discussed in Chapter 2. This much, however, is clear: by declaring that freedom of choice is not permissible, what he is interested in is to justify interventionism in the market by either the government or what he calls a social authority, whatever that may mean. If by social authority he means some extra-governmental authority, we have already met that in Chapter 6 in the context of discussing the contributions of another Islamic economist, and if it is another term for the government, then it is, at the very least, confusing.[18]

A number of other reasons are advanced for interventionism, particularly consumption of luxuries and profit maximization. But these arguments betray inconsistencies. We have already dealt with the issue of luxuries versus. necessities,[19] but what the Islamic economists say about profit maximization is not less confusing. Consider Siddiqi again. He begins by misleading an unwary reader by stating that

---

[18] One may note that Ibn Taymiyya's *muḥtasib* is supposed to be a part of the government, though it may be autonomous.

[19] Yet the following is quite irresistible. After declaring that "Islam has strictly forbidden indulgence in luxuries as this is foreign to the Islamic way of life" Siddiqi, one sentence later, continues: "A man is fully entitled to such comforts of life over and above necessaries, if they are not out of place in his own economy in general. Regarding the consumption of luxuries, the actual condition or the state of the society must be taken into consideration" (1979, p. 92).

conventional economics assumes profits to be "the only motive of producers" and asserts that such "is not acceptable" (1992, p. 16) in an Islamic economy. He goes on, in another place, to articulate his Islamic vision on the subject:

> A Muslim entrepreneur cannot always be motivated by the urge to maximize his pecuniary profits, due to the simple reason that he is possessed of a stronger urge to live up to the Islamic ideals of justice and benevolence. His case, with respect to "economic rationality," is similar to that of the consumer. Should a conflict occur between the dictates of "economic rationality" and Islamic *injunctions*, he is, by assumption, expected to decide in favour of the latter. His "economic rationality" becomes confined within the limits set by the Islamic *spirit*. Within these limits, *he may seek to maximize his profits as far as possible*. The realistic assumption is that he will. It may be urged that while the demands of justice are to a large extent determinate, those of benevolence know no bounds. That would mean that the confines within which profit maximization is *allowed* are not well defined.

And as though that is not enough, he continues:

> This objection contains some truth, but not the whole of it. So far as the principle that the entrepreneur *should* take the welfare of others into consideration is concerned, it must be regarded as a *well-defined obligation*. This demand of benevolence is a *duty* of the Muslim entrepreneur, the norm of his business policy" (1979, p. 102, emphasis added).

The first thing that strikes a reader is that profit maximization is not permissible but then it is permissible "as far as possible" within limits set by the "Islamic spirit," but then the "confines" of this spirit are not "well defined." Even so, it must be regarded as "well-defined obligation." It is difficult to make any sense of this vision, but let us give it a try. The ideals that a Muslim entrepreneur is supposed to live up to are justice, which we know ought to be related to the enforceable part of *fiqh*, and benevolence (*iḥsān*), which is purely voluntaristic, and therefore not enforceable, and as a matter of fact ought not be subject to coercive enforcement as per the discussion in Chapter 5. That is why Siddiqi opts to merge the two into "Islamic spirit." He seems to perceive the difficulty of defending his position when he says that the "demands of justice are to a large extent determinate," and "those of the benevolence know no bounds," but then fails to recognize that any social system, including the system of justice, is predicated on what is legally permissible and what is not. In other words, it is based upon the structure of property rights as enshrined in the legal corpus of a society. What is permissible is permissible, and if any economic agent wishes to go beyond that and show benevolence and altruistic behavior, it is entirely up to him, and such an act cannot be declared as an enforceable social duty and thus a "well-defined" legal "obligation." With regard to both the issue of luxuries versus necessities and that of profit maximization, a remarkable confusion arises when the voluntary self-abnegation of Ṣūfis is raised by fiqhnomics to the status of not just a moral but rather a legal imperative for the entire Muslim community without any foundation in *fiqh*.[20]

And let us not forget that Siddiqi imposes these moral obligations on the entrepreneur and not just the firm, and keep in mind that while the existence of firm is necessarily predicated on there being an entrepreneur, the existence of entrepreneur does not necessarily imply the existence of a firm. A firm is a legal entity, and it is quite possible that a small entrepreneur may not be accorded that recognition in the legal corpus of a society, as commonly happens in the informal sector in the less developed countries. As far as Siddiqi is concerned, if we use our analogy, all farmers and all herders are capitalist entrepreneurs, associated with large companies if not corporations. At the very least, he assumes that an Islamic economy—with all its distinct institutions as well as its distinct legal corpus and therefore the corresponding structure of property rights, as emphasized in the preceding chapters—will not be any different from the existing developed capitalist economies.

Then, after declaring that the perfectly competitive model is inadmissible because of its lack of realism, after throwing monopolistic competition into the same basket as oligopoly and monopoly, and after assuming that money capital will share profits with the entrepreneur,[21] he tells us:

> Two important points follow. First, the right element to introduce in cost accounting would not be a return to capital but an expected rate of profits. Given the ratio of profit-sharing which is predetermined and contractual, the firm will try to earn a rate of profit on capital invested

[20] One may add that if in all this he is merely underscoring Islam's moral imperatives, he is not saying anything new. But then, for a survey of how various Islamic imperatives are deployed in an inconsistent manner by the Islamic economists, see Kuran (1989).

[21] In his system, physical capital will receive a rate of rental rather than a rate of interest. See Chapter 8 for further discussion on this subject.

> in the firm which will yield a return on money capital that *satisfies* its suppliers. For example, if the entrepreneur has contracted for giving half of the profit of enterprise to the supplier of capital, and a rate less than 10 per cent would not *satisfy* the supplier of capital, the firm would *strive* to make a profit of 20 per cent. The second point to be noted is that even when it is introduced as an element of cost, it would remain a flexible item, whose magnitude can be decreased or increased in the short run. Even in the long run, the possibility of changing the ratio of profit-sharing so as to yield a *satisfactory* return on money capital as the expected rate of entrepreneurial profit changes, maintains this flexibility. Should the entrepreneur opt for a *strategy* which is not likely to yield more than 15 per cent profit, he can still *satisfy* the supplier of capital by contracting to give two thirds of the profit to the supplier of money capital (1992, p. 18, emphasis added).

There are a number of incongruities in this passage that need to be highlighted. First, the purpose of profit-sharing, as commonly understood in Islamic economics, is to make the capitalists share the risk of enterprise. To begin with, Siddiqi exempts the owners of physical capital from this risk by guaranteeing them a predetermined fixed rental. In his vision, it is the money capital (his "capital" and the circulating capital that we met in Chapter 4), which must not be guaranteed a fixed return as this would be the same thing as interest (*ribā*)—something which will come under extended discussion in the following chapters—but then he goes ahead to guarantee the owners of money capital a satisfactory return (note the added emphases in the citation above), by putting the entrepreneur (in the perspective of Islamic economics, an entrepreneurship is more or less equated to management that shares profits of the enterprise) at the service of the owner of money capital. If the rate of profit needs to be increased to satisfy the fancies of the owner of money capital, the entrepreneur must satisfy them by using some magic wand of a strategy to increase the profits in order to satisfy this demand, but other than that he must not increase profits for this would amount to profit maximization, which of course would be quite un-Islamic. Would this "satisfactory" profit, when expressed in terms of a rate, be less than the rate of interest? (More on that in Chapter 10). What guarantee is there that the owner of money capital will stop short of stripping the entrepreneur of any reward, and in that case who would wish to become an entrepreneur and expose himself to the risk that such a role necessarily implies? And why did the money capital not have an opportunity cost to begin with, but was then eventually admitted to be "an element of cost"? On top of that it was now conceived to be a flexible item, to be increased or decreased whenever the demands of the owners of money capital so required, and thus obviously not determined through the market mechanism. Conceived thus, this element of cost becomes analogous to the abnormal profits of economics, which is to be paid to the suppliers of money capital at the rate determined by their own whims and fancies. Should we then take it to mean that Siddiqi treats all profits- and remember these are to be shared by the entrepreneur and the suppliers of money capital- as abnormal profits? In that case, he obviously has trouble recognizing the implicit costs associated with entrepreneurship. At any rate, it is not the capitalist who is blameworthy in the much maligned capitalism but rather the entrepreneur, the entrepreneur who earns barely normal profits, at least under perfect competition.

In his 1979 book, from where the previous citation comes, Siddiqi begins by assuming perfect competition, but after a page or so of articulating his vision, he forgets that he was discussing perfect competition, goes on to introduce a three-point "Islamic vision" and quickly moves on to defend "big corporations" operating under that vision by saying that such a corporation will self-impose an upper limit on its profits in light of the "public view about its reputation" and that there will be a lower limit to profits "in the mind of the individual entrepreneur" (whoever that may happen to be in a corporation, as we saw in Chapter 4), "to insure him an average income necessary for living. This later objective, of earning an income sufficient to live an efficient living (whatever that means!), is the *minimum* which, *normally*, no economic agent is expected to sacrifice" (p. 106, emphasis added). Thus once the entrepreneur becomes "homo-Islamicus," there is no need to worry, competition or not. Subsequently, while explicitly discussing monopoly and monopolistic competition, he concludes: "1) The influence of the Islamic spirit would dissolve the monopoly and render the industry competitive[22] (in case the monopoly was artificial, its maintenance being dependent upon certain un-Islamic restrictive practices). 2) The monopolies which are spared [by whom? he does not say] would lose their antisocial character and use their market power to further the good of society. In such cases, prices would not be higher nor output

[22] By competitive, he means "cooperative" behavior by producers through which these monopolies will be dissolved. The issue of cooperation between producers is taken up later in this chapter.

smaller than under competitive conditions"[23] (p. 125, only larger brackets are added). But why could the monopoly not serve the "good of society" in the previous case and what became of the un-Islamic restrictive practices now? So, under the Islamic vision, monopoly is bad to begin with but then it is good because under Islamic spirit it will lead to the same output as under "competitive conditions." We scarcely know how to make sense of these so-called Islamic visions. (I spare the reader his Islamic visions with regard to oligopoly and monopolistic competition).

A similar sort of confusion emerges when we read Mannan (1992a, pp. 176–83) who thinks that price discrimination under monopoly will serve Islamic purpose through lowering of the prices for the poor—indeed he envisions perfect price discrimination when he shows the total revenues curve in his Figure 16.3 (p. 180). He does not explain the point any further. One may surmise that he is thinking about a sort of muti-part pricing scheme, just like a regulated natural monopoly, where the higher price charged from one group of consumers may compensate for the losses accruing due to marginal cost pricing for another group (even if he were not thinking on those lines, the second and third points below will remain valid). Again, there are a number of difficulties such a line of reasoning gives rise to. First, all monopolies are not the result of the decreasing costs phenomenon that leads to losses when marginal cost pricing is implemented through regulation, losses that are then supposed to be recovered through a higher price charged those who are willing to pay a higher price. Second, those who are willing to pay a higher price may not necessarily be only those falling in the rich class. In that case, his argument that the rich will subsidize the poor falls apart. Third, price discrimination cannot be practiced until a number of conditions for doing so are satisfied, as conventional economic analysis shows us. But in the muti-part pricing, such an outcome is imposed upon the monopolist through regulation. The monopolist will not do this voluntarily, for he may have a distorted image of his self-interest—an idea that has been dis-

[23] One wonders, how a person to whom Pareto did not mean a thing arrived at the conclusion that somehow the competitive output was better than the monopoly output from the society's point of view. A little earlier in the article, he puts it this way: "thus given the motive of profit maximization, the fact that an industry is working under monopoly *invariably* results in antisocial phenomenon of smaller supply and higher price. It is antisocial because it implies that with the given resources of the economy, a larger demand could be satisfied with lesser disutility to the consumers, but for the monopoly" (1979, p. 120). All that but no Pareto.

cussed at length in previous chapters; recall the discussion with regard to homo-Islamicus. And in view of that, what is the guarantee that the monopolist will not exploit the consumers in the name of price discrimination sanctioned by Islam as per the Islamic economists. It may be kept in mind that under perfect price discrimination, which of course is impossible to achieve, the monopolist is able to appropriate all the consumers' surplus. Let us return to the argument about perfect competition where we left it.

Since monopoly is bad because it produces an output less than perfect competition, one would think that Siddiqi would approve of perfect competition. One is then surprised, for a page or so further down, he suddenly remembers that he was discussing perfect competition, and writes:

> Given the conditions of perfect competition, each entrepreneur has to take the market prices as given. His interest would lie in producing the goods at the minimum costs that are possible and selling them at their market prices. The resulting order of production, allocation of resources, and distribution would be the same as that of a free-enterprise economy, the only difference being that the pattern of demand, the distribution of purchasing power among consumers, and their scale of preferences are now modified as to get the *approval* of the entrepreneur's sense of justice and benevolence (1979, p. 108, emphasis added).

Is the entrepreneur out of the woods once he is conceived of as giving everyone his "approval" with regard to "justice and benevolence"—or was it supposed to be when he has discharged his obligations with regard to justice and benevolence? We know that the owner of the money capital may not have left much profit at his disposal. Not quite, because there still may not be sufficient purchasing power with the poor, and there still may be luxuries being produced, and so on and so forth. At the end of the day, his verdict on the market economy, which he equates with capitalism following the general presumption of Islamic economics in this matter—see Chapter 3—represents the culmination of his Islamic vision, and is quite remarkable in light of our discussion here and in Chapters 5 and 6:

> The suggested remedy is a suppression of the market mechanism and conscious planning of the economy. Consumer needs are to be intelligently assessed and the various resources of the community are to be allocated to the production of required goods in preplanned manner. The produce is to be distributed according to the needs of the individuals. All this is to be done by a Central Authority" (1979, pp. 82–83).

But, then, what is his "Islamic" vision of that "social" or this time "central" authority? He does not have a single word to spare on the issue. Looking at the history of the past fourteen centuries, one could not escape the conclusion that if an Islamic society indeed had lexicographic orderings, orderings that were not restricted to just economic affairs—and there is no reason for us to assume any such thing—the first thing it would wish to put in order would be the institutional form of its government. Even if we restrict ourselves to economic affairs, as long as public goods are included in those preferences, we would arrive at the same conclusion. We may now turn to the second issue, relating to the place of competition in Islamic economics.

Islamic economists show an aversion to the idea of competition, for Muslim brothers are not supposed to compete with one another in worldly pursuits. They are rather supposed to cooperate with one another. This idea originated, as usual, with Siddiqi (1979), but then Kahf (1992) took it up, to present the world with the concept of free cooperation as an Islamic alternative to the Smithian sacrilege called perfect competition. More than anything else, the introduction of this new jargon creates the misperception that conventional economics opposes cooperation among economic agents. Such, of course, is far from true. What it recognizes is that such cooperation may lead to collusive behavior (Smith's famous dictum about the baker and the butcher on this account may be recalled here), leading to formation of cartels and monopoly behavior. Such behavior would amount to perfect cooperation, something in perfect accord with Islamic values as portrayed by Islamic economics. If it is pointed out that this is to misread Islamic economics, for that vision is predicated on the existence of all economic agents being homo-Islamicus, then, as pointed out in Chapter 1, economics becomes irrelevant, whether of the conventional or Islamic variety.

When Siddiqi proposes cooperation, he actually proposes a normative rule. What is forgotten is that no moral system will have any objection to cooperation for the sake of social good, and indeed an economic system is inherently an example of such cooperation. The study of this system, which is what economics is, must contend with ground realities; it must concern itself with "what is" before the question of what "ought to be" can be addressed. In other words, there is no point in presenting visions that do not conform to reality if the purpose is to understand the existing ground realities, and from there to figure out what the future course of events is likely to be. But the ironic thing is that those who dislike profit maximization because they feel that the maximized profits will always be excessive, also dislike the remedy, which reduces these maximized profits to zero, as would happen in the case of perfectly competitive long-run equilibrium. It is another matter whether in the value system of Islam there is any explicit injunction against maximization of profits regardless of their magnitude. And there is no point in reposing such a confidence in that cooperation in the context of imperfect competition when the ground reality does not suggest it to be the likely outcome, for remember, as was pointed out in Chapter 3, individuals always have an exaggerated sense of self importance, and it is not always possible for them to assess what their economic worth is, and therefore what the rules of this "cooperative" game would be.

It is in this light that we understand competition as an additional check on the play of self-interest. Let us put it this way to sum up the argument: the legal corpus of a society can only accord recognition to the general idea of exchange being a contract. It is generally beyond its competence to determine the precise exchange ratio in each and every act of exchange. That is to say, it is not possible for the legal corpus to determine what the exchange ratio between meat and wheat ought to be, particularly when there are thousands of other goods and services, and therefore exchange ratios, besides the one between those two. These exchange ratios are determined by the market mechanism. But would these market determined ratios be fair and just? It is here that competition as a check on the play of self-interest shows its worth by ensuring that no individual will is able to exploit the others. In the light of our discussion in Chapter 5, what it means is that an individual will can go astray and not that it will necessarily do so. And if that be so, no social system can be predicated on the assumption that this cannot happen. The Kahfian confusion in proposing free cooperation as an Islamic alternative to perfect competition resides in presuming not only that the rules of the game are perfectly clear—or in presuming that every entrepreneur knows what the maximum level of profit is that he is legitimately entitled to, an issue taken up by Kuran (1986)—but also that no individual will is corruptible under this cooperative spirit. No wonder then that in the writings of Islamic economists, any market form, be it monopoly, oligopoly, etc., turns out to be equally good, or equally bad. One may sum it up by saying that until their Utopia is established, Islamic economists will presumably continue to follow the way of regulation as shown by Ibn Taymiyya, a view which is perfectly in accord with what economics has to say on the issue. If that is granted, then a commitment to competition logically follows.

What would then need to be realized is that competition is not a hat to don and doff arbitrarily; it is an idea that requires institution through the legal corpus of a society, and thus will be reflected in the structure of a society's property rights.

Specification and Enforcement of Property Rights

We have discussed the issue of property rights at some length in Chapter 3 as well as in Chapter 5. In this chapter it has been emphasized that *fiqh* will have to come to terms with the requirements of the modern age in which it cannot remain aloof from the institutional form a government takes in an Islamic society, for it is the government which is supposed to enforce the given structure of a society's property rights. How this could be done is a matter of political science and thus beyond the scope of this work. But a little reflection identifies some of the fundamental difficulties involved. *Fiqh* does not have any armor to deal with the issue. As far as it is concerned, the institution of government does not exist. Yes, there may be a caliph, a sulṭān, an amīr, or whatever (to correspond to the Qur'ānic term *ūlī al-amr*), who issues orders that the Muslims are supposed to obey. But what are the responsibilities of such an office? And what happens if those responsibilities are not discharged? A *fiqh* where the only concept relating to collective dispensation turns out to be *farḍ al-kifāya* is not prepared to deal with contingencies where the government by itself may indeed be an instrument of oppression. Besides, when an institution that is supposed to enforce property rights and dispense justice does not discharge its obligations, it actually ends up committing an act of injustice for which there must be a retributive guidance from the system which claims to be a complete way of life. What does *fiqh*, and therefore fiqhnomics, have to say on this issue? A *fiqh* and fiqhnomics that consider business to be a *farḍ al-kifāya*—a quixotic and rather careless extension of the idea of *farḍ al-kifāya*, as though life could be possible without business, defined broadly to include production activity—have hardly anything to say on the subject except that the head of the state is responsible for everything that happens in his realm. What is to be done if that responsibility is not discharged, either willfully or through incompetence? Nothing. One almost has the temptation to conclude that as far as *fiqh* is concerned, governance is also a *farḍ al-kifāya*, a responsibility that someone from the community discharges without being held liable for the consequences. There is no penalty for not discharging the responsibility according to some given expectations. Even when an answer to the question of responsibility was forthcoming, which would require some novel *fiqh* conceptualizations, how sound in itself is the idea of holding one man responsible in the complex modern societies where the government is comprised of a vast bureaucracy and is supposed to perform myriad functions as discussed in Chapter 3? A reader may recall that at various places in the preceding chapters I have offered my observations in this respect.

In the end, in view of the importance accorded to what I have called fiqhnomics within the context of an Islamic economy, the following remarks are in order. From the point of view of economics, it is of utmost importance that the structure of property rights be as clearly defined as possible, and that it be as efficiently enforced as possible both to avoid the process of adverse selection, and thereby to avoid chaos in the society, and to keep the enforcement costs as low as possible. Both these things are emphasized in Chapter 3, but in the context of the process of adverse selection expounded there, consider the following scenario: assume a number of small, say retail, businesses, operating in one another's neighborhood, each making just the normal profits. Suppose one of them, whose self-interest degenerates into selfishness, is able in connivance with tax officials to get his tax liability reduced, or steals electricity from a state-owned natural monopoly, and therefore is able to increase his profits. Would the others be able to resist the temptation? If the others have a reasonably accurate idea of their worth and therefore of the Siddiqi's "minimum profits for an efficient living," the answer may be in the affirmative, although this would require a continuous renewal of that commitment to resist the temptation.

But now suppose the tax official who is not receiving a take from such scrupulous persons, having the required discretionary power increases their tax assessment; or imagine that the corrupt businessman reduces his prices in order to capture a larger share of business, since he can now afford to do so. The others will now be forced to follow suit or they will be forced out of business. The process of adverse selection now gets under way where those who have any Islamic scruples will be shunted out. This process is the result of either a misuse of the discretionary power, as exercised by the government functionaries, which amounts to incomplete specification of property rights, or lack of enforcement of discipline on them as in the case of electricity theft.

Again, consider the problem of public sector bribery so rampant in most Muslim countries. Webster's Dictionary defines a bribe as "money or favor given or promised in order to influence the judgment or conduct of a person in a position of trust." While a person in a position of trust could be a non-governmental person in a principal and agent relationship, most of the time, the instances of bribery as far as a common man is concerned relate to public servants (servants!). Consider, then, the very simple and straightforward case of an excludable public service demanded by an individual, let us say an identity document without which a person is not entitled to other public services. Suppose he submits the application; it is duly scrutinized and he is given a date when he may collect the document. When he presents himself on the given date, he is given another date, and then another date and so on and on, always receiving the same answer, that the document is not yet prepared. After wasting a considerable amount of his time and money, he eventually gets the hint and pays a certain amount of money to the public servant concerned and gets the job done. Is this a case of bribe?

The simplistic answer, the one commonly offered, is yes. But is it a bribe when looked at from the payer's point of view? If we recognize his right to have the identity paper, then we run into the problem of deeming a payment which was forced upon him to get his due right as a bribe. But if an answer is offered that yes, he had the right to get the identity paper but the structure of property rights did not specify the duration within which he was supposed to get his right delivered, then we run into the difficulty of incomplete specification of property rights, i.e. the case of discretionary power already noted. But then the question is on what basis was he given the delivery date at the time of his application, and why was he given another date, and another? Does the specification of property rights say anything on the responsibilities of the public official? If yes, was there any monitoring, or would it be that for every such infringement, the person will have to approach the courts, and bear the attendant costs, costs that are likely to be very high at least under the existing system of adjudication in most of the Muslim countries? Are all these things clarified in the structure of property rights? If not, what has *fiqh* to say on such matters?

And this is not the end of the story. Suppose an agent outside the office tells our applicant that if he pays him a certain amount of money, he will get the document prepared in time. Would this be a bribe? The answer would depend upon whether the structure of property rights accords recognition to such soliciting, and whether the soliciting fees are clearly spelled out. And whether these fees are meant to defray the cost of certain services that the agent was supposed to provide that the applicant himself could not manage or are they simply meant to grease the palm of the same public servant with whom the applicant could have dealt directly perhaps at a lower cost, i.e. without involving a third party? And if the system works regularly on a greasing of palms basis, why does the structure of property rights not institute a payment, a fee so to speak, for the "poor" public servants, and avoid the problem of bribery by making such payments legal? It all depends on how the property rights are defined.

Interestingly, the "poverty" of public sector workers, especially in the lower ranks in some Islamic countries, raises another pertinent issue. It is commonly observed that the society turns a blind eye to the serious problem of low wages paid to these workers. An important reason, if not the only one, for this phenomenon is that the public sector has been turned into an employment agency (this is obviously an instance of conflict between equity and efficiency) with the end result that where only one worker is needed there are usually four, and if the four do the work which only one could do, their combined wages could not be more than what would have been the wages of one, assuming that there is some correspondence between work and reward in the public sector. But is there? While it is difficult to answer that question, one thing is quite clear: public sector employment has now become a redistributive tool. Is this a good redistribution policy? Let us assume, for the sake of argument, that there are four workers instead of one and all four are paid what one would have been paid otherwise. Seemingly, this should not raise any concern, provided that we further assume that no work would have been available to the additional three otherwise. The answer under all these stringent and unrealistic assumptions is still in the negative. Such a policy promotes a culture of shirking and lethargy, such that when four are supposed to do the work of one, none actually does the work responsibly (which is the process of adverse selection in another guise). It promotes a culture of irresponsibility that spills over into the private sector. If the public sector is inefficient, the private sector can hardly be assumed to be otherwise in exactly the same way that a sick financial sector cannot spawn healthy industries. But let us go back to the beginning. From the point of view of an individual citizen who cannot get his due rights under a well-defined structure of property rights without greasing someone's palms is concerned, let us read the dictionary definition of extortion: "the act or practice of extorting, especially obtaining money or other property by coercion or intimidation; generally an offense committed by an official engaging in such practice."

These examples are offered merely for the sake of illustration, but they do point to the issues that *fiqh* and fiqhnomics will need to tackle within the context of an institution, the government, where often nobody seems to be responsible for anything. I may end this discussion by noting that in light of the Islamic doctrine of individual responsibility, the structure of government must be so decentralized as to make it possible to assign individual responsibility through a well defined code of rules and regulation (or the property rights pertaining to public service). And since government functionaries are subject to the temptations of free will, their discretionary powers must be kept to the minimum possible in this code of conduct, for just like an entrepreneurial free will, the bureaucratic free will can equally go astray. In the final analysis, we must not forget that the government, if we assume it to be of a representative variety, itself is a classic case of principle and agent problem subject to heavy pulls of moral hazard.

Finally, a few words about the issue of asymmetric information hinted at earlier. In view of the vast recent literature on the subject, I would only restrict myself to noting one important conclusion: informational asymmetries make it possible for some, especially the agent in a principle and agent relationship, to exploit the principles to their own advantage. The recent crises of corporate governance, be it Enron or WorldCom in the United States, or Parmalat in Italy, to name but a few, would have been highly unlikely had the legal corpus of those countries not turned a blind eye to the existence of glaring informational asymmetries between the principles, the shareholders, and the agents, that is to say the management, a management which exercised rather unlimited power over the assets of the principles. The situation is not any better in the Islamic realm as far as I can see. It may be admitted that the disclosure requirements may vary from case to case, which means that the legal corpus may not be able to handle the problem—recall our discussion with regard to the role of competition earlier. After all, we see an emphasis on ethics to rectify the situation. My point is that the laws pertaining to disclosure of information will not only be essential but perhaps more stringent in an Islamic economy than is the case in the capitalist economies.

CHAPTER EIGHT

FACTORS AND FACTOR REWARDS

A Perspective on the Theory of Distribution

The issue of factor rewards is one of the most complicated subjects in economics, and manifestly the one which is the source of most of the dissatisfaction felt by Islamic economists with regard to conventional economics. The complications of conventional analysis could not but spill over into Islamic economics, and since Islamic economics did not care much about the virtue of clarity, even in those areas where the conventional analysis was fairly transparent, the degree of confusion multiplied when the subject came under the pen of the Islamic economists. As far as the conventional analysis is concerned, the complications center around the well-known problems associated with either the aggregation issues, or the identification, and therefore the role and rewards, of entrepreneurship. There is a third problem, relating to drawing a distinction between physical and circulating varieties of capital, which the conventional analysis considers trivial but which forms the point of departure in some of the formulations of Islamic economics. It is the circulating capital that is most exposed to the charge of *ribā* when this is unequivocally equated to interest. In some formulations, fixed return on any form of capital is considered equivalent to *ribā*. It is thought that since capital is necessarily exposed to risk, its owners must bear the corresponding risk (here notwithstanding Siddiqi, as we saw in Chapter 7) and must not be allowed to pass it on to someone else, which is what is supposed to happen when a fixed interest is earned.[1] The panacea for most of these problems, it is argued, resides in profit-sharing in one form or another. We

[1] When a student of conventional economics reads this, the first thought that comes to mind is: but the real rate of interest, and thus the real return which is what counts, is not known *ex-ante*. As far as Islamic economists are concerned, this question is irrelevant. It may also be noted that this rationale for the prohibition of *ribā* has no origin in *fiqh* literature, see, for example, Razi's (d. 1209) discussion of this subject. Both these issues are discussed in Chapter 10.

are told that it is the idea of profit-sharing that represents the true Islamic perspective on the questions relating to distribution, particularly when the institution of interest is abolished. We are also given the impression that this approach is novel as far as the conventional economic analysis is concerned, and implicitly, for the relevant issues are hardly ever explicitly stated, it is also supposed to resolve the difficulties associated with the conventional conceptualization of entrepreneurial input. In the following pages we will explore these premises to see how judicious this agenda has turned out to be. Specific attention will focus on the authenticity of the profit-sharing as the true Islamic perspective as per the original sources of Islamic imperatives as well as the analytical integrity of what are offered as new perspectives on the distributional issues.

The conventional difficulties in the theory of distribution do not elicit much response from the Islamic economists, for much of the conventional analysis is wittingly or unwittingly disowned on the presumption that the Islamic perspective on all matters economic will necessarily be different. This vision has been held so firmly, as it turns out, that even when it was unwarranted, Islamic perspective was colored to make it look different. Be that as it may, we cannot fully understand what is being offered as the new dispensation until we know the backdrop against which it is being laid out. Besides, to determine what is novel and what is not in the new coloring, we require some knowledge of the mosaic on that backdrop. We would note that Chapter 4 was intended to provide the necessary elements of this backdrop. Some of those elements, those relating to entrepreneurial and circulating capital, now need to be recalled here in a summary form. We note that issues pertaining to aggregation, particularly of capital, were not discussed in that chapter. To the extent those become relevant in view of Islamic economics emphasis on the rate of return in contrast to the rate of interest, they will be taken up in what follows.

The Backdrop

In Smith, we saw two explicit factors of production, land and labor, and an implicit factor that was referred to as the capitalist-employer in Chapter 4. He was the residual claimant after wages and rent had been paid, and this residual was sometimes referred to as profit and sometimes interest, though with hindsight we can see that it included both of those elements. In the wake of the marginalist revolution, when entrepreneurship was recognized as a separate factor of production, we see the capitalist-employer transformed into an equity-capitalist-entrepreneur who was now the residual claimant after not only the wages and rent, but also the interest had been deducted from the receipts of the enterprise. The close association between capital and entrepreneurship is not without reason. The fourth factor of production, the entrepreneurship, has had a somewhat checkered history. At the practical level, since the entrepreneur can run into losses, he has to be a person of considerable means to weather the storms, and that obviously establishes the connection with the capitalist class. When losses do accrue, it is the value of the enterprise that is immediately effected, which in turn means that it is the property assets, i.e. physical capital and land, which take a direct hit. If the incidence of losses therefore falls to a considerable extent on the capital, it is natural to associate entrepreneurship with capital.

Then there was, and still is, the difficult issue of justifying the existence of the entrepreneur in the long-run equilibrium in the standard, perfectly competitive, model. Although the standard model allows normal profits to the entrepreneur, as its opportunity cost, it is not at all clear what the entrepreneur was supposed to do in that long-run equilibrium, and what those normal profits therefore were for. A related difficulty arises because of the fact that there is no objective way of determining the level of those normal profits. There is no market for entrepreneurial input. The standard routine in which the opportunity cost of entrepreneurial input is explained in terms of what the entrepreneur would get if he were to work somewhere else is clearly unsatisfactory, for what is thus being identified as the opportunity cost of entrepreneurship is actually the opportunity cost of his labor input and not the entrepreneurial input. There is no objective way of splitting the actual profits into the required "normal" and "abnormal" categories. The theory of profit does not draw any distinction between these categories, and the explanations offered implicitly focus on abnormal profits. No wonder then that these explanations justifiably assign a role to the entrepreneur out of equilibrium, and profits thus emerge as a dynamic surplus, as discussed in Chapter 4. What, however, we wish to note here is that because of these ambiguities, any amount of profit could be justified, and by the same token any amount of profit could be castigated. These issues become even more complicated in the next stage of capitalistic development.

In the trustified version of capitalism, or managerial capitalism, it is the dominant equity holders along with the management who become the controllers of residual. All, or a large part, of the residual is now shared by the equity holders (as dividend) and management (as bonuses), at the discretion of the residual controllers. If profit is retained, its use also remains at the discretion of the residual controllers. Who is a capitalist, and who is not, in this complex organizational and decision-making structure is not an easy question to answer. For it cannot be answered only on the basis of the formal ownership, and therefore risk bearing dimensions, of the enterprise. The formal owners, and thus the dividend receivers, now also include small shareholders who for all practical purposes have no say in the crucial decisions that influence the magnitude of profits. In Chapter 4, I have argued that the controllers of residual are the eminent members of the class called capitalist. That these capitalists now receive part of the profits (normal or abnormal, who knows?) is quite evident, but they may also receive interest income to the extent they supply the debt capital. However, it is also true that a large proportion of the suppliers of debt capital, and therefore receivers of interest income, are small savers, and these could hardly be labeled capitalists by any stretch of imagination. It is also noteworthy that while the residual controllers have a discretionary power over the distribution of dividends, they do not exercise similar power on the payment of interest. Thus we see that a part of the total profits and a part of total interest payments accrues to small stake holders. If ire is to be directed at the excesses committed by capitalism, say in the form of excessive profits made, or earning a fixed return in the form of interest regardless of whether the enterprise makes any profits—the favorite accusation leveled by the Islamic economists—this fact will need to be kept in mind. At any rate, if a culprit is to be identified, one could hardly escape the conclusion that this must include the management followed by the dominant equity holders, with the qualification that the latter group may indeed be a part of the former, that is, the controllers of residual. It may also be noted that in the case of losses, the residual controllers are able to protect their own interests by passing the losses on to the small equity holders, though not the holders of debt capital—including of course the small savers—because of their lack of discretionary powers over the required interest payments except in the extreme case of default.

Since profits are perfectly permissible in the Islamic outlook, we need to be clear about the conventional perspective about them. In that perspective, profits are supposed to be a reward for entrepreneurship. But who exactly is the entrepreneur in this new setting? We saw in Chapter 4 that as the size of a firm grew to take advantage of the economies of scale, it led to a divorce of ownership from control. Indeed more than that, in so far as the modern corporate form also implies a divorce of ownership from entrepreneurship. Not all the owners could be party to the crucial decisions determining the profitability of the firm simply because of the diffusion and dilution of ownership. In the beginning, the role of entrepreneur was assumed by the major shareholders, but eventually that role substantially passed on to professional management. Should therefore the salaries of these professional managers be reckoned as profits? To put the question in a slightly different way: should the professional managers be entitled to a share of the profits? Economic theory gave an affirmative answer to this question. It reasoned that due to the divorce of ownership from control, and the accompanying principal and agent problem, the solution to the moral hazard problem could be found in some sort of profit-sharing arrangement, thus aligning the interests of the managers (the agents) with those of the owners (the principals). Thereby evolved a spectrum of profit sharing arrangements; often the magnitude of profits to be shared was left unspecified, to be determined in the form of bonuses at the discretion of the residual controllers, and the payment of the bonuses was not just confined to the management; workers also received a part in the form of efficiency wages. Thus profits were not meant just for the entrepreneurs (however defined) but also for the wage recipients. Yet most of what was to be shared went, increasingly it would appear with the passage of time, to the management. The extreme case of this occurred in the American form of corporate governance before the Sorbanes-Oxley Act when the management was virtually given a blank check as to how those profits were to be distributed. The agent was thus supposed to resolve the principle and agent problem, ostensibly in the name of flexibility required for an efficient management. If the excesses of management in the form of the Ebbers, the Skillings, the Stewarts and the Lays of this capitalist world came to the surface now, they should not be considered isolated episodes. These excesses were to be expected given the powers vested with the management; it is only that these now became unsustainable due to a process of adverse selection that had been underway for quite some time—a process that is described in Chapter 3. The process, interpreted in the present context, would imply not only an ever-increasing number of unscrupulous hands in the top management but also an increasing quantum of funds spindled in each case. All of the foregoing issues need to be taken into consideration when it comes to evaluate the profit-sharing arrangements proposed by the Islamic economists. That we will do in due time. One thing may be noted right away, and that is the following puzzle: one is never quite sure what to make of the writings of Islamic economists when they defend the management (which is what the entrepreneur is called in their parlance, and leaving aside the confusion on that score as we saw in the case of Siddiqi in the previous chapter) who may exercise all the power noted above, and attack the capitalist who, even in their conceptualizations, may well be a small equity holder. Furthermore, since the entrepreneur in certain cases, specifically in small businesses, may be the same person as the capitalist, one can hardly make out who is being defended and who is being castigated.

The second set of issues revolves around the concept of capital as a factor of production and its reward, particularly with respect to the circulating capital. Since Islamic economists equate *ribā* with interest, the conceptualization of interest being a return for capital poses a special difficulty. Even in the conventional economic discourse, there is considerable confusion on this score, at least in terms of the terminology used. Is it the rate of interest or is it the rate of profit? Of course these turn out to be identical in the absence of uncertainty, or in a steady state equilibrium. But the real world never conforms to this steady state parable. Further confusion is created when profits are reckoned to be a reward for entrepreneurship and the rate of profit is reckoned to be the reward for capital, as the marginal product of capital. The idea of marginal product of capital cannot be easily divorced from the idea of transformation, the transformation of putty, finance, into clay, physical capital. When economics talks about the rate of profit, it does so on the presumption that finance, or financial capital, has undergone the required transformation. But when the same logic is extended to the institution of interest, and thereby to the rate of interest (i.e. by equating it to the rate of profit), it is done on somewhat tenuous grounds, for practically speaking no such presumption about transformation is strictly valid under the institutionalization of interest. When credit is extended under that system in the capitalist economies, the structure of property rights does not necessarily impose the conditionality of transformation. That is not to say that transformation does not occur, most of the time it does, but there is no legal stipulation that it must. In view of the necessity of the circulating capital for an enterprise, such a stipulation may seem too restrictive. But then, it is this anomaly which leads Islamic economists to presume that no transformation is implied or intended. For them, all capital is putty (call it money, liquidity, or finance) and all capitalists are debt capitalists, or holders of debt instruments (more on this a little later). Let us put it this way: if the conventional economic discourse takes the transformation for granted, Islamic economists implicitly proceed on the presumption that no such thing occurs. Yet it must be pointed out that this is not how the Islamic economists articulate the issue; evidence to this effect comes only indirectly from the way capital is treated, as we will see shortly. The usual way in which they proceed is to highlight that the rate of profit, or for that matter rate of return as they would have it, is not known *ex-ante* while the rate of interest is.[2] There is no gainsaying that economics concerns itself with the real rate of interest which is not known *ex-ante* (Islamic economics' response to the issue of real versus nominal rate of interest is discussed in Chapter 10 under indexation). For them any rate of return is perfectly permissible following the *Sharīʿa*, and this is because it is necessarily uncertain, whereas any rate of interest, small or large, is not so, no matter whether nominal or real. But how sound is the idea that rate of return is always uncertain? An answer to this question, besides having an obvious bearing on the position taken by Islamic economics, is also important from the perspective of an individual investor who may be concerned about the permissibility or otherwise of the various ways such returns may accrue from the *fiqh* point of view.

This issue is directly related to the conceptualization of factors of production and their rewards. When economics identifies four factors of production, it does so as a gross simplification of reality, and this conceptualization is marred by the attendant aggregation problems. Furthermore, when economics identifies wages as reward for labor services, interest as reward for capital services, rent as reward for land services, and normal profits as reward for entrepreneurial services, it glosses over a number of complications that render such a strict correspondence between the factor services and their rewards problematic from a puritan's point of view. One would confront serious practical

---

[2] In the cruder versions of such articulations, money's connection with finance is not recognized, and since money, *per se*, is barren, no return on finance is therefore justifiable.

difficulties if one wished to apportion rewards to various factors in a conceptually precise and impeccable manner. Consequently, what may appear like fixed wages may indeed be a fixed reward to investment in, let us say, human capital, or what may appear as fixed rent may indeed be return to investment in land from an individual recipient's point of view. The aggregation problems arise when one attempts to lump diverse things under one heading, generally to handle the real-life complexity that otherwise would render the analysis too abstruse at times and therefore seemingly of not much use, practically speaking. While economics from the very beginning did not feel encumbered by the diversity of goods and services it was called upon to handle, it shied away from doing the same on the factors side. Thus it is that the conceptual apparatus of economics began with merely two factors of production in Smith, at least explicitly; it added physical capital as it became increasingly important to the process of production, and then was forced to add entrepreneurship, as the nineteenth century wore on, to lend credence to the marginal productivity theory of distribution, as we saw in Chapter 4. Accordingly, labor was paid wages, land commanded rent, capital's contribution was rewarded by interest, and the entrepreneur ended up with the residual, a part of which was supposed to be normal profit, recognized as the opportunity cost of entrepreneurial services. But then the actual profit may in fact diverge from the normal profit, either up or down, to yield positive or negative abnormal profit that also went to the entrepreneur as part and parcel of the actual residual.

Consider labor. The iron law of wages that treated labor as some sort of homogenous input did perhaps make some sense at the time, towards the end of the eighteenth century, but as human capital became increasingly important to the process of production in the wake of technological change, the homogeneity assumption clearly became problematic; for now what went under the rubric of wages was quite clearly not the same thing as what wages denoted when human capital was not as important, in the pre-industrial revolution economy. The specialization of labor that accompanied technological change meant that what was paid to labor as wages partly included returns for what subsequently came to be known as human capital. In such a situation, there would be as many wage rates as kinds of labor. If economics lumps all forms of labor together and continues to talk about *the* wage rate, it obviously does so as a gross simplification of reality. Things turn out to be even more complicated when one considers capital. Even if the complications that arise due to working (or circulating) capital and inventory capital are disregarded, there is no satisfactory way of aggregating the diverse forms the physical capital assumes. Ever since her student Ruth Cohen pointed the problem out to Joan Robinson, which subsequently came to be referred to as the "Ruth Cohen Curiosum," and led to the so-called Cambridge controversies in capital theory, the problems relating to aggregation of capital have dogged economics, without any satisfactory resolution. Samuelson's (1962) answer, in his conceptualization of surrogate production function, while satisfactory for certain applications at the macro level, does not resolve the difficulty at the micro level where the issue of heterogeneity of capital cannot be fudged. At the micro level, Solow's (1963) argument that "the central concept in capital theory should be *the rate of return on investment*" (p. 16), subsequently further clarified by Pasinetti (1969), seem quite satisfactory, for while re-switching mars the process of measuring capital at the aggregate level in the *ex-post* sense, it does not pose the same level of difficulty at the time investment decisions are made, i.e. in the *ex-ante* sense. Putting it slightly differently, while it may be difficult to define *the* rate of interest, or for that matter *the* rate of profit, in a conceptually impeccable manner, it is quite appropriate to talk of the rate of return on investment, and there may exist a whole array of rates of return at any given time in a world of heterogeneous capital.

There is no doubt that process of arbitrage leads towards equalization of rewards to various categories of capital in the *ex-ante* sense once one assumes the existence of some reference rate of profit, say an average economy-wide rate of profit in the *ex-post* sense. But the arbitrage process never gets completely exhausted in the real world of flux, which never quite attains the stationary or steady state equilibrium. Out of that equilibrium, things become messy, as Joan Robinson (1953) noted: "We are accustomed to talk of the rate of profit on capital earned by a business as though *profits and capital were both sums of money*. Capital when it consists of as yet uninvested finance is a money, and the net receipts of a business are sums of money. But the two never co-exist in time. While the capital is a sum of money, the profits are not yet being earned. When the profits (quasi-rents) are being earned, the capital has ceased to be money and become a plant. All sorts of things may happen which cause the value of the plant to diverge from its original cost" (p. 87, emphasis added).[3] In a world of uncertainty when the *ex-ante* expectations about profits are not realized in the *ex-post* reality, the actual rate of return may diverge from the expected rate of return. It is in this world of reality that losses may indeed accrue to the entrepreneur, and thus secure a role for him in the process of production as seen in Chapter 4, a point taken up later.

The rate of return approach also facilitates our understanding of some other difficulties that arise when we look at the rewards for other factors of production where those rewards may be reckoned differently by the buyers of factor services as compared to the sellers (suppliers) of those services. But besides these supply side complications, there are the complications that arise when the demand side is introduced into the analysis. One of Ricardo's (1817) contributions to economic thought resides in introducing the demand side into the factor reward determination process. Land commands rent because it is supposed to be fixed in supply, and therefore rent arises due to its scarcity in relation to demand. By the same logic, other factors may command scarcity rent, the quasi-rent, because of changes in their relative scarcity as a result of continuing changes in product demand for all sorts of reasons. For instance, wages at times may include quasi-rent, besides being a reward for raw labor as well as returns for the human capital component. One would recognize that in the long-run equilibrium in a perfectly competitive industry, labor will be paid a wage rate equal to the value of its marginal product. If the long-run equilibrium is now disturbed following an increase in demand, the derived demand for labor will increase. Although the marginal physical product curve does not change, yet the value of the marginal product curve will shift upwards. When a firm now responds by increasing its output, this change in quantity supplied is subject to the law of diminishing returns. At the new short-run equilibrium, marginal physical product of labor is lower, yet the wage rate inclusive of the quasi-rent is higher, resulting in a higher component of producers' surplus accruing to labor. Similarly, in a heterogeneous capital world, some forms of capital may earn quasi-rent, positive or negative, during periods of disequilibrium.

---

[3] Joan Robinson is obviously not talking of the circulating capital here, a point which will become significant in our later discussion in this chapter.

Let us now turn to the issue raised above, and consider, for instance, land. A producer who pays for the land services reckons it as rent but from the point of view of seller who had bought that land as an investment, that rent is simply a return on his investment. Although from the society's viewpoint, a transaction involving an existing asset such as land represents a mere transfer of ownership—for that would be considered as an investment by one individual accompanied by disinvestment by another—from the individual's point of view there is no difference between the purchase of land and purchase of a new machine for leasing purposes. Rent, as a pure surplus, accrued to the original owners when the property rights in land were recognized, let us say, for instance, at the time of the enclosure movement in England. But as far as the subsequent owners are concerned, it simply represents a return on investment. Of course, from the social point of view, it retains its logical integrity as a pure surplus which accrues to anyone who acquires the property rights in it. An individual who has a certain amount of investable resources at his disposal would have a variety of options available to him. He may indeed use these funds to build up his own human capital in the expectation of earning a higher wage rate. What he may then receive in the form of higher wages will simply be a return on investment in human capital, an investment which this time corresponds to what would be strictly referred to as investment in the economic sense. In other words, there is no corresponding disinvestment, as happened in the case of a transfer of ownership of land. The point is that from the point of view of the seller of factor services, what accrues to him as wages, rent, and interest may not necessarily correspond to what these factor rewards denote in economics, strictly speaking. The arbitrage process will tend to equalize the rate of return on investment regardless of whether it shows up in the form of higher wages, rent, interest or profits, at the same time that all of these may partly reflect quasi-rent. Thus we see that what may appear as fixed wages, or rent may indeed include a fixed component as return on investment. At this stage we may specifically note that in an Islamic perspective a fixed rate of return is perfectly permissible irrespective of what it may be called. For instance, it may be paid as wages to labor (for the investment in human capital), to physical capital (rental), or to land (rent).

Returning to the issue of circulating capital, we note that it functionally seems to fit the bill of how Islamic economists conceive of capital, that is to say, it exists in the putty form. Conventional economics did not feel the need to scurtinize the distinction between rate of interest and rate of profit. Perhaps it was because of the complication of handling two forms of capital, the circulating and physical varieties, in a production process where both were indispensable, and where the financial capital could be used either way depending upon the requirements at hand, at least in the *ex-ante* sense. If physical capital was entitled to a return, so must be working capital, for physical capital could not produce anything without the complementary circulating capital. We can discern the thought process of the early exponents of economics on this issue thus: though not itself undergoing a transformation, working capital (Smith's wages fund) was intimately connected with the process of transformation such that there was no need to draw a distinction between it and physical capital. (This issue was addressed at some length in Chapter 4—Taussig's concerns). And as the process of capital deepening gathered steam, and as working capital continued to become a smaller and smaller proportion of the overall capital requirements of an enterprise, the issue of drawing such a distinction became of marginal importance. Eventually economics more or less assumed the distinction away, at least at the theoretical level.

However, one must note that the circulating capital may slush around the financial system as short term debt, looking for the highest returns, in the interim period when it may not be needed as a cushion. Admittedly, it may serve as circulating capital for those enterprises that run into difficulties and had not set aside enough funds to weather the storm, and therefore may be willing to pay a higher rate of interest. Nevertheless, it can invite a charge from someone concerned about money earning money. Although not articulated in so many words, one can discern that it is this perspective that forms the point of departure for the Islamic economists when they level the charge against debt capital, or articulate their concept of "time value of money." One may also note that a part, perhaps a significant part, of this debt capital comes from retained profits, their magnitude being determined at the discretion of the residual controllers.

Regardless of the way the Islamic economists articulate their disapproval, that it is this roving capital which is at the back of their minds is clear from the fact that they willingly accept the idea of fixed returns on property assets, though there may be differences of opinion on this count as we will see, be they physical capital or land, but they would call such returns rental income, an idea quite familiar to conventional economics. One could perhaps define a rental rate if one so wished, and this comes to more or less the same thing as rate of interest in the conventional economic thinking with the crucial difference that unlike the rate of interest, the rental rate necessarily implies transformation, and includes a depreciation component. But how do the Islamic economists propose to handle the issue of the necessary circulating capital? Their answer is that it ought to be achieved in the form of profit sharing. Here it suffices to note that the concepts of profit-sharing and returns on investment are not something new to economic discourse, introduced by Islamic economics, as seen above. We now turn to what the Islamic economists have to say on the issue of factors and their rewards in light of what they perceive as Islamic imperatives.

The Islamic Economists' Perspectives

In Siddiqi (1992), we observe the conventional classification of the factors of production with the difference that financial capital (he probably means circulating capital) is separately treated. The factor rewards are conventional as far as labor and land are concerned. Physical capital gets rental income, and circulating capital and entrepreneurship share profits according to a predetermined sharing ratio. Sadiq (1992), on the other hand, looks at the issue from an individual's point of view and lumps the physical capital and land under one heading, the property assets, a perspective that we encountered earlier in this chapter. He also keeps the circulating capital separate from physical capital, and has management instead of entrepreneurship. He allows wages for labor, grants a rental payment for property assets, and argues for a sharing of the residual, that he calls profits, between the two remaining factors, financial capital and management. In both of these formulations, profits are not split between the familiar conceptual categories, normal and abnormal profits. Implicitly, therefore, there is no recognition of a distinct opportunity cost of entrepreneurship. Either these profits, whatever their magnitude, are supposed to represent the opportunity cost of the entrepreneurship, a problematic notion in view of their open-ended nature, or else they are a pure surplus, and not a reward for any economic contribution. Either the opportunity cost of entrepreneurship is indeterminate or the entrepreneurship is a free factor. Both of these interpretations are problematic. Either any amount of profit is justified, or none is. Of course there is the other side of this problem, which is that if we consider profits to be an opportunity cost of entrepreneurship, how do we come to terms with the notion of negative opportunity cost when these profits turn out to be negative?

Then there is Zubair Hasan's (1986) conceptualization. In him we have the three conventionally defined factors: land, labor, and capital, the latter presumably of only physical variety. There is no entrepreneurship in his scheme of things, and thus the question of splitting the actual profits into the normal and abnormal categories does not arise. Land is allowed the conventional rent, labor is to be paid some maintenance (subsistence) wage, but then over and above that is conceived to share the surplus, i.e. profits, with capital according to some predetermined proportions. Capital is not to be allowed any fixed rental. Its reward is its share of the profits, which may turn out to be negative. There is no conceptualization of the opportunity cost of capital as in the previous writers. Both capital and entrepreneurship are free factors, the owners of which share the pure surplus, which by itself is openended. Again, in his formulation, any amount of profit is permitted by the *Sharīʿa*. Besides, in his conceptualization, there is no recognition of the circulating capital, and therefore no question of any returns on it. In a later paper, Hasan (1992) looks at the implications of his conceptualization for the equilibrium of the firm, which raises more questions than it answers, to which we will turn shortly. Then there is the conceptualization by Mustafa and Askari (1986) in which there is physical capital, land, and labor, with the entrepreneurial function entrusted to both capital and labor. They recognize the opportunity costs of all the three explicitly stated factors, and these are therefore to be paid the market determined wage rate, rent, and rental (in their terminology normal profits, a confusing one at the very least, but which, thankfully, they later clarify to be contractual rent, or in our terminology rental). Labor and capital are then to share the residual, which, rather peculiarly, they call abnormal profits. One may grant them their freedom of choice in the use of terminology—leaving aside the confusion this is likely to create in view of the conventional usage of these terms—but what labor then receives out of these profits is not for its work, but *qua* entrepreneur, and similarly what capital gets of these profits accrues to the owner of capital *qua* entrepreneur. In absence of any recognition of the opportunity cost of entrepreneurship, our previous remarks about the conceptual questions that arise are equally relevant in their case.

How ignoring the opportunity cost of an economic input gives rise to misleading conclusions is illustrated when we consider Hasan's (1992) use of his conceptualization to work out its implications for the output decisions of a firm. He uses an imperfectly competitive model, reduces the wage rate from the market determined one, W, to what he calls the maintenance wage rate, w, thereby reducing the explicit labor costs. He uses a cost function that yields linear average and marginal cost curves that both begin at the origin—so he does not have any fixed costs!—and ends up with a post reduction marginal cost curve that has a negative intercept. He then goes through the derivation of profit functions, one pre-, and the other post-reduction, to prove the obvious, that the post reduction profit, π^1 is greater than pre-reduction profit, π^*. The firm now produces a larger output, obviously because the explicit costs have gone down in the model, the explicit marginal cost curve shifts down. He tells us that the increase in profits is greater than the cost-saving due to decreased wage rate, perhaps implying that the labor can be more than compensated with these increased profits. But then since profits, including the additional component, are to be shared between the owners of capital and labor, it is not clear whether labor will come out any better now. He does not bother himself with this question and is content to show us that the new profits, that now include part of the opportunity cost of labor, are higher than before as though this, by itself, is necessarily a superior outcome from the Islamic point of view, and as though labor would necessarily be indifferent to this new outcome even when it is being exposed to risk, and does not even know whether it will receive the same compensation as it received before this profit-sharing went into effect. The only thing his model shows for sure is that the output of the firm will be higher, as though this is necessarily a good thing by itself, without appeal to some social criterion.

Let us put the question somewhat differently, and ask if these so-called higher profits represent an improvement from the social point of view. The real question is this: would the profits at the now higher output level once adjusted downwards for the now higher opportunity cost of labor (for the higher output would imply that one way or another more labor has been used) be higher than what they would be at that output level without the new dispensation of profit-sharing? The answer is obviously negative, for otherwise the firm was not maximizing its profits to begin with. If indeed the firm was not maximizing profits originally, was it because of shirking and relatively high monitoring costs? Hasan does not explore these questions, except to assert that "the non-fixity of returns to the productive agents" permits "the firm to be more venturesome by ensuring a wide risk spread and more of work effort on the part of productive agents" (p. 249). This is the sort of confusion that can arise when a scarce economic resource is treated as though it is free. There is no reason for us to assume that making an explicit cost implicit reduces its magnitude.

What Hasan in fact does is to take Vanek's (1965) argument, subsequently elaborated upon by Samuelson (1977), and then fully taken up in Weitzman's (1984) *The Share Economy* but then casts it in the context of a firm to support the same conclusions that Vanek and Weitzman draw at the macro level. Mario Nuti (1995), who has had a longstanding interest in the subject, evaluates those contributions and shows considerable skepticism about the results at the theoretical level as well as questioning their practical relevance. At the theoretical level, one of the difficulties he points out is related to what was said a little earlier about the reckoning of total rather than just explicit costs. Nuti writes; "First, firms should be well aware that, whatever their pay formula, they can only attract workers by offering the going rate for labour total pay and should regard this, and not the fixed element of pay, as marginal cost of labour" (p. 43). It is conceivable that the Vanek–Weitzman results would hold if the employers do not have information on the "going rate of labour," which will happen under the extreme condition where all firms follow the sharing arrangement. However, such a state of affairs is possible only if the sharing system is imposed by law. Nuti remarks that under a sharing system, "one way or another, additional employment would result from either lower profits or lower labour earnings or a combination of both, just as if a subsidy on additional employment was introduced and financed out of a tax on profits or on the wages of those currently employed. Neither arrangement would be introduced contractually and would have to be imposed by legislation" (p. 39). In an Islamic economy, since the *Sharīʿa* permits fixed wage contracts, it would not be possible to impose an economy-wide sharing system, exposing labor income to risk and uncertainty.

The issue of fixed returns versus variable returns cannot be fully appreciated until it is recognized that in the final analysis it boils down to a question of alternative specifications of property rights. According to the Coase theorem (Coase, 1960), as long as the property rights are clearly defined and transaction costs are negligible, the allocation of resources will be efficient regardless of the exact delineation of those rights. It is of course possible that different specifications of the property rights may have different transaction costs, in which case such costs may become an important consideration in specification of property rights. Furthermore, different specifications of property rights will lead to different distributions of benefits and costs. What this means is that in a particular situation, a society may prefer a particular specification of property rights in view of its distributional consequences even though the transaction costs may be low for an alternative specification of property rights. (This represents another instance of conflict between efficiency and equity, a subject covered in Chapter 2.) This point is of fundamental significance when the primary issue turns out be one of choosing between equally acceptable alternative specifications of property rights under a given system of values.

When we consider the fixed returns versus variable returns alternatives under this light, the following points draw our attention. First, if the transaction costs are assumed to be negligible under both the alternatives, the allocation of resources will not be effected by the specification of property rights. If one of those specifications of property rights is preferred on distributional grounds, the choice is quite clear cut in its favor. Second, if the transaction costs are not negligible, those will now need to be taken into consideration. For instance, barring distributional considerations, the specification that has lower transaction costs then becomes the obvious choice. If distributional considerations are important, the specification that has the lowest transaction costs but leads to the same distributional outcome should be preferred. There may be other such combinations that would require careful weighing of transaction costs against the accompanying redistributional benefits. The principle of reckoning the costs and benefits of a particular specification of property rights is by no means intended to rule out the possibility that sometimes a particular specification of property rights may be selected on distributional, or other societal values, considerations even though the transaction costs may be relatively high.

When we look at profit-sharing in Hasan's way, we cannot escape the fact that the transaction costs of instituting profit-sharing between capital and labor are likely to be quite high, simply because of the diverse forms labor assumes in view of the human capital component. There will have to be a different profit-sharing ratio for each type of labor, which will render the system cumbersome. But there is another serious problem that is usually not adequately, if at all, addressed. Even if we assume that labor is homogeneous—an assumption that could be more justifiably made in the case of capital, particularly of the circulating variety—the question now is how will the sharing ratio be determined? Islamic economists provide too simplistic an answer to this question in that the sharing ratio will be determined through mutual consent of the parties, which is to say that it will be determined through negotiations between the two parties. What is troubling is that it is then presumed that whatever sharing ratio is thus determined will necessarily be fair. This is like saying that since every exchange is voluntary, any price charged would necessarily be "just and fair." For some writers, the favorite alternative is a determination through a government fiat. For those who seemingly do not feel comfortable with the idea of leaving it to government, for it could fall short of their ideal, the ratio must be juridically determined, a veiled reference to determination through a *fatwā*.[4] In light of our discussion in Chapter 7, none of these answers is satisfactory, unless we interpret the determination through mutual consent to mean that it is determined through the market forces of demand and supply, and even there one must be aware that the outcome will be just only if no single party is able to exercise any influence on the sharing ratio so determined, i.e. is determined through a competitive market process. By taking a somewhat hostile position against even the competitive markets, Islamic economists put themselves in a straightjacket of always resorting to an omnipotent government to come to their rescue when answers elude them.

Theoretically, all factors of production could be conceived of as collaborating in the process of production on the basis of variable returns, with each distinct factor getting its reward according to its sharing ratio, with the sum of all the sharing ratios being equal to one. In this case, total revenue will show up as total profit. At the other extreme, all factors except the entrepreneur—being necessarily the residual claimant—could get fixed returns. In a world of perfect information, the outcome in both cases would turn out to be the same as Coase theorem would imply as long as the transaction costs for both specifications of property rights are the same. With these assumptions,

[4] See, for instance, Hasan (1992), p. 40.

any other specification of property rights, that is to say any intermediate position between these two extremes, gives the same results. In a world of uncertainty, the variable income recipients end up bearing the burden of the variability in returns, be that the conventional entrepreneur alone as in the latter case, or all the factors as in the former case where, in a sense, all factors become part entrepreneurs. It goes without saying that when those assumptions are not satisfied, the specification of property rights selected should depend upon the transaction costs of the alternative arrangements. It then becomes a question of economizing on those costs given the taste for uncertainty among the owners of different factors of production. Or alternatively, given the transaction costs, it would become a question of catering to the preferences of different factor owners with regard to uncertainty.

As far as the Islamic position on this issue is concerned, we must note that Islam does not impose variable returns on all factors of production, indeed on any of the factors of production that may derive their income under contractual arrangements. As we have seen, it permits fixed returns on land (regardless of whether we call it rent from the macro perspective, or rental from the micro perspective),[5] physical capital (regardless of whether we call it rental or interest, even under the strictest interpretations of *fiqh* as long as transformation occurs, or even if it is presumed to occur, as we will see in Chapter 10), and labor (wages that partly include returns on human capital). The return to entrepreneurship, by definition could not be fixed, and on this score, in principle, there is hardly any difference between the position taken by Islamic economists and conventional economics. Actually, according to the original sources of Islamic imperatives, variable returns to labor in particular may not even be permissible, for a well known *ḥadīth* report admonishes believers to pay the wages before the worker's sweat is dry.[6] It is also objectionable in view of the prohibition of *gharar* (ambiguity in the terms of a contract, which may be in

[5] Some Islamic writers on the issue of land ownership opt for a stretched interpretation of certain verses of the Qur'ān to argue for complete ownership of land by the state. As far as I can see there is no justification whatsoever for such interpolations, as our coverage in Chapter 6 has shown. In view of the confusion between state ownership and communal ownership, as pointed out there, one would hope that these writers are aware of the tragedy of the commons. At any rate, even when there is state ownership, the argument about rent as the opportunity cost of land will remain valid.

[6] Report No. 2891 in Ibn Māja, *Kitāb al-Sunan*.

terms of value, quality, or the time of delivery), leading to uncertainty about the distribution of benefits of an exchange.[7] Then there is the *fiqh* maximum, quite easily understood in the light of our exposition in Chapter 5, according to which whatever is not prohibited is permissible. And last, and by no means least, is the problem that the idea of profit-sharing is not even mentioned in either the Qurʾān or the vast *ḥadīth* literature. All of these issues are taken up in detail in Chapter 10. At the moment, we confine ourselves to the positions taken by the Islamic economists. As a concluding statement, we may now briefly turn to their most ardently advocated viewpoint, which is supposed to represent a panacea for all the evils relating to interest, and which is the idea of profit-sharing between capital and entrepreneurship. In this brief account, we will pay special attention to the context, fully explored in Chapter 4, in the background of which this vision is articulated.

The difference between conventional and Islamic economists' treatment of capital is crucially related to the treatment of circulating capital. Conventional economics has traditionally disregarded the distinction between circulating capital and physical capital, as a simplification on the presumption, often not explicitly articulated, that circulating capital is an indispensable ingredient for the smooth functioning of any business enterprise. The Islamic economists' implicit argument that circulating capital is used mostly for smoothing out the required business transactions—money as a medium of exchange does this for all economic agents, be they producers or consumers—and as such should not be entitled to a return at par with physical capital is not something that conventional economics ever entertained seriously, for the following implicit reasons. All businesses forego interest on their current account balances that are needed to avoid running into liquidity problems, for at times businesses may even go bankrupt if they are not careful to pay attention to their cash flows. In a sense, therefore, they forego interest on such balances to earn higher returns. Admittedly, it may be argued that the overall returns will have to be higher if they are reckoned on the basis of just the physical capital to the exclusion of the complementary circulating capital. For their part, if and when the Islamic economists recognize the merits of this argument, they feel

[7] *Fiqh* splits *gharar* into the following categories: *gharar fī al-ṣifa* (about characteristics of goods); *fī al-miqdār* (about quantity); *fī al-ajal* (about time of delivery); and *fī al-taslīm* (about delivery of the goods).

that the correct approach is to reward circulating capital through a sharing of the profits. Since circulating capital cannot be distinguished from money, it can always be used for speculative purposes, and thus is prone to fall under the sanction against *ribā*. If money is to serve the social purpose of easing transactions, it ought not serve as a means of making private gains through speculative activity. When it strictly serves as a circulating capital, it may earn a return but through the only alternative way possible, which is through sharing of profits. It then is necessarily associated with the process of transformation, and not sitting as a Keynesian predator in search of a prey.

More specifically, their answer is that either the enterprise provides its own working capital whereby its return will be included in the higher profits, or alternatively it arranges a financier on the basis of profit-sharing. At any rate, working capital is supposed to be entitled to a return but only from the profits. Thus profits are not for the entrepreneur only. They are to be shared on the basis of some predetermined sharing ratio at the very least with the circulating capital.[8] The origins of the idea of profit-sharing are to be found in the *fiqh* contract known as *muḍāraba* (originally called *qirāḍ* or *muqāraḍa*), which Kuran (2002) understandably identifies as the precursor to the modern corporate form of governance.[9] A detailed discussion about the evolution of *muḍāraba* and its applicability in the contemporary times is postponed until Chapter 10. Here we note only the points that are directly relevant to the discussion. Since it is a form of contract, *fiqh* has come to be quite specific about stipulating the conditions that must be satisfied for this contract to be valid. Some of these include: i) profits are to be shared by the financier (the *rabb al-māl* or *ṣāḥib al-māl*) and the manager (the *muḍārib* or *ʿāmil*, literally worker) according to a mutually agreed predetermined sharing ratio; ii) no finance is to be provided by the *muḍārib*; iii) the *rabb al-māl* is not allowed to interfere in the management of the enterprise by the *muḍārib*; iv) all financial loss is to be borne by the *rabb al-māl*; v) therefore, the loss of

---

[8] The presence of the various positions advocated by Islamic economists, and especially the emphasis on profit-sharing, has misled many a student of Islamic economics in understanding that the correct Islamic position is that all forms of capital will receive a reward through profit-sharing. It is under this misunderstanding, as we will see in Chapter 10, that some writers have advocated that an Islamic economy must be an entirely equity-based economy. See, for instance, Mahdi and Al-Asaly (1987), and Habibi (1987).

[9] Known as commenda in the West. See, for instance, Udovitch (1970).

the *muḍārib* is limited to the loss of his labor income. By virtue of (iii), *muḍāraba* becomes a principal and agent problem *par excellence*. As such, it becomes akin to the American form of corporate governance, as discussed earlier. That, along with (ii), makes it practically irrelevant in modern times. In addition, the problems identified above in the context of profit-sharing in general also become relevant in the present case. To be more specific on one issue, there is the question of the *muḍārib*'s labor income being subjected to uncertainty and therefore ambiguity (*gharar*). While *fiqh* writers are quite adamant that these stipulations must all be satisfied, the writings of the Islamic economists (see, for instance, Siddiqi, 1983) show some flexibility to make the contract relevant for the modern times. In the final analysis, the acceptance of the idea of profit sharing, and therefore the exclusive legitimacy of the *muḍāraba* contract as its peg, which is then to serve as the pivot of the financial system, crucially depends on the presumed equality between *ribā* and interest. We turn to that issue in the next chapter.

CHAPTER NINE

RIBĀ, INTEREST AND USURY

Introduction

It perhaps will not be lost on any student of Islam and economics, or Islamic economy, that the enterprise called Islamic economics began as a result of a very strong dislike of the institution of interest by its exponents on the presumption that it was precisely the same thing as *ribā*. So much so that one can even conclude that the enterprise stands or falls on the validity or otherwise of that presumption. In light of the importance of this subject, its coverage needs to be somewhat more comprehensive than has, admittedly, been the case for the other topics thus far covered in this work. In light of the volume of material, I have spread the coverage over two chapters. In the present chapter I focus on the meanings of the word *ribā* as these could be understood from the Qurʾānic exhortations, the meanings given it by the *fiqh* literature and the various issues attendant upon the fairly involved discourse that emerged. The *fiqh* understanding does not tie up neatly and easily with the Qurʾānic one, and this obviously raises the question as to why this discrepancy arose. This question is addressed in Chapter 10.

The Arabic word *ribā* literally means an excess or increase. In the Qurʾān it occurs in a number of verses that have come to be known as *ribā* verses. These leave no doubt that what is termed *ribā* is categorically prohibited. At the same time, it is also clear from the reading of the Qurʾān that not every increase in various economic transactions falls in the ambit of this prohibition, for otherwise the profit will also be prohibited. Which of the increases are prohibited, therefore, became a crucial question for Islamic jurisprudence, i.e., *fiqh*. When it came to address that question, *fiqh* came to the conclusion that the *ribā* verses were not sufficiently clear by themselves to provide a precise answer that it thought was required for its purpose, particularly in view of the severity of prohibition, or rather in light of the strong language used in its condemnation. In addition to these verses, there are a number of *ḥadīth* reports that were understood to reinforce the Qurʾānic prohibition. Regardless of whether the *ribā* verses were clear enough or not, *fiqh* must have felt obliged to take this additional evidence into consideration before articulating its position, if for no other reason than to present a picture that was consistent with respect to these two primary sources of juridical formulations according to the principles of jurisprudence in Islam, namely *uṣūl al-fiqh*. Although these principles require *fiqh* to first consult the Qurʾān (the *aṣl al-uṣūl*, the principle of principles, as the Qurʾān is referred to in the *fiqh* literature), and only then proceed to the *ḥadīth* literature to clarify any ambiguity that may seem to remain, *fiqh* has always taken the position that the Qurʾānic evidence needs to be corroborated by the *ḥadīth* evidence. When it attempted to formulate its position thus, the task turned out to be much more difficult than seemingly anticipated, for the *ḥadīth* reports presented a perspective that was quite different from what appeared to emerge from the Qurʾān. At that stage, *fiqh* decided to proceed on the assumption that the *ḥadīth* perspective was more general, and tried to reconcile the Qurʾānic perspective with it. In retrospect we can see that this task of reconciliation proved somewhat elusive, it seems primarily because of the way the *ḥadīth* perspective was interpreted. Relating *ribā* to what later came to be known as interest was one of the dimensions of this discourse, and the one that created the most problems in the path of the reconciliation, and it is this dimension that is the primary focus of the modern discourse, particularly what I have called fiqhnomics, i.e. *fiqh* when it is specifically applied to economic issues.

There is no doubt that there exists a connection between *ribā* and interest, though this connection is not as straightforward as it is made out to be, namely a strict equality between these two, particularly when it comes to this connection in the context of institutionalized credit in modern times. This unqualified and blanket interpretation, however, has created a serious difficulty for several reasons, as we shall see below as well as in the next chapter where *fiqh*'s response to the prohibition of *ribā* is explored more fully. *Fiqh* set off on its interpretation by assuming that Qur'an does not provide a sufficiently precise definition of *ribā* for legal purposes, and thus it was up to *fiqh* to do so. Soon after that journey began, the Qurʾānic exegetical works showed that the meaning of the word was so well understood by the Arabs of the time—even in its technical sense—as to need no elaboration by the Qurʾān, and therefore by implication by anybody else. Disregarding that evidence, *fiqh* continued apace on the course it had set for itself until the onset of the twentieth century. At this stage, the discourse on *ribā* took a rather peculiar turn, at least in the writings of an influential, and a rather vocal—and perhaps influential because vocal—group of modern *fiqh* writers. This group, on the one hand, has felt compelled to acknowledge the historical evidence presented in the exegetical works, but on the other has attempted to faithfully adhere to the classical interpretation that was based on the contrary position, namely that the meaning of *ribā* was not very clearly understood. By doing this they have added their own share of confusion to an already complicated subject. One of the major objectives of this and the next chapter is to evaluate the various strands of argument that led to the position taken by *fiqh* with a particular focus on the proposition that the Qurʾānic commandment was not clear enough to identify which "increase" it was that was being prohibited.

Unlike its lay usage, for even an uninformed Muslim is aware of the term and thinks that it has a unique meaning, one encounters a number of *ribā* terms in the *fiqh* literature. This is quite understandable in view of the differences between the perspective of the Qurʾān and that of the *ḥadīth* literature on the subject. At the fundamental level, there is the so called Qurʾānic *ribā*, which was originally known as *ribā al-jāhiliyya* (pre-Islamic *ribā*), and then there is what has been called *ribā al-ḥadīth*. This latter variety is given several names depending partly on the nature of transaction for which it is being defined, and partly upon the individual likings of the different *fiqh* scholars. There is, for instance, *ribā al-faḍl*, which is defined over spot but barter transactions; *ribā al-buyūʿ* which is *ribā* on barter transactions, be they spot or on deferred basis; *ribā al-dayn* or *duyūn* signifies transactions that will give rise to debt because the payment was to be made on deferred basis (though whether the term was exclusively applied to transactions that were conducted on barter basis, or also included payment in the form of cash is often not quite clear); and beyond all those there is *ribā al-nasīʾa*, originally defined on barter transactions on deferred payment basis, but subsequently extended to cover all transactions on deferred payment basis, and yet later to include monetary loan transactions. The interesting thing about this varied terminology is that it does not belong to the Prophetic times.

It would be natural for an uninitiated reader to think that the relevant *ḥadīth* literature, and thus *ribā al-ḥadīth*, was meant to explain the same thing as the Qurʾānic *ribā*. It is not difficult to understand that the point would not have been lost on the classical exponents of *fiqh*. But the perspective that emerged out of the *ḥadīth* reports was quite different from that of the Qurʾān. In view of this difficulty, *fiqh* was torn between two conflicting objectives; it wished to affect a separation between the two at the legal level at the same time that it attempted to establish some sort of principial connection between them. This task proved difficult as we observe in *Risāla* of Shāfiʿī (d. 820) where we see the term *ribā al-faḍl* for the first time, as far as I know.[1] Eventually, the form of *ribā al-ḥadīth* that was used to establish the necessary connection with the Qurʾānic *ribā* was *ribā al-nasīʾa*, and it is this term that came to be widely used in the *fiqh* literature. Exactly when this term became well-established is difficult to discern clearly but we see it being used in the thirteenth century by Rāzī (d. 1209) in his *Tafsīr al-kabīr*. Rāzī was not just an exegete but also a *faqīh* (*fiqh* scholar), and it is in that work that we clearly see an equivalence established between these two forms of *ribā*. The exposition in this chapter is based on the fundamental distinction between the two major perspectives, one emerging from the Qurʾān and the other from the *ḥadīth* literature, and the terms used for these are: *ribā al-jāhiliyya* and *ribā al-ḥadīth*.

The assumption of a perfect correspondence between *ribā* and interest, characteristic of the modern discourse on the subject, means that *ribā* is understood to be an increase over the principal amount in a loan contract involving money. Interpreted as such, it obviously involves a time dimension. It is plausible that by the time *fiqh* came around to formulate its position on the subject, a century or so after the Prophetic times, the term might have acquired such an association in the popular culture not only in light of the Qurʾānic perspective, but also in line with the Judeo-Christian interpretation of usury (we explore this hypothesis further in the next chapter). The predicament *fiqh* encountered was that when it turned to the *ḥadīth* literature, the time dimension did not seem to be an essential ingredient of what was termed *ribā* in that literature. Indeed, at the explicit and obvious level, these reports were not predicated on there being an essential time dimension for a transaction to involve *ribā*, as is attested by the term *ribā al-faḍl*—a point which will become clear as we proceed. It was only with some difficulty that the time dimension was forced into the interpretation, which led to the coining of the term *ribā al-nasīʾa*. Add to that the fact that there existed a certain number of *ḥadīth* reports (to be fully discussed below in the section on chronological issues) that

[1] This is understandable, for it is *fiqh* that had to deal with the issue of a formal interpretation, for legal purposes, more than any other branch of inquiry.

tell us that the Qur'ānic sanction against *ribā* was revealed more or less towards the end of the Prophet's life, and that he did not have enough time to explain the real meanings of the term, and you have a recipe for confusion. No wonder then that the issue of *ribā* has turned out to be one of the most difficult, perhaps the most difficult, subjects in *fiqh*, and no wonder, either that the connection between *ribā* and interest has turned out to be equally fraught with difficulties, difficulties that were amply demonstrated in the judicial proceedings in Pakistan in the case relating to the abolition of interest from the economy.

In the modern discourse on the subject, a number of additional complications have entered this already confusing mix as a result of the inevitable march of history. Two of these complications are especially noteworthy. First, the context, or the background conditions, in which the prohibition of *ribā* came down has undergone a drastic change with the passage of time, giving rise to the necessity of relating the rationale for the prohibition of *ribā* both in terms of its *ḥikma* (the Divine wisdom behind prohibition),[2] and, this is what gives rise to the second complication, *ʿilla* (the effective juridical cause) for the prohibition to become effective, where the classical position has become practically irrelevant due to the replacement of the commodity (or real) money—the essential ingredient of the classical discourse—with paper money. This latter complication has also given rise to the possibility of a wide divergence between the nominal and real values of various economic variables including those relating to *ribā*, or for that matter interest. The modern discourse on the subject, by both the influential and vocal *fiqh* experts (henceforth dominant *fiqh* group) and Islamic economists, has either not recognized these complications, as happens in the case of the first complication—or has by and large tended to ignore them as niceties, as happens in the case of the second complication, particularly as far as the divergence between the nominal and real values is concerned. When it came to the inevitable question of providing alternative modes of financing, the *fiqh* scholars from the very beginning were forced to sanction modes some of which looked peculiarly like interest except in name, while others seemed only a step or two removed from it. Such modes were sanctioned under the *fiqh* term *ḥīla* (a legal ruse) in recognition of the practical business

---

[2] Recall our discussion of the contextual effects in connection with the idea of social justice in Chapter 5.

requirements. However, *fiqh* never felt fully comfortable with these alternatives, neither originally, more than a millennium ago, nor now when it has been forced to rearticulate its position *vis-à-vis* interest in the wake of what has come to be known as the Islamic renaissance, with Islamic economics tagging along as an essential part of that renaissance.

This modern discourse brings forth the same issues that the classical *fiqh* scholars must have faced in their times, albeit now in a much more complex setting, and appears to be a sort of repeat of history. The main contours of this discourse can be summed up as follows: the dominant *fiqh* school has recognized the futility of asserting that the meaning of the term *ribā* was not clearly understood because of the unassailable evidence provided by the exegetical works. Its writers take their point of departure by asserting that the meaning of the term *ribā* was well understood at the time of the revelation—and it is here that they significantly differ from the classical *fiqh* expositions—but then they use the classical concept of *ribā al-nasī'a* to establish an equality between *ribā* and interest, all along giving the false impression that they are presenting the classical *fiqh* position. Part and parcel of their exposition is the presentation of alternative modes of financing that are supposed to be derived from the classical literature, and an impression is created that these were the universally acceptable modes in the early period of Islam. The twists and turns of this argument will come under discussion in Chapter 10. Here we note only the following points: there are those who, aware of the contradictions inherent in this line of reasoning, have expressed their disapproval of this blanket equation of *ribā* and interest. This group, which includes not only traditional *fiqh* scholars but also exegetes, has its origins in Al-Azhar University in Cairo but has come to include scholars from other parts of Islamic world. According to them the interest relating to modern banking transactions does not fall in the ambit of *ribā* prohibition. As far as the Islamic economists are concerned, they create the impression that they are actually following the exposition of the *fiqh* scholars belonging to the dominant group, but having themselves delved a bit into the classical *fiqh* literature, they seem to have influenced some of the directions taken by the dominant group. Theirs also seems to have been a voyage of discovery, and thereby also a repeat of history. They began by arguing for an abolition of interest from the financial system through an administrative fiat, without any regard to the need for presenting alternative modes of financing. Recognizing the futility of such a position, we then see them articulating the traditional modes of financing as available in the *fiqh* literature and insisting that the detailed contractual stipulations as enunciated originally—centuries ago—must be considered as binding, indeed rather sacrosanct. Due to the untenability of such a position in the changed circumstances, we now witness a third phase in this discourse in which some flexibility is evident both with regard to those detailed stipulations as well as acceptance of new financial instruments. The *ḥiyal* (legal ruses) have now reappeared but in new and more sophisticated forms.

One of the interesting dimensions of this modern discourse is the critical appraisals of the position taken by the dominant *fiqh* school concerning the equality between *ribā* and interest, with active participation by non-*fiqh* experts, some of them professional economists but some belonging to other academic disciplines. It would appear that these critical appraisals draw considerable strength from the deviations from the classical position taken by the dominant group of *fiqh* scholars. Admittedly most of these writings are of a journalistic nature, and therefore lack scholarly depth, yet they make their points in all earnestness. An impetus to these writings was provided by the appeal proceedings in the so called *ribā* case in the Federal Appellate Bench of the Supreme Court of Pakistan in 1999, and again in 2002, against the 1991 judgment of the Sharīʿa Court that declared institutionalized interest to be illegal, on the one hand, and by the *fatwā* rendered by the Grand Sheikh (Rector) of Al-Azhar University in December 2002 expressing a contrary opinion, on the other. It is significant to note that some of the most pertinent questions in this regard were posed during these proceedings by the legal experts, some of them quite well versed in *fiqh*, and not all of them representing the plaintiff. These hearings highlighted, as they were bound to, the most obvious age-old riddles relating to the issue of *ribā*, and have thereby underscored the importance of an objective assessment of the various positions relating to the issue. Yet the issues relating to *ribā* are so complex that even the proceedings of these hearings leave, in my view, a number of pertinent questions unaddressed.

The degree of complexity pertaining to the issue of *ribā* is so great that a logically consistent set of answers to an elementary, but fundamental, set of questions turns out to be impossible. Consider the following questions: If debt financing is problematic, for it is here that *ribā* is supposed to reside, can we then assume that an Islamic economy is *necessarily* a purely equity-based economy? An affirmative answer to this question could not be offered since both the Qur'ān and *ḥadīth* permit the institution of debt. But then notwithstanding the Qur'ānic position and the *ḥadīth* reports, a number of writers contributing to the Islamic economics discourse naively proceed on the presumption that the answer must be in the affirmative, for as far as they can see this is the only logically consistent way to proceed if the economy is to be an interest-free one (recall the discussion on this subject in Chapter 8). Pose that question from a slightly different, but equally important, perspective: if a fixed return on money is *ribā* and therefore not permissible, does it mean that an Islamic economy should be rendered as an equity-based economy which relies on profit-sharing for financing purposes, particularly in light of large financing requirements of a modern enterprise? According to some *ḥadīth* reports, the answer is no as we will see subsequently. Does it then mean that debt can be incurred but the payment against the debt must not involve any increase on the amount of (money) debt? Yes, for otherwise it would involve *ribā* as far as the *fiqh* is concerned, but then no according to some of the *ḥadīth* reports, as long as the increase is not predetermined. And in a somewhat similar context, since a loan may involve a real asset such as an animal, can the value of the asset used for discharging of the debt be higher than the value of the loaned asset? The answer is yes according to some *ḥadīth* reports. Similarly, if the Qur'ānic term *qarḍ ḥasan* (a beneficent loan) is interpreted as a *ribā*-free (interest-free, in the modern discourse) loan, what then is the difference between it and *qarḍ* in general, which could not be interest-bearing anyway? The *fiqh*, as far as I know, is silent on this question though in recent writings some sort of a fudge can be noted, as will become clear when we take up this matter again. Is the value of the principal that is supposed to be returned to the lender the same amount as the value of the loan? Yes, if the loan is in terms of money, but then not necessarily if it involves *bay' mu'ajjal* (deferred payment contract).[3] And such

[3] Much is made of the *bay' mu'ajjal* in fiqhnomics, though I am not clear at what stage in the evolution of *fiqh* it became a part of its terminological apparatus. It is not used in the *ḥadīth* literature, and thus it certainly does not belong to the Prophetic times. Most probably, the term is of relatively recent origin, coming out of the Fatāwa-e-Alamgīrī that belong to seventeenth-century India. During the Prophetic times, what is now denoted by this term was subsumed under *salaf*—a term found in the *ḥadīth* literature—though subsequently *fiqh* adopted the more or less equivalent term *salam*,

puzzling questions continue. To this must be added the carelessness in the use of modern economic terminology of "compound interest" to represent the crucial Qurʾānic clause *aḍʿāfan muḍāʿafa* (doubling and redoubling, of the principal amount) not only by non-economists, such as legal experts, but also by economists, which has led to further complications as far as the connection between *ribā* and interest is concerned. In what follows in this chapter, I have made an effort to provide a historical perspective on the interpretation of both forms of *ribā* to see if the current dominant *fiqh* position on the subject can be supported; historical in the sense that for *ribā al-jāhiliyya* I have resorted to the great works on Qurʾanic exegesis and for *ribā al-ḥadīth* to the relevant *ḥadīth* reports. The conclusion that emerges from this inquiry is that the dominant *fiqh* position that attempts to establish an unequivocal equality between *ribā* and interest cannot be supported.

Ribā al-jāhiliyya

While the prohibition of *ribā* could be viewed from several dimensions, the confusion that has come to surround it relates essentially to one fundamental issue; and that is whether the Qurʾān clearly defines, or at the very least provides an unambiguous hint at, what exactly is the thing that is being prohibited. A clear definition would be expected if an ordinance relating to something completely new, something unfamiliar and previously unknown, were being instituted. Alternatively, it would be natural to expect a very clear hint at what is being prohibited if the thing being prohibited was already a part of common knowledge. At this stage, a brief perspective on the subject of *uṣūl al-fiqh*, as covered in Chapters 5 and 6, is in order. We understand that when a Qurʾānic ordinance was related to something entirely new, as was true in the case of rituals, the minute details pertaining thereto when not explicitly stated in the Qurʾān were entrusted

---

and thus *bayʿ salam*, a term that in the modern discourse is reserved for advance payment for a contract involving deferred delivery. Under the barter system, which was common during the Prophetic times, and which forms the basis of *fiqh* discourse even now as far as the traditional *fiqh* scholars are concerned, it becomes difficult to distinguish between *bayʿ salam* and what has now come to be known as *bayʿ muʿajjal* as we will see below. In view of the focus on this term in the modern *fiqh* and fiqhnomics discourse, I have at times, but only at times, used it in the following pages instead of *salaf* or *salam* to identify the relevant issues.

to the Prophet in the form of an informal revelation—informal in the sense of not being included in the Qurʾān—as happened in the case of how the ritual prayer, the *ṣalāt*, was to be offered, or were left to his discretion, as happened, for instance, in the case of how certain detailed acts within the *ṣalāt* were to be performed. On the other hand, when the meanings of certain ordinances were commonly understood, one would surmise that the Prophetic traditions would reinforce those meanings for the sake of clarity. Therefore, *fiqh* would consult the Prophetic *Sunna*, which includes the *ḥadīth* reports, to arrive at its formulations. In absence of clarity in the Qurʾān, resort is made to the latter, and this of course is true for rituals as well as *muʿāmalāt* (public dealings). In cases where no explicit guidance could be had from either of those original sources, matters would be resolved through either *ijmāʿ* (which came to mean only the consensus of the Prophet's companions or their immediate followers) or *ijtihād* in which *qiyās* (analogical reasoning) may be used. We see that in the case of *ribā*, *fiqh* primarily relied on the relevant *ḥadīth* reports although when it came to *ribā al-jāhiliyya*, it had to resort to *qiyās* to bridge the gap that still remained. The exegetical position that the meaning of the term *ribā* was quite clearly understood is justified, and the contrary assertion that the Qurʾān did not provide a precise definition cannot be easily accepted, for the Qurʾān indeed gives us a precise, and a rather concise, hint at what it was that was being prohibited, and this precisely corresponds to how the term was commonly understood. In what follows, special attention will be paid first to what we can discern from the *ribā* verses, and second to what was the meaning attached to the term *ribā* by the Arabs of the Prophetic times.

The reason *fiqh* took the position it did will emerge as we proceed. One of the major difficulties *fiqh* encountered was related to a number of *ḥadīth* reports to the effect that the Qurʾānic verses relating to the prohibition of *ribā* were more or less the last verses to be revealed to the Prophet, and that he did not have enough time to explain their true meanings. These reports obviously contradict the hypothesis that the meaning of the term *ribā* was well understood. To have a correct perspective about these reports, we are obliged to go through the chronology of revelations relating to *ribā* on the presumption that if the chronology reveals that there was enough time between the time of the revelation and the Prophet's passing away, there would have arisen sufficient occasions for clarifications about such important an issue as *ribā*, in which case the reports that the meaning of the term *ribā* was not well understood require some investigation. If nothing else, we would need to understand the purport of such reports, with a particular eye as to whether these could be reconciled with the hypothesis that the meaning of the term *ribā* was well understood. We will see that a number of crucial *ḥadīth* reports relating to *ribā* can be looked more from the perspective of *gharar* (ambiguity), and once that is done the major difficulties are resolved and a number of other *ḥadīth* reports that might otherwise pose some difficulties become consistent with the overall perspective on *ribā* that then emerges. We now turn to the issue of chronology of the *ribā* verses.

Chronological Issues

Chronologically, the first revelation where the word *ribā* occurs is a verse in *sūra al-Rūm* (The Byzantines), which belongs to the middle Makkan period; it is said to have been revealed about six to seven years before the *Hijra*. It shows a disapproval of *ribā* in contrast to charity and reads as follows:

> And (remember:) whatever you give out in *ribā* (usury) so that it might increase through (other) people's possessions will bring (you) no increase in the sight of God—whereas all that you give out in charity, seeking God's countenance, (will be blessed by Him) for it is they, they (who seek His countenance) that shall have their recompense multiplied (30:39).

A look at various works on Qur'ānic exegesis and translation reveals two ambiguities in the interpretation of this verse: one relating to the interpretation of the term *ribā* itself, and the other, which is actually contingent upon the first, relating to whether it is addressed to the payers or receivers of *ribā*. Along with Muhammad Asad, as in the above translation, Muhammad Marmaduke Pickthall and A. J. Arberry interpret the term *ribā* as "usury" and interpret the opening part of the verse as being addressed to the givers: either "what" or "which" you give in usury. The Khan/Hilali translation, on the other hand, following most of the classical works on exegesis, particularly the magisterial work of Ṭabarī (d. 923), as well as of Bayḍāwī (d. 1280), and Suyūṭī (d. 1505), interpret the term *ribā* as gift (*hadīya* or *tabarru'*)[4] and

---

[4] It may be noted that the word *hadīya* is often used for a price where the price may not be quite commensurate with the intrinsic value of the product. The most common usage of this occurs in the case of the price of a copy of Qur'ān.

render the opening part as "And whatever you give in gift (to others), in order that it may increase (your wealth by expecting to get a better one in return from other people's property), has..." This seems to be the dominant interpretation as far as some of the important authorities of the first and second generations are concerned; Suyūṭī attributes it to Ibn ʿAbbās, Saʿīd Ibn Jubayr, Mūjahid (d. ca. 723), Ṭāwūs, Qatādah (d. ca. 735), Dhahhāk, and Ibrahīm al-Nakhaʿī (d. ca. 715). On the other hand, Fazlur Rahman (1964), following Ibn Qayyim (d. 1350), who in turn seems to represent the interpretation of Ibn Ḥanbal (d. 855), translates the opening part of the verse as "And whatever you invest by way of *ribā* so that it may..." and thus as addressed to the lenders, i.e. the receivers of *ribā*. It is, perhaps, this that leads ʿAbd Allāh Yūsuf ʿAlī to translate the opening part as "That which you lay out for increase through the property of (other) people..." If we accept the former interpretation, it makes this verse the only one addressed to the borrowers (the givers) in *ribā* transactions. Though in that case the "gift" interpretation seems somewhat surprising, for the giving of gifts is much recommended in both the Qurʾān and *ḥadīth* literature, and while one may interpret the verse as suggesting that gifts should not be given in the expectation of receiving one, or at least one of a higher value, in return, one would not expect disapproval of something simply on the basis of expectations that may never materialize. The pertinent question, which has yet to be addressed, is the following: why was the "gift" interpretation maintained by all those authorities (down to Suyūṭī in the sixteenth century) in the face of subsequent clear and categorical prohibition of *ribā*? A possible explanation may be the use of the phrase *fa-lā yarbū ʿinda ʾllāh* (does not increase with God) in this verse and *yarbī al-ṣadaqāt* (God increases *ṣadaqāt*) in 2:276 (see the translation of the latter verse below), both derived from the same root as the word *ribā*, although in the latter case the context makes it clear that the words are being used in a general sense to denote a reward from God. At any rate, modern commentators have not addressed this question—though they generally ignore this interpretation—except for Fazlur Rahman who comments, somewhat bitterly, that "A 'permissible' (*ḥalāl*) *riba* has been invented by these commentators and it has been asserted by them that this verse relates to that *riba*" (1964, p. 10).

Fazlur Rahman does not provide any evidence by way of examples for this remark. We can surmise that it is the "gift" interpretation which is the cause of his disenchantment. One can conjecture that the verse is addressed to the rich merchants of Makkāh to whom their less fortunate relatives and clansmen might have been used to entrusting their meager savings—alternatively it is possible that these rich merchants would raise finance from them on their own volition—for use in trading operations, particularly at the times when caravans left on trading journeys. These merchants would then pay them back something extra ("it may increase on other people's property," as Pickthall has it in his translation of the verse) from the profits thus generated. It is conceivable that they would give their clansmen the impression that they were doing them a favor by providing them the opportunity to invest their savings and thus providing them with a return which they themselves would not be able to earn (and thus the gift interpretation). By doing this they would be acting like modern financial intermediaries, and *fiqh* terminology readily recognized this as something akin to what has come to be known as a *muḍāraba* arrangement—and there is some evidence that such an arrangement was prevalent in Makkah of the Prophetic times, since Imām Mālik has a whole section on *qirāḍ* in his *al-Muwaṭṭa*ʾ (there is more on this in what follows, particularly in Chapter 10 in relation to Sarakhsī's inauguration of *muḍāraba* as an acceptable form of profit-sharing contract in *fiqh* at the turn of the twelfth century). What the verse then seems to underscore is the high-handed attitude of those who were wealthy, and to remind them that by making such a payment they were not doing their clansmen a favor, in contrast to *ṣadaqa*, which is also mentioned in the preceding verse. This represented a purely business transaction from which the wealthy equally profited. The verse does not portray a situation where a debtor was being forced to discharge his debt obligations even when he was in difficult economic circumstances. What is absolutely clear from the verse is that *ribā* is set in a sharp contrast to charity. Of all the *ribā* verses, this is the only verse in which the word *ribā* is used without a definite article *al*; when subsequent references are made to *ribā* with the definite article, the implication is that the same concept is being referred to. All of these points are taken up later in this chapter.

The second revelation, and a rather pivotal one, occurs in *sūra Āl-ʿImrān*, which belongs the early Medinan period, and it is generally agreed that this verse was revealed after the battle of Uḥud in 3 AH:

> O you who have attained to faith! Do not gorge yourselves on *ribā* (usury), doubling and redoubling it—but remain conscious of God, so that you might attain to a happy state (3:130).

It is in this verse that we meet the crucial qualifying clause *aḍʿāfan muḍāʿafa*. Asad and Arberry translate it as "doubling and redoubling," Pickthall as "doubling and quadrupling," while Yūsuf ʿAlī and Khan/Hilali have "doubled and multiplied." There is no doubt that the term on the whole implies manifold increase ultimately, and indeed comes from the same root as the last word of the first revelation, *muḍʿifūn*, signifing the multiplied reward promised to those who give charity. It is noteworthy that the prohibition of *ribā* is quite unequivocal in this verse, unlike the previous verse where only a strong disapproval of what it might have meant to the Makkans at the time is expressed.

The next, third revelation, the exact date of which is not quite certain, belongs to *Sūra al-Nisāʾ*, which is generally understood to date from 4 AH. It refers to the arguments the Jews used to have with the Prophet:

> So, then, for the wickedness committed by those who follow the Jewish faith did We deny unto them certain of good things of life which (aforetime) had been allowed to them; and (We did this) for their having so often turned away from the path of God, and (for) their taking *ribā* (usury) although it had been forbidden to them, and their wrongful devouring of other people's possessions. And for those from among them who (continue to) deny the truth We have readied grievous suffering (4:160–61).

The real significance of this verse is not that it forbids *ribā* to Muslims, for there were a number of things forbidden to Jews that were not forbidden to Muslims in the new dispensation, and the careful exegetes have never interpreted it in such a manner, but that it offers a logical continuity in the concept of *ribā*, which was forbidden in the previous dispensations: it implies that what was forbidden in those dispensations is precisely what was now being forbidden. The interesting question of course is what the Jewish interpretation of *ribā* (usury) was at the time of the Prophet, and whether it had remained faithful to the original prohibition. That, however, is not something that needs to detain us here.

After the third revelation, the chronology of the relevant revelation(s) becomes somewhat hazy. There are altogether five verses that occur together as a set in *sūra al-Baqara*, which are the subject of a great deal of controversy not only with regard to the timing of their revelation, which is considered by some to be particularly important for the issue at hand, but also as to whether they were all revealed at once, as one revelation, or whether they were part of more than one revelation occurring at different times. The translation of these verses, individually, is:

> Those who gorge themselves on *ribā* (usury) behave but as he might behave whom Satan has confounded with his touch; for they say, "Buying and selling is but a kind of *riba* (usury)"—the while God has made buying and selling lawful and usury unlawful. Hence, whoever becomes aware of his Sustainer's admonition, and thereupon desists (from *ribā*), may keep his past gains, and it will be for God to judge him; but as for those who return to it—they are destined for the fire, therein to abide! (275)
>
> God deprives usurious gains of all blessing, whereas He blesses charitable deeds with manifold increase. And God does not love anyone who is stubbornly ingrate and persists in sinful ways. (276)
>
> Verily, those who have attained to faith and do good works, and are constant in prayer, and dispense charity—they shall have their reward with their Sustainer, and no fear need they have, and neither shall they grieve. (277)
>
> O you who have attained to faith! Remain conscious of God, and give up all outstanding gains from *ribā* (usury), if you are (truly) believers; (278)
>
> For if you do it not, then know that you are at war with God and His Apostle. But if you repent, then you shall be entitled to (the return of) your principal: you will do no wrong, and neither will you be wronged. (279)
>
> If, however, (the debtor) is in straitened circumstances, (grant him) a delay until a time of ease and it would be for your own good—if you but knew it—to remit (the debt entirely) by way of charity. (280)
>
> And be conscious of the Day on which you shall be brought back unto God, whereupon every human being shall be repaid in full for what he has earned, and none shall be wronged. (281)

We may note at the outset that verses 2:277 and 2:281 do not directly relate to the issue at hand. I have included both of them here; the former because it reinforces the admonition for acts of charity occurring in 2:276 in the spirit of the first revelation on the issue cited earlier, while the rationale for the inclusion of 2:281 will become clear a little later.

To get a perspective on the issue of chronology of these verses, we begin, first, by noting that it is generally agreed that *sūra al-Baqara* is an early Medinan *sūra*. Marmaduke Pickthall cites in his introduction to the *sūra* Nöldeke's opinion that it was revealed in the first four years after the *Hijra*, although most of it was revealed in the first eight months. His own conclusion is that "the period of revelation is the years 1 and 2 AH. for the most part" with "certain verses of legislation being considered as of later date." Muhammad Asad concurs with Pickthall in saying that it was mostly revealed during the first two years after the *Hijra* except that he identifies the "verses of legislation" to be verses 275–81, and adds that these "belong to the last months before the Prophet's death (verse 281 is considered to be the very last revelation which he received)." There is, however, considerable disagreement not only about the timing of the revelation of these verses but also about whether the whole set was revealed at the same time. Fazlur Rahman (1964, p. 12) agrees with Asad that the whole set was revealed at once but does not agree with his timing framework, for he thinks that the whole set was revealed much earlier—some time after Uḥud but before 5 AH. Some other writers think that verses 275 and 276 were revealed in the third year of the *Hijra* shortly after the revelation containing 3:130 in *Sūra Āl-ʿImrān*,[5] while still others, though remaining silent about those two verses, concur with the former group of writers in contending that verses 278 and 279 were revealed in the 9 AH after the conquest of Makkāh, much earlier than the Prophet's death in 11 AH.[6] Broadly, one can discern two distinct strands of opinion relating to the chronology of these verses: some maintain that these verses belong to the last few months of the Prophet's ministry, and those who subscribe to this view rely primarily on a set of *ḥadīth* reports to support their stance. Some circumstantial evidence is also provided to buttress the claim. The second strand of opinion, that the verses were revealed earlier or perhaps much earlier, finds support primarily in strong circumstantial evidence, though some support is also found in a different set of *ḥadīth* reports.

The *ḥadīth* reports that have been the source of this controversy are narrated on the authority of such luminaries as ʿUmar Ibn al-Khaṭṭāb, the second caliph, and ʿAbd Allāh Ibn ʿAbbās, the Prophet's cousin. Consider the *ḥadīth* report attributed to Ibn ʿAbbās appearing in Bukhāri's *Kitāb al-tafsīr*, which reads: "the last verse sent down to the Prophet was the verse on *riba*."[7] Bukhārī, in his commentary on

---

[5] See, for instance, Report of the IIIE Workshop on Islamization of the Financial System, Islamabad: International Islamic University, 1997, p. 13.

[6] See Muhammad Taqi Usmani (2000, p. 25), who seems to attribute it to Ṭabarī's *Jāmiʿ al-Bayān*.

[7] *al-Jāmiʿ al-ṣaḥīḥ*, no. 4544.

verse 2:278 records that "Ibn ʿAbbās said that this was the last verse which was revealed upon the Prophet." Some of the writers, including Fazlur Rahman, have wondered why the singular *āya* (verse) is used for a set of verses, and fail to entertain the possibility that Ibn ʿAbbās might have meant the last verse from that set to be the last revelation. Others[8] draw on Ṭabarī's explanation that the verse under consideration is verse 281, the possible reasons for which will become clear a little later. This interpretation is problematic, for a reading of verse 281 shows that it could not be interpreted as a verse about *ribā*, strictly speaking, for it represents a common refrain of a general admonition that occurs at numerous places in the Qurʾān with slight change in the precise wordings. One could perhaps disregard this report, as the writers cited here do, were it not for the fact that there are other reports that corroborate it, and therefore make it quite difficult to conveniently ignore it. There are two reports, both attributed to the personality of none other than ʿUmar Ibn al-Khaṭṭāb, reported in various collections. Consider, first, the report in the Ṣaḥīḥ of Bukhārī in which he is said to have lamented that the details of three issues remained unexplained when the Prophet passed away; two of these pertained to inheritance and one to *ribā*.[9] Then there is the report in Sunan of Ibn Māja where ʿUmar is supposed to have declared that "the verse of *riba* was the last revealed verse and the Prophet passed away before explaining it in full terms."[10] Usmani (2000) discards this report by saying that *one* of its narrators, Saʿīd Ibn Abī ʿArūba "has been held by the experts of *ḥadīth* [reports] as a person who used to confuse one narration with the other" (p. 44). The difficulty is not fully resolved, for the same *ḥadīth* is reported in the Musnād of Ibn Ḥanbal on the authority of Saʿīd Ibn al-Musayyab, which Asad records in his commentary on verse 30:39 (p. 622, f.n) where ʿUmar is recorded as saying that "the last (of the Qurʾān) that was revealed was the verse on *riba*, and, behold, the Apostle of God passed away before having explained its meaning to us." Usmani (p. 45) feels that if there were any doubts in ʿUmar's mind, they related to only *ribā al-faḍl*. The trouble with this explanation is that the distinction between various forms of *ribā* did not exist at the time, and thus if we accept his point of view the doubts

---

[8] Such as Usmani (2000, p. 29).
[9] *Ḥadīth* report no. 5266.
[10] *Ḥadīth* report no. 2276 in *Kitāb al-tijāra*.

would then be equally applicable to *ribā al-nasīʾa*—which is the keystone of his elaborations on the subject, as we will see in Chapter 10.

The circumstantial evidence that is supposed to lend support to the foregoing position relates to the Prophet's sermon (*khutba*) at the farewell pilgrimage, in which the Prophet is reported to have prohibited *ribā* and "also declared that the *first riba* decreed to be void is the *riba* payable to his uncle ʿAbbās ibn Abu Muṭṭalib." Usmani, from whom this particular wording comes (p. 26), goes on to argue that to read it to mean that "the prohibition of *riba* was not effective before the last Hajj" (pilgrimage) is "misconceived." He thinks that the Prophet simply reminded people of an already instituted prohibition, just like a number of others injunctions, such as prohibition of liquor, maltreatment of women, etc. that he mentioned on the same occasion. That explanation would be fine were it not for the word "first"; if it was the first *ribā* that was declared void, then one wonders why it was not voided in the corresponding cases much earlier, that is to say, in the intervening years after Uḥud when the second revelation, that I have referred to as the pivotal one, belonging to *sūra Āl-ʿImrān* (verse 3:130), came. This raises another interesting question: if 3:130 belongs to period immediately after Uḥud, and I am not aware of any difference of opinion on that count, why did the issue of *ribā* prohibition center on the timings of the verses belonging to *sūra al-Baqara*? For the prohibition in verse 3:130 is quite unequivocal. It appears to me that part of the difficulty can be resolved when we pay a somewhat closer attention to verse 3:130 along with the nature of *qarḍ* transactions prevailing at the time. But before taking up those ideas, we need to look at the circumstantial evidence relating to the timing of the prohibition being earlier than the last months before the Prophet's passing away.

One piece of this evidence relates to debt relations between the tribes of Banū Thaqīf of Tāʾif and Banū Mūghīra of Makkāh, in which the latter carried considerable debt owed to the former. At the time the people of Tāʾif entered Islam in 9 AH, after the conquest of Makkāh, they entered into a treaty with the Prophet, one clause of which was supposedly, we are told, interpreted as giving them an exemption against the prohibition of *ribā*, such that they would continue to charge *ribā* from the Banū Mūghīra.[11] When the Banū Mūghīra protested against the

[11] Usmani (2000, p. 24) cites a *ḥadīth* reported in Sunan Abū Dāʾūd in support of this treaty clause. On the other hand, the text of this treaty as it appears in Ibn Isḥāq's

demands for the payment of *ribā*, and the Banū Thaqīf did not relent, the matter was brought to ʿAttāb bin ʿAsīd, the governor of Makkāh, for adjudication, who in turn referred it to the Prophet in Medina. According to Ṭabarī, it was on this occasion that verses 278 and 279 of *Sūra al-Baqara* were revealed, and accordingly, but not necessarily because of this particular revelation, if we assume that the prohibition against *ribā* already existed, the Prophet ruled against Banū Thaqīf. At any rate, this places the timing of *ribā* prohibition at a much earlier date than the last months before the Prophet's passing away.

The other piece of evidence relates to verse 5:3,[12] part of which reads "This day I have perfected your religion (*Dīn*) for you, and completed my blessings upon you," which, all authorities on Qurʾānic exegesis agree, was revealed on the Day of *ʿArafa* during the last pilgrimage of the Prophet. Accordingly, the date is Friday, 9 *Dhū al-ḥijja*, 10 *AH* (March, 632), which is 81 or 82 days before the death of the Prophet. The word *akmaltu* is translated as "perfected," and is taken by some authorities to mean "completion" in the legal sense, for Sūyūṭī then goes on to state that "no verse was sent down relating to permission (*ḥilla*) and prohibition (*ḥurma*)" after the revelation of that verse.[13] (One wonders if this was the reason why out of the set 2:275–281, the refrain verse 281 was deemed to be the verse of *ribā* by the exegetes as pointed out above, for it does not contain any legal stipulations.) ʿAbd Allāh Yūsuf ʿAlī, in his translation of the Qurʾān, thinks that this was the last revelation. There are others, such as Ṭabarī, who tend to interpret "perfected" somewhat differently as referring to the political victory of Islam upon the conquest of Makkāh, when the "idolaters

Sīrat Rasūl Allāh reads: "The text of the document the apostle wrote for them runs: 'In the name of God the Compassionate the Merciful. From Muhammad the prophet, the apostle of God, to the believers: The acacia trees of Wajj and its game are not to be injured. Anyone found doing this will be scourged and his garments confiscated. If he repeats the offence he will be seized and brought to the prophet Muhammad. This is the order of the prophet Muhammad, the apostle of God'. Khālid b. Saʿīd has written by the order of the apostle Muhammad b. Abdullah, so let none repeat the offence to his own injury in what the apostle of God Muhammad has ordered"; see Guillaume (1955, p. 617). The document was prepared in Medīna where a delegation of Banū Thaqīf had come to embrace Islam. The understanding that the treaty included a clause on *ribā* exemption may be attributed to a little-known work by Abū ʿUbayd bin Salām entitled *Kitāb al-amwāl*, which is supposed to reproduce the full text of the document and includes the said clause: "The sums due to them from the people—the Banū Thaqīf will get out of those only the principal (sums) advanced," as cited by Qureshi (1946, p. 61).

[12] Or verse 5:4 in some of the renditions of the Qurʾān.

[13] As cited by Fazlur Rahman (1964, p. 10).

had been eliminated from the holy city." This interpretation is probably based on the reference to the opposition of the Quraysh of Makkah to Islam in the verse. The full verse reads:

> Forbidden to you is carrion, and blood, and the flesh of swine, and that over which any name other than God's has been invoked, and the animal that has been strangled, or beaten to death, or killed by a fall, or gorged to death, or savaged by beast of prey, save that which you (yourselves) may have slaughtered while it was still alive; and (forbidden to you is) all that has been slaughtered on idolatrous altars. And (you are forbidden) to seek to learn through divination what the future may hold in store for you: this is sinful conduct. *Today, those who are bent on denying the truth have lost all hope of (your ever forsaking) your religion: do not, then, hold them in awe, but stand in awe of Me! Today have I perfected your religion for you, and have bestowed upon you the full measure of My blessings, and willed Islam to be your religion.* As for him, however, who is driven (to what is forbidden) by dire necessity and not by an inclination to sinning—behold, God is much-forgiving, a dispenser of grace (5:3).

Some support for Ṭabarī's conjecture is provided by the fact that one of the *ḥadīth* reports in Ṣaḥīḥ Muslim (*Kitāb al-tafsīr*) that provides evidence on the timing of the revelation of this verse is narrated on the authority of ʿUmar himself. In light of the *ḥadīth* reports attributed to ʿUmar on the timings of the prohibition of *ribā*, one must conclude that he did not see any contradictions in these reports, and therefore would not have interpreted 5:3 to be either the last revelation or as implying "completion" as far as *ḥilla* or *ḥurma* were concerned.

From the foregoing conflicting evidence it is clear that if we were to determine the exact timings of the prohibition of *ribā* on the basis of the set of verses in *sūra al-Baqara*, we would not be able to come to any definite conclusion. There is, however, the following point, which I have not seen being taken into consideration. If we place the timings of those verses at the end of the Prophet's life, we run into a rather unpalatable question, and that is: who exactly were the people who raised the question whether *ribā* was just like *bay*ʿ *(sale and purchase)*, to which the Qurʾān responded as noted earlier, at that late date when the whole Arabian Peninsula had accepted the message of Islam? One would presume that the question may have been raised by the Jews of Medina, but that would have happened before 5 AH, and one would not expect the Qurʾān to respond to the question several years later. It seems, therefore, that the relevant verses of *sūra al-Baqara* belong to the years before the departure of the Jews from Medina rather than to the months before the Prophet's death. In any case, in light of the uncontroversial timing of 3:130, the whole issue would seem to be inconsequential, except that when we look at it somewhat more carefully we run into another dilemma, a dilemma that comes in two parts: first, if the prohibition is placed at the earlier date, why was there so much controversy in the *fiqh* literature on the timing of these verses in *sūra al-Baqara*, and therefore its formulations about *ribā* prohibition? This question will be taken up in Chapter 10. Yet we may note that classical *fiqh* interpretation was based on the presumption that the prohibition came towards the end of the Prophet's life, whereas the interpretation of the dominant school in modern *fiqh* discourse, of whom Usmani is a representative, discards that presumption for reasons that will become clear as we proceed.

And the other part of the dilemma can be put in the following words: why was the *ribā* owed to ʿAbbās the "first" to be written off on the Day of *ʿArafa* in the Prophet's sermon on the occasion of the last pilgrimage when the prohibition had come so much earlier? A possible answer to this riddle is provided by a scrutiny of verse 3:130, specifically the words *aḍʿāfan muḍāʿafa*. That we will do towards the end of this section, but the subject will recur in several places, including Chapter 10, because it appears to me that the entire issue of *ribā* prohibition cannot be fully understood without a very close look at the significance of these words.

The other element without which the issue of *ribā* cannot be fully understood, and which interestingly again is intimately connected with the same words, is the rationale (*ḥikma*) for the prohibition of *ribā*, an element that *fiqh* acknowledges, particularly in its modern writings, but which it discounts to the maximum possible extent. Although more or less all the relevant verses hint at the underlying rationale, verse 2:279 makes it too obvious to leave any room for doubt on this account—"you will do no wrong, and neither will you be wronged (*lā taẓlimūn*a *wa-lā tuẓlamūna*). In the other verses, which presumably predate this explication, this premise is highlighted by the use of a number of exhortations: often by the general Qurʾānic term *taqwā* (usually rendered as God-fearing) as in 3:130, 2:278 and 2:281, but also by phrases such as "wickedness committed" (4:160), "confounded with Satan's touch" (2:275), and "stubbornly ingrate" (2:276). There is hardly any doubt that the Qurʾān considers transactions involving *ribā* as unjust. This unjustness is then, quite appropriately, set in sharp contrast to charity (*zakāh*, as in 30:39, *ṣadaqāt*, as in 2:276, and from the same root *taṣaddaqu*, as in 2:280). If there is a common theme that runs through all these verses, it is the contrast between *ribā* and charity. Indeed as far as the verses in *sūra al-Baqara* are concerned, where the denunciation of *ribā* is the strongest, the relevant exhortations are set right in the middle of a discourse on charity. This discourse begins with verse 2:261 (verses 2:261–72 were cited in Chapter 6 as the most comprehensive statement about charity in one place in the Qur'ān) and continues uninterrupted down to 2:275, where it comes to the subject of *ribā*. It continues thereafter to stress the charity dimension, with the summing up of the *ḥikma* dimension in 2:279, but then goes on to stress the dimension of justice in social relations involving loans in 2:282, finally culminating in 2:284. The *sūra* ends in a beautiful prayer, after a brief summing up of a few theological points, with verse 2:285.

Finally we may note that the dominant *fiqh* group's discourse on the subject takes its point of departure by drawing a distinction between *ribā* and *bay*ʿ (sale and purchase) transactions, and creates the impression that the problem of *ribā* essentially arises in loan transactions and not in *bay*ʿ transactions. This tendency originates in a specific reading of the verse 2:275 where the unbelievers are quoted as objecting to the prohibition by saying "buying and selling is but a kind of usury"[14] and the answer, that immediately follows, strongly asserts that these two things are not the same by any means, in so far as the first is permissible, from which gains can be derived, and the second is forbidden (*ḥarām*) for being unjust. And immediately after the answer has been offered, the point that it was meant to be an answer is substantiated by reminding people of the consequences: "whoever accepts the answer.., and those who do not accept it..." The verse by no means implies that debt could not arise in *bay*ʿ transactions. Indeed, a large part of the classical *fiqh* discourse, which was couched in terms of *bay*ʿ framework (no wonder that the relevant *ḥadīth* reports are mostly recorded in the respective *Kitab al-buyū*ʿ chapters of the *ḥadīth* collections), attempts to identify those *bay*ʿ transactions that would involve *ribā*. It does not directly deal with the loan transactions *per se*. Such transactions would fall in the ambit of *qirāḍ* and thus give rise to returns in the form of the so-called permissible *ribā* as we saw earlier. It is another matter that the term *qirāḍ* seemingly disappears from the classical *fiqh*

[14] The reference is, in fact, to buying and selling on credit.

discourse, a point which has important bearing on the discussion in Chapter 10. Let us now focus on the Qurʾānic perspective, and pay a closer attention to what I have called the pivotal verse, verse 3:130.

The Qurʾānic Perspective and the Historical Evidence

In this verse, our attention is naturally focused on the phrase *aḍʿāfan muḍāʿafa*, various renderings of which by different translators have already been noted. There is nothing unusual about this, for as far as the classical commentators (exegetes) are concerned, this was the focal point of their interpretation of the word *ribā* in its technical sense. In the contemporary discourse, on the other hand, there is a somewhat puzzling loss of focus on it. This may, admittedly, be the result of a thought process stretching back a few centuries, centuries that could not possibly be characterized as a time of intellectual ferment in the Islamic sciences.[15] Nevertheless, one of the things that requires our attention is the possible reasons for this tendency to discard the classical scholarly heritage. The qualifying clause *aḍʿāfan muḍāʿafa* occurs immediately after the word *ribā* in the verse. The inescapable question, therefore, is: what is the purport of this clause as far as the prohibition of *ribā* is concerned? If we reformulate the question in the language of *fiqh*, it becomes: does it have what is commonly referred to as a *Sharīʿa* value? That is to say: does it represent the *ʿilla* (the effective juridical cause) for the prohibition of *ribā*?[16] All the classical works on exegesis tacitly assume that it does, as we will see below; it is another matter that *fiqh* did not come to accord it that due recognition—an issue more fully taken up in Chapter 10. The words are immediately followed by "but fear God" with the obvious implication that if you do not avoid *aḍʿāfan muḍāʿafa*, then you are not God-fearing. What exactly was the nature of the process that led to *aḍʿāfan muḍāʿafa*, therefore, becomes the crucial issue, and it is here that we must consult the classical works on exegesis for an answer.

Consider what Qureshi (1946) states from Ṭabarī's *Jāmiʿ al-bayān* (vol. iv, p. 56):

[15] It should not come as a surprise that most of the relevant works cited in the discourse belong to the twentieth century.

[16] The complete *fiqh* term being *ʿillat al-ḥukm*, the effective cause of a decree.

> The manner in which *ribā* was acquired at Makkāh during the Pagan days, was quite similar to that prevailing in Tā'if, that is, when the time fixed for repayment of a loan arrived, the creditor would enquire whether the debtor was ready to repay his loan or was he ready to pay "the additional." If the debtor had the means, he immediately discharged his debt; otherwise he would procure "an easing-time" of another year for the repayment of debt.
>
> If a one year old she-camel was due, in the following year he would claim a two-year old she-camel, in the third year a three-year old she-camel, and so on. The same was true in money transactions, that is, if the debtor be unable to pay at the fixed time, he would be required to pay double the amount next year, and so on until the debtor cleared his entire debt.
>
> The creditor naturally demanded repayment of his debt at the appointed time, but if the debtor were unable to pay he would apply for another year's "extension," in return for an "addition." Both agreed; and that was the vogue of *aḍ'afan muḍa'afa*" (pp. 63–64).[17]

There are several words and phrases that draw our attention, such as "if the debtor had the means, he immediately discharged his debt," "easing time," and "unable to pay," to which we shall turn a little later. Qureshi also cites more or less similar passages from Bayhaqī as well as Suyūṭī with exactly similar phrases (pp. 64–65). For example, from Suyūṭī the following is cited:

> The *ribā* in Pagan Arabia lay in that the creditor demanded at the time fixed for payment of debt his dues from his debtor. If the latter complied, the principal advanced would be received and the debt discharged. But if the debtor was unable to pay, "easing time" was granted to him on consideration of an additional sum (p. 65).

We are then provided the following statement from Ṭabarī:

> The type of *ribā* forbidden by God is the one in which the debtor agreed to pay to his creditor a fixed additional amount in consideration of the "easing time" (p. 65).

Though it is not clear from these reports what the terms of the original loan contract were—a subject taken up later—it is quite clear that *ribā* cannot be divorced from *aḍ'āfan muḍā'afa* which in turn is associated with an inability to pay the principal amount upon maturity. A defi-

[17] Qureshi uses the term 'compound interest' instead of *aḍ'āfan muḍā'afa*, as though Ṭabarī had used the term. His inappropriate, rather careless, use of a modern term to underscore *aḍ'āfan muḍā'afa* has created much confusion in the contemporary discourse on the issue—a point to which we shall return shortly.

nite statement as to what *aḍʿāfan muḍāʿafa* meant comes to us on the authority of Mujāhid (d. 723), as reported by Ṭabarī:

> Muhammad bin ʿAmr reported to us, he said that Abū ʿĀsim related to him from ʿIsā, he from Ibn Abū Najīh, who said that concerning the Qurʾānic verse "O you who believe, do not devour *riba* with continued re-doubling," Mujāhid said, "This is the *riba al-jāhiliyya*."[18]

Or consider the following *ḥadīth* report appearing in the venerable *Muwaṭṭa*ʾ of Mālik (d. 795) on the authority of the famous *tabīʿī* commentator, Zayd bin Aslam (d. 754):

> *Riba* of *Jāhiliyya* operated in this manner: if a man owed another a debt, at the time of its maturity the creditor would ask the debtor: "Will you pay up or will you increase [*am turbī*—from *riba*]"?. If the latter paid up, the creditor received back the sum; otherwise the principal was increased on stipulation of a further term.[19]

These reports do not leave any doubt about the intimate connection between ribā and the process of *aḍʿāfan muḍāʿafa*. Such reports, and similar ones, leave the terms of the original loan contract unexplained. For our purpose, it is not sufficient to know that a debt existed; we also wish to know exactly how that debt arose, and attained a specific value. For instance, was it comprised of only the principal amount or did it include something over and above the principal amount, something that we would now understand to be interest, or the permissible ribā? And if it was comprised of only the principal amount, were there any periodic payments in the interim, i.e. from the date the loan was contracted to the maturity period when the principle amount became due?

About the nature, or the terms, of the original loan contract, Mawdudi (1961, p. 258, n. 2) argues that the loan was made without any demand for payment during the duration of the loan or any increase on the loaned amount at the time of repayment. On the other hand, a contemporary of Mawdudi, Muhammad Shafi is reported as stating, "The prevailing practice in Arabia was that a certain amount of money was advanced for a fixed period at a fixed rate of interest. If the debtor paid the loan within the prescribed time, the matter was settled on the payment of interest, otherwise he had to pay more interest"

[18] See Fazlur Rahman (1964, p. 7).
[19] As rendered ibid., p. 5.

(Rahman, 1964, p. 6).[20] Now let us evaluate these modern interpretations with what we get from the classical works on exegesis. Consider, for instance, what Rāzī has to say on the subject in his Tafsīr al-kabīr.[21] By the time Rāzī wrote, or because of what he wrote, the *fiqh* distinction between two forms of *ribā* had crystallized, and he used those terms in his commentary. About *ribā al-nasī'a*, which he now equates with *ribā al-jāhiliyya*, notwithstanding the fact that originally *fiqh* did not interpret it in this manner (no wonder, therefore, that the modern discourse on the issue by the dominant school invariably takes Rāzī's position as their point of departure, as though nothing had been said on the issue in the previous five, if not six, centuries), he wrote:

> Know that *ribā* is of two kinds—*ribā al-nasī'a* and *ribā al-faḍl*. As regards *ribā al-nasī'a*, it is the same thing that was well known and prevalent in Pagan days. It lay in that the creditors advanced loans on condition that they would receive every month a certain fixed sum, without diminishing thereby their principal sums advanced. When the time for repayment of loan expired, they demanded their dues: if the debtor was unable to pay, they increased their dues and extended the time of repayment. This is what was known as *ribā* which was practiced in Pagan days.[22]

This statement tells us about two kinds of increases relating to a loan: the monthly payment that does not decrease the amount of the principal, and the other that is added because of the inability of the debtor to discharge his obligation at the time the principal payment becomes due. It is this which has been referred to as *aḍ'āfan muḍā'afa* in the earlier narrations, though Rāzī, being not only an exegete but also a jurist (*faqīh*) does not use those words, but it is quite clear that he is referring to *ribā al-jāhiliyya*. While keeping silent on the issue of the first type of increase, but implying its acceptability, he is indeed saying that if upon the expiry of the loan period set in the contract, the principal amount is returned, there will be no charge of *ribā* against the parties involved, this being the so called *halāl ribā*. It must be emphasized that his description of *ribā al-nasī'a* begins in the second

[20] It may be kept in mind that Shafi used the Urdu word *sūd* (literally benefit or profit); although the word is originally Persian, it is also used in Urdu to denote interest. What was the term used in original sources from which he draws his conclusions in not clear.

[21] Originally titled *Mafātiḥ al-ghayb*, but commonly known as Tafsīr al-kabīr (The great exegesis).

[22] As rendered by Qureshi (1946, p. 77). The same is also rendered, with slight change in words but without altering the substance, by Usmani (2000, p. 33).

last sentence with the words "When the time," and therefore does not cover the first form of increase, namely the monthly payments made before the date of repayment. Any lingering doubts about the original terms of the loan contracts is removed by the *ḥadīth* report narrated on the authority of Zayd bin Aslam in *Muwaṭṭa'*, about which Fazlur Rahman (1964) records that, "the statement of Zayd bin Aslam, which is recorded not only by Mālik but also by Bayhaqī, Razīn [Razī?] and other *Muhaddithûn* and *fuqahâ'*, shows that the initial interest itself was not usurious and, therefore, not considered *riba*" (p. 6). The confusion over the issue of *ribā* is then demonstrated by his lashing out at the classical exegetes, "such as Ṭabarī, Bayḍāwi, Suyūṭī, and others" for "inventing a *halâl riba*" (p. 10), when a couple of pages earlier (p. 7) he had argued that interest relating to bank transactions was not *ribā*.

The interesting thing is that in general the reports that mention *aḍʿāfan muḍāʿafa* do not clarify the nature of original loan contracts, and the reports that do so fail, at least explicitly, to relate it to *aḍʿāfan muḍāʿafa*.[23] For example, while the statement of Rāzī clarifies that the original loan contract stipulated "fixed monthly payments," it leaves the question open as to what would happen if the debtor was unable to discharge even his monthly payment obligations. One would surmise that in that case the process of *aḍʿāfan muḍāʿafa* would have become immediately operative. Surely if a person is unable to pay an installment, he could not possibly discharge the principal amount. Beyond that, there is another question that remains unanswered in these reports. It is not clear whether the loan was in cash or kind, for we know it was quite common in those days to sell goods on credit, and indeed in the original *fiqh* formulations, *ribā al-nasī'a* was defined over such transactions. While this may seem a trivial detail, in light of the subsequent developments in *fiqh* relating to the distinction between *ribā* transactions (that necessarily involve a loan as long as it is of the *nasī'a* and not *faḍl* variety) and *bay'* transactions (that *may* involve a loan if they are of *muʿajjal*-deferred payment-variety) it does not remain trivial any more. It then means that we face a situation where a loan falls under either a *ribā* or *bay'* contract, with the possibility of each variety having its own legal conditions that may not be mutually

[23] Or at least that is the impression one gets when one reads the English renderings, as well as the secondary sources. Admittedly, this may be the result of selective culling, an issue that will come under discussion in Chapter 10.

consistent. We know that this is exactly what happened in reality, and we will return to this issue a little later, but at this juncture, the more immediate question is whether we can trace this confusion back to the time period under consideration.

From the historical records we know that there were cash loans, there were loans of animals, and there were loans that related to sales on deferred payment basis. Ṭabarī reports on the authority of Qatadāh: "The *ribā* of *jahiliyya* was a transaction whereby a person used to sell a commodity for a price payable at a future specific date, thereafter when the date of payment came and the buyer was unable to pay, the seller used to increase the amount due and give him more time" (Usmani, 2000, p. 36). It is this transaction which has now come to be known as *bayʿ muʿajjal* and it therefore is clear that such a *bayʿ* could also lead to *aḍʿāfan muḍāʿafa*. To avoid any confusion, it must be kept in mind that the deferred payment price used to be higher than the spot price (and *fiqh* recognizes this quite well, and sanctions it because it is supposed to be related to a *bayʿ* transaction). Since the Qurʾān recognizes the right of the creditor to his *raʾs al-māl* (generally translated as the amount of principal), it is therefore important to find out what the *raʾs al-māl is* in these transactions. First, it is quite clear that in the case of cash loans, the *raʾs al-māl* would be the amount given to the debtor at the time of extending the loan, and this is precisely the amount that ought to be paid back at the time of repayment, although in the meantime there may be periodic payments made according to the terms of the loan contract that would correspond to the permissible *ribā*, which is exactly the same as the modern usage of the term interest. But what exactly would the *raʾs al-māl* be in a loan involving a sale on a deferred payment basis? Would it be the spot price, which is what the creditor in fact surrenders, or would it be the higher amount (the higher price) that was to be ultimately paid by the debtor?

Before discussing the classical *fiqh* position on the subject, let us note the following theoretical possibilities with regard to a comparison of these two loan contracts:

i. If what the debtor pays in the deferred payment loan is taken to be the *raʾs al-māl*, then the two loan contracts turn out to be exactly the same; in the deferred payment loan, the creditor would get what would technically be called his principal amount along with an increase that would correspond to interest. For instance, consider a $100 loan at a 10 percent rate of interest leading to a repayment of

$110 after one year, comprised of $100 as the principal amount and $10 as the interest payment. This will be exactly the same thing as a sale of goods on a deferred payment basis for $110, the spot price of which was $100 and the payment were to be made after one year;

ii. If, on the other hand, the *ra's al-māl* in the deferred payment sale was to be deemed as the spot price of the goods, i.e. $100, and that was to be the amount returned after one year, but no interest payment was to be made, the two loan contracts would not be equal.

iii. And if in the cash loan case, no interest payments are to be made, the two loan contracts, namely cases (ii) and (iii), are equal.

iv. And, finally, if no interest payment is to be made in the cash loan but a higher payment than spot price is to be made in the deferred payment loan, the two loan contracts turn out to be different.

Let us now consider each one of these cases from the dominant *fiqh* school's point of view. In (i), the equivalence is not recognized because one contract is considered to be a *bay*ʿ and the other a loan contract, never mind even if the $100 amount is to be used to buy the same goods as would be bought in the other case. The former is permissible while the latter is not. The presumption is that people somehow take out loans just to keep money in their pockets. In (ii), the *bay*ʿ contract is permissible except that such is implicitly assumed to be practically irrelevant, and the money loan with interest would be impermissible as per point (i). In (iii), the *bay*ʿ contract is permissible as per (ii), and when it is a money loan, it is permissible and is commonly referred to as *qarḍ ḥasan*, but it could equally be called *qarḍ*, which is also supposed to be interest-free. Case (iv) is the one which is supposed to represent the true *Sharīʿa* position, notwithstanding the interpretations of the classical scholars of Qurʾānic exegesis down to the sixteenth century (to Suyūṭī's times). What is important to note is that in these permissible cases, it is the payment to be made by the debtor in the deferred payment loan (which is permitted to be higher than the spot price) which is being considered as the *ra's al-māl*. This issue will occupy us most of the remaining part of this section.[24] At this stage, we may turn again to verses 2:278–80 in light of what has gone so far.

[24] It is interesting to note that in the early ninth century, Shāfiʿī worried about this issue, and argued that *rā's al-māl* is the original (and therefore) spot price of the goods in the case of deferred payment in a credit sale. See the English translation of his Risāla by Khadduri (1987, pp. 127, 157, and 190–91). It is another matter that

When we pay close attention to what the specific words and phrases occurring in the *ribā* verses meant to the Arabs at the time these verses were revealed, the substance of these verses can be put thus: O you who believe; fear God by giving up what a debtor has come to owe you due to *ribā*, that is, through the process of *aḍʿāfan muḍāʿafa*. Know that "if the debtor had the means," he would have "immediately discharged his debt" and made the required payment to you. And although you are entitled to your *raʾs al-māl*, for this is what justness demands, yet you must grant an "easing time" to him if at the moment he is "unable to pay" the required amount due to economic hardship which obviously is beyond his control. And as such, it is only just that you do not inflict any additional hardship on him. And indeed, in view of his economic hardship, which may not ease any time soon, you *may* remit the *raʾs al-māl* by way of charity, for that will be much better for you, if you but knew it, for God will give you a manifold reward for such an act of charity.

Two other points that emerge from this analysis must be noted. The first is the inescapable connection between debtor's inability to pay and the process of *aḍʿāfan muḍāʿafa*, and the second is the creditor's legal claim to his *raʾs al-māl*. Both of these relate to *lā taẓlimūna wa-lā tuẓlamūn*. To sum up the point, while the term *aḍʿāfan muḍāʿafa* does not occur in the later set of verses belonging to *sūra al-Baqara*, it is implied therein, and this is how the classical scholars of exegesis have interpreted these verses, as has been shown above, for otherwise these verses could not be connected to the rationale for the prohibition of *ribā*, that is to the injustice inflicted on a weaker party in a contract involving debt.

The Rationale for the Prohibition

Consider the first point. It is the "straitened circumstances" mentioned in verse 2:280 that led to the failure of timely restitution by the debtor and thus start the process of *aḍʿāfan muḍāʿafa*. In modern parlance, it amounts to a default or bankruptcy and what, therefore, *fiqh* needed to do was to focus on the rules relating to bankruptcy, or bankruptcy protection, for those debtors who were in economic hard-

because of practical difficulties in its enforcement, the issue was subsequently ignored in the *fiqh* literature.

ship, something it hardly ever paid any attention to. Indeed the idea of bankruptcy scarcely occurs even in the contemporary *fiqh* writings or writings on fiqhnomics, although traditional *fiqh* covers it under the topic of *ḥijr*; which actually covers the legal restrictions on minors, the deranged, or bankrupts but only with regard to the disposal of their property. It is in this context that one appreciates the wisdom of the Qurʾānic sanction for the use of *zakāh* funds for discharging the debts of those who are in "straitened circumstances" as we saw in Chapter 7, for this not only relieves the debtors of their obligations but also ensure the payment of *raʾs al-māl* to the creditors consistet with *lā taẓlimūna wa-lā tuẓlamūn*.

A slight digression is in order at this stage. While the word interest is of relatively recent origin, it is derived from the Latin word *interesse*. We earlier made a reference to Judeo-Christian traditions in respect to usury, and it will be useful to have a brief look at those traditions. Don Patinkin (1972) tells us:

> Etymologically, *interest* stems from the medieval Latin word *interesse*, although the meaning of *interesse* was sharply distinguished by the medieval canonists from what is now denoted by *interest*. In particular, the canonists used *interesse* to refer to the compensation made by a debtor to his creditor for damages caused to the creditor as a result of default or delay in the repayment of a loan; as such the compensation evolved from the *quod interest* of Roman law, which was the payment for damages arising from the nonfulfillment of any contractual obligation. The canonists considered *interesse* to be conceptually distinct from the payment for the use of a loan, which they (and Roman law) denoted by the term *usura*. Since canon law permitted *interesse* but forbade *usura*, the reason for the evolvement of the modern term *interest* is clear (p. 118).

The meaning attached to the term *interesse* by the canonists precisely coincides with *ribā* as explained above in so far as it could imply nonfulfillment of payment obligations due to straitened economic circumstances, and thus *aḍʿāfan muḍāʿafa*. Since the term *interesse* belongs to medieval Latin, it evolved after the ninth century, and therefore coincides with the evolution of *fiqh*. Did the discourse on *ribā* influence the interpretation given to the term *interesse*? It is significant that the canonists took a position that would seem just the opposite of the position that emerges out of the classical works on exegesis as seen earlier: while *interesse* was permitted, periodic payments on loan were prohibited. One wonders if this was part of a reaction (that subsequently became somewhat customary) of Christianity to Islam during the fateful centuries marked by the Crusades and their aftermath. Yet it did not work out very well, for eventually the derived term, interest, came to acquire the meaning which was the opposite of the meaning of its root word—notwithstanding Patinkin's "reason for evolvement" of the term being "clear"—and came to be equivalent to what we have seen as the permissible *ribā*. But there is another question that perhaps needs to be explored: was the *fiqh* interpretation in the subsequent centuries influenced by the canonical position on *usura*? Although I will take up some of the strands relating to these questions in the next chapter, their fuller treatment will have to wait for another time. Yet I will note the following remarks by Marshall Hodgson relating to either the late Ummayad or early ʿAbbāsid times in connection with the evolution of *fiqh*:

> In the law of contracts, the Sharīʿah insisted more on substance than on form. A contract was not binding unless it involved some sort of real equivalence in an exchange, for instance. On the whole it was expected that most human relations, outside of close friendship and family ties, would take the form of contract relations rather than be determined in advance by status; yet many provisions attempted to guarantee those who were weak in one way or another against the strong taking great advantage of them. Perhaps rather naively, for instance, contracts that called for taking interest were banned: a position that was becoming stronger in the monotheistic traditions, and that the Muslim legists now tried to make absolute by interpreting a certain Qurʾānic word as covering any money payment for money (Hodgson, 1974 vol. 1, pp. 338–39).

More than anything else what this makes clear is that Qurʾānic exegesis and *fiqh* parted ways very early on as far as the interpretation of the word *ribā* was concerned, with exegesis becoming the custodian of the pristine Medinan tradition, and protecting that tradition down the centuries up to Suyūṭī's time, while *fiqh* shows the scars and bruises dealt it by the earthly reality; a reality that *inter alia* involved an extensive contact with well-established religio-cultural traditions of the time in their home territories, particularly in Egypt, Syria and Iraq. This understandably involved accommodation and adjustment. The compromises with reality took the form of *ḥiyal* (sing. *ḥīla*), and these were particularly pronounced in the area of finance. One specifically observes that ever since that time, *fiqh* has lived with the difficulties of its own making in what could be called a regime of *ḥiyal*, as we will see below, but more fully in the next chapter.

In the contemporary discourse, the term *aḍʿāfan muḍāʿafa* has taken on a rather peculiar meaning. While the dominant group has, faithfully in this case, followed the classical tradition in disregarding the significance of the term, an economist, Anwar Iqbal Qureshi, whom we have met earlier, started that peculiar interpretation by equating it to compound interest. Qureshi was aware of the exegetical works and as such could not ignore the term, and his became a fairly common interpretation among those who felt obliged to take it more seriously than the dominant group. It seems to have begun with an effort to translate *aḍʿāfan muḍāʿafa* into English—the vernacular in which he wrote—with some justification, for the clause does imply a process of compounding. When he used the prefix "compound" with *ribā*, it yielded the term "compound *riba*." By the time this happened, the term *ribā* had already been transformed into "interest," and thus we end up with the term "compound interest" to represent *ribā al-jāhiliyya*. It is another matter that after having done that, he decided to ignore it all the same, and focused instead on the issue of abolition of interest from the economy. He forgot that the compounding in compound *ribā* was necessarily occasioned by the inability of the debtor to discharge his debt obligations, and therefore the connection he established was in fact one of compounding occasioned by bankruptcy. At any rate the correct way if the word compounding is to be used is that it is actually the compounding of the principal amount due to *ribā*.

While Qureshi used the word "compounding" in its literal sense, it was natural that it would end up being mixed with its technical meaning and usage in economics, and being a trained economist, he should have known better. Since the concepts of compounding and, its inverse, discounting, more often the latter, are used in economics for inter-temporal comparison of values, and since rate of interest is used for such compounding or discounting purposes—although it could equally be the rate of profit—and since theoretically this rate could assume any value, it was a short step to eliminate compound from the term "compound interest" to associate interest not only with *ribā al-jāhiliyya* but also with the idea of compounding and discounting. In this way a purely technical usage of the rate of interest now became associated with injustice in Islamic economics. In addition, in economics, simple rate of interest and compound rate of interest can be used interchangeably depending upon the context. The connection between these two rates is of course very intimate. Any simple rate of interest can be converted into a compound rate, and vice versa, through the use of compounding, or for that matter discounting, equation.[25] Thus we observe a misplaced logical sequence in the discourse on *ribā*, where compound *ribā* quickly becomes compound interest, then transforming itself into compound rate of interest, which then becomes simple rate of interest, eventually leading to simple interest taking the place of compound *ribā* in the arguments, as a legitimate representation of the Qurʾānic concept of *aḍʿāfan muḍāʿafa*, and thus the injustice implied thereby. One may note in passing that the confusion so created eventually led to the rejection of rescheduling of bank loans caused by temporary liquidity problems—a point to which we will return in the context of *murābaḥa* in the next chapter.

With regard to the second point, relating to the legal claim of the creditor to his *raʾs al-māl*, the important question is whether this claim is to be understood as a claim in nominal or in real terms. The practical implications of this theoretical distinction have become important but only in recent times, historically speaking. The gradual shift away from real money to paper money has meant that price level can change drastically in a short span of time. Although paper money has been with us for centuries, as long as there was a system of gold backing in place, the vagaries of paper money remained in check. Gradually as the system of backing was eroded, and the gold standard yielded to the pure paper standard in the second half of the twentieth century, the possibility of nominal values becoming vastly different from their real counterparts assumed a worrying dimension, and not without cause

[25] Consider the compounding equation:

$$FV = PV\ (1+i)^n$$

Where FV is future value, PV is present value, i being the rate of interest, and n the number of periods. Assume i to be 12%, PV to be 1, and n to be 1 (one year), in which case the FV turns out to be 1.12. Suppose for this simple interest case we want to know what the compound rate will be on quarterly basis. Substituting n = 4 in the equation, and calculating i when the future value is held at 1.12, we get 2.87% [from the equation $(1+i)^4 = 1.12$]. Thus the simple interest is converted into a compound one when the duration for i is reckoned in quarters instead of a year. Similarly, if we assume a month to be the duration for specification of i, and assume the monthly rate to be 1%, this simple rate can be converted into a compound rate for a year, and in this case we get 12.68% from the equation $FV = 1(1+0.01)^{12}$. What this means is that if the rate of interest is specified in monthly terms, but the payment is not made until the end of the year, the 1% simple rate will turn out to be equivalent to 12.68% compound rate after a period of twelve months. In principle, therefore, there is no conceptual difference between simple interest and compound interest. On the other hand, compounding in the case of *ribā*, in principle, is occasioned by economic hardship or bankruptcy.

if the recent evidence from various countries is anything to go by. It would plainly be unrealistic to expect any discussion on this issue in the classical writings; indeed even modern *fiqh* writers have hardly begun to tackle this issue. Whatever meager fare is available is so intertwined with the issue of interest that the real substance of the question is lost in the fog surrounding it—more on this in Chapter 10.

Fiqh's Interpretation

A natural point of departure in the present context is to consider *fiqh*'s terminology relating to what the word loan means to see what light this could shed on the issues that have been discussed so far. There are four *fiqh* terms that draw our attention, and these are: *qarḍ, qarḍ ḥasan, dayn*, and *qirāḍ*. The first three of these words directly occur in the Qur᾽ān, and the fourth is a turn on the plural of the first, qurūḍ. Since all these words were vested with specific meanings by *fiqh*, we need to understand to what extent these *fiqh* meanings are consonant with their corresponding Qur᾽ānic meanings. That inquiry will be relevant for the three of those words that occur in the Qur᾽ān, but for the fourth one we need to ask why *fiqh* needed a term which is the same as the first, except being related to its plural form. Ordinarily the word *qarḍ* translates as loan, and that is how the Qur᾽ān uses it. And that is how *fiqh* interpreted it except that it gave it somewhat restricted meanings that have two ingredients: first, that it represented a *ribā*-free, or an interest-free, loan; and second, to make sure that the foregoing condition was satisfied, that it must be repaid in kind, that is to say in terms of the same good that was originally loaned, but then it could not involve the goods that were the subject of *ribā al-faḍl*—a point which will become clear only when we come to that subject under *ribā al-ḥadīth* below.[26] However, we are not quite sure whether these conditions, particularly the second one (and therefore by implication the first one too), can be traced back to the Prophetic times. We know there was *salaf*, a term that comes to us from the *ḥadīth* reports, and in place of which *fiqh* later popularized an equivalent

[26] This originally included only six goods explicitly mentioned in the relevant *ḥadīth* reports, though subsequently various schools of *fiqh* extended the scope of prohibition to include a large number of other goods, except the Ẓāhirī school. The original goods are noted below in the section on *ribā al-faḍl*.

term, *salam*, which essentially involved loan, and in which there could be an increase in the quantity returned.[27] To avoid the obvious problem this posed, *fiqh*, when it came to articulate its position subsequently, thought the problem could be solved by deeming these to be *bayʿ* contracts, and thus to distinguish them from *qarḍ* contracts, and imposed the arbitrary requirement that the payment must be made in terms of goods different from the goods originally loaned (which in its conceptualization turned the transaction into a sale) as will become clear a little later. The result was that there was an increase, but one that was not considered *ribā*.[28]

So, if *qarḍ* was an interest-free loan, what was *qarḍ ḥasan*? The modern *fiqh* discourse defines it as, again, an interest-free loan. But the roots of this interpretation go far back in time. Islamic economists trace it back to Māwardī who lived in the eleventh century. To put the question slightly differently, if the *qarḍ ḥasan* is an interest-free loan, why is it distinguished from qarḍ? Since *qarḍ ḥasan* is a Qurʾānic term, we are well advised to consult that original source for a clarification. The Qurʾān mentions the term in six different places: verses 2:245, 5:12, 57:11, 57:18, 64:17 and 73:20.[29] Of these, verses 2:245, 57:11, 57:18 and 64:17 do not leave any doubt that what is meant is

[27] Subsequently, Ḥanafī *fiqh* used the term *salaf* for *ribā*-free loans. I have already pointed out in an earlier footnote (no. 3) that *salaf*, *salam*, and *bayʿ muʿajjal* turn out to be identical in the case of a barter transaction. But more on that below.

[28] One may note that a *qarḍ* may arise in the case of *ʿāriya*, which is a loan of goods where only usufruct rights are transferred, and the good is to be returned to the owner according to the time frame agreed upon. Originally it involved borrowing of household utensils or small implements from neighbors.

[29] The translation of these verses is: "Who it is that will offer up unto God a goodly loan, which He will amply repay, with manifold increase?" (2:245).

"And God said: 'Behold, I shall be with you! If you are constant in prayer, and spend in charity, and believe in my apostles and aid them, and offer up unto God a goodly loan, I will surely efface your bad deeds and bring you into gardens through which running water flows" (5:12).

"Who is it that will offer up unto God a goodly loan, which He will amply repay? For, such (as do so) shall have a noble reward" (57:11)

"Verily, as for the men and women who accept the truth as true, and who (thus) offer up unto God a goodly loan, they will be amply repaid, and shall have a noble reward (in the life to come)" (57:18).

"If you offer up to God a goodly loan, He will amply repay you for it, and will forgive you your sins: for God is ever responsive to gratitude, forbearing" (64:17).

"Recite, then, (only) as much of it as you may do with ease, and be constant in prayer, and spend in charity, and (thus) lend unto God a goodly loan: for whatever good deeds you may offer up in your own behalf, you shall truly find it with God—yea, better, and richer in reward" (73:20).

a loan given to God, or rather given in the name of God, which is to be repaid by Him and therefore is not to be claimed back from the individual recipients. Here, it turns out to be another name for charity. However, this interpretation gives rise to a pertinent question: is there a purpose behind the use of *qarḍ ḥasan* rather than charity, especially if the word charity (*zakāh*) is also mentioned in the same breath alongside it in 5:12 and 73:20? Verse 5:12 is addressed to Banū Isrāʾīl and represents a historical account. One could, therefore, regard it as just that, i.e. a historical narrative not necessarily having a *Sharīʿa* value in the new dispensation, just like 4:160–61 in the context of *ribā*. But, then, we read 73:20 in which the same two words, *zakāh* and *qarḍ ḥasan*, recur, a verse which begins by addressing the Prophet directly in the context of his long nightly vigils reciting the Qurʾān, and then seems to generalize the point in view of the various other preoccupations that the believers would be likely to have in their daily routines. Although Asad and Pickthall translate it as a qualifying clause for *zakāh*, so it is the *zakāh* itself that is what *qarḍ ḥasan* means, others, including Yūsuf ʿAlī, Khan and Hilali, and Arberry, interpret the two as separate items.

It seems to me that there is a purpose behind the use of two distinct words to denote charity, where *qarḍ ḥasan* is intended to underscore the straitened circumstances that may be perceived as transitory, circumstances that may be the result of a temporary setback, but then in reality they may not turn out to be so. While the lender could not claim the loan amount back as a matter of legal right, for the circumstances of the loan recipient may not improve—and thus from his perspective the loan must be viewed as charity, a beneficent loan—the use of the word *qarḍ* may be interpreted as directed at the recipient of the loan, urging him to repay the loan if his circumstances improve and thus make it possible for him to do so, for the lender may at times himself be in need. Read thus, *qarḍ ḥasan* is either an outright grant, or a loan to be repaid at the discretion of the recipient. Correspondingly, it could also be interpreted as remission of the *raʾs al-māl* as of 2:280, which of course would be an act of charity. What these verses make clear is that a *qarḍ ḥasan* could not be interpreted as an interest-free loan, for in that case the lender has a legal claim to his *raʾs al-māl*. So what imperatives led *fiqh* to place a different interpretation on the term *qarḍ ḥasan* from the Qurʾānic interpretation? The existence of the term "interest-free loan" cannot be understood without the existence of its counterpart, and the obvious candidate for that would be the case of a loan that commanded a return in what has previously been noted as permissible *ribā*.[30]

Before we say more on that subject, let us look at the meanings of the third Qurʾānic term *dayn*. *Fiqh* has reserved this term for debts associated with *bayʿ* contracts, such as *bayʿ muʿajjal, bayʿ salam*, and possibly *murābaḥa* as it is interpreted now. But this interpretation is also arbitrary, for it is not supported by the Qurʾānic meanings of the word as we will see shortly. While these contracts could be interpreted as involving a *qarḍ*, as we saw above, *fiqh* wishes to keep a very strict separation between a *qarḍ* and a *bayʿ* contract, and all of the aforementioned contracts are deemed to be *bayʿ* contracts. The only difference between *qarḍ* and *dayn* is that the latter literally means debt while the former means loan, but then we also know that any loan as soon as it is contracted becomes a debt. But how justified is the *fiqh* distinction between *qarḍ* and *dayn* bearing in mind the Qurʾānic use of the term *dayn*? A careful look at the relevant verses makes it clear that such a distinction is not justified. The term *dayn* occurs five times in the Qurʾān, once in 2:282, and four times in 4:11–12, and while all the translators have translated it as debt, the interpretation could not be restricted to debt arising out of *bayʿ* contracts. This is because in 4:11–12, it is used in the context of retiring the debt of a deceased person from his property before the issue of inheritance can be settled, and since the term *qarḍ* is not separately mentioned in those verses, it is clear that the term implies all debt, regardless of the way it had been contracted. By interpreting the term *dayn* in a peculiar way, *fiqh* permitted an increase over and above the principal amount, for the spot payment (price) could be lower than the deferred payment (price), but would not allow such an increase under any circumstance for a *qarḍ*. But then when it came to default, the two cases were treated identically, as we will see below.

---

30 In the relatively recent *fiqh* writings, we see another fudge through the introduction of the term *qarḍ al-ʿām* presumably in view of the dilemma posed by the question under consideration. The difference between these two is that, unlike in the former case, the banks are entitled to charge a service fee for providing the *qarḍ al-ʿāṃ* (interest-free loan). One need not offer any comments on the viability of such wild proposals, but one would like to point out that this could not possibly be an interpretation derived from classical writings when the banking system, as we know it today, did not even exist. See Tahir al-Qadri, "The Alternative to Interest-bearing Financial System" (in Urdu), Fortnightly Tehreek (Lahore), Special Supplement, vol. 3, no 20, (October 15–30), 1992, who is the author of this proposal.

The subject of debt is treated with considerable attention to detail in 2:282, immediately after the verses on *ribā* in *sūra al-Baqara*, details that pertain to the care that must be taken at the time of entering into such contracts, for it is rightly presumed that if these details are not adhered to, disputations may arise later that may lead to an injustice being inflicted on one of the parties. One of the longest verses of Qurān, perhaps the longest as far as I can determine, says:

> O you who have attained to faith! Whenever you enter into a contract of debt for a stated term, set it down in writing. And let a scribe write it down equitably between you; and no scribe shall refuse to write as God has taught him: thus shall he write. And let him who contracts the debt dictate; and let him be conscious of God, his Sustainer, and not weaken anything of his undertaking. And if he who contracts the debt is weak of mind or body, or is not able to dictate himself, then let him who watches over his interests dictate equitably. And call upon two of your men to act as witnesses; and if two men are not available, then a man and two women from among such as are acceptable to you as witnesses, so that if one of them should make mistake, the other could remind her. And the witnesses must not refuse (to give evidence) whenever they are called upon. And be not loath to write down every contractual provision, be it small or great, together with the time at which it falls due; this is more equitable in the sight of God, more reliable as evidence, and more likely to prevent you from having doubts (later). If, however, (the transaction) concerns ready merchandise which you transfer directly unto one another, you will incur no sin if you do not write it down. And have witnesses whenever you trade with one another, but neither scribe nor witness must suffer harm; for if you do (them harm), behold, it will be sinful conduct on your part. And remain conscious of God, since it is God who teaches you (herewith)—and God has full knowledge of everything (2:282).

The emphasis on not just having witnesses but having a written contract with all the provisions, *small or great*, recorded therein is simply remarkable at a time when only a few individuals were literate (and writing materials were not very handy either), and that explains the statement that no one who is capable of writing a contract would refuse to do so. However, one wonders why in view of the rather unequivocal nature of this commandment no written debt contracts have reached us; that would have made it possible to see what the relevant provisions, "small or great," actually were.[31] This is particularly

[31] There are detailed accounts of what *ribā* meant, accounts that explain the process of *aḍʿāfan muḍāʿafa* in considerable details, such as recorded by not only by towering

so if we understand, as is commonly done, that the relevant verse (2:282) belongs to the early Medinan period. But then the verse may not belong to that period, for it occurs immediately after the set of *ribā* verses (2:275–281), the timings of which have been a matter of controversy, as we saw earlier, though as far as I can see no one has included this verse in the controversy about the timings of the *ribā* verses. At any rate, in view of the difficulties of preparing written contracts at the time, it was, perhaps, more in anticipation of the times to come that the guidance was vouchsafed.[32] Though no written contract belonging to the Prophetic period has come down to us, an interesting incident during the caliphate of ʿUmar sheds some light on the nature of *qarḍ* transactions prevailing at the time, though the term used is *qirāḍ*, the last element in the aforementioned list.

The term *qirāḍ* became a purely *fiqh* term. But since it is related to the plural of the word *qarḍ*, which itself was a *fiqh* term, one wonders what were the specific needs that *qarḍ* did not provide that necessitated the introduction of its plural form as a distinct and separate term. We know that *fiqh* decided to reserve it for a sort of profit-sharing contract. It is another matter that it did not feel very comfortable with it and thus some of *fiqh* schools, the Ḥanafī and Ḥanbalī, introduced, though much later, an entirely new term, *muḍāraba*, to replace it. But since the evidence shows that the term existed during the period immediately after the Prophetic times, and in all likelihood during those times, the question is what meanings were attached to it at the time. This is clarified by a story reported in the *Muwaṭṭa*ʾ of Mālik,[33] on the authority of

figures such as Mālik and Ṭabarī, but also by commentators such as Bayhaqī, Razīn, etc., on the authority of the famous *tābiʿī* (meaning a companion of the Companions of the Prophet) Zayd bin Aslam, but no record of any written contract of debt, as far as I am aware.

[32] It may be noted that while the term "ready merchandizing" (*tijārat al-ḥaḍra*), for which an exemption from written contracts is given, may possibly be interpreted as encompassing what subsequently came to be known as *bayʿ muʿajjal* because the merchandise is transferred at the time of sale, one would readily see that it more appropriately refers only to spot sales. What this means is that exemption from committing the contracts to writing (with small or large conditions) could, if at all, apply to debt arising out of *bayʿ muʿajjal* and not debt arising out of a *qarḍ* (loan) contract. Yet no historical evidence is available for these, as noted.

[33] Book 32, Number 32.1.1. It may be noted here, pending further discussion in the next chapter, that Imām Mālik does not cite very many *ḥadīth* reports in his lengthy chapter on *qirāḍ*. He presents his own opinions on the issue, in his struggle to come to terms with the situation as it prevailed towards the end of the eighth century, which itself is quite telling.

Zayd bin Aslam (d. ca. 754), which goes something like this: two sons of Caliph ʿUmar, ʿAbd Allāh ibn ʿUmar and ʿUbayd Allāh ibn ʿUmar had gone to the lands of Iraq with a military expedition. When the expedition was returning to Medina, it passed through Basra where the two brothers met with the governor of Basra, Abū Mūsa al-Ashʿarī. The governor had to send some tax revenues (*māl Allāh*) to Medina, which he wanted to entrust to them. However, he expressed the desire that he would give the amount to them as a *qarḍ* rather than as an *amāna* so that they could buy merchandize with the money and thus derive some profit from it. To this the brothers agreed, and made a profit by selling the merchandize in Medina. When the father came to know about it, his sense of equity immediately prompted him to ask whether Abū Mūsa had entrusted the money to all members of the expedition or specifically to the two brothers. Upon finding out that he had entrusted it specifically to the two of them, he exclaimed: "The governor did it because you were the sons of the Caliph" (actually *amīr al-muʾminīn*, the title he preferred). His sense of fairness led him to order that the original amount as well as all the profit be deposited in the *bayt al-māl* (the treasury). ʿAbd Allāh acquiesced, but ʿUbayd Allāh protested, arguing that they were the guarantors of the amount (it being a *qarḍ* and not an *amāna*), and had anything happened to the merchandize, they would have been liable to restore the amount to the *bayt al-māl*. We are told that ʿUmar did not pay much attention to this line of argument, and repeated his orders. When ʿUbayd Allāh continued his protest, someone from the audience interjected by pleading with ʿUmar that the case be considered as one of *qirāḍ*. At this stage, ʿUmar is supposed to have said: "Alright, consider it a matter (*muʿāmala*) relating to *qirāḍ*," and half of the profit was surrendered to *bayt al-māl* while the remaining half was left with the two brothers, and that is how the issue was resolved.[34]

There are several points that are noteworthy. Some of these are related to the issue of profit-sharing, and these will be taken up in the next chapter when we come to discuss *muḍāraba*. Yet one very

[34] There is another *ḥadīth* report in *Muwaṭṭaʾ* which tells us that ʿUthmān, the third caliph, made a loan to a person on the basis of *qirāḍ* and shared the resulting profits with him. Further, Bukhārī reports that the famous companion of the Prophet, Zūbayr ibn al-ʿAwwām left a huge debt upon his death because he used to take loans from people to invest them in real estate on the basis of *qirāḍ*. He was a very wealthy merchant. It must be noted that in none of these reports there is any mention of loss-sharing.

important thing that draws our attention is related to the question of loss-sharing, for had there been a loss, the loan guarantee was quite clearly understood to be the return of the full loan amount (the *ra's al-māl*) without any reduction to take account of the losses. Far clearer evidence on this score is provided by Ṭabarī in his Tārīkh al-Ṭabarī where he narrates a story about Hind, the wife of Abū Sufyān. She received a loan (*qirāḍ*) of 4,000 dirhams sanctioned by ʿUmar from the *bayt al-māl* for trading purposes in the last year of ʿUmar's life (23 AH).[35] In all likelihood this happened after the event recorded in the Muwaṭṭaʾ, and it is quite likely that that event might have prompted this loan demand. Although Hind, a person of considerable means herself, could have been taken as the guarantor of the loan, ʿUmar, being a very prudent man, took the additional precaution of insisting on taking a guarantee from Abū Sūfyān. We are told that Hind suffered a loss in the trade, and protested to ʿUmar that he should reduce the amount of the loan. ʿUmar plainly refused, saying that the money belonged to all the Muslims, adding that had it been his private money, he might have considered the request more seriously. He called Abū Sūfyān to his presence and did not let him go until Hind had returned the full amount. In the present context though, what is noteworthy is the way the meaning of the word *qirāḍ* was understood by all. It is obvious that it was not something new; for there is not the slightest hint that the settlement worked out represented an entirely new arrangement.[36] But what was this profit share called? Sewharvi (1959, p. 286) mentions another *fiqh* term *ribah*, calls it permissible profit (as though profit could by itself be impermissible), and naturally associates it with *salaf*, *salam*, etc. And was it a contractually fixed percentage of the *qarḍ* amount, making it the same thing as interest or permissible *ribā*? If it was, it would support my conjecture with regard to the interpretation of the first revelation, that is to say verse 30:39, earlier in this chapter. After all, we also see a strange *fiqh* term, somewhat defunct now, *ʿaqd al-tabarruʿ*, a contractual gift payment; the idea of an involuntary giving of a gift seems quite unique to Islamic jurisprudence. But in light of the gift interpretation of the verse 30:39, as we saw earlier in this chapter, it all falls into place.

---

[35] Tārīkh al-Ṭabarī, vol. 5, Incidents of 23 AH.

[36] There is a *ḥadīth* report in Ibn Māja that tells us that the Prophet blessed *salam* and *muqāraḍa*, the latter being another name for *qirāḍ*, but the chain of narration is weak.

Fiqh's divergent interpretation of the term *ribā* as compared to the interpretation of the classical exegetes eventually led to difficulties that became more and more pronounced with the passage of time, and are nowhere near any resolution. The resorting to *ḥiyal* to get around the problem was never quite convincing. We will come to a somewhat detailed treatment of that question in Chapter 10. For the moment we need to do some stock-taking and ask whether *fiqh* could from the very beginning have avoided those difficulties had it taken the same route as the exegetes took.

Such an approach would have gone a long way towards avoiding the pitfalls *fiqh* eventually ran into, provided some of the issues were seen in their proper perspective at the time. This can be explained with the help of the seeming contradictions in the two perspectives on the timings of the prohibition that the foregoing pages have highlighted. Let us begin by a brief summary statement of these contradictions. If we assume that the prohibition of *ribā* came a bit too late for the Prophet to explain its true meanings, we run into the following difficulties. First, the notion that the Qurʾān would prohibit something, and denounce it rather as strongly as conceivable, without really explaining what exactly it was that was being prohibited and denounced, is rather problematic. This would go against an unequivocal Qurʾānic claim where God says "For clearly, most clearly, have *We spelt everything*!" (17:12). Surely, therefore, one could scarcely expect a categorical prohibition, such as on *ribā*, remaining unexplained in the Qurʾān. And then there is the related problem of verse 3:130 that is generally agreed to belong to the early Medinan period, and which quite categorically prohibits *ribā*. If we assume the timing of 3:130 is correctly understood, and we do not have any divergence of opinion on that score, and therefore place the prohibition in the early Medinan period, we run into the difficulty of not only explaining the purport of those *ḥadīth* reports that are understood as saying that the Prophet did not have enough time to explain the true meanings of the term *ribā*, but also the lacuna arising out of the indubitable reference to the first *ribā* being written off in the Prophet's sermon at the occasion of the farewell pilgrimage. An explanation of these apparent contradictions is resolved only when we focus more acutely on the qualifying clause *aḍʿāfan muḍāʿafa* in 3:130, something that was well understood at the time, but subsequently disregarded in most of the *fiqh* interpretations of the term *ribā*. Why *fiqh* did what it did is a question for Chapter 10. But now consider how this increased focus resolves some of the apparent contradictions. Let us begin by looking at the issue of the first *ribā* being written off at the time of the farewell pilgrimage.

Recall that *aḍʿāfan muḍāʿafa* necessarily involves two things: first, that there is an inability to pay on the part of the debtor as a result of the straitened circumstances, and second, that there is a disregard of these circumstances on the part of the creditor in so far as he increases the *raʾs al-māl*—doubled and then redoubled, and so on.[37] And now consider whether a situation like that would be likely to arise in the Medina of the Prophetic times, particularly after the 5 AH when all the Jews had already left the city. The Prophetic times are in general unusual times, and this was particularly true of Medina during those ten fateful years. It is clear from a large number of *ḥadīth* reports that loans were indeed contracted in the post 3:130 period. But if both of these conditions were satisfied simultaneously, at least in some cases, it would provide some clues as to why no condoning of the loans occurred before the last pilgrimage. The evidence suggests that the first condition was satisfied in a number of cases, which is to say that hardship cases did arise, but it appears that things did not go as far as the second stage as is made clear by a number of *ḥadīth* reports. For instance, Ṣaḥīḥ Muslim has five reports of the Prophet intervening, two of those seemingly relating to a single incident but reported through somewhat different chains of reporters, one of which reads: "Kaʿb bin Mālik reported that he made a demand for the repayment of the debt that Ibn Abī Hadrad owed to him. There was an altercation between them, until their voices became loud. There happened to pass by them the Prophet of God and he said: O Kāʿb, and pointed out with his hand in such a way as he meant half. So he got half of what he (Ibn Abū Hadrad) owed to him and remitted the half."[38] Notice that while there was a condoning of debt involved in this, it did not amount to a writing off of *ribā*, for there is no evidence to suggest that *aḍʿāfan muḍāʿafa* had occurred. It was perhaps a writing off of part of the principal amount as an act of charity. In addition, there are a number of *ḥadīth* reports in which the Prophet is supposed to have highlighted the merits of those who remit debts of those who are in straitened cir-

[37] We have historical accounts of instances where people ended up in slavery as a result of the unbearable burden thus occasioned.

[38] Report No. 3781. A similar report (No. 3779) is reported on the authority of ʿĀʾisha, the Prophet's wife.

cumstances.[39] It therefore appears that the Prophet's presence deterred any loan reaching the stage of *aḍʿāfan muḍāʿafa*.

Then there was the tradition of paying somewhat more than the amount of the principal. The Prophet, we are told, himself took a loan, and at the time of its discharging paid an extra amount. In the case of the Prophet, such a payment would have to be voluntary. According to the relevant *ḥadīth* report, appearing in the Sunan of Abū Dāʾūd: "Muḥārib reported that he heard Jābir bin ʿAbd Allāh saying that the Prophet owed him some money and at the time of repayment of the loan the Prophet added (some money) in excess of the principal borrowed."[40] It is rightly understood that the additional amount was paid voluntarily; and it is not difficult to understand that it would be so, for Jābir would scarcely demand even his principal amount in deference to the Prophet, especially in view of his perception of the Prophet's economic circumstances at the time this incident occurred. But then loans contracted in Makkāh before its conquest would be an altogether different matter. Qureshi (1946, p. 62) records from Tafsīr Khāzin that the Prophet's uncle ʿAbbās "used to participate in interest-transactions." ʿAbbās, about three years senior to the Prophet and a childhood companion, embraced Islam after the Battle of Badr, though history records that he entertained much sympathy for the Prophet during the hardship years in Makkāh. After embracing Islam, he returned to his home in Makkāh but a few years later decided to move to Medina, just about at the time of the conquest of Makkāh. It is quite possible that he was dealing in the permissible *ribā* transactions during that period, and when he moved to Medina some of the loans, including perhaps the periodic payments, may have remained unsettled in his absence, and might have been found by the Prophet to represent genuine cases of hardship (*aḍʿāfan muḍāʿafa*), and it must have been these that occasioned his remarks at the farewell pilgrimage. It must also be kept in mind that the Prophet specifically used the words *ribā al-jāhiliyya* in his sermon. Needless to say that this also explains the

---

[39] See, for instance, Ṣaḥīḥ Muslim, *Ḥadīth* reports nos. 3788 to 3795.

[40] In *Kitāb al-buyūʿ*, *Bāb ḥusn al-qaḍāʾ*. It also appears in the Musnad of Ibn Ḥanbal. There are a number of *ḥadīth* reports recommending a better repayment of loan in the case of animal loans; see, for instance, Ṣaḥīḥ Muslim, *Kitāb al-buyūʿ*, *Ḥadīth* reports nos. 3896 to 3900. Some of the *fiqh* writers tend to restrict such increase to cases involving animal loans only, contrary to the previous report, and it is not difficult to see why.

Banū Thaqīf versus Banū Mughīra affair referred to earlier. There is no contradiction between *ribā* having been forbidden earlier and the first *ribā* having been cancelled at the time of the farewell pilgrimage, for the forbidden *ribā* necessarily involved *aḍʿāfan muḍāʿafa*, and not every loan gave rise to it.

We are left with those *ḥadīth* reports that tell us that the Prophet did not have enough time to explain the real significance of the *ribā* prohibition. There may be two possible reasons for this impression. First is the absence of the qualifying *aḍʿāfan muḍāʿafa* in the set of verses in *sūra al-Baqara*, at least some of which are supposed to have been revealed quite late in the Prophet's life. This may have raised questions in some minds that perhaps the commonly-understood definition of *ribā* had gone through a change—after all, this is precisely the basis of subsequent confusion on the issue relating to the precise legal definition of the term in *fiqh*. But then the well-known maxim *al-Qurʾān yufassiru baʿduhu baʿḍ* (one part of the Qurʾān explains another) should have led to the clarification that a more specific meaning must have a precedent over the general meaning, particularly when it comes to establishing the legal definition. The intricacies of the *fiqh* discourse on this subject are covered in Chapter 10. And the second reason, which may have reinforced that impression, was the use of the term *ribā* by the Prophet in certain instances that would not be understood to involve *ribā* in the common apprehension of that term. It is these instances, which subsequently occasioned the distinction between *ribā al-jāhiliyya* and what came to be known as *ribā al-ḥadīth*, specifically of the *faḍl* variety, to which we now turn.

Ribā al-ḥadīth

There are a fairly large number of *ḥadīth* reports that relate to the subject of *ribā*, but there are only a handful that are specific enough for us to derive any inference as to what *ribā* might be, or what transactions would fall in the ambit of *ribā*. And it is only a subset of these that has formed the basis of the various categories into which *ribā al-ḥadīth* was divided by the subsequent developments in *fiqh*. Though the nomenclature is somewhat varied, as noted at the outset of this chapter, there are essentially two variants into which these developments can be divided, *ribā al-faḍl* and *ribā al-nasīʾa*. At the center of these developments stand two *ḥadīth* reports, each appearing in a number of variants with regard to the details included, and all of these are narrated on the authority of four eminent companions of the Prophet: ʿUmar ibn al-Khattāb, Abū Hurayra, Abū Saʿīd al-Khudrī, and ʿUbāda bin al-Samīṭ. These reports appear in all major collections. Take, for instance, the most cited:

> Abū Saʿīd al-Khudrī reported God's Messenger as saying: Gold is to be paid for by gold, silver by silver, wheat by wheat, barley by barley, dates by dates, salt by salt, like for like, transaction to be made "hand to hand." If anyone gives more or asks for more he shall deal in *ribā*. The receiver and the giver are equally guilty.[41]

The variant reported by ʿUbāda bin al-Samīṭ includes all six goods but does not include the last two sentences (*Ṣaḥīḥ Muslim*, No. 3853); the one reported on the authority of Abū Hurayra includes only four goods to the exclusion of gold and silver (*Ṣaḥīḥ Muslim*, No. 3856), but then another one attributed to him includes only gold and silver (*Ṣaḥīḥ Muslim*, No. 3857), and in yet another variant, dinars (gold coins) and dirhams (silver coins) are mentioned (*Ṣaḥīḥ Muslim*, No. 3858) with no mention of *ribā*. This last appears with slight change in words in another variant reported on the authority of ʿUthmān bin ʿAffān, the third caliph, again without any mention of *ribā*, which reads: "Do not sell a dinar for two dinars and one dirham for two dirhams" (*Ṣaḥīḥ Muslim*, No. 3849, also in Bukhārī).[42] Further, it may be noted that in the Muwaṭṭaʾ, Mālik reports a similar *ḥadīth* but this time the word *ribā* is replaced by the word *rama*, and it is added that *rama* is the same thing as *ribā*.[43] It has already been pointed out that time is not an essential, or even apparent, dimension of *ribā al-ḥadīth*; what is under consideration here relates to spot transactions, conducted on the basis of barter. Much was subsequently made of the words *yadan bi-yad* (hand to hand) by *fiqh*, and more or less all the confusions

---

[41] Bukhārī, Muslim, Nasāʾī and Dārimī in their respective *Kitāb al-buyūʿ* and *Bāb al-ribā*; and Ibn Māja in his *Abwāb al-tijāra*. In Bukhārī, it is reported on the authority of ʿUmar ibn al-Khaṭṭāb.

[42] In al-Muwaṭṭa[ʾ, Mālik narrates this *ḥadīth* report on the authority of two companions, ʿUthmān and Abū Hurayra. In Bukhārī, a report to a similar effect appears on the authority of Abū Saʿīd al-Khudrī: "Sell not two *ṣāʿ* of dates for one *ṣāʿ* nor exchange two dirhams for one dirham." *Ṣāʿ* is a measure of weight equalling 2.175 kgs.

[43] The full text of this report from *Kitāb al-buyūʿ*, Number 31.16.34, is: Yahya related to me from Mālik from Nāfiʿ from ʿAbd Allāh ibn ʿUmar that ʿUmar ibn al-Khaṭṭāb said, "Do not sell gold for gold except like for like, and do not increase one part over another part. Do not sell silver for silver except like for like, and do not increase one part over another part. Do not sell silver for gold, one of them at hand and the other to be given later. If someone seeks to delay paying you until he has been to his house, do not leave him. I fear *rama* for you." *Rama* is usury.

subsequently arose because of that, as we will see, but since *ribā al-faḍl* was defined on the basis of spot transactions, one would need to ask the crucial question: why would wheat be exchanged for wheat, and salt exchanged for salt, etc.? In other words, if one already possessed wheat, why would one wish to conduct an exchange in wheat? The mystery is only resolved when one looks at another set of *ḥadīth* reports that specifically focus on the exchange of dates for dates to discover that what is being highlighted is the fact that goods were not always of homogeneous quality. Consider the following report:

> Abū Saʿīd al-Khudrī reported: Dates were brought to the Messenger of God, and he said: These dates are not like our dates, whereupon a man said: We sold two *sā*ʿs of our dates for one *sā*ʿ of these (fine dates), whereupon the Messenger said: That is *ribā*; so return these dates and get yours back; then sell those for money and use the money to buy the fine quality dates (Ṣaḥīḥ Muslim, No. 3872).

In another variant of this report, attributed again to the same narrator, the person who is supposed to have brought the dates was the famous Bilāl (Ṣaḥīḥ Muslim, No. 3871). Two other *ḥadīth* reports, one of which is narrated on the combined authority of not only the former reporter but also Abū Hurayra, and the other on the authority of the latter only, relate to dates that were supposed to have been brought from Khaybar, and upon the Prophet's inquiry as to whether such fine quality dates had indeed come from Medina, he was told that the Medinan ones had been exchanged for the superior quality Khaybar ones; then follows the same admonition from the Prophet, but this time the word *ribā* is not used, or more appropriately, that part of the *ḥadīth* report which makes the exchange equivalent to *ribā* is absent (*Ṣaḥīḥ Muslim*, Nos. 3869 and 3870). It is not difficult to see that the real purport of these reports lies in avoidance of unequal exchange, for the common thread that runs throughout all of them is to emphasize exchange of a good for money and then using the proceeds to purchase another—thus necessitating a reliance on the market determined evaluations (prices) of the goods under consideration. It is obvious that market determined evaluations are therefore considered to be fair, a point emphasized earlier in Chapter 6. The Prophet discouraged barter exchanges because of the inherent ambiguity (*gharar*) in the values being exchanged at a given time, since prices are subject to change at any time, and thus encouraged the use of money because of the inherent transparency of the values being exchanged. By removing the ambiguity, the use of money ensured an equitable exchange.

That the purport of these *ḥadīth* reports was to eliminate the possibility of unequal exchange due to ambiguity is further supported by the following reports: Jābir bin ʿAbd Allāh is reported to have said that the Messenger of God forbade the sale of a heap of dates the weight of which is unknown in accordance with the known weight of dates;[44] and Abū Hurayra's report in which the Messenger of God said, "He who bought food grain should not sell it until he has measured it."[45] Or consider the following report, which is quite explicit as to the purpose of such reports, but which also indicates that the point was not fully appreciated by all, for there seems to be some difference of opinion as to what it all meant: Abū Nadra reported, "I asked Ibn ʿAbbās about the conversion (of gold and silver for silver and gold). He asked: is it hand-to-hand exchange? I said: yes, whereupon he said: There is no harm in it." The narrator is then reported to have relayed the story to Abū Saʿīd al-Khudrī, who responded by saying: "We will soon write to him (Ibn ʿAbbās), and he will not give you this *fatwā*," and continued: "By God, some of the boy servants of the Prophet brought dates, but he refused to accept them because they did not seem to be dates of our land. Upon inquiry the servant said: Something had happened to the dates of our land, or our dates. So I got these dates (in exchange by giving) excess (of the dates of our land), whereupon the Prophet said: you made an addition for getting the fine dates (in exchange) which is tantamount to *ribā*; don't do that. Whenever you find some *doubt* about (the quality of) your dates, sell them and then buy the dates you like."[46]

Let us put the matters somewhat differently, and ask what the words "like for like" (*mithlan bi-mithl*) signify in these reports. *Fiqh*'s use of the term "same genus" is not very helpful here, for different varieties of dates would qualify as falling under the same genus. Did the Prophet use the term *mithlan bi-mithl* to underscore goods of the same genus that could be heterogeneous, in the parlance of economics, or did he mean homogeneous goods? If he implied by the same genus heterogeneous goods, whose values could be different, equal weight would not necessarily imply justness in exchange. But if he meant homogeneous goods, the exchange would be in terms of equal value, and thus just. When we look at these *ḥadīth* reports, it becomes clear that by

---

[44] *Ṣaḥīḥ Muslim*, report no. 3654.
[45] *Ṣaḥīḥ Muslim*, report no. 3651.
[46] *Ṣaḥīḥ Muslim*, report no. 3874.

the term *mithlan bi-mithl*, the Prophet meant homogeneous goods. Had that not been the case, he would have directed his companions to return the extra quantity of dates, so that one *sāʿ* would then get exchanged for one *sāʿ*, and thus there would be no imperative to direct them to sell one variety for money and then to buy the other from the proceeds. There is no escaping the fact that the purpose of these reports was to ensure equal value in exchange for the sake of justness.

While it is easy to understand the possible heterogeneity of goods in the case of wheat, barley, dates and salt—though a little difficulty does apparently arise in the case of salt, yet there could be quality differences between the sea and rock salts—but heterogeneity in the case of gold and silver is not easy to comprehend, especially when the issue of possible adulteration is not explicitly stated, or not even necessarily implied, in these reports. This point is further strengthened by the *ḥadīth* report about the exchange of one dīnār for two dīnārs etc. narrated on the authority of ʿUthmān. But the real question is why an exchange of one dinar for two dinars was even contemplated. We know that the dirham (the silver coin) and dinar (the gold coin) served as money in the Arabian economy of the day and it is therefore even more puzzling to read about the possibility of one unit of money exchanging for two units of the same money. It must be kept in mind that our focus at the moment is on what later came to be known as *ribā al-faḍl*. Had these reports been interpreted as specifically pertaining to exchanges involving a time dimension (*nasāʾ*), there would have been no reason for *fiqh* to develop the concept of *ribā al-faḍl*.

The puzzle cannot be resolved until we look, however sketchy the historical evidence that has come down to us, at the monetary system used in Arabia at the time. Although the Arabs did not have a currency of their own, coins were in circulation. These coins actually belonged to the neighboring empires: the Byzantine and Persian empires. Though the circulation of these coins was somewhat limited, it is also clear that coins from both empires were in circulation.[47] Besides these coins, small pieces of gold and silver, though not of uniform weight, were also used to conduct transactions.[48] The use of these pieces was obviously cumbersome, for it is clear that every time they were to be

[47] Balādhurī, in his *Futūḥ al-buldān* mentions three varieties of coins, the third perhaps belonging to the Egyptian realm.

[48] Encyclopedia of Islam, article on Mecca.

used, their weight and contents would need to be ascertained, thus putting a premium on the use of, and thus demand for, coins. This problem is discussed by Māwardī, whom we met earlier in Chapter 6, particularly with reference to the Ummayyad period, and it is easily understandable that the problem would have existed in Arabia during the Prophetic times with equal if not greater severity. This suggests several possibilities as to why there could be unequal exchange of gold for gold, and silver for silver. The possibility that readily suggests itself is that of people surrendering more than the metallic contents of coins to acquire them for the ease of their use. But this could not be the whole explanation, for it fails to explain as to why there could be an exchange of one dirham for two dirhams.

Following upon Māwardī, Qureshi (1946, p. 70) and Sewharvi (1959, p. 279), to mention but two, provide evidence as to why this could be so. First, the Arabs used to trade with both the Persian and Byzantine empires, and the dominance of one over the other effected these trade relations. When the Byzantines overwhelmed the Persians, as predicted by the Qur'ān in the opening of *sūra al-Rūm* (The Byzantines), which more or less coincided with the Battle of Badr, the demand for Byzantine coins might have increased. It is this that might have led to trading of coins on unequal terms. The second reason is related to the debasing of the coins. For one, it is understandable that some of the coins in circulation will lose a part of their metallic contents through normal wear and tear, prompting an exchange at an unequal level, which may have been expressed idiomatically as exchange of one dirham for two dirhams. But more than that there also might have been the problem of clippage: Māwardī specifically notes the clippage of the Persian coins.[49] Be that as it may, the inescapable conclusion is that these exchanges were deemed to be unjust in a world of real money where the coins had their own intrinsic values determined by their metallic contents. It was this unequal exchange, prompted by speculative activity, which must have been the focus of these *ḥadīth* reports.

When it comes to the other form of, or rather term for, *ribā al-ḥadīth*, the *ribā al-nasī'a*, its source can be traced to a number of *ḥadīth* reports where the word *nasī'a* occurs, although they do not explain the exact nature of transactions to which it was applicable.

[49] In Sunan Abū Dā'ūd there is a report to the effect that the Prophet forbade breaking of the coins except for some defect, though it is not clear whether this necessarily refers to the clippage problem. See his *Kitāb al-ijāra*, Report no. 3442.

These *ḥadīth* reports, recorded in more or less all the canonical collections, such as Bukhārī, Muslim, Nasāʿī, Dārimī, Ibn Māja, and Ibn Ḥanbal, emphasize that *ribā* involves *nasīʾa* (deferment, and therefore loans).[50] For instance, in Bukhārī we read: "there is no *riba* except in deferment [*nasīʾa* i.e. on loans]"; or in Mūslim: "there is no *riba* when payment is made on spot," or then again in his collection, somewhat more meaningfully, on the authority of Ibn ʿAbbās: "there *can be* an element of *riba* in loans [emphasis added]."[51] But what was the nature of the transactions on which these reports were applicable? In view of the widespread prevalence of *ribā al-jāhiliyya*, which necessarily involved a time dimension, one would think that the reason for these reports was to underscore the Qurʾānic prohibition. But then that is not how the classical *fiqh* interpreted them. In view of its focus on the previous set of *ḥadīth* reports, it opted to interpret *nasīʾa* by focusing on the words *yadan bi-yad*. These words were not interpreted as an admonition for prompt payment once the delivery had been affected, or prompt delivery once the payment had been made, as would seem natural, but rather as signifying prohibition of sale on deferred payment basis, originally, it must be specifically noted, involving barter transactions. What this was taken to mean was that those six goods when they were to be transacted on non-spot basis must be transacted on the same principles as spot transactions. Therefore, their quantities could not be different when they were exchanged, each for itself, when a time duration was involved. But then the quantities, and by implication the values, could be different when the exchange did not involve the same goods, whether spot or deferred did not matter. Obviously the scope of *ribā* prohibition under this original interpretation was quite limited, and therefore *fiqh* extended its scope subsequently as we will see in Chapter 10. But for the moment, let us see what it implied when *yadan bi-yad* was vested with this, the usual, *fiqh* interpretation.

To begin with, let us disregard the later *fiqh* developments with regard to the distinction between *qarḍ* and *salam*. In this case, we would note that whether we call the relevant transactions *qarḍ* or *bayʿ* (of *salam* or *muʿajjal* variety) does not matter one way or the

[50] Except for Ibn Ḥanbal, in their respective chapters on *Riba*, as noted in n. 41. For Ibn Ḥanbal, see his Musnad, V: 200, 202, 204, 206, 208, and 209.

[51] For the last cited report, see Muslim, *Ḥadīth* report No. 3877. The same phrase recurs in Reports Nos. 3876, and 3879, as we will see below. *Ḥadīth* reports to this effect also occur in all other major collections including Nasāʾī, Ibn Māja, Dārimī, and Ibn Ḥanbal.

other. Consider someone giving one *ṣā*ʿ of wheat (let us say as seed) in exchange for one and a quarter *ṣā*ʿ of wheat to be paid upon harvest. Is this *bay*ʿ *salam* or *muʿajjal*? For the person who paid one *ṣā*ʿ, it is *salam* since he is making an advance payment for goods that are to be delivered later. But for the person who got that one *ṣā*ʿ, it is a *bay*ʿ *muʿajjal*, since he bought the seed on a deferred payment basis. Mind you, this conclusion will not change if it was an exchange of wheat for dates or whatever else as long as it is a barter exchange. No wonder then that during the Prophetic times, the term used was *salaf* (though the term *salam* meant the same thing) and the term *muʿajjal* did not exist. And since the distinction between *qarḍ* and *salam* did not exist, the transaction was also a *qarḍ* transaction. And regardless of what name we give the transaction, an increase due to the time dimension would be quite permissible. But under the *fiqh* interpretation of *yadan bi-yad*, when the imperatives of spot transactions were extended to loan transactions, the quite permissible *salam* had to be somehow exempted from the scope of prohibition. *Fiqh*'s answer was that the payment for *salam* must involve goods different from the goods to be received. This solved the problem because the term *qarḍ* was now restricted to the inter-temporal exchange of same goods. That of course would mean that there could not be a *qarḍ* contract in any of the six goods, some of them bare necessities (wheat, barley, dates, if not salt), that would be the object of routine borrowing by the poor, as indeed we know they were. One can see *fiqh* responding to this incongruity by saying that they could meet their needs through *bay*ʿ *salam*. At any rate, *bay*ʿ or no *bay*ʿ, the end result would be a debt contracted. We may sum up the intricacies of the interpretation of *yadan bi-yad* by noting: *yadan bi-yad* did not mean what it readily, or literally, implies—which is a prompt payment or a prompt delivery, as noted above—but that when the *ribā* goods are the subject of inter-temporal exchange, the terms of exchange must be the same as those for spot transactions, and keep it in mind that two of those goods, gold and silver, served as money.

It will perhaps be worthwhile to look at the *ḥadīth* reports relating to *salaf*. Muslim lists four of them, and all four are more or less the same, except for minor differences in wording. Consider the one narrated on the authority of ʿAbd Allāh ibn ʿAbbās: "Those who pay in advance [the Arabic word used is *aslaf*, from *salaf*) for anything must do so for a specified weight and for a definite period" (No. 3906). There is nothing in this report which could possibly be interpreted as supporting the later *fiqh* distinctions between *qarḍ* and *salam*, and that the *salam* transactions must involve different goods, etc. If anything, one can again notice a strong emphasis on clarity in the terms relating to the underlying transactions, and therefore an absence of *gharar*, which is quite consistent with our reading of the other *ḥadīth* reports earlier.

A brief stock-taking is in order at this stage: we see that the way *fiqh* came to interpret these *ḥadīth* reports, to tie them up to its own conceptualization of *ribā al-faḍl* and *ribā al-nasīʾa*, means that unequal exchanges of non-like goods in terms of quantities, and therefore values, was perfectly permissible regardless of whether they were on spot (*al-faḍl*), or deferred (*nasīʾa*) basis, and regardless of whether they involved money or not (there are explicit *ḥadīth* reports that permit this, e.g. gold could be exchanged for silver, etc., though admittedly it is not clear from these reports, or at least the direct reports from the Prophet, whether this permission was restricted to spot transactions). One then wonders what happened to the Prophetic insistence that money must be used in exchanges to avoid *ribā*. It would appear that all these difficulties can be avoided if the *ḥadīth* reports using the word *nasīʾa* are interpreted as reinforcing the prohibition against *ribā al-jāhiliyya*, as pointed out earlier. What we are then left with are those reports discussed at the outset of this section that gave rise to the interpretation known as *ribā al-faḍl*. I have suggested that *ribā al-faḍl* must be interpreted as directed against ambiguity (*gharar*), and therefore the attendant possibility of injustice, in spot transactions. This obviously gives rise to the uncomfortable feeling that this interpretation may actually run counter to the Prophetic ordinance on the subject.

If such a predicament is to be avoided, we need to further explore the reason behind the use of the word *ribā* in these reports. As we know, the word *ribā* can be used in either its lexical or technical sense, and thus the first issue to address is whether the meaning of the word *ribā* in these reports is to be understood in its lexical sense or interpreted in its technical meanings. It should be obvious that it could not possibly be understood in its lexical sense, for then we run into the problem that any gain, including profits, would be declared *ribā*, although this is precisely how it has eventually come to be interpreted by some writers, though they condemn only excessive profits (but who would define how excessive is excessive?). It is obvious that, in that case, we also run into the problem of interpreting the Qurʾānic verses where an increase in the form of profit seems to have been sanctioned. It is therefore clear that we must concentrate on the technical meanings. The technical meanings of course relate to its prohibition, and these can be read at two levels: one relates to the *cause*, (the *ʿilla*, in the parlance of *fiqh*, though I would hasten to add that I am using the term in a somewhat broader, or theoretical, way rather than its specific use in *fiqh* relating to the issue of *ribā*), which essentially focuses on the process occasioned by the straitened economic circumstances of the debtor that gives rise to *ribā*, through the process of *aḍʿāfan muḍāʿafa*, and therefore his inability to discharge the debt. This necessarily involves a time dimension and it is this which must yield the needed legal definition of the term as per the Qurʾānic perspective. It may be added that a legal meaning is necessarily technical, but a technical meaning may not necessarily have a legal import. The other technical meaning relates to the *effect*, and in this case the focus is on the injustice that it *necessarily* entails, and this effect precisely being the rationale, the *ḥikma*, for its prohibition; the *lā taẓlimūna wa-lā tuẓlamūn*, as discussed earlier. What this means is that *ribā* in the lexical sense does not necessarily imply injustice whereas *ribā* in the technical sense, whether relating to the cause or effect, necessarily does.

We can now turn to the question as to whether the Prophet used the term *ribā* in the legal or just the technical sense in the aforementioned *ḥadīth* reports. It was noted earlier that he used the term *ribā* in only some of those instances, and not in others that were otherwise identical. If he had meant to use the term in the legal sense, he would have used the term in all instances. Instead, what it means is that he used a term that was commonly understood to imply injustice to forbid instances of exchange that might be unjust. Remember that that is exactly what he meant in the identical instances where he did not use the term *ribā* yet forbade those exchanges. Once we recognize this, we can easily discard the conclusion reached by Fazlur Rahman (1964) who writes: "It appears that the *riba* described in the above-quoted *ḥadīth* [he is referring to the *ḥadīth* report by al-Khudrī, noted earlier], which is known by the technical name of *riba al-faḍl* is a later innovation. Eminent Companions of the Prophet, like Muʿāwiyah, Usāma bin Zayd, Zayd bin Arqam, ʿAbd Allāh ibn ʿAbbās and ʿAbd Allāh bin ʿUmar, were unaware of it" (p. 13). The evidence for their unawareness, according to him, is the fact that none of the *ḥadīth* reports relating to the *ribā al-faḍl* is narrated on their authority. Needless to say that is a *non sequitur*, for it could be argued that this was simply because these companions were unaware of the term *ribā al-faḍl* since the term did not exist at the time.[52] During the lifetime of the Prophet, there was

---

[52] It may be noted that Fazlur Rahman uses the term *ribā al-faḍl* as equivalent to what I have called *ribā al-ḥadīth*.

only one term and that was *ribā*, commonly understood to relate to *ribā al-jāhiliyya*.

Yet it is not difficult to see that some of the companions of the Prophet might have been a little puzzled by the use of the word *ribā* in the context of spot transactions—not because they did not understand the technical meanings of the word but because they understood it all too well, and had by now come to understand it even in the legal sense. We get a hint that something was felt to be amiss by the companions in a dialogue recorded in two *ḥadīth* reports that are related to those cited earlier on the authority of Ibn ʿAbbās. The first of these reads:

> Abū Ṣāliḥ reported: I heard Abū Saʿid al-Khudrī said: Dinar (gold) for gold and dirham for dirham can be (exchanged) with equal for equal; but he who gives more or demands more in fact deals in *ribā*. I said to him: Ibn ʿAbbās says otherwise, whereupon he said: I met Ibn ʿAbbās and said: Do you see what you say; have you heard it from the Messenger of God, or found it in the Book of God, the Glorious and Majestic? He said: I did not hear it from the Messenger of God, and I did not find it in the Book of God, but Usāma bin Zayd narrated to me the Messenger of God said: There can be an element of *ribā* in loans (Muslim, No. 3876).[53]

And the other one narrates, perhaps, the same incident with slightly different words but hints more clearly at the underlying irony:

> ʿAtāʾ bin Abū Rabāḥ reported: Abū Saʿīd al-Khudrī met Ibn ʿAbbās and said to him: What do you say in regard to the conversion (of commodities or money); did you hear it from the Messenger of God, or is it something which you found in the Book of God, Majestic and Glorious? Thereupon Ibn ʿAbbās said: I do not say that. So far as the Messenger of God is concerned, you know him better, and so far as the Book of God is concerned, I do not know it (more than you do), but Usāma bin Zayd narrated to me the Messenger of God having said this: Beware, there can be an element of *ribā* in loans (Muslim, No. 3879).

The obvious question that these reports raise is that if *ribā al-ḥadīth* could be easily interpreted as *ribā al-nasīʾa*, why did *fiqh* feel obliged to develop the concept of *ribā al-faḍl*? Indeed, as we will see in Chapter 10, in the beginning *fiqh* actually developed the concept of *ribā al-faḍl*, and only subsequently came to the idea of *ribā al-nasīʾa*. One can surmise that this may have been the result of those *ḥadīth* reports that tell us that the Prophet passed away before explaining the meanings of the term *ribā*.

---

[53] In Bukhārī, this incident is narrated in Report No. 1355.

One would readily understand that it was *fiqh* that had to face the full brunt of this dilemma more than any other branch of Islamic sciences, but then, for reasons to be fully discussed in Chapter 10, it ended up taking a wrong turn, as a result of the various compulsions it operated under, by primarily focusing on *ribā al-faḍl* for explaining the prohibition of *ribā* and making *ribā al-jāhiliyya* incidental to it. As time progressed, the discourse became increasingly complex as more and more incongruities were introduced into the complicated mix. The most significant of these incongruities is related to the modern extension of the scope of *ribā al-nasīʾa*, that originally included only six goods (the *amwāl al-ribāwiyya*), to loan transactions to arrive at the conclusion that any nominal increase, however small it may happen to be, and regardless of whether one could infer any injustice therein, was *ribā* in the legal sense. It thus ended up throwing overboard the Qurānic emphasis on *aḍʿāfan muḍāʿafa* as well as the rationale, the *ḥikma*, of the prohibition. It was not that an increase *may* involve an injustice, as would happen in the case of economic hardship leading to the process of *aḍʿāfan muḍāʿafa*, which therefore must be considered forbidden, but rather that any increase was *necessarily* unjust regardless of whether or not one could discern any injustice in the relevant loan or financing contracts. In the modern discourse, as it turns out, the periodic interest payments in all financing contracts are deemed to be *ribā*. Not only that, but any payment above and beyond the nominal principal amount, even when it in fact represented a decrease in the principal amount in real terms, has now come to be seen as *ribā*, and therefore unjust though, admittedly, the issue of justness or otherwise does not explicitly enter into their discourse. How *fiqh* ended up in this predicament, where instead of being the upholder of justice (*ʿadl*), it actually started to defend a position that could patently involve injustice, is the subject matter of the next chapter. At this stage, we need to highlight the important points that emerge from what has gone so far on this subject.

Conclusion

Following the foregoing discussion, we can define *ribā* as an increase on *raʾs al-māl*, involving either a loan or a deferred payments sale, which is contingent upon an inability to pay on the part of the debtor, and leads towards a perpetual increase in debt over the *raʾs al-māl* through the process of *aḍʿāfan muḍāʿafa*.[54] It should be obvious that this definition does not conform to an equation of *ribā* with either interest, as is common in the predominant modern discourse on *fiqh* and Islamic economic, or with usury, as in the work of some writers who are not well-disposed to accepting the former point of view. Much has been said earlier, directly or indirectly, on the issue of equality between *ribā* and interest. At this stage, we would briefly note the difference between *ribā* and usury. It is well recognized that no precise definition of usury, as it has come to be interpreted in the contemporary discourse, is possible—and that seems to be the reason that the *fiqh* scholars are rightly weary of accepting its equality with *ribā*—but it is generally understood to be a high rate of interest.[55] Any attempt to define what is high is bound to be marred by difference of opinion, as well as the complications that arise from the possible divergence between real and nominal values. It goes without saying that this makes it impossible to define it in any precise manner with respect to the nominal rate of interest, or rather the observed rate of interest to satisfy the legal requirements. In the case of *ribā*, this issue does not even arise. When it comes to a connection between *ribā* and interest, it is not a question of high or low rate of interest, for any rate of interest could, in a particular instance, give rise to the process of *aḍʿāfan muḍāʿafa* once the debtor is incapable of making the required payments. Theoretically this rate could even be negative in the real sense as long as it is nominally positive (which it is bound to be), and therefore has the built-in tendency to lead to the compounding of the *raʾs al-māl*. However, it is clear that the higher the rate of interest, the greater the likelihood that a debtor will run into difficulties in discharging his obligations, leading to genuine hardship, and therefore default. It should also be clear that no such rate could be defined as a unique rate applicable to all loan contracts, for given any particular rate of interest, as long as it is not so exorbitant as to be practically irrelevant, some borrowers may be able to discharge their payment obligations while others may not be able to do so.

[54] One would admit that this definition does not cover *ribā al-faḍl*, but then *ribā al-faḍl*, even when we extend its scope beyond the original six goods, became practically irrelevant long ago, and at any rate the relevant issues can be handled under the gharar provisions of *fiqh*.

[55] Although one would note that most of the English translations of the Qurʾān use the term usury for *ribā*.

Earlier we have used the term bankruptcy to underscore this contingency, i.e. inability to discharge debt obligations. One thing, however, should be noted lest a misunderstanding arise: bankruptcy is a relatively recent term that implies not only hardship but a little more than that in the legal sense. It implies writing off of the not only interest obligations but also of the principal amount. In the case of *ribā*, no writing off of the principal amount could be implied. That is to say, the law (*fiqh*) cannot, and indeed does not in its coverage under *ḥijr*, impose the burden implied by the writing off of the principal amount on the creditor. Such writing-off is purely voluntary, though strongly urged in the verses we have studied earlier, and as such would remain an act of charity, or *iḥsān*. However, the law (*fiqh*) may, or perhaps must, in view of modern impersonal business dealings, cater to provisions with regard to the "easing time" if such are not voluntarily forthcoming. And after those provisions have been exhausted, in the case where the principal amount remains un-discharged by the debtor, either partly or fully, because of his continuing straitened circumstances, the state must discharge the principal from the *zakāh* funds as sanctioned by the Qurʾān. Obviously there is the practical difficulty of ascertaining legitimate cases of hardship in contrast to willful default, but that need not stand in the way of establishing the principles that are under consideration here. But what exactly is the amount of the principal, the *raʾs al-māl*, that must be discharged? The answer is not as simple as it may sound in light of the complications that arise in the case of the so-called *bayʿ muʿajjal*.

First, we note that in the case of a money loan, the *raʾs al-māl* represents what is commonly understood to be the principal amount in a loan contract. This amount remains intact in the face of intervening periodic payments, i.e. interest, or permissible *ribā* as defined in the classical works on Qurʾānic exegesis, and it is this amount which the creditor is entitled to receive upon the bankruptcy of the debtor, if that compact term may be used to be consistent with its modern usage, for in modern usage it also arises essentially out of economic hardship. What this means is that whenever the inability to pay arose, whether during the term of the contract or at its expiry, sanction against *ribā* will become operative, and thus provisions relating to bankruptcy protection will have to be enforced. The determination of *raʾs al-māl* in the case of *bayʿ muʿajjal*, however, is somewhat complicated. Pending further discussion in Chapter 10, let us briefly note the following: since the spot price of the goods under consideration may, and indeed will, be different from the price charged under *bay' mu'ajjal*, which one of these should be considered the *ra's al-māl*? We have earlier noted Shāfi'ī's opinion on the issue in favor of the spot price, though *fiqh* never took up his lead, and the question has remained dormant. In current writings, it is presumed that it will be the deferred (*mu'ajjal*) price, rather than the spot price prevailing at the time the contract was entered into. It may be recalled that it was this that drove the wedge between a loan contract and the *bay' mu'ajjal* contract, and thus the basis of much discontent among modern readers not enamored of the subtleties of *fiqh*. But *fiqh*, seemingly confident of its invincibility, remains unfazed by any such charges of inconsistency. Suppose the spot price of a good is $100, and a person takes a loan at 5 percent annual rate of interest, purchases the good, and after one year pays the creditor $105. This is deemed a *ribā* transaction by *fiqh*. Now consider the same person buying the good under *bay' mu'ajjal* from the seller and agreeing to pay $110 after one year. This is perfectly acceptable as far as *fiqh* is concerned, for it represents a *bay'* contract, and as such approved by *fiqh*, a *fiqh* that is not in the least bothered by the fact that a *bay'* contract can be as unjust as a *ribā* contract. At any rate, according to the *fiqh* position, it is this amount that is deemed to be *ra's al-māl*, the amount that must be returned in the case of bankruptcy. But then there is the complication that arises because of the extension of *bay' mu'ajjal* to sales on installment basis, and thus we are back to square one, for we again do not know exactly what the *ra's al-māl* would be in such cases. In addition, there is the question of whether the *ra's al-māl* is to be returned in nominal or real terms, a question that was raised earlier in this chapter but to which we have not yet paid any attention. Since this question has become pertinent only in recent times, there was no reason to introduce the complication in the preceding coverage which is all based on the presumption that all values were reckoned in real terms. All these complications form a part our discussion in Chapter 10.

CHAPTER TEN

FIQH'S RESPONSE TO THE PROHIBITION OF *RIBĀ*: FROM CLASSICAL TO CONTEMPORARY TIMES

Classical Times

The fundamental point that emerges out of the exposition of the previous chapter on the issue of *ribā* is that the process of *aḍʿāfan muḍāʿafa* must form an integral part of its legal definition. As to its link with interest, one can see that the process of *aḍʿāfan muḍāʿafa* cannot operate unless the nominal rate of interest is assumed to be positive. This in turn means that any rate of interest *could* become *ribā*, and therefore unjust, depending upon, and this is crucial, the economic circumstances of the debtor. However, when it came to establishing a connection between interest and *ribā*, or the legal interpretation of interest, *fiqh* came to the surprising conclusion that since any rate of interest *could* be unjust, it must be deemed as *necessarily* unjust, and therefore *ribā*. Since the question as to how it came to this conclusion is hardly ever discussed explicitly, one requires a little stealth to discover the different factors that may have contributed to establishing this identity. Some of the factors that might have contributed to this turn of interpretation have been hinted at in the previous chapter, but those factors, such as the Judeo-Christian interpretations and what was noted as the contextual effects in Chapter 5, got woven into what appears to me a more fundamental characteristic of Islamic jurisprudence that came to serve as a common denominator in the *fiqhī* formulations. This common denominator could be referred to as erring on the side of caution.

Here we may recall a point that has been made earlier in this work. Since evolution of *fiqh* was essentially the result of individual efforts, it does not require a leap of imagination to see that those engaged in it would individually feel quite constrained on account of what others might subsequently come to regard as too liberal an interpretation of a particular Divine injunction. In other words, since there was no formal sharing of responsibility as far as a specific interpretation went, the individual interpreters could not find any relief or support that is characteristic of a group decision-making process where a person may feel a measure of satisfaction in the knowledge that he is not alone in having a specific outlook on a particular issue.

We know that Abū Ḥanīfa tried to resolve this difficulty by sharing his views with others in a somewhat open forum where a particular issue, often a hypothetical one, would be discussed for hours before some sort of consensus would emerge, and we also know that his liberalism—which usually was associated with the hypothetical nature of a query posed, but could equally be associated with the involvement of a whole group in this process—became a focal point of attack on his system of interpretation. The dissatisfaction of the other leading *fuqahā'* against the *ahl al-ray'*, or the so-called Kūfāh school of jurisprudence, which is associated with the name of Abū Ḥanīfa, succeeded in large measure in the sense that subsequently the rules of jurisprudence developed by Shafi'i were accepted by all. This did yield the positive result of imposing some sort of discipline on the framework within which *fiqh* evolved but it must be kept in mind that this discipline was achieved at the expense of flexibility. Particularly, it made the individual interpreters much more cautious in rendering their legal opinions (the *fatwās*).

One would also recognize that this cautious approach, which is quite understandable in light of the Qur'ānic charge against the Jews for their taking liberties with interpretation of the scriptures, as noted earlier in Chapter 5, gave rise to what I have referred to as erring on the side of caution, and it is this that led over time to a process of accretion resulting in an accumulation of caution. While this is a tendency that pervades *fiqh*, it is particularly pronounced in the context of its formulations on the subject of *ribā*. The tendency, in this case, may indeed have begun with a *ḥadīth* report narrated on the authority of 'Umar ibn al-Khattāb. This report is more or less identical to the one cited in the previous chapter, again on his authority, as reported in the Sūnan of Ibn Mājah, where he is supposed to have declared that "the verse of *ribā* was the last revealed verse and the Prophet passed away before explaining it in full terms;" with the following words added "so leave aside *ribā* and *rībah* (doubtful)". This report is cited not only by Ibn Mājah but also by Ibn Hanbal, Bayhaqī as well as, with a great deal of stress, understandably in the present context, by a number of later compilers of *ḥadīth* reports.[1] It is this framework of caution in which

[1] See Fazlur Rahman (1964), p. 8.

fiqh evolved, serving as an integral backdrop of the stage on which the *fuqahā'* operated, to which were added a number of contributing factors that, with the passage of time, in this case the first few centuries of Islam, established *fiqh*'s position on *ribā*. I submit that it is only in this perspective that we can hope to understand the developments in *fiqh* over time, eventually leading to the current controversies, as we will see below.

The Ground Realities

Consider, first, the social background in which *fiqh* began its evolution. Within a score of years after the death of the Prophet, the Muslims had established their sovereignty over vast areas of the well-established religio-cultural traditions of the time, not only in North Africa, and the contemporary Middle East, but much beyond. It is well-known that the Muslim rulers of the time, once they were firmly established at Damascus—the Ummayyads—did not encourage, indeed rather discouraged, the conversion of the 'People of the Book' to the new faith. There was an interlude, during the brief reign of ʿUmar II, when some encouragement seems to have been fostered, but overall, as a result, the process of conversion was quite slow and gradual. In regard to dealings with non Muslims subjects, the Muslims rulers followed the pattern set by the Prophet himself in Madīna, whereby the regulation of the internal affairs of the People of the Book was to be left at their own disposal, to be adjudicated upon by whatever authorities those communities chose on the basis of their respective *Sharīʿa*. The economic affairs of the areas that came under the sovereignty of Damascus were left uninterrupted under the local populations. For the Muslims, the Peninsula ʿArabs, apart from a small proportion who lived in the new capital city, were mostly engaged in military expeditions, and were supposed to live in the garrison towns that were exclusively built for them at the outer fringes of the Central ʿArab lands, such as Basra, Kūfāh and further away al-Fustāt in Egypt. The internal economic life of these garrison towns, mostly merchandizing but some long distance trading,[2] was of course regulated by the Muslims themselves, and it

[2] Recall from Chapter 9 the incident of a loan extended to ʿAbd Allāh ibn ʿUmar and ʿUbayd Allāh ibn ʿUmar by Abū Mūsa al-Ashʿarī, the governor of Basra, for trading purposes.

would be reasonable to infer that it was regulated by the patterns well-known to the ʿArabs—the patterns primarily set in Madīna of the Prophet's time.

As the process of conversion proceeded, and as the ʿArabs themselves grew in numbers, not only in the garrison towns but also beyond those in the settled lands, an increasing sphere of economic affairs came under the purview of the then evolving *fiqh*. The two major centers of such activity beyond Madīna itself were Kūfāh, where Abū Ḥanīfa—the founder of the Ḥanafī School (*madhhab*)—lived (though later on Baghdad after its inauguration about the middle of the 8th Century continued that tradition) and Damascus though Damascus became less significant in the aftermath of the Abbasīd victory over the Ummayads. It is then that Baghdad became the prime centre of intellectual activity in the Islamic realm. By the time *fiqh* came to address economic issues, particularly the issue of *ribā*, certain societal expectations must have come to be associated with the possible responses that could be offered, expectations that must have been influenced by the Judeo-Christian perspective in a society where the Muslims formed a minority. And this for two reasons: not only that those who now converted to the new faith naturally carried their older psychological makeup with them, a temperament that was supposed to be rooted in earlier revelations, but also because the new dispensation was rightly viewed as a continuation of the earlier revelations not only by the new adherents but also the older ones, the Muslims themselves, as the Qurʾān makes clear in numerous places.[3] We have already seen in the previous chapter Marshall Hodgson noting that the Judeo-Christian tradition by this time had come to consider interest as falling under the religious prohibition. This outlook was strongly influenced by the institution

[3] Thus we observe the elements known as 'Israeliats' in Islamic literature, and hence also in its folklore. This cross influence is well recognized. For instance, Hamilton Gibb (1962, p. 324) writes: "..the civilization of the Middle East and that of the so-called Western world are closely related; both before and after the rise of Islam there has been interpenetration between them.... Medieval Christianity and medieval Islam, thanks to common heritage and their *common problems*, were linked by a bond of both common spiritual and intellectual affinity" (emphasis added). And in light of the point about the integrity of the Islamic methodology, we may note that Gibb continues, "But, while the Arab world was an integral part of the Western world in the broad sense of that term, we must not lose sight of the fact that it has always remained an independent part; it has taken from the common heritage what it desired or needed, and fused it with the principles of its own culture."

of moneylending. If Christ condemned the class of moneylenders, it obviously was in view of their heartlessness in charging exorbitant rates of interest that more often than not led to the process of *aḍʿāfan muḍāʿafa*. Clearly, it was the injustice associated with the institution of moneylending that occasioned its condemnation. And quite apart from the fact that we don't hear much on the issue of *ribā* during the Ummayyad and early Abbasīd periods, but later at the time when *fiqh* began to evolve, its formal exponents now, as also their precursors, could hardly have remained unconcerned about the underlying injustice, and this concern was bound to temper the evolution of *fiqh*. But then it also needs to be noted that not every loan contracted by the moneylenders would end up leading to *aḍʿāfan muḍāʿafa*. To the extent the institution of moneylending began to permeate among the Muslims, and this regardless of whether the class of moneylenders included any Muslims or not, with the passage of time, *fiqh* would be expected to address the excesses associated with it. The important question, however, would have been: how?

Had *fiqh* paid a close attention to the process of *aḍʿāfan muḍāʿafa* in its legal definition, it would have had to face the tricky problem of distinguishing between the legitimate cases of straitened circumstances, or should we say cases of genuine default, from the spurious ones, where unscrupulous elements in the society could misuse the rulings to their personal advantage. Equating *ribā* to interest resolved that difficulty at the same time that it met the prevailing societal expectations. It is important to keep in mind that these societal expectations were closely influenced by the excesses committed by the class of moneylenders.[4] What perhaps was not realized at the time was that if ascertaining the legitimate cases of hardship was difficult, enforcing the prohibition against interest was going to be equally fraught with difficulties. When the forces of demand are either influenced by an irresistible prospect of profit, or are based on the desperation of those who need to make the two ends meet, and when these are matched by an equally powerful motive on the supply side to make as much gain as possible out of those economic realities, it is not difficult to see what the enforcement authorities will be up against. But then the

---

[4] It may be kept in mind that there is no contradiction between the business of moneylending and *fiqh*'s response in terms of its *bayʿ* framework in the context of real (commodity) money, gold and silver, a point noted in Chapter 9.

issue of enforcement was not something that *fiqh* much bothered itself with for reasons that are not difficult to understand. The relationship between those who felt called upon to formulate *fiqh* and the state was by no means a congenial one, and this had an unintended consequence.

Those who were engaged in the formulation of *fiqh*, and this was always done in their private capacity, felt compelled to keep a distance between themselves and the state because of the disquiet that pious Muslims in general felt about the *fitan* (sing. *fitan* strife) that led to the establishment of the state after the first four caliphs, though admittedly the first *fitan* began during the later times of the third caliph, ʿUthmān. This unique feature of Islamic jurisprudence meant that state was not a part of the *fiqh* formulations. In general, when legislative enactments are carried out under the auspices of the state, one would expect some attention to be paid to the difficulties, or the costs, of enforcement. But the way *fiqh* evolved, there could not have been any prior expectation on the part of those who were engaged in its formulation that their individual opinions would necessarily be enforced through the state machinery. A large part of *fiqh* relates to private affairs, and the corresponding provisions could not be effectively enforced through the state machinery; indeed these were not meant to be so enforced, as discussed in Chapters 5 and 6. While one would recognize that in the case of *ribā*, with its unequivocal prohibition and the necessarily social dimension of this prohibition, the individual formulators could legitimately anticipate some sort of enforcement response from the state, yet such a response could not be taken for granted. At any rate, as seen in Chapter 6, *fiqh* never drew a distinction between its enforceable and non-enforceable elements, and therefore by default never quite emphasized, at least in formal terms, the enforcement role that the state was supposed to play in an Islamic polity. It was left to the state to pick and choose whatever components of *fiqh* it wished to enforce even as, at times, some of the leading *fuqahā*ʾ came to be associated with the court during the Abbāsid era as *qāḍī*s (judges).[5]

In a sense, by doing this, *fiqh* inadvertently contributed to its own marginalization as far as its enforceable parts were concerned. It must, however, be admitted that it is easier to see this point in retrospect

[5] For instance, the famous Abū Yūsuf, a student of Abū Ḥanīfa, in the early Abbāsid period, or Māwardī in the middle Abbāsid period.

than to have clearly anticipated it in the first place, at the time. The social milieu that formed the integral background for the evolution of *fiqh* rendered such anticipations out of place. In small communities that were primarily based upon personal relationships, the climate of solidarity fostered by a vibrant faith reduced the importance of enforcement. Such a perspective, however, becomes irrelevant in the case of a cosmopolitan society which is regulated more by impersonal relations. But then, interestingly, *fiqh* retained that original imprint, of being articulated in an atmosphere regulated by personal relationships, down the centuries to the present time. It is quite another matter that in modern times, particularly in the post-colonial era, and in a political atmosphere over-saturated with nationalism, a segment of its exponents suddenly discovered the significance of state power for enforcement, particularly of those of its formulations that have not elicited the sympathy of the ordinary adherent. The new found activism of this school has looked out of place to Muslims outside its own circles, and particularly to those who are aware of, and therefore worry about, the intellectual challenges modernity, for better or for worse, has thrown their way. All this because i) it has scarcely paid any attention to the issue of what ought to be enforced through the coercive power of the state, and what ought to be left to the individual discretion, and ii) it is totally oblivious to the issues that modern technology continuously brings forth, and not just for the non-Muslims in this global village. *Fiqh* cannot continue to ignore these issues, a subject discussed in Chapter 6, for it would do so on the pain of becoming practically irrelevant. More on this later, but at the moment let us return to the subject of how the original *fiqh* position on the subject of *ribā* developed.

It appears that all three elements noted above (the societal expectations arising out of the misuses relating to the institution of money-lending, the difficulty of separating the legitimate cases of default from the spurious ones, and the peculiar way *fiqh* evolved) contributed to the equation of what we now know as interest with *ribā*. It is also clear that whatever position *fiqh* would take will have to be grounded in its own original sources following the *usūl al-fiqh*, namely the Qur᾽ān and *ḥadīth*. In retrospect we can see, as in Chapter 9, that this task proved more difficult than might have been anticipated, for the position coming out of *ḥadīth* reports did not quite neatly tie up with the corresponding position as it emerged out of a careful reading of Qur᾽ān. The efforts to reconcile either of these two to interest in a straightforward way under the compulsions mentioned above introduced so many contradictions that in the end it became difficult to discern any consistent relationship between those perspectives themselves, i.e. the perspective of the Qur'ān and the one that was thought to emerge from the *ḥadīth* reports. This, idiomatically speaking, amounted to a struggle to circle a perfect square, and down the centuries the struggle has continued without yielding any satisfactory result. When one corner of the square is pushed in the other pops out, with the end result that *fiqh* has kept on going in circles around this deformed square of its own making.

As we have seen in the previous chapter, the efforts to reconcile the Qur'ānic position on *ribā* with interest, one way or another revolved around detaching the Qur'ānic term *aḍ'āfan muḍā'afa* from *ribā*, and thereby belittling its significance in the *fiqhī* (legal) definition of *ribā*. This was done either by resorting to the uncertainty relating to the timing of revelation of the verses in *sūra al-Baqara* along with a corresponding neglect of the undisputed timing of the crucial verse in *sūra Āl-'Imrān* (3:130), which categorically prohibits *ribā*, and in which the term *aḍ'āfan muḍā'afa* occurs, or disregarding the rationale for the prohibition of *ribā*, namely the injustice that it implied (which was often done by contrasting *ribā* transactions to *bay'* transactions, as though *bay'* transactions could never be unjust), or both. What this ultimately amounted to was to put *ribā al-ḥadīth* at the centre stage, and thereby assigning the Qur'ānic *ribā*, or *ribā al-jāhiliyya*, a secondary, indeed an incidental, role in *fiqh* formulations (so much so that even in the present times when a traditional *fiqh* scholar takes up the issue of *ribā*, his exposition hardly ever goes beyond the terms of reference set around *ribā al-ḥadīth*). But when *ribā al-ḥadīth* was made the pivot for formulating *fiqh* pronouncements on interest, *fiqh* confronted insurmountable difficulties. The discourse that followed over the centuries is so involved and intricate that it becomes difficult to pick out the individual threads running through it. However, when we keep an eye on the sequence (if not the exact chronology, for that is not very consequential now) of the important developments in this discourse, we can begin to see how the various pieces of this jigsaw puzzle fit together. Accordingly, we can divide those difficulties into the following classes:

1. Justification for focusing on *ribā al-ḥadīth* at the expense of *ribā al-jāhiliyya*.

2. The scope of *ribā al-ḥadīth*, centering primarily on the issue of *ʿillā*. This in turn has several elements, as we will see.
3. Identification or formulation of the alternative modes of financing.

Focus on Ribā al-Ḥadīth

The background material that *fiqh* used to build its position with regard to this first element has already been presented in Chapter 9. The conflicting evidence on the chronology of the revelation of the relevant verses of *sūra al-Baqara* now formed the point of departure for *fiqh* formulations, notwithstanding the fact that there is hardly any dispute about the time of revelation of the verse 3:130, which unequivocally prohibits *ribā*. It is at this stage that we see the primary reliance on the *ḥadīth* reports, and the consequent introduction of the new nomenclature, specifically in the form of *ribā al-faḍl*, and *ribā al-nasīʾa*, though we are not quite sure exactly when these terms became precise *fiqh* terms. All intricacies of *furūʿ al-fiqh* (the procedure relating to derivation of specific *fiqh* rules) came into play to detach the adjective *aḍʿāfan muḍāʿafa* from *ribā*. Roughly it can be summed up by the following sequence of deductive reasoning (the chain leading to the final outcome with regard to *ribā* is noted in bold). The words, on which the *fiqh* rules were supposed to be based, could be ***naqliyya*** (coming from the Qurʾān, *Sūnna*, or *Ijmāʿ* of the companions), or *ʿaqliyya* (roughly rational, based upon *ijtihād* which in turn may use *qiyās*, logic, theology, linguistic analysis etc.). When the words are *naqliyya*, they may be *qatʿī* (definite) or ***zanni*** (speculative).[6] Furthermore, these could be split into *ʿām* (general), or *khāṣṣ* (specific) categories. As far as the *khāṣṣ qatʿī* (definite and specific) words are concerned, no interpretation (*taʿwīl*) is permissible. The *zanni* words, on the other hand, may become quickly

[6] It is interesting to note that when the Qurʾān charges the Jews for attributing "their own lying innovations" to God, as we saw in Chapter 5, it uses the word *zann*, which is more appropriately translated as conjecture, though one can see that a conjecture could be thought of as speculation. At any rate, *fiqh* did end up with elaborations that were *zannī*, it is another matter that this time these were used in a restrictive sense rather than taking liberties with the Divine injunctions as the Jews are commonly thought to have done. But then the Qurʾānic charge against them, as far as I can see, does not necessarily imply that it might have always been a case of taking liberties.

clarified through *ijtihād*, in which case they become clear (*muṭlaq*), or remain ***muqayyad*** (unclear, or subject to qualifications, and keep in mind that these could be either *ʿām* or *khāṣṣ*).

The unclear (*muqayyad*) words are further split into four classes: *khafi* (obscure); to be subjected to *ijtihād*); *mushkil* (difficult, again to be subjected to *ijtihād*); ***mujmal*** (ambiguous, to be clarified by resorting to Qurʾān, *Sūnna*, and *ijmāʿ*); and *mūtashābih* (intricate, that cannot even be clarified through *ijtihād*). At this stage, things apparently become a little hazy. For instance, the *mujmal* words may be further split into **homonyms** (those that have more than one probable meanings), or those where what would appear to be their literal meanings in the Qurʾān would be different than the juridical meanings that were supposed to be vested in them. These, in turn, could be classified as ***mūfassar*** (when Qurʾān/*Sūnnah* clarify them, and in such cases no further interpretation would be required), or can be made ***khāṣṣ*** (specific) through *qiyās* (e.g. *zakāh*). As far as the distinction between *ʿām* (general) and *khāṣṣ* (specific) is concerned, for some *fiqh* writers a Qurʾānic *ʿām* can be converted into a *khāṣṣ* through a solitary *ḥadīth* report, while for others this is not acceptable—in the sense that, for them, there must be at least two witnesses for this to happen to satisfy the Qurʾānic requirements.

Within this general framework, there were differences of opinion when it came to the route followed to define *ribā*. For some, the Qurʾānic word *ribā* was a general (*ʿām*) and speculative (*ẓannī*) term, which must be made specific (*khāṣṣ*) through *ḥadīth* reports. Others went a little further into the fore-mentioned framework to say that it was a *mujmal* word, and among these there were some who thought it was *khāṣṣ mujmal* (Ḥanafīs), while others maintained it was an *ʿām mujmal* (the remaining *fiqh* schools, though it must be noted that not all experts belonging to a particular school agreed to the general outlook of their respective schools, e.g. Rāzī, a Shafiʿī, and Ibn Rushd, a Mālikī took the same position as Ḥanafīs). We can now see that the implications of *aḍʿāfan muḍāʿafa* could be circumvented by declaring the Qurʾānic word *ribā* a general (*ʿām*) term, which is what the schools other than the Ḥanafī school did, and which could be made specific (*khāṣṣ*) through *ḥadīth* reports (even a solitary one, in principle). But, at the same time it was maintained that the general (*ʿām*) could be restricted to certain specific forms. The end result of this was that the meanings of the word *ribā* were interpreted at two levels: at one level, its meanings got clarified through *ḥadīth* reports, which led to the classifications *ribā al-faḍl* and *ribā al-nasīʾa*, and at the other, the Qurʾānic *ribā*, and therefore eventually interest in the case of institutionalized credit, fell under the prohibition through the use of *qiyās* (analogical reasoning) when *ribā al-nasīʾa* was connected to *ribā al-jāhiliyya.*

The Ḥanafīs took a slightly different route. The difficulties arose due to their principial position that a general (*ʿām*) rule applies to all parts, and since this represented a difficulty in the case of *ribā*, for not all increases were to be prohibited, it was considered to be a *khāṣṣ* (specific) term. This obviously led to the difficulty with respect to circumvention of the specificity arising out of *aḍʿāfan muḍāʿafa*. Thereupon, the Ḥanafīs proceeded on the assumption that a *khāṣṣ* of the Qurʾān specifies the *ʿām* of the Qurʾān only if the revelations are chronologically parallel. This essentially means that the rule would be applicable to only those cases where in a particular revelation, i.e. a revelation that came down at a specific time, containing perhaps a number of verses though not necessarily, in which the specific and general occur at the same time. In the present case, this implies that the specificity arising out of 3:130 does not carry to the general, that is to say the verses belonging to *sūra al-Baqara*. The linguistic rules pertaining to the definite and indefinite articles, about which the Arabic language is very particular and careful, somewhat like English, where the prefix 'al' is the definite article just like 'the' in English, were also disregarded in the present case. It is fascinating to note that in the first revelation on the subject, verse 30:39, the word *ribā* occurs without the 'al', whereas in all of the subsequent revelations, it is invariably used with the addition of the definite article, meaning thereby that the same concept is under consideration that has occurred earlier, beginning with 3:130.[7]

Now consider verse 3:130, which categorically prohibits *ribā*. The prefix 'al' signifies that it is the same concept that occurrs in the earlier verse 30:39. But there it was not prohibited, though sharply contrasted with charity (recall our discussion about that in the last chapter). The new revelation (i.e. 3:130) now categorically prohibited it. The crucial question now is whether the prohibition is applicable

[7] For a somewhat detailed, yet concise, statement of the intricacies of the discourse on *furūʿ al-fiqh* on the subject under consideration, see Nomani (2002).

to precisely the same form as in verse 30:39 or not? If the answer is yes, then there would be no need to add the qualifying adjective *aḍʿāfan muḍāʿafa*. And if the need was felt to add the qualification, there had to be a reason behind it. That is what has been discussed as the rationale (the *ḥikma*) behind the prohibition in Chapter 9. There are those, particularly as far as the modern *fiqh* discourse is concerned, who are convinced that *aḍʿāfan muḍāʿafa* does not represent a qualification, and that it is there just to underscore the severity of the consequences of *ribā* in their extreme. But, consider the verses belonging to *sūra al-Baqara*, in which the adjective clause does not occur. Should the word *ribā* in these verses now be read in the light of 30:39, that is in general terms, or should it be read in specific terms in light of the verse 3:130? We cannot read it in the former terms, for it was not yet prohibited, and therefore when we read it in the light of the latter, we cannot escape the specificity arising out of *aḍʿāfan muḍāʿafa*. As far as *fiqh* position is concerned, disregarding this imperative could be seen as a part of its disposition of erring on the side of caution. By the end of the day, the Ḥanafī school reached the same conclusions as the other schools, which is that there was the *ribā al-faḍl*, and *ribā al-nasīʾa* of the *ḥadīth* reports, about which there were no doubts, but then as far as *ribā al-jāhiliyya* was concerned, there were doubts, and these could be removed by analogical reasoning. In other words, the scope of *ribā* was confined to the *bayʿ* (sale) contracts. No wonder, then, that in the canonical collections of the *ḥadīth* reports, the subject of *ribā* falls under their respective chapters on *buyūʿ* (Kitāb al-Buyūʿ of each collection except for Ibn Mājah where the title is Tijāra). Exactly when these two forms, and their respective names, got fully crystallized is not clear, and perhaps not very germane to the argument at hand which relates to the next stage in the *fiqhī* developments. And this brings us to the second element in the fore mentioned list.

Expansion in the Scope of Ribā al-Ḥadīth

Thus it is that *fiqh*'s original formulations defined *ribā* on the basis of *bayʿ* transactions involving six goods, the *amwāl al-ribawiyya*, mentioned in the *ḥadīth* reports. These are: gold, silver, wheat, barley, salt, and dates. Later developments show that *fiqh* did not feel comfortable with this restricted list for this seriously circumscribed the scope of *ribā* prohibition, and therefore felt the need to expand the list. This compulsion must have been a reflection of societal expectations. This process of expanding the scope of prohibition has two very distinct dimensions: one relating to *ribā al-faḍl*, and the other to *riba al-nasī'a*. The expansion relating to the former was accomplished rather quickly, but the other was a somewhat protracted affair, as we will see, and it is this that was crucial to expand the scope of *ribā* to interest. All schools of *fiqh* used *qiyās* (analogical reasoning) to extend the scope of prohibition, and while there were areas of agreement, there were also differences relating to details as to the way analogy was to be applied. Interestingly, as far as the connection between *ribā* and interest was concerned, they all arrived at the same conclusions. Leaving aside the minor details, the different schools can be split into two groups. In one group belong the Ḥanafīs, and the Ḥanbalīs (H and H), and in the second the Shāfiʿīs and Mālikīs (S and M). Both groups divided the *amwāl al-ribawiyya* into two categories: gold and silver belonged to the first category, and the remaining four fell into the second. Essentially, this division was motivated by the necessity of according a separate identity to money, the subject of financial loans, and therefore interest.

Consider the H and H group,[8] which made weight and volume the distinguishing criteria for the division: the goods whose value was measured on the basis of weight, such as gold and silver, were thus put into one category, as though gold and silver could never be valued in terms of volume, the remaining four were supposed to be valued according to their volume, and thus were put in the second category, as though these could not be valued according to their weights, and as though they would for all time be valued by volumes. Now by analogy, the scope of the second category was extended to other goods that were supposed to be valued by volume, such as rice, beans, raisins, seeds, iron, copper, etc., to which the *ribā* ordinance was now applicable. On the other hand, goods such as bricks, tools, swords, eggs, etc., were not supposed to be valued by volume, and therefore were deemed to be exempt from the ordinance. One may ask if the same ordinance was to be applicable to both categories, what was the need to draw the distinction in the first place.

---

[8] *Fiqh J'āfarīa*, as far as I am aware, uses the same categorization.

The answer is that the goods belonging to the first category were supposed to serve as money *par excellence* (in light of some *ḥadīth* reports), and therefore the remaining form of money, which was made of material other than gold and silver, at the time called *fulūs*, was deemed to be exempt from the *ribā* ordinance.

The S and M group was somewhat more careful, though the division of the six goods was again rendered into two categories: the second category, that again included the same four goods, was predicated on those being food items, indeed staple food. The scope of this category was extended by including other staple food items such as rice, beans, corn, etc. This avoided the inconsistencies of the H and H group but clearly restricted the scope of expansion. In the first category fell the remaining two goods, though the criterion this time was that these were *nuqūd*: roughly money, but more appropriately liquidity. But then not all forms of money in circulation were included. Of course gold and silver were included but again to the exclusion of *fulūs*. In this all schools of *fiqh* concurred. Historically these developments belong to the latter half of the eighth and first half of the ninth century, for these are associated with the names of Shaybānī (d. 805) for Ḥanafī *fiqh* and Shāfiʿī (d. 820) to name only two.[9] Occurring against the backdrop of spot transactions, or in the framework of *ribā al-faḍl*, these developments had hardly any practical relevance. At any rate, by this time, due to the ever-increasing monetization of the economies, the original *ribā al-ḥadīth* became irrelevant, though it remained, as it still does, a theoretical curiosity. It is not very difficult to see that these developments, divorced as they were from the time dimension, or from the issues relating to loans, could not quite meet the societal expectations that were the *raison d'être* for all these revisions to begin with. Let us see what these revisions meant as far as the issue of loans, or for that matter financing requirements of the economy, was concerned.

We can see that until such time that *fiqh* worked out its distinction between *qarḍ* (to be paid back in the same good) and *salam* (a *qarḍ* not to be paid back in the same good), a loan could be arranged in the form of the same good under the pretext of *bayʿ salam*. After that distinction was made, it could be arranged in the form of silver to

[9] The Ẓāhirī school of *fiqh* did not approve of *qiyās*, and therefore stuck to the original six goods to define *ribā*.

be paid in gold, or *vice versa*, or for that matter in terms of any two goods. And after *fiqh* took the position that both gold and silver were *nuqūd* (money), ruling out the first of the foregoing possibilities, the second yet remained. And then there was *fulūs*, which was exempt from the *ribā* restrictions. (Paradoxically, the money that was used for small transactions, and therefore more often used by the poor, was thus exempted from the ambit of *ribā* restrictions.) Was it one of the famous *ḥiyāl* (ruses) meant to circumvent the prohibition? Perhaps, but then equally it may have been inspired by a number of *ḥadīth* reports in which the Prophet considered gold and silver as money *par excellence*. (We have already noted that he encouraged the use of money, at times explicitly, but then at other times by discouraging barter transactions).

Even when the scope of the *ribā* prohibition was extended, and even when money was formally included in its scope, the *fiqh* formulations remained wedded to the idea of *ribā* being applicable to only the *bayʿ* transactions in the context of a barter regime, and not to loan transactions *per se*, though admittedly a *bayʿ* transaction involving a time dimension, *salam*, could hardly be set apart from a loan transaction. In other words, the focus was on *yadan bi-yad* (terms of the loan must be the same as spot transactions) and therefore on *ribā al-faḍl*. It should not come as a surprise then to see that the traditional *fiqh* scholars have maintained their faithfulness to that perspective down to the present times. For instance, a well known Indian *fiqh* scholar of the twentieth century permitted the sale of a 10-rupee note for 12 rupees to be paid after a period of time (though it may be noted that no further increase in the case of non-compliance, or lack of payment, is admissible, for such will be considered as *ribā* because it would involve compounding. This of course is quite consistent with the Qurʾānic perspective on *ribā* but the argument was never linked to the straitened circumstances of the debtor. More on this issue of non-compliance in the context of modern banking later. And here we are not talking about some charlatan, but a very influential and respectable scholar—albeit one disregarded by the dominant *fiqh* school; indeed a whole school of religious thought, the Barelavī school, is named after him. One can also see that as the scope of *ribā* prohibition was extended, the use of *ḥiyāl* would increase, such as the use of *bayʿ al-ʿīna* (a buy-back contract) in the Ḥanafī school. Be that as it may, these developments not only left societal expectations unfulfilled, for nothing in these developments could deter the institution of moneylending, but must have also caused discomfort among those who could not see, with considerable justification, these ruses except in a negative light. We also know that some schools of *fiqh*, for instance the Mālikī school, rejected the idea of *ḥiyāl*. In any case, once *fiqh* had decided that the Qur'ān does not provide adequate guidance on the question of the legal definition of *ribā*, and embarked on its journey on the basis of *ribā al-ḥadīth*, there was no turning back for a very long period of time; it was the end of the nineteenth century that would herald the modern *fiqh* discourse on the subject.

Let us go back to the beginning of the ninth century to pick up the story from where we left it a short while ago. It is at this time that because of discontent with the *fiqhī* developments thus far, we can discern a shift in their focus away from the peculiar interpretation given to *yadan bi-yad* that formed the basis of *ribā al-faḍl*, to *mithlan bi-mithl*, which resulted in the formulation of the second form of *ribā al-ḥadīth*, namely *ribā al-nasī'āh*. The term *yadan bi-yad*—with its obvious meaning that in an exchange, when the delivery of the good has been affected, the corresponding payment must be made promptly, or *vice versa*, to avoid any injustice—was now interpreted to mean that even when the contract involved a *qarḍ*, the condition in its revised form, linking it now to *mithlan bi-mithl* must be observed. The distinction between a *qarḍ* and *bay' salam*, as noted, was an obvious part of this development. But it took considerable time for *fiqh* to firmly articulate its position on the *nasī'a* dimension to establish *riba al-nasī'a* as the primary focus of its discourse on the subject of *ribā*. For we see it formally expounded by Jassās (d. circa 1000)[10] roughly two centuries after Shaybānī's times, in the latter part of the tenth century. When what I have earlier called the dominant group of (contemporary) *fiqh* writers wishes to lend support to its position on the equality between *ribā* and interest, the farthest it can manage to reach back into *fiqh* developments is the position Jassās articulated on *riba al-nasī'a*, but that was roughly four centuries after the Prophetic times.

[10] Nobody quite knows the exact date of death of Jassās: Fazlur Rahman mentions 370 AH. Usmani mentions 380 AH. in his part of the Judgment on the so called Ribā Case, while the main Judgment records it as 390 AH. A complete reference to the judgment is provided below.

Reading Jassās is illuminating but from a slightly different angle, for it illustrates the background of the discourse on *ribā* at the time. That questions would be raised on the *fiqh* position on *qarḍ* is quite obvious from the account presented here. One may also note that the use of *qirāḍ*—profit but no loss sharing—would have become more prevalent and cast a shadow on the discourse that neglected the issue of loan financing as such, though whether by that time the concept had undergone any change from its original position at the time of ʿUmar, as we saw in Chapter 9, is not clear. We only know that it did undergo a transformation but a couple of centuries later. One interesting question that was being asked at the time, and probably had been asked for quite some time, as is clear from Jassās's response, was: if a larger quantity (read amount) could not be claimed for a *qarḍ*, for that would amount to *ribā*, could the lender offer a discount for an early payment? Jassās's answer is a definite no. He interprets verses 2:278–279 to mean, in his example, that if 1000 dirhams were due to a person, he *could not* accept 500 dirhams, for such would amount to a "counter value" (a favorite phrase in the *fiqh* discourse to signify deviations from equal value in exchange, as per *mithan bi-mithl*) "in lieu of period". Thus, according to him, even the principal amount could not be remitted voluntarily before time. To appreciate this remark, it should be kept in mind that he was talking about *salam*, in which the due payment, the deferred price, would be larger than the spot price, and therefore the 1,000 dirhams would include this difference. And thus while the counter value in lieu of time was quite permissible at the time the transaction occurred, a reduction in that amount 'in lieu of a reduced time period' was impermissible, not even as a condition at the time the original contract was negotiated. He then adds, "As for those among the ancestors [he means Ibn ʿAbbās and Ibrāhīm al-Nakhʿī, whom he explicitly mentions earlier in his exposition] who permitted the transactions based upon "hasten the payment and I will reduce the amount", they probably did so because it had not been stipulated as a condition, that is, the discount was being offered without any conditions being stipulated and the other party also hastened the payment without any condition" (pp. 7–8).[11]

[11] All citations to Jassās's work come from the translation of excerpts by Imran Nyazee. See info@nyazee.com.

It must be pointed out explicitly, although it is obvious from the reference to *salam*, that Jassās's exposition was couched in the conventional *fiqh* context provided by the concept of *bayʿ* rather than loans. His objective seems to be to shift the focus away from *ribā al-faḍl* to what was now being expounded as *riba al-nasīʾa*. He refers to the *ḥadīth* reports that emphasize the *nasīʾah* dimension of *ribā*, as reported in Chapter 9, and specifically focuses on the *ḥadīth* report attributed to ʿUmar that *ribā* remained unexplained at the time of the passing away of the Prophet, and concludes that *ribā* was a *mujmal* term and therefore required an elaboration (*bayān*) through *ḥadīth* reports and presumably also *qiyās*. He goes on to argue that, "in the tradition [*ḥadīth* report] of Usamāh bin Zayd, which was related from him by ʿAbd al-Rahman ibn ʿAbbās, that *ribā* exists in *nasīʾah alone*, and in some version it is reported as: "There is no *ribā except* in *nasīʾah*." This proved that the term *ribā* in the *Sharʿ* is applied *some times* to *tafadūl* (from *faḍl*) and at *other times* to *nasāʾ*" (p. 5, emphasis mine). He does not see any contradiction in the conclusion that he draws, and goes on to tell us that "Ibn ʿAbbās, when he came to know about the *ḥadīth* report about *tafadūl*, [which one, we are not told] retracted his views that *ribā* was only in *nasīʾah*. To support this assertion, he tells us on the authority of some Jābir ibn Zayd that "Ibn ʿAbbās (also) withdrew his opinion about *sarf* as well as his view about *mutʿah*". After having said all that, and having said that *ribā* was a *mujmal* term, he equates *ribā al-ḥadīth* to *ribā al-jāhiliyya* by saying that "And the *ribā* that the Arabs knew and practiced was a loan of dirhams or dinars for a certain term with an increase on the amount of loan on which they mutually agreed."[12]

The striking thing about this definition is that it presents only half of the explanation that comes out of the classical works on exegesis, the unimportant half, as we have seen in the previous chapter. In selecting this half as the definition, Jassās completely ignores the well-known authoritative accounts of *ribā al-jāhiliyya* by none other than the likes of Zayd bin Aslam, Mālik, and Ṭabarī. No wonder then that two hundred years later, Rāzī (d. 1209), himself no lesser an authority on *fiqh* by any means, completely ignored him and reiterated the well-established meaning of *ribā al-jāhiliyya*. Nevertheless, it must be noted that it was Rāzī who used the term *riba*

[12] Ahkām al-Qurʾān, vol. 1, p. 465.

al-nasīʾa as a substitute term for *ribā al-jāhiliyya*. At any rate, one should not be surprised to find Jassās becoming the authority on the subject of *ribā* definition for the so-called dominant school of *fiqh*, and therefore fiqhnomics, in the modern discourse on the subject, for his definition fits the bill of equating *ribā* to interest perfectly.

At this stage, a brief stock-taking may be in order, even at the pain of some repetition, relating to the first two points. Notwithstanding all the problems noted, *fiqh* opted to hold firmly to its position, a position which, while never quite articulated in so many words, can be summed up thus: since any rate of increase (interest) could possibly lead to the process of *aḍʿāfan muḍāʿafa*, and since under the dominant institutional set up relating to provision of credit prevailing at the time, that is to say under the institution of moneylending, such was not so uncommon an occurrence, it was quite all right to equate interest to *ribā*. More than anything else, this may be a reflection of the sway the institution of moneylending held on the imagination of *fiqh*. But what the foregoing discussion also shows is that *fiqh* had to throw a great deal overboard to insist on what could be called a simple solution to a somewhat complex problem, and interestingly after all those centuries it distinctly retains that tendency even today. And the serious thing about this tendency, particularly as far as the issue under consideration is concerned, is that what could be regarded as a simple solution in the circumstances prevailing at that time turns out to be a rather *simplistic* one in contemporary times in light of the changes that have taken place, particularly on the institutional front. Viewed from a slightly different angle, the simple solution may be attributed to erring on the side of caution. But since this erring on the side of caution was not a one-time affair, we observe there has been an accumulation of caution over time as a result of various *fiqh* scholars contributing their own bits of interpretation in response to a change in circumstances, with the end result that the original picture has been distorted beyond recognition.

Before turning to the next issue, we must take account of the classical response to one important dimension of *ribā* prohibition, and this relates to the *ḥikma* of prohibition. The classical literature does not seem to address this issue until the time of Rāzī. Indeed it could not, for the framework it selected to expound the issue of *ribā* did not allow such an excursion. In that perspective both parties to the transaction were deemed to be equally guilty. Rāzī could address the issue but only because he did not confine the interpretation of *riba al-nasīʾa* to just the *ḥadīth* perspective, but rather connected it to *ribā al-Qurʾān*. In the Qurʾānic position, there is clearly one party who inflicts injustice on the other in a *ribā* transaction. No such identification is possible in the case of *ribā al-ḥadīth*, nor did the relevant *ḥadīth* reports examine the issue of any such identification. When one *ṣāʿ* of superior quality dates was exchanged for two *ṣāʿ* of inferior quality dates, without ascertaining of their respective values through their corresponding prices, who ended up gaining and who ended up losing as a result of the exchange remains unclear. Even the parties involved remain ignorant as to who gained and who lost unless they resort to a spot inquiry about the corresponding prices. It goes without saying that once such an inquiry had been conducted, and the exchange turned out to be unequal, one of the parties would not enter into the exchange anyway. We have discussed these *ḥadīth* reports at some length in Chapter 9.

All we need to note at this juncture is that these reports needed to be interpreted in light of the *gharar* involved, and that is precisely why the Prophet admonished his Companions against such barter exchanges, and instead advised them to use money. In the case of a transaction involving *gharar*, one of the two parties is likely to suffer an injustice. But then what is baffling is that some of those reports equate both the parties to the exchange as far as the penal consequences are concerned. In other words, we end up with a situation where in an exchange, both parties are deemed to be aggressors, and therefore quite explicitly according to some *ḥadīth* reports, as guilty as if they had committed incest. Surely this perspective goes contrary to the Qurʾānic perspective of *lā tazlamūna wa lā tuzlamūn*, according to which the charger of *ribā* is clearly a *zālim* (unjust), and if there is a *zālim*, there has to be a *mazlūm* (on whom the injustice is inflicted). The only way one could conceive the two parties to be equally guilty would be in the context of a willful promotion of barter exchanges which would institutionalize *gharar*. And that may well be the reason the Prophet so strongly admonished against such transactions.

Once Rāzī, at the end of the twelfth century, had established a connection between *riba al-nasīʾa*, as it evolved in *fiqh* out of *ribā al-ḥadīth*, and *ribā al-jāhiliyya*, he could articulate the *ḥikma* of its prohibition. He offered several supposedly rational explanations, in each case emphasizing the possible social disruption that may ensue as a result of charging of *ribā*. These included: i) it means appropriating another person's property without giving him anything in return (unequal exchange; the example offered is the *ḥadīth* report prohibiting the spot exchange of one dirham for two dirhams, as cited in Chapter 9); ii) it prevents people from working to earn money; iii) it prevents people from doing good to one another; and iv) it is contrary to the spirit of charity, for the lender is likely to be a rich person and the borrower poor.[13] Whatever the cogency of these arguments (and we will come to the issue a little later, for his arguments have been repeated ad-nauseam by most of the *fiqh* writers trying to rationalize the prohibition) they are decidedly cast in the context of the institution of moneylending. We may now turn to the third point in our list.

The Financing Alternatives

Once what we now know as interest had been declared the same thing as *ribā*, *fiqh* faced the question of how the genuine financing requirements of an economy that was becoming increasingly complex were to be met. The first response took the form of *ḥiyāl* (ruses) where any financing arrangement was supposed to be legitimate provided a tangible asset (usually consumer goods) was involved in the transaction. This took several forms, but in each case the end result was that a purely financial transaction, a loan contract, was converted into a *bay*ʿ contract. For instance, when A wanted a loan from B, he would sell some good to B through a fictitious spot sale, receive the amount of loan, and at the same time will buy the good back from B at a higher price which was to be paid later. This way a fictitious spot sale was combined with a sale on deferred payment basis (*salam*, or in the parlance of the dominant *fiqh* group, *bay*ʿ *mūʿajjal*) to convert what was considered to be a *ḥarām* loan transaction into a *ḥalāl bay*ʿ transaction, all the while no good had actually changed hands for all practical purposes. Such ruses were introduced by, and therefore quite commonly used in, the Ḥanafī *fiqh* but the other *madhāhab* were not immune to their use. While *fiqh* insisted that some good must be involved, that the first transaction (the spot sale) must be genuine, it is not difficult to see that this would happen

[13] About Rāzī's *Tafsīr al-Kabīr*, Suyūtī (d. 1505) commented in his exegesis (Itqān) that there is in it every thing but a Qurʾān commentary. It is interesting to note that no one cites Zamakhsharī (d. 1143), the rationalist (he was a professed Muʿatazilī in his theology), in the *ribā* discourse.

just on paper, so to speak, and no good would change hand while the finance would be provided on interest. One can also understand that even if a good had to be involved, it could easily be done and therefore for all practical purposes there could hardly be any difference between a *salam* transaction and the interest based financing. It is also not difficult to see that *fiqh* would have noticed this anomaly, and the difficulty of enforcing such a system, but there was no way out of this dilemma. There were those, for instance Shāfiʿī, who imposed the condition that a third party be involved in such buy-back arrangements, but surely when the two parties to a transaction would find it fruitful, they could always arrange a third party for that purpose without much difficulty to satisfy the *fiqh* requirements.

In light of these difficulties, *fiqh* was forced to search for alternative solutions that would meet the legitimate financing requirements of business. Some of the relevant developments occurred quickly while others took a fairly long period of time. The loop hole in *salam* was the first to be plugged by requiring that the payment be in form of a different good (money) than the good under consideration. But this was not accomplished without introducing a contradiction with another set of *ḥadīth* reports that were a variant of the ones that formed the basis of defining *ribā al-ḥadīth*, or more appropriately *ribā al-faḍl*. Consider the following report:

> Abū Saʿīd al-Khudrī reported Allah's Messenger as saying: Do not sell gold for gold, except like for like (*mithlan bi-mithl*), and do not increase something of it upon something; and do not sell silver unless like for like, and do not increase something of it upon something, *and do not sell for ready money something to be given later* (Mūslim No. 3845, emphasis mine).

In a variant of this report the last sentence reads; "and do not increase something of it upon something, *and do not sell for ready money something not present, but hand-to-hand* (*yadan bi-yad*)" (Mūslim No. 3846, emphasis added for comparison). These reports provide an opportunity to link the discussion here with that in Chapter 9. Several points need to be noted: first, while these reports are similar to the ones that formed the basis of defining *ribā al-faḍl*, there is no mention of the word *ribā* in these reports. Second, while the wordings of these reports, identical with those cited in the previous chapter, except the last sentence, could form the basis of defining *ribā al-faḍl*, they cannot be easily extended to define *riba al-nasīʾa*. The words *mithlan bi-mithl* and *yadan bi-yad* do not leave any doubt on that score. One can, therefore, understand why *fiqh's* formulations about *ribā al-ḥadīth* started with what came to be known as *ribā al-faḍl*. When it eventually came to define *ribā al-nasīʾa*, *fiqh* now kept the *mithlan bi-mithl* and *yadan bi-yad* stipulations for the *bayʿ* transactions involving a time dimension, that is to say the *salam* transactions. But the variant last sentence of the reports cited posed a difficulty when this was done, and it is for this reason that *fiqh* required the deferred payment to be made in terms of a different good, as noted above. Third, and this is what is relevant for the issue at hand, when this was done, it is not difficult to see that odds would turn against the use of *qirāḍ*, for it obviously made the extension of credit difficult. The institution of *qirāḍ* was resurrected but under a different name, and it took a long period of time.

In the meantime we see the development of various forms of *shirka* (partnership), such as *mūʿāwada, ʿinān, mufāwada, sanaʿ, wujūh,* etc. Yet *shirka* could not be considered a pure mode of financing, for more than anything else it represented a pooling of resources, and in general all the participants were supposed to be more or less directly involved in the business undertaken. The mode that represented a pure financing arrangement ultimately came to be known as *muḍāraba*. This is because it is the only contractual arrangement in *fiqh* which recognizes, though not in so many words, the functional distinction between the surplus units (the lenders) and the deficit units (the borrowers), which is the foundation of the modern theory of finance. The roots of this contractual arrangement are commonly traced back to pre-Islamic Arabia. It is said that it was one of the arrangements for raising finance for trading purposes, or alternatively it is viewed as an arrangement adopted by those who did not, or could not, undertake the trading journeys themselves, especially the women traders. Some writers speculate that the Prophet himself worked for his wife Khadīja, prior to their marriage, under this arrangement, and whether or not that was the case, it is argued that at the very least this arrangement commanded the Prophet's tacit approval.[14] It is clear,

[14] Certain *ḥadīth* reports are anxiously pressed into service to make this point. See Khafīf, p. 63. In their zeal to connect *muḍāraba* (a term that does not belong to the Prophetic period) to the Prophet, one of the writers on Islamic economics cites the following *ḥadīth* report from *Sūnan* Abū Dāʾūd (Kitāb al-buyūʿ): "ʿUrwaʾ ibn ʿAli al-Jaʿd reported that the Apostle of God gave him a dinār to purchase for him a sacrificial animal or a goat. He purchased two goats. He sold one of the two for a dinār and came to him with a goat and a dinār, and the Prophet prayed for his business...."

however, that the term itself does not belong to that period. The contractual stipulations pertaining to this mode, as these are enunciated by the dominant *fiqh* group, took a fairly long time to crystallize. What is more significant at this juncture is the fact that its roots go back to those times but only through *qirāḍ*, a term that can be traced back to ʿUmar's time, if not any earlier.

We know that *qirāḍ*, or something akin to it, had existed in pre-Islamic times in Arabia as well as during the Prophetic times, though in absence of any direct *ḥadīth* evidence, we are not quite sure about what it was called at the time. It is clear that the legal meaning given to *qirāḍ* (which is to say when it eventually became a *fiqh* term) was developed later by *fiqh* to distinguish it from *qarḍ*. This, however, must have happened fairly early on, for we read about it in the Mūwattaʾ of Mālik. The return which was permissible on *qirāḍ* was probably called *ribah*,[15] and since it was necessarily based on the profits earned in the trading mission undertaken, at some stage in *fiqh* developments it simply came to be associated with a share of the profits. We have noted two things earlier in relation to *qirāḍ* that we now need to recall. First, it is not clear from the historical evidence whether the profit share was a proportion of the profits or a proportion of the finance provided.[16] Secondly, from the evidence it is clear that originally there was no stipulation of loss-sharing as far as the finance providers were concerned. As time progressed, the issues surrounding *qirāḍ* became more and more complicated and controversial, notwithstanding the

---

He also cites the next report in Abū Dāʾūd which has more or less the same wordings, except this time the report is narrated on the authority of Hākim bin Hizām (whom we will meet later in the context of *qirāḍ* dealings) who was the one sent to purchase the sacrificial animal. See Muhammad Akram Khan (1989), *Economic Teachings of Prophet Muhammad*, Islamabad: International Institute of Islamic Economics, and Institute of Policy Studies, pp. 72–73.

[15] Sewharvi (1959, p. 286) uses this term (r-b-h) to denote what he calls legitimate profits.

[16] Interestingly Muhammad Yusufuddin (1984, pp. 44–50) notes that in pre-Islamic Arabia, each tribe, or even a clan, acted somewhat like a business firm, sort of an investment company, for trading purposes, in which individual members, and sometimes even members of other tribes and clans, contributed with their funds as loans either on the basis of profit-sharing or interest. One wonders whether there were two distinct terms prevalent at the time, one for profit-sharing and the other for something that subsequently came to be known as interest. At any rate, this supports my conjecture in the previous chapter with respect to the existence of a permissible *ribā* in context of the interpretation of verse 30:39.

contrary impression created by the modern discourse in favor of its successor, namely *muḍāraba*.

Consider, for instance, Māwardī (d. 1058) who did not approve of it, following, it is readily admitted by its proponents, the majority of the *fuqahā'*.[17] Why was the majority of *fuqahā'* opposed to an arrangement which can be traced back to more or less the Prophetic times, in the reports about the *qarḍ* contracted by ʿAbd Allah ibn ʿUmar and ʿUbayd Allah ibn ʿUmar, as well as the corresponding reports about ʿUthmān ibn ʿAffān, and Zūbayr ibn ʿAwwām? It is only in light of what we have seen earlier that we can begin to understand this displeasure with *qirāḍ*. Efforts were now underway to transform it into something more in tune with *fiqh*'s perspective on *ribā*. One should not be surprised to see that such efforts by themselves may not be approved by those who do not like to see any tampering with what existed in the pristine Madīna, and this may explain the disapproval of what came to be known as *muḍāraba*, as we will see in the latter part of this chapter. [18]

Let us return to the main argument. Interestingly, at this stage of the discourse, we observe popularization of a weak (*daʿīf*) *ḥadīth* report by Bayhaqī (d. 1077) narrated on the authority of one Fudāla bin ʿUbayd, a report which did not find its way into any of the canonical collections, and which reads: "Every loan from which *some* profit accrues to the creditor is *one of the forms* of *ribā* (emphasis added)." Indeed Bayhaqī has a whole chapter entitled "Every loan from which some profit accrues is *ribā*." The way this *ḥadīth* is reported leaves hardly any doubt as to its purport: it is squarely directed against the profit-sharing that had prevailed under *qirāḍ*.[19] Subsequently this report went through a sort of evolution to rid it of the uncertainties associated

---

[17] In his Hāwī, a part of which has been published under the title 'Al-Mudārabah' by Abd al-Wahhab al-Siba'ī in Cairo. Siddiqi (1992, p. 74) writes, "Māwardi does not allow it, following the majority of the jurists", but then goes on to note that it is "more suitable for answering the needs of our times."

[18] Yet it may be noted that most of the conditions attached to the new variant are derived from *Muwaṭṭā'* of Mālik. It may be of some interest to note that the *Muwaṭṭā'*, which is more of a legal text than a *ḥadīth* collection, focused more on the *ʿamal* (practice, from ta'āmul, see n. 17 in Chapter 5) of Madina even to the neglect of some explicit *ḥadīth* reports. For a detailed discussion on this issue, see Dutton (1999). One can understand the displeasure of such as Shafi'īe with such neglect.

[19] Yet, it must be noted that Bayhaqī remained faithful to the original *fiqh* position, for he devotes a whole chapter in his *Sunan* to argue that there is no *ribā* except in articles of food, gold and silver.

with some of the words used in it. Fazlur Rahman (1964, pp. 22–24) goes through this process of evolution, whereby first the highlighted words, namely "some" and "one of the forms" disappear, and second the *ḥadīth* is declared '*hasan li-ghayrihi*' (good on the basis of supporting evidence). And thus we see the reformed version of the report forming a strong support in the discourse of the so-called dominant school of *fiqh* in modern times. We can now understand why the word *qirāḍ* had to undergo a metamorphosis to become *muḍāraba*, and why even when some of the schools of *fiqh* did not quite like the change in terminology at the expense of *qirāḍ*, the modern discourse scarcely ever mentions the word *qirāḍ*.[20]

At this time, shortly after Māwardī, we see Sarakhsī (d. 1090) coming to the rescue of *muḍāraba* by providing hitherto unknown, or perhaps neglected, evidence.[21] He notes a number of incidents form the Prophetic times, and some from the times immediately following. Some of these incidents have already been cited, such as the incident of *qirāḍ* relating to the two sons of ʿUmar, and those relating to ʿUthmān ibn ʿAffān, and Hind, the wife of Abū Sūfyān. Sarakhsī now provides additional evidence: ʿUmar entered into a *qirāḍ* contract with one Zayd ibn Khūlaydā, and that he used to give out savings of orphans on such contracts so that these savings might grow. He tells us that one Qāsim bin Muhammad reports: "we had deposited some of our savings with ʿĀisha [Prophet's wife] who used to lend those out on *qirāḍ*. Indeed he provides evidence that such things definitely happened in the life-time of the Prophet. We are told that the Prophet himself entered into a similar contract with one Sāʾib ibn Sharīk during the Makkan period, and that when he met with him later in Madīna, he recollected the incident and mentioned it with approval. We are also told that ʿAbbās, the Prophet's uncle, engaged

---

[20] Incidentally, following Bayhaqī and other *fiqh* exponents of this doctrine, Islamic economics makes much of the dictum "No gain (profit) without risk" (*al-ghunm bi-al-ghurm*) at the same time that it asserts "No risk for gains" in line with *fiqh*'s position on *gharar* and *maysir*.

[21] It has been noted, as for instance Kuran (2002) points out, that *muḍāraba* arrangement was the precursor of the modern corporate form of governance. Also one cannot help but notice the similarities between *muḍāraba* and *muzāraʿa* (share-cropping). Indeed this may explain why the latter became a favorite mode of land cultivation in contrast to leasing of land, although there are conflicting *ḥadīth* reports approving both the forms. It may also be noted that Sarakhsī remained faithful to the original *fiqh* framework for defining *ribā*, unlike Jassās a century earlier.

in *qirāḍ* deals, with certain conditions (we are not told what these conditions were),[22] and that when the Prophet came to know about this fact, he expressed his approval; and that Hākim ibn Hizām also engaged in similar dealings. Sarakhsī also tells us that one day a man came to the Prophet and said, "I work at the market and my partner engages himself in prayers in the mosque", whereupon the Prophet said, "Probably the prosperity of your business is due to this fact", and that the Prophet said, "A man who is bringing up three daughters is like a prisoner; so O slaves of God, do *qirāḍ* with that man, *lend* him."[23] One can readily see that what Sarakhsī did was only to press *qirāḍ* in the service of *muḍāraba*. At any rate, there is no escaping the fact that once *fiqh* had taken a position on what a *qarḍ* was supposed to be, it simply could not reconcile it with the evidence on *qirāḍ*.

To be fair to Sarakhsī, his exposition could equally be interpreted, notwithstanding the terminology used, as a defense of *qirāḍ*, for he does not say anything about the treatment of losses. The real break between *qirāḍ* and *muḍāraba* had to wait for another hundred years. Thus a century after Sarakhsī, Kasānī (d. ca. 1190) attempted to provide an answer by connecting *qirāḍ* with the Ḥanafi conceptualization of *shirkat al-ʿinān* (in which, incidentally, the shares of the partners are not necessarily in proportion to their capital contributions thus reserving a share of the profits for one who may be the *āmil*), and this

---

[22] It is interesting to note that these reports did not appear in the canonical collections. To what extent the position that *fiqh* took on the issue of *ribā* contributed to this omission, if indeed it amounted to such, remains to be explored. It must be kept in mind that by the time the canonical collections came to be compiled close to the middle of the ninth century, *fiqh* had already taken a stand on what *ribā* was supposed to be, as we saw earlier. There is also the fascinating question about politics influencing the reports that were in currency at a given time. To what extent the Abbasīd power contributed to restoring the image of ʿAbbās that had been somewhat tarnished by the reports, earlier in circulation, that allege that he used to practice *ribā*, is not a subject that we can explore here. Indeed the whole issue becomes irrelevant in view of the permissible *ribā*, as we saw in the previous chapter. At any rate, Sarakhsī records this report at the end of the eleventh century when the 'Abbāsīd power was well past its zenith. But since the work is entitled al-Mabsūt (extended) implying an extension of the works of Abū-Yūsuf (d. 799) and Muhammad al-Shaybānī (d. 805), whose work itself was entitled al-Mabsūt (though now *al-asl*, or the original, is added to distinguish it from Sarakhsī's Mabsūt), it is not clear to me whether those reports are mentioned by them, though it is usually understood that the written work attributed to the two was actually done by Shaybāni. At any rate what those two said is supposed to primarily represent the opinion of Abū Ḥanīfa, their teacher.

[23] All these incidents are reported in his al-Mabsūt, vol. 22, pp. 18–19, except the one related to the Prophet himself, which is narrated in vol. 11, p. 151.

he did by somehow providing a new dictum, "No gain without the risk of loss."[24] An interesting piece of evidence on how secure the foundation of this dictum was is provided by a paper on the subject of profit-sharing presented by Siddiqi, the most ardent exponent of the idea in the modern discourse on the subject, at the second of the seminars on the subject of 'Monetary and Fiscal Economics of Islam' in Islamabad in January 1981. In one of the initial versions of the paper, which was published in his "Issues in Islamic Banking: Selected Papers" (1983), he had this to say but only in a footnote about that dictum: "Traditions [*ḥadīth* reports] to this effect appear in Abū Dā'ūd: Sunan Kitāb al-Buyū', and also in the Sunans of Tirmidhī, Nasa'ī, and Ibn Māja, as well as in the Musnad of Imām Ahmad Ibn Hanbal", and then adding that "A good exposition of the principle [he means the dictum, but which in the text he calls "the Islamic principle"] is found in Kāsānī's Badā'i' al-Sanā'i'."[25] In the revised version of the paper, this time published in the proceedings of that seminar later the same year, the dictum is present but the footnote disappears.[26] We also know that there was considerable controversy on the subject of profit-sharing in the first of those two seminars held in Makkāh in October, 1978. And it may not be out of place here to note that in the 1981 Seminar, a paper dealing with the subject of *mūdāraba* in Islamic jurisprudence by Zia ul-Haq, presumably a student of Fazlur Rahman at the University of Chicago, was included in the program but was not permitted to be presented.[27] It may also be mentioned that writers such as Muhammad 'Abdūh, Rashīd Riḍā, and 'Abd al-Wahhāb al-Khallāf did not approve of the *muḍāraba*.[28] The reason usually offered for such disapproval is stated

[24] See f. n. 19. Some writers trace the fuller articulation of *muḍāraba* contract to the Hambalī jurist and Sūfi Ibn Qūdāma (d. 1223), who was a contemporary of Rāzī and Kasānī. See his *al-Mūghnī*, vol. iii.

[25] The reference is to Jamali Press Cairo, 1910, vol. vi, pp. 62–63.

[26] See his paper in Ziauddin Ahmed et al. (eds.), *Fiscal Policy and Resource Allocation in Islam*, (1983).

[27] See the programme of the seminar, in ibid, pp.359–363. It may also be noted that the papers presented in such seminars are either invited or assigned. This means that if at all a specific viewpoint emerges out of the proceedings, which usually is then presented as a consensus, it is nothing more than consensus of the like-minded.

[28] Writing on the subject in 1960, Yūsuf al-Qardāwi adds the following footnote: "In his treatise, al-Islām wa mushkilātinā al-Mu'asirah [Islam and contemporary problems] Dr. Muhammad Yusuf Musa quotes Sheikh Muhammad 'Abdūh and Sheikh 'Abd al-Wahhāb as disagreeing with the jurists concerning (such) partnership contracts. They argue that this has no basis in the Qur'ān and *Sunnāh*" (Qardawi, 1960, p. 272).

quite succinctly, and that is that there simply is no basis for it in the Qur'ān and *Sunna*. In the present case, one can surmise that it may have to do with the divergence between what *qirāḍ* originally meant and what *muḍāraba* eventually came to signify, starting perhaps with Kasānī. We know that some sort of profit-sharing arrangement was prevalent in pre-Islamic Arabia, but we have no evidence to substantiate that this was based on a pre-determined sharing ratio. The possibility that the sharing was based on a pre-determined rate of return, the permissible *ribā*, as we saw in the context of a possible interpretation of the first revelation on the subject in *sūra al-Rūm*, cannot be ruled out. At any rate, *muḍāraba* as it finally came to be articulated was based on a strict separation between the provider(s) of finance (*sāhib al-māl* pl. *ashāb al-māl*, or *rab al-māl* pl. *arbāb al-māl*) and *mūdārab* or *ʿāmilūn* (worker sing. *ʿāmil*), and the implications arising therefrom. We may note three things in particular, (the *fiqh* stipulations will be discussed as we proceed, instead of stating them here for the sake of economy).

First, there is the problem of uncertainty (*gharar*) with respect to labor income, that is to say the income of the *mūdārab*, as was pointed out in Chapter 8. It may be kept in mind that the way *muḍāraba* came to operate in Baghdad and other cities of the Islamic realm was primarily related to merchandizing as opposed to *qirāḍ* which was primarily associated with long-distance trading. Unlike the latter case, where small savers would entrust their savings to a leading merchant going with a trade caravan, in the case of *muḍāraba*, we observe a well-off financier entrusting his business affairs to somebody who might have previously been employed as a worker in the relevant business.[29] And this may well be one of the reasons for the change in terminology from *qirāḍ* to *muḍāraba*. In economic parlance, one can easily understand that this would primarily be motivated by high monitoring costs. Alternatively, one can view this as the well recognized profit-sharing solution to the moral hazard problem arising out of a principal-agent situation. Second, and more in tune with the original spirit behind the use of *qirāḍ*, is the problem of loss-sharing by the small savers. And, interestingly, this is an issue that is as fresh and relevant in modern times as it was during the

[29] Jazīrī's Kitab al-fiqh 'ala al-madhāhib al-arbaʿa, vol.ii, gives the definite impression that the arrangement was primarily used for cloth merchandizing.

Prophetic times, and one may add, as it would have remained down the centuries. It is another matter that *fiqh*, concerned as it was with the predicament of the small borrower (and not small lenders), did not pay much attention to it. But such an attitude is puzzling to say the least in modern times.

And then, third, there is an even more serious issue, and this is related to protection of the *rā's al-māl*, which is side-stepped in the discourse on *muḍāraba*. Profits are reckoned only after the original amount of *māl*, usually called capital, has been accounted for. If there are losses, i.e. a diminution of capital, these are supposed to be borne by the *sāhib al-māl*, whereas the *'āmil* loses the reward due for his labor. One can easily understand how this arrangement would have worked in the long distance trading of the Makkans, since a *qirāḍ* contract would automatically come to an end upon the return of the caravan and the disposal of the wares it brought. The next trade caravan would be a wholly new affair. Profits would be distributed, though exactly in what manner remains unclear. If there were losses, the small savers might have got their *rā's al-māl* back, though it is conceivable that disputations may have arisen on the accounting issues, as a particular trader may have dealt with more than one good and some of those goods may have fetched profits while others might have occasioned losses. Nevertheless, under the foregoing trading scenario, one can understand what Sarakhsī, and possibly some earlier *fiqh* authorities, would mean by the protection of the original capital.[30]

But what would happen when the *muḍāraba* was instituted on a perpetual basis, as would happen in the case with a cloth merchandizing business? The interests of the *sāhib al-māl* and *'āmil*, which were supposed to have been brought into harmony through the profit-sharing arrangement, would now diverge sharply on the issue of the duration after which the profits are to be reckoned and distributed. The *sāhib al-māl* would wish the duration to be as as short as possible, for this protects his capital from losses if and when they occur. In other words, as long as profits are being made, his share is protected, but if there are losses, these will have to be recovered through future profits (rather than being offset through the existing pool of undistributed

[30] Sarakhsī discusses the issue in al-Mabsūt, vol. 22, p. 105, but the point originally comes from the *Muwaṭṭā'* of Mālik.

profits) without any compensation being paid to the *ʿāmil*, following one of the relevant stipulations of *fiqh*.

On the other hand, when it comes to the interest of the *ʿāmil*, the situation is not very clear. At one level, he would wish this period to be as long as possible, for if losses accrue, they will be recovered from the accumulated profits, but then he will not have any regular income for wherewithal. On the other hand, if he opts for a short period for the distribution of profits, he may get regular income, but in that case if losses accrue, depending upon their magnitude, he may have to work for a long time to recover those losses before he can claim any reward for his labor. Thus there may be a conflict between the two parties about the duration after which the profits are to be distributed. *Fiqh* hardly ever bothers about such issues, for it simply assumes that the two parties will agree on a time period for the sharing of the profits. This conflict of interest cannot be simply ignored especially in light of the other stipulations of *muḍāraba* as we will see below. But while *fiqh*'s assuming away the problem is excusable, more so in the initial times of relative simplicity, one would hardly expect such a response from fiqhnomics. But that is precisely what it does.

Consider, for instance, Siddiqi (1985) who writes, "In a running business losses will be made good by profit till the business comes to a close and accounts are settled finally. At the time of the settlement of accounts, the original capital will first be set apart. Any amounts left after that will be deemed profits or, in case of shortage, loss" (p.16). Having said that, he totally forgets to address the implications of this stipulation for a running business. He probably would be happy to impose a liquidation on the business even every month (keep in mind that strictly speaking, in a *muḍāraba*, the capital is to be contributed in the form of liquidity, and so is it to be received back), if somehow that could be the agreed time frame for sharing of the profits, as long as his conceptualization of the profit-sharing (i.e. *muḍāraba*) survives. But would it really? And since his primary focus is on a financial system that is to be erected on the principle of *muḍāraba*, how such a condition of frequent liquidation would be imposed on the perpetual business that a financial institution happens to be is beyond comprehension.

But coming back to issue of conflict of interest with regard to the duration: How would those conflicting interests with respect to the duration after which the profits are to be distributed be resolved? Siddiqi, perhaps, would gladly assign the responsibility to the government, or to be more specific, to the central bank of the country. But then through what process are the sharing ratios to be determined? Since the market mechanism and competition are alien Western concepts, the responsibility must again be assigned to the government, and in this Islamic economists are quite explicit. If we disregard the complication arising out of liquidation of the bank every time it has to share profits with its *muḍāraba* depositors, is the bank going to impose the stipulation on all the businesses to *which* it provides the finances? Let us assume the answer to be negative in the name of flexibility, for Islam is supposed to be flexible, how are then the capital gains, one of the important sources of profits in modern times, to be handled?

Siddiqi confines his analysis to only the operating profits as far as the *muḍāraba* depositors, usually the small savers, are concerned. But who would end up with the accrued capital gains if the business is not to be liquidated? As soon as such gains accrue, the *ʿāmil* (read management of the business) would wish to discharge the bank obligations on the basis of operating profits (keep in mind that as per the *fiqh* rules, any party can terminate the contract at any time), and thus appropriate the capital gains that rightfully belonged to those depositors. Would this be considered a just outcome by the proponents of *muḍāraba*? It is not an issue that troubles Siddiqi. And this is by no means the end of such questions. The bottom line is that either the businesses are periodically liquidated to ensure a just outcome, which is practically impossible, or the classical *fiqh* stipulation is ignored in the name of flexibility, but then a just outcome cannot be guaranteed. What might have worked quite well in the case of long-distance trading, but note, under the original *qirāḍ* arrangement, and quite possibly in the case of cloth merchandizing on the basis of personal relations between the two parties under *muḍāraba*, becomes irrelevant when it comes to modern business organization.

Two additional pertinent points must be noted before we leave this subject. First, the modern exposition of *muḍāraba*, particularly as it comes out in the writings on fiqhnomics, distorts the original *fiqh* position with respect to the rights of *sāhib al-māl*. It is insisted that he does not have anything to do with the enterprise once he has handed over his capital to the *ʿāmil*. It is the *ʿāmil* who now does whatever he wishes with the capital entrusted to him. This, of course, renders *muḍāraba* a principal and agent scenario *par excellence*, perhaps even worse than the American system of corporate governance. A reading of the various *fiqh* schools on the issue, for instance in Jazīrī, does not at all support this blanket vesting of power with the agent. All sorts of conditions can be imposed by the *sāhib al-māl* at the time the contract is entered into, though *fiqh* insists on some types of restrictions that he may not impose on the *ʿāmil* in view of protecting his interests.

The fiqhnomics' stand on the issue is primarily a recognition of the impracticality of according the relevant rights in the case of instituting *muḍāraba* at a financial institution, such as a bank. And this leads to the second point: if its vision of *muḍāraba* is to be instituted at only the financial institutions, what is the point of insisting on the loss-sharing—which is what primarily draws a wedge between *muḍāraba* and *qirāḍ*, in context of a diversified portfolio that these institutions would be supposed to hold? The only possibility of loss that one would need to worry about then would arise in the event of a bank failure. Would fiqhnomics insist on inflicting the losses on all depositors, a vast majority of whom will be small savers? And beyond that what about the Qurʾānic injunction about the protection of the *rāʾs al-māl* once Kasānī's dictum, or Siddiqi's Islamic principle is deemed an innovation pure and simple? Fiqhnomics may not quite worry about such issues in its zeal to promote its vision of Islamic financing, but if and when such a system is instituted in the name of Islam and some institutions run into trouble, as they are bound to, it would lead to serious psychological consequences for the trusting ordinary adherents of Islam who do not understand the intricacies of this discourse.

The Brave New World

We can now turn to the modern discourse on *ribā* prohibition. There are several features that set this discourse apart from the classical one. First, in this discourse, only *ribā al-faḍl* is associated with the *ribā al-ḥadīth*, and following Rāzī, *riba al-nasīʾa* is associated with the Qurʾānic *ribā*. Second, and flowing directly from the previous point, the idea that the Qurʾān does not provide enough clarity on what is meant by *ribā* for legal purposes, that it was a *mujmal* term that needed to be explained through *qiyās*, has been abandoned. Third, the confusion about the chronology of the revelation of the *ribā* verses in *sūra al-Baqara*, which was pivotal in the formulation of the classical *fiqh* position, has now been recognized to lead nowhere, particularly in light of the clarity about the timing of the revelation of verse 3:130. Yet, those verses are, or continue to be, given a precedence over verse 3:130 (where the qualification *aḍʿāfan muḍāʿafa* occurs) when it comes to provide a legal definition of the term, thus nullifying the logical implications of their recognition. Fourth, since this definition implies that finance must be made available at a zero rate of interest, and since it is realized that a financial system could not be erected on such a foundation, alternative modes of financing are proposed, and an attempt is made to root them in the framework of the *ribā al-ḥadīth* or, failing that, in the classical *fiqh* discourse—a glimpse of which we have seen above. Doing so results in similar contradictions that we have discussed earlier, but now these become even more serious under an entirely new institutional setting characterizing the modern financial system, and the contextual changes. Thus the efforts to circle a perfect square continue apace.

As far as I can see, in modern times the first attempt to explore the connection between *ribā* and interest was made by the modernist Muhammad Abduh (d.1905), at one time the Grand Mufti of Egypt, and a member of the administrative council of Al-Azhar University. He argued that the institution of interest, the interest as it relates to the modern financial system, was not the same thing as *ribā*. Abduh, who was steeped in classical Islamic learning as well as exposed to the currents of modernity, for he had spent some time in Paris, must have felt that the context of *ribā* prohibition as such scarcely applied to the modern financial system. Further he must have been aware of the permissible *ribā*, whatever it was called. After him, his student, the Syrian Rashīd Rīdā (d. 1935) maintained the same position. Rīdā (1960) shunned the inconsistencies of *fiqh* aside and interpreted *ribā* as it emerged out of the classical works of exegesis and thus related it to the straitened circumstances of the debtor, as we saw in Chapter 9. He maintained that it was this *ribā* which was prohibited by the Qurʾān. Rīdā did not mince any words and roundly criticized the jurists of the past for appropriating the Divine prerogative of determining what was *ḥalāl* and what was *ḥarām*. At about the same time, in the sub-continent, Abdullah Yusuf Ali, in his translation of the Qurʾān, opined in a footnote to verse 2:275, that bank interest was not the same thing as *ribā*. Since this translation was very well received, and became a common reference in English, it was quite widely published, by anyone interested in disseminating the message of the Qurʾān (it may be noted that *fiqh* has no conceptualization equivalent to the copyright). A few decades after its original publication, when it was published under Saudi auspices, its publishers did something quite offensive—indeed in modern scholarship it would be deemed intellectual dishonesty. The part of the footnote that expressed the opinion about interest was expunged (self-professed piety has its own way of committing excesses), and to top it all, an addition was made at the beginning, without any warning to the reader. Here is the original footnote, with the expunged portion enclosed in brackets:

> Our ʿUlama, ancient and modern, have worked out a great body of literature on Usury, based mainly on economic conditions as they existed at the rise of Islam. [I agree with them on the main principles, but respectfully differ from them on the definition of Usury. As this subject is highly controversial, I shall discuss it, not in the Commentary, but on a suitable occasion elsewhere. The definition I would accept would be: undue profit made, not in the way of legitimate trade, out of loans of gold and silver, and necessary articles of food, such as wheat, barley, dates and salt (according to the list mentioned by the Holy Apostle himself). My definition would include profiteering of all kinds, but exclude economic credit, the creature of modern banking and finance] (footnote no. 324).[31]

Then in the middle of the twentieth century, Anwar Iqbal Qureshi, whom we have met earlier, wrote a treatise on the subject in which he forcefully argued for abolition of interest through an administrative fiat. He was an admirer of Keynes; for his reading of some obscure passages from the *General Theory* led him to believe that Keynes advocated, or at least contemplated, that the institution of interest could be abolished from the economy. It may well have been a misreading of the liquidity trap arguments, or perhaps those relating to the exposition of the classical economics' worry about stationary state, as we saw in Chapter 4, which might have contributed to the error in his understanding. Nevertheless Qureshi was convinced that once the

[31] The addition at the beginning reads: "Usury is condemned and prohibited in the strongest possible terms. There can be no question about its prohibition. When we come to the definition of usury there is room for difference of opinion. Caliph ʿUmer, according to Ibn Kathīr, felt some difficulty in the matter, as the Apostle left this world before the details of the question were settled. This was one of the three questions on which he wished he had had more light from the Apostle, the other two being Khilāfat and Kalālat." One wonders how much of classical Islamic work may have gone through such "corrections".

government abolished interest from the economy, it would usher in a golden Islamic state, be it stationary or steady.

On the other side of the *fiqh* divide, at about the same time Qureshi wrote as an economist, two influential *fiqh* scholars from Pakistan, Mawdudi, and Muhammad Shafi, also wrote on the issue. Both of them made a u-turn from the classical '*mûjmal*' framework, emphasizing that the Qur'ān was absolutely clear about what it prohibited, but nevertheless put the verses of *sūra al-Baqara* at the centre of their exposition, and arrived at the conclusion that what it prohibited was precisely the same thing as interest (*sūd*, in Urdu). Mawdudi (1961), for instance, did not even discuss *ribā al-faḍl* in his main chapter on *ribā*. He relegated it to another chapter entitled *Sūd kay Mut'allaqāt* (The adjuncts of interest), and argued that the objective of Prophetic prohibition of *ribā al-faḍl* (which is what was explicitly left of the *ribā al-ḥadīth* after its *nasī'ah* variety was associated with Qur'ānic *ribā* by Rāzī), was nothing more and nothing less than to make sure that "people did not even come near interest" (p. 149). Thus the essential vehicle of the classical *fiqh* exposition of *ribā* now simply became an adjunct to the explanation. There were some dissenting voices, admittedly less influential, of writers such as Jafar Shah Phulwarwi, Sayyid Yaqub Shah, but then again of Fazlur Rahman, but these were either ignored or more or less drowned in the din of the betrayal-of-Islam charge leveled against some of them. In the past decade or so, the main exponent of the Mawdudi-Shafi line of argument is the same Muhammad Taqi Usmani, who served as a judge in the famous *ribā* case in the Sharī'a Appellate Bench of the Supreme Court of Pakistan, and who is associated with the same Institute in Karachi (the Idaratul Ma'arif) with which Muhammad Shafi was associated. It is this school of thought that I have referred to as the dominant *fiqh* group. The ascendancy of this school can be attributed to two interrelated developments that occurred more or less concurrently in the late 1970s.

The Process of Islamization

The first of these was the establishment of Islamic Development Bank (IDB) in Jeddah in 1975. It appears that the conservative Saudi climate did not like the *apparently* liberal views on at least some issues, including *ribā*, associated with Al-Azhar University which was supposed to be the premier institution of higher learning in the Sunnī realm of Islam. The conservative elements in Pakistan's *fiqh* establishment, on the other hand, seemed to them to be a more favorable option, a kind of confluence of the like-minded. A few years later the International Centre for Research in Islamic Economics was established at King Abdulaziz University, Jeddah, and in the early 1980s, the IDB established the Islamic Research and Training Institute (IRTI), as its research wing, and these became the primary spawning grounds for Islamic economics, and thus fiqhnomics. This, in turn, added to the influence of the Pakistani *fiqh* vision. But then the second fortuitous development for this group occurred in Pakistan, and this was the emergence of the Zia ul-Haq regime in July 1977, a regime that co-opted this group to launch its program of Islamization of the economy. It was this development that to a considerable extent determined the subsequent course of the so-called Islamic economics and Islamic banking throughout the world, particularly the Sunnī realm of Islam.

In Pakistan, the issue of the connection of interest with *ribā* came to a head when the matter was brought to the Sharīʿa Court (commonly referred to as the Shariat Court) in 1991. A judgment prohibiting interest from the financial sector was delivered in 1992, which was challenged in the Sharīʿa Appellate Bench of the Supreme Court of Pakistan, which did not hear the appeal until 1999, and which upheld the decision of the Sharīʿa Court. When it seemed that the matter had been settled for good, the Appellate Bench being the final arbiter in the adjudication process, the case was once again appealed against in the Sharīʿa Appellate Bench in 2002, and not surprisingly this time the appeal was upheld, and the case referred back to the Sharīʿa Court for reconsideration. And that is where matters rest as far as Pakistan is concerned. But more or less at the same time, the issue was referred to the Rector (the Grand Shaykh) of Al-Azhar University in October, 2002, for a *fatwa*, and the *fatwa* was delivered in December 2002 by Muhammad Sayyid Tantāwī, who upheld the Abduh-Rīda position. Tantāwī had already been known to hold the position which was reflected in his *fatwa*, and indeed that position may have contributed to the second referral to the Sharīʿa Appellate Bench in Pakistan. It appears to me that we can better understand the controversies surrounding the issue of *ribā* and interest by focusing on the developments relating to Islamization of the economy in Pakistan, particularly its financial system. But before we do that, we must note the institutional changes that had occurred since classical

Islamic times, the changes that provide the contextual background to which these controversies must relate.

As far as the general economic background is concerned, the world has undergone profound changes since those times, and particularly in the past two and a half centuries beginning with the industrial revolution, and so has systematic economic thought beginning with Smith's *Wealth of Nations* in 1776, incidentally more or less coinciding with the industrial revolution. From then on, the world has gone through one revolution after another in the field of technology be that related to steam engine, electricity, telephone, internal combustion engine, jet engine, nuclear technology, transistor, laser, information technology, microbiology, etc. The world GNP per capita has increased from roughly US $500 to over $5,500 in the past two hundred years, causing a remarkable and unprecedented improvement in the living conditions of even workers, notwithstanding the fact that pockets of misery persist throughout the world, and particularly in the Islamic countries. How economic thought responded to some of these changes was the subject of Chapters 2, 3, and 4. Here, in the context of the subject at hand, we will note two things in the backdrop of what has been said in those chapters, particularly Chapter 4. Both the changes that we wish to focus on here relate to the transformation that has occurred in the area of finance, and primarily relate to the institutional changes in that area.

One of these changes concerns the preponderance of small savers, in terms of numbers, that are now able to participate in the process of financing, and the other relates to shift from direct to indirect financing. It goes without saying that a healthy financial sector is a *sine qua non* of a healthy economy. Correspondingly, the functions that financial intermediaries must perform are well recognized in economic theory, and among other things these include: i) to facilitate the process of investment through a coordination between the surplus and deficit units; ii) in view of the foregoing, to economize on information and transaction costs; and iii) in the light of the foregoing, to make it possible for a small saver to have a claim on a diversified portfolio, and thereby reduce his exposure to risk. (One perhaps would not need to belabor these issues had it not been for the confusion prevailing in Islamic economics on these elementary subjects).

More to the point, what this has meant is that the conventional institution of moneylending, call it loan sharking or whatever, though it survives to this day, has lost its significance as far as the overall financing magnitudes in a modern economy are concerned. One may indeed add that the less developed the financial system of an economy, the greater the reliance on the age-old institution of moneylending. If the worry of the classical exponents was an exploitation of the poor borrowers by the rich moneylenders, the overwhelming worry under the modern institutional form of finance is the possibility of exploitation of the low income lenders (depositors) by the rich borrowers and/or financial intermediaries, a subject touched upon in Chapter 4.

The second important thing that needs to be noted is that the modern financial system is built on the principle of indirect, rather than direct, financing, although there is more to it than just that as we will see a little later. What this has meant is that the possible exploitation of the poor by the rich and powerful has become impersonal in nature, rather than being personal as would be the case under the institution of moneylending. The possibility of exploitation primarily arises out of lack of sufficient competition, which in turn is attributed to the economies of scale. Thus we end up with the principal and agent problem not only because the industry deals with funds that belong to someone else but also by virtue of it being run under a corporate form of governance. The solution to this dilemma has been sought primarily through regulation, a subject that has been much discussed in the literature. What has often not been discussed, at least explicitly, is that the structure of property rights that has evolved in relation to the financial intermediaries has accorded legal recognition to both the pure and impure intermediation. In the latter case, the intermediaries were allowed to hold their won assets and liabilities. That is to say, the deposits were recognized as the liabilities of the intermediary regardless of what happened on the assets side of the balance sheet of an intermediary. This can be viewed in both negative and positive lights.

On the negative side, this may in principle lead, as it often does in reality, to a rich intermediary earning huge profits on the basis of assets that were created with the deposits of the low income savers. On the positive side, since some of the loans of an intermediary go sour, the arrangement ensures that a particular small saver gets a return on its deposit regardless of what happens to some of the specific assets of the intermediary. The overall health of an intermediary is supposed to be insured by the government through regulation. Needless to say that government itself is a principal and agent scenario, and this time the agent happens to hold monopoly power, at least until the next elections (but this obviously under a republican form of political dispensation). The purpose of highlighting these elementary issues is to see whether these have drawn the attention of the Islamic economists. The answer will become clear as we proceed.

Let us return to Zia ul-Haq's Islamization in Pakistan, and the collaboration of the dominant school of *fiqh* in this enterprise. On assuming power on 5 July 1977, Zia ul-Haq promised that he would hold elections within 90 days and transfer power to the elected government. Quickly thereafter he underwent a change of heart, for we know that on 29 September 1977 he mandated the Council of Islamic Ideology (CII, a constitutional body established to make sure that no law enacted was repugnant to the spirit of Islam; we may note that its chairmanship at the time was entrusted to one Tanzilur Rahman, who played a prominent role in the subsequent course of developments) to prepare a blueprint of an interest-free economic system. In November 1977, the CII appointed a panel of economists and bankers to prepare a report to the same effect. The panel submitted its report in February, 1980, and the CII adopted the report, after some modifications to make it *Sharīʿa* compliant, so to speak, in June 1980. This report was entitled "Elimination of Interest from the Economy." What followed thereafter can best be summed up as a twenty-year struggle in which the dominant *fiqh* group attempted to come up with a viable alternative to interest for the financial system, and failed, as the 2002 judgment of the Sharīʿa Appellate Bench testifies. In this struggle we see the dominant group groping with a new set of *ḥiyāl* (ruses) that would not only meet the financing requirements of the modern business but also command general acceptance within its own group, and thereafter other sections of society. It is an interesting story in which we see intra-group differences on what is acceptable as an alternative to interest, particularly in view of the difficulties of enforcement of the various alternative modes devised under the new ruses, for unlike the classical times, in this new world, the issue of an effective enforcement could not be ignored. After all, the group was a part of the government of the time when it all started, and besides its philosophy happened to be a top-down enforcement of *fiqh* stipulations through the power of the state. The following discussion pays special attention to these two themes: the new ruses, and an anticipation of enforcement through the state machinery.

The Issue of Permissible Alternatives

It seems that the panel of economists recommended ten alternative modes of financing to replace interest, out of which the CII rejected two and accepted the remaining eight. It pointed out that the "ideal" alternatives to interest were profit/loss sharing and *qarḍ ḥasan*, but in view of the "practical" difficulties of adopting these modes in "certain spheres, the Council has endorsed the recommendations of the Panel of Economists and Bankers" for a number of other alternatives. We will turn to the "ideal" alternatives a little later after listing the remaining modes along with brief, but pertinent, remarks (I have added emphasis, through italics or brackets):[32]

a) Lending on the basis of service charge: Disapproved with the following comments: "although this solution may appear to meet the requirements of *Sharīah* in the literal sense" but, among other things, "interest-free loaning with service charge would in essence mean providing capital resources at a very *low* cost", and that "since financial institutions would cease to earn any income except that for meeting their own administrative expenses, there would be no *incentive* to set up such institutions in the private sector as no return on the share capital would be available," and that under this system "the strong and affluent would be the gainers while the weak and needy would be the losers."
b) Indexation of Bank Deposits and Advances: The Panel made this recommendation in view of the fact that if loans were to be interest-free, at least the principal amount must be guarded against inflation, following the Qur'ānic exhortation *lā tazlimūna wa lā tuzlamūn*. The Council rejected this recommendation by noting that the prices do not increase by the same proportion in all sectors of the economy, and then went on to offer the following gem of logical deduction: "agriculture sector is likely to suffer because agricultural prices are often *controlled by the government* or determined by international demand and supply factors. If the increase in the prices of agricultural products is *less* than the rise in the general price level,

[32] All citations in this discussion come from CII (1983) which includes comments by two invited commentators as well as the discussion that followed the presentation of the report.

indexation, of banks advances will place the agricultural sector in a disadvantageous position" (p. 115), as though government must be assumed to remain blind to the fact of inflation in determining the agricultural prices, and as though the rules of Islamic finance being articulated were to be confined to only Pakistan. But then, more seriously, what about the indexation of deposits? So the strong and affluent must gain, after all, at the expense of the weak. Beyond that, the argument, as it continues, harks back to the classical *fiqh*'s *bayʿ* framework, for we are told that, "under *Sharīʿah*, currency transactions are not treated differently from commodity transactions in as far as *lending and borrowing* are concerned" (p. 116), and this implies that the same nominal amount must be returned, for in the context of the profit-sharing by depositors, it notes that "finance provided on the basis of *Bai Muajjal* cannot be treated as loan" (pp. 147–148). More on this when we return to the issue of indexation below.

c) Leasing: There is nothing new in this, for leasing is a universally recognized arrangement for capital rental.
d) Investment Auctioning: A pure ruse, for there is nothing that would lead one to believe that arbitrage under it will lead to results any different from the arbitrage in the case of interest.
e) *Bayʿ Mūʿajjal*. A variant of classical *salam* in view of the fact that money is no longer a commodity by itself, and thus it has been felt prudent to differentiate between deferred payment (*bayʿ mūʿajjal*) and deferred delivery (*bayʿ salam*), and thus the former term has been culled from Fatawa-i Alamgīri compiled in the seventeenth century in India on behest of Mughal Emperor Aurangzeb Alamgīr. At any rate there is nothing new in it as far as modern finance is concerned. A price higher than the spot one in the case of deferred payment is universally recognized to represent interest. Much is made of the condition that in the case of *bayʿ mūʿajjal*, the deferred payments could not be increased due to default in payment. A detailed discussion of how the issue of default is handled in this framework follows a little later. On the other hand, *bayʿ salam* is also permitted in the case of agricultural financing.
f) Hire Purchase: Similar to *bayʿ mūʿajjal*, except that the property rights (ownership) will not be fully transferred to the buyer until the maturity of the contract.
g) Financing on the Basis of Normal Rate of Return: A pure ruse, for that is what interest rate happens to be, provided government does not break the link between the rate of return and rate of profit as

discussed in Chapter 4. Interestingly, the Council envisions such rate to be quite industry specific, and thus leaves it to the government (a specialist public agency, it says) to figure these rates out. One wonders what happened to the process of market arbitration, but then the Council may not have a market system as its point of reference. In that case, in light of our discussion in Chapter 6, we have a right to ask why this would be so assumed. But then one can also raise a question: if this rate is not to be uniform across different industries, for that would look too much like rate of interest, why stop at the industry level? The rate of return, following the Council's own logic, could vary from firm to firm.

h) Time Multiple Counter-loans: This is perhaps a new idea. What it means simply is that if a person takes an interest-free loan of 300 for one year, he must keep an interest-free deposit of say one third of the amount (100) for a duration three times as long as the duration of his loan (time multiple, which means three years in the present case) at the same financial institution. Theoretically a neat idea, for it can be related to both the life cycle hypothesis as well as the inter-temporal utility maximization model, but practically difficult to implement because an individual would remain a deficit unit for a fairly long period of time (in the early part of his life cycle) and would not be able to immediately put in a realistic amount to service his loan after he becomes a surplus unit (in the middle part of his life cycle). No wonder then that the idea disappeared in the subsequent articulations of the Islamic modes of financing.

i) Special Loans Facility: Same as *qarḍ ḥasan*, but this time to signify loans taken only by the government for the "general welfare of the community" (p. 121). Thus the impracticality of *qarḍ ḥasan* as a business financing mode was not lost on the Council, though it thought efforts should be made to extend such loans to the agricultural sector.

When it came to articulate its vision of the "ideal" mode of financing, i. e. the profit/loss sharing, the Council was ambiguous to say the least. It was not sure whether to relate it to *muḍāraba* or *mushāraka* (p. 122), probably in view of the difficulties relating to the former (needless to say that some of those difficulties will also relate to the latter), and also because its own vision about the determination of the sharing ratio violated the corresponding *fiqh* rules, for it delegated that power to the government, saying that "the division of profits between the financial institutions and business and industrial enterprises should not be left to be decided by the two parties but should be regulated by the central bank of the country" (p. 122). In view of these difficulties, it decided to call it neither, hence the coining of the term profit/loss sharing. This new vision relates to those classical forms only conceptually, since it violates most of the detailed stipulations of *fiqh* relating to profit-sharing contracts. One of the reasons, it seems, the Council delegated the power of sharing ratio determination to the government was that once it recognized the rights of the two parties in determination of the ratio, as *fiqh* would actually require, in the second tier of Siddiqi's two-tiered *muḍāraba*, it could not deny the same rights to the depositors in the first tier of that *muḍāraba*, something it was not willing to contemplate (No prize for guessing as to how these ratios, since there could be more than one of these, were to be determined). In line with the philosophy of fiqhnomics, as discussed at some length in Chapters 6 and 7, the Council simply could not contemplate any role for market mechanism (arbitration) in the determination of these sharing ratios. It was the central bank of the country that was to figure out what these ratios were supposed to be. One wonders if the central bank was supposed to determine everything as far as the returns on loans were concerned, what would be wrong with the central bank directly determining the rate of interest, or an economy-wide (normal) rate of profit, in the first place?[33] Needless to say, though, that the divergence

[33] The distribution of the profits to the depositors, the Council suggested, was to be worked out on the daily product basis. The Council used a hypothetical example to illustrate how this was to work. While one could not take the numbers used in the example too seriously, they could be considered as suggestive, especially when the chairman of the panel of economists that worked out the illustrations in the report (and indeed who was one of the two persons who presented the report of the Council at the seminar, the proceedings of which form the basis of the present discussion) was no other than the Deputy Governor, State Bank of Pakistan at the time (he subsequently served as the Governor, State Bank of Pakistan, and upon his retirement from the State Bank, served as the Director General of International Institute of Islamic Economics, International Islamic University, Islamabad). We note only two incongruities from the illustration provided (p. 147): first, the reserves of the bank, presumably the required ones—but then banks at times can end up with excess reserves—are lumped with the capital of the bank, as though it will always be the capital of the bank which will be set aside to meet the reserve requirements, for sharing purposes. This means that the reserves will be entitled to profits at par with the capital of the bank, and these profits will accrue to the owners of the bank. Second, the capital and reserves portion was assigned a weight of 1 in the proposed scheme of distribution. Thus, the capital of the owners does not suffer any reduction in profits due to the required

between actual and market determined rate of profit (or interest) in capitalist economies is the result of governmental interference in the market mechanism through the institution of central bank, as we saw in Chapter 4.

Even within this cohesive group, that took charge of the Islamization process, there were differences of opinion,[34] for what the panel (of economists and bankers) submitted in its report was considerably revised in the final CII report, in light of the criticism leveled by some members within this group against either some of the proposed modes of financing, or the way some (other) modes were articulated. Evidence to this effect comes from the comments of the invited experts, published alongside the report. While the report of the panel was also published immediately after the CII report as Appendix I, unfortunately the portion (labeled as Paragraph 1, a long one though with a number of sub-paragraphs) which was the cause of discontent was expunged from this publication (see p. 201). We are forced to rely on indirect evidence from what the commentators wrote in this context. For instance, Siddiqi (pp. 224–229) did not like the way the profit/loss-sharing mode was worked out, nor did he like the idea of investment auctioning.[35] He did not approve of the *murābaḥa* mode

reserve condition, and all reduction is passed on to the depositors, except the holders of time deposits with more than 5-year maturity period. And since the weights are ascending with respect to the time duration of the deposits, proportionately greater onus of reduced profits, the profits left after the portion of the owners' share has been deducted, falls on savings and the short-term deposit holders as compared to the long-term deposit holders. This may be justified if the required reserve ratios are lower on long-term deposits as compared to short-term deposits, and are as finely calibrated as the sharing weights used in the report. But then we note that the sharing weights used in the report are: capital and reserves (1); savings and time deposits up to 6 months (0.3); 6–12 months (0.4); 1–2 years (0.6); 2–3 years (0.7); 3–4 years (0.8); 4–5 years (0.9); and 5 years and above (1). And if a central bank were to use these numbers, the returns to capital, reserves, and deposits with maturity period more than 5 years would be 320% higher than the returns to the savings deposits and the deposits up to 6 months maturity. Well, so much for the gains to the weak, who would normally be the short term deposit holders, versus gains to the 'strong and affluent."

[34] On the subject of conflicting opinions among Islamic economists in general, see Kuran (1989).

[35] In the light of our discussion about *muḍāraba* earlier, I have thought it better to let the reader see what he has to say here: "It is gratifying to note that the Council has duly modified the 'new system' of sharing profits and losses proposed by the Panel in paragraph 1.27 of its Report (as also contained in the Committee Report on Interest Free Banking). It has stated categorically that 'the loss would, however, be shared strictly proportionately to the respective contributions' (Council Report, 1.23). The system proposed in the other two Reports violated the *Sharīʿa* and went against the

as proposed by the panel, and appreciated that, "The Council has done well in modifying *murabaha*, which is based on a particular juristic opinion not shared by many eminent jurists, to *Bai Muajjal* which has relatively more secure foundations, despite the fact that it remains *controversial*" (p. 226, emphasis added). Scarcely a page later he changes his mind about *bay*ʿ *mūʿajjal* for then he says, in a rather authoritative manner: "I would prefer that *Bai Muajjal* is removed from the list of permissible methods altogether" (p. 227). It seems that if Siddiqi had had his way he would remove every mode of financing other than his favorite, the *muḍāraba*. And after having approved of the Council's vision of profit/loss sharing where every sharing ratio is determined by the government, in his own paper on the subject of profit-sharing, presented at the same seminar (Siddiqi, 1983), he suddenly realizes that market mechanism can strengthen his arguments and thus goes on to write, "Competition ensures that entrepreneurship pushes forward in all possible directions till the rate of profit is equal [sic] on the margin—an ideal situation being always approached but never reached" (p. 179).[36]

The traces of another point on which differences of opinion between the panel of economists and the hawkish members of the group can

---

Islamic approach to the respective roles of capital and enterprise in the productive process. Any departure from this approach, which regards losses as an erosion of equity (i.e. decrease in capital) and profits as a joint result of and reward for capital and enterprise, will lead us astray from the justice ordained by the *Shariʿah*" (p. 224). And again: "It is gratifying to note that the Council did not endorse the method of 'Investment Auctioning' as formulated by the Panel (Panel Report, 1.14). According to this formulation 'the offer of the needed long term/medium term finance' is part of the package being 'sold' on deferred payment. But an offer to finance is not a valid object of sale in *Shariʿah*. It would be an exchange of a smaller sum of money for a larger sum of money to be paid later—a clear case of the prohibited *riba*" (pp. 227–228). No wonder, there were inconsistencies in the CII report on the issue of loans, as noted above under the mode 'Indexation of Bank Deposits and Advances'. He also had objections to the term "Profit/Loss Sharing," for he wanted it to be called just "Profit-sharing." Where the losses would fall can be seen from the first citation in this note. But then there he is talking only about financial losses, and does not recognize the loss of the *muḍārib's* unrewarded labor.

[36] Similar confusion is also found in Chapra (1985) who besides approving this position also argues that these ratios may be determined through custom. One could pursue the question of how Siddiqi's profit-sharing, a principal and agent situation *par excellence* given that the principal is supposed not to have any say as to how the business is run, would work in a market economy, but in view of the fact that market mechanism has hardly any role to play in this vision, one can perhaps leave that subject out at the moment.

be discerned relates to the stability of the system erected on the basis of profits/loss-sharing. The Panel was of the view that depositors should be protected through some sort of government guarantee, sort of a deposit insurance, a point that the hawkish group did not want to concede. For such, they thought, might compromise their insistence on loss-sharing. The final CII Report did accept the proposal with some reservations as is clear from the following words, "...the government may continue the guarantee at present provided to deposits of nationalized commercial banks for a transitional period of, say, two years", and is compelled to add: "However, this guarantee would be in the nature of a moral obligation on part of the government but it cannot be enforced legally." And this because, the Report continues, "In this connection it is pertinent to note that the underlying spirit of the Islamic system in so far as it pertains to investment is that any one who wishes to earn a profit in business should also accept the risk of loss. Therefore, this guarantee should be for a short period as recommended and should not be allowed to continue indefinitely" (p. 148).

What is interesting to note is the way the Report seems to feel compelled to somehow justify even this temporary recommendation. At the end of the foregoing citation, the Report adds a footnote (n. 6) to justify the recommendation. This footnote refers to the famous incident (described fully in Chapter 9) involving *qirāḍ* and Caliph ʿUmar's two sons as recorded in the *Muwaṭṭaʾ* of Mālik, from which the following conclusion is drawn: "Caliph Umer declared this transaction as *mudarabah* and recovered fifty percent of profit from them (his sons), which was paid to *Bayt al-Māl*. The Caliph took this decision not in the capacity of a lender but in that of a *Walī al-amr* (the Ruler). Hence, if the government provides the guarantee of this type in its capacity as a Walī al-amr, then it would not be in the nature of interest" (p. 148). One fails to understand what guarantee was provided by ʿUmar in that incident, for if there was any mention of the word guarantee, it was by ʿUbayd Allāh, one of his sons, who argued that they (the two brothers) were the guarantors of the loan had there been a loss in trading. And there is a total disregard of the fact that ʿUmar agonized over the issue before someone mentioned that it could be considered as a case of *qirāḍ* (and not *muḍāraba*, it must be noted), whereupon he reluctantly agreed to an idea that, surely because of its ready acceptance, was well known at the time. And he agonized about it not because he was instituting something new but about the propriety of giving a private loan from the public treasury, the *bayt al-māl*; subsequently he had to concede a similar loan to Hind, one of the wealthiest persons of the time. If what the Report makes of that incident appears to be a self-serving interpretation, wait until we come to what Usmani, another member of the hawkish sub-group, does with it, a little later.

The exclusive focus on profit-sharing is motivated by the possibility of "back-door" entry of interest into the system, an over-used term that, more than anything else, betrays a lack of confidence in what is promoted as a true Islamic vision of a financial system (no writing of this school of *fiqh* goes without expressing apprehensions about the back-door entry of interest). It is the difficulties of enforcing what this dominant group of *fiqh* writers proposes that always lurk at the back of their mind. When they cast a glance at the society around them, their homo-Islamicus, that social agent par excellence 'imbued' with the spirit of Islam, a vision they so dearly hold in their writings, was nowhere to be found. What they in fact saw could only be described as the "jungle out there," and it is in this jungle that they took on the onerous task of creating some sort of order. Little was realized, or at the very least acknowledged, that the jungle out there was primarily the result of a lack of enforcement of property rights motivated by the rent-seeking behavior of the government functionaries.

The attention of the dominant *fiqh* group in the process of Islamization was squarely fixed at the abolition of interest, for in their vision, once that was accomplished, and the "ideal" financial system put in place, all other problems would simply disappear from this new landscape. And this was to be achieved through the power of the state, through the government (a government that was part of the problem to begin with, in the light of what I have called the process of adverse selection in Chapter 3). If, in the changed circumstances, the government did not concur in this process, as happened in Pakistan, and tried to evade the enforcement of the new vision, it was to be hauled to the courts of law to ensure its compliance. All this was happening when the government of the day was regularly flouting the judicial orders with regard to enforcement of a number of existing laws, and there were massive regulatory failures, one after another, to say the least, in the financial sector of the economy as attested to by the scandals involving finance companies, cooperatives, prize bonds, and the Taj Company, to list only the prominent examples.[37] And all along, the eyes that were fixed on the issue of abolition of interest did not see that for most of the time under consideration, the real rate of interest, in the system inaugurated in 1980 under the CII Report with a financial system dominated by the banks that had been nationalized in the previous decade, was negative at least as far

---

[37] The finance companies scandal began in Karachi—historically a bastion of the dominant group, though by that time in the mid 1980s, a student leader was well on his way to wrestling political power from the group. The finance companies lured the simple-minded small savers to entrust their savings to them by offering exorbitant rates of interest (7% per month was not uncommon). From there, these companies mushroomed throughout Pakistan in a flash. For a short time, they paid the monthly dues from the funds so generated. Eventually, when the government could not help but take notice of what was going on, instead of nabbing the culprits unawares, started a campaign of warning the public through full-page advertisements in the newspapers. No wonder then that the culprits managed to flee the country; none could be apprehended. Were these cases referred to Interpol? The cooperative scandal a few years later was not any different, though this time some assets of these companies were seized, for they were not as illusive as the finance companies. Thereafter followed the prize bonds scandal in the mid 1990s. Prize bonds are an interest-free financing instrument used by the government, in which the prospect of winning a prize, through a lottery-like draw, serves as the bait. The ingenuity of some unscrupulous minds led them to begin selling shares in a bond (for example a hundred rupee bond would be split into 20 five-rupee allotments with the same number) with the promise that each holder would get one-twentieth of the prize if the corresponding number came up in the draw (it was not uncommon to sell much larger number of coupons bearing the same serial number than the twenty shares, as implied). The scandal lay not only in selling an indefinite number of *tickets*, as these were called, under a given prize bond number, but also converting the game into a pure lottery where the ticket money (say the five rupees) was not refundable. Thus if a person sold twenty 5-rupee tickets against a prize bond of Rs 100, he ended up swindling the amount (and perhaps much more than Rs 100) from others while retaining the original bond which could be returned to the government or sold for its face value of Rs 100. Outlets doing this business sprang up overnight in all parts of the country, skimming money from the poorest of savers who could not afford to buy even the lowest denominations of these bonds. When a massive number of the poorest of the poor were so skimmed, even the children of the poor sections were not spared from the sale of these tickets, and the situation became very precarious, the government woke up to shut these outlets down. But it is reported that the activity still goes on in some of the far-flung areas of the country. All this was topped by the Taj Company scandal, a company exclusively dealing in the printing and publication of Qur'ān. The company used to raise funds on profit-sharing basis—and many devoted Muslims were attracted to the proposition not only because they thought it saved them from dealing in *ribā* but also because of the noble business the company was engaged in, never suspecting that a company that engaged in that noble business could swindle them and that the perpetrators would disappear, again, into thin international air. And no less significant is the collapse of the Ihlas Finans, a Turkish Islamic finance house, in 2001, in which $1.3 billion of depositors' money was swindled by the owners of the company. For this last case, see Economist, 17 February 2001.

as the small depositors were concerned, and that the resulting financial repression, as a result of the implementation of the new vision, might have a lot to do with one scandal after another that became the defining characteristic of the time. Were any voices raised against these scandals by the dominant group? None whatsoever, for as far as this group was concerned, the more this alien financial system ran into trouble, the more support there would be for their vision of things to come.

This psychology was part of a mindset according to which Islam had nothing to do with whatever modernity had wrought, and thus the resulting social problems were not for them to address. And thus if the roads and streets become killing fields as a result of the lack of enforcement of the relevant rules and laws, it was all part of what the modernity had wrought. At the end of the day, it was the same government mindset that was to be relied upon to enforce their vision, through judicial orders if necessary, and never mind the fact that this government mindset was quite used to disregarding such orders whenever doing so was convenient and in the self-serving interests of the government functionaries. Although my focus is on Pakistan, for after all the whole drama of Islaimization was enacted on that stage, the situation was hardly any different in most of the other Islamic countries. Let us then return to the next act in that drama.

The report of the CII was implemented, in stages, beginning in 1980, and the process continued until the end of June 1985, by which time the Islamization of the banking system in line with the Report was complete. But even before the completion of that process, worries about "back-door" entry of interest through *bayʿ mūʿajjal* had been impressed upon the Council by the same sub-group that, as we saw, was not in its favor. On 20 June 1984, the State Bank issued a circular in which it enumerated twelve permissible modes of financing,[38] and thereupon the Council decided to review its position on *bayʿ mūʿajjal*, after which it disallowed its use by saying, "There is a genuine fear among Islamic circles that if interest is largely substituted by 'mark-up' [though the Council used the term *bayʿ mūʿajjal*, in practice it could

[38] These modes (BCD Circular No. 13) included: i) Loans on the basis of service charge; ii) *Qard-e-hasan*; iii) *bayʿ muʿajjal* or *murābaḥa*; iv) buy-back agreement [the famous ruse in the form of *bayʿ al-ʿīna*, as we saw earlier]; v) property development loans on service charge [= i]; vi) purchase of trade-bills; vii) leasing; viii) hire-purchase; ix) *mushāraka*; x) share-purchase; xi) participation term certificates and *Mūḍāraba* certificates; and xii) rent-sharing redeemable partnership.

not be distinguished from *murābaḥa*—which explicitly uses the term mark-up] under the PLS (Profit/Loss Sharing) operations, it would represent a change just in name rather than in substance. PLS under the mark-up system was in fact the perpetuation of the old system of interest under a new name." But the recommendation was not enforced by the government.

The Adjudication Dilemmas

However, the dominant group, which by this time had left the government, could not be that easily deterred. It now decided to approach the Sharīʿa Court, set up under the Islamization program by Ziaul-Haq. But it had to wait until 1989 in line with the constitutional provision enacted by Zia ul-Haq in 1979 under the auspices of the dominant *fiqh* group, according to which the fiscal laws of the country could not be challenged in the courts for the next ten years, presumably to protect his relevant Islamization enactments from any challenges, though as it paradoxically turned out, it was the dominant group itself that felt the need to mount such a challenge to the implementation of its own vision. Yet the challenge was delayed for a couple of years to ensure a suitable ambiance. For it was quite clear that once the matter came to the courts, things would become much more complicated. *Ribā* would now have to be precisely defined before any judgment on interest could be rendered. The opportunity arose when the former chairman of CII, Tanzilur Rahman, became the Chief Justice of the Sharīʿa Court. The hearing began in 1991, the verdict was rendered in November 1991, and the judgment published in early 1992.

In this judgment interest was unequivocally equated to *ribā*, and the mark-up system deemed the same thing as the interest system. In the mean time, in 1991, the government set up a commission, the Commission for Islamization of the Economy (CIE), to assess the permissibility of the various modes of financing consistent with the State Bank Circular, and the Commission submitted its report in 1992 (Report on Banks and Financial Institutions), upholding the *fiqh* permissibility of the mark-up mode, call it *bayʿ mūʿajjal* or *murābaḥa*.[39] It should

[39] This Commission had twelve members: the Governor of the State Bank of Pakistan (chairman), one *Sharīʿa* scholar, three politicians, one senior advocate of the Supreme Court of Pakistan, one retired civil servant, two economists, one chartered accountant, and two bankers, one of whom served as the secretary of the Commission.

not come as a surprise then that some time later the Commission was reconstituted under the chairmanship of a different person. This new Commission submitted its report in August 1997, but its findings on the issue of mark-up were not any different. After the Sharīʿa Court's judgment, the decision was appealed against in the Sharīʿa Appellate Bench of the Supreme Court of Pakistan, at the behest of the government. The hearing of the case, as we noted above, did not begin until 1999, until an opportune time, and thus the financial system continued to function in line with the State Bank circular. The case was taken up for hearing in February 1999, the verdict was rendered on 23 December 1999, and the judgment published in early 2000. The new judgment in one sense upheld the verdict of the earlier judgment but in another sense overturned it. It agreed with the definition of *ribā* that equated it with interest, but overturned the earlier decision regarding the impermissibility of the mark-up mode. However, in light of its acceptance of the equality of *ribā* to interest, it ordered a drastic overhaul of the existing laws. What is of direct interest to us in these two judgments is the definition of *ribā*, and we will turn to that subject in a short while. Before that we note a few details regarding the judgment and what transpired thereafter.

The bench delivered an 1,100-page judgment: the leading judgment (550 pages) was written by the Chief Justice, Khalil-ur-Rehman Khan, to which one of three other Judges, Munir A. Sheikh, concurred without any qualifications. The third Judge, Wajihuddin Ahmed endorsed the judgment but felt it necessary to add a lengthy note (98 pages) of his own. The fourth Judge, Muhammad Taqi Usmani, endorsed the judgment but felt compelled to present his own version of the judgment (250 pages), which he proudly published as a monograph entitled "Historic Judgment on Interest," a work already referred to, and to which we will return shortly.[40] This decision represented the culmination of the due process of law, but then it was once more appealed more or less at the end of the time period that the Judgment had specified for the revision of a whole set of laws, and surprisingly the Court accepted the appeal. This

It may be noted that five of the members thus selected were contributors to the CII Report.

[40] The Bench originally included another Judge, an ad-hoc member, Mahmood Ahmed Ghazi, who left in the middle of the hearings to take up another government assignment.

time the bench was comprised of the following judges: Shaikh Riaz Ahmad, Chief Justice of the Supreme Court; Munir A. Sheikh, who was a signatory to the previous judgment; Qazi Muhammad Farooq; Khalid Mahmood; and Rashid Ahmad Jallundari, the last two being ad-hoc members, as *fiqh* experts. The hearing began on 6 June 2002 and continued intermittently up to 22 June, and the Judgment was announced on 24 June. This time the court upheld the appeal, on the grounds that are presented a little later, and referred the original judgment back to the Sharīʿa Court for reconsideration and clarification, explicitly stating that any additional evidence will be admissible. (Interestingly one of the judges, rather paradoxically, was a signatory to both the judgments).

In the meanwhile, complying with an explicit directive given in the 1999 judgment, the government set up a commission to control and supervise the process of transformation of the financial system (Commission on Transformation of Financial System, but commonly known as the Hanafi Commission) under the chairmanship of Imtiaz A. Hanafi, at the time the Governor of the State Bank of Pakistan. The Commission submitted its 207-page report, just at the time of the new hearings, which endorsed, this time, only seven modes of financing, though including the mark-up mode, the *murābaḥa*.[41] It is noteworthy that by this time, CII's great expectations about *qarḍ ḥasan* becoming the workhorse of the Islamic financial system had evaporated, and there is no mention of it in the Hanafi Commission's report. Even Usmani (1999) does not care to mention it as a mode of finance in an Islamic economy. Equally though, the idea of financing on the basis of normal rate of return also disappeared, indeed it disappeared after the report of the CIE in 1992. Once *ribā* was equated with interest, it should not come as a surprise that none of the Commissions could contemplate dispensing with the mark-up mode. It replaced the classic *bayʿ al-ʿīna* as the leading *hīla* (ruse). It may be worthwhile at this stage to digress a little to explore its origins in *fiqh*.

We first note that *murābaḥa* is essentially a form of *bayʿ*, and the only thing that distinguishes it from other forms of *bayʿ* contracts, in

[41] The other approved modes included: ii) *mūsawama* (general sale on a stipulated price, whatever that meant); iii) *ijāra* and leasing; iv) *salam*; v) *mushāraka*; vi) *muḍāraba*; and vii) *istiṣnā* (same thing as *salam* but specific to situations where an order is placed for manufacturing of machinery or equipment, etc.

the words of Usmani, is "that the seller in *murābaḥa* expressly tells the purchaser how much cost he has incurred and how much profit he is going to charge in addition to the cost" (1999, p. 96). This in contrast to the other general category of *bay*ʿ, called *bay*ʿ *musāwama* in which no such information needs to be revealed. In the *fiqhī* conditions pertaining to *murābaḥa*, Usmani enumerates the following: "*Mūrābahāh* is valid only where the exact cost of a commodity can be ascertained" (p. 103). The important question now is if the buyer knows that he is to pay a higher price, and he also ascertains it, why would he not buy the commodity from the other seller from whom he had ascertained the price? In another place, Usmani (2000, p. 141) offers us the following gems as possible reasons: "the atmosphere of the shop of the seller is cleaner and more comfortable," the "seller is more courteous," the "seller is more trustworthy", and "the shop is nearer to the buyer". Unlike his exposition of the other modes of financing, at no place in his exposition of this mode does he provide any classical reference concerning its origins, or its exposition by any classical *fiqh* writer. As far as I am aware, Shafiʿī uses the term, probably in his Risāla. Amini (1975, p. 281) mentions it as one of the prevailing forms of *bay*ʿ in Arabia at the time of the Prophet, and implying that it was not prohibited by him contrary to a number of others that were. Yet it is a fact that we rarely hear about it in the classical *fiqh* writings, and it is not difficult to see that the disclosure requirements listed earlier would hardly make it a favorite form of business activity, particularly in the presence of the *salam* (now commonly known as *bay*ʿ *mūʿajjal*). So why has it been put right at the centre stage of Islamic finance, again in preference to the latter? The answer is not very difficult to imagine: it requires the financial institutions to disclose their mark-up unlike the *fiqh* protection against such disclosure as far as *bay*ʿ *mūʿajjal* is concerned. The fact remains that once it is brought to the field of finance from its natural *bay*ʿ habitat, it becomes a pure *hīla*, regardless of how many conditions, usually impractical—for they are notoriously difficult to enforce—its proponents may like to attach to it to avoid its misuse, or the backdoor entry of interest. It represents a back-door that cannot be closed without closing the front door. We now turn to some specifics of the famous *Ribā* Case.

At the 1999 hearings, the views of the opposing group of *fiqh* scholars were also presented. These views coincide with those described earlier in reference to Muhammad ʿAbduh, Rashīd Riḍā. Some of them were eminent: Muhammad Sayyid Tantāwī Abd al-Razzāq Sanhūrī, ʿAbd Allāh Draz (from Egypt), ʿAbd al-Wahhāb Khallāf, Marouf Daoualibi (from Syria), and Jafar Shah Phulwarwi, Syed Yaqub Shah, and Qadeeruddin Ahmed (from Pakistan). In the judgment, these views were dismissed. But what is interesting is that while the leading judgment by Khalil-ur-Rehman Khan records these views, Muhammad Taqi Usmani in his separate Judgment, does not even care to mention these names. These names are taboo as far as the dominant *fiqh* school is concerned, and their works are never referred to in fiqhnomics and Islamic economics. In the following discussion specific attention is paid to the position taken by the arch exponent of the dominant *fiqh* group on the subjects under consideration, Muhammad Taqi Usmani.

Consider the definition of the term *ribā*. Usmani abandons the classical *fiqh*'s *mujmal* framework by asserting that what the Qur'ān prohibited was so well understood that there was no need for it to provide a word by word definition of what was being prohibited. Not only that, he actually turns the classical *fiqh* discourse upside down by claiming that if there was any ambiguity, it related to *ribā al-faḍl*, i.e. *ribā al-ḥadīth*. Referring to the *ḥadīth* reports attributed to Caliph ʿUmar, he opines that a deeper study of these "reveals that he [ʿUmar] was doubtful only about the *ribā al-faḍl* mentioned in the *ḥadīth* cited above [actually the cited *ḥadīth* report does not use the word *al-faḍl*, for had it been so, there would not have been any ambiguity in the statement, and remember the term *ribā al-faḍl* does not belong to the Prophetic times], and not about the original *ribā* which was prohibited by the Holy Qur'an and as was practiced by the Arabs of *Jahiliya* in their transactions of loan and non-barter [?] sales" (2000, p. 43). If in this reading, he seems right to a point, it is thanks to Ibn Qayyim (d. 1350) who actually took the first daring step in this direction, in a story that we have narrated earlier up to the time of Rāzī. Realizing the problems of inconsistencies that *fiqh* had created for itself, Ibn Qayyim shifted the focus away from *ribā al-faḍl* to *ribā al-jāhiliyya*. This he did by introducing the strange concept of *ribā al-khafī*, i.e. hidden *ribā*. He argued that there is a *ribā al-jalīy*, the manifest *ribā*, which was the *ribā al-jāhiliyya*, or *riba al-nasī'a* (recall that the latter, which in its original formulation was one of the versions of *ribā al-ḥadīth*, had by the time of Rāzī become associated with *ribā al-jāhiliyya*), and, in contrast to that, *ribā al-faḍl* was actually *ribā al-khafī*.

As far as I can see, he was the first *fiqh* scholar who cast a doubt on *fiqh*'s approach to the issue of *ribā*, though one is surprised to find a mind like his introducing the concept of hidden-ness involving open transactions in which there could hardly be anything hidden. He must have thought this was the only route available to counter the historical weight of the relevant *fiqh* formulations.[42] Following that lead, Usmani emphasizes that if there was any *mujmal*-ness associated with the concept of *ribā*, it lay in *ribā al-ḥadīth*. But then he does not address the natural question as to why the centuries of classical discourse squarely hung on to the idea of *mujmal*-ness of the Qur'ānic term *ribā* down to the time of Ibn Qayyim in the 14th Century, and even thereafter to the present times at least in certain circles. For once we accept the new position, the entire classical discourse becomes redundant and irrelevant. So did he throw that discourse overboard? We shall seek an answer in what follows.

To begin with, let us turn to what he makes of the newly discovered clarity about what the Qur'ān prohibited. This issue can be pursued on two levels. First, what we can directly infer from the Qur'ānic verses, and second, what was the commonly understood meaning of the term *ribā*. This was the approach we followed in Chapter 9, and to avoid repetition, the reader is asked to recall that discussion. Usmani cites more or less all the reports cited there (Ṭabarī from Ibn Jurayj, Suyūtī, Ṭabarī again, but this time from Mujāhid, Mālik from Zayd bin Aslam, and Rāzī, in that order), but he opts to ignore that the *ribā al-jāhiliyya* was clearly related to the second parts of those reports, rather than the whole of them. In doing this, he actually follows Jassās, and that is why he ignores what Abduh and Riḍā had to say on the matter.

Thus his justification for asserting that the prohibition related to what was very well understood at the time is not quite true, and he is aware of this inconsistency, and that is why he turns to the verses in *sūra al-Baqara*. Being well-versed in Islamic sciences, he recognizes the futility of appealing to the late revelation of the verses in *sūra al-Baqara* to justify the classical *mujmal*-ness of the Qur'ānic term *ribā*,

[42] It may, however, be noted that in a fairly lengthy treatise Ibn Qayyim hardly devotes a page or so to this issue. See the Delhi edition (1367 AH), vol. I, p. 200.

particularly in view of the undisputed timing of the revelation of verse 3:130, and therefore rightly concludes that the prohibition, in accordance with 3:130, came around the second year of the Hijra at the time of the Battle of Uhud. But he decides to disregard the *aḍʿāfan muḍāʿafa* implications of that verse. He asserts that these words "are not intended to qualify the prohibition of *ribā* with doubling and redoubling. They are only meant to emphasize the added severity of the sin if the interest charged is so exorbitant or excessive. This intention of the verse of the Holy Qurʾan is quite evident in the light of the verse of *sūra al-Baqara* already quoted above" (p. 67). Therefore, he feels that verse 3:130 must be interpreted in the light of a verse (note: not the entire set of verses) of *sūra al-Baqara*.

But which verse is he referring to? His mindset could hardly be expected to connect *aḍʿāfan muḍāʿafa* to the straitened circumstances of the debtor, leading to consequences that might become increasingly difficult for the debtor to bear, as underscored in verse 2:280. Before we turn to that question, note the contradiction of what he says next with what he had said earlier about the ambiguity of *ribā al-faḍl*. He continues: "Secondly, the interpretation of the Holy Qurʾan should *always* be based on the explanation given by or *inferred* from the *aḥadīth* of the Holy Prophet and his noble *companions* who were the direct recipients of the revelation and were *fully familiar* with the context of the verse and the environment in which it was revealed. From this aspect as well, it is *certain* that the prohibition of *ribā* was never meant to be restricted to a particular rate of interest. The prohibition was meant to cover every amount charged in excess of the principal, however small it may be" (p. 67, emphasis added). Never mind what we are supposed to make of what he said about the ambiguity about *ribā al-faḍl* a little earlier).[43]

The verse he has in mind is 2:278, which admonishes believers to "give up whatever remains of *ribā*." He goes on to cite part of 2:279, which establishes the entitlement of creditors to the principal amount. He fails to point out the connection between charity and *ribā* emphasized in 2:276, and indeed which was the subject of the discourse that began with 2:262 and ended with 2:281; disregards the focus on straitened circumstances that are supposed to give rise to

[43] He goes on to cite a *ḥadīth* report from Tafsīr Ibn Abī Ḥātim, and says it is sufficient to prove the point.

ribā as noted in 2:280, and feels the meaning of the word *ribā*, that he needs to use in his translation of 2:278, is provided not by the exegetes but by an obscure *ḥadīth* report that he finds in the *Tafsīr* of Ibn Abī Ḥātim. The interesting, and rather pertinent, question now is that when he already had given the definition that he actually needed from Jassās, why did he now need to resort to a relatively unknown *Tafsīr* to find one to the same effect? Usmani realizes that Jassās's definition, coming from the first part of the relevant exegetical reports, would be subject to an easy demolition, and as such he must have felt the need for a reinforcement. This he found, but it is unlikely that a categorical statement on the prohibition of *ribā* could have gone unnoticed by all the Companions of the Prophet and the generations following them all the way down to his source in Ibn Abī Ḥātim.

After committing himself to that definition, and then laying great emphasis on the *ḥadīth* report reaching us through Bayhaqī, that "every loan that yields a profit to the creditor is *ribā*" (p. 70 in the Hyderabad edition, 1352 AH), one wonders how he will extract himself from all the reports about *qirāḍ*? It is here that we see a surprising lack of consistency and an evasion of the real issues. First, he manages to postpone a mention of the term for a long time, and when he eventually comes to it, he simply notes that *qirāḍ* (his *qiraz*) is an alternative term for *muḍāraba* (p. 121). Nevertheless, he is unable to avoid all the reports relating to *qirāḍ* without a loss of credibility. He cleverly uses the term commercial loans in its place when he comes to deal with them, but then avoids the issue of profit-sharing mechanism under such loans. He seizes on an unguarded presentation of one of the appeal lawyers, who argued that most of loans in the times of *jāhiliyya* were consumption loans, and spends pages refuting the argument, narrates the history of commercial credit in pre-Islamic Arabia, and then finally come to the relevant cases, and the way he manages to evade the real issue is quite fascinating. Consider the following cases in the light of what has already been noted about them in Chapter 9, and also keep in view what has been said earlier from Sarakhsī:

- The case of Zubayr ibn ʿAwwām: He states that Zubayr ibn ʿAwwām was one of the richest companions of the Prophet, etc. and that he used to invest peoples' money in trade, and concludes that "the manner in which he used to receive deposits and invest them in trade is very similar to a private bank" (isn't that wonderful, so the present day Islamic banks could learn a thing or two from his example, and operate on the same basis). But just when one thought he was going to tell us something about how that bank operated, he abruptly finishes by adding that "It is reported by Imam Bukhari that his liabilities toward his depositors were calculated, at the time of his death, to be two million and two hundred thousand, and all this amount was invested in commercial projects" (pp. 61–62).

- The Hind case: He states that she took a loan of 4000 dirhams from ʿUmar (no mention of *bayt al-māl* from where the money came) for trading, and concludes by saying, "She invested this money in purchasing goods and selling them in the market of the tribe of Kalb" (p. 62). So what happened to the rest of the story?
- The ʿAbd Allāh ibn ʿUmar and ʿUbayd Allāh ibn ʿUmar incident: He narrates the whole of the report from Mālik, and concludes that it was declared a *muḍāraba*, as though that term belonged to that period, and fails to note that even if we consider it as such, there was not to be any loss-sharing for that is what ʿUbayd Allāh implied when he said that "we [the two brothers] would have been liable to return the principal amount had there been a loss" (pp. 63–64).
- The ʿUthmān ibn ʿAffān case: He mentions the case, and concludes that it was not a consumption loan. So what happened to the profits earned if it was a commercial loan?

We may now turn to some of the other issues, including those relating to indexation, and the *ʿilla* versus *ḥikma* of *ribā* prohibition, and note that the court proceedings relating to the latter two are also covered where needed.

Beyond the Adjudication Dilemmas

On the whole, one may note that Usmani does not quite follow other writers of his group whose favorite line of argument, after they have disregarded the essential dimension of injustice associated with *aḍʿāfan muḍāʿafa*, and therefore verse 3:130—this is usually done by either not mentioning it at all, or starting the discourse with verse 2:275—is to focus on that part of verse 2:275 which responds to the question raised by the unbelievers that *ribā* is the same thing as *bayʿ*, whereby the Qurʾān says that these are two different things altogether.

This issue has been discussed in Chapter 9, but it would be fruitful to see how the modern discourse—which exclusively focuses on it—makes use of it. The inconsistencies of the modern discourse based on this distinction have been pointed out earlier in various places, yet it seems appropriate to touch on them to present a concise summary of the arguments. The modern *fiqh* discourse that emphasizes this distinction (not as an answer to a question raised by the Jews, as it was, but as a matter of distinction in principle), proceeds on the following assumptions: first, that a *bayʿ* contract is *ḥalāl*, and therefore it could not possibly involve an injustice (never mind if it may appear to be so), and second—and by the same token—that *ribā*, which of course is *ḥarām*, is essentially related to loan contracts, and is necessarily unjust regardless of whether we can infer the inherent injustice by using the faculty of our reason.

We come back to the issue of justice shortly when we take up the issue of indexation. Here we note that this line of argument would make sense only if we could make a clear distinction between the two forms of contracts under either a barter regime of exchange or a commodity money system. We have seen, both here and in the previous chapter in the context of *salaf* or for that matter *salam*, that under any of these systems it is not possible to draw a distinction between a loan contract and a *bayʿ* contract involving a time dimension. Classical *fiqh* wrestled with this problem, and eventually arrived at a very restrictive definition of loan in which the goods must be the same at both ends of the transaction. The modern discourse, regardless of the severance of its connection with the classical *fiqh* discourse, nevertheless feels it necessary to maintain a continuity with the classical tradition by noting that in a modern loan contract the required homogeneity condition is satisfied, for both sides of the contract involve money. This way paper currency is deemed to be at par with commodity money, namely gold and silver. Never mind that classical *fiqh* (all schools) excluded even a commodity such as *fulūs* (copper money) from the ambit of *ribā* prohibition.

The qualifying clause *aḍʿāfan muḍāʿafa* could be disregarded by the dominant group but could not be dismissed altogether. But since it was severed from its context, that is to say from the straitened circumstances of the debtor, its treatment posed additional difficulties. Here we will distinguish its treatment by the traditional *fiqh* writers on one hand and the dominant group on the other. The traditional writers, remaining faithful to the classical *bayʿ* framework, argue that once the price of a good has been determined, say in a *salam* or a *bayʿ mūʿajjal* contract, it could not be increased in the case of non-compliance with the payments as stipulated in the contract. Whether such non-compliance occurrs through willful default or straitened circumstances does not matter—the question is never posed, though admittedly those who sympathized with this position could read the straitened circumstances implied in the argument. And since paper money is just like *fulūs*, it can be sold at a higher price on deferred basis, but no further increase was to be allowed, for such would imply *aḍʿāfan muḍāʿafa*. But what happened thereafter is no concern of *fiqh*, or at least to the person issuing the *fatwā*—no enforcement worries need to be entertained, as we noted earlier.

When it comes to the dominant group of *fiqh* writers, it turns out to be an altogether different matter. They did not, and indeed could not, conceive of themselves as merely expressing a legal opinion. For they were trying to institute an entirely new system, a new paradigm, that was supposed to solve all humanity's ailments, including of course the economic ones. One must sympathize with the noble sentiment, but at the same time it must be pointed out that remedies cannot be advanced through wishful thinking or by hiding behind ruses. The ruse that dominated the Islamic financial system turned out to be the mark-up mode. These writers tried to erect fences around it, which need not detain us here, but experience showed them that the fences were too weak. Thereafter they tried to banish the mode from the system, but the weight of *fiqh* history would not allow this to happen, as we saw above. As regards the treatment of *aḍʿāfan muḍāʿafa* in this new system, they follow the same approach as followed by the traditional *fiqh* writers up to the point of non-compliance. The pertinent issue for the viability of the system was what was now to be done in the case of non-compliance, or in the modern familiar terminology: what was to be done in the case of a default. The default could be due to either genuine economic hardship—straitened circumstances—or it could be willful. Since in their framework *aḍʿāfan muḍāʿafa* is not connected to straitened circumstances, their attention could not turn to the issue of genuineness or otherwise of the case; for them it was all the same. It may be noted that when at times these writers do acknowledge default, they do so under the modern bankruptcy conceptualization, and not under *fiqh*'s *hijr* provisions: indeed the term *hijr* never occurs in these writings.

In his other publication, Usmani (1999, pp. 131–40), goes over the issue. Briefly this is how the argument proceeds: it will not be a problem in countries where all financial institutions are run on Islamic principles because "the government may develop a system where such defaulters may be penalized by depriving them from obtaining any facility from any financial institution"; however, such a solution is not possible where "majority of the financial institutions run on the basis of interest," because the defaulter "can approach the conventional institutions" (as though those other institutions are always heedless of the credit worthiness of their clients). He records that some of the contemporary scholars have suggested that the deliberate defaulters "should be made liable to pay compensation to the Islamic bank for the losses it may have suffered on account of default," and that such amount "may be equal to the profit given by the bank to its depositors during the period of default" but this concept of compensation "is not accepted by the majority of the present day scholars, including the author,"[44] because it "neither conforms to the principles of *Shariah* nor is it able to solve the problem of default" because such an "additional amount charged from a debtor is *riba*"; and though a grace period may be permitted in the cases of genuine hardship, this will be difficult in practice "because every debtor may claim that his default is due to his financial inability" (recall what I said about the *fiqh* dilemma of coming to grips with the cases of genuine default); and then goes on to conclude his argument by saying: "Obviously, insolvency is a rare phenomenon, and in this rare situation, even the interest-based banks cannot normally recover interest from the borrower. Therefore, the suggestion leaves no *practical and meaningful* difference between an interest based financing and an Islamic financing" (the added emphasis need to be kept in view when reading his solution a little later).

He presents a confused discussion in which he suggests that the imposed penalty on the defaulters will amount to a private penalty, for it is supposed to be imposed by the bank (as though no property rights,

[44] He refers to Resolution no. 53, 5th Annual Session of the Islamic Fiqh Academy, Jeddah, in support of this position. These sessions represent the assembly of the like-minded, and the resolutions thus passed are then presumed to have a binding force for all Muslims as though such a course of action is rooted in *Sharīʿa*, or has some democratic legitimacy.

or laws existed on the subject—a reflection of the same mindset of *fiqh* as pointed out a little earlier); and that if such a penalty is based on what the bank paid to the depositors, it will encourage default.[45] He further asserts that the imposition of such a penalty will amount to recognizing the concept of opportunity cost of money (not finance!),[46] after which he uses *qiyās* to sum up his position and offers us the following pearls of wisdom: "The one who defaults in payment of debt is, at the most [what is the least?], like a thief or usurper [note the blatant disregard of the possible straitened circumstances, and as though every instance of usurpation could be deemed theft]. But the study of the rules prescribed for theft and usurpation would show that a thief has been subjected to very severe punishment of amputating his hand, but he was never asked to pay an additional amount to compensate the victim of theft. *Similarly*, if a person usurped the money of another person, he may be punished by way of *taʿzīr* [he means amputation of hand], but no Muslim jurist has ever imposed on him a financial penalty to compensate the owner" (pp. 135–136, emphasis). No comments need be added, except that by imposing amputation on the defaulter, he gives the impression of being charitable to the defaulter; after all he saves him from a financial penalty through a mere amputation of one of his hands!

But then he feels a bit troubled by that solution, and goes on to offer an alternative one to this vexing problem, which he says is derived from the opinions of "some Maliki jurists" and in which the "debtor *may* undertake to give some amount in charity in case of

[45] This, in his thinking, is because the rate of profit earned by a bank's borrowers will be higher than the rate paid by the bank to depositors, and this will encourage the *murābaḥa* clients to renege on their payments in order to pay a lower rate as penalty, as though the penalty rate could not possibly be equal to what the bank was supposed to receive from those borrowers, which needless to say would be more realistic in view of the intermediation costs.

[46] In his Judgment, he tries his hand at economics. He thinks money is purely a medium of exchange and nothing else. Though he records Ghazālī's (d. 1111) views on the matter (pp. 91–93), in which one can clearly discern him also emphasizing the unit of account function, as well as a store of value function (his conceptualization is that it is a generalized purchasing power). He fails to notice the store of value function, the crucial one as far as finance is concerned. He introduces a concept around which he weaves his argument in the economic analysis portion of the judgment, the concept of *intrinsic* utility (in the present context, of money), whatever that means!

default" (but why would a willful defaulter opt for such an undertaking to begin with?), and continues that, "this is, in fact, a sort of *Yamin*, a vow, which is a self-imposed penalty to keep oneself away from default. Normally, such vows create a moral or religious obligation and are not enforceable through courts. However, some Maliki jurists allow [he means they leave room for him to maneuver] to make it justifiable, and there is nothing in the Holy Qur'an or in the *Sunnah* of the Holy Prophet which forbids making this vow enforceable through the courts of law," but then no part of this penalty should accrue as "income of the bank in any case, nor can it be used to pay taxes or to set-off any liability of the financier" [the bank, but presumably also its depositors], but since the penalty "is not deserved by the financier as his income" it must go to a charity. And since it is supposed to go to charity, "it may be any amount willfully [sic, he means willingly] undertaken by the debtor," and "it can also be determined on *per cent per annum basis*" (p. 139, emphasis added). Thereafter he gives a sample wording of this self-undertaken vow, but which is now to be enforced through the courts of law. But the financial institutions and their depositors are not entitled to these proceeds, proceeds that accrue because their funds have been blocked, for these proceeds represent something which is *ḥarām* (*ribā*) as per his interpretation of *aḍʿāfan muḍāʿafa*, an interpretation which runs diametrically opposite to the Qur'ānic conceptualization, essentially linking it to the straitened circumstances of the debtor. These are to be used for the noble cause of charity, and thus while the owners of the funds are saved from the vagaries of *ḥarām*, it is alright for the poor charity recipients to consume that *ḥarām* income![47]

At this juncture, it may be useful to summarize the developments in Pakistan's financial sector in light of the various modes of financing recommended by different commissions. The financial system in Pakistan has come to be constructed on what is known as the "mark-up" system, which in turn is supposed to be based on the

[47] As a result of this line of reasoning, this *fiqh* school is quite comfortable, for never a word is uttered against these practices, with 11.3% and 10% monthly fines (surcharges) imposed by the government owned utilities (electricity and gas respectively) in Pakistan. In annualized terms, these penalty rates turn out to be 260% and 214% respectively, but then it is comforting to know that we are saved from the vagaries of interest! And no need to guess which charity this money goes to.

contractual arrangement known as *murābaḥa*. But *murābaḥa* alone could not serve the purpose of financing that a business required, for there is no inherent stipulation of deferred payment in that contract. For instance, a bank could import a machine and sell it to a business at a mark-up of 10%, but that is not what a business requires. If it has the investment so needed, it will import the machine itself at a cost 10% lower than what it will end up paying to the bank. In light of this problem, *murābaḥa* was now combined with *bayʿ mūʿajjal* so that the necessary finance could be provided to the business and the higher price would now have to be paid in installments over an agreed period of time. In light of its similarity to the interest-based arrangement, much was made of the *fiqh* stipulation that the machine, or whatever wares, must come under the possession of the bank, even for a moment. This was supposed to satisfy the requirement that the bank is undertaking a risk to justify the return that it would receive through the marked-up price. It is, however, clear that such financing could be worked out only for physical capital (or merchandizing), and a number of other arrangements such as leasing could equally be used for this purpose, and a fixed return would be perfectly permissible in those instances as we saw in Chapter 8. What is noteworthy is that such arrangements could not be used to satisfy the circulating capital requirements of a business. It is in light of this difficulty that Siddiqi insisted on profit-sharing arrangement through *muḍāraba*. But we know from the above discussion that *muḍāraba* is not only controversial but creates more problems than it solves. In the end, the arrangement that worked satisfactorily turned out to be what was called the "mark-up" system in which the possession requirements of *murābaḥa* were ignored for all practical purposes. When all is said and done, one may ask what is the *practical and meaningful* difference between the interest-based financing and the mark-up system based on *murābaḥa* and *bayʿ mūʿajjal*? It is all a matter of words rather than substance, and that is what *ḥiyāl* (ruses) are all about.

The Issue of Indexation

Let us now turn to the issue of indexation. It is here that the modern *fiqh* discourse faced the real challenge to its ingenuity, for no explicit guidance was to be had on the issue from the classical sources down to modern times. For the necessary condition (the existence of paper money), which occasions the problems addressed by indexation, could not by definition exist under a commodity money regime. The same would logically be true under a paper money regime that was backed by a commodity such as gilt, a standard the world more or less adhered to from the introduction of paper money to the latter half of the twentieth century. But as the world entered the pure paper standard, as a result of the erosion of gold backing and its eventual elimination from the greenback in 1971, the issue of indexation became crucially important, at least in principle, if not in practice, the latter to the extent that achieving a stable value of paper currency was maintained as an overriding policy goal in a particular country. One would recognize that the issue of indexation would not assume a serious dimension in an all-equity economy as far as financial sector transactions are concerned. This is because an increase in goods prices would be accompanied by an increase in equity prices, and in that case one may ignore the issue of indexation from the point of view of financial (this time, equity) transactions, but at the pain of ignoring the specific re-distributional effects arising out of relative price changes. But an Islamic economy is not necessarily an all-equity economy, for we know debt financing, and the accompanying hypothecation (*rahn*) of assets, are permissible in the original sources of Islamic jurisprudence, namely the Qur'ān (2:283) and *Hadīth.* As a result, *fiqh* could hardly escape addressing the question, and thereby providing the necessary guidance. But when it came to responding to the challenge, *fiqh* found itself in a quandary, and at a loss for words. But the exponents of Islamic economics, or fiqhnomics are supposed to know better. It was here that they were supposed to help *fiqh* get out of its real, or commodity, money framework and extend its scope to the pure paper standard. This task could not be expected to be easy in light of the rigidity of *fiqh* exponents. No wonder, then, that some of the most heated exchanges in the gatherings of Islamic economics occurred when the issue came under discussion.

Unfortunately, if *fiqh* did not acquit itself well on this count, it was once again because of its concern with that back-door entry of interest. In a sense its exponents always felt as though they had been left alone in trying to guard something precious in a house, encircled by a sea of malcontents who were constantly pushing and shoving at the doors—no need to guess who these malcontents were supposed to be. And they did not have the wherewithal to guard the two entry points at the same time. It was the door in the dark back alley that was always thought to be more vulnerable. Leaving aside this world of parables, let us look at what the defenders had to say on the issue. The first reaction, and a rather hasty one, came in the CII Report cited earlier. Let us read what it had to say in this context: "Under *Shariʿah* [more appropriately *Fiqh*], currency transactions [read transactions involving gold and silver to the exclusion of fulūs] are not treated differently from commodity transactions [keep in mind that it is talking about commodity money] in as far as lending and borrowing are concerned [and recall the context in which *bayʿ* transactions could hardly be set apart from loan transactions, notwithstanding the later *fiqh* refinements setting them apart]. The basic principle is that the same quantity, or units, should be returned as were borrowed [making it a *qarḍ*, and not *salam*, following the later *fiqh* refinements] even though the price of the commodity may have changed in the meantime [note that price is immaterial as long as what is returned is the same good, the real value of which remains unchanged]. For example, if one *maund* [a measure of weight] of wheat has been borrowed, the borrower will have to return one *maund* of wheat even though the price of one *maund* of wheat may have risen from Rs 30 to Rs 50 per *maund* or fallen to Rs 15." So far so good, but then from there, it extrapolates to arrive at the conclusion: "Similarly, if the borrowing consisted of a specified amount of money, say Rs 1000 [as though a switch from real money to paper money must be inconsequential], the borrower will have to repay the same amount of money even if the value of rupee in terms of other goods and services [due to inflation primarily as a result of a change in the supply of money by the government] may have changed during the period" (p. 116). So we are supposed to suspend reason altogether in the name of Islam, the Islam which categorically insists on the protection of *rāʾs al-māl*, even in the case of a genuine default, under the fundamental imperative of justice: *lā tuẓlāmūna wa lā tuẓlāmūn*, as we saw in the previous chapter.

As far as Islamic economics is concerned, the issue could be ignored as far as equity financing, and therefore profit-sharing was concerned, but it could not be evaded when it came to *qarḍ* (call it an interest-free loan, if you like), or *qarḍ ḥasan* (which is the same thing), or the special loan facility. In light of what the CII said, it is not surprising to see Islamic economists offering flimsy apologies to defend CII position such as: that if there is inflation, it is not the "fault of the borrower," or perhaps the cost of inflation can be "shared equally by the two parties," or that a person who has advanced a *qarḍ* to help his brother would "not mind bearing the cost of inflation," etc. When one Islamic economist suggested that the interest-free bank deposits may be indexed according to the rate of inflation to protect their real value, the proposal was shot down for "it will open the floodgates to interest," and that it "gives a privilege to the lender which the one who decides to hold his money does not enjoy" (all citations from Siddiqi, 1983a, p. 44).[48] As far Siddiqi concerned, hoarding (which is strictly a leakage from the circular flow) and savings entrusted to a financial intermediary are the same things. Being an economist, he should have been more cautious, but then he must have felt obliged to close the backdoor, a door that this time will also let the flood waters in.

Two decades later, when the issue came under formal legal scrutiny in the 1999 hearings at the Sharīʿa Appellate Bench, the court in its leading Judgment noted that it is a "complicated issue" in view of the fact that sometimes the rate of inflation may exceed its "natural limit" [on what that limit would be, the court had nothing to say], and it argued that in the case where the rate of inflation remains within its natural limits, nothing needs to be done and "all transactions, payment and repayment will have to be made on the basis of its face value". But when the rate of inflation goes beyond its natural limit, "and enters the province of hyper-inflation," it will be taken to cause "*Ghaban Fahish* [which it translates as: excessive loss] to the creditor," and therefore "steps should be taken for the protection of the rights of the creditor. Here, the principle developed by the jurists in respect of *fulūs* seems to be applicable. They have concluded that if the circulation of the copper coins is stopped or the value of the *fulūs* substantially falls as compared to their face value, they will lose their status as medium of exchange and stock of value and will no more be considered as *Thaman Istilahi* or legal tender. In such a case the original value of the *fulūs* as prevalent at the time of the transaction shall have to be paid" (p. 490, and recall our discussion with regard to *fulūs* earlier). According to this explanation, the paper money will have to lose its status as legal tender before any compensatory action could be taken. Never mind by whom; for such a situation will be result of an irresponsible increase in the supply of money by the government to begin with.

[48] However, not all Islamic economists concur with Siddiqi on this score.

Usmani, on the other hand, did not quite agree with this principle, reads the court proceedings somewhat differently, and in his own version of the judgment begins by noting that "some appellants have tried to justify the interest charged and paid by the banks on the ground that since the value of money is decreasing constantly, the interest should be taken as a compensation for the erosion of the value of money during the period of borrowing. The financier, according to them, should have a right to claim at least the same amount in real terms as he had advanced to the borrower," and concludes that "this argument is without force because the rates of interest are thought as a major cause of inflation among other factors, they are not based on rate of inflation," and continues that "this suggestion is not practical so far as the banking transactions are concerned. The reason is obvious. The concept of indexation of loans is to give the real value of the principal to the financier based on the rate of inflation, and therefore, there is no difference between depositors and borrowers in this respect. It means that the bank will receive from its borrowers the same rate as it will have to pay its depositors" (as though borrowers and depositors are the same individuals, or, perhaps more likely in view of his following conclusion, as though the borrowing and lending rates are the same), and this naturally leads him to conclude—without realizing that in that case no bank can survive, indexation or not—that, "nothing will be left for the banks themselves, and no bank can be run without a profit" (pp. 113–15). Having dismissed indexation as far as the banking system is concerned, he softens up a bit, and notes that "however, the question of erosion of the value of money is certainly relevant to the individual loans and unpaid debts." He does not say whether he is concerned about interest-free loans (one can surmise that he is, but then what about the interest-free loans by the banks?), and notes that "several suggestions have been offered by various quarters such as i) indexation; ii) loans tied to gold; iii) loans tied to a hard currency like dollar; iv) apportioning of the loss between the borrower and the lender on half and half basis" (both citations from p. 116). Thereafter, he arrives at the following interesting conclusion: "having held that this question does neither justify interest nor provides a substitute for it in the banking transactions, we do not have to resolve this issue in this case, nor does the decision about the laws under challenge depend on it. We, therefore, leave the question open for further study and research"

(p. 117). And he conveniently remarks that bodies such as CII and CIE may deliberate on this issue.

As noted, the 1999 Judgment was once again appealed, the hearings were held in June 2002, and the verdict upholding the appeal, and thereby remitting the case back to the Sharīʿa Court, was announced on 24 June 2002. The court notes a number of weaknesses in the earlier judgments: "there are errors floating on the surface of record," and *inter alia* points out that "banks in Pakistan are working within the framework of banking instruments prescribed by the State Bank, with the approval of the CII, as valid Islamic instruments"; that "the bank interest does not fall under the *ribā* prohibition as per an alternative juristic opinion" (and refers to the names of those writers we have noted earlier); that "apart from *mūshārakāh*, all other modes are *hiyāl*"; and that "the injustice in the relevant transaction was not considered as the effective cause, *ʿillah*, in defining *ribā*." Interestingly, the court saw it fit to record the following observations from one of the appeal lawyers in these words: "He [the lawyer] contended that he had raised at least 33 propositions in the course of the hearings, which were not attended to by the Sharīʿa Appellate Bench. He argued that the judgment of the Federal Sharīʿa Court is biased inasmuch as Mr. Justice Dr. Tanzilur Rahman, C.J. had delivered the judgment with a predetermined mind because while delivering the judgment he had placed reliance on a report of the Council of Islamic Ideology of which he happened to be the chairman at the relevant time...The Sharīʿa Appellate Bench also proceeded to rely upon the said report and the writings of Dr. Tanzilur Rahman" (from the Short Order of the court published in various Dailies). In October of the same year, the issue of bank interest's connection with *ribā* was referred to the Rector of Al-Azhar University, Muhammad Sayyid Ṭanṭāwī, who issued a *fatwā* on 2 December 2002. I have thought it appropriate to record the relevant portions of the *fatwā* in the Appendix to this chapter for the interested reader.

Concluding Observations

In the following summing up, specific attention will be paid to the rationale (*ḥikma*) for the prohibition of *ribā*, and *fiqh*'s conceptualization of the *ʿilla* of its prohibition. It should not come as a surprise to see from the way *fiqh* evolved, which is to say the way it developed a framework in which the question of *ribā* prohibition focused squarely on *bay*ʿ contracts—and thereby the way its discourse centered around defining *bay*ʿ contracts in such a way that they would not cross the permissibility limits—that its formulation of the required *ʿilla* would be geared precisely to accomplish that objective. And this discourse began its journey at a time when a *bay*ʿ contract could not be quite effectively set apart from a loan contract. And with the passage of time when it had to confront the issue of pure loan as a distinct contract, *fiqh* defined the loan contract in such a way as to make it consistent with its framework, and called it *qarḍ*, and after having done that agonized over the issue of *qirāḍ*. It eventually, ended up transforming the latter into a conceptualization that predominantly came to be known as *muḍāraba*. In this way, it accomplished the following: first, a *bay*ʿ contract could not be deemed as a *qarḍ* contract, even when it led to debt, and a *qarḍ* contract could not be called a *bay*ʿ contract, and even when the initial principal amount was the same in both the cases, these two led to different amounts of debt. And second, the debt arising out of *qirāḍ* could be pushed aside under the rubric of profit and loss-sharing. The *ʿilla* of *ribā*, therefore, became any nominal increase over the principal amount but only in what would be deemed a *qarḍ* contract.

And this precisely represents the dilemma that the modern discourse faces, for it wishes to proudly carry the weight of history, but has to deal with an institutional setting that is drastically different from the institution of moneylending (which formed the essential back-drop to the classical discourse), in which the fundamental issue is how to make use of a large proportion of savings generated by small savers so that these will not remain buried under mattresses, so to speak, and are used for the betterment of the society. The Qurʾānic focus on justice now needs to be articulated in a setting where the surplus units (call them lenders, savers, depositors or what have you), could be, as indeed they are in reality, relatively less well-off as compared to the deficit units (call them borrowers, investors, entrepreneurs, or whatever). It is in the performance of this task that *fiqh*, and fiqhnomics, is found lacking, regardless of the rhetoric to the contrary, particularly in the writings in the latter genre. But this rhetoric, good at swaying sentiments, as rhetoric is supposed to do, could not escape coming under a closer scrutiny, as happened in the *Ribā* Case. But how well the judgment that emerged took cognizance of this scrutiny given the proceedings in the court, we will see in a moment.

It is noteworthy that *fiqh* has always found it difficult to establish a connection between the injustice, which is the *raison d'etre*, or *ḥikma*, of *ribā* prohibition and what it defined as the effective cause, the *ʿilla*, of enforcing the prohibition. Generally one would expect the *ʿilla* of a particular legal injunction to be rather unequivocally related to the rationale behind the legal injunction. We recall from Chapter 9 that the Qurʾān is absolutely clear about the rationale behind its prohibition of *ribā*, for it contrasts the virtue of charity with the evil of *ribā*, *ribā* which essentially arises out of the straitened circumstances of the debtor, circumstances that are beyond the control of the debtor. And beyond that, in light of the sanctity of private property that it enunciated, it protected the rights of the creditor even when the debtor was in straitened circumstances, though it ordained that an easing time must be granted to him to discharge his obligations, and beyond that it recommended that the debt may be forgiven as an act of charity, which means that it did not impose the forgiving as incumbent upon the creditor, if nothing else, in view of the human frailty. It was to be a voluntary charity, an act of *ihsān*, which was not to be legally imposed upon the creditor. The reasons why *fiqh* could not establish a connection between the *ʿilla* and the *ḥikma* are not difficult to see in light of our discussion here and Chapter 9. At this point, we may only recall that it was the severance of the essential connection between *aḍʿāfan muḍāʿafa* and the straitened circumstances of the debtor (and thereby classical *fiqh*'s assumption that the Qurʾānic term *ribā* was "*mûjmal*," which needed to be expounded through *qiyās* by relying on the evidence that came through the relevant *ḥadīth* reports), that led to the difficulties. For *fiqh*, *ʿilla* was all that it needed to focus on to discharge its juridical obligations.

In a sense, then, it is surprising that *fiqh* would even address the issue of *ḥikma* at all, as Rāzī did, though only after a passage of five centuries, towards the end of the twelfth century. But then he was not just a *fiqh* scholar. The reasons (i.e. the rationale for the prohibition) that he offered, and those were listed earlier in this chapter, have often been noted by the modern *fiqh* discourse. There was also another, more important, reason for the modern discourse to take this issue into consideration, and that had to do with its abandoning of the classical "*mujmal*" framework. Once the "mujmal-ness of the Qurʾānic term *ribā*" hypothesis had been forsaken, the *fiqh* now had to derive the rationale of the prohibition from the relevant Qurʾānic verses that formed the pivot of its explanation, and connect it to the *ʿilla* of prohibition. This proved difficult.

To put the matters in another way, we can see that since it could not shed the weight of history, it could not proceed through a straight forward linking of the *aḍʿāfan muḍāʿafa* to the straitened circumstances of the debtor. A search then led it to a part of verse 2:275 which answers a question raised by the unbelievers about *bayʿ* being the same thing as *ribā*. If the Jews of Medīna mischievously asked a nasty question, they were bound to receive an equally stern answer, in the form of a snippet in the middle of the verse. They knew well what they were asking, and they knew exactly what they got back. The modern discourse has used that answer on the one hand to sanctify *bayʿ* contracts, as though no *bayʿ* contract, even if we consider only the *fiqh*-approved ones, could ever be unjust, and on the other to assume that every loan that gave rise to a pre-determined fixed return is *ribā*, regardless of whether we are able to discern any injustice in it. Thus we are told that a loan that yields interest is unjust because no counter value is returned in lieu of interest, and thus it reduces the debtor to poverty in Rāzī's terms, without adding that Rāzī was actually explaining the Qurʾānic *ribā*, which he called *ribā al-nasīʾa*, and without any regard to the fact that this argument cannot be advanced in an unqualified manner in the context of the modern institutionalized credit. There may be pensioners and widows among the low-income depositors who may depend upon the returns earned on their life-time savings to make ends meet. We are also told that interest income is an unearned income. The creditor is conceived of as having no past, his money thus comes as manna from heaven, and since he himself has no opportunity to invest his money, he should not be entitled to any return on this manna unless he accepts the risk of loss, regardless of the fact that someone may be quite willing to pay him out of the profits earned through the utilization of this manna, and regardless of the fact that the borrower may be endowed with more of the same manna than the lender. And we are told that the prohibition is meant to encourage charity in provision of interest-free loans, never mind if the beneficiaries of that charity may happen to be much richer than the givers.

Thus when the issue came under scrutiny in the court hearings, as it was bound to, small wonder that the court, even after being forced to take notice of the afore-mentioned points, decided to ignore them all the same and came to the conclusion that it is a mistake to argue that the rationale of the *ribā* prohibition is the elimination of injustice (*ẓulm*) following verse 2:279 (p. 467). Usmani, in his part of the judgment, did not leave it at that. With regard to the use of human reason in determining the rationale of prohibition, he notes that "*zulm* (injustice) is a relative and rather ambiguous term the exact definition of which is very difficult to ascertain. Every person may have his own view about what is or what is not *zulm*"(p. 82), and "whenever the Holy Qur'an and *Sunnah* gave a specific command or prohibition in these areas, they did not rely on the rational assessment of the people, nor did they leave these transactions at the *mercy of human reason* to decide whether or not they have an element of *zulm*", and that "the Holy Qur'an and *Sunnah* were cognizant of the fact that human reason, despite its wide capabilities, cannot claim to have unlimited power to reach the truth" (p. 86, emphasis added). Thus he requires us to suspend our God-gifted faculty of reason in such matters despite the fact that the Qur'ān exhorts us in numerous places[49] to do precisely the opposite, and at one stage actually admonishes us not to abandon reason when reading what God has sent down in words (in a *sūra* that is appropriately named *al-Furqān*—The standard of true and false) that are blindingly clear about their purport: "And (know that true servants of God are only) those who never bear witness to what is false, and (who), whenever they pass by (people engaged in) frivol-

[49] The Qur'ān uses two words in this context; *taʿqilūn* (or *yaʿqilūn*), from *ʿaql* (the mental faculty of reasoning, and therefore those who use this faculty); and *tafakkarūn*, from *fikr* (reflection, and therefore those who reflect). The Qur'ān uses '*taʿqilūn* in at least 35 different verses scattered throughout its length, and *tafakkarūn* at another 10 places. These verses, along with the *diverse* contexts in which it exhorts us to use our reason, are: 2:164 (nature, cosmos); 2:164 (social relations); 3:65 (addressed to believers in earlier revelations); 3:118 (caution against enemies); 5:103 (shirk); 6:32 (worldly life); 6:151 (social relations); 7:169 (prevailing attitude of the Jews); 8:22 (cited above, in what follows); 10:16 (general, addressed to Makkans); 10:100 (faith, blessing of God); 11:51 (general, addressed to People of ʿĀd); 12:2 (Qur'ān revealed in your tongue so that you may understand it); 12:109 (general, addressed to Makkans); 13:4 (nature, i.e. *Sunnat-Allāh*); 16:12 (cosmos); 21:10 (Qur'ān containing all that you ought to bear in mind); 21:67 (what Abraham said to his people, about shirk); 23:80 (omnipotence of God); 24:61 (family and social relations); 26:28 (Moses' admonition to Pharaoh); 28:60 (ephemeral nature of worldly life); 29:35 (the doings of the people of Lot); 29:63 (Nature: the renewal of life on earth); 30:24 (same as the previous verse); 30:28 (nature, cosmos, His creative power; culminating verse of a lengthy discourse); 36:62 (in context of Satan leading people astray); 36:68 (human life as a gift); 37:138 (destruction of the people of Lot); 39:43 (shirk); 40:67 (stages in the creation of human life, growth of the embryo); 45:5 (nature); 49:4 (etiquettes in addressing the Prophet); 57:17 (natural renewal of life on earth); 59:14 (addressed to hypocrites of Madīna). For *tafakkarūn*: 2:266 (exhortation for charity); 6:50 (Prophetic missions); 7:176 (addressed to unbelievers in general); 13:3 (nature, life on earth); 16:11 (same as the previous verse); 16:44 (clarity of Qur'ānic message, addressed to the believers in previous revelations); 16:69 (God's bounties through nature); 39:42 (God's power over life and death); 45:13 (God's bounties through nature); 59:21 (Qur'ānic parables).

ity, pass on with dignity; and who, whenever they are reminded of their Sustainer's messages, do not throw themselves upon them (as if) blind and deaf" (25:72–73). And equally sternly at another place: "Verily, the vilest of all creatures in the sight of God are those deaf, those dumb ones who do not use their reason" (8:22). To not push the human reason in an attempt to grasp the ultimate metaphysical truths, *a lā* Ghazālī is one thing, but to abandon the use of reason in determining justness, or otherwise, in social dealings, the *muʿāmalāt*, is quite another. But then, having said all that, a few pages later Usmani continues, "A detailed account of the *rationale* of the prohibition of *riba* would, in fact, require a separate volume, but for the purpose of brevity we would concentrate on three aspects of the issue" (p. 89, emphasis added). Thereafter he devotes 28 pages of his incoherence in the name of economic reasoning, covering areas such as the nature of money, and the effect of interest on allocation of resources and distribution of income, to convince us that interest must be *replaced by profits* (as though this would by itself make any significant difference in the economic outcomes, a point extensively explored in economic theory—recall our discussion in Chapter 4) to save mankind from, what according to the "wide capabilities" of his reason, would be an unmitigated disaster. And beyond that, does he have anything to say on the excesses of capitalism, in which the financial institutions, and not the depositors, are the main players, as we noted in Chapter 4? Not a word.

One must not be too enamored with human frailty for, according to the Qurʾān man was created weak, provided such a frailty does not claim for itself a position of self-righteousness. In light of what has gone so far in this work, I would end by noting what Schuon, notwithstanding the excesses of his Shankerian metaphysics, had to say on the issue of human margins;

> Christ, in rejecting certain rabbinical prescriptions as 'human' and not 'Divine', shows that according to God's measurement there is a sector which, while being orthodox, and traditional, is none the less human in a certain sense; this means that the Divine influence is total only for the Scriptures and for the essential consequences of the Revelation, and that it always leaves a 'human margin' where it exerts no more than an indirect action, letting ethnic or cultural factors have the first word. It is to this sector or margin that many of the speculations of exoterism belong. Orthodoxy is on the one hand homogeneous and indivisible; on the other hand it admits of degrees of absoluteness and relativity…What is surprising in most cases, though not always equally so, is the vehement desire to pin

> oneself and others down on questions which are not of crucial importance, and the incapacity to allow a certain latitude as regards things which the Revelation did not deem it indispensable to be altogether precise about" (1976, pp. 36–37).

In the next chapter I sum up the arguments with a view to present the salient features of an Islamic economy as discussed in this work. Special attention is paid to the issue of similarities and differences between such an economy and capitalism, both being primarily market economies.

APPENDIX TO CHAPTER 10

The al-Azhar Fatwā

Office of the Grand Imam, Rector of Al-Azhar

Investing funds with banks that pre-specify profits

Dr. Hasan Abbas Zaki, Chairman of the Board of Directors of the Arab Banking Corporation, sent a letter dated 22/10/2002 to H.E. the Grand Imam Dr. Muhammad Sayyid Tantawi, Rector of Al-Azhar. Its text follows:

H.E. Dr. Muhammad Sayyid Tantawi,
Rector of Al-Azhar:

Greetings and prayers for Peace, Mercy, and blessings of Allah. Customers of the International Arab Banking Corporation forward their funds and savings to the Bank to use and invest them in its permissible dealings, in exchange for profit distributions that are pre-determined, and the distribution times are likewise agreed-upon with the customer. We respectfully ask you for the legal status of this dealing.

[Here a sample text of an account agreement is reproduced in the fatwa]

His Excellency, the Grand Imam, has forwarded the letter and its attachment for consideration by the Council of the Islamic Research Institute in its subsequent session. The Council met on Thursday, 25 Shaʿban 1423 A.H., corresponding to 31 October 2002 A.D., at which time the above-mentioned subject was presented. After the members' discussions and analysis, the Council determined that investing funds in banks that pre-specify profits is permissible under Islamic Law, and there is no harm therein.

Due to the special importance of this topic for the public, who wish to know the Islamic Legal ruling regarding investing their funds with banks that pre-specify profits (as shown by their numerous questions in this matter), the Secretariat General of the Islamic Research Institute decided to prepare an official fatwa, supported by the Islamic

Legal proofs and a summary of the Institute members' statements. This should give the public a clear understanding of the issue, thus giving them confidence in the opinion.

The General Secretariat presented the full fatwa text to the Islamic Research Institute Council during its session on Thursday, 23 Ramadan 1423, corresponding to 28 November 2002, A.D. Following the reading of the fatwa, and noting members' comments on its text, they approved it.

This is the text of the Fatwa:

Those who deal with the International Arab Banking Corporation Bank—or any other bank—forward their funds and savings to the bank as an agent who invests the funds on their behalf in its permissible dealings, in exchange for a profit distribution that is predetermined, and at distribution times that are mutually agreed-upon...

This dealing, in this form, is permissible, without any doubt of impermissibility. This follows from the fact that no Canonical Text in the Book of Allah or the Prophetic Sunnah forbids this type of transaction within which profits or returns are pre-specified, as long as the transaction is concluded with mutual consent.

Allah, transcendent is He, said: "Oh people of faith, do not devour your properties among yourselves unjustly, the exception being, trade conducted by mutual consent...." (Al-Nisa': 29).

The verse means: Oh people with true faith, it is not permissible for you, and unseemly, that any of you devour the wealth of another in impermissible ways (e.g. theft, usurpation, or usury, and other forbidden means). In contrast, you are permitted to exchange benefits through dealings conducted by mutual consent, provided that no forbidden transaction is thus made permissible or vice versa. This applies regardless of whether the mutual consent is established verbally, in written form, or in any other form that indicates mutual agreement and acceptance.

There is no doubt that mutual agreement on pre-specified profits is Legally and logically permissible, so that each party will know his rights.

It is well known that banks only pre-specify profits or returns based on precise studies of international and domestic markets, and economic conditions in the society. In addition, returns are customized for each specific transaction type, given its average profitability.

Moreover, it is well known that pre-specified profits vary from time period to another. For instance, investment certificates initially specified a return of 4%, which increased subsequently to more than 15%, now returning to near 10%.

The parties that specify those changing rates of returns are required to obey the regulations issued by the relevant government agencies.

This pre-specification of profits is beneficial, especially in this age, when deviations from truth and fair dealing have become rampant. Thus, pre-specification of profits provides benefits both to the providers of funds, as well as to the banks that invest those funds.

It is beneficial to the provider of funds since it allows him to know his rights without any uncertainty. Thus, he may arrange the affairs of his life accordingly.

It is also beneficial to those who manage those banks, since the pre-specification of profits gives them the incentive for working hard, since they keep all excess profits above what they promised the provider of funds. This excess profit compensation is justified by their hard work.

It may be said that banks may lose, thus wondering how they can pre-specify profits for the investors.

In reply, we say that if banks lose on one transaction, they win on many others, thus profits can cover losses.

In addition, if losses are indeed incurred, the dispute will have to be resolved in court.

In summary, pre-specification of profits to those who forward their funds to banks and similar institutions through an investment agency is legally permissible. There is no doubt regarding the Islamic Legality of this transaction, since it belongs to the general area judged according to benefits, i.e. wherein there are no explicit Texts. In addition, this type of transaction does not belong to the areas of creed and ritual acts of worship, wherein changes and other innovations are not permitted.

Based on the preceding, investing funds with banks that pre-specify profits or returns is Islamically Legal, and there is no harm therein, and Allah knows best.

Rector of Al-Azhar
Dr. Muhammad Sayyid Tantawi
27 Ramadam 1423 A.H.
2 December, 2002 A.D.

CHAPTER ELEVEN

SUMMING UP

The Basic Issues

Contrary to the heavily dirigistic stance taken by Islamic economists, this work clearly shows that an Islamic economy is necessarily a free market economy. Islamic economists' mistrust of, if not aversion to, market system is primarily motivated by their dissatisfaction with capitalistic system. Unfortunately, in expressing their displeasure with capitalistic system, they were unable to avoid a trap inadvertently created by the mainstream economic discourse where generally no distinction is drawn between a market system and capitalism. It is thus that in their exposition, disapproval of capitalism, unwittingly or otherwise, becomes a disapproval of the market system. This in turn is taken to mean that Islamic economics must be conceived of as an entirely new paradigm in the area of economics. The discipline of what is called conventional economics is then deemed irrelevant for an Islamic economy, and consequently the rich and varied economics literature is thrown overboard. Any endeavor to explore fresh avenues of economics for an Islamic economy is laudable, provided what is offered represents an internally consistent set of postulates, and provided, since what is offered is supposed to represent an Islamic vision, it is firmly grounded in the fundamental values of Islam as they emerge from the Qur'ān and *Sunna*. The exposition in this work shows that the new paradigm fails on both these counts.[1] This exposition shows that once the misunderstanding created by Islamic economics is cleared, a greater part of the conventional economic paradigm becomes relevant to an Islamic economy.

Two points need to be emphasized in this summing up: First, the conventional economic discourse is essentially predicated on the existence

[1] Instead of repeating which issues have been dealt with and in which chapters, I would refer an interested reader to Chapter 1 (Introduction) which presents a fairly detailed chapter-wise synopsis of the coverage of these issues.

of a representative form of government. This presumption is important not only for expression of individual freedom of choice in both economic and political arenas, but also in recognition of the important role assigned to government in view of market failure. Yet, if market failure is to be rectified by an appeal to the institution of government, governmental failure, on the other hand, may lead to economic breakdown and eventually to anarchy. If, on the basis of the Western experience, the so-called conventional economics takes its point of departure the existence of a reasonably efficient and representative form of government, no such presumption can justifiably be made by the proponents of Islamic economics. Even when the new paradigm cannot be maintained, the question about the appropriate institutional form of government of an Islamic society requires serious consideration, for if an Islamic economy is to be a market economy, the boundaries of governmental action in it need to be clearly spelled out. This issue has been addressed at various places throughout this work, yet it requires further attention in this summing up.

And second while an Islamic economy is a market economy, it is not necessarily the same thing as capitalism. This I have pointed out earlier in this work in a number of chapters. What needs to be explored somewhat further is how far this economy will be different from capitalism, the dominant form of market economy in the contemporary world. These two subjects are taken up in the second section of this chapter. There, I have supplanted my summary of what has been said earlier in this work with a number of additional observations that, in my view, indicate the avenues where further explorations are needed. Here, I present a brief summary of the pertinent points that emerge from the exposition of the various subjects, other than those two, covered in this work. In this summary, it would seem appropriate to follow the same arrangement that has been followed earlier, which is to relate it to the fundamental characteristics of a market economy.

The institution of private property is not only sanctioned but rather sanctified by Islam. We can also see a sanctioning of communal property, though only through a single *ḥadīth* report. There, however, is no evidence of state property during the Prophetic times, nor do we see it in the subsequent centuries up to modern times. Many of the collective functions that would require the state ownership of property were performed through either the *waqf* property (an institution that emerged in the immediate post-Prophetic period, during the caliphate of ʿUmar), the communal property, or the private property of the rulers. Several implications flow from this property ownership structure: i) the institution of private property commands higher degree of respect than is accorded to it in the Western system of values. This means whenever private property rights are infringed in public interest (e.g. for public works), compensation payments must be made, in other words, it is not sufficient to implement a change on the basis that the required compensation payments *could* be made. In exceptional cases, a departure from this rule must be justified, which is to say that an inability to affect compensation payments must be explicitly defended; ii) communal property needs to be regulated to avoid the tragedy of the commons, just as economics argues, for otherwise the institution may become defunct; iii) the institution of *waqf* property needs to be restored to its rightful place in the structure of property rights in an Islamic society: since it is a part of the cultural ethos of the Muslims, it can perform the functions it has historically performed in Islamic lands and reduce some of the burden that the state will otherwise have to carry in provision of public goods; and iv) the institution of state ownership of property can be accommodated in the flexible system of Islamic values wherever this may be deemed essential, as indeed it would be for a consistent provision of public goods in contemporary times. However, the confusion between communal ownership and state ownership, as prevailing in most of the Muslim countries as discussed in Chapter 5, must be rectified.

Second, the institution of private property ownership remains devoid of any substance without the attendant freedom of choice exercised with respect to it, and this freedom of choice is naturally guided by self-interest. Three points need to be noted about the idea of freedom of choice: i) contrary to a strong tendency for it to degenerate into selfishness, it is not necessarily the same thing as selfishness. Human will is free, and while it is corruptible it is also provided guidance for right conduct at both personal (individual man) and social (collective man) levels. Further, an important element of this guidance is the enunciation of corresponding laws that, in turn, require an implementation of a retributive system (of justice) to ensure that the instances of degeneration of self-interest do not go unnoticed, for a neglect on this score may lead to what I have called the process of adverse selection in Chapter 3. On the other hand, the degree to which self-interest degenerates into selfishness depends on the lack of restraints it may otherwise be obliged to respect. This highlights the crucial importance of the legal corpus of a society that defines the boundaries of the freedoms associated with the use of property, which places the concept of property rights at the center stage of economic discourse. The legal corpus of a society reflects the values held by that society. In an Islamic society, these values are primarily derived from the Qur'ān and *ḥadīth* reports. It, therefore, ought to be clear that the individual freedoms sanctioned by these fonts of Islamic values must be respected, and reflected in the legal corpus of an Islamic polity. I have argued that Islamic economists' exposition of consumer and production theories is not well thoughtout, and thereby is, at the very least, inconsistent with these values. I have emphasized that any infringement of these freedoms, if and when required, must be subject to a close scrutiny, and must be worked out through an institutional mechanism established for this purpose—more on this a little later. It is equally important that the additional prohibitions incorporated into the legal corpus be not treated at par with the *ḥarām* elements enunciated in the Qur'ān. Thus there may be actions that are illegal yet not *ḥarām*, and these additional elements must be understood to be subject to revision over time and space. This is what has been noted as the Divinely ordained flexibility in the sphere of *muʿāmalāt* earlier in this work. Finally, the structure of property rights must be effectively enforced; a persistent neglect on this score amounts to an absence of property rights and thus an invitation to chaos. The disenchantment of some of the Islamic economists with the working of the market system, in my view, is the result of exploitation of the poor by those in positions of power because of a lack of effective property rights enforcement. It is another matter that they miss this point in their expositions.

Third, the legal corpus of any society, Islamic or otherwise, cannot cope with every possible perversion of free will, and thus every instance of freedom of choice degenerating into selfishness. Economics implicitly assumes that an additional check on the play of self-interest in the form of competition goes a long way in eliminating the economic excesses that might otherwise occur, as shown in Chapter 3. The Islamic economists' reading of the idea of competition, as necessarily engendering hostility and thus implying a lack of cooperation among economic agents, is unwarranted. This additional check on the play of free will is in no wise contrary to either cooperation or Islamic values, and needs to be viewed in its proper perspective, as something that reduces the possibility of exploitation of the weak by the strong. Contrary to the position taken by Islamic economics, an Islamic economist may actually look at the exceptions to competition in the form of government licenses with suspicion. Indeed, every exception to competition incorporated in the structure of property rights of an Islamic economy must be subjected to a rigorous scrutiny.

Fourth, Islamic economists' exclusive focus on the issue of equity at the neglect of efficiency is misplaced for several reasons: i) a society cannot consume more than it produces. This in turn implies that the equity issues cannot be appropriately addressed without addressing the ones relating to efficiency. Neglecting the size of the pie may mean a smaller share of the pie for those that Islamic economists wish to concern themselves with, whereas that share may be larger if efficiency conditions are satisfied though, admittedly, with the possibility of a somewhat higher degree of inequality across different recipients; ii) Islamic economists create the impression that their preoccupation with equity represents the true Islamic perspective in the context of issues that may involve a trade-off between efficiency and equity. This may be the result of an absence of any specific discussion about this trade-off in *fiqh* literature. Any such expectation from classical *fiqh* discourse is out of place; even in conventional economics this issue crystallized only in the twentieth century. Nevertheless, one can clearly discern a concern with efficiency in *fiqh* literature when efficiency is interpreted broadly as doing the best in given circumstances, as I have shown in Chapter 5. There, it was argued that Pareto's conceptualization of efficiency can be traced back to a number of *fiqh* stipulations, and that an Islamic economy will be quite comfortable with the application of Pareto criterion wherever doing so may help it in charting a more efficient, or the optimal, course of action; iii) When Islamic economists argue for all sorts of collective redistributive schemes over and above the compulsory redistribution through *zakāh*, they fail to establish the presumed inadequacy of *zakāh* redistribution. It ought to be clear that no amount of redistribution can be adequate if the overall size of the pie is small relative to the size of the population. There is no discussion on whether the presumed inadequacy arises because the *niṣāb*, which determines the entitlement to receive *zakāh* funds, is too high, or because the *zakāh* rates are too low to generate enough funds, or both. These parameters have remained pegged at the level as determined during the Prophet's time as indicated by the relevant *ḥadīth* reports, for the Qur'ān is not explicit about their values. They were left at the discretion of the Prophet, and *fiqh* down the centuries has felt that there is no need for any revision in them. This outlook was justified until the advent of modernity, since the standard of living across the world remained more or less constant during all that time. It is only in the aftermath of the industrial revolution that the standards of living in the West started to improve, around the turn of the nineteenth century. Across the Muslim countries, the effect started to be felt but only in the twentieth century; much of it indeed only in the recent decades. This has altered societal expectations about the minimum standard of living an individual ought to be entitled to. It seems that Islamic economists' overriding concern with the question of equity is a reflection of these changed expectations. I have discussed this issue at some length in Chapter 7. There, it is pointed out that an Islamic government may deem the redistribution under the existing *niṣāb* and *zakāh* rates inadequate (more on that, a little later). At this stage, all we need to note is that this is a political question, and thus the Islamic economists' case for additional compulsory redistribution lacks substance. I have also argued that any additional redistribution, if and when necessary, must be direct, in the spirit of *zakāh*, rather than through market interference.

Fifth, *fiqh*'s interpretation of the Qur'ānic prohibition of *ribā* ran into problem quite early, indeed as early as the beginning of the *fiqh* itself. The revision of that interpretation in the modern times, beginning with the middle of the twentieth century, which is attributed to what I have called the dominant *fiqh* group, has proved to be even more problematic. Two lengthy chapters, Chapters 9 and 10, were devoted to this subject, for it is quite clear that the basic motivation behind developing the new paradigm, Islamic economics, resides in this revised interpretation where *ribā* is unequivocally equated to interest. The exposition in those chapters shows that while there is a connection between interest and *ribā, ribā* cannot be unequivocally equated to interest. I have integrated my concluding observations on this issue with the second subject of the next section, which is: how far would an Islamic economy differ from capitalism? In my assessment, the departures of an Islamic economy from capitalism are more or less determined by the differences between its financial system and that of capitalism.

The Substantive Issues

I have pointed out at a number of places in this work that one of the important omissions in *fiqh* literature relates to a complete absence of exposition of the appropriate institutional form of an Islamic government. It is not sufficient to enunciate a theory of state without offering any details as to how that state is to be functionally organized. An important element of this elaboration, relates to specification of limits to the power the state functionaries, including the head of government, may exercise. The traditional refrain that rulers come from God is clearly as unsatisfactory now, as it ever was. The Qur'ānic obligation of *sūra* (42:38) cannot be left at the discretion of rulers to be used when it may be convenient. One may find instances where this was complied to satisfactorily by this or that ruler, but such an *ad hoc* deployment of a fundamental governance imperative is clearly unacceptable. The initial encounters of *fiqh* with state power, notably during the times of Mālik and Ibn Ḥanbal, culminated in a truce whereby power was exercised by rulers but authority was enjoyed by *'ulamā'*,[2] resulting in a status quo that has prevailed to the present (though in modern times we see instances of erosion of that authority in certain places). By virtue of the authority they could bring to bear on the conduct of rulers, the *'ulamā'* were at times successful in circumventing the blatant excesses of rulers and others in positions of power. We see the appearance of a large number of treatises, beginning with the early 'Abbāsid period, offering advice to rulers, whoever they may happen to be, for the right conduct of state affairs, but not much was offered to the ruled by way of remedial action in instances where the rulers ignored those strictures. If anything, the masses were advised to obey their rulers even if they appeared to be unjust, presumably to prevent instability. A revolt against even an unjust ruler was deemed a *fitna*. The arrangement seems to have worked well for both the parties; indeed it appears that the *'ulamā'* were quite happy with it, for otherwise the status quo could not have endured for so long.

In a sense, this status quo was thought to be the second best arrangement in view of the hopeless task, practically speaking, of reviving the ideal caliphate (*khilāfa*), governance by the pious, the only arrangement that was supposed to be readily acceptable to Muslims. Right from the beginning, the Muslim thinkers were aware of the Greek ideas relating to governance, but they never took them seriously. For them, governance was a matter of discharging a personal responsibility, and thus the idea of corporatism represented by the republicanism of the Greek did not quite fit in with their memory of the Prophetic times and the times of the rightly guided caliphs. At any rate, the arrangement that came to prevail was quite in line with the spirit of its age;

---

[2] In this summing up, I have used the general term *'ulamā'* instead of *fiqh* scholars, since not all who belong to the former category, influential though they may be in the present context, would fall in the latter category.

the republicanism of the Greeks had been defunct for quite some time, and contrary to what happened elsewhere, it did facilitate the rise of a brilliant civilization. It is thus that *fiqh* never insisted on the institutionalization of *sūra*. In the arrangement that came to prevail, *sūra* was treated as a prerogative of the rulers, and left to their discretion as to when, and in what form, it was to be sought. Often it was interpreted by both the parties (the rulers and the *ʿulamāʾ*) as nothing more than an informal consultation of rulers with *ʿulamāʾ*.

Apart from the matters relating to who was to be included in the process of *sūra*, and what form this process was to take, the institutionalization of *sūra* would have raised another question: how binding on the rulers the outcome of the *sūra* process was to be? The Qurʾānic exhortation to the Prophet to consult his Companions, arrive at a decision, and then leave matters to God (3:159), was interpreted correctly in so far as the Prophet's acceptance or otherwise of a particular viewpoint was concerned, but it was perhaps not very prudent to extend the same privilege to every ruler; for no ruler, however wise and pious he may be, can possibly be treated as equal to the Prophet. Prophetic personalities are endowed with extraordinary insight as well as unmatched farsightedness, and thus it is quite understandable that at times they may not accept the opinions of ordinary mortals, even when these may include exceptional personalities such as ʿUmar. Since the *ʿulamāʾ* themselves came to prominence not as a result of some institutional process of selection but through contest, it suited those who came to such prominence to exercise a greater degree of authority on behalf of their fraternity, and thus the status quo continued to prevail through the centuries.

In this relationship, power was exercised by individuals with various titles, such as caliph, sulṭān, amīr, etc., in a more or less unencumbered manner. The *ʿulamāʾ* felt comfortable with the arrangement because this meant that implementation of any policy or a change required convincing just one individual. There were certain advantages to this arrangement: for instance, to the extent the *ʿulamāʾ* represented the conscience of the community, injustice and repression associated with state power could be checked, and any advantageous change could be quickly implemented. What is noteworthy about this arrangement, and this cannot be over-emphasized, is that with the passage of time, it became a part of the Islamic social ethos, an ingrained part of Muslim psyche, quite contrary to the Qurʾānic injunction concerning *sūra*. As long as Muslims were politically autonomous, this *modus operandi* did not cause any serious problems apart from those caused by periodic struggle for political power among competing groups. For an ordinary Muslim, life went on as usual except for the hardship that might have been caused by those political upheavals every few generations. However, with the ascendency of West in the last few centuries, this arrangement has become problematic. What it now meant was that the West needs to manipulate one person to achieve its objectives, and it is this that has caused enormous problems in the relationship between the Islamic world and the West, particularly in the recent past. While on the one hand, West insists that the Islamic world must follow in its footsteps and introduce democratic norms—this, it is argued, will help Muslims get rid of the repressive regimes—on the other, it consistently negates that rhetoric by following a policy which disrupts, if sabotages be too strong a word, the evolution of representative forms of government wherever doing so suits its geopolitical objectives.

The conformism historically fostered by the *ʿulamāʾ* and the resultant social ethos means that Muslims came to tolerate even the most repressive of their rulers. Evidence to this effect is amply available even in the recent past, evidence which, paradoxically, shows that, at times, even the *ʿulamāʾ* themselves were on the receiving end of state repression. Yet, the *ʿulamāʾ*, on their part, have not wholeheartedly lent any support to the cause of democracy for this is perceived, correctly to some extent, as a threat to their long-standing authority. Of course, they could contest for power under a democratic arrangement but are not quite sure if it will yield results to their liking; the sway of their authority on the imagination of Muslim political sentiment has eroded in the recent years. The long-standing dichotomy between *dīn* and *dunyā*, as discussed in Chapter 6, may have contributed to this erosion. Thus there are both internal and external difficulties on the way to adopting a representative form of government in Islamic world, though in my view it is the internal difficulties that pose a more serious hindrance. In a social ethos where political parties hardly ever feel the need to hold party elections at the grass root level, and where personality cults matter more than personal integrity, implementation of democratic norms even in the egalitarian climate of Islam has become extremely difficult.[3]

---

[3] It is somewhat ironic that the personality cult in politics may actually be a throwback to similar cults in the religious arena, particularly relating to the posthumous veneration of saints in institutionalized sufism.

Regardless of these difficulties, Muslims must now come to terms with the Qur'ānic imperative of *sūra* by building the required institutional framework. What form this may take is beyond the scope of this work. Nevertheless, since such an undertaking will have important implications for the institutional form the governance will assume, few points relating to basic principles may be recalled as discussed earlier, in various chapters. First, the institution of *sūra* should not be innocuous: it should form an abiding process of legal formulations in the sphere of *mu'āmalāt* where no explicit Qur'ānic legislation is available, and where the new legal formulations do not violate the spirit of *sunna*. Second, in light of Islam's emphasis on individual responsibility, state power must be devolved to the lower levels to the maximum extent possible, but since self-interest can degenerate into selfishness (human will is corruptible), the governing functionaries must be held fully accountable for the misdemeanors associated with exercise of power vested in their offices. This is important in view of the unavoidable discretionary powers vested in those offices. However, to keep the discretionary power to a minimum, the procedural rules must be laid down in detail and be transparent. This, in turn, means that procedural justice will be a prominent part of the justice system of an Islamic polity.[4] Third, once *sūra* has been institutionalized and, as a result, a representative government put in place, the economic literature on the subject of the economic role of government becomes relevant within the purview of the corresponding structure of property rights of that society. This structure of property rights, or the legal corpus, may vary across time and space in view of not only the different *fiqh* schools but also the Divinely ordained flexibility as elaborated upon in Chapters 5 to 8. (In this regard, certain reservations with respect to stabilization policy will be discussed a little later). Fourth, while it is obvious that *zakāh* would be an integral part of the taxation system, I am aware of a section of *fiqh* writers who feels that *zakāh* is the only tax that an Islamic state can impose. This position is probably based on the fact that *zakāh* revenues can be spent under diverse heads. Yet, to the extent the inflexibility of both

[4] One notes with dismay that during Zia ul-Haq's Islamization in Pakistan, procedural law was exempted from the process, for it could not be challenged in the *Sharī'a* courts.

niṣāb and the *zakāh* rates is maintained (though, it was noted that some of the contemporary *fiqh* scholars seem to be favorably disposed to the idea of revision in these parameters), *zakāh* revenues may not be sufficient given the magnitude of government expenditures in modern times. The *zakāh* revenues then may be supplanted through other taxes, preferably in the form of user fees and corrective taxes. This caveat is important in view of the fact any property or income tax can be conceived of as *zakāh* from the payer's point of view since *zakāh* was the only tax imposed by the state during the Prophet's times, and in principle it ought to be the first tax imposed by an *Islamic* government.

We now turn to the important question relating to the differences between capitalism and an Islamic economy. The distinguishing characteristics of capitalism, over and above those that characterize a market economy, were discussed at some length in Chapter 4, and were again touched upon in Chapter 8. In Chapter 4, note was also taken of how economics dealt with the theoretical issues relating to those characteristics. The salient points of that story can be summarized here for ready reference. What transforms a market economy into capitalism is the commoditization of money and thence the instrumentalization of interest as a result of governmental interference in the capital markets in the name of stabilization policy. The end result of this process is the severance of link between rate of interest and the expected rate of profit as determined in the real sector of the economy. It is the severance of this link which makes interest a purely monetary phenomenon, which in turn gives rise to some of the excesses associated with capitalism. This severance, in the final analysis, is not sustainable but can be prolonged for a fairly extended period of time by the government, which can defray the attendant cost by virtue of its fiduciary and taxation powers. If money (especially when it is easily borrowed) and financial instruments can be juggled around by economic agents to appropriate the largesse distributed by government through its interest rate policy, ostensibly in the name of stabilizing the economy, no one could resist the temptation to make the quick (and perfectly legal) gains. The ultimate result of this commoditization of money, and thereby of financial instruments, is that these instruments are not viewed as means of undertaking investment but purely a means to exploiting the opportunities of windfall gains offered by the fluctuations in the rate of interest.

The other important cause of capitalism's excesses, intimately connected with the foregoing, is related to the divorce of ownership from control that transformed capitalism into what I have referred to as the trustified capitalism. This represents the culmination of the process that began with the institution of limited liability, which in the new environment facilitated transformation of the age-old principal-agent relationship into an uncontrollable problem. The attendant moral hazard now pervades the corporate sector of the capitalist economies, including the financial one, so thoroughly that the expected gains through the economies of scale look only a mixed blessing. As the size of enterprise increased to take advantage of these economies, increasing reliance came to be placed on not just the equity capital, contributed by an ever-increasing number of share holders, but also debt capital contributed in part by a large number of small savers. The control of the enterprise was now vested in a few hands that may, and usually did, not have any stake in the outcome of their decisions. The agent in this principal-agent relationship could raise funds in capital markets—for expansion of the enterprise, new acquisitions, leverage, or whatever else—markets that were themselves inhabited by intermediaries that represented a principal-agent relationship. These intermediaries, in turn, acquired an increasingly larger amount of their funds from another breed of intermediaries—the pension, retirement, and mutual funds, etc.—that again were run by agents on behalf of the principals, and the entire system was to be overseen and regulated by a government that itself represented a principal-agent relationship, this time a monopoly agent, even if it could be changed on occasions as a result of elections. It is clear that the severity of moral hazard in a principal–agent relationship crucially depends on the leeway an agent may come to enjoy either in the name of required flexibility, the lack of adequate vigilance, or because of informational asymmetries. As noted in Chapter 4, it is the American form of corporate governance that has afforded the greatest degree of leeway to the agents—I have called them the residual controllers—and thus it is no surprise that the excesses committed by them have now created enormous difficulties for the world economy, and threaten to destabilize the system.

Earlier in this work I have noted that Islamic economists' displeasure with market economy is the result of their discontent with capitalism's excesses. In light of the exposition in this work, we can see that their primary cause was the commoditization of money. This, however, is not how the Islamic economists articulate their displeasure. Instead, following the dominant *fiqh* school's interpretation of *ribā*, they proceed to unequivocally equate *ribā* to interest. This has amounted to climbing the wrong tree. On the other hand, as far as the principal-agent problems are concerned, they have failed even to acknowledge them. Indeed they do not seem to be concerned with them at all; their own articulations especially relating to *muḍāraba* profit-sharing, as a substitute for interest-based transactions, are based on the principal-agent relationship. But then *muḍāraba* itself is a controversial contractual arrangement in *fiqh*. What is offered beyond *muḍāraba* represents either well-known financing arrangements, even under capitalism, or arrangements that are more or less the same thing as interest-based arrangements except in name, as is shown in Chapter 10.

At this stage, a brief review of the rationale for the sanction against interest as understood by the Islamic economists, primarily following Rāzī's exposition is in order, for much is made of this rationale. Interest is considered to be unearned income, for according to an old adage money is supposed to be barren. It is never recognized that money is barren only if it remains money and does not undergo a transformation. But that presumption is hardly ever true, for nobody borrows money to, idiomatically speaking, simply put it under a mattress. Money, being a store of value, is generalized purchasing power. It is putty which can be readily converted into any other asset (clay). When it is converted into consumer goods, it directly yields utility, and in that case *fiqh* and Islamic economics has no problem in accepting a compensation for it in the form of higher deferred payments as compared to the corresponding spot prices, as is clear from their articulations on *bayʿ muʿajjal*. On the other hand, when it is converted into productive assets it creates surplus, and now the question is who is entitled to this surplus if the savers and investors happen to be two different groups of individuals, or more appropriately two different economic entities? The argument that since savers cannot invest their money on their own—thus for them it is barren—they should not be entitled to any part of the returns occasioned by the transformation of their savings into productive assets (the surplus) is not very convincing, to say the least. If we put the argument on its other leg, the investors, who in their scheme of things will be entitled to the entire surplus, would not be able to earn any returns if those savings were not made available to them. This will, of course, mean that socially productive investment opportunities will be wasted—the savings will not be transformed into productive assets—and as a result society will be worse off. At any rate, to deprive savers the rewards accruing as a result of the transformation of their savings and to argue that all of those rewards must go to investors is plainly unjust.

It is argued that the institution of interest destroys social cohesion; it is a manifestation of greed when interest is charged for the use of money. Now imagine a society where a large number of small savers are deprived of any reward for their savings because all such rewards must go to those who have access to these savings. Imagine also that there are retirees, pensioners, widows, and other deprived members of the society whose life-time savings are now to be put at the service of those who are in a position, for reasons that are irrelevant here, to exploit the productive opportunities available to society, and argue that this will promote social cohesion, and you have a sure recipe for disaster at the societal level. But the Islamic economists, who present this vision, remain unfazed; this in their view, is required to institute the social justice, (the *ʿadl*), of Islam.

A similar sort of confusion arises when it is argued, still following Rāzī, the first exegete to discuss the rationale of *ribā* prohibition and who somehow reached the conclusion, that charging interest somehow stifles the circulation of wealth. There is a logical inconsistency in this argument. Even when we look at it in the background of Rāzī's own times, it is difficult to see how a withholding of money by the moneylender because he cannot charge interest will boost the circulation of wealth. And at any rate the issue is irrelevant in the context of a modern financial system where savings are entrusted to financial intermediaries for converting them into investment, and as long as productive investment opportunities are available, the leakages will be injected back into the circular flow. But if nothing is paid to the savers, there is a greater chance that savings will be stashed away as hoarding, and as a result will not be injected back into the circular flow. The circular flow will shrink to the detriment of society.

Beyond the rationale of *ribā* prohibition, much is also made of the issue of risk taking, risk attendant upon the transformation of savings into investment, for the future is unknown. It is argued, this time citing Bayhaqī as the authority, as we saw in Chapter 10,[5] that a saver is not

[5] See n. 20 in Chapter 10.

entitled to any return unless he bears the risk associated with investment. And since interest is a sure return, it therefore is not permissible, and therefore the same thing as *ribā*. This argument has several flaws relating not only to modern finance but also relating to *fiqh*'s perspective on risk in the context of investment. Consider the flaws relating to the former. First, interest is a sure return only in nominal terms, and not in real terms. Real rate of interest is not known at the time the contracts are entered into; it simply cannot be known ex-'ante, for the rate of inflation cannot be known with certainty. Second, risks relating to default and those arising from the fluctuations in the rate of interest in the case of bonds, if they have to be redeemed before their maturity date (the so called market risk), cannot be avoided. Third, the theory of the risk structure of interest rates takes the varying degrees of risk associated with different businesses into consideration, with the end result that risky enterprises end up paying a higher rate of interest and thus bear the cost of risk. If it is argued that lenders (the depositors) do not bear the risk of these enterprises because they are paid a uniform rate of interest on specific forms of deposits, the following, fourth point, may be noted. In a diversified portfolio, held by an intermediary on behalf of a large number of savers, the risk is spread over all those savers, and thus savers end up bearing the risk, for it is a part of the cost of intermediation.[6]

As far as *fiqh* position is concerned, it allows all sorts of risk-free returns to various forms of investment as has been discussed in Chapter 8. Islamic economists, thereby, are left with only circulating capital to attack. In the context of the issue at hand, *fiqh* never raised the question of risk bearing in the context of its elaborations with regard to *ribā*, until Bayhaqī's time, several centuries later. Thus the cue taken from Bayhaqī seems more of an afterthought in the increasingly complex discourse on the subject of *ribā* prohibition, as we saw in Chapter 10.

Coming back to the question: how far will an Islamic economy, or rather its financial system, differ from a capitalist one? The answer

[6] A skeptic may point out that this explanation is largely irrelevant in the case of government bonds. It will, however, not be lost on the reader that I have dealt with that issue quite extensively in Chapter 4, under instrumentalization of interest, and more will be said later in this chapter. At any rate, the cost of risks that governments take is spread over all the citizens.

depends on a number of things. To begin with, it depends on the Islamic position on the characteristics of the capitalist financial system as summarized earlier, for whether the Islamic system can avoid the pitfalls relating to those characteristics, and thus the excesses of capitalism, crucially depends on that position (we come to this a little later). But above all the answer depends on the correct meaning of the Qurʾānic term *ribā*, and thus its relation to interest. In Chapter 9, after a careful consideration of the relevant literature, I offered the following definition of *ribā*:

> We can define *ribā* as an increase on *rāʾs al-māl*, involving either a loan or a deferred payments sale, which is contingent upon an inability to pay on part of the debtor, and leads towards a perpetual increase in debt over the *rāʾs al-māl* through the process of *aḍʿāfan muḍāʿafa*.

According to this definition, *ribā* is equivalent to neither interest nor usury in any straightforward manner. But then, it is also related to interest, or for that matter usury, in so far as any rate of interest may give rise to the process of *aḍʿāfan muḍāʿafa*. The crucial thing that renders any rate of interest *ribā* is the inability on part of debtor to discharge the contractual payment obligations because of his straitened circumstances. *Riba*, therefore, is the burden that will be imposed on him due to circumstances beyond his control by a perpetual increase in the amount of debt as a result of the compounding of the principal amount, the *rāʾs al-māl*. According to this definition, it is not interest *per se* which is *ribā* and therefore prohibited; it is any rate of interest that in individual circumstances beyond the control of the debtor makes it impossible for him to discharge his debt obligations according to the contractual provisions. It is thus that *ribā* prohibition provides protection in the case of a legitimate default, or bankruptcy. Is it then equivalent to bankruptcy protection as conceptualized in the Western legal frameworks? The answer is a definite "no"; unlike the Western legal provisions, the Qurʾān explicitly provides protection of the principal amount, although it ordains the granting of an easing time, a respite, to the debtor for its payment contingent upon improvement in his economic circumstances. However, it does not specify any duration for this easing time.

It is stipulations relating to this definition that, in my view, need to be implemented to begin with to establish a *ribā*-free financial system, but this is not an easy task; indeed this was one of the reasons why *fiqh* ended up with the difficulties of its own making in its interpretation of *ribā*, as discussed in Chapters 9 and 10. The challenges are daunting; yet Muslims, in my view, have no choice but to come to grips with them. Several points can be noted for further explorations. First, an institutional, and therefore property rights, framework must be put into place to distinguish between genuine and spurious cases of default, to provide protection in the legitimate cases of hardship and to make sure that the black sheep of society, who will wish to take advantage of this provision by declaring willful default, are adequately, rather harshly, dealt with, for otherwise such sabotage may lead to the collapse of the system. Second, minimum provisions with regard to granting of easing time to the debtor may also be incorporated into the property rights structure rather than leaving it to the individual creditor's discretion, although individual discretion with respect to granting of additional time, beyond the one envisioned in those provisions, may be acknowledged. The easing time may not be universally the same in all cases, and thus factors that may be taken into consideration in this regard will need to be explored. Third, implementation of the foregoing provisions will require specification of the private assets that may be exempted from the burden of discharging the principal amount of debt to ensure decent standard of living for the debtor. Again, while there may or may not be a universal list of such assets, it is clear to me that some flexibility will be required in terms of the value of exempted assets, for the valuation of the same assets may vary across time and space. Also, the individual needs may vary from person to person. Fourth, if after the easing time, the debtor is unable to discharge his obligations, the state may discharge them on his behalf from the *zakāh* funds as allowed by the Qurʾān. This raises the question of whether this amount should be deemed recoverable if the circumstances of the debtor subsequently improve? All these issues and questions require considerable further exploration. Fifth, should the principal amount to be discharged be reckoned in real terms or nominal terms? Theoretically, the principal should be discharged in real terms, for all the relevant Islamic principles were enunciated at the time when all values were expressed in real terms. In the present context, two points need to be noted: i) it is possible that the easing time in some, if not all, of the cases may be fairly long, and two, whatever the easing time, the rate of inflation during that time may turn out to be quite high in a world of pure paper standard. Both these points highlight the significance of the question: should there be an indexation of the principal amount? If the principal is to be discharged in real terms, the answer will be in the affirmative. This means that the principal amount should be either adjusted for inflation, or be reckoned in terms of the value of some commodity—such as gold or perhaps a basket of commodities—on the day the default occurs. The foregoing points also highlight, in my view, one dimension of the concept of limited liability in Islam, enunciated a long time ago, but never quite articulated due to a lack of its relevance in a commodity money system.

We now turn to the two remaining issues, relating to the commoditization of money and the moral hazard arising out of the principal-agent relationship. We have noted that the dominant *fiqh* school's interpretation, whereby interest is equated to *ribā*, is heavily influenced by its exponents' twentieth-century experience where a diverse variety of financial instruments—commoditized, it may be recalled—were traded in a manner that did not inspire any confidence that the returns earned on them were by any means related to the rate of profit in the real sector of the economy (thus the charge that these returns were "unearned"). It is true that often huge returns did accrue to capital (though usually in the form of capital gains), and it was difficult for the exponents of that school to see how the rate of profit could be so high as to make this possible. Someone unfamiliar with the idea of the capitalization of future stream of expected profits that results in such capital gains can hardly escape the impression of these being unearned gains. These capital gains can be very large during a Schumpeterian upheaval particularly in the industries directly effected by the technological change. Yet, there is a point to this charge but one which hardly draws their attention. Often capital gains (and losses) are the result of speculative activity, an activity which is closely linked to governmental interference in the capital markets, at times in the form of policy statements that may have an important bearing on the largesse distribution, as explained in Chapter 4, enlisting a response from those who could thus make quick gains. The asset price bubbles, in the final analysis, are the result of loose monetary policy. It is thus that the governments in the capitalist economies end up responding to the crises of their own making, and on both occasions expend tax-payers' money in a zero-sum redistribution of income game whose main beneficiaries are the controllers of residual at the expense of ordinary taxpayers.

I do not see any justification for such interference by government in the capital markets in an Islamic economy. The problem of commoditization of money can be considerably reduced if there is no instrumentalization of interest. This implies government's non-capital borrowing privileges must be considerably constrained. Borrowing for capital budget ordinarily must be earmarked to specific projects carefully assessed under a cost-benefit analysis, and their costs defrayed through levying of user charges wherever such may be feasible. Additional precautions may include a greater degree of earmarking of private borrowing to specific projects and an upper limit on the funds that can be borrowed for working capital in line with the assessed requirements of the business under consideration instead of offering it open lines of credit as is often done under the capitalist financial system. To hold the self-interest of the financial institutions in check, a greater degree of competition in the financial industry must be ensured. No institution should be allowed to become "too large to fail" under the pretext of the economies of scale and thus pose systemic risk.

As far as the principal-agent problem is concerned, its roots can be traced back to the early centuries of Islam. But those were different times and the principal-agent arrangement was fairly simple and, based as it was on personal relationship, not too prone to the pulls of moral hazard. It is one thing for a cloth merchant in Baghdad to get help for his business and pay a reward based on the performance of the agent and quite another where an agent represents thousands of principals not even known to him, each one of whom may have a very small stake in the enterprise, on the basis of an impersonal relationship that has come to characterize the corporate sector in modern times. When *fiqh* discussed the issue, it meticulously expounded the provisions relating to the rights and responsibilities of each party, and incorporated these in the corresponding contract to ensure a just relationship between the two parties. While the individual provisions relating to such contracts may not be applicable in the changed times and circumstances, the spirit behind them must be kept in view to ensure that the agent does not misuse the power vested in him to enrich himself at the expense of the principals, especially when for a vast majority of the principals an effective monitoring may not be possible because of either relatively high transaction costs or lack of required expertise. The industry must be closely monitored; regulatory regimes must be chalked out and these, including the disclosure requirements, must be effectively enforced. Here an Islamic economy will essentially confront the same dilemmas faced by capitalism.

It is clear that lessons can be learnt from capitalism's experience in recent years. Volumes will be needed to evaluate this experience. It is not possible to delve into this vast world of derivatives, swaps, futures, etc. in any substantive way here. But one brief glimpse to highlight the point: we see banks trying to shift risk on to home owners, for one, under the umbrella of asset backed securities, which were bundled together, packaged and repackaged, and sold to other financial intermediaries such that nobody could accurately assess the risk associated with these packages. The possibility of default on these, and other similarly opaque financial instruments, was insured through another set of financial intermediaries, the insurance companies (a principal-agent scenario, again), that themselves did not quite understand the risk of what they were insuring, notwithstanding the complex mathematical models used to arrive at the corresponding decisions. One thing is clear: all this was happening at the time when the property bubble was inflating and it was clear that one day it will burst, and possibly cause a systemic failure. No amount of risk spreading, and juggling it around, could eliminate it from the economy, as the regulators should have known. And so it happened that capitalism ran aground, for the regulators were, so to speak, fast asleep at the steering wheel, having turned on the auto pilot as suggested by the efficient markets theory. Much could be said, as indeed will be, over the coming years, perhaps decades, about the collapse of 2008, but one thing is certain: capitalism's financial system along with its corporate governance is up for a drastic revision. Whether that revision will successfully circumvent its blatant excesses in future is a question that only time will answer.

What this means is that the corporate sector of an Islamic economy, and especially its financial sector, which like the financial sector of any other economy in modern times, is prone to a higher degree of moral hazard because of relatively low capital requirements, must be tightly regulated. The issue of regulation is quite complex, for it requires input from diverse academic disciplines. Here, the likely overhauling of the regulatory regimes in capitalist economies may have an important bearing on similar regulation in Islamic economies in a world of integrated finance. One lesson, however, may be explicitly stated. The financial industry in an Islamic economy must not be allowed to devise financial instruments that are so opaque to make monitoring and regulation difficult and thus very costly, if not impossible. It probably will be preferable to define a set of permissible instruments instead of leaving it to financial institutions and their clever legal advisors to devise any instrument of their own fancy so long as it does not seem to violate the letter of the law, and made opaque to dodge the regulators. One other thing may be noted; this relates to the moral hazard contingent upon the system of deposit insurance instituted by the government. There is considerable merit in this as far as the protection of small depositors is concerned, but obviously there is a downside to it whereby the financial intermediaries become less careful in their lending operations. Without going into details, I feel in an Islamic economy such protection may be linked to the overall wealth position of a depositor, to protect the less fortunate in the society. The practical difficulties relating to the specification of property rights to institute such an arrangement will need to be explored.

In conclusion, it may be noted that the institution of interest in the final analysis is an institution of surplus sharing. This surplus manifests in two forms; the consumers' and producers' surpluses. Profits of an enterprise are directly related to the latter form of surplus, and in that sense, they can be viewed as forming the basis of profit sharing regardless of the specific form this sharing may take: the institution of interest being one, and the most commonly used, form of this surplus sharing. (The word for interest in Urdu, coming from Persian, is *sūd*, which literally means benefit—and thus ties up neatly with the economic idea of surplus—though it is commonly translated as profit.) We may end this discussion with two observations: first, the link between profits and interest may break as a result of the commoditization of money but more so through the instrumentalization of interest.[7] But it is equally true that such a severance of link is not sustainable, for interest cannot be paid indefinitely in absence of profits. And finally, the terms of trade in any exchange, including the one involving interest, crucially depend on the power, economic or political, that may be brought to bear on that exchange. The possibility of exploitation of one party by the other crucially depends on this power. It is readily recognized that both parties to an exchange gain as a result of the exchange, but the proportion of gains appropriated by one party may be disproportionately high, thus leading to the charge of exploitation, as we saw in Chapter 7. Such exploitation is the function of the structure of property rights of the society, as well as whether or not the

[7] The classical economists were fairly clear about the importance of this link, as has been shown in Chapter 4. Even though governments used to borrow at that time, those borrowings were supposedly for undertaking public works projects that would lead to an increase in productivity. At any rate it surely was not the same thing as an increase in the supply of money in an era of paper money.

given structure is effectively enforced. And beyond that, it depends on the degree of competition prevailing in the relevant sphere, or industry, which by itself is related to the property rights structure. It is not a question of interest or no interest, for such exploitation can arise under any institutional arrangement if the corresponding conditions with respect to the structure of property rights and competition are not satisfied. And the regulatory regime of a society is a crucial part of its structure of property rights.

This puts the issue of devising an appropriate structure of property rights squarely at the center stage of the task of constructing an Islamic economy. In view of the crucial role of the government in defining and enforcing property rights, it ought to be clear that an economy will be Islamic only to the extent its government is, and if it is a representative government, how far the majority of the Muslims care about, and show an abiding commitment, to Islamic values enshrined in the Qurʾān and *Sunna*. No amount of rhetoric and wishful thinking can resolve the difficulties in this process; it can only create confusion that makes it difficult to address the relevant issues.

BIBLIOGRAPHY

In CC: In common circulation in various editions throughout the Islamic world.

Abū Yūsuf, Yaʿqūb ibn Ibrāhīm (1962), *Kitāb al-Kharāj*, Cairo: al-Matbaʿah al-Ṣalafiyya.

Abū Dāʿūd Sūlaymān al-Ashʿath al-Sijistānī (d. 889), *Kitāb al-Sūnan.* In CC.*

Ahmad, Ausaf (1992), "Macroconsumption Function in an Islamic Framework: A Survey of the Current Literature," in Ausaf Ahmad and Kazim Raza Awan (eds.), *Lectures on Islamic Economics*, Jeddah: IRTI, Islamic Development Bank, pp. 245–76.

Amīnī, Muḥammad Taqī (1975), *Fiqh Islāmī ka Tarīkhī Pasmanẓar* (Urdu, Islamic fiqh in historical perspective), Lahore: Islamic Publications.

Aquinas, Thomas (d. 1274), *Summa Theologiae*, 2–2, q. 77, art. 1.

Arrow, Kenneth J. (1963), *Social Choice and Individual Values*, 2nd ed., New York: Wiley.

Barelvi, Ahmad Raza Khan (n.d.), *Kifl al-Faqīh al-Fāhim.* In CC.

Baydawī, ʿAbd Allah ibn ʿUmer al- (d. 1280), *Anwār al-Tanzīl wa-Asrār al-Taʾwīl.* In CC.

Bayhaqī, Abu ʾl-Fadl, al-, (1077), *Sunan al-Kubra.* In CC.

Bentham, Jeremy (1781), *An Introduction to the Principles of Morals and Legislation*, ed. J. H. Burns and H. L. A. Hart, London: The Athlone Press, 1970.

Bergson, Abram (1938), "A Reformulation of Certain Aspects of Welfare Economics," *Quarterly Journal of Economics*, February, pp. 310–34.

Bohm-Bawerk, Eugen von (1889), *Capital and Interest*, vol. 2, The *Positive Theory of Capital*, trans. George D. Huncke, South Holland, Ill.: Libertarian Press, 1959.

Buchanan, James M. (1986), *Liberty, Market and State: Political Economy in the 1980s*, New York: New York University Press.

Būkhāri, Muhammad bin Ismaīl al- (d. 870), *Al-Jāmiʿ al-Sahīh.* In CC.

Chapra, Muhammad Umer (1985), *Towards a Just Monetary System*, Leicester: The Islamic Foundation.

—— (1992), *Islam and the Economic Challenge*, Leicester: The Islamic Foundation.

—— (1993), *Islam and Economic Development*, Islamabad: Islamic Research Institute.

—— (1996), *What is Islamic Economics?*, Jeddah: Islamic Development Bank & IRTI.

Clark, John Bates (1899), *The Distribution of Wealth*, New York: Macmillan.

Coase, Ronald H. (1937), "The Nature of the Firm," *Economica*, vol. 4 (November), pp. 386–405.

—— (1960), "The Problem of Social Cost," *Journal of Law and Economics*, vol. 3 (October), pp. 1–44.

—— (1998), "The New Institutional Economics," *American Economic Review*, vol. 88, no. 2, (May), pp. 72–74.

Council of Islamic Ideology (1983), "Report on Elimination of Interest from the Economy," in Ziauddin Ahmed et al. (eds.), *Money and Banking in Islam*, Islamabad: Institute of Policy Studies, pp. 103–257.

Crum, W. L. (1938), "Corporate Earnings on Invested Capital," *Harvard Business Review*, 16 (Spring), pp. 340–41.

Dārimī, Abū Muhammad ʿAbd Allāh al- (d. 894), *Kitāb al-Sunan.* In CC.

Debreu, G. (1959), *Theory of Value*, New York: Wiley, Ch. 4.

Demsetz, Harold (1967), "Towards a Theory of Property Rights," *American Economic Review*, vol. 57, no. 2, (May 1967), pp. 347–59.

Dutton, Yasin (1999), The Origin of Islamic Law: The Qur'ān, the Mūwatta' and Madinan 'Amal, Richmond, Surrey: Curzon.

Elster, Jon (1992), *Local Justice: How Institutions Allocate Scarce Goods and Necessary Burdens*, NY: Russell Sage Foundation.

Faridi, F. R. (1983), "A Theory of Fiscal Policy in an Islamic State," in Ziauddin Ahmed et al. (eds.), *Fiscal Policy and Resource Allocation in Islam*, Jeddah: International Centre for Research in Islamic Economics, pp. 27–58.

Fisher, Irving (1907), *The Rate of Interest*, New York: Macmillan.

—— (1930), *The Theory of Interest*, New York: Kelly.

Ghazālī, Abū Hāmid Muḥammad al- (d. 1111), *Ihyā' 'ulūm al-dīn*, Cairo: Dār al-Salām, 2003.

Gibb, Hamilton A. R. (1962), *Studies on the Civilization of Islam*, Princeton: Princeton University Press.

Guillaume, Alfred (1955), *The Life of Muhammad: A Translation of Ibn Ishaq's Sirat Rasul Allah*, Oxford: Oxford University Press.

Habibi, Nader (1987), "The Consequences of Islamic Banking in a Macro-Economic Framework," in Proceedings of Economic Discipline Council's Seminar on Islamic Economics, Association of Muslim Social Scientists and International Institute of Islamic Thought, Washington, D.C., pp. 106–53.

Hameedullah, Muhammad (1992), *Khutbat-e-Bahawalpur* (Urdu) (Bahawalpur Lectures); Islamabad: Islamic Research Institute.

Hasan, Zubair (1986), "Distributional Equity in Islam," in Munawar Iqbal (ed.), *Distributive Justice and Need Fulfilment in an Islamic Economy*, Islamabad: International Islamic University, pp. 25–54.

—— (1992), "Profit Maximization: Secular versus Islamic," in, Sayyid Tahir et al. (eds.), *Readings in Microeconomics: An Islamic Perspective*, Petaling Jaya: Longman Malaysia, pp. 239–255.

Hicks, John R. (1936), "Mr. Keynes' Theory of Employment," *Economic Journal*, 46 (June), p. 246.

—— (1939), *Value and Capital; An Enquiry into Some Fundamental Principles of Economic Theory*, Oxford: Clarendon Press.

—— (1940), "The Valuation of Social Income," *Economica*, vol. vii, pp. 105–24.

—— (1944), "The Four Consumer's Surpluses," *Review of Economic Studies*, vol. xi, pp. 31–41.

—— (1956), *A Revision of Demand Theory*, Oxford: Clarendon Press.

Hockman, Harold and James Rodgers (1969), "Pareto Optimal Redistribution," *American Economic Review*, vol. 57, pp. 542–57.

Hodgson, Marshall, G. S. (1974), *The Venture of Islam: Conscience and History in World Civilization*, 3 vols.; Chicago: The University of Chicago Press.

Holland, Muhtar (1982), *Public Duties in Islam*, Translation of Ibn Taymiyya's *al-Hisbah fī al-Islām*: Leicester, England: Islamic Foundation, 1982.

Ibn Ḥanbal, Aḥmad ibn Muḥammad (d. 855), *al-Mūsnad*. In CC.

Ibn Khaldun, Abū Zayd 'Abd al-Raḥman (1332–1406), *Muqaddima*, London: Routledge and Kegan Paul, 1967.

Ibn Māja, Muḥammad ibn Yazīd (d. 886), *Kitāb al-sunan*. In CC.

Ibn Nujaym, Zayn al-'Abidīn Ibrahim (d. 1573), *al-Ashbāh wa al-Naẓā'ir*, Damascus: Dar al-Fikr, 1983.

Ibn Qayyim, Abū 'Abd Allāh Muḥammad (d. 1350), *I'lām al-muwaqqi'*, Delhi, 1313 AH.

Ibn Qudāma, 'Abd Allah Ibn Ahmad Ibn Muhammad (d. 1223), *al-Mughnī*. In CC.

Ibn Taymiyya, Aḥmad ibn ʿAbd al-Ḥalīm (d. 1328), *al-Hisbah fī al-Islām*, Cairo: Dār al-Shaʿb, 1976.

Jassās, Abū Bakr al- (d. circa1000), *Ahkām al-Qurʾān*. In CC.

Jaziri, Abd al-Rahman bin Muhammad al- (d. 1941), *Kitāb al-Fiqh ʿalʿl Madhahab al-Arbaʿa*, Cairo, 1938 (Arabic). Published in Urdu under the title *Kitab al-Fiqh*, (2nd ed.), Lahore: Government of Punjab, Auqaf Department, 1978.

Jevons, W. Stanley (1870), "Economic Policy," in *Report of the British Association for the Advancement of Science*, Journal of the Royal Statistical Society, Vol. 33.

Kahf, Monzer (1978), *The Islamic Economy: An Analytical Study of the Functioning of the Islamic Economic System*, Plainsfield, Ind.: MSA of US and Canada.

—— (1980), "A Contribution to the Theory of Consumer Behaviour in an Islamic Society," in K. Ahmad (ed.), *Studies in Islamic Economics*, Leicester: The Islamic Foundation. Reprinted in Sayyid Tahir et al. (eds.), *Readings in Microeconomics: An Islamic Perspective*, Petaling Jaya: Longman Malaysia, 1992, pp. 90–104.

—— (1992), "Market Structure: Free Cooperation," in Sayyid Tahir et al. (eds.), *Readings in Microeconomics: An Islamic Perspective*, Petaling Jaya: Longman Malaysia, 1992, pp. 146–56.

Kaldor, N. (1939), "Welfare Propositions and Interpersonal Comparisons of Utility," *Economic Journal*, vol. xlix, pp. 549–52.

Keynes, John Maynard (1930), *A Treatise on Money*, London: Macmillan.

—— (1936), *The General Theory of Employment, Interest and Money*, London: Macmillan.

—— (1937), "Alternative Theories of the Rate of Interest," *Economic Journal*, 47, (June), pp. 246–48.

Khadduri, Majid (2002), *The Islamic Conception of Justice*, Baltomore: Johns Hopkins University Press.

Khafif, Ali al- (n. d.), *Al-Skirkak fiʾl-Fiqh al-Islami*, Cairo: Dar al-Nashr.

Khallāf, ʿAbd al-Wahhāb (n.d.), *al-Fiqh ʿala al-Madhāhib al-Arbaʿa*, Maṭbaʿ al-Shaʿab.

Khan, M. Fahim (1992), "Theory of Consumer Behaviour in an Islamic Perspective," in Ausaf Ahmad and Kazim Raza Awan (eds.), *Lectures on Islamic Economics*, Jeddah: IRTI, Islamic Development Bank, pp. 169–81.

Knight, Frank H. (1921), *Risk, Uncertainty and Profit*, Boston: Houghton Mifflin.

Konow, James (2003), "Which is the Fairest of All? A positive Analysis of Justice Theories," *Journal of Economic Literature*, Vol. XLI (December), pp. 1188–1239.

Kuran, Timur (1986), "The Economic System in Contemporary Islamic Thought: Interpretation and Assessment," *International Journal of Middle East Studies*, vol. 18, pp. 135–64.

—— (1989), "On the Notion of Economic Justice in Contemporary Islamic Thought," *International Journal of Middle East Studies*, vol. 21: pp. 171–91.

—— (2001), "The Provision of Public Goods under Islamic Law: Origins, Impact, and Limitations of the Waqf System," *Law and Society Review*, vol. 35, pp. 84–197.

—— (2002), "The Islamic Commercial Crisis: Institutional Roots of Economic Underdevelopment in the Middle East," Los Angeles: USC Center for Law, Economics & Organization, Research Paper no. C01–12.

Little, I. M. D. (1957), *A Critique of Welfare Economics* (2nd ed.), Oxford: Oxford University Press.

Mahdi, Syed Iqbal, and Saif Al-Asaly (1987), "A Model of Income Determination in an Interest Free Islamic Economy," in Proceedings of Economic Discipline Council's Seminar on Islamic Economics: Association of Muslim Social Scientists and International Institute of Islamic Thought: Washington, D.C., pp. 58–105.

Mālik ibn Anas (d. 795), *al-Muwaṭṭaʾ*. In CC.

Mannan, M. A. (1992), "Islamic Perspectives on Market Prices and Allocation," in Sayyid Tahir et al. (eds.), *Readings in Microeconomics: An Islamic Perspective*, Petaling Jaya: Longman Malaysia, 1992, pp. 193–219.

—— (1992a), "Islamic Perspectives on Market Imperfections with Special Reference to the Theory of Monopoly," in Sayyid Tahir et al., (eds.), *Readings in Microeconomics: An Islamic Perspective*, Petaling Jaya: Longman Malaysia, 1992, pp. 176–83.

Marshall, Alfred (1890), *Principles of Economics*, 8th ed. (1920), London: Macmillan.

Masud, Muhammad Khalid (1991), "A History of Islamic Law in Spain: An Overview," *Islamic Studies*, Vol. 30, No. 1–2: pp. 7–35.

Māwardī, Abū-al-Ḥasan ʿAlī ibn Muḥammad ibn Ḥabīb al-Basṛ ī al- (d. 1058), *al-Aḥkām al-sulṭāniyya wa-al-wilāyāt al-dīniyya*, Beirut: Dar-al-Fikr, 1983.

——, *Kitāb adab al-dīn wa-al-dunyā*, Beirut: Dar Ihyāʾ al-Tūrāth al-ʿArabī, 1979.

Mawdudi, Sayyid Abul Ala (1961), *Sud* (Urdu), Lahore.

Mill, John Stuart (1848), *Principles of Political Economy*; London; Longmans, Green and Co, and various later editions.

Muslim ibn al-Ḥajjāj al-Nīshāpūrī (d. 875), *Kitāb al-Ṣaḥīḥ*. In CC.

Mustafa, Ahmad H. and Hossein G. Askari (1986), "Economic Implications of Land Ownership and Land Cultivation in Islam," in Munawar Iqbal (ed.), *Distributive Justice and Need Fulfilment in an Islamic Economy*, Islamabad: International Islamic University, pp. 85–128.

Naqvi, Syed Nawab Haider (1981), *Ethics and Economics: An Islamic Synthesis*; Leicester: The Islamic Foundation.

Nasaʾī, Aḥmad ibn Shuʿayb (d. 915), *Kitāb al-Sunan*. In CC.

Noldeke, Theodor (1860), *Geschichte des Qorâns*, Gsschichte Verlag der Dieterichschen Buchhandlung.

Nomani, Farhad (2002), "The Interpretative Debate of the Classical Islamic Jurists on Riba (Usury)," *Topics in Middle Eastern and North African Economies*, vol. 4, the online journal of MEEA.

Nozick, Robert (1974), *Anarchy, State, and Utopia*, NY: Basic Books.

Nuti, D. Mario (1995), *The Economics of Participation*, Jeddah: IDB and IRTI Eminent Scholars' Lecture Series No. 11.

Ohlin, Bertil (1937), "Some Notes on the Stockholm Theory of Savings and Investment," *Economic Journal*, 47, (March and June), pp. 53–69, 221–40.

Paley, William (1785), *The Principles of Moral and Political Philosophy*, New York: B & S Collins (1835), Chapter VII, (Virtue).

Pasinetti, Luigi L. (1969), "Switches of Technique and the 'Rate of Return' in Capital Theory," *Economic Journal*, vol. 79, pp. 508–31.

Patinkin, Don (1972), *Studies in Monetary Economics*, New York: Harper and Row.

Pigou, A. C. (1920), The Economics of Welfare, London: Macmillan and Co., Ltd.

Posner, Richard A. (1991), *The Economics of Justice*, Cambridge: Harvard University Press.

Qaradāwī, Yūsuf al- (1960), *Al-Hilal wal Haram Fil Islam*, Qatar: Department of Shariah Courts and Islamic Affairs. Reprinted in English translation as "The Lawful and the Prohibited in Islam", Indianapolis: American Trust Publications (n. d.).

—— (1969), *Fiqh al-zakāh*, Beirut: Dar al-Irshad.

Qureshi, Anwar Iqbal (1946), *Islam and the Theory of Interest*, Lahore: Shaikh M. Ashraf.

Rahman, Fazlur (1964), "*Riba* and Interest," *Islamic Studies*, vol. 3, (March), pp. 1–43.

Rashid, Salim (1987), "Islamic Economics: A Historico-inductive Approach," in Proceedings of Economic Discipline Council's Seminar on Islamic Economics: Association of Muslim Social Scientists and International Institute of Islamic Thought: Washington, D.C., pp. 37–56. Also published in *Journal of Islamic Banking and Finance*, 1:89, pp. 33–44.

Rawls, John (1971), *A Theory of Justice*, Cambridge: Harvard University Press.

Rāzī, Abū al-Fadl Muhammad Fakhr al-Dīn al- (d. 1209), *Mafātih al-Ghayb*, Cairo. In CC.
Ricardo, David (1817), *On the Principles of Political Economy and Taxation*, London: John Murray.
Riḍā, Rashīd (1960), *al-Ribā wa-al-Muʿāmalāt fī al-Islām*, Cairo: Maktabat al-Qāhira.
Robbins, Lionel (1930), "On a Certain Ambiguity in the Conception of Stationary Equilibrium," *Economic Journal*, 40 (June), pp. 194–214.
—— (1932), *An Essay on the Nature and Significance of Economic Science*, London: Macmillan and Co., Ltd. , Ch. vi.
Robertson, Dennis R. (1933), "Saving and Hoarding," *Economic Journal*, 43, (September), pp. 399–413.
—— (1940), *Essays in Monetary Theory*, London: King and Son.
Robinson, Joan (1953), "The Production Function and the Theory of Capital," *Review of Economic Studies*, vol. 21, pp. 81–106.
Rosenthal, Franz (1967), *The Muqaddimah*; London: Routledge and Kegan Paul.
Saʿdī, ʿAbd Allāh Jamʿān Saʿīd al- (1986), *Fiscal Policy in the Islamic State*, trans. Ahmed al-Anani, Newcastle under Lyme: Lyme Books.
Sadeq, Abul Hasan M. (1992), "Factor Pricing and Income Distribution from an Islamic Perspective," in Sayyid Tahir et al. (eds.), *Readings in Microeconomics: An Islamic Perspective*, Petaling Jaya: Longman Malaysia, pp. 272–86.
Salama, Abidin Ahmed (1983), "Fiscal Policy of an Islamic State," in Ziauddin Ahmed et al. (eds.), *Fiscal Policy and Resource Allocation in Islam*, Jeddah: International Centre for Research in Islamic Economics, pp. 99–118.
Samuelson, Paul A. (1943), "Dynamics, Statics, and the Stationary State," *Review of Economic Statistics*, 25:1 (February), pp. 58–68.
—— (1962), "Parable and Realism in Capital Theory: The Surrogate Production Function," *Review of Economic Studies*, vol. 39, pp. 193–206.
—— (1977), "Thoughts on Profit-Sharing," *Zuitschrift fur die Gesamte Staatswissenschaft*, vol. 133 (Special Issue on Profit-Sharing), pp. 9–18.
Sarakhsī, Abū Bakr Muhammad bin al-Sahl al- (d. 1090), *Al-Mabsūt* , 30 vols., Cairo: 1323 AH.
Schumpeter, Joseph A. (1928), "The Instability of Capitalism," *Economic Journal*, 38 (September), pp. 361–86.
—— (1942), *Capitalism, Socialism and Democracy*, New York: Harper.
Schuon, Frithjof (1963), *Understanding Islam*; London: George Allen and Unwin.
—— (1969), *Dimensions of Islam*; London George Allen and Unwin.
—— (1976), *Islam and the Perennial Philosophy*, London: George Allen and Unwin.
Scitovsky, T. (1941), "A Note on Welfare Propositions in Economics," *Review of Economic Studies*, vol. ix (1), pp. 77–88.
Sewharvi, Muhammad Hifzur Rehman (1959), *Islām kā Iqtiṣādī Niẓām* (Urdu, Economic system of Islam), New Delhi; repr. Lahore: Idara-e-Islamiat, 1984. The citations are from the Lahore edition.
Shafi, Muhammad (1960), *Masʾalah sud* (Urdu), Karachi: Idaratul Maʿarif.
Shāfiʿī, Muḥammad ibn Idrīs al- (d. 820) (1987), *al-Im Khṇammad ibn Idris al-Shāfiī's al-Risbn Idriṣṣūal-Risbn I Treatise on the foundations of Islamic jurisprudence, trans. (with introduction, notes and appendices)* Majid Khadduri, 2nd ed., Cambridge: Islamic Texts Society.
Siddiqi, Muhammad Nejatullah (1979), *Economic Enterprise in Islam*, 2nd ed., Delhi: Markazi Maktaba Islami, first published 1972.
—— (1983), "Economics of Profit-Sharing," in Ziauddin Ahmed et al. (eds.), *Fiscal Policy and Resource Allocation in Islam*, Islamabad: Institute of Policy Studies, pp. 163–201.
—— (1983a), *Issues in Islamic Banking: Selected Papers*, Leicester: The Islamic Foundation.

—— (1985), *Partnership and Profit-Sharing in Islamic Law*, Leicester: The Islamic Foundation.
—— (1992), "Some Notes on Teaching Economics in an Islamic Perspective," in Sayyid Tahir et al. (eds.), *Readings in Microeconomics: An Islamic Perspective*, Petaling Jaya: Longman Malaysia, pp. 1–39.
—— (1992), "History of Islamic Economic Thought," in Ausaf Ahmad and Kazim Raza Awan (eds.), *Lectures on Islamic Economics*, Jeddah: Islamic Development Bank, pp. 69–83.
Simon, Herbert (1957), "A Behavioral Model of Rational Choice," in *Models of Man, Social and Rational: Mathematical Essays on Rational Human Behavior in a Social Setting*, New York: Wiley.
—— (1991), "Bounded Rationality and Organizational Learning," *Organization Science*, vol. 2, no. 1 (February), pp. 125–34.
Smith, Adam (1776), *The Wealth of Nations*, New York: Random House, Modern Library Edition, 1937.
Smyth, R. L. (1963), *Essays in Economic Method*, New York: McGraw Hill.
Solow, R. M. (1963), *Capital Theory and the Rate of Return*, Amsterdam: North-Holland Pub. Co.
Strauss, J. H. (1944), "The Entrepreneur: The Firm," *Journal of Political Economy*, 52 (June), pp. 112–27.
Suyūṭī, ʿAbd al-Rahmān Jalāl al-Din al- (d. 1505), *Al-Itqān fī ʿUlūm al-Qurʾān*. In CC.
Ṭabarī, Abū Jaʿfar Muḥammad ibn Jarīr al- (d. 923), *Jāmiʿ al-bayān fī tafsīr al-Qurʾān*, (30 vols.), Cairo, 1903; also in CC.
—— *Tārīkh Ṭabarī*. In CC.
Tahir, Sayyid, et al. (eds.) (1992), *Readings in Microeconomics: An Islamic Perspective*, Petaling Jaya: Longman Malaysia.
Taussig, Frank W. (1908), "Capital, Interest, and Diminishing Returns," *Quarterly Journal of Economics*, 22 (May), pp. 333–63.
Tyser, C. R. et al. (1967), *The Mejelle*, Lahore: All Pakistan Legal Decisions.
Udovitch, Abraham L. (1970), *Partnership and Profit in Medieval Islam*, Princeton: Princeton University Press.
Usmani, Muhammad Taqi (1999), *An Introduction to Islamic Finance*: Karachi: Idaratul Maʿarif.
—— (2000), *The Historic Judgment on Interest Delivered in the Supreme Court of Pakistan*, Karachi: Idaratul Maʿarif.
Vanek, Jaroslav (1965), "Workers' Profit Participation, Unemployment and the Keynesian Equilibrium," *Weltwirtschaftliches Archiv*, vol. 94, no. 2, pp. 206–14.
Ward, A. W. and A. R. Waller (eds.) (1907–27), *The Cambridge History of English Literature*, Cambridge: The University Press.
Warr, Peter (1982), "Pareto Optimal Redistribution and Private Charity," *Journal of Public Economics*, vol. 19, pp. 131–38. Webster's Dictionary of the English Language (1988 ed.), New York: Lexicon Publications.
Weitzman, Martin L. (1984), *The Share Economy*, Cambridge, Mass.: Harvard University Press.
Wicksell, Knut (1935), *Lectures on Political Economy*, London: Routledge and Kegan Paul.
Williamson, Oliver E. (1998), "The Institutions of Governance," *American Economic Review*, vol. 88, no. 2, pp. 75–79.
Winch, David M. (1971), *Analytical Welfare Economics*, Hammondsworth: Penguin.
Yusufuddin, Muhammad (1984), *Islām kā muʿāshī naẓariyya* (Urdu, Economic doctrines of Islam), Karachi.

Zaman, Asad (1992), "Towards Foundations for an Islamic Theory of Consumer Behaviour," in Sayyid Tahir et al. (eds.), *Readings in Microeconomics: An Islamic Perspective*, Petaling Jaya: Longman Malaysia, 1992, pp. 81–89.

Zarqa, Muhammad Anas (1992), "Distributive Justice in Islam," in Ausaf Ahmad and Kazim Raza Awan (eds.), *Lectures on Islamic Economics*, Jeddah: IRTI, Islamic Development Bank, pp. 145–61.

INDEX